ALL·IN·ONE

Sun® Certified Solaris™ 9.0 System and Network Administrator

EXAM GUIDE

ALL·IN·ONE

Sun® Certified Solaris™ 9.0 System and Network Administrator

EXAM GUIDE

Paul Watters

McGraw-Hill/Osborne

New York • Chicago • San Francisco • Lisbon
London • Madrid • Mexico City • Milan • New Delhi
San Juan • Seoul • Singapore • Sydney • Toronto

The McGraw-Hill Companies

McGraw-Hill/Osborne
2600 Tenth Street
Berkeley, California 94710
U.S.A.

To arrange bulk purchase discounts for sales promotions, premiums, or fund-raisers, please contact **McGraw-Hill**/Osborne at the above address. For information on translations or book distributors outside the U.S.A., please see the International Contact Information page immediately following the index of this book.

Sun® Certified Solaris™ 9.0 System and Network Administrator All-in-One Exam Guide

1234567890 DOC DOC 019876543

Book p/n 0-07-222531-9 and CD p/n 0-07-222532-7
parts of
ISBN 0-07-222530-0

Publisher
Brandon A. Nordin

Vice President & Associate Publisher
Scott Rogers

Editorial Director
Gareth Hancock

Project Editor
Monika Faltiss

Acquisitions Coordinator
Jessica Wilson

Technical Editor
William Shamblin

Copy Editor
Dennis Weaver

Proofreaders
Mike McGee
Paul Medoff

Indexer
Jack Lewis

Computer Designers
Kathleen Fay Edwards
George Toma Charbak
Lucie Ericksen

Illustrators
Michael Mueller
Melinda Moore Lytle
Lyssa Wald

Series Design
Peter F. Hancik

Cover Design
Greg Scott

This book was composed with Corel VENTURA™ Publisher.

DEDICATION

This book is dedicated to my new daughter Nellie

ABOUT THE AUTHOR

Paul A. Watters received his PhD in computer science from Macquarie University. He also has degrees from the University of Cambridge, the University of Tasmania, and the University of Newcastle. He has worked in both commercial and R&D organizations, designing systems and software on the Solaris platform. His commercial interests are focused on Java, Web Services, and e-commerce systems in the enterprise. His research areas include virtual enterprises, secure distributed storage, and complex systems. He has previously written *Solaris 9: The Complete Reference* and *Solaris 9 Administration: A Beginner's Guide*, both published by Osborne/McGraw-Hill.

ABOUT THE TECHNICAL EDITOR

William Shamblin is currently a senior systems programmer at Duke University's Department of Computer Science. He has been working with a variety of Internet technologies over the last eight years as a systems administrator, and has worked with Solaris since SunOS 4.0.

CONTENTS AT A GLANCE

CONTENTS

ACKNOWLEDGMENTS

I would like to acknowledge the professionalism and support of the team at McGraw-Hill/Osborne. Gareth Hancock and Jessica Wilson worked very hard to ensure that this certification title arrived on the market in a timely fashion, but also with a strict commitment to quality. Monika Faltiss and Elizabeth Seymour provided valuable insight and feedback on each chapter, while Dennis Weaver politely but thoroughly corrected every typo and error in the manuscript. The technical editor, Joe Shamblin, was tough but fair. Thanks Joe!

To everyone at my agency, Studio B, thanks for your past and continued support. To Neil Salkind, my agent, thanks for your wisdom and pragmatic advice.

To Bill Moffitt, at Sun Microsystems, thanks for your continued support of my publishing efforts.

Finally, thanks to my family, especially my wife Maya, for always being there, through good times and tough times.

INTRODUCTION

Putting your skills to the test in a certification exam is not an easy task. In the field, you can use your trusty man pages or AnswerBook to look up command options, recall procedures, or ask a colleague for advice. During a certification exam, it's just you, the computer, and the exam questions. Even the most experienced and qualified system administrators rightly feel nervous heading into exams! After all, certification exams exist to sort sheep from goats and novices from experts, and by achieving certification you'll be recognized as an industry professional with up-to-date skills. This will make your resumé infinitely more marketable to recruiters and potential employers.

There are several largely unwritten rules about certification exams that it pays to know, especially when taking either of the exams covered in this book. First, remember that the certification exam is going to test your knowledge of the Solaris product *as released by Sun*. Thus, there's not much point reviewing material about non-Sun software for the exams, even if it forms an integral part of your daily sysadmin routine. For example, while you may be asked to interpret a Bourne shell script in the exam, you won't be asked to analyze a PHP script even though you might use PHP more often in real life. Second, it pays to memorize pesky and seemingly trivial command options for all of the common commands—many a test candidate has been stumped trying to recall a largely unused parameter for a command that they use regularly. Having said that, certification exams do not deliberately try and mislead you, and by examining the table of contents for this book, you'll see that many of the topics are familiar. Third, it pays to practice: use the review questions in the book after reading each chapter to see if you can accurately recall material appropriately, and use the testing tool provided on the CD-ROM to put your skills to the test in real time. Only by simulating actual exam conditions will you truly be able to evaluate your readiness to attempt a certification exam.

PART I

Solaris 9 Operating Environment, Exam I

Introduction to Solaris 9

In this chapter, you will

- Cover the Solaris operating environment and the SunOS operating system
- Learn about different types of Solaris certification exams available
- Learn about the optional Solaris courses available through Sun Educational Services
- Be given an overview of the exam's target material
- Cover the certification process
- Learn exam tips and tricks

Operating systems are the building blocks of computer systems and provide the interface between user applications and computer hardware. Solaris 9 is a multiuser, multitasking operating system developed and sold by Sun Microsystems (**http://www.sun.com/**), and is one implementation of the UNIX operating system that draws on both the System V (AT&T) and Berkeley (BSD) systems. It has risen from little more than a research project to become the dominant UNIX operating system in the international marketplace today. Solaris 9 is the latest in a long line of operating environment releases based around the SunOS operating system, which is currently in version 5.9. Solaris is commonly found in large corporations and educational institutions that require concurrent, multiuser access on individual hosts and between hosts connected via the Internet. However, it is also rapidly being adopted by small businesses and individual developers through Sun's promotion of the "Free Solaris" program. In this book, when we refer to "Solaris 9," many of the commands and procedures will apply equally to earlier versions of Solaris 2.*x*. Commands for Solaris 1.*x* are specified only where relevant.

Many desktop computer users have never heard of the word "Sun" in the context of computing, nor are they usually familiar with the term "Solaris" as an operating environment. However, almost every time that an Internet user sends an e-mail message or opens a file from a networked server running Sun's Network File System (NFS) product, Solaris 9 is transparently supporting many of today's existing Internet applications. In the enterprise computing industry, Sun is synonymous with highly available, highly reliable performance hardware, while Solaris 9 is often the operating environment of choice to support database servers and application servers. Sun's hardware solutions are based around the SPARC and UltraSPARC integrated circuit technologies, which currently support more than 64 processors in a single E10000 server system.

In recent times, two of Sun's innovations moved the spotlight from the server room to the desktop. First, Sun's development of the Java programming language, which promises "write once, read anywhere" application execution across any platform that supports the Java Virtual Machine, has revolutionized the development of networked applications. In addition, Java "applets" now appear on many web pages, being small encapsulated applications that execute client side, while "servlets" power the back end of many three-tier applications, such as CRM and complex HR applications.

Secondly, Sun is promoting a "free" version of Solaris 9 for the SPARC hardware platform. However, the release of a new version of Solaris for the Intel platform has been delayed. This means that organizations that have previously committed to using Microsoft Windows or Caldera/SCO OpenServer on the Intel platform, for example, can reuse the servers currently deployed with these operations by installing Solaris 8 for Intel, and upgrading when Solaris 9 becomes available. Sun has also made Solaris 9 more accessible for desktop users, offering the StarOffice productivity suite for free, or for a limited cost, shown in Figure 1-1. StarOffice is a product that is competitive with Microsoft Office—it contains word processing, spreadsheet, presentation, and database components that are fully integrated. In addition, StarOffice runs on many different platforms and in eight languages, meaning that a user on a Sun SPARCstation can share documents seamlessly

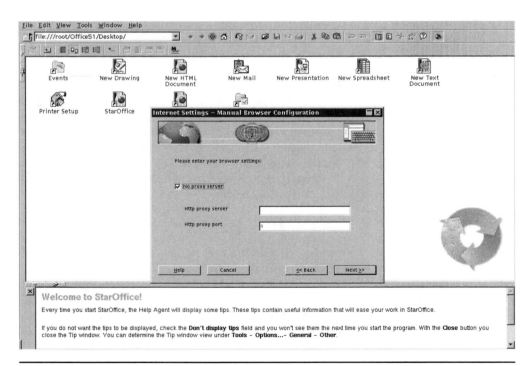

Figure 1-1   The StarOffice productivity suite

with users on Linux and Microsoft Windows. The combination of a solid operating system with a best-of-breed productivity suite has given Solaris new exposure in the desktop market.

This book is a complete guide to the Solaris 9 operating environment, and for the SunOS 5.9 operating system, meaning that we will try to cover, in detail, the operational aspects of Solaris and SunOS. If you simply need to look up a command's options, you can usually make use of Sun's own online "manual pages," which you can access by typing **man** *command*, where *command* is the command for which you require help. Or, you can retrieve the text of man pages and user manuals online by using the search facility at **http://docs.sun.com/**. This reference will be most useful when you need to implement a specific solution, and you need practical tried-and-tested solutions. Although Solaris 9 comes with a set of traditional, unsecured remote access tools and servers by default, these are not always the best tools, in terms of security, that you should use in a production environment. For example, although ftp is fine for transferring files around a local area network, you should conduct remote exchanges of data using a secure file transfer system, such as sftp, which is a new utility supplied with the OpenSSH package. In outlining a solution to a problem, we generally introduce Sun-supplied software first, and then discuss the installation and configuration of third-party alternatives. You can also use this book as a reference for previous versions of Solaris, since much of the command syntax remains unchanged across operating system releases. Command syntax is typically identical across different platforms as well (SPARC and Intel).

If you've been keeping track of recent press releases, you may be wondering why Solaris has a version number of "9," while SunOS has a revision level of 5.9. Since the release of Solaris 7 (SunOS 5.7), Sun has opted to number its releases sequentially with a single version number, based on the old minor revision number. This means that the release sequence for Solaris has been 2.5.1, 2.6, 7, 8, and now 9. Thus, many sites will still be running Solaris 2.6 without feeling too far left behind, especially if they don't require the 64-bit functionality for the UltraSPARC processors provided with Solaris 7 and beyond. Sun does provide "jumbo patches" for previous operating system releases, which should always be installed when released to ensure that bugs (particularly security bugs) are resolved as soon as possible. Thus, most of the commands and topics covered in this book for Solaris 9 are equally applicable to Solaris 7, 8, and all previous releases of SunOS 5.*x*.

However, wherever possible, we have also included references to the SunOS 4.*x* operating system, which was retrospectively labeled the Solaris 1.*x* platform. This is because many installations have just started using SunOS 5.*x* in the past few years, and until Y2K problems emerged with SunOS 4.*x*, many sites still ran legacy applications on this platform (especially if they prefer the BSD-style SunOS 4.*x* to the System V–style SunOS 5.*x* operating system). Many Internet firewalls, mail servers, and news servers still run on SPARC architecture CPUs, and some of these models are not supported by the SunOS 5.*x* operating system.

 CAUTION Making the decision to upgrade from SunOS 4.*x* to SunOS 5.*x* was tough for many Sun installations.

Fortunately, with the release of Solaris 7, 8, and 9, 64-bit computing has arrived, and a stable platform has been established. Many of the changes between Solaris 7, 8, and 9 may appear cosmetic; for example, Larry Wall's Perl interpreter has been included since the Solaris 8 distribution, meaning that a new generation of system administrators will no longer have the pleasure of carrying out their first postinstallation task. However, other quite important developments in the area of networking and administration may not affect all users but be particularly important for the enterprise.

In this chapter, we cover the background to the Solaris 9 operating environment, which really begins with the invention and widespread adoption of the UNIX operating system. In addition, we also cover the means by which Solaris 9 can run cross-platform applications; for example, Solaris for Intel is capable of running Linux binary applications by using an application called *Lxrun*, which is freely available from Sun. Although earlier attempts to emulate other operating systems were largely unsuccessful (for example, WABI for emulating Microsoft Windows), Sun's development of Java can be seen as a strong commitment to cross-platform interoperability. In addition, Solaris 9 provides many network management features that allow a Solaris 9 server to act as a primary or backup domain controller to manage Windows NT clients using Samba—for example, if you want the reliability of Solaris 9 coupled with the widespread adoption of Microsoft Windows as a desktop operating system.

Finally, we review some of the many sites on the Internet that provide useful information, software packages, and further reading on many of the topics that we cover in this book.

What Is UNIX?

UNIX is not easily defined, because it is an "ideal" operating system that has been instantiated by different vendors over the years, in some quite nonstandard ways. However, there are a number of features of UNIX and UNIX-like systems (such as Linux) that can be readily described. UNIX systems have a core kernel that is responsible for managing core system operations, such as logical devices for input/output (such as */dev/pty*, for pseudoterminals), and allocating resources to carry out user-specified and system-requisite tasks. In addition, UNIX systems have a hierarchical file system that allows both relative and absolute file path naming, and is extremely flexible. UNIX file systems can be mounted locally, or remotely from a central file server. All operations on a UNIX system are carried out by processes, which may spawn child processes or other lightweight processes to perform discrete tasks.

 TIP　Processes can be uniquely identified by their process ID (PID).

Originally designed as a text processing system, UNIX systems share many tools that manipulate and filter text in various ways. In addition, small, discrete utilities can be easily combined to form complete applications in rather sophisticated ways. These applications are executed from a user shell, which defines the user interface to the kernel.

 CAUTION Although GUI environments can be constructed around the shell, they are not mandatory.

UNIX is multiprocess, multiuser, and multithreaded. This means that more than one user can execute a shell and applications concurrently, and that each user can execute applications concurrently from within a single shell. Each of these applications can then create and remove lightweight processes as required.

Because UNIX was created by active developers, rather than operating system gurus, there was always a strong focus on creating an operating system that suited programmer's needs. A *Bell System Technical Journal* article in 1978 lists the key guiding principles of UNIX development:

- *Create small, self-contained programs that perform a single task.* When a new task needs to be solved, either create a new program that performs it or combine tools from the toolset that already exists to arrive at a solution. This is a similar orientation to the current trend towards encapsulation and independent component building (such as Enterprise JavaBeans), where complicated systems are built from smaller interacting but logically independent modules.

- *Programs should accept data from standard input and write to standard input;* thus, programs can be "chained" to process each other's output sequentially. Avoid interactive input in favor of command-line options that specify a program's actions to be performed. Presentation should be separated from what a program is trying to achieve. These ideas are consistent with the concept of piping, which is still fundamental to the operation of user shells. For example, the output of the ls command to list all files in a directory can be "piped" using the | symbol to a program such as grep to perform pattern matching. The number of pipes on a single command-line instruction is not limited.

- *Creating a new operating system or program should be undertaken on a scale of weeks, not years: the creative spirit that leads to cohesive design and implementation should be exploited.* If software doesn't work, don't be afraid to build something better. This process of iterative revisions of programs has resurfaced in recent years with the rise of object-oriented development.

- *Make best use of all the tools available, rather than asking for more help.* The motivation behind UNIX is to construct an operating system that supports the kinds of toolsets required for successful development.

This is not intended to be an exhaustive list of the characteristics that define UNIX, but these features are central to understanding the importance that UNIX developers often ascribe to the operating system. It is designed to be a programmer-friendly system.

The History of UNIX

UNIX was originally developed at Bell Laboratories as a private research project by a small group of people starting in the late 1960s. This group had experience with a number of different operating systems research efforts in the previous decade, and their goals with the UNIX project were to design an operating system to satisfy the objectives of transparency, simplicity, and modifiability, with the use of a new third-generation programming language. At the time of conception, typical vendor-specific operating systems were extremely large and all were written in assembly language, making them difficult to maintain. Although the first attempts to write the UNIX kernel were based on assembly language, later versions were written in a high-level language called C, which was developed during the same era. Even today, most modern operating system kernels, such as the Linux kernel, are written in C. After the kernel was developed using the first C compiler, a complete operating environment was developed, including the many utilities associated with UNIX today (for example, the visual editor, vi). In this section, we examine the timeline leading to the development of UNIX, and the origins of the two main "flavors" of UNIX: AT&T (System V) and BSD.

Origins of UNIX

In 1969, Ken Thompson from AT&T's Bell Telephone Labs wrote the first version of the UNIX operating system, on a DEC PDP-7. Disillusioned with the inefficiency of the Multics (Multiplexed Information and Computing Service) project, Thompson decided to create a programmer-friendly operating system that limited the functions contained within the kernel and allowed greater flexibility in the design and implementation of applications. The PDP-7 was a modest system on which to build a new operating system—it had only an assembler and a loader, and it would allow only a single-user login at any one time. It didn't even have a hard disk—the developers were forced to partition physical memory into an operating system segment and a RAM disk segment. Thus, the first UNIX file system was emulated entirely in RAM!

After successfully crafting a single-user version of UNIX on the PDP-7, Thompson and his colleague Dennis Ritchie ported the system to a much larger DEC PDP-11/20 system in 1970. This project was funded and charged with the requirement of building a text processing system for patents, the descendents of which still exist in text filters such as troff. The need to create application programs ultimately led to the development of the first C compiler by Ritchie, which was based on the B language. C was written with portability in mind—thus, platform-specific libraries could be addressed using the same function call from source code that would also compile on another hardware platform. Although the PDP-11 was better than the PDP-7, it was still very modest compared to today's scientific calculators—it had 24K of addressable memory, with 12K reserved for the operating system. By 1972, the number of worldwide UNIX installations had grown to ten.

The next major milestone in the development of UNIX was the rewriting of the kernel in C, by Ritchie and Thompson, in 1973. This explains why C and UNIX are strongly related—even today, most UNIX applications are written in C, even though other programming languages have long been made available. Following the development of the C kernel, the owners of UNIX (being AT&T) began licensing the source code to educational institutions within the U.S. and abroad. However, these licenses were often restrictive, and the releases were not widely advertised. No support was offered, and no mechanism was available for officially fixing bugs. However, because users had access to the source code, the ingenuity in hacking code—whose legacy exists today in community projects like Linux—gathered steam, particularly at the University of California at Berkeley. The issue of licensing and AT&T's control over UNIX would determine the future fragmentation of the operating system in years to come.

In 1975, the first distribution of UNIX software was made by the Berkeley group, and was known as the BSD. Berkeley was Ken Thompson's alma mater, and he teamed up with two graduate students (Bill Joy and Chuck Haley) who were later to become leading figures in the UNIX world. They worked on a UNIX Pascal compiler that was released as part of BSD, and Bill Joy also wrote the first version of vi, the visual editor, which continues to be popular even today.

In 1978, the seventh edition of the operating system was released, and it supported many different hardware architectures, including the IBM 360, Interdata 8/32, and an Interdata 7/32. The version 7 kernel was a mere 40K in size, and included the following system calls: _exit, access, acct, alarm, brk, chdir, chmod, chown, chroot, close, creat, dup, dup2, exec*, exit, fork, fstat, ftime, getegid, geteuid, getgid, getpid, getuid, gtty, indir, ioctl, kill, link, lock, lseek, mknod, mount, mpxcall, nice, open, pause, phys, pipe, pkoff, pkon, profil, ptrace, read, sbrk, setgid, setuid, signal, stat, stime, stty, sync, tell, time, times, umask, umount, unlink, utime, wait, write. Indeed, the full manual for version 7 is now available online at **http://plan9.bell-labs.com/7thEdMan/index.html**.

With the worldwide popularity of UNIX version 7, AT&T began to realize that UNIX might be a valuable commercial product, and attempted to restrict the teaching of UNIX from source code in university courses, thereby protecting valuable intellectual property. In addition, AT&T began to charge license fees for access to the UNIX source, for the first time. This prompted the UCB group to create their own variant of UNIX—the BSD distribution now contains a full operating system in addition to the traditional applications that originally formed the distribution. As a result, version 7 forms the basis for all the UNIX versions currently available. This version of UNIX also contained a full Brian Kernighan and Ritchie C compiler, and the Bourne shell. The branching of UNIX into AT&T and BSD "flavors" continues even today, although many commercial systems—such as SunOS—which are derived from BSD have now adopted many System V features, as discussed next.

The most influential BSD versions of UNIX were 4.2, released in 1983, and 4.3, released in 1987. The DARPA-sponsored development of the Internet was largely undertaken on BSD UNIX, and most of the early commercial vendors of UNIX used BSD UNIX rather than paying license fees to AT&T. Indeed, many hardware platforms even today—right up to Cray super computers—can still run BSD out of the box. Other responses to the commercialization of UNIX included Andrew Tanenbaum's independent solution, which was to write a new UNIX-like operating system from scratch that would be compatible with UNIX, but without even one line of AT&T code. Tanenbaum called it Minix, and Minix is still taught in operating systems courses today. Minix also played a crucial role in Linus Torvald's experiments with his UNIX-like operating system, known today as Linux.

Bill Joy left Berkeley prior to the release of 4.2BSD, and modified the 4.1c system to form SunOS. In the meantime, AT&T continued with their commercial development of the UNIX platform. In 1983, they released the first System V Release 1, which had worked its way up to Release 3 by 1987. This is the release that several of the older generation of mainframe hardware vendors, such as HP and IBM, based their HP-UX and AIX systems upon, respectively. At this time, Sun and AT&T also began planning a future merging of the BSD and System V distributions. In 1990, AT&T released System V Release 4, which formed the basis for the SunOS 5.x release in 1992—this differed substantially from the previous SunOS 4.x systems, which were entirely based on BSD. Other vendors, such as IBM and DEC, eschewed this new cooperation and formed the Open Software Foundation (OSF).

In recent years, a new threat has emerged to the market dominance of UNIX systems: Microsoft's enterprise-level computing products, such as Windows NT and Windows 2000, are designed to deliver price-competitive alternatives to UNIX on inexpensive Intel hardware. In the same way that UNIX outgunned the dominant mainframe vendors with a faster, leaner operating system, Microsoft's strategy has also been based on arguments concerning total cost of ownership (TCO), and a worldwide support scheme for an enormous installed base of desktop Microsoft Windows clients. However, the increasing popularity of Linux and the release of Solaris for Intel have forced Microsoft to defend their platform publicly, and the future of enterprise operating systems is not clear. UNIX will have an important role to play in the future, however. As desktop computing systems rapidly become connected to the Internet, they will require the kinds of services typically available under operating systems such as Solaris 9. As part of their territorial defense of the UNIX environment, many former adversaries in the enterprise computing market, such as IBM, HP, and Sun, have agreed to work towards a Common Open Software Environment (COSE), which is designed to capitalize on the common features of UNIX provided by these vendors. By distributing common operating system elements such as the Common Desktop Environment, based on X11, these vendors will be looking to streamline their competing application APIs, and to support emerging enterprise data processing standards, such as the Object Management Group's CORBA object management service.

Features of BSD

Solaris was originally derived from the BSD distribution from the University of California. Thus commands in SunOS 4.x were very similar to those found in other BSD distributions, although these changed significantly in SunOS 5.x when System V Release 4 was adopted. For example, many veteran system administrators would still find themselves typing ps aux to display a process list, which is BSD style, rather than the newer ps –eaf, which is correct for SVR4. Before AT&T commercialized UNIX, the BSD distribution required elements of the AT&T system to form a fully operational system. By the early 1990s, the UCB groups had removed all dependencies on the AT&T system. This led to the development of many of the existing BSD systems available today, including FreeBSD and NetBSD.

The innovations pioneered at UCB included the development of a virtual memory system for UNIX, a fast file system (which supported long filenames and symbolic links), and the basic elements of a TCP/IP networking system (including authentication with Kerberos). The TCP/IP package included support for services such as telnet and ftp, and the sendmail mail transport agent, which used the Simple Mail Transfer Protocol. In addition, alternate shells to the default Bourne shell—such as the C shell, which uses C-like constructs to process commands within an interpreted framework—were also first seen in the BSD distribution, as were extensions to process management, such as job control. Standard terminal management libraries such as termcap and curses also originated with BSD. Products from other vendors were also introduced into BSD, including NFS clients and servers from Sun Microsystems. Later releases also included support for symmetric multiprocessing, thread management, and shared libraries.

It is often said that the BSD group gave rise to the community-oriented free software movement, which underlies many successful software projects being conducted around the world today. However, BSD is not the only attempt to develop a "free" version UNIX. In 1984, Richard Stallman started developing the GNU (GNUs Not UNIX) system, which was intended to be a replacement for UNIX that was completely free. The GNU C and C++ compilers were some of the first to fully support industry standards (ANSI), and the GNU Bourne again shell has many more features than the original Bourne shell. You can find more information about the GNU project at **http://www.gnu.org/**.

 TIP   Several versions of BSD are still freely distributed and available, such as FreeBSD.

Features of System V Release 4

Solaris 9 integrates many features from the AT&T System V releases (including support for interprocess communication) that were missing in the BSD distributions. As we discussed earlier, many legal battles were fought over the UNIX name and source. System V was developed by the UNIX System Laboratories (USL), which was still majority owned by AT&T in the early 1980s. However, Novell bought USL in early 1993. Eventually, USL sold UNIX to Novell, which ultimately sold it to X/Open. In 1991, the OSF-1 specification was released, and although DEC is the only major manufacturer to fully implement the standard, there is much useful cross-fertilization between System V and other operating systems. Since Sun joined OSF in 1994, there has been new hope of standardizing UNIX services and APIs across platforms.

The major contributions of System V to the UNIX platform are as follows:

- Enhancement of the Bourne shell, including shell functions
- The STREAMS and TLI networking libraries
- Remote file sharing (RFS)
- Improved memory paging
- The Application Binary Interface (ABI)

The major differences between SVR4 and BSD UNIX can be summarized as follows:

- **Boot scripts**   */etc/init.d* in System V, */etc/rc.d* in BSD
- **Default shell**   Bourne shell in System V, C shell in BSD
- **File system mount database**   */etc/mnttab* in System V, */etc/mtab* in BSD
- **Kernel name**   */unix* in System V, */vmunix* in BSD
- **Printing system**   *lp* in System V, *lpr* in BSD
- **String functions**   *memcopy* in System V, *bcopy* in BSD
- **Terminal initialization**   */etc/inittab* in System V, */etc/ttys* in BSD
- **Terminal control**   *termio* in System V, *termios* in BSD

The Solaris Advantage

Sun Microsystems was formed by former graduate students from Stanford and Berkeley, who used Stanford hardware and Berkeley software to develop the workstation market in the enterprise. It aimed to compete directly with the mainframe vendors by offering CPU speed and a mature operating system on the desktop, which was unprecedented. For a given price, greater performance could be obtained from the Sun workstations than was ever possible using mainframes. From one perspective, this success destroyed the traditional client/server market, which used very dumb terminals to communicate with very clever but horrendously expensive mainframe systems. The vendors of some proprietary systems, such as HP and DEC, saw their market share rapidly decline in the enterprise market because Sun delivered more "bang per buck" in performance. By 1986, UNIX was the dominant force, at the expense of operating systems like VAX/VMS, although VMS would later come back to haunt UNIX installations in the form of Windows NT. When users could have a workstation with graphics instead of a dumb terminal, there were few arguments about adopting Sun.

However, Sun's innovation enabled departments and workgroups to take control of their own computing environments and to develop productively with the C programming language. Sun took BSD and transformed it into a commercial product, adding some useful innovations (such as NFS) along the way. This was similar in some ways to the approach of Linux companies that create distributions of useful software packages and bundle them with the Linux kernel. However, one significant difference between Sun and Red Hat Linux is that Sun has always been a company with a hardware focus—its systems were designed with the SPARC chipset and more recently the UltraSPARC chipset in mind. This has enabled Sun to create very fast workstations and servers with typically lower CPU speeds than Intel, but faster and more efficient bus performance. Sun invests heavily in hardware design and implementation for an expected commercial reward, all the more so now that Sun gives away the Solaris operating system.

The major innovations of SunOS 4.*x* can be summarized as follows:

- Implementation of the Network File System (NFS version 2.0, running over UDP)

- The OpenWindows 2.0 graphical user environment, based on X11
- The OpenBoot monitor
- The DeskSet utilities
- Multiprocessing support

The major innovations of SunOS 5.*x* can be summarized as follows:

- Support for symmetric multiprocessing of up to 64 processors in a single server
- The OpenWindows 3.0 graphical user environment and OpenLook. Integration with MIT X11R5, Motif, PostScript, and the common desktop environment (CDE)
- The Network Information Service (NIS+)
- Kerberos integration for authentication
- Support for static and dynamic linking
- Full-moon clustering, ensuring high availability
- The ability to serve NT clients as a primary domain controller
- Tooltalk
- Java
- POSIX-compliant development environment, including single threads, multithreading, shared memory, and semaphores
- Real-time kernel processing
- X/OPEN-compliant command environment
- Compliance with UNIX 95 and UNIX 98 standards
- Support for very large (> 2G) files
- Microsoft Windows emulation on the desktop with WABI
- Advanced volume management (`vold`)
- Standardized package administration and deployment tools
- Standardized patch management and integration
- Software-based power management
- Access control lists for resource authorization
- Support for centralized management of user home directories using the automounter
- Improvements to NFS (version 3), running over TCP
- Support for advanced networking, such as ATM, frame relay, and Gigabit Ethernet
- JumpStart customization of local site installation and deployment
- A 64-bit kernel architecture with Solaris 7 and later

- Simplified backup and restore procedures
- Simplified site administration with the AdminSuite toolkit

Hardware Support (SPARC and x86)

The classic CPU for Sun systems is the SPARC chip. Many systems in deployment today, including SPARC 5, 10, and 20, use different versions of the SPARC chip, with processor speeds of around 40–60 MHz. Later systems, which use the UltraSPARC chipset, have processor speeds (as of this writing) of up to 900 MHz. Although this may not seem fast, the bus architectures of Sun systems are much faster than their PC counterparts, more than making up for apparently slower chip speeds. Many SPARC systems are still supported in Solaris 9, although it is advisable to check with Sun to determine whether older machines such as IPCs and IPXs will be supported in future releases. Sun 4 machines and older are no longer supported by Sun, but they may run one of the BSD releases or Linux. Some older machines, such as Classics, have a very loyal support base and are still actively supported.

With the introduction of Solaris 2.1 came support for the Intel platform, supporting ISA, EISA, MCA, and PCI bus types. This performed adequately on high-end 486 systems. Given the significant variation in types and manufacturers of PC hardware, not all devices are currently supported under Solaris 9. Newer innovations, such as the Universal Serial Bus (USB), have only been recently supported. Solaris 9 for Intel runs very fast on modern Pentium-II and Pentium-III systems, meaning that Intel devotees now have a wider choice of operating system if they don't want to buy Sun hardware. There was also a single port of Solaris to the PowerPC platform (with version 2.5.1), but this failed to impress MacOS users and was deprecated in Solaris 2.6.

Solaris for Intel users will require the Hardware Compatibility List (HCL) to determine whether their particular system or their peripheral devices are supported. You can find this list at **http://access1.sun.com/drivers/hcl/hcl.html**. The HCL lists all tested systems, components, and peripherals that are known to work with Solaris for Intel. Chances are, if your hardware is not listed, it won't be supported. However, many Intel-based standards have been adopted by Sun, including the PCI bus, which is now integrated in the desktop Ultra workstations.

Cross-Platform Interoperability

Solaris supports several different kinds of cross-platform interoperability. For example, Sun recently released a product called *lxrun*, which allows Linux binaries to be run under Solaris for Intel. This is very handy, as many database vendors, for example, have given away free versions of their database management products for Linux, but not for Solaris. Being able to exploit a free offer for one platform and make use of it on Solaris is a very handy cost saver indeed.

Sun also includes a binary compatibility package in Solaris that allows Solaris 1.x applications to run without modification. However, success can depend on whether the application is statically or dynamically linked. It is not clear whether binary compatibility will continue to be supported in future releases of Solaris.

Of course, the greatest hope for the interoperability of different operating systems lies with the Java programming language, developed by Sun. Starting life as the "Oak" project, Java promises a "write once, run anywhere" platform, which means that an application compiled on Windows NT, for example, can be copied to Solaris 9 and executed without modification and without recompilation. Even in the 1970s, when C was being implemented far and wide across different hardware platforms, it was often possible to transfer source and recompile it without modification, but binary compatibility was never achieved. The secret to Java's success is the two-stage compile and interpretation process, which differs from many other development environments. Java source is compiled on the source platform to an intermediary bytecode format, which can then be transferred to any other platform and interpreted by a Java Virtual Machine (JVM). Many software vendors, including SunSoft and Microsoft, have declared support for the Java platform, even though some vendors have failed to meet the specifications laid out by Sun. Until a standard is developed for Java, Sun will retain control over its direction, which is a risk for non-Solaris sites especially. However, Solaris 9 installations should have few qualms about integrating Java technology within their existing environments. With the release of free development tools, development in Java is becoming easier for C and experienced UNIX developers. For example, the Solaris Management Console, covered in Chapter 29, uses Java technology to build its interface, shown in Figure 1-2. Java is the best attempt yet at complete binary compatibility between operating systems and architectures.

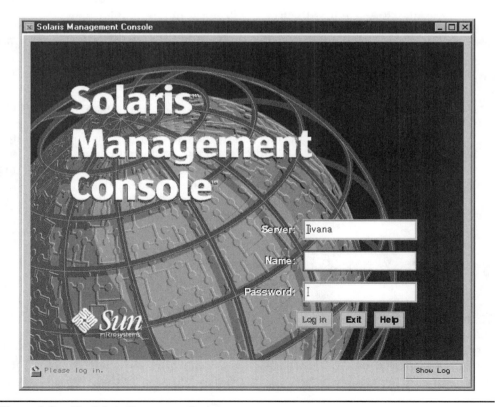

Figure 1-2   The Solaris Management Console

Recent Solaris Innovations

Recent Solaris releases have contained many enhancements and new features compared to earlier versions, on both the client and server side—and specifically for administrators. For example, StarOffice is now included with the operating system distribution, as well as providing support for integration between personal organization applications and the new generation of "Palm computing" devices. On the server side, Solaris now ships with the Apache web server installed, and runs Linux applications through *lxrun*. Security is overhauled with the inclusion of Kerberos version 5, OpenSSH, and IPSec for both IPv4 and IPv6, which are also supported, making it easy to create virtual private networks through improved tunneling and encryption technologies. Developers will appreciate the inclusion of a Perl interpreter, other popular tools released under the GNU license, and the Java 2 SDK.

New Client Tools

Solaris has always been known as a server-based operating system. Its history and involvement with powering the Internet and providing a reliable platform for database servers and client/server applications are the characteristics that most administrators would associate with Solaris. However, Solaris 9 has brought about many improvements on the desktop as well, with further integration and support for standards-based, CDE-based applications (in contrast to the old proprietary OpenWindows system). Further support for multimedia is also provided, with facilities for MIDI audio and streamed video supporting many popular formats. CDE support for interfacing with productivity applications hosted on mobile computing devices, such as Palm, is also provided in conjunction with CDE.

Of course, the biggest desktop announcement of 1999 was Sun's purchase of the StarOffice suite from Star Division, and their decision to both ship it for free to the general public and to include it as an integral part of Solaris 8. StarOffice is now distributed by Sun for a much cheaper price than equivalent office productivity suites. In addition, Sun is promoting the Sun Ray client as a cost-effective alternative to desktop computing based around legacy PC architectures, with clients centrally managed by a departmental server (such as an E450). This approach promises to revolutionize the way that many organizations currently (and often inconsistently) manage software updates, patches, and distribution.

 TIP With the security and reliability of Solaris on the server side, the Solaris desktop will continue to see innovation in Solaris 9 and beyond.

StarOffice

StarOffice is a complete office productivity suite, including integrated word processing, spreadsheet, database, presentation, formula rendering, image processing, and web page design applications. A big advantage is the capability to import existing documents from office packages distributed by other vendors (including Microsoft Office products). The interoperability between StarOffice and competing products is also reflected in the cross-platform implementation of the product. In addition to running on Solaris, it is also available for OS/2, Linux, and Microsoft Windows computers. Reflecting its European roots, StarOffice natively supports many different languages, including Dutch, English, French, German, Italian, Portuguese, Spanish, and Swedish.

Creating a new "StarBase" database is easy: Just select the appropriate option from the menu, and a Database Design Wizard appears. Using a wizard makes creating a database very easy for novice users, and although the StarOffice database is not an industrial strength server, it is perfectly adequate for routine administrative tasks such as creating customer contact and product description tables.

StarOffice has some advantages over competing products. For example, it has the capability to render quite complex formulas through an innovative formula painter. You can simply select the appropriate function and enter the appropriate arguments. In addition, you can combine more than one predicate to form complex expressions. For example, you can construct a combined cubic root and exponential function expression in just a few keystrokes.

StarOffice also has the capability to design and publish web pages as new documents or to export existing documents. In fact, you can create an entire site by using the wizards that are supplied as part of the HTML editing package. The first web site wizard screen demonstrates the wide variety of templates available through the program.

Although StarOffice comes with complete online documentation and help, you can find further information regarding StarOffice at the StarOffice web center (**http://www.sun .com/staroffice**).

Mobile Computing

The Solaris Operating Environment includes a number of enhancements to the common desktop environment (CDE). Personal digital assistant (PDA) support synchronizes data (using PDASync) from most Palm computing devices with the CDE textpad, calendar, mail, and address book. This enables Palm users to transfer data seamlessly between the desktop and the palmtop, previously a feature of traditionally desktop-oriented operating systems. PDASync is based around 3Com's HotSync technology, making synchronization possible with a single click.

Sun has also released the "K" Java Virtual Machine (KVM), which will allow Java developers on Solaris to easily port their Java 2 applications to mobile computing platforms, including Palm. The KVM forms part of the Java 2 Micro Edition suite, and has a small memory and disk footprint (that is, less than 128K RAM). For further information regarding interoperability between Solaris and mobile computing devices using Java, see the KVM home page at **http://java.sun.com/products/kvm/**.

PC Support

Although Solaris 8 was coreleased for SPARC and Intel platforms at the same time, Sun has indicated that Solaris 9 for SPARC will be released on a different schedule than Solaris 9 for Intel. Thus, Intel users may need to wait before they can upgrade from Solaris 8 to Solaris 9. However, PC networks that require a reliable server system for web, database, file, and application serving can make use of proven Solaris reliability and high availability by using Solaris 9 on a SPARC server. In addition, Solaris for Intel provides a cost-effective alternative to SPARC hardware, and can act as a "drop-in" replacement for other server operating systems that also use Intel hardware. For example, the Samba software running on a Solaris server provides many key networking services to PCs, which are normally provided by NT server systems. These services include the following:

- Primary and backup domain control, enabling centralized sharing of user and resource database for department-sized workgroups

- Security and authentication using security identifiers for generating genuinely unique accounts

- Support for legacy networking protocols, such as NetBIOS, and naming services such as WINS

- NT file and print services

With the reliability and scalability of Solaris providing these basic network services for existing PC networks, many organizations are centralizing their server software around Solaris, because the same server can provide Samba services to PCs while performing other tasks (such as database serving).

There are several good reasons for using Solaris 9 as a server platform for PCs. First, viruses written for a PC platform are both physically and logically ineffective against Solaris, because the compiled code base is different for both operating systems. In addition, even if the same code base was shared (for example, a rogue Java application executed from a remote shell), the Solaris authentication and identification system does not permit unprivileged users to write to system areas, preventing any malicious damage from occurring to the server. Second, Solaris provides packet-filtering technology that prevents network intruders from browsing internal networks, whereas PCs may freely broadcast and exchange information between each other.

One of the most exciting innovations in the new collaborative technology that accompanies Solaris 9 is WebNFS, literally "network file serving" through the Web. WebNFS provides a standard file system for the World Wide Web, making it easy for users within the same building, or across the globe, to exchange data in a secure way, using industry standard clients. In fact, existing applications can be "webified" by gaining access to virtual remote file systems, by using an extension of Sun's original NFS system.

Server Tools

As always, Sun has released a new batch of server-side products to improve on the existing functionality of Solaris. Of interest to those in the data center will be the new 3.0 release of Sun's "Cluster" product, which offers high system availability through management of hardware redundancy. This offering caters largely to the corporate world, but developers who are more interested in championing open source technologies will also be pleased with the inclusion of *lxrun*, a platform for binary compatibility between Linux applications and the Solaris operating environment. Originally developed for UNIX systems distributed by the Santa Cruz Operation (SCO), *lxrun* allows applications developed for

Linux, and released with a binary-only code base, to be executed natively on the Solaris Intel platform without recompilation or modification. This will ultimately lead to a greater exchange of technology and ideas between Solaris and Linux users.

Clustering Technology

Increased performance is often gained by the use of hardware redundancy, which can be achieved on a file system-by-file system basis, by using a software solution, such as DiskSuite, or a hardware-based solution, such as an A1000 or T3 RAID appliance. This allows partitions to be actively mirrored so that in the event of a hardware failure, you can rapidly resume service restore missing data.

This approach is fine for single-server systems that do not require close to 100-percent uptime. However, for mission-critical applications, where the integrity of the whole server is at stake, it makes sense to invest in clustering technology. Quite simply, clusters are what the name suggests—groups of similar servers (or "nodes") that have similar function, and that share responsibility for providing system and application services. Clustering is commonly found in the financial world, where downtime is measured in hundreds of thousands of dollars, and not in minutes. Large organizations need to undertake a cost-benefit analysis to determine whether clustering is an effective technology for their needs. However, Sun has made the transition to clustering easier by integrating the Cluster product with Solaris 9.

Solaris 9 ships with Cluster 3.0, which features a clustered virtual file system, and cluster-wide load balancing. For more information on introducing clustering technology using Sun Cluster 3.0, see Paul Korzeniowski's technical article at **http://www.sun.com/ clusters/article/**.

lxrun

One of the advantages of Solaris for Intel over its SPARC companion is the greater interoperability between computers based on Intel architectures. This means that there is greater potential for cooperation between Linux, operating on Intel, and Solaris, also operating on Intel. This potential has been realized recently with the efforts of Steve Ginzburg and Solaris engineers, who developed *lxrun*, which remaps system calls embedded in Linux software binaries to those appropriate for the Solaris environment. This means that Linux binaries can run without recompilation or modification on Solaris. In some ways, *lxrun* is like the Java Virtual Machine in that Linux applications execute through a layer that separates the application from the operating system. This means that your favorite Linux applications are now directly available through Solaris, including the following:

- KDE
- Gnome
- WordPerfect 7 and 8
- Applix
- Quake 2
- GIMP

For more information on *lxrun*, see its home page at **http://www.ugcs.caltech.edu/~steven/lxrun/**.

Security Innovations

Security is a major concern for Solaris administrators. The Internet is rapidly expanding with the new IPv6 protocol set to completely supersede IPv4 sometime in the next few years. This will make many more addresses available for Internet hosts than are currently available. It also means that the number of crackers, thieves, and rogue users will also increase exponentially. Solaris 9 prepares your network for this "virtual onslaught" by embracing IPv6, not only for its autoconfiguration and network numbering features, but also because of the built-in security measures that form part of the protocol. In particular, authentication is a key issue after the many highly publicized IP-spoofing breaches reported in the popular press over the past few years. A second layer of authentication for internal networks and intranets is provided in Solaris 9 by the provision of Kerberos version 5 clients and daemons. Previous releases, such as Solaris 7, included support for Kerberos version 4 only. OpenSSH is a key development in the remote access arena.

Kerberos Version 5

Kerberos is the primary means of network authentication employed by many organizations to centralize authentication services. As a protocol, it is designed to provide strong authentication for client/server applications by using secret-key cryptography. Recall that Kerberos is designed to provide authentication to hosts inside and outside a firewall, as long as the appropriate realms have been created. The protocol requires a certificate granting and validation system based around "tickets," which are distributed between clients and the server. A connection request from a client to a server takes a convoluted but secure route from a centralized authentication server before being forwarded to the target server. This ticket authorizes the client to request a specific service from a specific host, generally for a specific time period. A common analogy is a parking ticket machine that grants the drivers of motor vehicles permission to park on a particular street for one or two hours only.

Kerberos version 5 contains many enhancements over Kerberos version 4, including ticket renewal, removing some of the overhead involved in repetitive network requests. In addition, there is a pluggable authentication module, featuring support for RPC. The new version of Kerberos also provides both server- and user-level authentication, with a role-based access control feature that assigns access rights and permissions more stringently, ensuring system integrity. In addition to advances on the software front, Solaris 9 also provides integrated support for Kerberos and Smart card technology using the Open Card Framework (OCF) 1.1. More information concerning Kerberos is available from MIT at **http://web.mit.edu/network/kerberos-form.html**.

IPv6

IPv6, described in RFC 2471, is the replacement IP protocol for IPv4, which is currently deployed worldwide. The Internet relies on IP for negotiating many transport-related transactions on the Internet, including routing and the Domain Name Service. This means that host information is often stored locally (and inefficiently) at each network node. It is clearly important to establish a protocol that is more general in function, but more centralized for administration, and can deal with the expanding requirements of the Internet.

One of the growing areas of the Internet is obviously the number of hosts that need to be addressed; many subnets are already exhausted, and the situation is likely to get worse. In addition, every IP address needs to be manually allocated to each individual machine on the Internet, which makes the use of addresses within a subnet sparse and less than optimal. Clearly, there is a need for a degree of centralization when organizing IP addresses that can be handled through local administration, and through protocols like Dynamic Host Configuration Protocol (DHCP). However, one of the key improvements of IPv6 over IPv4 is its autoconfiguration capability, which makes it easier to configure entire subnets and to renumber existing hosts. In addition, security is now included at the IP level, making host-to-host authentication more efficient and reliable, even allowing for data encryption.

One way that this is achieved is by authentication header extensions: this allows a target host to determine whether a packet actually originates from a source host. This prevents common attacks, such as IP spoofing and denial of service, and reduces reliance on a third-party firewall by locking in security at the packet level. Tools are also included with Solaris 9 to assist with IPv4 to IPv6 migration.

What's New in Solaris 9

Each new release of Solaris brings about changes at the client, server, and system level. These changes affect users, administrators, and developers in different ways. For example, Solaris 9 introduces a completely new multithreading library. This will affect users of multithreaded applications, such as Java servlets, by increasing response time and reducing errors. It will affect system administrators, who will need to update *LD_LIBRARY _PATH* variables and check the dependencies of existing libraries. It will also affect developers, who will need to recode some existing multithreaded applications as well as adjust to coding with a new API.

The following sections discuss products and services released for the first time with Solaris 9.

Resource Manager

The Resource Manager extends a number of existing tools that provide for monitoring and allocation of system resources to various tasks and services. This is particularly useful in high-end systems, where a large pool of resources can be allocated to specific processes. Although the existing `nice` command allows priorities to be set on specific processes, and prstat displays the resources used by each process, the Resource Manager is an integrated toolkit, featuring a scheduler, and accounting and billing tools. Again, although accounting tools are supplied as part of the standard Solaris toolkit, they have never been integrated with useful real-time monitoring tools. The Resource Manager also features a command-line interface and optional GUI for configuring and monitoring resource allocation and usage.

Linux Compatibility Tools

In addition to the *lxrun* binary execution environment for Solaris Intel, a number of libraries are now provided as part of the standard Solaris distribution to ensure that Linux applications can be linked and executed under Solaris. These libraries include glib, GTK+, JPEG, Tcl/Tk, libpng, libtif, and libxml12. These enhancements will improve interoperability between Linux and Solaris SPARC systems.

iPlanet Directory Server

The iPlanet Directory Server (iDS) is a commercial-grade LDAP solution for providing directory storage and access for hundreds and thousands of users. LDAP extends traditional Solaris directory service tools, such as NIS+, by using the standard LDAP protocol. iDS provides developers with C and Java APIs to create LDAP-compatible applications, so that they can maintain a single repository of authentication and identification data. In addition, iDS can be integrated with other iPlanet products, such as the proxy server, to ensure that Internet users have managed, rather than unfettered, access to the Internet during work hours.

Volume Manager

Although software RAID support has been previously provided in Solaris through Solstice Disk Suite (SDS), this product has now been superseded by Volume Manager (VM). VM supports RAID levels 0, 1, and 5, and allows a wide range of mirroring and striping facilities. Cross-grade and migration tools are also available to assist SDS users who are currently using metadevices as their primary virtual file systems for boot and nonboot disks and their associated slices.

Live Upgrade

Live Upgrade allows a Solaris system to continue running while components of its operating system are upgraded. This is particularly useful in production environments, where system downtime costs money and customers, particularly on shared platforms like the StarFire. A separate boot environment is constructed during runtime, after which the system is rebooted with the new configuration, thereby minimizing downtime.

Smaller Installation Footprint

In a move that defies the trend towards bloatware, Sun has actually reduced the size of the minimal installation, so that the system can be installed faster and with fewer of the optional features installed. This is particularly important where single- or limited-purpose servers are concerned, because they require only the base operating system packages, and one or two options that may be installed at a later time.

Virtual Memory Sizing

Improvements have been made in the processes used to allocate virtual memory by swapping to disk. The previous 8K limit has now been removed—basically, any page size that is supported by your hardware will be supported under Solaris. This means that memory-intensive applications should see improved performance, particularly where they used virtual memory to support their operations.

New Multithreading Library

Solaris provides advanced lightweight process support in the form of threads. Threads are used by multithreaded applications, such as the Java Virtual Machine (JVM), to support many small parallel operations being performed simultaneously, without requiring the spawning of multiple processes. The new *libthread* supersedes previous versions, improving speed, and making the most of modern multitasking CPUs.

Internet Key Exchange (IKE)

Virtual private network (VPN) technology is also provided with Solaris 9, using IPSec. IPSec is compatible with both IPv4 and IPv6, making it easier to connect hosts using both new and existing networking protocols. IPSec consists of a combination of IP tunneling and encryption technologies to create sessions across the Internet that are as secure as possible. IP tunneling makes it difficult for unauthorized users (such as intruders) to access data being transmitted between two hosts on different sites. This is supported by encryption technologies and an improved method for exchanging keys, using the Internet key exchange (IKE) method. IKE facilitates interprotocol negotiation and selection during host-to-host transactions, ensuring data integrity. By implementing encryption at the IP layer, it will be even more difficult for rogue users to "pretend" to be a target host, intercepting data with authorization.

Open Secure Shell (OpenSSH)

Although secure shell (SSH) has been provided for several years at **www.ssh.com** for Solaris, Sun has finally released OpenSSH, which is integrated into Solaris 9. OpenSSH allows terminal sessions to be encrypted using public-key cryptography to ensure that packets exchanged across the network cannot be easily decrypted, even if they are intercepted by a hostile third party. OpenSSH is a vast improvement over traditional remote access tools, such as telnet, and all sites should now switch off telnet in favor of OpenSSH.

Web-Based Enterprise Management (WBEM)

Solaris provides WBEM tools to ease the administrative burden of managing multiple servers and networks in a production environment. WBEM tools make use of Internet protocols and data descriptors, like HTTP and XML, to ensure that networks and servers can be managed using a unified, single method.

Sources for Additional Information

In this chapter, we have so far examined the history of UNIX and what distinguishes UNIX systems from other operating systems. We have also traced the integration of both "flavors" of UNIX into the current Solaris 9 release. With the ever-rising popularity of Solaris 9, there are many web sites, mailing lists, and documentation sets that new and experienced users will find useful when trying to capitalize on an investment in Sun equipment or the latest Solaris 9 operating environment. In this section, we present some pointers to the main Internet sites where you can find reliable information about Solaris 9.

Sun Documentation/Sun Sites

Unlike some operating systems, Solaris 9 comes with a complete set of online reference manuals and user guides on the AnswerBook CD-ROM, which is distributed with all Solaris 9 releases (Intel and SPARC). The AnswerBooks are in PDF format, and cover a wide range of system administration topics, including the following:

- Binary compatibility guide
- JumpStart guide
- Mail server guide
- Naming services guide
- NFS administration guide
- NIS+ guide
- SunShield security guide
- System administration guides
- TCP/IP guide
- Troubleshooting guides

A set of user guides is also available on AnswerBook:

- OpenWindows user guide
- CDE user guide
- CDE transition guide
- Power management user guide

Developers will also be pleased with the AnswerBook coverage for development issues:

- A 64-bit developer's guide
- Device drivers guide

- Internationalization guide
- SPARC assembly language guide (yes, it is still included for the adventurous)
- STREAMS guide
- Source compatibility guide
- WebNFS developer's guide

Hardware maintenance and technical staff will find the hardware reference guides invaluable.

The best thing about the AnswerBook series is that they are available for download and interactive searching through **http://docs.sun.com/**. This means that if you are working in the field and you need to consult a guide, you don't need to carry around a CD-ROM or a printed manual. Just connect through the Internet and read the guide in HTML, or download and retrieve a PDF format chapter or two.

The two main Sun sites for Solaris 9 are at **http://www.sun.com/solaris** (for SPARC users) and **http://www.sun.com/intel** (for Intel users). Both of these pages contain internal and external links that will be useful in finding out more information about Solaris 9 and any current offerings. The Sun Developer Connection is a useful resource that users can join to obtain special pricing and to download many software components for free.

Web Sites

Many third-party web sites are also available that deal exclusively with Sun and Solaris 9. For example, if you are looking for a Solaris 9 FAQ, or pointers to Sun information, try the Sun Help site (**http://www.sunhelp.org/**). If it's free precompiled software that you're after, check the Sun Freeware site (**http://www.sunfreeware.com/**) or one of the many mirrors. Here you can find the GNU C compiler in a precompiled package (Sun dropped the compiler from Solaris 1.*x* to Solaris 8, leading to the most frequently asked question on many Solaris 9 forums: "Why doesn't the Solaris C compiler work?"). For Solaris for Intel users, there is also an archive of precompiled binaries available at **ftp://x86.cs.duke.edu/pub/solaris-x86/bins/**.

In case you are interested in seeing what the pioneers of UNIX are doing these days, check out the home pages of these famous UNIX developers:

- **Brian Kernighan**   **http://cm.bell-labs.com/cm/cs/who/bwk/index.html**
- **Dennis Ritchie**   **http://cm.bell-labs.com/cm/cs/who/dmr/index.html**
- **Ken Thompson**   **http://cm.bell-labs.com/who/ken/**

A list of Solaris resources for this book is maintained at **www.cassowary.net/solaris**.

USENET

USENET is a great resource for asking questions, finding answers, and contributing your skills and expertise to help others in need. This is not necessarily a selfless act—there will always be a Solaris 9 question that you can't answer, and if you've helped others before, they will remember you. The **comp.unix.solaris** forum is the best USENET group for Solaris 9 information and discussion. The best source of practical Solaris 9 information is contained in the Solaris FAQ, maintained by the legendary Casper Dik. You can always find the latest version at **http://www.wins.uva.nl/pub/solaris/solaris2/**. For Solaris for Intel users, there is the less formal **alt.solaris.x86** forum, where you won't be flamed for asking questions about dual booting with Microsoft Windows, or mentioning non-SPARC hardware. For Solaris Intel, the best FAQ is at **http://sun.pmbc.com/faq/**. For both SPARC and Intel platforms, there is a **comp.sys.sun.admin** group that deals with system administration issues, which also has a FAQ available at **ftp://thor.ece.uc.edu/pub/sun-faq/FAQs**.

Mailing Lists

Mailing lists are a good way of meeting colleagues and engaging in discussions in a threaded format. The Sun Manager's List is the most famous Sun list, and contains questions, answers, and (most importantly) summaries of previous queries. All Solaris-related topics are covered. Details are available at **ftp://ftp.cs.toronto.edu/pub/jdd/sun-managers/faq**. In addition, there is a Solaris for x86 mailing list archived at **http://www.egroups.com/group/solarisonintel/**, which has some great tips, tricks, and advice for those who are new to Solaris 9, or who are having difficulties with specific hardware configurations.

Solaris Certification Exams

Now that we've examined what Solaris is, we'll look at the certification process for Solaris. The three exams we will cover in this book are

- Sun Certified System Administrator for the Solaris 9 Operating Environment Part I (310-014)
- Sun Certified System Administrator for the Solaris 9 Operating Environment Part II (310-015)
- Sun Certified Network Administrator for the Solaris 9 Operating Environment Part II (310-016)

These exams were also available for Solaris 8 and previous releases. The exams will be referred to as Sysadmin I, Sysadmin II, and Network Admin throughout this book. It's important to note that a pass on both Sysadmin I and Sysadmin II is required for full certification as a system administrator. These two exams are prerequisites for taking the Network Admin exam.

There are several ways to book a test. You must contact Sun Educational Services through one of the following ways and purchase a voucher:

- Snail: UBRM12-175, 500 Eldorado Blvd., Broomfield, CO 80021
- Phone: (800) 422-8020 or (303) 464-4097

- Fax: (303) 464-4490
- WWW: http://suned.sun.com/USA/certification/

Once you have a voucher for the test you wish to take, you need to contact a Prometric Test Center at a location convenient to you. You can register online with Prometric at **http://www.2test.com/**. Once you have attended the center and taken both Sysadmin I and Sysadmin II, you'll be certified immediately as a system administrator if you have passed both exams. Of course, you don't need to take them on the same day: it makes sense to attempt Sysadmin I and pass it before attempting Sysadmin II. Since Sysadmin I is a prerequisite for Sysadmin II, you won't be able to book a sitting for Sysadmin II until your Sysadmin I results are certified. Once you have completed the two exams, and you have become a certified system administrator, you'll need to take the Network Admin exam to become certified as a network administrator.

The current cost for attempting each exam is $150. Sysadmin I has 57 questions, comprising multiple choice, free response, and drag-and-drop types. You will need a score of at least 64 percent to pass the test, and you will only have 90 minutes in which to complete it. Sysadmin II has 58 questions, comprising multiple choice, free response, and drag-and-drop types. You will need a score of at least 65 percent to pass the test, and you will only have 90 minutes in which to complete it. Network Admin has 41 questions, comprising multiple choice, free response, and drag-and-drop types. You will need a score of at least 68 percent to pass the test, and you will only have 120 minutes in which to complete it.

Solaris Exam Preparation Courses

There are three preparation courses available for Solaris certification:

- Solaris 9 System Administration I (SA-238)
- Solaris 9 System Administration II (SA-288)
- Solaris 9 Operating Environment TCP/IP Network Administration (SA-389)

Let's examine what material is covered in each exam.

Fundamentals of Solaris 9 Operating Environment for System Administrators (SA-118)

If you're completely new to Solaris, you may benefit from taking one or more of the exams that do not lead to a specific certification test. The Fundamentals of Solaris 9 Operating Environment for System Administrators (SA-118) is one such course. It is designed to endow up and coming administrators with basic UNIX skills, including the following:

- Navigating the hierarchical file system
- Setting file permissions
- Using the vi visual editor

- Using UNIX shells
- Understanding Solaris network facilities

After completing the course, students should feel confident performing the following tasks:

- Change settings in configuration files
- Create new directories
- Create new text files and edit existing files using vi
- Identify and send signals to user processes
- Move around mounted file systems
- Set permissions on existing files
- Use a shell to execute commands
- Use the Common desktop environment (CDE)

Solaris 9 System Administration I (SA-238)

The SA-238 course aims to build a set of core skills required to administer stand-alone Solaris systems. Typically, these are the skills required to install and run a single Solaris system, including:

- Management of disks, file systems, and partitions
- Backup and restore techniques
- User and group administration
- Hardware device configuration
- Process management and operations

The course lasts for five days and costs $2,495. After completing the course, newly skilled sysadmins should feel confident performing the following tasks:

- Add users and groups to a system
- Add new packages
- Back up a system, and recover a lost file system
- Change a system's run level (init state)
- Configure hardware devices
- Control user and system processes
- Manage system printing
- Mount file systems
- Patch existing packages

- Recover damaged file systems using fsck
- Review disk layout using format
- Secure a system
- Set up system-wide shell configurations
- Shut down a system
- Understand client/server architectures
- Understand the root file system and the UNIX directory structure
- Use eeprom to set boot parameters
- Use file permissions to implement file security

The course consists of 17 different modules, including the following topics:

- Module 1: Introduction to Solaris 9 Operating Environment Administration
- Module 2: Adding Users
- Module 3: System Security
- Module 4: The Directory Hierarchy
- Module 5: Device Configuration
- Module 6: Disks, Slices, and Format
- Module 7: Solaris ufs File Systems
- Module 8: Mounting File Systems
- Module 9: Maintaining File Systems
- Module 10: Scheduled Process Control
- Module 11: The Print Service
- Module 12: The Boot PROM
- Module 13: System Initialization of the boot process
- Module 14: Installing the Solaris 9 Operating Environment on a Stand-alone System
- Module 15: Installation of Software Packages
- Module 16: Administration of Software Patches
- Module 17: Backup and Recovery

Solaris 9 System Administration II (SA-288)

The SA-288 course aims to build a set of core skills required to administer networked Solaris systems. Typically, these are the skills required to install and run multiple Solaris systems, and Solaris networks. The course lasts for five days and costs $2,495. After completing the course, newly skilled network admins should feel confident performing the following tasks:

- Centralize home directory access using the automounter
- Configure the major naming services
- Installation of multiple Solaris client systems using JumpStart
- Installation of Solaris server systems
- Manage systems remotely
- Share disks using the Network File System (NFS) protocol
- Use the system log facility
- Using the admintool
- Volume management

The course consists of 13 different modules, including the following topics:

- Module 1: The Solaris 9 Network Environment
- Module 2: Network Models
- Module 3: Solaris syslog
- Module 4: Introduction to Virtual Disk Management
- Module 5: Introduction to Swap Space and Pseudo File Systems
- Module 6: Configuring the NFS Environment
- Module 7: CacheFS File Systems
- Module 8: Using Automount
- Module 9: Naming Services Overview
- Module 10: NIS Configuration
- Module 11: Solstice AdminSuite
- Module 12: JumpStart
- Module 13: System Administration Workshop

Solaris 9 Operating Environment TCP/IP Network Administration (SA-389)

The SA-389 course aims to build a set of core skills required to administer Solaris networks. Typically, these are the skills required to install and run networks that are based around Solaris systems. The course lasts for five days and costs $2,795. The course consists of 14 different modules, including the following topics:

- Module 1: Network Models
- Module 2: Introduction to Local Area Networks

- Module 3: Ethernet Interface
- Module 4: ARP and RARP
- Module 5: Internet Layer
- Module 6: Routing
- Module 7: Transport Layer
- Module 8 Client-Server Model
- Module 9: DHCP
- Module 10: Introduction to Network Management Tools
- Module 11: Domain Name System
- Module 12: Network Time Protocol (NTP)
- Module 13: Network Troubleshooting
- Module 14: IPv6

Exam Tips and Tricks

A comprehensive strategy is required to ensure success in passing the Solaris certification exams. This strategy should be based around at least some of the following components:

- Take the preparatory courses
- Practice your skills on a Solaris system and/or network
- Read books on Solaris (including this book)
- Read man pages
- Practice the questions in this book
- Sign up for a simulated exam service

Without a study plan, even experienced Solaris system administrators may fail the certification exam. This is because the exams are based on the "official" Sun line on many system administration issues, which may differ substantially from what is used in the field. For example, many sites don't use the Internet super daemon inetd to provide remote access facilities and other network services.

Taking at least some of the preparatory courses ensures that you are familiar with most of the material that is found in the certification exams. This material is prepared by Sun Educational Services, the same group who develops the exams. Thus, a certain degree of overlap should be anticipated between course materials and exam contents. However, it should be noted that not all of the course material will be examined, and that some process-based questions can only be effectively answered by practical experience using and administering Solaris systems.

This is why it is critical that, as a prospective Solaris administrator, you gain access to Solaris as a user, and preferably as an administrator. Even supervised administrative access, with a senior staff member or colleague assisting you, will give you the experience and perspective you need to be able to answer questions on operational issues.

 EXAM TIP You cannot expect to pass the exams if you've never used a Solaris system in real life.

You should also read widely on Solaris. This includes companion volumes such as *Solaris 9: The Complete Reference, Solaris 9 Essential Skills,* and *Solaris Administration: A Beginner's Guide,* all published by Osborne/McGraw-Hill. These books touch on some of the same material as this book, but cover some topics in more depth and contain longer and more detailed examples.

Reading man pages is an essential review process for memorizing command options. This is because some exam questions may not just pertain to the Solaris command set, but also to the multitude of options available for each command. You should consult the man pages when you're using commands to ensure that you're using the most appropriate options for a specific command. However, if you'd like to consult man pages offline, *UNIX in a Nutshell,* published by O'Reilly, contains many annotated man pages. Note that these are not Solaris-specific, and some options may not work on Solaris 9.

It's important to attempt the questions contained in this book as if you were taking the exam. Sitting for several two-three hours sessions under exam conditions will help you to develop strategies for best answering the questions contained in the test. In addition to the practice questions contained in this book, it may be useful for you to purchase a subscription to one of the "online" certification practice tests, offered at the following sites:

- http://networkessentials.com/certified/sca/
- http://www.inlink.com/~hoechstj/solaris/
- http://www.solariscert.com/
- http://www.solarisprep.com/
- http://www.sunguru.com/
- http://www.learnsolaris.com/

One excellent way to determine whether your skills are up to speed is to join the **comp.unix.solaris** USENET forum, and see whether you can answer some of the more frequently asked questions there!

The Internet also has some great sites. "Learn more about Solaris" is from the Sun Microsystems home page for Solaris (**http://www.sun.com/solaris**). Some key documents within the Sun site for Solaris include the following:

- Solaris overview (**http://www.sun.com/software/solaris/ds/ds-sol8oe/**)
- Solaris downloads (**http://www.sun.com/software/solaris/downloads.html**)
- Solaris support (**http://www.sun.com/software/solaris/support.html**)
- Solaris education (**http://www.sun.com/software/solaris/education.html**)
- Solaris clustering (**http://www.sun.com/software/fullmoon/**)
- Solaris Intel platform (**http://www.sun.com/software/intel**)

Possibly the most important link on the Sun site is the documentation (**http://docs .sun.com/**). Here, you can interactively search or browse all of the Sun documentation and/or download entire manuals in PDF format.

How to Find Out More

The main site for all Sun technologies is **http://www.sun.com/**. For further information on Java technologies, users should browse Sun's Java site at **http://java.sun.com/**. If you prefer an independent evaluation of Sun technologies, check out the Sun World site at **http://www.sunworld.com**, or Java technologies at **http://www.javaworld.com/**.

Summary

This chapter was intended to introduce the main features of the Solaris 9 operating environment and the SunOS 5.9 operating system. Solaris has been at the forefront of change in enterprise computing for many years, and has continued to improve and enhance its features while maintaining consistency in its core operations.

System Concepts

In this chapter, you will
- Understand the role of the kernel, shell and file system
- Review commonly used Solaris shells
- Investigate the distinction between a multiuser system and a multitasking system
- Explore the role of clients and servers
- Define hosts, hostnames, networks, and IP addresses
- Explore the range of SPARC and Intel hardware supported by Solaris

Understanding what makes Solaris different from other operating systems is critical to appreciating why it is the environment of choice for high-availability client/server environments. In this chapter, we review the terms used to describe Solaris systems and major components, as well as networking terminology associated with Solaris networks. Understanding these terms will ensure that you understand some of the concepts discussed in later chapters. Much Solaris terminology is particular to the context of Solaris systems, and some generic terms may have one meaning in Solaris but another meaning for other operating systems. For example, while the term *host* may be used generically to identify any system attached to a network, it may be used in Solaris, to refer to *multihomed hosts*.

The Kernel

Operating systems are the building blocks of computer systems, and they provide the interface between user applications and computer hardware. Solaris is a multiuser, multitasking operating system developed and sold by Sun Microsystems (**http://www.sun.com/**), and it is one implementation of the UNIX operating system that draws on both the System V (AT&T) and Berkeley (BSD) systems. Solaris has evolved from little more than a research project to become the dominant UNIX operating system in the international marketplace.

Solaris 9 is the latest in a long line of operating environment releases that are based around the SunOS operating system, which is currently in version 5.9. Solaris is commonly found in large corporations and educational institutions that require concurrent, multiuser access on individual hosts and between hosts connected via the Internet.

Many desktop computer users have never heard of the word *Sun* in the context of computing, nor are they usually familiar with the term *Solaris* as an operating environment.

However, almost every time that an Internet user sends an e-mail message or opens a file from a networked server running Sun's Network File System (NFS) product, Solaris is transparently supporting the Internet applications that allow these things to happen. In the enterprise computing industry, Sun is synonymous with highly available, highly reliable performance hardware, while Solaris is often the operating environment of choice to support database servers and application servers. Sun's hardware solutions are based around the SPARC and UltraSPARC integrated circuit technologies, which can currently support more than 64 processors in a single server system, such as the E10000 StarFire configuration.

UNIX is hard to define because different vendors have historically introduced different features to arrive at the entities that most users would think of as UNIX. However, it is easy enough to list the fundamental characteristics that are common to all UNIX and UNIX-like systems:

- They have a *kernel*, written in the C programming language, which mainly manages input/output processing rather than being a complete operating system. The kernel has ultimate responsibility for allocating system resources to complete various tasks.

- They have a hierarchical file system, which begins with a root directory and from which the branches of all other directories (and file systems) are mounted.

- System hardware devices are represented logically on the file system as special files (such as */dev/pty*, for pseudoterminals).

- They are process-based, with all services and user shells being represented by a single identifying number (the process ID, or PID).

- They share a set of command-line utilities that can be used for text and numeric processing of various kinds, such as *troff*, *col*, *cat*, *head*, *tbl*, and so on.

- User processes can be spawned from a shell, such as the Bourne shell, which interactively executes application programs.

- Multiple processes can be executed concurrently by a single user and sent into the background by using the & operator.

- Multiple users can execute commands concurrently by logging in from pseudoterminals.

Note that a graphical user interface (GUI) is not necessarily a defining feature of UNIX, unlike other desktop operating systems, which place much stock in "look and feel." Although CDE remains the default desktop for Solaris 9, Sun plans to integrate the GNOME window manager (**http://www.gnome.org/**) into future maintenance releases. GNOME is currently the leading desktop of Linux users. Integrating GNOME into Solaris 9 will lead to greater interoperability between Solaris and Linux systems, particularly in terms of GUI application development. It will also make porting GUI applications between Solaris and Intel easier, because Linux back-end applications have been able to be executed on Solaris Intel for some time by using *lxrun*.

The reasons for this distinction are largely historical and related to the UNIX design philosophy. For operating systems that are not layered, changing the window manager or even the look and feel involves rewriting significant portions of back-end code. In the Solaris environment, where the interface and display technologies are appropriately abstracted from the underlying kernel, moving from CDE to GNOME involves simply changing the command to initialize the X11 display manager; the kernel remains unmodified. The layering of the various components of a UNIX system is shown in Figure 2-1.

Broadly speaking, a UNIX system is layered according to applications that are invoked through user shells, which are managed by a kernel—which in turn uses file systems to create a persistence storage mechanism. Because the kernel provides the interface between shells and the file system, (and by extension, between applications and the file system), it is considered the central part of UNIX technology.

Solaris kernels can trace their origins to both the System V and BSD variants of UNIX, while Microsoft NT was based on the Virtual Memory System (VMS) kernel originally developed for the high-end VAX systems. Most kernels during the 1960s were written using assembly language or machine (binary) code, so the development of a high-level language for writing kernels (the C language) was one of the founding ideas of UNIX. This level of abstraction from hardware meant that kernels could be ported to other hardware platforms without having to be completely rewritten. The tradition of writing kernels in C continues today, with the Linux kernel (for example) being written in C. Obviously, a kernel alone is not a complete operating environment, so many additional applications (such as the visual editor, vi) were later added to what UNIX users would recognize as the suite of standard UNIX tools.

All UNIX systems have a kernel, which is the central logical processor that provides an interface between the system hardware, the system services, and the user shells that directly enable applications. For example, support for network interfaces is provided in the form of a kernel module and a device file that logically represents the physical device. Services are defined in the services database, and network daemons provide the final layer for supporting applications that use the network to transmit data. Since UNIX kernels are typically written in the C programming language, many systems-level applications and daemons are also written in C.

Of course, UNIX systems share some common characteristics with other operating systems, including the use of a hierarchical file system in which special files called *directories* are used to arrange related files logically. But UNIX has some distinctive features as well: explicit permissions to read, execute, and modify files on the UNIX file system can

Figure 2-1
Components of
a UNIX system

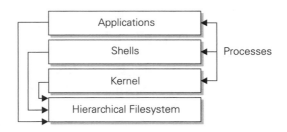

be granted to specific users or groups of users, making it easy to share work and collaborate with other users on the system.

Because UNIX was created by active developers, rather than by operating system gurus, the focus was on creating an operating system that suited a programmer's needs. A *Bell System Technical Journal* article in 1978 lists the following key guiding principles of UNIX development:

- Create small, self-contained programs that perform a single task. When a new task needs to be solved, either create a new program that performs it or combine tools from the toolset that already exists to arrive at a solution. This is a similar orientation to the current trend toward encapsulation and independent component building (such as Enterprise JavaBeans), where complicated systems are built from smaller interacting but logically independent modules.

- Programs should accept data from standard input and write to standard output; thus, programs can be "chained" to process each other's output sequentially. Interactive input should be avoided in favor of command-line options that specify a program's actions to be performed. Presentation should be separated from what a program is trying to achieve. These ideas are consistent with the concept of piping, which is still fundamental to the operation of user shells. For example, the output of the `ls` command to list all files in a directory can be "piped" using the "|" symbol to a program such as `grep`, to perform pattern matching. The number of pipes on a single command-line instruction is not limited.

- Creating a new operating system or program should be undertaken on a scale of weeks, not years—the creative spirit that leads to cohesive design and implementation should be exploited. If software doesn't work, don't be afraid to build something better. This process of iterative revisions of programs has resurfaced in recent years with the rise of object-oriented development.

- Make best use of all the tools available, rather than asking for more help. The motivation behind UNIX is to construct an operating system that supports the kinds of toolsets that are required for successful development.

This is not intended to be an exhaustive list of the kernel-oriented characteristics that define UNIX; however, these features are central to understanding the importance that UNIX developers often ascribe to the operating system. It is designed to be a programmer-friendly system.

The Shell

A key Solaris concept is the functional separation between the user interface and the operating system. This distinction means that a user can access a Solaris system by using either a terminal-based character user interface (CUI) or a high-resolution graphical user interface (GUI) without modifying the underlying operating system.

With so much attention paid to GUI, why are CUI environments still important to Solaris? Are they just a historical hangover that Windows has managed to overcome? Or are they simply the tools of choice for long-haired network administrators who have never used a mouse? In fact, mastering the Solaris command line is one of the effective tools available under any UNIX environment, and the good news is it's not that difficult to learn. Using the command line (or *shell*) has several advantages over GUI environments.

The shell is essential for programming repetitive tasks that can be performed laboriously through a GUI. For example, searching a file system for all document files that have changed each day and making a copy of all these files (with the extension *.doc*) to a backup directory (with the extension *.bak*) takes time.

The shell can be used to search for, modify, edit, and replace Solaris configuration files, which are typically storied in text format. This is much like the approach taken with Windows *.ini* configuration files, which were text-based. However, after Windows 95, Windows versions store configuration information in the Registry in a binary format, making it impossible to edit manually. All Solaris configuration files, including the startup scripts, are text-based.

The shell has a number of built-in commands that typically mirror those provided in the C programming language. This means that it is possible to write small programs as shell statements that are executed as sequential steps, without having to use a compiler (just like MS-DOS batch files are interpreted without requiring a compiler).

The shell can be used to launch applications that use a CUI, which is especially useful for logging onto a remote system and enabling access to the commands an administrator can use on the console, a valuable point in this era of global information systems. While Windows applications like Symantec's pcAnywhere can be used for remote access to the Windows Desktop, they don't easily support multiuser access (or multiuser access where one user requires a CUI and another a GUI).

The shell can be used to execute commands for which no equivalent GUI application exists. Although many operations could conceivably be performed using a GUI, it is usually easier to write a shell script than create a completely new GUI application.

Many applications in Solaris, Linux, and Windows are now available through a GUI interface. If you feel more comfortable using GUI interfaces, there is little reason to stop using them as long as you can find the tools to perform all of the tasks you need to undertake regularly, such as monitoring resource usage, setting process alarms and diagnostics, and/or remote access. However, if you want to make the most of Solaris and competently administer the system, you will need to become familiar with the shell and command-line utilities.

In keeping with the philosophy that different administrators have different needs and styles, Solaris makes several different shells available:

- **Bourne shell (sh)** The original UNIX shell used to write all system scripts by convention.

- **Korn shell (ksh)** Provides enhanced input/output features, including the `print` and `read` commands.

- **C shell (csh)** Offers a command syntax similar to the C programming language.

- **The Cornell shell (tcsh)**   Includes improved terminal handling compared to the original C shell.
- **Bourne Again shell (bash)**   An open source, much improved version of the Bourne shell.

Exercise 2-1

Find out if these shells are installed on your system, and what others might be supported. Precompiled binary shells can be downloaded from **www.sunfreeware.com**.

The File System

UNIX also features a hierarchical file system that makes it easy for you to separate related files logically into directories, which are themselves special files. While MS-DOS and similar operating systems feature a hierarchical file system with simple file access permissions (such as read only), UNIX has a complete user-based file access permission system. Like process management, each file on the system is "owned" by a specific user, and by default only that user can perform operations on that file. *Privileged* users can perform all operations on all files on the file system. Interestingly, a special file permission allows *unprivileged* users to execute certain commands and applications with *superuser* privileges (such as `setuid`).

The following file system types are supported by the kernel:

- **cachefs**   The CacheFS cached file system
- **hsfs**   The High Sierra file system
- **nfs**   The Network File System (NFS)
- **pcfs**   The MS-DOS file system
- **tmpfs**   A file system that uses memory
- **ufs**   The standard UNIX File System (UFS)

The default local file system type is contained in the */etc/default/fs* file, while the default remote file system type is contained in the */etc/default/fstypes* file.

Multiuser vs. Multitasking

Operating systems like MS-DOS are single-user, single-task systems; they are designed to be used by a single user who wishes to execute a single program from the shell. However, with advances in CPU technology, even the humble MS-DOS shell was expanded to allow multitasking, where more than one application can execute concurrently. This approach was extended with Microsoft Windows, which allows several applications to be executed concurrently in a GUI environment. In addition, Microsoft Windows has support for multiple users, although it is generally possible for only a single user to initiate a console session, limiting its concurrency—unless some third-party product is installed (such as Symantec's pcAnywhere, or Terminal Server with Windows 2000/XP).

UNIX provides the best of both worlds, because it is designed from the ground up to permit multiple users to initiate multiple shells, which in turn can execute multiple applications. In addition, Solaris supports lightweight processes such as threads, which allow the traditional concept of multitasking to be generalized to execute multiple threads within a single process. Solaris also supports symmetric multiprocessing, meaning that the physical execution of processes, threads, and user applications may occur on one of many different supported processors.

Client/Server Networks

While PC operating systems were designed in response to the waning of client/server systems, Solaris and other UNIX systems are firmly designed as client/server systems. While a PC is designed to run many high-powered applications using the local CPU, a client/server network is designed around the concept of multiple *thin* clients that access data and execute applications on a *fat* centralized server, or on a number of servers that are dedicated to one particular purpose. For example, a typical Solaris network might consist of hundreds of Sun Ray thin client systems, which are supported on the front line by several E450 departmental servers, as well as a set of rack-mounted 420R systems that run database, web server, and development systems.

The client/server topology is also reflected in the structure of UNIX services: client applications running on client systems are designed to connect through to server applications running on server systems. Sun was instrumental in initiating key distributed computing technologies, such as the Remote Procedure Call (RPC) technology used in the Network File System (NFS) protocol. In addition, the Remote Method Invocation (RMI) technology developed as part of the Java networking and distributed computing APIs allows objects to be passed around the network as seamlessly as RPC.

Basic Networking Terminology

A Solaris network consists of a number of different hosts that are interconnected using a switch or a hub. Solaris networks connect to one another via routers, which can be dedicated hardware systems, or Solaris systems, which have more than one network interface. Each host on a Solaris network is identified by a unique hostname; these hostnames often reflect the function of the host in question. For example, a set of four FTP servers may have the hostnames *ftp1*, *ftp2*, *ftp3*, and *ftp4*.

Every host and network that is connected to the Internet uses the Internet Protocol (IP) to support higher-level protocols such as Transmission Control Protocol (TCP) and User Datagram Protocol (UDP). Every interface of every host on the Internet has a unique IP address that is based on the network IP address block assigned to the local network. Networks are addressable by using an appropriate netmask that corresponds to a class A (255.0.0.0), class B (255.255.0.0), or class C (255.255.255.0) network.

Solaris supports multiple Ethernet interfaces that can be installed on a single machine. These are usually designated as */etc/hostname.hmen*, where *n* is the interface number and *hme* is the interface type. Interface files contain a single unqualified domain name or IP address, with the primary network interface being designated with an interface number of zero. Thus, the primary interface of a machine called *ftp* would be defined by the file */etc/hostname.hme0*, which might contain the unqualified domain name "ftp", or the IP address *203.17.64.28*. A secondary network interface, connected to a different subnet, might be defined in the file */etc/hostname.hme1*. In this case, the file might contain the unqualified domain name "mail", or the IP address *10.17.65.28*.

The decision to use unqualified domain names or IP addresses rests largely with the naming service used by the system, which is defined by the file */etc/nsswitch.conf*. If this file does not allow hostname resolution from the */etc/hosts* because the Domain Name System (DNS) is used exclusively, using unqualified domain names in */etc/hostname.** files can lead to a failure of local hostname resolution. However, because IP addresses can change from time to time (particularly if Dynamic Host Configuration Protocol, or DHCP, is used), some administrators may need to use unqualified domain names.

Enabling multiple interfaces is commonly used in organizations that have a provision for a failure of the primary network interface or to enable load balancing of server requests across multiple subnets (for example, for an intranet web server processing HTTP requests). A system with a second network interface can act either as a router or as a multihomed host. Hostnames and IP addresses are locally administered through a naming service, which is usually DNS for companies connected to the Internet, and the Network Information Service (NIS/NIS+) for companies with large internal networks that require administrative functions beyond what DNS provides, including centralized authentication.

It is also worth mentioning at this point that it is possible for you to assign different IP addresses to the same network interface; this configuration can be useful for hosting "virtual" interfaces that require their own IP address, rather than relying on application-level support for multihoming (for example, when using the Apache web server). You simply create a new */etc/hostname.hme*X:Y file for each IP address required, where *X* represents the physical device interface and *Y* represents the virtual interface number.

The subnet mask used by each of these interfaces must also be defined in */etc/netmasks*. This is particularly important if the interfaces lie on different subnets, or if they serve different network classes. In addition, it might also be appropriate to assign a fully qualified domain name to each of the interfaces, although this will depend on the purpose to which each interface is assigned.

System Configuration

Solaris provides a simple way to view all the hardware devices on your system. This in formation can be used to configure your system. For example, by identifying the disk devices on your system, you can correctly select targets for formatting.

The `prtconf` command is used for displaying system information:

```
prtconf
System Configuration:  Sun Microsystems   sun4u
Memory size: 128 Megabytes
```

This section shows the hardware architecture (sun4u, which means that this is a Sun 4 system with an UltraSPARC CPU) and that it has 128MB of RAM.

The following section identifies the terminal emulator, keyboard, and UFS. These devices are necessary to boot a Solaris system.

```
System Peripherals (Software Nodes):
SUNW,Ultra-5_10
    packages (driver not attached)
        terminal-emulator (driver not attached)
    disk-label (driver not attached)
        SUNW,builtin-drivers (driver not attached)
        sun-keyboard (driver not attached)
        ufs-file-system (driver not attached)
```

The next section shows the OpenBoot PROM (programmable read-only memory), physical memory, and virtual memory monitor devices:

```
    chosen (driver not attached)
    openprom (driver not attached)
        client-services (driver not attached)
    options, instance #0
    aliases (driver not attached)
    memory (driver not attached)
    virtual-memory (driver not attached)
```

The final section displays devices attached to the first PCI local bus. This includes an Integrated Device Electronics (IDE) hard disk, IDE hard drive, and network interface:

```
pci, instance #0
        pci, instance #0
            ebus, instance #0
                auxio (driver not attached)
                power, instance #0
                SUNW,pll (driver not attached)
                se, instance #0
                su, instance #0
                su, instance #1
                ecpp (driver not attached)
                fdthree, instance #0
                eeprom (driver not attached)
                flashprom (driver not attached)
                SUNW,CS4231 (driver not attached)
            network, instance #0
            SUNW,m64B (driver not attached)
            ide, instance #0
                disk (driver not attached)
                cdrom (driver not attached)
                dad, instance #0
                sd, instance #30
```

 NOTE Obviously, the specific devices installed on each system vary, and so will the configuration displayed when using prtconf.

Processes

Processes lie at the heart of all modern multiuser operating systems. By dividing system tasks into small, discrete elements that are uniquely identified by a process identifier (PID), Solaris is able to manage all the applications that may be concurrently executed by many different users. In addition, individual users may execute more than one application at any time. Each Solaris process is associated with a UID and a GID, just like a standard file. This means that only users may send signals to their own processes (except for the superuser, who may send signals to any process on the system). Signals are typically used to restart or terminate processes. The multiuser, multitasking process model in Solaris ensures that system resources can be shared equally among all competing processes or allocated preferentially to the most important applications. For example, a firewall application would probably take precedence over all other system processes. Individual users and the superuser may allocate a priority level to active processes in real time.

Solaris provides a number of command-line tools that can be used to manage processes. In addition, APIs are provided for C programmers to allow them to operate directly on processes—spawning, managing, and killing as necessary. Solaris also provides lightweight processes (LWPs) that don't require as much overhead to operate as "normal" processes.

Naming Services

Every computer connected to the Internet must have an IP address, which identifies it uniquely within the network. For example, *192.18.97.241* is the IP address of the web server at Sun. IP addresses are difficult for humans to remember, and they don't adequately describe the network on which a host resides. Thus, by examining the fully qualified domain name (FQDN) of *192.18.97.241*—**www.sun.com**—it's immediately obvious that the host, *www*, lies within the **sun.com** domain. The mapping between human-friendly domain names and machine-friendly IP addresses is performed by a distributed naming service known as the *Domain Name Service* (DNS). DNS is the standard protocol used by UNIX systems (and other operating systems) for mapping IP addresses to hostnames, and vice versa.

Although Solaris provides complete support for DNS, it uses its own domain management and naming system, known as the Network Information Service (NIS). NIS is not only responsible for host naming and management, but it is a comprehensive resource management solution that can be used to structure and administer groups of local and remote users.

NIS uses a series of maps to create namespace structures. Sometimes administrators ask why this extra effort is required to manage hosts and naming, because DNS already provides this for Internet hosts by converting computer-friendly IP addresses to human-friendly "names." However, NIS does not just provide naming services; a NIS server also acts as a central repository of all information about users, hosts, Ethernet addresses, mail aliases, and supported Remote Procedure Call (RPC) services within a network. This information is physically stored in a set of maps that are intended to replace the network configuration files usually stored in a server's /etc directory, ensuring that configuration data within the local area network (LAN) is always synchronized. Many large organizations use NIS alongside DNS to manage both their Internet and LAN spaces effectively. Linux also supports NIS.

In the past, Sun introduced an enhanced version of NIS known as NIS+. Instead of a simple mapping system, it uses a complex series of tables to store configuration information and hierarchical naming data for all networks within an organization. Individual namespaces may contain up to 10,000 hosts, with individual NIS+ servers working together to support a completely distributed service. NIS+ also includes greater capabilities in the area of authentication, security (using DES encryption), and resource access control.

Recently, Solaris has begun a transition to Lightweight Directory Access Protocol (LDAP) directory services as an alternative source of authoritative information for naming, identification, and authentication. LDAP is based on the original Directory Access Protocol (DAP), which provided X.500-type services for centralized directory lookups. Like NIS and NIS+, LDAP performs lookups, given a token, and returns a result. However, the query is much more generalized than what can be returned from NIS or NIS+: text, sounds, and graphics can all be associated with an entry in the directory.

LDAP does not provide any kind of programmatic query language, like SQL, to query the directory, so its use is still limited. However, because it works directly over TCP/IP, and it can support directory services for clients on different operating systems, LDAP is often viewed as the future central naming and directory service for Solaris.

Server-Side Java

Java is a new programming language that is often used to create platform-independent GUIs that a user can interact with in complex and sophisticated ways. However, Java *applets*—the bits of code that are transmitted over the Internet and executed on the user's machine—are only one side of the whole Java story. This section will focus on the *server* side of Java.

Java applications that execute on the server are called *servlets*, and they have their own standard API specification that has now been widely implemented in web server extension products known as servlet *runners* (such as Apache's Tomcat server). Servlets are useful in developing web-enabled, Solaris-based enterprise applications.

Increasingly, applications in the enterprise are being implemented using web interfaces, partly in response to the persistent heterogeneity of computing platforms within organizations that span cities, states, and even nations. Accepting platform diversity does not mean losing control of standards, however. Sun Microsystems has pioneered a platform-independent programming language in which applications run on top of a logical Java Virtual Machine (JVM) that presents a consistent API for developers. Most major hardware platforms and operating systems now have virtual machines implemented, including (obviously) Solaris. In fact, the Solaris JVM produced by Sun has been highly optimized in its production release series. JVMs have also been integrated into popular web browsers, so that Java programs can be downloaded from a server and executed within these browsers. (HTML has an `<applet>` tag that facilitates this process.) Applets have increased the complexity of web-based user interfaces from simple arrays of buttons and forms to dynamic interaction with the user in a way that is similar to a normal desktop application.

Although Java has been successful in improving the client side of web-based computing, it has been slower to make an impact on the server side (this is as much a result of the excitement surrounding applets as any deficit in the servlet API). However, many people believe that the server side is where Java has its greatest potential. The notion of having platform-independent enterprise applications that run through a standard web interface promises to change the way that users, developers, and software interact. The "write once, run anywhere" philosophy means that servers with totally different operating systems and hardware can be replaced with newer systems, without concern for application stability and porting. Commonly used Java classes can be bundled as *beans* that can provide rapid implementation for a client's business logic. Full access to the Java API and database servers is also provided for Java servlets, using the Java Database Classes (JDBC) supplied by Oracle and other major vendors. These features ensure that today's Java server-side programs will not become tomorrow's legacy applications.

How does server-side Java compare to web-based client/server techniques such as the combination of a Common Gateway Interface (CGI) and a non-object-oriented language such as C? Although a compiled language like C is faster on a byte-per-byte basis than an interpreted language like Java, performance increases for Java can be gained by the combination of optimizing "just-in-time" (JIT) compilers for specific platforms and by reducing the process and memory overhead associated with the CGI. For example, if you wrote a search application in Perl that was accessed by 1,000 web users per hour, that would mean an extra 1,000 invocations of Perl that the server has to deal with, unless a specialized module was used. Of course, if you are running on an E10000, this would probably result in a negligible system strain. For other systems, invoking a Java servlet that occupies only a single process after being loaded into memory, and which *persists* across sessions, is both memory and process efficient. Servlets are therefore more appropriate for applications that are constantly being executed by multiple users, by taking advantage of Java's multithreading and synchronization capabilities.

On the flip side, CGI programs are often better suited to single-user, infrequently used, and numerically intensive applications that might only be invoked once per hour. In addition, CGI programs written in C are logically isolated from each other in the server's memory space: if Java servlets are executed using a single instance of a service manager (for example, Live Software's Jrun), an unhandled exception arising from malformed or unexpected input could potentially impact all servlets running through the manager, especially if the JVM crashes.

SPARC Hardware

Sun has developed a wide range of hardware systems over the past few years, many of which are still supported by Solaris 9. These systems are based on the Scalable Processor

ARChitecture (SPARC), which is managed by a SPARC member organization (**http://www.sparc.org/**). In addition to Sun Microsystems, Fujitsu (**http://www.fujitsu.com/**) and T.Sqware (**http://www.tsqware.com/**) also build SPARC-compliant CPU systems. System vendors that sell systems based on SPARC CPUs include Amdahl Corporation (**http://www.amdahl.com/**), Tatung (**http://www.tatung.com/**), Tadpole (**http://www.tadpole.com/**), and Toshiba (**http://www.toshiba.com/**). Vendors of system boards and peripherals for SPARC CPU–based systems include Hitachi (**http://www.hitachi.com/**), Seagate (**http://www.seagate.com/**), and Kingston Technology (**http://www.kingston.com/**).

Although media critics and competitors often paint SPARC systems from Sun as stand-alone, vendor-specific traps for the unwary, the reality is that a large number of hardware vendors also support the SPARC platform. It should also be noted that software vendors such as Red Hat also support SPARC versions of Linux, which proves that Solaris is not the only operating system that powers the SPARC platform. The SPARC standards can be downloaded free of charge from **http://www.sparc.org/standards.html**.

Often, administrators of Linux and Microsoft Windows systems who are used to "PC" hardware are incredulous to discover that some supported systems (such as the SPARCclassic) have CPUs that run below 100 MHz. This must seem a slow CPU speed in the age of Intel CPUs and their clones reaching the 1-GHz mark. However, CPU speed is only one component that contributes to the overall performance of a system—SPARC systems are renowned for their high-speed buses and very fast I/O performance. In addition, many SPARC systems were designed for continuous operation—it is not unheard of for systems to have several years of uptime, compared to several days for some operating systems. The many impressive features of the Solaris operating systems were developed with the SPARC hardware platform as a target, and these systems naturally have the best performance. The following is an actual uptime reported by the technical editor:

```
$ uptime
1:36pm up 718 day(s), 22:44, 1 user, load average: 0.23, 0.15, 0.13
```

However, Sun has not ignored hardware developments and emerging standards—in recent years, Sun has created the Ultra series of workstations and servers that feature a PCI local bus and compatibility with Super Video Graphics Array (SVGA) multisync monitors commonly sold with PC systems. Of course, SPARC systems have always supported the SCSI standard, and all SCSI devices will work with Solaris. At the same time, Sun has proceeded with innovations, such as the 64-CPU Enterprise 10000 system, which can operate as a single system with massively parallel computational abilities, or it can be logically partitioned to act as up to 64 different systems. Imagine being able to control an entire application service provider (ASP) with no apparent "shared hosting" to the client, which is actually being serviced by a single physical system. Although the up-front cost of an E10000 far exceeds that required for 64 systems running Linux or Microsoft Windows, only one administrator is required to manage an E10000, while 64 different systems might require more than one administrator.

Supported Platforms

SPARC systems have an application architecture and a kernel architecture: most modern Sun systems have an application architecture of type 4, while the latest UltraSPARC systems have a kernel architecture of type *u*. Thus, UltraSPARC systems are known as *sun4u* systems. One of the great advantages of SPARC is that systems with the same application architecture can run the same binaries; thus, the binary of an application compiled on an Ultra 1 should work on an E10000. However, the kernel architecture has changed significantly over the years, so that systems with different kernel architectures cannot boot the same kernel. While an Ultra 1 and E-450 can boot from the same sun4u kernel, a SPARCstation 5 must boot from a sun4m kernel.

Table 2-1 shows a list of common application and kernel architectures for some type 4 Sun systems.

You will need a Sun-4 architecture system to run Solaris 9, or any kind of modern UNIX kernel for that matter. (Your old 3/60 really does belong in a museum!) Even some Sun-4 architectures have had support deprecated in Solaris 9, mainly because of the requirement for a minimum of 96MB of RAM. The following SPARC systems are supported under Solaris 9:

SPARCclassic	SPARCstation LX	SPARCstation 4	SPARCstation 5
SPARCstation 10	SPARCstation 20	Ultra 1 (including Creator and Creator 3D models)	Enterprise 1
Ultra 2 (including Creator and Creator 3D models)	Ultra 5	Ultra 10	Ultra 30
Ultra 60	Ultra 450	Enterprise 2	Enterprise 150
Enterprise 250	Enterprise 450	Enterprise 3000	Enterprise 3500
Enterprise 4000	Enterprise 4500	Enterprise 5000	Enterprise 5500
Enterprise 6000	Enterprise 10000	SPARCserver 1000	SPARCcenter 2000

Some popular systems are no longer supported, particularly those in the sun4c family. Often, these systems can be upgraded with a firmware or CPU change to be compatible with Solaris 9. In addition, a minimum of 96MB of RAM is required to install Solaris 9—

Table 2-1	Application	Kernel	Architecture	System Name
Common Application and Kernel Architectures for Sun-4 Systems	4	C	sun4c	SPARCstation 1
	4	C	sun4c	SPARCstation IPX
	4	M	sun4m	SPARCstation 5
	4	M	sun4m	SPARCstation 10
	4	D	sun4d	SPARCserver 1000
	4	D	sun4d	SPARCcenter 2000
	4	U	sun4u	UltraSPARC 5
	4	U	sun4u	Enterprise 220R

the Web Start Wizard will not let you proceed unless it can detect this amount of physical RAM, so be sure to check that your system meets the basic requirements before attempting to install Solaris 9.

 NOTE Some machines listed in Table 2-1 will support Solaris 9, but only in 32-bit mode.

System Components

A typical Solaris SPARC workstation consists of the following components:

- Base unit (aka "pizza box"), which contains the motherboard, SCSI controller, and SBUS cards
- Frame buffer or graphics card
- SCSI or IDE units connected by SCSI or IDE cables to the SCSI or IDE controller in the pizza box
- CD-ROM drive, internal or external (SCSI or IDE)
- DVD-ROM drive, internal on newer systems
- Speaker box and microphone, external
- Two serial ports (A and B)
- A parallel port
- A tape drive, internal or external (DAT/DDS/QIC and so on)
- Mouse (mechanical or infrared) and keyboard (type 4 or type 5)

As noted, most desktop workstations come in a "pizza box" chassis, although earlier Internetwork Packet Exchange (IPX) and similar systems had a "lunch box" chassis. Both of these designs were more compact than their PC counterparts. Servers generally come in two versions: stand-alone or rack-mountable. The version numbers on servers also differ with their chassis type. The 220R, for example, is the rack-mounted version of the stand-alone E-250, while the 420R is the rack-mounted version of the stand-alone 420. The 220R and E-250 have two CPUs each, while the 420R and E-450 have four CPUs each.

Let's examine two SPARC systems in detail; a workstation (UltraSPARC 5) and a server (UltraSPARC E-450). The UltraSPARC 5 system is a popular, low-end desktop model. Although it has been replaced in this category by the new, lower-cost Sun Blade 100 (available for around $1,000), it remains a popular workstation for business and home use. It supports UltraSPARC-IIi CPUs with speeds ranging from 270 to 400 MHz. Internally, it features 16KB instruction and data caches, while it supports from 256KB to 2MB of external cache memory. In terms of memory and disk capacity, the system supports up to 512MB of physical RAM, a CD-ROM, a 1.44MB floppy disk, and two hard drives, making it possible to enable volume management. The system has three peripheral ports—two serial and one parallel—and it has a built-in Ethernet adapter and supports 10–100-Mbps transmission rates. The system also features a PCMCIA bay, which allows a wide variety of PC-type hardware to be connected.

While the UltraSPARC 5 is comparable in performance to desktop PCs, the E-450 is a workgroup-level server that features symmetric multiprocessing, larger numbers of disks, fast buses, hot swapping, and more cache RAM per CPU. The E-450 supports up to four UltraSPARC-IIi CPUs, operating at 250–480 MHz. Internally, it features 16KB instruction and data caches per CPU, and up to 4MB of external cache per CPU—for a four-CPU system, that's a total of 16MB of external cache. The system also features two UPA buses operating at 100 MHz, supporting up to two CPUs on each bus. With respect to mass storage and memory, the system accepts up to 16 dual inline memory modules (DIMMs), giving up to 4GB of physical RAM. Some 20 slots for hard disks provide a large pool of hot-swappable volumes on a fast SCSI-3 bus. A CD-ROM and floppy disk drive are also supplied, and a DDS-3 internal digital audio tape (DAT) drive for backups. In addition, hot-swappable power supplies can be installed into the chassis, enabling two different power sources to be utilized.

Intel Hardware

If Solaris was originally designed to run on SPARC hardware, and if SPARC hardware is where Sun makes its money, why would Sun support an Intel version? For starters, many more Intel systems exist in the world than SPARC systems. Sun also has a historical relationship with Intel, which supported SunOS 4.*x* for several 80386 and 80486 systems. At this point, however, Sun introduced the SPARC range of CPUs, which were the forerunners of the current UltraSPARC series. Intel-based systems are also suitable for workstation environments, and were (until the recent release of the Sun Blade 100) much cheaper than SPARC systems. Since Sun is primarily in the server hardware business, it made sense to develop a reliable operating system for Intel workstations that was supported by its high-end servers.

For many potential Solaris users, SPARC systems are still prohibitively expensive, even though these users want the features of the UNIX operating system. Often, organizations need to make best use of their existing investment in PC hardware. However, some PC operating systems may not currently meet their needs. While PCs have become the de facto standard for desktop computers, investments in PC-based solutions have sometimes met with dissatisfaction from users because some PC operating systems lack stability—particularly regarding application-specific issues, although operating systems have also caused concern. Some of the problems included the perceived lack of reliability of operating systems that were prone to crash during important business operations. Although Intel CPUs featured modes that should logically isolate such failures to the operation that causes them (such as protected mode), this requires operating system support that was never fully perfected by some vendors. In other words, PC hardware is up to the task, but operating systems have not taken full advantage of the PC's abilities.

Perhaps more frustratingly, errors in existing PC operating systems could not be corrected by talented developers, because most PC operating systems are proprietary—in some instances, operating system vendors actually charged users to report operating system bugs, only refunding the charge if the bug was verified. In addition, frustration was often caused by so-called "standard" hardware, which often had incompatibilities with application and server software. For example, at the time when 80286 CPU systems were being touted as "IBM compatible," most were using an ISA bus, while IBMs were actually using the Micro Channel Architecture (MCA) as the bus on their PS/2 systems. However, PC hardware has converged on a number of standards, such as the PCI bus, which have vastly improved the performance figures for data throughput on PCs.

There are some key benefits to using Solaris for Intel over SPARC hardware: For a start, "plug and play" devices are supported, meaning that explicit device configuration is often not required. In addition, you can get access to modern bus architectures like PCI without having to purchase an UltraSPARC system. This point relates to overall system cost: If SPARC systems are going to use PCI for the foreseeable future, why use SPARC when PCI is supported by Intel systems at a smaller cost? In addition, Solaris for Intel supports multiple CPUs, each of which are much cheaper in cost than the equivalent SPARC CPUs.

There are, however, some limitations to using Solaris for Intel. These may be specific to Solaris, but some relate to the architecture itself. For example, while some versions of Microsoft Windows support up to four Enhanced Integrated Drive Electronics (EIDE) controllers, Solaris will see only the first two. Granted, EIDE disks and controllers are generally less favorable than SCSI-3 drives, but they do exist and they are cheap. In addition, support for the universal serial bus (USB) is still experimental, making it harder to add new devices that don't use the serial port for connection. Many new modems also won't work on anything but Windows (so-called "Winmodems") because they rely on Windows to control the modem hardware rather than having a built-in controller.

Because Sun makes no direct revenues from Solaris Intel, the bottom line is that, with the growing popularity of Linux for the Intel platform, continued development of the Solaris Intel edition may receive less attention than the SPARC edition. This doesn't mean that you shouldn't continue to use Solaris Intel, though, because it is a mature and stable product. In terms of contemplating future server purchases, however, it might be wiser to go with SPARC.

The Hardware Compatibility List (HCL), which is available at **http://soldc.sun.com/ support/drivers/hcl/index.html**, is the definitive guide to all hardware devices supported by the Solaris Intel platform. If a device does not appear in the HCL, it is unlikely that it will be supported under Solaris Intel—with some exceptions: motherboards, for example, often follow fairly loose standards, with clone boards usually working correctly under Solaris even if they don't appear in the HCL. The most common compatibility issue occurs with video cards—many are not supported at all, or if they are, their full feature set is unsupported. For example, some video cards have hardware support for receiving TV signals. While their graphical rendering ability will be supported, the TV functions will generally not work with Solaris.

Fortunately, if your video card is not supported, it is possible to replace the X server provided by Solaris with the XFree-86 X server (**http://www.xfree.org/**). This server is functionally equivalent to any other server that supports the X11R6 standard, meaning that the common desktop environment (CDE) and all other Solaris GUI applications will run if you have installed XFree. The main advantage of using XFree-86 is that it supports a much larger array of hardware devices than the Solaris X server.

Devices Supported Under Solaris Intel

This section reviews some of the families of devices supported under Solaris Intel and examples of products that are likely to be supported. Most common motherboards are supported, including those developed by Acer, ASUS, EPoX, and Intel. Some examples are the Acer M9N MP, the ASUS A7V, and the EPoX EP-MVP3G. In addition, motherboard support has been established for many prebuilt systems, including the Acer AcerAcros T7000 MT, Bull Information Systems Express5800-HX4500, and Compaq Deskpro EN 6400. Many symmetric multiprocessing (SMP)-capable motherboards are also supported. No special configuration is required to support SMP devices—they are plug and play—and some popular models include the Dell PowerEdge 6300, the Fujitsu TeamSERVER-T890I, and the Gateway 8400.

Video cards from many different manufacturers are supported, including those operating from ISA, PCI, or AGP buses. Five display resolutions are supported:

- 800 × 600 pixels
- 1024 × 768 pixels
- 1152 × 900 pixels
- 1280 × 1024 pixels
- 1600 × 1200 pixels

Both 8- and 24-bit color are supported in all of these modes, depending on the chipset and onboard memory. Many cards are supported, including the ATI 3D RAGE, the Boca Voyager 64, and the Chips & Technology 65540. All multisync monitors are supported. However, the *kdmconfig* application used for setting up the display does not show 14-inch monitors in its selection list: in most cases, you will be able to use the 15-inch setting, as long as the frequency specified is supported by your monitor. Fixed-sync monitors should work as long as their frequency is supported by the video card at the resolution you require. Serial, bus, and PS/2 mouse devices are supported under Solaris. In addition, many third-party pointing devices are supported, including the MicroSpeed MicroTRAC trackball, the LogiTech MouseMan cordless, and the Kraft Systems MicroTrack.

In terms of SCSI host adapters, both standard and ultra-wide SCSI support is included for the most popular host adapters, including the Adaptec AHA-2940/2940W, AMD PCscsi, and the Compaq 32-bit Fast-Wide SCSI-2. Many Iomega Jaz/Zip devices are supported under Solaris, including the SCSI devices 2250S Zip drive (250MB) and the V2008I Jaz drive (2GB), as well as the ATAPI and IDE Z100A Zip drives (100MB).

Many different types of network adapters are supported, including 10-Mbps and 100-Mbps data transfer rates. Supported adapters include the 3Com EtherLink III PCI Bus Master, the Adaptec ANA-6901, and the AMD PCnet-PCI.

For laptops, common PCMCIA devices are generally supported, such as modems and network adapters, including the ATI Technologies 14400 ETC-EXPRESS, the Compaq SpeedPaq 192, and the Hayes 5361US.

Summary

In this chapter, we have examined some of the key concepts that underlie the Solaris Operating Environment and the SunOS Operating System. From the kernel to the shell to different file system types, Solaris provides a number of sophisticated methods for managing systems and deploying applications in the enterprise.

Questions

1. Which of the following best describes Solaris?

    A. Single user, single process

    B. Single user, multiprocess

    C. Multiuser, single process

    D. Multiuser, multiprocess

2. What is the main responsibility of the kernel?

    A. Allocating system resources to complete assigned tasks

    B. Displaying graphics using X11

    C. Managing applications

    D. Choosing the appropriate shell

3. What sort of native file system does Solaris support?

    A. A flat file system, which begins with a C:\ directory

    B. A hierarchical file system, which begins with a root directory

    C. A flat file system, which begins with a root directory

    D. A hierarchical file system, which begins with a C:\ directory

4. How are hardware devices logically represented on Solaris hosts?

    A. As special files

    B. As database entries

    C. As device plug-ins

    D. On the Control Panel

5. How are processes distinguished in Solaris?

   A. By process names

   B. By command names

   C. By process IDs

   D. By session variables

6. Which of the following file systems is *not* supported by Solaris?

   A. High Sierra

   B. Joliet

   C. UFS

   D. MS-DOS

7. Which of the following subnets matches with a class B network?

   A. 255.0.0.0

   B. 255.255.0.0

   C. 0.255.255.255

   D. 255.255.255.255

8. What might the file */etc/hostname.hme0* contain (choose two only)?

   A. The hostname of interface *hme0*

   B. The IP address of interface *hme0*

   C. The netmask of interface *hme0*

   D. The ethernet address of interface *hme0*

9. What video card bus types are supported by Solaris Intel?

   A. ISA

   B. AGP

   C. PCI

   D. All of the above

10. What system architecture is recommended for running a Solaris 9 system on SPARC?

    A. Sun-4

    B. Sun-3

    C. Sun-5

    D. Sun-60

Answers

1. **D.** Solaris is a multiuser, multiprocess operating system.

2. **A.** The main role of the kernel is to allocate system resources to complete assigned tasks.

3. **B.** Solaris supports a hierarchical file system, which begins with a root directory.

4. **A.** Hardware devices are logically represented on Solaris hosts by special files.

5. **C.** Processes are distinguished in Solaris by Process IDs (PIDs).

6. **B.** The Joliet file system is *not* supported by Solaris.

7. **B.** 255.255.0.0 is the subnet mask for class B networks.

8. **A, B.** */etc/hostname.hme0* might contain a hostname or IP address.

9. **D.** Solaris Intel supports ISA, PCI, and AGP buses.

10. **A.** The Sun-4 architecture system is recommended for Solaris 9.

The OpenBoot PROM

In this chapter, you will
- Analyze host setup details using OpenBoot commands
- Change the default boot device
- Test system hardware
- Create device aliases using nvalias
- Remove custom devices using nvunalias
- Diagnose and troubleshoot booting problems
- Halt a hung system

One of the main hardware differences between SPARC systems that run Solaris and PC systems that run Linux or Microsoft Windows is that SPARC systems have an OpenBoot PROM monitor program, which can be used to modify firmware settings prior to booting. In this chapter, we examine how the monitor can be used to boot a system and troubleshoot hardware problems.

The OpenBoot PROM Monitor

The OpenBoot PROM monitor is based on the Forth programming language, and can be used to run Forth programs that perform the following functions:

- Booting the system, by using the `boot` command
- Performing diagnostics on hardware devices by using the `diag` command
- Testing network connectivity by using the `watch-net` command

The OpenBoot monitor has two prompts from which commands can be issued: the ok prompt, and the > prompt. In order to switch from the > prompt to the ok prompt, you simply need to type **n**:

```
> n
ok
```

Commands are typically issued from the ok prompt. These commands include `boot`, which boots a system from the default system boot device, or from an optional device specified at the prompt. Thus, if a system is at run level 0, and needs to be booted, the `boot` command with no options specified will boot the system:

```
ok boot
SPARCstation 20, Type 5 Keyboard
ROM Rev. 2.4, 256 MB memory installed, Serial #456543
Ethernet address 5:2:12:c:ee:5a HostID 456543
Rebooting with command:
Boot device: /iommu@f,e0000000/sbus@f,e0001000/espdma@f,400000/esp@f,8...
SunOS Release 5.9 Version Generic 32-bit
Copyright (c) 1983-2002 by Sun Microsystems, Inc.
configuring IPv4 interfaces: hme0.
Hostname: Winston
The system is coming up. Please wait.
checking ufs filesystems
/dev/rdsk/c0t0d0s1: is clean.
NIS domainname is Cassowary.Net.
starting rpc services: rpcbind keyserv ypbind done.
Setting netmask of hme0 to 255.255.255.0
Setting default IPv4 interface for multicast: add net 224.0/
4: gateway Winston
syslog service starting.
Print services started.
volume management starting.
The system is ready.
winston console login:
```

Alternatively, if you have modified your hardware configuration since the last boot and you want the new devices to be recognized, you should always reboot using this command:

```
ok boot -r
```

This is equivalent to performing a reconfiguration boot using the following command sequence in a shell as the superuser:

```
# touch /reconfigure; sync; init 6
```

or

```
# reboot -- -r
```

So far, we've looked at automatic booting. However, sometimes it is desirable to perform a manual boot, using the command `boot -a`, where parameters at each stage of the booting process can be specified. These parameters include:

- The path to the kernel that you wish to boot
- The path to the kernel's modules directory
- The path to the system file
- The type of the root file system
- The name of the root device

For example, if we wished to use a different kernel, such as an experimental kernel, we would enter the following parameters during a manual boot:

```
Rebooting with command: boot -a
Boot device: /pci@1f,0/pci@1,2/ide@1/disk@0,1:a File and args: -a
Enter filename [kernel/sparcv9/unix]: kernel/experimental/unix
Enter default directory for modules [/platform/SUNW,Sparc-20/kernel
/platform/sun4m/kernel /kernel /usr/kernel]:
Name of system file [etc/system]:
SunOS Release 5.9 Version Generic 64-bit
Copyright (c) 1983-2002 by Sun Microsystems, Inc.
root filesystem type [ufs]:
Enter physical name of root device
[/pci@1f,0/pci@1,2/ide@1/disk@0,1:a]:
```

To accept the default parameters, simply press ENTER when prompted. Thus, to only change the path to the experimental kernel, we would enter **kernel/experimental/unix** at the Enter filename prompt.

Analyzing System Configuration

To view the OpenBoot release information for your firmware, as well as the system configuration, use the following command:

```
ok banner
SPARCstation 20, Type 5 Keyboard
ROM Rev. 2.4, 256 MB memory installed, Serial #456543
Ethernet address 5:2:12:c:ee:5a HostID 456543
```

Here, we can see the system is a SPARCstation 20, with a standard keyboard, and that the OpenBoot release level is 2.4. There are 256MB of RAM installed on the system, which has a hostid of 456543. Finally, the Ethernet address of the primary Ethernet device is 5:2:12:c:ee:5a.

Changing the Default Boot Device

To boot from the default boot device (usually the primary hard drive), you would enter the following:

```
ok boot
```

However, it is also possible to boot using the CDROM by using this command:

```
ok boot cdrom
```

The system may be booted from a host on the network by using this command:

```
ok boot net
```

Alternatively, if you have a boot floppy, the following command may be used:

```
ok boot floppy
```

Because many early Solaris distributions were made on magnetic tape, it's also possible to boot using a tape drive with the following command:

```
ok boot tape
```

Instead of specifying a different boot device each time you want to reboot, it is possible to set an environment variable within the OpenBoot monitor, so that a specific device is booted by default. For example, to set the default boot device to be the primary hard disk, you would use the following command:

```
ok setenv boot-device disk
boot-device = disk
```

To verify that the boot device has been set correctly to disk, the following command can be used:

```
ok printenv boot-device
boot-device disk
```

In order to reset the system, to use the new settings, you simply use the `reset` command:

```
ok reset
```

To set the default boot device to be the primary network device, you would use the following command:

```
ok setenv boot-device net
boot-device = net
```

This configuration is commonly used for diskless clients, such as Sun Rays, which use RARP and NFS to boot across the network. To verify that the boot device has been set correctly to net, the following command can be used:

```
ok printenv boot-device
boot-device net disk
```

To set the default boot device to be the primary CD-ROM device, you would use the following command:

```
ok setenv boot-device cdrom
boot-device = cdrom
```

To verify that the boot device has been set correctly to cdrom, the following command can be used:

```
ok printenv boot-device
boot-device cdrom disk
```

To set the default boot device to be the primary floppy drive, you would use the following command:

```
ok setenv boot-device floppy
boot-device = floppy
```

To verify that the boot device has been set correctly to floppy, the following command can be used:

```
ok printenv boot-device
boot-device floppy disk
```

To set the default boot device to be the primary tape drive, you would use the following command:

```
ok setenv boot-device tape
boot-device = tape
```

To verify that the boot device has been set correctly to tape, the following command can be used:

```
ok printenv boot-device
boot-device tape disk
```

Testing System Hardware

The test command is used to test specific hardware devices, such as the loopback network device. This device could be tested by using the following command:

```
ok test net
Internal Loopback test - (OK)
External Loopback test - (OK)
```

This indicates that the loopback device is operating correctly. Alternatively, the watch-clock command is used to test the clock device:

```
ok watch-clock
Watching the 'seconds' register of the real time clock chip.
```

```
It should be ticking once a second.
Type any key to stop.
1
2
3
```

TIP   Timing results can be cross-checked against a reliable timing device for accuracy.

If the system is meant to boot across the network, but a boot attempt does not succeed, it is possible to test network connectivity using the watch-net program. This determines whether or not the system's primary network interface is able to read packets from the network it is connected to. The output from the watch-net program looks like this:

```
Internal Loopback test - succeeded
External Loopback test - succeeded
Looking for Ethernet packets.
'.' is a good packet. 'X' is a bad packet.
Type any key to stop
......X.........XXXX.......XX............
```

In this case, a number of packets are marked as bad, even though the system has been connected successfully to the network.

In addition to the `watch-net` command, the OpenBoot monitor can perform a number of other diagnostic tests. For example, all of the SCSI devices attached to the system can be detected by using the `probe-scsi` command. The `probe-scsi` command displays all of the SCSI devices attached to the system. The output of `probe-scsi` looks like this:

```
ok probe-scsi
Target 1
Unit 0 Disk SUN0104 Copyright (C) 1995 Sun Microsystems All rights reserved
Target 1
Unit 0 Disk SUN0207 Copyright (C) 1995 Sun Microsystems All rights reserved
```

Here, we can see that two SCSI disks have been detected. If any other disks or SCSI devices were attached to the chain, they have not been detected, indicating a misconfiguration or hardware error.

TIP   If you are using a PCI system, then SCSI devices may or may not appear.

Creating and Removing Device Aliases

The OpenBoot monitor is able to store certain environment variables in nonvolatile RAM (NVRAM), so that they can be used from boot to boot, by using the `nvalias` command. For example, to set the network device to use RARP for booting, we would use the following command:

```
ok nvalias net /pci@1f,4000/network@1,1:rarp
```

This means that booting using the net device, as shown in the following example, would use the /pci@1f,4000/network@1,1 device to boot the system across the network:

```
ok boot net
```

However, if we wanted to use the Dynamic Host Configuration Protocol (DHCP) to retrieve the host's IP address when booting, instead of using RARP, we would use the following command:

```
ok boot net:dhcp
```

To remove the alias from NVRAM, you simply use the nvunalias command:

```
ok nvunalias net
```

This would restore the default value of net.

Troubleshooting Booting Problems

If a system fails to start correctly in multiuser mode, it's likely that one of the scripts being run in /etc/rc2.d is the cause. In order to prevent the system from going multiuser, it is possible to boot directly into single-user mode from the ok prompt:

```
ok boot -s
...
INIT: SINGLE USER MODE
Type Ctrl-d to proceed with normal startup,
(or give root password for system maintenance):
```

At this point, the root password can be entered, and the user will be given a root shell. However, not all file systems will be mounted, although individual scripts can then be checked individually for misbehaving applications.

If the system will not boot into single-user mode, the solution is more complicated because the default boot device cannot be used. For example, if an invalid entry has been made in the /etc/passwd file for the root user, the system will not boot into single- or multiuser mode. To recover the installed system, the host needs to be booted from the installation CD-ROM into single-user mode. At this point, the default root file system can be mounted on a separate mount point, the /etc/passwd file edited, and the system rebooted with the default boot device. This sequence of steps is shown next, assuming that /etc is located on /dev/dsk/c0t0d0s1:

```
ok boot cdrom
...
INIT: SINGLE USER MODE
Type Ctrl-d to proceed with normal startup,
(or give root password for system maintenance):
# mkdir /temp
# mount /dev/dsk/c0t0d0s1 /temp
# vi /temp/etc/passwd
# sync; init 6
```

Using eeprom

Solaris provides an easy way to modify the values of variables stored in the PROM through the `eeprom` command. The `eeprom` command can be used by the root user when the system is running in either single- or multiuser mode. The following variables can be set, as shown next with their default values:

```
# /usr/sbin/eeprom
tpe-link-test?=true
scsi-initiator-id=7
keyboard-click?=false
keymap: data not available.
ttyb-rts-dtr-off=false
ttyb-ignore-cd=true
ttya-rts-dtr-off=false
ttya-ignore-cd=true
ttyb-mode=9600,8,n,1,-
ttya-mode=9600,8,n,1,-
pcia-probe-list=1,2,3,4
pcib-probe-list=1,2,3
mfg-mode=off
diag-level=max
#power-cycles=50
system-board-serial#: data not available.
system-board-date: data not available.
fcode-debug?=false
output-device=screen
input-device=keyboard
load-base=16384
boot-command=boot
auto-boot?=true
watchdog-reboot?=false
diag-file: data not available.
diag-device=net
boot-file: data not available.
boot-device=disk net
local-mac-address?=false
ansi-terminal?=true
screen-#columns=80
screen-#rows=34
silent-mode?=false
use-nvramrc?=false
nvramrc: data not available.
security-mode=none
security-password: data not available.
security-#badlogins=0
oem-logo: data not available.
oem-logo?=false
oem-banner: data not available.
oem-banner?=false
hardware-revision: data not available.
last-hardware-update: data not available.
diag-switch?=false
```

Halting a Hung System

If a system is hung, and commands cannot be entered into a shell on the console, then the key combination STOP-A can be used to halt the system and access the OpenBoot PROM monitor.

 CAUTION   If the system is halted and rebooted in this way, all data that has not been written to disk will be lost, unless the go command is used to resume the system's normal operation.

An alternative method of accessing a system if the console is locked is to *telnet* to the system as an unprivileged user, using the su command to obtain superuser status, and kill whatever process is hanging the system. Normal operation can then be resumed.

STOP Commands

The STOP commands are executed on the SPARC platform by holding down the special STOP key located on the left-hand side of the keyboard, and another key that specifies the operation to be performed. The following functions are available:

STOP	Enters the POST environment.
STOP-A	Enters the PROM monitor environment.
STOP-D	Performs diagnostic tests.
STOP-F	Enters a program in the Forth language.
STOP-N	Initializes the nonvolatile RAM settings to their factory defaults.

Boot Commands

You can use the boot command with any one of the following options:

net	Boots from a network interface.
cdrom	Boots from a local CD-ROM drive.
disk	Boots from a local hard disk.
tape	Boots from a local tape drive.

In addition, you can specify the name of the kernel to boot by including its relative path after the device specifier. Or, you can pass the -a option on the command line to force the operator to enter the path to the kernel on the boot device.

Summary

The OpenBoot PROM monitor is one of the outstanding features of the SPARC architecture. It allows a wide range of system parameters to be configured using a high-level programming language that is independent of the installed operating system. A wide range of diagnostic and testing applications are included with OpenBoot.

Questions

1. How can the default boot device be set to CD-ROM from the OpenBoot PROM monitor?

   A. `setenv boot-device cdrom`

   B. `set boot-device cdrom`

   C. `set boot cdrom`

   D. `setenv bootdevice cdrom`

2. How can the default boot device be set to disk from the OpenBoot PROM monitor?

   A. `setenv boot-device disk`

   B. `set boot-device disk`

   C. `set boot disk`

   D. `setenv bootdevice disk`

3. How can the default boot device be set to net from the OpenBoot PROM monitor?

   A. `setenv boot-device net`

   B. `set boot-device net`

   C. `set boot net`

   D. `setenv bootdevice net`

4. How can the default boot device be set to tape from the OpenBoot PROM monitor?

   A. `setenv boot-device tape`

   B. `set boot-device tape`

   C. `set boot tape`

   D. `setenv bootdevice tape`

5. How can the default boot device be set to floppy from the OpenBoot PROM monitor?

   A. `setenv boot-device floppy`

   B. `set boot-device floppy`

   C. `set boot floppy`

   D. `setenv bootdevice floppy`

6. How can a reconfiguration boot be performed from the OpenBoot PROM monitor?

   A. `boot -configure`

   B. `boot -configure`

   C. `boot -reconfigure`

   D. `boot -r`

7. How can a manual boot be performed from the OpenBoot PROM monitor?

   A. `boot -manual`

   B. `boot -man`

   C. `boot -a`

   D. `boot -m`

8. How can the system clock be tested from the OpenBoot PROM monitor?

   A. `watch-time`

   B. `watch-clock`

   C. `test-clock`

   D. `test-time`

9. How can the network connection be tested from the OpenBoot PROM monitor?

   A. `watch-network`

   B. `watch-net`

   C. `test-net`

   D. `test-network`

10. How can a reconfiguration boot be performed from a shell?

    A. `touch /reconfigure; init 6`

    B. `init 5`

    C. `shutdown`

    D. `startup`

Answers

1. **A.** The `setenv` command must be used in conjunction with the boot-device variable for the token cdrom.

2. **A.** The `setenv` command must be used in conjunction with the boot-device variable for the token disk.

3. **A.** The `setenv` command must be used in conjunction with the boot-device variable for the token net.

4. **A.** The `setenv` command must be used in conjunction with the boot-device variable for the token tape.

5. **A.** The `setenv` command must be used in conjunction with the boot-device variable for the token floppy.

6. **D.** The `boot` command must have the -r (reconfigure) option passed.

7. **C.** The `boot` command must have the -a (manual) option passed.

8. **B.** The `watch-clock` command can be used to "watch" the system clock.

9. **B.** The `watch-net` command can be used to "watch" the packets on the primary network interface.

10. **A.** You must create the */reconfigure* file before giving the `reboot` command.

Solaris 9 Installation

In this chapter, you will
- Learn how to perform preinstallation planning
- Estimate disk space requirements for installation
- Perform a Web Start Wizard installation
- Configure a Solaris system for first time operation

Solaris 9 provides more installation methods than ever before. These include the Web Start Wizard, JumpStart, *suninstall*, and Live Upgrade. The Web Start Wizard is the easiest method used to install Solaris 9: it uses a Java-based front end that presents a series of configuration choices. For those who prefer a command-line installation, the suninstall program is also available. This is particularly useful for installing servers that are attached to a simple terminal on the console port, using *tip*, rather than a high-resolution monitor. Large organizations are more likely to create a JumpStart configuration to install a standard operating environment (SOE) on all Solaris 9 systems. Using JumpStart ensures that all systems have an identical installation base, making it easy to manage patches and maintain production systems. Live Upgrade is a new innovation, which minimizes the downtime of production servers: a new boot environment is constructed while the server is still operating under its existing operating environment release. Once the second boot environment has been installed, the system is quickly rebooted into the new operating environment, and the previous version is uninstalled in the background.

Preinstallation Planning

The basic process of installing Solaris remains the same, regardless of the installation method selected. A number of planning tasks must be performed prior to installation. These tasks include:

- Choosing the appropriate installation method from the Web Start Wizard, JumpStart, suninstall, and Live Upgrade.
- Deciding whether or not to upgrade an existing installation or install the operating system cleanly. If your system is currently running Solaris 2.6, 7, or 8, an upgrade can be performed. If your system is running Solaris 2.5.1 or earlier, or if it is not running Solaris at all, you need to perform an initial installation.

An upgrade preserves many of the system settings from a previous installation, and generally takes less time to complete than a completely new install. If an upgrade is being performed, the current system should be backed up by using ufsdump or something similar so that it can be restored in the event of an upgrade failure.

- Analyzing your existing hardware devices to determine whether or not Solaris 9 will run on your system without an upgrade. For example, Solaris 8 on SPARC would run with only 64MB RAM, but at least 96MB of RAM is required to run Solaris 9. To perform an upgrade installation, extra RAM would need to be added to an existing Solaris 8 system with only 64MB RAM.

- Determining whether your storage devices have sufficient capacity to install Solaris 9 and all required third-party applications. A complete Solaris 9 installation requires 2.4GB of disk space, if OEM support is included, and 2.3GB if OEM support is excluded. A Developer installation requires at least 1.9GB, while the End User installation requires 1.6GB. In addition, an amount of swap space equivalent to twice your physical memory should be factored into the sum, along with third-party and user disk space requirements. This is not a requirement, but a sound practice.

- Choosing an appropriate installation medium. Possibilities include a JumpStart, CD-ROM, DVD-ROM, or net-based installation from a remotely mounted CD-ROM or DVD-ROM drive. For large organizations, it's often convenient to set up a single network server with an NFS-exported DVD-ROM or CD-ROM drive that is publicly available for mounting. In addition, large organizations might also choose a customized JumpStart installation, which also requires network access to a centralized boot server. Smaller organizations will almost certainly use a CD-ROM or DVD-ROM drive attached to the local system to be installed.

- Gathering all of the necessary system configuration information. This includes the system hostname, IP address, subnet mask, name service type, name server IP address, default router IP address, time zone, locale, and proxy server IP address. These values, and when they are required, will be discussed next.

By undertaking a comprehensive preinstallation review, a successful installation can be assured. In addition to making decisions about the installation type and gathering basic system data, it's important to understand the network context in which the system will operate. The network context can be defined by answering several key questions:

- Will the system be networked? If so, you will need an IP address, subnet mask, and default router (unless the system itself is intended to be a router).

- Will the system use the Dynamic Host Configuration Protocol? If so, you will not need to supply an IP address, as a lease over an IP address will automatically be granted to you at boot time.

- Will the system use IPv6, the newest version of the Internet Protocol?

- Will the system form part of a Kerberos v5 realm, to allow centralized authentication? If so, you will need the name of the realm, the administration server's IP address, and the address of the primary KDC.

- Will the system use the Domain Name Service (DNS)? If so, you will need the IP address of a primary and secondary DNS server, which is authoritative for the local domain.

- Will the system use Network Information Service (NIS) or NIS+? If so, the IP address or the hostname of the local NIS or NIS+ server will need to be supplied.

- Will the system make use of the Lightweight Directory Access Protocol (LDAP) for centralized authentication and authorization? If so, you will need to supply the profile server's IP address or hostname.

- Will the system use a proxy server to access the Internet? If so, the IP address or hostname of the proxy server will be required.

Answers to these questions will be required to completely configure the system during installation.

Disk Space Planning

The question of how much disk space you require to install Solaris 9 can only be answered by examining the purpose of the server. For a SPARC system, with 512MB RAM, a complete installation will require 2.6GB for software and 1024MB for swap, as well as space for user data and applications. Extra disk space must be set aside for special features, such as internationalization, and an estimate needs to be made of the size of print and mail spooling directories which lie under /var. Although the default size of /var is usually small in the installation program, mail and print servers will need to increase this, by allowing for a reasonable allocation of spooling space per user.

 CAUTION   Since a full /var file system caused by a large print job can affect other tasks such as mail, it's important to overestimate rather than underestimate the size of /var.

In terms of applications, an Oracle database server, for example, will require at least 1–2GB of disk space, for software packages, mount points, and table data. For a development system with multiple users, a projection based on the maximum quota for each user should be computed. For example, if 50 users are allowed 100MB disk space each, then at least of 5GB of disk space must be available for their exclusive use—as a rule, if users have quotas imposed on them, they should always be guaranteed access to that space. If data on a server is mission critical, consideration should be given to installing some volume management software, as described in Chapter 21.

In terms of specific layouts, the typical file system layout for a SPARC architecture system follows a set of customary, although not required, disk slice allocations. Slice 0 holds the root partition, while slice 1 is allocated to swap space. For systems with changing virtual memory requirements, it might be better to use a swap file on the file system, rather than allocating an entire slice for swap. Slice 2 often refers to the entire disk, while */export* on slice 3 traditionally holds older versions of the operating system, which are used by client systems with lower performance (for example, Classic or LX systems that use the trivial FTP daemon, tftpd, to download their operating system upon boot). These systems may also use slice 4 as exported swap space. Export may also be used for file sharing using the Network File System (NFS). Slice 5 holds the */opt* file system, which is the default location under Solaris 9 for local packages installed using the pkgadd command. Under earlier versions of Solaris, the */usr/local* file system held local packages, and this convention is still used by many sites. The system package file system */usr* is usually located on slice 6, while */export/home* usually contains user home directories on slice 7. Again, earlier systems located user home directories under */home*, but because this is used by the automounter program in Solaris 9, some contention can be expected.

The typical file system layout for an Intel architecture system also follows a set of customary, although not required, disk slice allocations. Slice 0 again holds the root partition, while slice 1 is also allocated to swap space. Slice 2 continues to refer to the entire disk, while */export* on slice 3 again holds older versions of the operating system, which are used by client systems, and slice 4 contains exported swap space for these clients. The local package file system */opt* is still located on slice 5, and the system package file system */usr* is again located on slice 6. Slice 7 contains the user home directories on */export/home*. However, the two extra slices serve very different purposes: boot information for Solaris is located on slice 8, and is known as the "boot slice," while slice 9 provides space for alternative disk blocks, and is known as the "alternative slice."

Device Names

Among the most challenging aspects of understanding Solaris hardware are the device names and references used by Solaris to manage devices. Solaris uses a very specific set of naming conventions to associate physical devices with instance names on the operating system. In addition, devices can also be referred to by their device name, which is associated with a device file created in the */dev* directory after configuration. For example, a hard disk may have the physical device name/pci@1f,0/pci@1,1/ide@3/dad@0,0, which is associated with the device file */dev/dsk/c0t0d0*. The benefit of the more complex Solaris device names and physical device references is that it is easy to interpret the characteristics of each device by looking at its name. For the disk example given above, we can see that the IDE hard drive is located on a PCI bus at target 0. When we view the amount of free disk space on the system, for example, it is easy to identify slices on the same disk by looking at the device name:

```
# df -k
Filesystem           kbytes      used   avail capacity  Mounted on
/proc                     0         0       0     0%    /proc
/dev/dsk/c0t0d0s0   1982988    615991 1307508    33%    /
fd                        0         0       0     0%    /dev/fd
```

```
/dev/dsk/c0t0d0s3     1487119   357511  1070124     26%   /usr
swap                   182040      416   181624      1%   /tmp
```

Here, we can see that */dev/dsk/c0t0d0s0* and */dev/dsk/c0t0d0s3* are slice 0 and slice 3 of the disk */dev/dsk/c0t0d0*. If you're ever unsure of which physical disk is associated with a specific disk device name, the `format` command will tell you:

```
# format
Searching for disks...done
AVAILABLE DISK SELECTIONS:
0. c1t3d0 <SUN2.1G cyl 2733 alt 2 hd 19 sec 80>
        /pci@1f,0/pci@1/scsi@1/sd@3,0
```

Here, we can see that physical device /pci@1f,0/pci@1/scsi@1/sd@3,0 is matched with the disk device */dev/dsk/c1t3d0*. In addition, a list of mappings between physical devices to instance names is always kept in the */etc/path_to_inst* file. More information on device naming conventions can be found in Chapter 18.

SPARC Preinstallation

Prior to installing or upgrading Solaris on a SPARC system, it is suggested that a few basic checks of the system be performed, to obtain data necessary for installation (such as the device name of the boot disk) and to verify that all system components are functional. The three most commonly performed tasks are checking network connectivity, checking the disks that have been detected on the SCSI bus, and reviewing how much memory is installed.

If you are booting over a network, or if your system needs to access a DNS, NIS/NIS+, Kerberos, or LDAP server, and you want support for these services to be installed, your network connection will need to be operational. In order to ensure that packets are being sent and received to your system, you can use the `watch-net` command:

```
ok watch-net
Internal Loopback test - succeeded
External Loopback test - succeeded
Looking for Ethernet packets.
'.' is a good packet. 'X' is a bad packet.
Type any key to stop
......X.........XXXX.......….XX............
```

If a large number of packets are showing as bad, then you should check for hardware errors on your network cable, and/or use a packet analyzer to determine if there is a structural fault on the local area network. In order to check whether or not all of the disk devices attached to the system have been correctly detected, you can use the `probe-scsi` command to print a list of available devices.

Intel Preinstallation

To install Solaris Intel, the first step is to switch on the system and insert the Solaris 9 Installation CD-ROM into the drive. If you have a high-resolution graphics monitor attached to the system, the GUI-based Configuration Assistant will start. Alternatively, if you are using a low-resolution terminal to connect, the Configuration Assistant will be text-based.

After the BIOS messages have been displayed, the following message will be displayed:

```
SunOS Secondary Boot
Solaris Intel Platform Edition Booting System
Running Configuration Assistant...
```

The Configuration Assistant is responsible for performing a number of preinstallation tasks, and must be executed prior to the Web Start Wizard or any other installation program. At the opening screen, simply press F2 to proceed with the installation, unless you are performing an upgrade.

The first task performed by the Configuration Assistant is determining the bus types supported by your system, and collecting data about the devices installed in your system. During this process, the following message will be displayed on your screen:

```
Determining bus types and gathering hardware configuration data ...
```

After all of the devices have been discovered by scanning, a list of identified devices is printed on the screen:

```
The following devices have been identified on this system. To identify
devices not on this list or to modify device characteristics, choose Device
Task. Platform types may be included in this list.

    ISA: Floppy disk controller
    ISA: IDE controller
    ISA: IDE controller
    ISA: Motherboard
    ISA: PS/2 Mouse
    ISA: PnP bios: 16550-compatible serial controller
    ISA: PnP bios: 8514-compatible display controller
    ISA: PnP bios: Audio device
    ISA: System keyboard (US-English)
```

If you are satisfied that the devices required for installation have been correctly detected (for example, video card and RAM size), you may press F2 again to proceed with booting. Alternatively, you may perform several other tasks on this screen, including:

- Viewing and editing devices
- Setting the keyboard type
- Saving the current configuration
- Deleting a saved configuration
- Setting the default console device

If your system does not already have a UFS file system installed, or if it is a completely new system, you will need to use fdisk to create new partitions at this point so that your system may be installed. However, if you have an existing Linux system that you wish to dual boot with Solaris, you must ensure that the Linux swap partition is not confused with a Solaris UFS device, because they have the same type within fdisk. You should be able to distinguish Linux swap partitions by their maximum size (127MB). The following page will be displayed during booting and prior to the execution of fdisk:

```
<<< Current Boot Parameters >>>
Boot path: /pci@1,0/pci-ide@6,1/ide@2/sd@1,0:a
Boot args: kernel/unix
<<< Starting Installation >>>
SunOS Release 5.9 Version Generic 32-bit
Copyright 1983-2001 Sun Microsystems, Inc. All rights reserved.
Configuring /dev and /devices
Using RPC Bootparams for network configuration information.
Solaris Web Start installer
English has been selected as the language in which to perform the install.
Starting the Web Start Solaris installer
Solaris installer is searching the system's hard disks for a
location to place the Solaris installer software.
No suitable Solaris fdisk partition was found.
Solaris Installer needs to create a Solaris fdisk partition
on your root disk, c0d0, that is at least 395 MB.
WARNING: All information on the disk will be lost.
May the Solaris Installer create a Solaris fdisk [y,n,?]
```

You should heed the warning that all data will be lost if you choose to overwrite it with fdisk.

Disk Partitions

If you consent to using fdisk, you will see a screen similar to the following:

```
Total disk size is 2048 cylinders
Cylinder size is 4032 (512 byte) blocks
Cylinders
Partition   Status   Type   Start   End    Length   %
=========   ======   ====   =====   ====   ======   ===
1                    UNIX   0       1023   1024     50
2                    DOS    1024    2047   1024     50
SELECT ONE OF THE FOLLOWING:
1. Create a partition
2. Specify the active partition
3. Delete a partition
4. Exit (update disk configuration and exit)
5. Cancel (exit without updating disk configuration)
Enter Selection:
```

In this example, we can see that there are two existing partitions occupying 1,204 cylinders each. Partition 1 is a UNIX partition (perhaps from SCO UNIX), while partition 2 is an MS-DOS partition. If we want to use the entire disk for Solaris, we would need to select option 3 on this menu twice, to delete each existing partition in turn. Alternatively, if we wished to retain the UNIX partition but delete the MS-DOS partition, we would use option 3 only once, and select partition 2 for deletion.

After you have freed up space, if necessary, you will be required to select option 1 to create a partition. You will then be required to select option A from the following menu to create a Solaris partition:

```
Select the partition type to create:
1=SOLARIS 2=UNIX 3=PCIXOS 4=Other
5=DOS12 6=DOS16 7=DOSEXT 8=DOSBIG
A=x86 Boot B=Diagnostic 0=Exit?
```

Note that it is not possible to run Solaris from a non-UFS partition; however, it is possible to mount non-Solaris file systems after the system has been installed. Next, you need to specify the size of the partition, in either the number of cylinders or the percentage of the disk to be used. In this example, we would enter either **100%** or **2048** cylinders:

```
Specify the percentage of disk to use for this partition
(or type "c" to specify the size in cylinders).
```

Next, you will need to indicate whether or not the target partition is going to be activated. This means that the system will attempt to boot the default operating system loader from this partition. If you are going to use the Solaris boot manager, you may activate this partition. However, if you are using Boot Magic or LILO to manage existing Microsoft Windows or Linux partitions, and you wish to continue using either of these systems, you should answer no.

After you have created the partition, the fdisk menu will be updated and displayed as follows:

```
2 Active x86 Boot 8 16 9 1
Total disk size is 2048 cylinders
Cylinder size is 4032 (512 byte) blocks
                              Cylinders
Partition  Status  Type      Start  End   Length  %
=========  ======  ========  =====  ====  ======  ===
2          Active  x86 Boot  0      2047  2048    100
SELECT ONE OF THE FOLLOWING:
1. Create a partition
2. Specify the active partition
3. Delete a partition
4. Exit (update disk configuration and exit)
5. Cancel (exit without updating disk configuration)
Enter Selection:
```

At this point, you should select option 4. You will then be prompted with the following message:

```
No suitable Solaris fdisk partition was found.
Solaris Installer needs to create a Solaris fdisk partition
on your root disk, c0d0, that is at least 395 MB.
WARNING: All information on the disk will be lost.
May the Solaris Installer create a Solaris fdisk [y,n,?]
```

Since you've just created the appropriate partition using fdisk, you should type **n** here. You will then see the following message:

```
To restart the installation, run /sbin/cd0_install.
```

After restarting the installer, you will see the formatting display shown in the next section.

Disk Formatting and Virtual Memory

If your system already has a UFS partition, or if you have just created one, you will see a screen similar to the following:

```
<<< Current Boot Parameters >>>
Boot path: /pci@1,0/pci-ide@6,1/ide@2/sd@1,0:a
Boot args: kernel/unix
<<< Starting Installation >>>
SunOS Release 5.9 Version Generic 32-bit
Copyright 1983-2001 Sun Microsystems, Inc. All rights reserved.
Configuring /dev and /devices
Using RPC Bootparams for network configuration information.
Solaris Web Start installer
English has been selected as the language in which to perform the install.
Starting the Web Start Solaris installer
Solaris installer is searching the system's hard disks for a
location to place the Solaris installer software.
The default root disk is /dev/dsk/c0d0.
The Solaris installer needs to format
/dev/dsk/c0d0 to install Solaris.
WARNING: ALL INFORMATION ON THE DISK WILL BE ERASED!
Do you want to format /dev/dsk/c0d0? [y,n,?,q]
```

At this point, you simply enter **y**, and the disk will be formatted as required, so that new partitions may be created. You will then be prompted to enter the size of the swap partition:

```
NOTE: The swap size cannot be changed during filesystem layout.
Enter a swap partition size between 384MB and 1865MB, default = 512MB [?]
```

You will then be asked to confirm that the swap slice can be installed at the beginning of the partition:

```
The Installer prefers that the swap slice is at the beginning of the
disk. This will allow the most flexible filesystem partitioning later in the
installation.
Can the swap slice start at the beginning of the disk [y,n,?,q]
```

After creating the swap partition, the other slices can be created on the target disk, since the installation program requires a UFS file system to install correctly. However, the system must first be rebooted clean to perform the layout:

```
The Solaris installer will use disk slice, /dev/dsk/c0d0s1.
After files are copied, the system will automatically reboot, and
installation will continue.
Please Wait...
Copying mini-root to local disk....done.
Copying platform specific files....done.
Preparing to reboot and continue installation.
```

```
Need to reboot to continue the installation
Please remove the boot media (floppy or cdrom) and press Enter
Note: If the boot media is cdrom, you must wait for the system
to reset in order to eject.
```

After you press the ENTER key, you will see the standard Solaris shutdown messages, including:

```
Syncing file systems... 49 done
rebooting...
```

Boot Manager

After ejecting the installation CD-ROM from your drive, you will see the standard Solaris boot manager menu:

```
SunOS - Intel Platform Edition Primary Boot Subsystem
Current Disk Partition Information
Part#    Status    Type       Start    Length
=======================================
1        Active    X86 BOOT   0        2048
Please select the partition you wish to boot:
```

After you enter **1** and hit the ENTER key, you will see the following message:

```
SunOS Secondary Boot
Solaris Intel Platform Edition Booting System
Running Configuration Assistant...
Autobooting from boot path: /pci@1,0/pci-ide@6,1/ide@2/sd@1,0:a
If the system hardware has changed, or to boot from a different
device, interrupt the autoboot process by pressing ESC.
```

A few seconds later, the boot interpreter is initialized:

```
Initializing system
Please wait...
<<< Current Boot Parameters >>>
Boot path: /pci@0,0/pci-ide@7,1/ata@1/cmdk@0,0:b
Boot args:
Type b [file-name] [boot-flags] <ENTER> to boot with options
or i <ENTER> to enter boot interpreter
or <ENTER> to boot with defaults
<<< timeout in 5 seconds >>>
Select (b)oot or (i)nterpreter:
SunOS Release 5.9 Version Generic 32-bit
Copyright 1983-2001 Sun Microsystems, Inc. All rights reserved.
Configuring /dev and /devices
Using RPC Bootparams for network configuration information.
```

Next, you will need to use kdmconfig to set up your graphics card and monitor, so that the Web Start Wizard can display its windows correctly. To start kdmconfig, press F2, after which you will be taken to the kdmconfig introduction screen. After pressing F2 again, you will be asked to perform the kdmconfig view/edit system, configuration window. Here, you can make changes to the settings detected for your system. If your system is listed on the Hardware Compatibility List (HCL), you won't have any problems with hardware detection.

Web Start Wizard Installation

To use the Web Start Wizard installer using a local DVD-ROM or CD-ROM drive, you need to bring the system to run level 0 so that commands can be entered into the PROM boot monitor (for more information about the boot monitor, see Chapter 3). The following command can be used from a root shell to bring the system to run level 0:

```
# sync; init 0
```

Once the system has reached init level 0, the following prompt will be displayed:

```
ok
```

Next, you need to place the Solaris 9 Installation CD-ROM or DVD-ROM into the local drive, and type the following command:

```
ok boot cdrom
```

Note that the command is the same whether a DVD or CD-ROM is used as the source. If you have a Solaris Intel system, you cannot upgrade from 2.6 and 7 to 9 by using the Web Start Wizard from the CD-ROM: you must use either a DVD-ROM, JumpStart, or net-based installation. In addition, your BIOS and hard disk controller for the boot device must support logical block addressing (LBA) to work with Solaris 9.

Soon after the system has started booting, you will see output similar to the following:

```
Boot device: /sbus/espdma@e,8400000/esp@e,8800000/sd@6,0:f File and args:
SunOS Release 5.9 Version Generic 32-bit
Copyright 1983-2001 Sun Microsystems, Inc. All rights reserved.
Configuring /dev and /devices
Using RPC Bootparams for network configuration information.
Solaris Web Start installer
English has been selected as the language in which to perform the install.
Starting the Web Start Solaris installer
Solaris installer is searching the system's hard disks for a
location to place the Solaris installer software.
Your system appears to be upgradeable.
Do you want to do a Initial Install or Upgrade?
1) Initial Install
2) Upgrade
Please Enter 1 or 2 >
```

If the following message appears in the boot messages, you may elect to perform an upgrade of the existing Solaris installation. However, most administrators would back up their existing software, perform a fresh install, and then restore their data and applications once their system is operational. In this case, we will choose to perform an Initial Install, which will overwrite the existing operating system.

After you enter **1** and hit ENTER, you will see a message like this:

```
The default root disk is /dev/dsk/c0t0d0.
The Solaris installer needs to format
/dev/dsk/c0t0d0 to install Solaris.
WARNING: ALL INFORMATION ON THE DISK WILL BE ERASED!
Do you want to format /dev/dsk/c0t0d0? [y,n,?,q]
```

Formatting the hard drive will overwrite all existing data on the drive—you must ensure that if you previously installed an operating system on the target drive (c0t0d0), you have backed up all data that you will need in the future. This includes both user directories and application installations.

After entering **y**, the following screen will appear:

```
NOTE: The swap size cannot be changed during filesystem layout.
Enter a swap slice size between 384MB and 2027MB, default = 512MB [?]
```

Just hit the ENTER key to accept the default on 512MB if your system has 256MB physical RAM, as the sample system has. However, as a general rule, you should only allocate twice the amount of physical RAM as swap space; otherwise, system performance will be impaired. The swap partition should be placed at the beginning of the drive, as the following message indicates, so that other slices are not dependent on its physical location:

```
The Installer prefers that the swap slice is at the beginning of the
disk. This will allow the most flexible filesystem partitioning later in the
installation.
Can the swap slice start at the beginning of the disk [y,n,?,q]
```

After entering **y** to this question, you will be asked to confirm the formatting settings:

```
You have selected the following to be used by the Solaris installer:
Disk Slice : /dev/dsk/c0t0d0
Size : 1024 MB
Start Cyl. : 0
WARNING: ALL INFORMATION ON THE DISK WILL BE ERASED!
Is this OK [y,n,?,q]
```

If you enter **y**, the disk will be formatted and the mini root file system will be copied to the disk, after which the system will be rebooted and the Web Start Wizard installation process can begin:

```
The Solaris installer will use disk slice, /dev/dsk/c0t0d0s1.
After files are copied, the system will automatically reboot, and
installation will continue.
Please Wait...
Copying mini-root to local disk....done.
Copying platform specific files....done.
Preparing to reboot and continue installation.
Rebooting to continue the installation.
Syncing file systems... 41 done
rebooting...
Resetting ...
```

```
SPARCstation 20 (1 X 390Z50), Keyboard Present
ROM Rev. 2.4, 256 MB memory installed, Serial #456543
Ethernet address 5:2:12:c:ee:5a HostID 456543
Rebooting with command: boot /sbus@1f,0/espdma@e,8400000/
  esp@e,8800000/sd@0,0:b
Boot device: /sbus@1f,0/espdma@e,8400000/esp@e,8800000/sd@0,0:b
  File and args:
SunOS Release 5.9 Version Generic 32-bit
Copyright 1983-2001 Sun Microsystems, Inc. All rights reserved.
Configuring /dev and /devices
Using RPC Bootparams for network configuration information.
```

Configuration

The Web Start Wizard proceeds by asking a number of configuration questions that are used to determine which files are copied to the target drive, and how the new system's key parameters will be set. Many of the questions involve network and software configuration, because these are the two foundations of the Solaris installation. In the following sections, we will review each of the configuration options and cover examples of appropriate settings.

Network Support

The Network Support screen gives users the option to select a networked or non-networked system. Some examples of non-networked systems include stand-alone workstations and offline archives. If you don't want or need to install network support, however, you will still need a unique hostname to identify the localhost.

DHCP Server

Network users must first identify how their system is identified using the IP. One possibility is that the system will use Dynamic Host Configuration Protocol (DHCP), which is useful when IP addresses are becoming scarce on a class C network. DHCP allows individual systems to be allocated only for the period during which they are "up." Thus, if a client machine is only operated between 9:00 A.M. and 5:00 P.M. every day, it is only "leased" an IP address for that period of time.

 TIP   When an IP address is not leased to a specific host, it can be reused by another host. Solaris DHCP servers can service Solaris clients, as well as Microsoft Windows and Linux clients.

Hostname

A hostname is used to uniquely identify a host on the local network, and when combined with a domain name it allows a host to be uniquely identified on the Internet. Solaris administrators often devise related sets of hostnames that form part of a single domain. For example, names of the planets, minerals, and jewels are commonly used. Alternatively, a descriptive name, such as "mail," can be used to describe systems with a single purpose, such as mail servers.

IP Address

If your network does not provide DHCP, you will need to enter the IP address assigned to this system by the network administrator. It is important not to use an IP address that is currently being used by another host, because packets may be misrouted. Like a hostname, the IP address needs to be unique to the local system.

Netmask

You will next need to enter the netmask for the system, which will be 255.0.0.0 (class A), 255.255.0.0 (class B), or 255.255.255.0 (class C). If you're not sure, ask your network administrator.

IPv6 Support

Next, you need to indicate whether IPv6 needs to be supported by this system. The decision to use or not to use DHCP will depend on whether your network is part of the mbone, the IP-v6-enabled version of the Internet. As proposed in RFC 2471, IPv6 will replace IPv4 in the years to come, as it provides for many more IP addresses than IPv4. Once IPv6 is adopted worldwide, there will be less reliance on stopgap measures like DHCP. However, IPv6 also incorporates a number of innovations above and beyond the addition of more IP addresses for the Internet—enhanced security provided by authenticating header information, for example, will reduce the risk of IP spoofing and denial of service attacks succeeding. Since IPv6 support does not interfere with existing IPv4 support, most administrators will want to support it.

Kerberos Server

Kerberos is a network authentication protocol that is designed to provide centralized authentication for client/server applications by using secret-key cryptography, which is based around tickets. Once a ticket has expired, the trust relationship between two hosts is broken. In order to use Kerberos, you'll need to identify the name of the local KDC.

Name Services

A name service allows your system to find other hosts on the Internet or on the local-area network. Solaris supports several different naming servers, including the Network Information Service (NIS/NIS+), the Domain Name Service (DNS), or file-based name resolution. Solaris supports the concurrent operation of different naming services, so it's possible to select NIS/NIS+ at this point, and set up DNS manually later. However, since most hosts are now connected to the Internet, it may be more appropriate to install DNS first, and install NIS/NIS+ after installation.

DNS Server

The Domain Name Service maps IP addresses to hostnames. If you select DNS as a naming service, you will be asked to enter a domain name for the local system. This should be the fully qualified domain name (for example, **cassowary.net**). If you selected DNS, you will either need to search the local subnet for a DNS server or enter the IP address of the primary DNS server that is authoritative for your domain. You may also enter up to two secondary DNS servers that have records of your domain. This can be a useful backup if your primary DNS server goes down. It is also possible that, when searching for hosts with a hostname rather than a fully qualified domain name, you would want to search multiple local domains. For example, the host **www.buychapters.com** belongs to the **buychapters.com** domain. However, your users may wish to locate other hosts within the broader **cassowary.net** domain by using the simple hostname, in which case you can add the **cassowary.net** domain to a list of domains to be searched for hosts.

NIS/NIS+ Server
NIS/NIS+ is a network information service that is used to manage large domains by creating maps or tables of hosts, services, and resources that are shared between hosts. NIS/NIS+ centrally manages the naming and logical organization of these entities. If you choose NIS or NIS+ as a naming service, you will need to enter the IP address of the local NIS or NIS+, respectively.

LDAP Server
LDAP is the Lightweight Directory Access Protocol, which provides a "white pages" service that supersedes existing X.500 systems and runs directly over TCP/IP. The LDAP server is used for managing directory information for entire organizations, using a centralized repository. If you wish to use an LDAP server, you will need to provide both the name of your profile and the IP address of the LDAP server.

Router
To access the local area network and the Internet, you will need to supply the IP address of the default router for the system. A router is a multihomed host that is responsible for passing packets between subnets. More information about routers is provided in Chapter 35.

Time Zone and Locale
The next section requires that you enter your time zone, as specified by geographic region, the number of hours beyond or before Greenwich Mean Time (GMT), or by time zone file. Using the geographic region is the easiest method, although if you already know the GMT offset and/or the name of the time zone file, you may enter that instead. Next, you are required to enter the current time and date, with a four-digit year, a month, day, hour, and minute. In addition, you will need to specify support for a specific geographic region in terms of locales, if required.

Power Management
Do you want your system to switch off automatically after 30 minutes of inactivity? If you can honestly answer yes to this question (for example, because you have a workstation that does not run services), then you should enable power management, because it can save costly power bills. However, if you're administering a server, you'll definitely want to turn power management off. A case in point: once your server has shut down in

the middle of the night, and your clients cannot access data, you'll understand why disabling power management is so important.

Proxy Server

A proxy server acts as a buffer between hosts on a local network and the rest of the Internet. A proxy server passes connections back and forth between local hosts and any other host on the Internet. It usually acts in conjunction with a firewall to block access to internal systems, thereby protecting sensitive data. One of the most popular firewalls is squid, which also acts as a caching server. To enable access to the Internet through a proxy server, you need to enter the hostname of the proxy server and the port on which the proxy operates.

64-bit Support

Solaris 9 provides support for 64-bit kernels for the SPARC platform. By default, only a 32-bit kernel will be installed. For superior performance, a 64-bit kernel is preferred because it can natively compute much larger numbers than the 32-bit kernel. In the 64-bit environment, 32-bit applications run in compatibility mode. The installation program will automatically select the appropriate kernel for your system.

Disk Selection and Layout

If you are performing an upgrade or installing a new system, you will need to decide whether or not to preserve any preexisting data on your target drives. For example, you may have five SCSI disks attached, only one of which contains slices used for a previous version of Solaris. Obviously, you will want to preserve the data on the four nonboot disks. However, partitions on the boot disk will be overwritten during installation, so it's important to back up and/or relocate files that need to be preserved. Fortunately, if you choose to perform an upgrade rather than a fresh installation, many system configuration files will be preserved.

The Web Start Wizard will also ask you if you want to autolayout the boot disk slices, or if you want to manually configure them. You should be aware that the settings supplied by the installation program are very conservative, and trying to recover a system that has a full root file system can be time-consuming, especially given the low cost of disk space. It's usually necessary to increase the size of the / and /var partitions by at least 50 percent over what the installer recommends. If you have two identical disks installed, and you have more space than you need, you can always set up volume management to ensure high availability through root partition mirroring—thus, if your primary boot disk fails, the system can continue to work uninterrupted until the hardware issue is resolved.

Finally, some client systems use NFS to remotely mount disks on central servers. While this can be a useful way of accessing a centralized home directory from a number of remote clients (by using the automounter), database partitions should never be remotely mounted. If you need to access remote partitions via NFS, you can nominate these partitions during the installation program.

Root Password

An important stage of the installation process involves selecting the root password for the superuser. The root user has the same powers as the root user on Linux, or the administrator account on Windows NT. If an intruder gains root access, he or she is free to roam the system, deleting or stealing data, removing or adding user accounts, or installing Trojan horses that transparently modify the way that your system operates.

One way to protect against an authorized user gaining root access is to use a difficult-to-guess root password. This makes it difficult for a cracker to use a password-cracking program to guess your password to be successful. The optimal password is a completely random string of alphanumeric and punctuation characters.

In addition, the root password should never be written down, unless it is locked in the company safe, nor should it be told to anyone who doesn't need to know it. If users require levels of access that are typically privileged (such as mounting CD-ROMs), it is better to use the sudo utility to limit the access of each user to specific applications for execution as the superuser, rather than giving out the root password to everyone who asks for it. Role-based access control (RBAC) can also be used for this purpose.

The root password must be entered twice—just in case you should happen to make a typographical error, as the characters that you type are masked on the screen.

Software Selection

After all of the configuration settings have been entered, the following message will be seen on the screen:

```
Please wait while the system is configured with your settings...
```

The installation kiosk will then appear on the screen. The kiosk is primarily used to select the type of installation that you wish to perform. To begin the software selection process, you need to eject the Web Start CD-ROM, and insert the Software (1) CD-ROM. Next, you have the option of installing all Solaris software using the default options or customizing your selection before copying the files from the CD-ROM. Obviously, if you have a lot of disk space and a fast system, you may prefer to install the entire distribution, and delete packages after installation that you no longer require. This is definitely the fastest method. Alternatively, you can elect to perform a customized installation.

You are then presented with a screen of all the available software groups. Here, you may select or deselect individual package groups, or package clusters, depending on your requirements. For example, you may decide to install the Netscape Navigator software, but not install the NIS/NIS+ server for Solaris. After choosing the packages that you wish to install, you are then required to enter your locale based on geographic region (the U.S. entry is selected by default). You may also elect to install third-party software during the Solaris installation process—this is particularly useful if you have a standard operating environment that consists of using the Oracle database server in conjunction with the Solaris operating environment, for example. You would need to insert the product CD-ROM at this point so that it could be identified.

After selecting your software, you will need to lay out the disks. This involves defining disk slices that will store the different kinds of data on your system. The fastest configuration option involves selecting the boot disk and allowing the installer to automatically lay out the partitions according to the software selection that you have chosen. For example, you may wish to expand the size of the */var* partition to allow for large print jobs to be spooled, or web server logs to be recorded.

Finally, you will be asked to confirm your software selections and proceed with installation. All of the packages will then be installed to your system. A progress bar displayed on the screen indicates which packages have been installed at any particular point, and how many remain to be installed. After you have installed all of the software, you will have to reboot the system. After restarting, your system should boot directly into Solaris unless you have a dual-booting system, in which case you will need to select the Solaris boot partition from the Solaris boot manager.

After installation, the system will reboot and display a status message when starting up, which is printed on the console. A sample console display during booting will look something like this:

```
ok boot
Resetting ...
SPARCstation 20 (1 X 390Z50), Keyboard Present
ROM Rev. 2.4, 256 MB memory installed, Serial #456543
Ethernet address 5:2:12:c:ee:5a HostID 456543
Boot device: /iommu/sbus/espdma@f,400000/esp@f,800000/sd@1,0
File and args:
SunOS Release 5.9 Version generic [UNIX(R) System V Release 4.0]
Copyright (c) 1983-2001, Sun Microsystems, Inc.
configuring network interfaces: le0.
Hostname: server
The system is coming up. Please wait.
add net default: gateway 204.58.62.33
NIS domainname is paulwatters.net
starting rpc services: rpcbind keyserv ypbind done.
Setting netmask of le0 to 255.255.255.0
Setting default interface for multicast: add net 224.0.0.0: gateway client
syslog service starting.
Print services started.
volume management starting.
The system is ready.
client console login:
```

By default, the CDE login screen is displayed.

Network Installation

Although we've looked in detail at CD-ROM and DVD-ROM installation from a local drive, it's actually possible to set up a single install server from which installation clients read all of their data. This approach is quite useful where a number of different clients will be using the same disk to install from, and/or if installation is concurrent. Thus, it's possible for a number of users to install Solaris from a single server, which can be very useful when a new release of Solaris is made. For example, the Solaris 9 beta was distributed in a form suitable for network installation, allowing multiple developers to get their systems running as quickly as possible. For existing install servers, this reduces administration overhead, because different versions of Solaris (Solaris 8 and 9, for example) can be distributed from the same server.

The install server reads copies of the installation CD-ROMs and DVD-ROMs and creates a distributable image, which can then be downloaded by remote clients. In addition, it's possible to create images for both SPARC and Intel versions that can be distributed from a single system; thus, a high-end SPARC install server could distribute images to many Intel clients. The install server uses DHCP to allocate IP addresses dynamically to all install clients. Alternatively, a name server can be installed and used for allocating permanent IP addresses to install clients.

To create SPARC disk images on the install server, the `setup_install_server` command is used. For a SPARC DVD-ROM or CD-ROM, this command is located in */cdrom/cdrom0/s0/Solaris_9/Tools*. For an Intel DVD-ROM or CD-ROM, this command is located in */cdrom/cdrom0/Solaris_9/Tools*. The only parameter that needs to be supplied to the command is the path where the disk images should be installed. You should ensure that the path can be exported to clients, and that the partition selected has sufficient disk space to store the images.

When creating Intel disk images, the same command is used, but the path is different: for a SPARC DVD-ROM or CD-ROM, the command is located in */cdrom/cdrom0/ Solaris_9/Tools*, while for an Intel DVD-ROM or CD-ROM, the command is located in */cdrom/cdrom0/s2/Solaris_9/Tools*.

To set up individual clients, the `add_install_client` command must be executed on the install server—once for each client. You need to specify the name of the client to be installed, as well as its architecture. For a sun4m system named pink, you would use the following command:

```
# /export/install/boot/Solaris_9/Tools/add_install_client pink sun4m
```

On the client side, instead of using `boot cdrom` at the ok prompt, you will need to enter the following command:

```
ok boot net
```

suninstall Installation

To boot with the suninstall program, you don't use the Solaris 9 Installation CD-ROM; rather, the Solaris 9 Software 1 CD-ROM, which is bootable, should be employed. The suninstall program has the advantage of not requiring high-resolution graphics to complete installation: thus, a low-resolution monitor or terminal can be used. It requires a minimal amount of RAM, and allows you the greatest flexibility in configuring your system prior to installation (including internationalization). However, it does not allow you to install third-party software as part of the installation process, like the Web Start Wizard. The order of questions and procedures followed are generally the same as for the Web Start Wizard.

When installing Solaris Intel, using the suninstall method is more reliable than the Web Start Wizard, because it relies less on graphic cards and displays that may not be compatible with the Solaris X11 server.

JumpStart

JumpStart is an installation technology that allows a group of systems to be installed concurrently, using a standard file system layout and software package selection. For sites with hundreds of systems that are maintained by a small group of staff, it is the ideal tool for upgrading or reinstalling systems. For example, when a staff member leaves, his or her workstation can be simply reinstalled by using JumpStart, rather than assuming that no system software was modified or that a Trojan horse was not installed. By enforcing a standard operating environment (SOE), there is no need to individually configure every system that needs to be installed, greatly reducing the administrative burden on system administrators.

When using JumpStart on a large number of clients, installation can be expedited by using a *sysidcfg* file, which defines a number of standard parameters for installation. The *sysidcfg* file can contain configuration entries for the following properties:

- Current date and time
- DHCP server IP address
- Local domain name
- Graphics card
- Local hostname
- Local IP address
- IPv6 support
- Locale
- Security policy
- Monitor type
- DNS server
- NIS/NIS+ server
- LDAP server
- Netmask
- Network interface
- Pointing device
- Power management
- Root password
- Security policy

- Terminal type

- Time zone

The following is a sample *sysidcfg* file:

```
system_locale=en_US
timezone=US/Eastern
timeserver=192.168.34.3
network_interface=le0 {netmask=255.255.255.0 protocol_ipv6=yes}
security_policy=NONE
terminal=dtterm
name_service=NONE
root_password=5fg48;r3f
name_service=NIS {domain_name=cassowary.net name_server=nis(192.168.44.53)}
```

Here, we can see that the system locale has been set to standard U.S. English, the time zone set to the U.S. East coast, the time server set to 192.168.34.3, and the network interface running IPv6 is set to */dev/le0*. While the default terminal and root password are also set, the name service and security policy have not been set, because these might change from system to system. In addition, the name service selected is NIS, with the NIS server set to **nis.cassowary.net** (192.168.44.53). More details on JumpStart are given in Chapter 30.

Live Upgrade

All of the installation methods reviewed so far require an existing system to be brought to run level 0 in order to start the installation process. In addition, any system undergoing upgrade can expect to be in single-user mode for a matter of hours while distribution files are copied and third-party software is reinstalled. This kind of downtime may be unacceptable for a production server. While many departmental servers will no doubt have a backup server, which can take their place during upgrading and installation testing, many high-end servers, such as the StarFire, are logically divided into domains that run on a single system. A second standby system may not be available to replace a high-end server just for the purpose of an upgrade. While it's possible to configure each domain individually, many sites would prefer to keep all servers at the same release level.

In such cases, Solaris now offers a Live Upgrade facility. This allows a separate boot environment to be created, with the distribution of the new operating system files installed to an alternative location. Once the installation of the new boot environment has been completed, the system needs only to be rebooted once to allow the system to run the new operating environment. If the new boot environment fails for some reason (such as a missing driver or hardware incompatibility), the old boot environment can be reinstated as the default, and the system can be rebooted into its previous state. This allows operations to resume as quickly as possible in the event of a failure.

One of the nice features of Live Upgrade is that the file system layout and configuration can be quite different from your existing installation. This allows you to fine-tune your existing settings before upgrading. For example, if print and mail jobs have continually caused the /var partition to overfill on a regular basis, the size of the /var partition can be increased in the new boot environment. Changes can be made to the /, /usr, /var, and /opt partitions. Other file systems continue to be shared between the existing and new boot environments unless otherwise specified.

In order to create a new boot environment, a separate partition must be identified and formatted before the procedure can begin. This partition must have sufficient disk space to install the new boot environment. The current contents of /, /usr, and /opt are then copied to the new partition prior to upgrade. Alternatively, if you have a second disk installed on the system, the existing files can be copied to the appropriate slices on the new disk. Once these files are in place, the new boot environment is ready to be upgraded. All of these processes can occur without interfering with the current boot environment.

Upgrading typically involves overwriting the files stored on the new boot environment in /, /usr, and /opt. Once this has been completed, the new boot environment can be activated and the system booted into the new environment.

Live Upgrade operates through a terminal-based menu that allows the following operations to be performed:

- **Activate** Activates a newly installed boot environment.
- **Cancel** Cancels a file transfer operation.
- **Compare** Checks for differences between the new and current boot environments.
- **Copy** Begins a file transfer operation.
- **Create** Initializes a new boot environment.
- **Current** Prints the name of the current boot environment.
- **Delete** Uninstalls a boot environment.
- **List** Displays the file systems in a boot environment.
- **Rename** Modifies the name of a new or existing boot environment.
- **Status** Prints the condition of any boot environment.
- **Upgrade** Begins the upgrade process on the new boot environment.
- **Help** Prints the help menu.
- **Exit** Quits the program.

Summary

In this chapter, we have examined how to perform preinstallation planning, and how to estimate the amount of disk space requirements for installation. In addition, we have walked through how to perform a Web Start Wizard installation, and how to configure a Solaris system for first time operation. These techniques must be employed whenever a Solaris system is installed.

Questions

1. Which of the following Solaris 9 installation types requires the greatest amount of disk space?

   A. Entire Distribution without OEM Support

   B. Entire Distribution plus OEM Support

   C. Developer System

   D. End User System

2. The acronym SPARC stands for which of the following names?

   A. Super Processor ARChitecture

   B. Super Processor Adaptable Recurrent Computation

   C. Scalable Processor ARChitecture

   D. Special ARChitecture

3. What are the main advantages of the SPARC architecture (choose two only)?

   A. A high-speed bus

   B. Fastest available CPU speeds

   C. Fast I/O performance

   D. Compatibility with Intel CPUs

4. Which of the following SPARC systems are supported under Solaris 9 (choose two only)?

   A. SPARCclassic

   B. SPARCstation LX

   C. SPARCstation 1

   D. SPARCstation 2

5. What is the minimum amount of RAM required to run Solaris 9?

   A. 16MB

   B. 32MB

   C. 96MB

   D. 128MB

6. Which is a valid physical device for /pci@1f,0/pci@1,1/ide@3/dad@0,0?

   A. */dev/dsk/c0t0d0*

   B. */dev/dsk/c0t0d1*

   C. */dev/dsk/c1t0d0*

   D. */dev/dsk/c0t1d0*

7. What is a hostname?

   A. A network name that identifies a group of hosts

   B. A special username that has superuser privileges

   C. A unique name that is associated with a system

   D. A network name that identifies an entire network

8. What is an IP address?

   A. A network address that identifies a group of hosts

   B. A number that is used to locate hosts on the same local subnet

   C. A unique name that is associated with a system

   D. A network number that identifies a single host

9. What is a domain name?

   A. An IP address that identifies a group of hosts

   B. A number that is used to locate hosts on the same local subnet

   C. A unique name that is associated with a system

   D. A network name that identifies a group of hosts

10. What is a subnet mask?

   A. An IP address that identifies a group of hosts

   B. A number that is used to locate hosts on the same local subnet

   C. A unique name that is associated with a system

   D. A network name that identifies a group of hosts

11. What is a root password?

   A. An authentication token for the superuser

   B. A hacking tool used to crack low-level accounts

   C. A password that cannot be used to gain indirect access to the nobody account

   D. A network name that identifies a group of hosts

12. What is DHCP?

   A. A protocol for permanently assigning IP addresses to hosts

   B. A protocol for leasing IP addresses to hosts

   C. A method for invoking superuser privileges

   D. A protocol for identifying a group of hosts

Answers

1. **B.** Entire Distribution plus OEM Support requires the greatest amount of disk space.

2. **C.** SPARC stands for Scalable Processor ARChitecture.

3. **A, C.** The SPARC architecture features a high-speed bus and fast I/O performance.

4. **A, B.** SPARCclassic and SPARCstation LX are supported under Solaris 9.

5. **C.** 96MB is the minimum amount of RAM required to run Solaris 9.

6. **A.** /dev/dsk/c0t0d0 is a valid physical device for /pci@1f,0/pci@1,1/ide@3/dad@0,0.

7. **C.** A hostname is a unique name that is associated with a system.

8. **D.** An IP address is a network number that identifies a single host.

9. **D.** A domain name is a network name that identifies a group of hosts.

10. **B.** A subnet mask is a number that is used to locate hosts on the same local subnet.

11. **A.** A root password is an authentication token for the superuser.

12. **B.** DHCP is a protocol for leasing IP addresses to hosts.

System Run Levels

In this chapter, you will

- Learn how to start up a Solaris system
- Learn how to shut down a Solaris system
- Discover the role of run levels/init states
- Review the role of the `init` command
- Learn how to write startup scripts

Solaris 9 uses a flexible boot process that is based on the System V Release 4.0 specification for UNIX systems, making it easier to create and customize startup and shutdown procedures that are consistent across sites and systems. This is in contrast to the simpler BSD-style boot process used by Solaris 1, which lacked a differentiated organization of startup scripts corresponding to distinct system states. The aim of this chapter is to introduce readers to the basic terminology and initialization elements that play an important role in bringing a Solaris system to single- and multiuser "run levels" or "init states," which are mutually exclusive modes of operation. Transitions between init states are managed by the init process. After reading this chapter, Solaris 9 administrators should feel confident in tailoring the startup and shutdown of their own systems, and should have a clear understanding of the boot sequence dependencies when upgrading legacy Solaris 1 systems.

Startup and Shutdown

In many respects, Solaris startup and shutdown is similar to many other systems. However, it is important to recognize and appreciate the distinguishing features of the Solaris operating system from other servers. One of the outstanding facilities for SPARC hardware is the firmware monitoring system, discussed in Chapter 3, which is responsible for key prebooting tasks such as:

- Starting the Solaris operating system by typing **ok boot** at the OpenBoot prompt, which boots the Solaris kernel (on Solaris x86, the `boot` command must be issued through the Primary Boot Subsystem menu).

- Setting system configuration parameters, such as the boot device, which could be one of the hard disks (specified by a full device path name or device alias), another host on the network, or a CD-ROM.

- Watching network traffic by issuing the `ok watch-net` command at the OpenBoot prompt.

- Performing simple diagnostic tests on system devices (for example, testing the termination status of a SCSI bus, or the power-on self test, POST, tests).

Rather than just being a simple operating system loader, like the LILO Linux Loader supplied with many Linux distributions, OpenBoot also permits programs written in the stack-based Forth programming language to be written, loaded, and run before booting commences. This is very useful for customizing servers in large organizations, where a corporate logo must be displayed on boot rather than the default Sun logo. This task can be achieved by creating a Forth array with the appropriate pixel values, and executing the `oem-logo` command.

 TIP Variables can also be set postboot during single- and multiuser init states by using the `eeprom` command as superuser.

For example, eeprom can be used to change the amount of RAM self-tested at boot to 64MB:

```
server# eeprom selftest-#megs=64
```

On Solaris x86 systems, the firmware does not directly support this kind of eeprom functionality—every PC manufacturer has a different "BIOS" system, making it difficult. Instead, storage is simulated by variables set in the *bootenv.rc* file.

To view the OpenBoot release information for your firmware, use the following command:

```
ok banner
SPARCstation 10, Type 5 Keyboard
ROM Rev. 2.4, 64 MB memory installed, Serial #6745644
Ethernet address 6:3:10:a:cc:4a HostID 5767686
```

If the prompt for OpenBoot is not "ok" (for example, it is displayed as ">"), then simply type **n** to return to the "ok" prompt:

```
>
n
ok
```

A second distinguishing feature of the Solaris operating system is the aim of maximized uptime, through efficient kernel design and the user application model. In some non-Solaris server environments, the system must be rebooted every time a new application is installed. Alternatively, a kernel rebuild might be required to change a configuration. Fortunately, rebooting is rarely required for Solaris systems, as applications are logically isolated from system configuration options, and many system-level configuration options can be set in a superuser shell. For example, many TCP/IP options can be set dynamically using the following command:

```
# ndd /dev/tcp
```

NOTE   In some newer hardware configurations, it is not even necessary to reboot to install new hardware. These are the kinds of benefits that will be a welcome relief to new Solaris administrators.

Initialization

Upon booting from OpenBoot, Solaris has several different modes of operation, which are known as "run levels" or "init states"—so called because the init command is often used to change run levels, although init-wrapper scripts (such as shutdown) are also used. These init states can be single- or multiuser, and often serve a different administrative purpose, and are mutually exclusive (that is, a system can only ever be in one init state). Typically, a Solaris system designed to "stay up" indefinitely will cycle through a predefined series of steps in order to start all the software daemons necessary for the provision of basic system services, primary user services, and optional application services. These services are often only provided when a Solaris system operates in a multiuser run state, with services being initialized by run control (rc) shell scripts. Usually, one run control script is created to start each system, user, or application service. Fortunately, many of these scripts are created automatically for administrators during the Solaris installation process. However, if you intend to install third-party software (such as a database server), it will be necessary to create your own run control scripts in the */etc/init.d* directory to start up these services automatically at boot time. This process is fully described later in this chapter.

If the system needs to be powered off for any reason (for example, a scheduled power outage), or switched into a special maintenance mode to perform diagnostic tests, there is also a cycle of iterating through a predefined series of run control scripts to kill services and preserve user data. It is essential that this sequence of events be preserved so that data integrity is maintained. For example, operating a database server typically involves communication between a server-side, data-writing process and a daemon listener process, which accepts new requests for storing information. If the daemon process is not stopped prior to the data-writing process, it could accept data from network clients and store it in a cache while the database has already been closed. This could lead to the database being shutdown in an inconsistent state, potentially resulting in data corruption and/or record loss.

CAUTION   It is essential that Solaris administrators apply their knowledge of shell scripting to rigorously managing system shutdowns as well as startups using run control scripts.

Run Levels

In terms of system startup, Solaris has some similarities to Microsoft Windows and Linux. Although it doesn't have an *AUTOEXEC.BAT* or *CONFIG.SYS* file, Solaris does have a number of script files that are executed in a specific order to start services, just like Linux. These scripts are typically created in the */etc/init.d* directory as Bourne shell scripts, and are then symbolically linked into the "run level" directories. Just like Microsoft Windows has "safe modes," Solaris supports a number of different modes of operation, from restricted single-user modes to full multiuser run levels. The complete set of run levels, with their respective run control script directories, is displayed in Table 5-1.

Each run level is associated with a run level script, as shown in Table 5-2. The run level script is responsible for the orderly execution of all run level scripts within a specific run level directory. The script name matches the run level and directory name.

When a Solaris system starts, the init process is spawned, which is responsible for managing processes and the transitions between run levels. You can actually switch manually between run levels yourself by using the `init` command, as shown in the following example:

```
# init 3
```

Control Scripts and Directories

Every Solaris init state (such as init state 6) has its own run level script directory (for example, */etc/rc6.d*). This contains a set of symbolic links (like shortcuts in Microsoft Windows) that are associated with the service startup files in the */etc/init.d* directory. Each linked script starts with a letter *S* ("start") or the letter *K* ("kill"), and is used to start or kill processes, respectively. When a system is booted, processes are started. When a system is shut down, processes are killed. The start and kill links are typically made to the same script file, which

Run Level	Description	User Status	Run Control Script Directory
0	Hardware maintenance mode	Console access	/etc/rc0.d
I	Administrative state; only root file system is available	Single user	/etc/rc1.d
2	First multiuser state; NFS resources unavailable	Multiuser	/etc/rc2.d
3	NFS resources available	Multiuser	/etc/rc3.d
4	User-defined state	Not specified	N/A
5	Power down state	Console access	/etc/rc5.d
6	Operating system halted and reboot	Multiuser	/etc/rc6.d
S	Administrative tasks and repair of corrupted file systems	Console access	/etc/rcS.d

Table 5-1   Solaris Run Levels and Their Functions

Run Level	Run Control Script
0	/etc/rc0
I	/etc/rc1
2	/etc/rc2
3	/etc/rc3
4	N/A
5	/etc/rc5
6	/etc/rc6
S	/etc/rcS

Table 5-2   Solaris Run Level Scripts

interprets two parameters: "start" and "stop." The scripts are executed in numerical order, so a script like /etc/rc3.d/ S20dhcp is executed before /etc/rc3.d/ S21sshd. If you're curious about what kind of scripts are started or killed in Solaris during startup and shutdown, Table 5-3 shows the startup scripts in /etc/rc2.d, while Table 5-4 shows the kill scripts found in /etc/rc0.d. It's important to realize that these will change from system to system.

Script	Description
S05RMTMPFILES	Removes temporary files in the /tmp directory.
S20sysetup	Establishes system setup requirements, and checks /var/crash to determine whether the system is recovering from a crash.
S21perf	Enables system accounting using /usr/lib/sa/sadc and /var/adm/sa/sa.
S30sysid.net	Executes /usr/sbin/sysidnet, /usr/sbin/sysidconfig, and /sbin/ifconfig, which are responsible for configuring network services.
S69inet	Initiates second phase of TCP/IP configuration, following on from the basic services established during single-user mode (rcS). Setting up IP routing (if /etc/defaultrouter exists), performing TCP/IP parameter tuning (using ndd), and setting the NIS domain name (if required) are all performed here.
S70uucp	Initializes the UNIX-to-UNIX copy program (UUCP) by removing locks and other unnecessary files.
S71sysid.sys	Executes /usr/sbin/sysidsys and /usr/sbin/sysidroot.
S72autoinstall	Script to execute JumpStart installation if appropriate.
S72inetsvc	Final network configuration using /usr/sbin/ifconfig after NIS/NIS+ have been initialized. Also initializes Internet Domain Name Service (DNS) if appropriate.
S80PRESERVE	Preserves editing files by executing /usr/lib/expreserve.
S91leoconfig	Configuration for ZX graphics cards (if installed).
S92rtvc-config	Configuration for SunVideo cards (if installed).
S92volmgt	Starts volume management for removable media using /usr/sbin/vold.

Table 5-3   Typical Multiuser Startup Scripts Under Solaris 9

Script	Description
K00ANNOUNCE	Announces that "System services are now being stopped."
K10dtlogin	Initializes tasks for the CDE (Common Desktop Environment), including killing the dtlogin process.
K20lp	Stops printing services using */usr/lib/lpshut*.
K22acct	Terminates process accounting using */usr/lib/acct/shutacct*.
K42audit	Kills the auditing daemon (*/usr/sbin/audit*) .
K47asppp	Stops the asynchronous PPP daemon (*/usr/sbin/aspppd*) .
K50utmpd	Kills the utmp daemon (*/usr/lib/utmpd*).
K55syslog	Terminates the system logging service (*/usr/sbin/syslogd*).
K57sendmail	Halts the sendmail mail service (*/usr/lib/sendmail*).
K66nfs.server	Kills all processes required for the NFS server (*/usr/lib/nfs/nfsd*).
K69autofs	Stops the automounter (*/usr/sbin/automount*).
K70cron	Terminates the cron daemon (*/usr/bin/cron*).
K75nfs.client	Disables client NFS.
K76nscd	Kills the name service cache daemon (*/usr/sbin/nscd*).
K85rpc	Disables remote procedure call (rpc) services (*/usr/sbin/rpcbind*).

Table 5-4   Typical Single-User Kill Scripts Under Solaris 9

Boot Sequence

Booting the kernel is a straightforward process, once the operating system has been successfully installed. The Solaris kernel can be identified by the pathname /platform/PLATFORM_NAME/kernel/unix where PLATFORM_NAME is the name of the current architecture. For example, sun4u systems boot with the kernel /platform/sun4u/kernel/.

NOTE   Kernels can be alternatively booted from a CD-ROM drive or through a network connection (by using the `boot cdrom` and `boot net` commands from the OpenBoot PROM monitor, respectively).

When a SPARC system is powered on, the system executes a series of basic hardware tests before attempting to boot the kernel. These power-on self tests (POSTs) ensure that your system hardware is operating correctly. If the POST tests fail, you will not be able to boot the system.

Once the POST tests are complete, the system will attempt to boot the default kernel using the path specified in the firmware. Alternatively, if you wish to boot a different kernel, you can press STOP+a, enter **boot kernel/name** and boot the kernel specified by "kernel/name." For example, to boot a kernel called newunix, you would use the command `boot kernel/newunix`.

Systems either boot from a UFS file system (whether on the local hard disk or a local CD-ROM drive) or across the network. Two applications facilitate these different boot types: ufsboot is responsible for booting kernels from disk devices, while inetboot is responsible for booting kernels using a network device. While servers typically boot themselves using ufsboot, diskless clients must use inetboot.

The ufsboot application reads the bootblock on the active partition of the boot device, while inetboot performs a broadcast on the local subnet, searching for a trivial FTP (TFTP) server. Once located, the kernel is downloaded using NFS and booted. Once located, a bootable image is downloaded from the TFTP server and the bootparam server sends information on where to find the NFS mount point for the kernel.

System Startup

There are three kinds of boots that administrators should be aware of. In addition to a normal reboot, which is initiated by the command

```
# shutdown
```

from a superuser shell, a reconfiguration boot involves reconstructing device information in the /dev and /devices directories, while a recovery boot involves saving and analyzing crash dump files if a system does not respond to commands issued on the console. A reconfiguration boot is commonly undertaken in older SPARC systems when new hard disks are added to the system, although this may not be necessary with newer systems, such as the E450, which have hot-swapping facilities. This kind of boot can be initiated by typing

```
# boot -r
```

at the OpenBoot monitor prompt, or by issuing the command

```
# touch /reconfigure
```

prior to issuing a shutdown command from a superuser shell. A recovery boot is a rare event on a Solaris system—although hardware failures, kernel module crashes, and incorrect kernel parameters can sometimes result in a hung system. A stack trace is usually provided if a system crash occurs, which can provide vital clues to tracking the source of any system problems using the kernel debugger (kadb).

Although Solaris has eight init states, only five are commonly encountered by administrators during normal operations. The first is run level S, which is a single-user init state used for administrative tasks and the repair of corrupted file systems, using the following command:

```
# /usr/sbin/fsck
```

Also encountered are run level 2, where the init state changes to multiuser mode for the first time, with the exception of NFS exported network resources; run level 3, where all users can log in, and all system and NFS network resources are available; run level 6, which halts the operating system and initiates a reboot; and run level 0, during which the operating system is shut down, ensuring it is safe to power down. In older

SPARC systems, it is necessary to bring the system down to run level 0 to install new hardware, such as disk drives, peripheral devices, and memory modules. However, newer systems, such as the E450, are able to continue to operate in multiuser init states while disks are hot-swapped into special drive bays. This means that these machines may not have a need to enter - run level 6. Further, uptimes of many months or years are not uncommon.

The Solaris software environment provides a detailed series of run control (rc) scripts to control run level changes. In this section, we will examine each of the control scripts in turn, and highlight the improvements and innovations from the old BSD-style Solaris 1.*x* control scripts. Each run level has an associated rc script located in the */sbin* directory, which is also symbolically linked into the */etc* directory: rc0, rc1, rc2, rc3, rc5, rc6, and rcS. */sbin/rc0* is responsible for:

- Executing all scripts in */etc/rc0.d*, if the directory exists.
- Terminating all system services and active processes, initially using `/usr/sbin/killall` and `/usr/sbin/killall 9` for stubborn processes.
- Syncing all mounted file systems, using `/sbin/sync`.
- Unmounting all mounted file systems, using `/sbin/umountall`.

/sbin/rc5 and */sbin/rc6* are just symbolic links to */sbin/rc0*, and do not need to be maintained separately, whilst */sbin/rc1* is responsible for executing all scripts in the */etc/rc1.d* directory, if it exists. This terminates all system services and active processes, initially using `/usr/sbin/killall`, and `/usr/sbin/killall 9` for stubborn processes. The differences between */etc/rc0* and */etc/rc1* are that the latter brings up the system into single-user mode after shutting down all processes in multiuser mode, and does not unmount any file systems.

In run level 2 state, */sbin/rc2* executes all scripts in the */etc/rc2.d* directory, bringing the system into its first multiuser state. Thus, all local file systems listed in */etc/vfstab* are mounted, disk quotas and file system logging are switched on if configured, temporary editor files are saved, the */tmp* directory is cleared, system accounting is enabled, and many network services are initialized. These services are described in more detail in Table 5-2.

In run level 3 state, */sbin/rc3* executes all scripts in the */etc/rc3.d* directory, bringing the system into its final multiuser state. These services are mainly concerned with shared network resources, such as NFS, but Solstice Enterprise Agents and other SNMP-based systems may also be started here. */sbin/rcS* executes all scripts in the */sbin/rcS.d* directory, to bring the system up to the single-user run level. A minimal network configuration is established if a network can be found; otherwise, an interface error is reported. Essential system file systems (such as /, */usr*, and */proc*) are mounted if they are available, and the system name is set.

Under Solaris 1.*x*, there were two main BSD-style control scripts: */etc/rc* and */etc/rc.local*. Typically, vendor-provided daemons were initialized from */etc/rc*, while customized and locally installed daemons were executed from */etc/rc.local*. For example, */etc/rc* was responsible for mounting file systems, enabling quotas, adding swap space, and starting the Internet super daemon (inetd). Alternatively, */etc/rc.local* was responsible for later innovations, such as web servers and authentication services, as well as printer drivers. A general rule of thumb when upgrading legacy systems from Solaris 1.*x* to Solaris 2.*x* is to cross-check all of the required services in */etc/rc*, and ensure that they are enabled in either */etc/rc1.d* or */etc/rc2.d*, and to add any local customizations from */etc/rc.local* to a System V–style startup script in */etc/rc2.d*. Alternatively, shared network resource scripts can be added to */etc/rc3.d*.

 TIP Many Solaris 1.*x* applications will run in binary compatibility mode under Solaris 2.*x*, but your software vendor should be contacted for the latest versions of third-party software.

To the superuser on the console, the transition between run levels is virtually invisible: most daemons, whether starting in a single-user or multiuser init state, display a status message when starting up, which is echoed to the console. A sample console display during booting will look something like this:

```
ok boot
Resetting ...
SPARCstation 20 (2 X 390Z50), Keyboard Present
ROM Rev. 2.4, 128 MB memory installed, Serial #6745644
Ethernet address 6:3:10:a:cc:4a HostID 5767686
Boot device: /iommu/sbus/espdma@f,400000/esp@f,800000/sd@1,0
File and args:
SunOS Release 5.9 Version generic [UNIX(R) System V Release 4.0]
Copyright (c) 1983-2002, Sun Microsystems, Inc.
configuring network interfaces: le0.
Hostname: server
The system is coming up. Please wait.
add net default: gateway 10.16.27.1
NIS domainname is subdomain.mydomain.com
starting rpc services: rpcbind keyserv ypbind done.
Setting netmask of le0 to 255.255.0.0
Setting default interface for multicast: add net 224.0.0.0: gateway server
syslog service starting.
Print services started.
volume management starting.
Starting Apache webserver...done.
The system is ready.
server console login:
```

When booting into single-user mode, there will obviously be fewer messages displayed on the console, as multiuser init state processes are not started. The single-user run level messages will appear as something like this:

```
ok boot -s
SunOS Release 5.9 Version [UNIX(R) System V Release 4.0]
Copyright (c) 1983-2001, Sun Microsystems, Inc.
configuring network interfaces: le0.
Hostname: server
INIT: SINGLE USER MODE
Type Ctrl-d to proceed with normal startup,
(or give root password for system maintenance):
```

At this point, the password for the superuser account should be entered (it will not be echoed to the display). Assuming that the correct password is entered, the display will then proceed with another banner and a Bourne shell prompt:

```
Sun Microsystems Inc. SunOS 5.9 November 2001
#
```

After maintenance is complete, simply exit the shell by using CTRL-D, and the system will then proceed with a normal multiuser boot.

The /sbin/init daemon is responsible for process control initialization, and is a key component of the booting process. While it is not significant in many day-to-day operations after booting, its configuration for special purposes can be confusing for first-time users. In this section, we will examine the initialization of init using the */etc/inittab* file, and explain in detail what each entry means. The primary function of init is to spawn processes, usually daemon processes, from configuration information specified in the file */etc/inittab* in ASCII format.

 NOTE Process spawning always takes place in a specific software context, which is determined by the current run level.

After booting the kernel from the OpenBoot monitor, init reads the system environment variables stored in */etc/default/init* (for example, the time zone variable *TZ*), and sets them for the current run level. init then reads the */etc/inittab* file (described more completely in the next section), setting the init level specified in that file by the initdefault entry. In most multiuser systems, this entry will correspond to run level 3, and the entry will look like this:

```
is:3:initdefault:
```

If the file */etc/inittab* does not exist during booting, the superuser will be asked to manually enter the desired run level for the system. If this event ever occurs unexpectedly for a multiuser system, it is a good strategy to enter single-user mode (by typing **s**) to perform maintenance on the */etc/inittab* file. Another potential problem (which is discussed later) is if */etc/inittab* does contain an empty rstate value in the initdefault entry: the system will go to firmware and continuously reboot! If this occurs, exit from the operating system into the OpenBoot monitor by holding down the STOP key, and pressing A. You can now boot directly into single-user mode, and add an appropriate rstate entry to the */etc/inittab* file. There are safeguards built into init, however: if the system discovers that any entry in */etc/inittab* is respawning rapidly (that is, more than five times per minute), init assumes that a typographical error has been made in the entry, and a warning message is printed on the system console. init will then not respawn the affected entry until at least five minutes has elapsed since the problem was identified.

After entering a multiuser run level for the first time since booting from the OpenBoot monitor, init reads any appropriate boot and bootwait entries in */etc/*

inittab. This provides for basic initialization of the operating system, such as mounting file systems, which is generally performed before users may be allowed to operate on the system.

In order to spawn processes specified in */etc/inittab*, init reads each entry and determines the process requirements for the commands to be executed. For example, for entries that must be respawned in the future, a child process is created using `fork()`. After reading all entries and spawning all processes, init simply waits until it receives a signal to change the system's init state (this explains why init is always visible in the process list). */etc/inittab* is always reread at this point to ensure that any modifications to its specified behavior are used. In addition, init can be initialized at any time by passing a special parameter to force rereading of */etc/inittab*:

```
# init q
```

When init receives a valid request to change run levels, a warning signal is sent to all affected processes, and it waits five seconds before forcibly terminating any processes that do not behave well, and then exits by sending a kill signal. Affected processes are those that will be invalid under the target init state (for example, when going from multiuser to single-user mode, daemons started in multiuser mode will be invalid). Since five seconds may not be sufficient to shut down an entire database server and close all open files, it is best to ensure that such activities precede any change of state that affects the main applications running on your system (for example, by executing the appropriate command in */etc/init.d* with the `stop` parameter).

/sbin/init can only be executed by a superuser, as changes in the system's init state executed by a normal user could have serious consequences (for example, using init to power down a live server). Thus, it is always wise to ensure that file permissions are correctly set on the /sbin/init binary.

Shutdown

A Solaris system is designed to stay up continuously, with as few disruptions to service through rebooting as possible. This design is facilitated by a number of key high-availability and redundancy features in Solaris, including:

- Dual power supplies, where a secondary supply can continue to power the system if the primary power supply fails.

- Mirroring of disk data, meaning that the system can generally continue to operate even in the face of multiple disk failure.

- Hot-swappable disks, meaning that a faulty disk can be removed and replaced while the system is still online. The new disk can be formatted and used immediately, especially when DiskSuite is used.

- The use of domains on E10000 systems, where maintenance performed on one "virtual" host can be performed while a second domain acts in its place.

However, there are a number of situations where a Solaris system must be halted by the superuser, such as:

- Performing a reconfiguration boot
- Powering down the system

Note that the `drvconfig` command can be used to recognize most new hardware devices, further reducing the need for rebooting. A number of different commands are available to shut down and halt a system, and which one is used depends on the specific situation at hand. For example, some commands cycle through a series of shutdown scripts that ensure that key applications and services, such as databases, are cleanly shut down. Others are designed to ensure that a system is powered down as rapidly as possible. For example, if a storm strikes out the main power system and you're only left with a few minutes of battery backup, it might be wise to perform a rapid power down to protect equipment from further damage. We'll investigate the following commands: `init`, `shutdown`, `poweroff`, `halt`, and `reboot`.

Shutting Down the System

The `shutdown` command is used to change a system's state, performing a similar function to init as described previously. However, shutdown has several advantages over init, for instance:

- A grace period can be specified, so that the system can be shut down at some future time, rather than immediately.
- A confirmation message requires the superuser to confirm the shutdown before it proceeds. If an automated shutdown is to be executed at some future time, the confirmation message can be avoided by using the `-y` option.
- Only init states 0, 1, 5, 6, and S can be reached using the `shutdown` command.

For example, to shut down the system to run level 5 so that the system can be moved, the following command would be used, giving 60 seconds notice:

```
# shutdown -i 5 -g 60 "System will be powered off for maintenance. LOGOUT NOW."
```

This will print the following messages at 60 and 30 seconds, respectively:

```
Shutdown started.    Thu Jun   21  12:00:00 EST  2001
Broadcast Message from root (pts/1) on cassowary Thu Jun    21
   12:00:00 EST  2001...
            The system will be shut down in 1 minute
System will be powered off for maintenance. LOGOUT NOW.
Shutdown started.    Thu Jun   21  12:00:30 EST  2001
Broadcast Message from root (pts/1) on cassowary Thu Jun    21
   12:30:00 EST  2001...
            The system will be shut down in 30 seconds
System will be powered off for maintenance. LOGOUT NOW.
```

Once the countdown has been completed, the following message will appear:

```
Do you want to continue? (y or n):
```

If you type **y**, the shutdown will proceed. If you type **n**, the shutdown will be cancelled and the system will remain at the current run level.

Rebooting

The `reboot` command is used to reboot the system, from the current run level to the default run level, and not to change to any other run level. The `reboot` command has several options: the `-l` flag can be used to prevent the recording of the system halt in the system log, which it normally attempts before halting the CPU, while the `-n` option prevents the refreshing of the superblock, which is performed by default to prevent damage to mounted file systems. The most extreme option is `-q`, which does not attempt any kind of fancy actions before shutting down.

In addition, reboot accepts the standard parameters passed to the `boot` command, if they are preceded by two dashes and are placed after the reboot parameters described above on the command line.

For example, to perform a configuration reboot without recording an entry in the system log, the following command could be used:

```
# reboot -1 -- -r
```

Reconfiguration Boot

Performing a reconfiguration boot involves updating the hardware configuration for the system. If new hardware is added to the system, other than a disk, the system must be brought down to the hardware maintenance state (level 0) before the new device can be inserted. In addition, the system must be notified of a reconfiguration reboot by either booting from the OpenBoot PROM monitor with the command `boot -r`, or by creating an empty file called *reconfigure* in the root directory before changing to run level 0. This can be achieved by using the command `touch /reconfigure`. Be sure to remove the */reconfigure* file after the system has been reconfigured if not rebooting!

Powering Down

The `poweroff` command is used to rapidly shut down the system, and switch off power (like switching to run level 5), without cycling through any intermediate run levels, and executing the kill scripts specified for those run levels. This ensures that a very fast shutdown can be achieved when emergency situations dictate that the system cannot remain live, even with the risk of data loss. For example, if a system is under a denial of service attack and the decision is made to pull the plug on the service, the `halt` command will do so much faster than `init` or `shutdown`. The CPU is halted as quickly as possible, no matter what the run level.

The `poweroff` command has several options: the `-l` flag can be used to prevent the recording of the system halt in the system log, which it normally attempts before halting the CPU, while the `-n` option prevents the refreshing of the superblock, which is performed by default to prevent damage to mounted file systems. The most extreme option is `-q`, which does not attempt any kind of fancy actions before shutting down.

Halting the System

The `halt` command is used to rapidly shut down the system, to the OpenBoot PROM monitor, without cycling through any intermediate run levels, and executing the kill scripts specified for those run levels. This ensures that a very fast shutdown can be achieved when emergency situations dictate that the system cannot remain live, even with the risk of data loss. For example, if a system is under a denial of service attack, and the decision is made to pull the plug on the service, `halt` will do so much faster than `init` or `shutdown`. The CPU is halted as quickly as possible, no matter what the run level.

The `halt` command has several options: the `-1` flag can be used to prevent the recording of the system halt in the system log, which it normally attempts before halting the CPU, while the `-n` option prevents the refreshing of the superblock, which is performed by default to prevent damage to mounted file systems. The most extreme option is `-q`, which does not attempt any kind of fancy actions before halting.

Writing Control Scripts

For a multiuser system, the most important control scripts reside in the */etc/rc2.d* and */etc/rc3.d* directories, which are responsible for enabling multiuser services and NFS network resource sharing, respectively. A basic script for starting up a web server looks like this:

```
#!/bin/sh
# Sample webserver startup script
# Should be placed in /etc/rc2.d/S99webserver
case "$1" in
    'start')
        echo "Starting webserver...\c"
        if [ -f /usr/local/sbin/webserver ]; then
            /usr/local/sbin/webserver start
        fi
        echo ""
        ;;
    'stop')
     echo "Stopping webserver...\c"
        if [ -f /usr/local/sbin/webserver ]; then
            /usr/local/sbin/webserver stop
        fi
        echo ""
   ;;
   *)
        echo "Usage: /etc/rc2.d/S99webserver { start | stop }"
        ;;
    esac
```

This file should be created by root (with the group sys) and placed in the file */etc/rc2.d/S99webserver*, and should have executable permissions.

```
# chmod 0744 /etc/rc2.d/S99webserver
# chgrp sys /etc/rc2.d/S99webserver
```

This location of the file is a matter of preference. Many admins treat the web server similar to an NFS server—in this respect, the system's run level 3 represents a "shared" state. Since a web server is a shared service, it could also be started from a script in */etc/rc3.d*. When called with the argument `start` (represented in the script by "$1"), the script prints a status message that the web server daemon is starting, and proceeds to execute the command if the web server binary exists. The script can also act as a kill script, since it has a provision to be called with a `stop` argument. Of course, a more complete script would provide more elaborate status information if the web server binary did not exist, and may further process any output from the web server by using a pipe (for example, mailing error messages to the superuser).

One of the advantages of the flexible boot system is that these scripts can be executed to start and stop specific daemons without changing the init state. For example, if a web site was going to be updated and the web server needed to be switched off for a few minutes, the command

```
# /etc/rc2.d/S99webserver stop
```

would halt the web server process, but would not force the system back into a single-user state. The web server could be restarted after all content was uploaded by typing this command:

```
# /etc/rc2.d/S99webserver start
```

In order to conform to System V standards, it is actually more appropriate to create all the run control scripts in the */etc/init.d* directory, and create symbolic links back to the appropriate *rc2.d* and *rc3.d* directories. This means that all scripts executed by init through different run levels are centrally located and can be easily maintained. With the web server example, a file could be created in */etc/init.d* with a descriptive filename:

```
# vi /etc/init.d/webserver
```

After adding the appropriate contents, the file could be saved, and the appropriate symbolic link could be created using the symbolic link command `ln`:

```
# ln -s /etc/init.d/webserver /etc/rc2.d/S99webserver
```

Using this convention, kill and startup scripts for each service can literally coexist in the same script, with the ability to process a `start` argument for startup scripts, and a `stop` argument for kill scripts. In this example, you would also need to create a symbolic link to */etc/init.d/webserver* for K99webserver.

Writing Kill Scripts

Under System V, kill scripts follow the same convention as startup scripts, in that a `stop` argument is passed to the script to indicate that a kill rather than a startup is required, in which case a `start` argument would be passed. A common approach to killing off processes is to find them by name in the process list. The following script kills the asynchronous PPP daemon, which is the link manager for the asynchronous data link protocol. This daemon is started using aspppd—thus, the script generates a process list that is piped through a grep to identify any entries containing "aspppd," and the process number is extracted using awk. This value is assigned to a variable ("$procid"), which is then used by the `kill` command to terminate the appropriate process. Alternatively, the `pgrep` or `pkill` command could be used:

```
procid=`ps -e | grep aspppd | awk '{print $1}'`
if test -n "$procid"
then
      kill $procid
fi
```

Alternatively, sed could be used to match the process name:

```
procid=`/usr/bin/ps -e |
   /usr/bin/grep aspppd |
   /usr/bin/sed -e 's/^  *//' -e 's/ .*//'`
```

When multiple processes are to be terminated using a single script (for example, when the NFS server terminates), a shell function (`killprocid()`) can be written that takes an argument and searches for it in the process list, terminating the named process if it exists:

```
killprocid() {
procid=`/usr/bin/ps -e |
        /usr/bin/grep -w $1 |
        /usr/bin/sed -e 's/^  *//' -e 's/ .*//'`
    [ "$procid" != "" ] && kill $procid
}
```

A more modern way of finding and killing processes involves using the `pgrep` and `pkill` commands, respectively.

Individual processes can then be terminated using the same function:

```
killproc nfsd
killproc mountd
killproc rpc.boot
killproc in.rarpd
killproc rpld
```

However, there are two problems with these approaches to process termination. Firstly, there is an ambiguity problem in that different daemons and applications can be identified by the same name. For example, a system may be running the Apache web server, which is identified by the process name httpd, as well as a web server from another vendor (such as NCSA) that is also identified by httpd. If a script was written to kill the Apache web server, but the first process identified actually belonged to the NCSA web server, the NCSA web server process would be terminated. One solution to this problem is to ensure that all applications are launched with a unique name, or from a wrapper script with a unique name. The second problem is that for a system with even a moderately heavy process load (for example, 500 active processes), executing the ps command to kill each process is going to generate a large CPU overhead, leading to excessively slow shutdown times. Alternative solutions to this problem are provided in the previous section.

Displaying eeprom Variables

To examine the default values used by your system for booting the kernel, and the default boot devices, simply use the /usr/sbin/eeprom command:

```
# /usr/sbin/eeprom
tpe-link-test?=true
scsi-initiator-id=7
keyboard-click?=false
keymap: data not available.
ttyb-rts-dtr-off=false
ttyb-ignore-cd=true
ttya-rts-dtr-off=false
ttya-ignore-cd=true
ttyb-mode=9600,8,n,1,-
ttya-mode=9600,8,n,1,-
pcia-probe-list=1,2,3,4
pcib-probe-list=1,2,3
mfg-mode=off
diag-level=max
#power-cycles=50
system-board-serial#: data not available.
system-board-date: data not available.
fcode-debug?=false
output-device=screen
input-device=keyboard
load-base=16384
boot-command=boot
auto-boot?=true
watchdog-reboot?=false
diag-file: data not available.
diag-device=net
boot-file: data not available.
boot-device=disk net
local-mac-address?=false
ansi-terminal?=true
screen-#columns=80
screen-#rows=34
silent-mode?=false
use-nvramrc?=false
nvramrc: data not available.
security-mode=none
security-password: data not available.
security-#badlogins=0
oem-logo: data not available.
oem-logo?=false
oem-banner: data not available.
oem-banner?=false
hardware-revision: data not available.
last-hardware-update: data not available.
diag-switch?=false
```

You can also change the values of the boot device and `boot` command from within Solaris by using the `eeprom` command, rather than having to reboot, jump into the OpenBoot monitor, and set the values directly.

Shutting Down the System

In order to manually change run levels, the desired init state is used as an argument to /sbin/init. For example, to bring the system down to a single-user mode for maintenance, the following command can be used:

```
#  init s
INIT: New run level: S
The system is coming down for administration. Please wait.
Print services stopped.
syslogd: going down on signal 15
Killing user processes: done.
INIT: SINGLE USER MODE
Type Ctrl-d to proceed with normal startup,
(or give root password for system maintenance):
Entering System Maintenance Mode ...
#
```

The system is most easily shut down by using the new `/usr/sbin/shutdown` command (not the old BSD-style `/usr/ucb/shutdown` command discussed later). This command is issued with the form

```
# shutdown -i run-level -g grace-period -y
```

where `run-level` is an init state different than the default init state S (that is, one of the run levels 0, 1 2, 5, or 6). However, most administrators will typically be interested in using the `shutdown` command with respect to the reboot or power-down run levels. The `grace-period` is the number of seconds before the shutdown process is initiated. On single-user machines, the superuser will easily know who is logged in and what processes need to be terminated gracefully. However, on a multiuser machine, it is more useful to warn users in advance of a power down or reboot. If the change of init state is to proceed without user intervention, it is useful to include the `-y` flag at the end of the `shutdown` command; otherwise, the message

```
Do you want to continue? (y or n):
```

will be displayed, and y must be entered in order for the shutdown to proceed. The default grace period on Solaris is 60 seconds, so if the administrators wished to reboot with 2 minutes warning given to all users, without user intervention, the command would be

```
# shutdown -i 5 -g 120 -y
```

The system will then periodically display a message warning all users of the imminent init state change:

```
Shutdown started. Mon Jan 10 10:22:00 EST 2001
Broadcast Message from root (console) on server Mon Jan 10 10:22:00...
The system server will be shut down in 2 minutes
```

The system will then reboot without user intervention, and does not enter the OpenBoot monitor. If commands need to be issued using the monitor (that is, an init state of 0 is desired), the following command can be used:

```
# shutdown -i0 -g180 -y
Shutdown started. Mon Jan 10 11:15:00 EST 2001
Broadcast Message from root (console) on server Mon Jan 10 11:15:00...
The system will be shut down in 3 minutes
.
.
.
INIT: New run level: 0
The system is coming down. Please wait.
.
.
.
The system is down.
syncing file systems... [1] [2] [3] done
Program terminated
Type help for more information
ok
```

There are many ways to warn users in advance of a shutdown. One way is to edit the "message of the day" file (*/etc/motd*) to contain a warning that the server will be "down" and/or rebooted for a specific time. This message will be displayed every time a user successfully logs in with an interactive shell. The following message gives the date and time of the shutdown, expected duration, and a contact address for enquiries:

```
System server will be shutdown at 5 p.m. 2/1/2001.
Expected downtime: 1 hour.
E-mail root@system for further details.
```

At least 24 hours notice is usually required for users on a large system, as long jobs need to be rescheduled. In practice, many administrators will only shut down or reboot outside business hours to minimize inconvenience; however, power failure and hardware problems can necessitate unexpected downtime.

This method works well in advance, but since many users are continuously logged in from remote terminals, they won't always read the new "message of the day." An alternative approach is to use the "write all" command (`wall`), which sends a message to all terminals of all logged-in users. This command can be sent manually at hourly intervals prior to shutdown, or a cron job could be established to perform this task automatically. An example command would be

```
# wall
System server will be shutdown at 5 p.m. 1/10/2001.
Expected downtime: 1 hour.
E-mail root@system for further details.
^d
```

After sending the `wall` message, a final check of logged-in users prior to shutdown can be performed using the `who` command:

```
# who
root        console     Jan 10 10:15
pwatters      pts/0      Jan 10 10:15      (client)
```

A message can be sent to the user pwatters on pts/0 directly to notify him of the imminent shutdown:

```
# write pwatters
Dear pwatters,
Please logout immediately as the system server is going down.
If you do not logout now, your unsaved work may be lost.
Yours Sincerely,
System Administrator (root@system)
^d
```

Depending on the status of the user, it may also be fruitful to request a talk session by using this command:

```
# talk pwatters
```

If all these strategies fail to convince the user pwatters to log out, there is nothing left to do but proceed with the shutdown.

Changing init States

In addition to being the process spawner, init can be used to switch run levels at any time. For example, to perform hardware maintenance, the following command would be used:

```
# init 0
```

To enter the administrative state, the following command would be used:

```
# init 1
```

To enter the first multiuser state, the following command would be used:

```
# init 2
```

To enter the second multiuser state, the following command would be used:

```
# init 3
```

To enter a user-defined state, the following command would be used:

```
# init 4
```

To power down the system, the following command would be used:

```
# init 5
```

To halt and reboot the operating system, the following command would be used:

```
# init 6
```

To enter the administrative state, with all of the file systems available, the following command would be used:

```
# init S
```

Before using init in this way, it's often advisable to precede its execution with a call to sync. The sync command renews the disk superblock, which ensures that all outstanding data operations are flushed and the file system is stable before shutting down.

/etc/inittab

After the kernel is loaded into memory, the /sbin/init process is initialized, and the system is bought up to the default init state, which is determined by the initdefault value contained in */etc/inittab*, which controls the behavior of the init process. Each entry has the form

```
identifier:runlevel:action:command
```

where `identifier` is a unique two-character identifier, `runlevel` specifies the run level to be entered, `action` specifies the process characteristics of the command to be executed, and `command` is the name of the program to be run. The program can be an application or a script file. The run level must be one of the following: s, a, b, c, 1, 2, 3, 4, 5, or 6. Alternatively, if the process is to be executed by all run levels, no run level should be specified.

The following is a standard inittab file:

```
ap::sysinit:/sbin/autopush -f /etc/iu.ap
ap::sysinit:/sbin/soconfig -f /etc/sock2path
fs::sysinit:/sbin/rcS sysinit           >/dev/msglog 2<>/dev/msglog
</dev/console
is:3:initdefault:
p3:s1234:powerfail:/usr/sbin/shutdown -y -i5 -g0 >/dev/msglog 2
<>/dev/msglog
sS:s:wait:/sbin/rcS                     >/dev/msglog 2<>/dev/msglog
</dev/console
s0:0:wait:/sbin/rc0                     >/dev/msglog 2<>/dev/msglog
</dev/console
s1:1:respawn:/sbin/rc1                  >/dev/msglog 2<>/dev/msglog
</dev/console
s2:23:wait:/sbin/rc2                    >/dev/msglog 2<>/dev/msglog
</dev/console
s3:3:wait:/sbin/rc3                     >/dev/msglog 2<>/dev/msglog
</dev/console
s5:5:wait:/sbin/rc5                     >/dev/msglog 2<>/dev/msglog
</dev/console
s6:6:wait:/sbin/rc6                     >/dev/msglog 2<>/dev/msglog
</dev/console
fw:0:wait:/sbin/uadmin 2 0              >/dev/msglog 2<>/dev/msglog
</dev/console
```

```
of:5:wait:/sbin/uadmin 2 6                    >/dev/msglog 2<>/dev/msglog
</dev/console
rb:6:wait:/sbin/uadmin 2 1                    >/dev/msglog 2<>/dev/msglog
</dev/console
sc:234:respawn:/usr/lib/saf/sac -t 300
co:234:respawn:/usr/lib/saf/ttymon -g -h -p "`uname -n` console
login: " -T sun
-d /dev/console -l console -m ldterm,ttcompat
```

This */etc/inittab* file only contains entries for the actions sysinit, respawn, initdefault, wait, and powerfail. These are the common actions found on most systems; however, Solaris provides a wide variety of actions which may be useful in special situations (for example, when powerwait is more appropriate then powerfail). Potential actions are identified by any one of the following:

- **initdefault** This is a mandatory entry found on all systems, which is used to configure the default run level for the system. This is specified by the highest init state specified in the rstate field. If this field is empty, init interprets the rstate as the highest possible run level (run level 6), which will force a continuous reboot of the system. In addition, if the entry is missing, the administrator must supply one manually on the console for booting to proceed.

- **sysinit** This entry is provided as a safeguard for asking which run level is required at boot time if the initdefault entry is missing. Only devices required to ask the question are affected.

- **boot** This entry is only parsed at boot time, and is mainly used for initialization following a full reboot of the system after power down.

- **off** This entry ensures that a process is terminated upon entering a particular run level. A warning signal is sent, followed by a kill signal, again with a five-second interval.

- **once** This entry is similar to boot, but more flexible in that the named process runs only once and is not respawned.

- **ondemand** This entry is similar to the respawn action.

- **powerfail** Runs the process associated with the entry when a power fail signal is received.

- **powerwait** Similar to powerfail, except that init waits until the process terminates before further processing entries in */etc/inittab*. This is especially useful for enforcing sequential shutdown of services that are prioritized.

- **bootwait** This entry is parsed only on the first occasion that the transition from single-user to multiuser run levels occur after a system boot.

- **wait** This entry starts a process and waits for its completion on entering the specified run level; however, the entry is ignored if */etc/inittab* is reread during the same run level.

- **respawn** This entry ensures that if a process that should be running is not, it should be respawned.

The */etc/inittab* file follows conventions for text layout used by the Bourne shell: a long entry can be continued on the following line by using a backslash (\), and comments can only be inserted into the process field by using a hash character (#). There is a limitation of 512 characters for each entry imposed on */etc/inittab*; however, there is no limit on the number of entries that may be inserted.

Summary

In this chapter, we have examined the different processes and techniques involved in initializing and booting a Solaris system. Once a system has been installed, many applications and services require startup scripts to be written and maintained, so it's critical that administrators understand the sequence of boot and shutdown scripts before modifying existing files.

Questions

1. What is the purpose of run level 0?

   A. First multiuser state

   B. Administrative state

   C. Hardware maintenance state

   D. Power off

2. What is the purpose of run level 1?

   A. First multiuser state

   B. Administrative state

   C. Hardware maintenance state

   D. Power off

3. What is the purpose of run level 2?

   A. First multiuser state

   B. Administrative state

   C. Hardware maintenance state

   D. Power off

4. What is the purpose of run level 5?

   A. First multiuser state

   B. Administrative state

   C. Hardware maintenance state

   D. Power off

5. What user access is granted at run level 0?

   A. Console access

   B. Single-user access

   C. Multiuser access

   D. Not specified

6. What user access is granted at run level 1?

   A. Console access

   B. Single-user access

   C. Multiuser access

   D. Not specified

7. What user access is granted at run level 2?

   A. Console access

   B. Single-user access

   C. Multiuser access

   D. Not specified

8. What user access is granted at run level 4?

   A. Console access

   B. Single-user access

   C. Multiuser access

   D. Not specified

9. What are the most commonly found entries in */etc/inittab*?

   A. `sysinit, respawn, initdefault, wait,` and `powerfail`

   B. `sysinit, respawn, initdefault, wait,` and `poweron`

   C. `sysdown, respawn, initdefault, wait,` and `powerfail`

   D. `sysinit, despawn, initdefault, wait,` and `powerfail`

10. If the administrator wished to reboot with two minutes warning given to all users, without user intervention, what `shutdown` command would be used?

    A. `shutdown -i 6 -g 120 -n`

    B. `shutdown -i 6 -g 120 -y`

    C. `shutdown -i 6 -g 2 -y`

    D. `shutdown -i 6 -g 2 -x`

Answers

1. **C.** Run level 0 is the hardware maintenance state.

2. **B.** Run level 1 is the administrative state.

3. **A.** Run level 2 is the first administrative state.

4. **D.** Run level 5 is the power off state.

5. **A.** Only console access is available at run level 0.

6. **B.** Single-user access is available at run level 1.

7. **C.** Multiuser access is granted at run level 2.

8. **D.** Access at run level 4 is user-defined.

9. **A.** The `sysinit`, `respawn`, `initdefault`, `wait`, and `powerfail` entries are most commonly found in */etc/inittab*.

10. **B.** The `shutdown -i 6 -g 120 -y` command will perform a reboot with two minutes warning given to all users, without user intervention.

Managing Users

In this chapter, you will
- Understand the concepts of users and groups
- Discover Solaris password management facilities
- Learn how to create users and groups using the CLI
- Review the management of users and groups using the admintool GUI

The concept of the user is central to Solaris—all processes and files on a Solaris system are owned by a particular user, and are assigned to a specific user group. No data or activities on the system may exist without a valid user or group. Managing users and groups as a Solaris administrator can be a challenging activity—you will be responsible for assigning all of the privileges granted or denied to a user or group of users, and many of these permissions carry great risk. For example, a user with an inappropriate privilege level may execute commands as the superuser, causing damage to your system. In this chapter, we will learn how to add users to the system, and add and modify groups. In addition, the contents and structure of key user databases, including the password, shadow password, and group files, are examined in detail. Finally, we introduce the admintool, which is a GUI-based user administration tool designed to make user management easier under Solaris.

Users

All users on a Solaris system have a number of unique identifiers and characteristics that can be used to distinguish individual users from each other, and also to logically group related users. Most physical users of a Solaris system will have a unique "login" assigned to them, which is identified by a username with a maximum of eight characters. Once a user account is created, it can be used for the following purposes:

- Spawning a shell
- Executing applications interactively
- Scheduling applications to run on specific times and dates
- Accessing database applications and other system services

In addition to user accounts, Solaris also uses a number of system accounts (such as root, daemon, bin, sys, lp, adm, and uucp) to perform various kinds of routine maintenance, including:

- Allocation of system resources to perform specific tasks
- Running a mail server
- Running a web server
- Process management

Users may access a Solaris system by accessing the console, or through a remote terminal, in either graphical or text mode. In each case, a set of authentication credentials is presented to the system, including the username and password. When entered, a user's password is compared to an encrypted string stored in the password database (*/etc/passwd*) or the shadow password database (*/etc/shadow*). Once the string entered by the user has been encrypted, it is matched against the already encrypted entry in the password database. If a match is made, authentication occurs and the user may spawn a shell. A Solaris username may have a maximum of eight characters, as may a Solaris password. Since the security of a Solaris system relies heavily on the difficulty of guessing passwords, user policies should be developed to either recommend or enforce the use of passwords containing random or semirandom character strings. The authentication sequence is shown in Figure 6-1.

User Characteristics

There are a number of other user characteristics that are associated with each user, in addition to a username and password. These features include:

- The user ID (UID), which is a unique integer that begins with the root user (UID=1), with other UIDs typically (but not necessarily) being allocated sequentially. Some systems will reserve all UIDs below 1023 for system accounts (for example, the apache user for managing the Apache web server), while those UIDs above 1024 are designated for ordinary users. The UID of 0 designates the superuser account, which is typically called "root".

Figure 6-1
Solaris
authentication
sequence

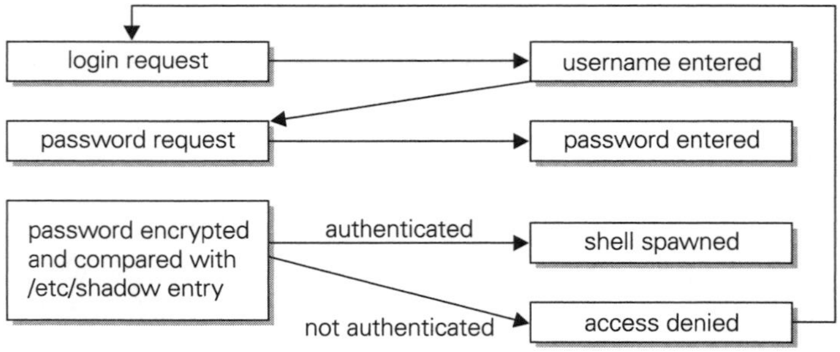

- A flexible mechanism for distinguishing different classes of users, known as groups. Groups are not just sets of related users: the Solaris file system allows for group-designated read, write, and execute file access for groups, in addition to permissions granted to the individual user and to all users. Every UID is associated with a primary group ID (GID); however, UIDs may also be associated with more than one secondary group.

- A home directory, which is the default file storage location for all files created by a particular user. If the automounter is used, home directories may be exported using NFS on */home* or other directories. When a user spawns a login shell, the current working directory will always be the home directory.

- A login shell, which can be used to issue commands interactively, or to write simple programs. A number of different shells are available under Solaris, including the Bourne shell (sh), the C shell (csh), the Bourne again shell (bash), and the Cornell shell (tcsh). The choice of shell depends largely on personal preference, user experience with C-like programming constructs, and terminal handling.

- A comment, which is typically the user's full name, such as "Paul Watters". However, system accounts may use names that describe their purpose (for example, the command `WebServer` might be associated with the apache user).

Adding Users

Adding a user to a Solaris system is easy, but this operation may only be performed by the root user. There are two options: the first option is to edit the */etc/passwd* file directly, incrementing the UID, adding the appropriate GID, adding a home directory (and remembering to physically create it on the file system), inserting a comment, and choosing a login name. In addition, a password for the user must be set using the `passwd` command. The second is to use the built-in command-line interfaces to create accounts.

 TIP Does adding a user on the command line sound difficult? If so, you should consider using the automated `useradd` command, which will do all of the hard work for you as long as you supply the correct information.

The `useradd` command has the following format:

```
# useradd -u uid -g gid -d home_directory -m -k /etc/skel -s path_to_shell -c comment login_name
```

Let's add a user to our system, and examine the results:

```
# useradd -u 1004 -g 10 -d /opt/www -m -k /etc/skel -s /bin/sh -c "Web User" www
```

Here, we are adding a "Web User" called "www" with the UID 1004, GID 10, with the home directory */opt/www*, and the Bourne shell as their login shell. At the end of the `useradd` script, an appropriate line should appear in the */etc/passwd* file:

```
# grep www /etc/passwd
www:x:1004:10:Web User:/opt/www:/bin/sh
```

However, the `useradd` command may fail under the following conditions:

- The UID that you specified has already been taken by another user. UIDs may be recycled as long as precautions are taken to ensure that a previous owner of the UID no longer owns files on the file system.
- The GID that you specified does not exist. Verify its entry in the groups database (*/etc/group*).
- The comment contains special characters, like double quotes " ", exclamation marks "!", or slashes "/".
- The shell that you specified does not exist. Check that the shell actually exists in the path specified, and that the shell has an entry in the shells database (*/etc/shells*).

Modifying User Attributes

Once you have created a user account, it is possible to change any of its characteristics by directly editing the password database (*/etc/passwd*), or by using the `usermod` command. For example, if we wanted to modify the UID of the www account from 1004 to 1005, we would use this command:

```
# usermod -u 1005 www
```

Again, we can verify that the change has been made correctly by examining the entry for www in the password database:

```
# grep www /etc/passwd
www:x:1005:10:Web User:/opt/www:/bin/sh
```

Remember that if you change a UID or GID, you must manually update existing directory and file ownerships by using the `chmod`, `chgrp`, and `chown` commands where appropriate.

Once a user account has been created, the next step is to set a password, which can be performed by the `passwd` command

```
# passwd user
```

where user is the login name for the account whose password you wish to change. In all cases, you will be required to enter the new password twice—if you happen to make a typing error, the password will not be changed and you will be warned that the two password strings entered did not match. Here's an example for the user www:

```
# passwd www
New password:
Re-enter new password:
passwd(SYSTEM): They don't match; try again.
New password:
Re-enter new password:
passwd (SYSTEM): passwd successfully changed for www
```

After a password has been entered for a user, such as the www user, it should appear as an encrypted string in the shadow password database (*/etc/shadow*):

```
# grep www /etc/shadow
www:C4dMH8As4bGTM:::::::
```

TIP Once a user has been granted an initial password, they may then enter a new password of their own choosing by using the `passwd` command with no options.

Exercise 6-1

Create a user account called "jbloggs" using the `useradd` command and check that a password entry is created in the shadow password database (*/etc/shadow*).

Deleting Users

Now imagine that one of your prized employees has moved on to greener pastures unexpectedly—although you will eventually be able to change the ownership on all of her files, you cannot immediately restart some production applications that must be available 24×7. In this case, it is possible to temporarily disable logins to a specific account by using a command like

```
# passwd -l natashia
```

This command would lock Natashia's account until the root user once again used the `passwd` command on this account to set a new password. A locked account can be identified in the password database by the characters LK:

```
# grep natashia /etc/shadow
natashia:*LK*:::::::
```

Once all of the user's files have been backed up, and any active processes have been killed by the superuser, the user account may be permanently deleted by using the `userdel` command. For example, to delete the user account natashia, and remove that user's home directory and all of the files underneath that directory, you would use the command

```
# userdel -r natashia
```

Alternatively, you could edit both the password and shadow password databases, and remove the appropriate lines containing the entries for the user natashia. You would also need to manually remove the user's home directory, and all of her files underneath that directory.

 TIP There are several system accounts that should remain locked at all times to prevent interactive logins, including adm, bin, listen, nobody, lp, sys, and uucp.

Exercise 6-2

Delete the user account called jbloggs using the `userdel` command and check that its password entry has been removed from the shadow password database (*/etc/shadow*).

Groups

Solaris provides a facility for separating sets of related users into groups. Each user is associated with a primary group ID (GID), which is associated with a name. The group name and GID can be used interchangeably. In addition, users can also be associated with one or more secondary groups. This flexibility means that while a user might have a primary group membership based on their employment or organizational status (for example, staff or managers), they can actively share data and system privileges with other groups based on their workgroup needs (for example, sales, engineer).

Group Characteristics

Information about groups in Solaris is stored in the groups database (*/etc/group*), but the local groups database may also be supplemented by the NIS/NIS+ or LDAP databases. Let's examine a typical set of groups:

```
# cat /etc/group
root::0:root
other::1:
bin::2:root,bin,daemon
sys::3:root,bin,sys,adm
adm::4:root,adm,daemon
uucp::5:root,uucp
mail::6:root
tty::7:root,tty,adm
lp::8:root,lp,adm
nuucp::9:root,nuucp
staff::10:paul,maya,brad,natashia
postgres:a.mBzQnr1ei2D.:100:postgres, paul
daemon::12:root,daemon
sysadmin::14:
nobody::60001:
noaccess::60002:
nogroup::65534:
```

We can see that the lower group numbers are associated with all of the system functions and accounts, such as the bin group, which has the members root, bin, and daemon, and the sys group, which has the members root, bin, sys, and adm. Higher-numbered groups, such as staff, contain several different users, such as paul, maya, brad, and natashia. Notice also that paul has a secondary group membership in the postgres group, giving him database access privileges. A group password can also be set for each group, although most groups don't use this facility. In this group database, we can see that the postgres group is the only group that has an encrypted password (a.mBzQnr1ei2D.).

You can obtain a list of all groups that a user belongs to by using the `groups` command. For example, to view all of the groups that the root users belongs to, we use the command

```
# groups root
other root bin sys adm uucp mail tty lp nuucp daemon
```

You can also see the converse, who belongs to a particular group using the command:

```
# getent group groupname
```

For example:

```
# getent group root
root:*:0:root
```

Adding Groups

To add a new group to the system, you may either manually edit the */etc/group* file or use the `groupadd` command, which has the following syntax:

```
/usr/sbin/groupadd -g gid  group_name
```

Thus, to add a group called managers to the system, with a GID of 500, we would use the command

```
# groupadd -g 500 managers
```

We would then be able to verify the new group's existence by searching the groups database:

```
# grep management /etc/group
managers::500:
```

 CAUTION The `groupadd` command will fail if the GID that you specify has already been allocated to an existing group, unless you use the −o option, or if the group_name is greater than eight characters.

Managing Groups

If you want to change your group from the primary to the secondary during an interactive session, to ensure that all of the files that you create are associated with the correct GID, you need to use the `newgrp` command. For example, the root user has the following primary group membership:

```
# id
uid=0(root) gid=0(root)
```

However, if the root user wishes to act as a member of another group, such as sys, the following command would have to be used:

```
# newgrp sys
```

The effective GID would then change to sys:

```
# id
uid=0(root) gid=3(sys)
```

Any operations that the root user performs after using `newgrp`, such as creating files, will be associated with the GID of 3 (sys) rather than 0 (root). For example, if we created a new file with the primary group, the group associated with the new file would be GID 0:

```
# touch root.txt
# ls -l root.txt
-rw-r--r--   1 root     root     0 Oct 12 11:17 root.txt
```

However, if the root user then changes groups to sys and creates a new file, then the group associated with the file will be sys rather than root:

```
# newgrp sys
# touch sys.txt
# ls -l sys.txt
-rw-r--r--   1 root     sys      0 Oct 12 11:18 sys.txt
```

Passwords

All Solaris users have a username and password associated with their account, except where a user account has been explicitly locked (designated *LK*), or where a system account has been specified not to have a password at all (NP). Many early exploits of Solaris systems were associated with default passwords used on some system accounts, and the most common method of gaining unauthorized access to a Solaris system remains password cracking and/or guessing. In this section, we examine the password database (*/etc/passwd*), and its more secure counterpart the shadow database (*/etc/shadow*), and examine strategies for making passwords safer.

The standard password database is stored in the file */etc/passwd*, and looks like this:

```
# cat /etc/passwd
root:x:0:1:Super-User:/:/sbin/sh
daemon:x:1:1::/:
bin:x:2:2::/usr/bin:
sys:x:3:3::/:
adm:x:4:4:Admin:/var/adm:
lp:x:71:8:Line Printer Admin:/usr/spool/lp:
```

```
uucp:x:5:5:uucp Admin:/usr/lib/uucp:
nuucp:x:9:9:uucp Admin:/var/spool/uucppublic:/usr/lib/uucp/uucico
listen:x:37:4:Network Admin:/usr/net/nls:
nobody:x:60001:60001:Nobody:/:
noaccess:x:60002:60002:No Access User:/:
nobody4:x:65534:65534:SunOS 4.x Nobody:/:
postgres:x:1001:100:Postgres User:/usr/local/postgres:/bin/sh
htdig:x:1002:10:htdig:/opt/www:/usr/local/bin/bash
apache:x:1003:10:apache user:/usr/local/apache:/bin/sh
```

We have already seen some of the fields shown here when adding users to the system:

- The username field, which has a maximum of eight characters
- The encrypted password field, which in a system using shadow passwords is crossed with an *x*
- The user ID field, which contains the numeric and unique UID
- The primary group ID field, which contains the numeric GID
- The user comment, which contains a description of the user
- The path to the user's home directory
- The user's default shell

In older versions of Solaris, the encrypted password field would have contained an encrypted password string like "X14oLaiYg7bO2". However, this presented a security problem, as the login program required all users to have read access to the password file:

```
# ls -l /etc/passwd
-rw-r--r--   1 root      sys          605 Jul 24 11:04 /etc/passwd
```

Thus, any user with the lowest-form privilege would be able to access the encrypted password field for the root user, and could attempt to gain root access by guessing the password. A number of programs were specifically developed for this purpose, such as *crack*, which takes a standard Solaris password file and uses a dictionary and some clever lexical rules to guess passwords.

 CAUTION   Once a root password has been obtained, a rogue user may perform any operation on a Solaris system, including formatting hard disks, installing Trojan horses, launching attacks on other systems, and so forth.

The cryptographic algorithm used by Solaris is not easy to crack—indeed, a brute force guess of a password composed of a completely random set of characters would take many CPU years to compute. The task would be made even more difficult (if not impossible) if the root password was changed weekly, again with a random set of characters. However, the reality is that most users enter passwords that are easily guessed from a dictionary, or from some knowledge about the user. Since we are constantly required to use PINs and passwords, people generally choose passwords that are easy to remember. However, easily remembered passwords are also the easiest to crack.

Solaris has reduced the chances of a rogue user obtaining the password file in the first place by implementing a shadow password facility. This creates a file called */etc/shadow*, which is similar to the password file (*/etc/passwd*), but is only readable by root, and contains the encrypted password fields for each UID. Thus, if a rogue user cannot obtain the encrypted password entries, it is impossible to use them as the basis for a crack attack.

pwck

The `pwck` command is used to verify the accuracy of the password file. It reads */etc/passwd*, and it verifies that the expected number of fields exist for each entry in the file and validates the contents of the username, UID, and GID fields. It also checks whether the home directory exists and whether the default shell noted is a valid shell.

grpck

The `grpck` command is similar to the `pwck` command; you can use it to verify the accuracy of the group file. It reads */etc/group* and verifies that the expected number of fields exist for each entry in the file, and it validates the contents of the group name and GID fields. It also creates a list of usernames defined in the group and checks that these are contained in the */etc/passwd* file. If not, an error is reported, because an old user account may have been deleted from */etc/passwd* but may still be listed in a group.

pwconv

You can use the `pwconv` command to convert systems that do not have a shadow password file to use password shadowing. Most (if not all) modern systems would use password shadowing. However, if the */etc/shadow* file does not exist, the encrypted password is stripped from */etc/passwd*, and is replaced by *x*, indicating that the password for each user is shadowed. A shadow password file would then be created using the encrypted passwords extracted from the password file.

However, a more common use of *pwconv* is to update the shadow password file with entries that have been created manually in */etc/passwd*. Although this is not the recommended method of adding users to the system, some sites have scripts that create blocks of new user accounts by generating sequential usernames with generic group and password information. In such cases, it would be necessary to run *pwconv* after the script has been executed to ensure that entries created in */etc/passwd* are correctly transferred to */etc/shadow*.

Managing Users and Groups with admintool

So far, we have only examined user and group administration by using command-line tools, such as *useradd* and *groupadd*. Fortunately, Solaris also provides an easy to use administrative interface for adding users and groups to the system called admintool. The admintool interface is shown in Figure 6-2. The interface shown is for user management, displaying the username, UID, and user comment. In addition to managing users and groups, admintool is also useful for managing hosts, printers, serial ports, and software.

Figure 6-2
The Solaris
admintool

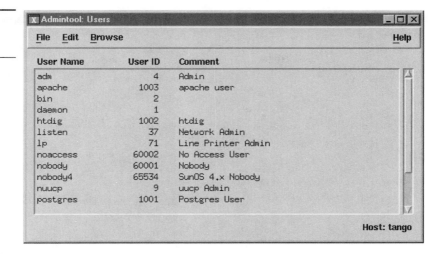

Each management option has its own interface, which is accessible from the Browse menu. When an interface is selected, such as the printers interface, administrators may then add, modify, or delete the entries that exist in the current database (in this case, administrators may add, delete, or modify the entries for printers).

Let's examine how to modify existing user information using the admintool, as shown in Figure 6-3. First, select the user whose data you wish to modify (for example, the adm user, one of the preconfigured system accounts that is created during Solaris installation). Next, select the Modify option from the admintool Edit menu. The user entry modification window is shown in Figure 6-3 for the adm user. Here, it is possible to modify the following options:

- The username
- The primary group
- All secondary groups
- The user comment
- The login shell, which is selected from a drop-down menu containing all valid shells defined in the shells database (/etc/shells)
- The minimum and maximum days required before a password change
- The maximum number of inactive days for an account
- An expiry date for the user's account
- The number of days warning to give a user before their password must be changed
- The path to the user's home directory

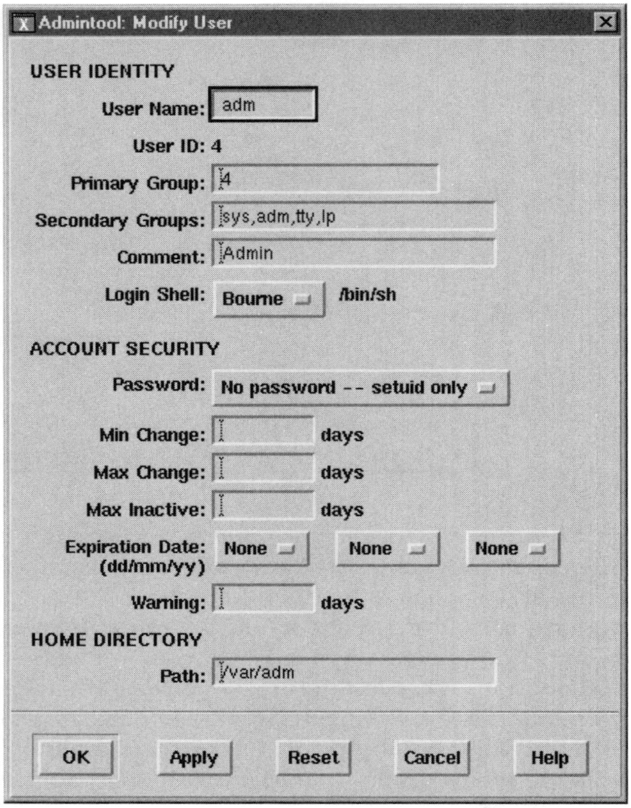

Figure 6-3

Modifying user details with admintool

Of course, all of this information can be set on the command line by using the `passwd` command. However, the admintool interface is easier to use, and provides some additional functionality. For example, it is impossible to enter an invalid expiration date, because the day, month, and year are selected from drop-down boxes. In addition, if there are any problems encountered during modification, no changes will be recorded.

Adding a user to the system involves entering data into the same interface used for modifying user details, as shown in Figure 6-4. The UID is sequentially generated, as is a default primary group, user shell, password option (not set until first login), and the option to create a new directory for the user as their home directory. Again, admintool has advanced error-checking facilities that make it difficult to damage or overwrite system files with invalid data.

Admintool can also be used as a group administration tool. Groups may be created, and users added to specific groups or removed from groups. In addition, groups may also be deleted using admintool. The group administration interface is shown in Figure 6-5. Here, five groups are shown: the adm group (GID 4) has three members: root, adm, and daemon. To add a user to the group, simply select the adm group and click the Add entry

Figure 6-4
Adding user
details with
admintool

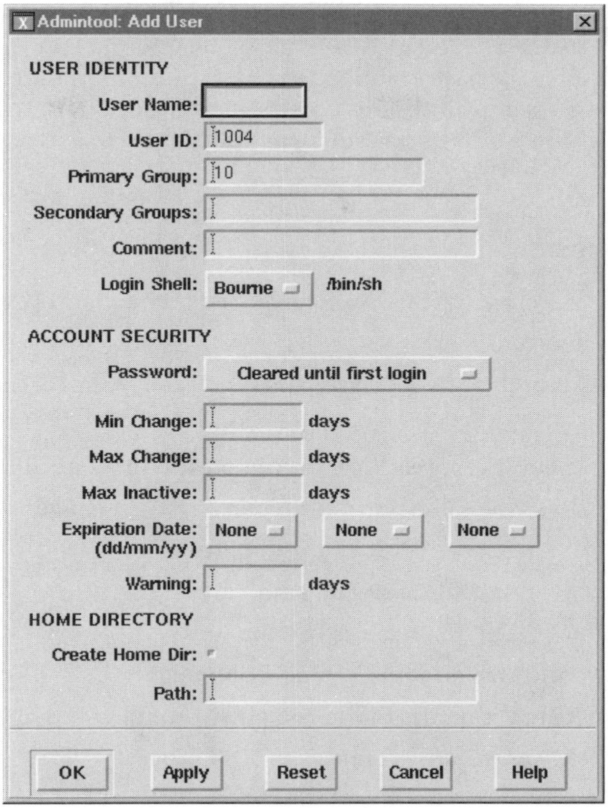

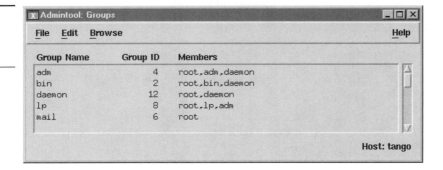

in the Edit menu. A comma-delimited list of users in the group would then be displayed. The bin user could be added to the adm group by inserting a comma after the last entry and adding the name "bin" to the list.

Figure 6-5
Adding group
details with
admintool

Summary

In this chapter, we have examined the basic procedures for managing users and groups on a Solaris system. Since all processes and threads are executed with a real or effective user and group ID, it's important for administrators to understand how to manage these entities effectively.

Questions

1. What are the typical uses for a Solaris user account (choose two only)?

   A. Spawning a shell

   B. Connecting networks together

   C. Performing hardware maintenance

   D. Scheduling applications to run on specific times and dates

2. Which of the following groups contains only default system accounts?

   A. root, daemon, bin, sys, lp, adm, www

   B. root, samba, bin, sys, lp, adm, uucp

   C. root, daemon, bin, sys, lp, adm, uucp

   D. oracle, daemon, bin, sys, lp, adm, uucp

3. What are the names of the two password files used by Solaris?

   A. /etc/passwd, /etc/secure

   B. /etc/password, /etc/secure

   C. /bin/passwd, /etc/group

   D. /etc/passwd, /etc/shadow

4. Which of the following users has a default UID of 0?

   A. bin

   B. root

   C. sys

   D. adm

5. Which of the following `useradd` commands is valid?

   A. `useradd -u abc -g 10 -d /home/abc -m -k/etc/skel -s /bin/sh -c "ABC" abc`

   B. `useradd -u 1023 -g abc -d /home/abc -m -k/etc/skel -s /bin/sh -c "ABC" abc`

    C. useradd -u 1023 -g 10 -d /home/abc -m -k/etc/skel -s /bin/sh
-c "ABC" abc

    D. useradd -u abc -g abc -d /home/abc -m -k/etc/skel -s /bin/sh
-c "ABC" abc

6. Which of the following usermod commands would change the UID of the
www account from 1004 to 1005?

    A. usermod -u 1005 www

    B. usermod -u 1004 -n 1005 www

    C. usermod www -n 1005

    D. usermod www 1004 1004

7. A locked account can be identified in *letc/passwd* by which of the following
entries?

    A. *LOCKED*

    B. LOCKED

    C. *LK*

    D. *

8. Which of the following userdel commands would delete account melissa
(UID 1002)?

    A. userdel -r melissa

    B. userdel -u 1002

    C. userdel -uid melissa

    D. userdel -r 1002

9. Which of the following groupadd commands is valid?

    A. groupadd -g 100 staff

    B. groupadd -g 100 -s staff

    C. groupadd staff -gid 100

    D. groupadd -g staff 100

10. Which of the following characteristics cannot explicitly be set using admintool?

    A. The primary group

    B. The login shell

    C. An expiry date for the user's account

    D. File permissions for the home directory

Answers

1. **A or D.** Most users log in with a shell and use it to launch applications.

2. **C.** www, samba, and oracle are common accounts on Solaris, but they are user-installed.

3. **D.** The passwd file doesn't contain passwords anymore, but retains all user details.

4. **B.** The root user has a default UID of 0, but this can be modified.

5. **C.** UIDs and GIDs must be numeric.

6. **A.** Only the UID needs to be identified with the –u parameter.

7. **C.** *LK* indicates a locked account.

8. **D.** UIDs must be used when deleting accounts.

9. **A.** UIDs must be used when adding groups.

10. **D.** admintool can be used to set the primary group, login shell, and an expiry date, but cannot perform normal shell tasks.

Security

In this chapter, you will

- Learn how to secure hosts from attack
- Identify common vulnerabilities for networked systems
- Discover how to protect sensitive files
- Create access control lists

Security is a central concern of system administrators of all network operating systems, because all services may potentially have inherent flaws or weaknesses revealed through undetected bugs that can compromise a system. Solaris is no exception, and new Solaris administrators will find themselves visiting issues that they may have encountered with other operating systems. For example, Linux, Microsoft Windows, and Solaris all run database systems that have daemons that listen for connections arriving through the Internet. These servers may be shipped with default user accounts with well-known passwords that are not inactivated by local administrators after configuration and administration. Consequently, exploits involving such services are often broadcast on USENET newsgroups, cracking mailing lists, and web sites.

Some security issues are specific to Solaris. For example, username and password sniffing while a remote user is using telnet to spawn a local shell is unique to Solaris and other UNIX systems, because PC-based products that provide remote access (such as Symantec's pcAnywhere product) encrypt the exchange of authentication credentials by default.

This chapter will lay the groundwork to help you understand the vulnerabilities of the Solaris operating system, as well as detail the techniques used by Solaris managers to reduce the risk of a successful attack by a rogue user. Our starting point will be the single host, which can be secured from both internal and externals threats by strict administration of user accounts and groups and their corresponding entries within standard password and shadowed password files.

It is critical that you maintain access to various files and directories by setting user and group ownership on those files. Once a user and group have been assigned ownership of a file or directory, they are free to determine which other users (if any) are able to read or write to that file—or for a directory, whether any files can be created under that directory. An exception to user- and group-based access control is the special "superuser" account (also known as the "root" user), who has global read, write, and create access on all files on a Solaris system. This includes normal files as well as directories and device files.

Finally, we'll examine how to keep tabs on all active users on a Solaris system, so that their behavior and activities can be monitored to ensure that only authorized activities are being conducted at all times.

User and Group Security

The concept of the user is central to Solaris—all processes and files on a Solaris system are "owned" by a particular user and are assigned to a specific user group. No data or activities on the system may exist without first establishing a valid user or group. Managing users and groups as a Solaris administrator can be a challenging activity—you will be responsible for assigning all the privileges granted or denied to a user or group of users, and many of these permissions carry great risk. For example, a user with an inappropriate privilege level may execute inappropriate commands as the superuser, causing damage to your system.

You can determine which user you are currently logged in as from a terminal session by using the id command:

```
$ id
uid=1001(natashia) gid=10(dialup)
```

The output shows that the currently logged-in user is natashia, with UID=1001. In addition, the current group of natashia is a dial-up group with GID=10. It is possible for the user and group credentials to change during a single terminal session. For example, if the su facility is used effectively to "become" the superuser, the UID and GID associated with the current terminal session will also change:

```
$ su root
Password:
# id
uid=0(root) gid=1(other)
```

Here, the root user (UID=0) belonging to the group other (GID=1) has spawned a new shell with full superuser privileges.

You can obtain a list of all groups that a user belongs to by using the groups command. For example, to view all the groups that the root user belongs to, we use the following command:

```
# groups root
other root bin sys adm uucp mail tty lp nuucp daemon
```

Protecting the Superuser Account

We've just examined how to use the su facility to invoke superuser privileges from an unprivileged account. The user with UID=0 (typically the root user) has unlimited powers to act on a Solaris system. The root user can perform the following potentially dangerous functions:

- Add, delete, or modify all other user accounts

- Read and write all files, and create new ones

- Add or delete devices to the system

- Install new system software

- Read everyone's e-mail

- Snoop network traffic for usernames and passwords of other systems on the local area network (LAN)

- Modify all system logs to remove all traces of superuser access

- Pretend to be an unprivileged user and access their accounts on other systems where login access is authenticated against a username

These powers combine to make the root account sound rather sinister; however, many of these activities are legitimate and necessary system administration routines that are undertaken daily. For example, network traffic can be snooped to determine where network outages are occurring, and copying user files to backup tapes every night is generally in everyone's best interest. However, if an intruder gains root access, he or she is free to roam the system, deleting or stealing data, removing or adding user accounts, or installing Trojan horses that can transparently modify the way that your system operates.

One way to protect against an authorized user gaining root access is to use a hard-to-guess root password. This makes it difficult for a cracker to use a password-cracking program to guess your password successfully. The optimal password is a completely random string of alphanumeric and punctuation characters.

 TIP The root password should never be written down unless it is locked in the company safe, nor should it be told to anyone who doesn't need to know it. The root password must usually be entered twice—just in case you should happen to make a typographic error, as the characters that you type are masked on the screen.

The root user should never be able to log in using telnet: instead, the su facility should be used by individual users to gain root privileges where necessary. This protects the root account since at least one other password is required to log in, unless the root user has access to the console. In addition, the su command should be owned by a sysadmin group (or similar) so that only those users who need access to the root account should be able to obtain it. Once su has been used to gain root access, the root user can use su to spawn a shell with the effective ID of any other user on the system. This is a security weakness, because the root user could pretend to be another user and perform actions or modify data traceable to the effective user and not root.

The /etc/passwd and /etc/shadow Password Files

Solaris has reduced the chances of a rogue user obtaining the password file in the first place by implementing a shadow password facility. This creates a file called */etc/shadow* that is similar to the password file (*/etc/passwd*) but is readable only by root and contains the encrypted password fields for each UID. Thus, if a rogue user cannot obtain the encrypted password entries, it is impossible to use them as the basis for a crack attack.

A shadow password file corresponding to the password file shown previously looks like this:

```
# cat /etc/shadow
root:YTS88sd7fSS:10528::::::
daemon:NP:6445::::::
bin:NP:6445::::::
sys:NP:6445::::::
adm:NP:6445::::::
lp:NP:6445::::::
uucp:NP:6445::::::
nuucp:NP:6445::::::
listen:*LK*::::::
nobody:NP:6445::::::
noaccess:NP:6445::::::
nobody4:NP:6445::::::
security:*LK*::::::
natashia:hY72er3Ascc::::::
```

If a system is correctly installed, the */etc/passwd* file should be readable by all users, but it should contain no passwords. Conversely, the */etc/shadow* file should be readable only by root and should contain the encrypted password strings traditionally stored in */etc/passwd*.

Remote Access Tools

Remote access is the hallmark of modern multiple-user operating systems like Solaris and its antecedents, such as VAX/VMS. Unlike the single-user Windows NT system, users can concurrently log into and interactively execute commands on Solaris server systems from any client that supports Transmission Control Protocol/Internet Protocol (TCP/IP), such as Solaris, NT, and Macintosh. Single-user remote access has now been made possible on Windows NT Server also, using TCP/IP through products like Symantec's pcAnywhere; however, remote logins prevent concurrent console logins on NT. This is not the case with Solaris, which can support hundreds and thousands of interactive user shells at any one time, constrained only by memory and CPU availability.

In this section, we will examine several popular methods of remote access, such as telnet, which have been popular historically. We will also outline the much-publicized security holes and bugs that have led to the innovation of secure remote access systems, such as Secure Shell (SSH). These "safer" systems facilitate the encryption of the contents of user sessions and/or authentication sequences and provide an important level of protection for sensitive data. Although remote access is useful, the administrative overhead in securing a Solaris system can be significant, reflecting the increased functionality that remote access services provide.

Remote Access Risks

One of the unfortunate drawbacks of the telnet system is that usernames, and especially unencrypted passwords, are transmitted in cleartext around the network. Thus, if you were using a telnet client to connect from a cyber café in Paris to a server in New York, your traffic might pass through 20 or 30 routers and computers, all of which can be programmed to "sniff" the contents of network packets. A sample traceroute of the path taken by packets from AT&T to Sun's web page looks like this:

```
$ traceroute www.sun.com
Tracing route to wwwseast.usec.sun.com [192.9.49.30]
over a maximum of 30 hops:
  1    184 ms    142 ms    138 ms   202.10.4.131
  2    147 ms    144 ms    138 ms   202.10.4.129
  3    150 ms    142 ms    144 ms   202.10.1.73
  4    150 ms    144 ms    141 ms   ia4.optus.net.au [202.139.32.17]
  5    148 ms    143 ms    139 ms   202.139.1.197
  6    490 ms    489 ms    474 ms   sf1.optus.net.au [192.65.89.246]
  7    526 ms    480 ms    485 ms   gn.cwix.net [207.124.109.57]
  8    494 ms    482 ms    485 ms   core7.SanFrancisco.cw.net [204.70.10.9]
  9    483 ms    489 ms    484 ms   core2.SanFrancisco.cw.net [204.70.9.132]
 10    557 ms    552 ms    561 ms   xcore3.Boston.cw.net [204.70.150.81]
 11    566 ms    572 ms    554 ms   sun.Boston.cw.net [204.70.179.102]
 12    577 ms    574 ms    558 ms   wwwseast.usec.sun.com [192.9.49.30]
Trace complete.
```

That's a lot of intermediate hosts, any of which could potentially be sniffing passwords and other sensitive data. If the network packet that contains the username and password is sniffed in this way, a rogue user could easily log into the target account using a telnet client. This risk has led to the development of Secure Shell (SSH) and similar products that encrypt the exchange of username and password information between client and server, making it difficult for sniffers to extract useful information from network packets.

TIP   OpenSSH is now supplied with Solaris for the first time with the release of Solaris 9.

Although rlogin is the fastest kind of remote login possible, it can be easily exploited on systems that are not trusted and secure. Systems that are directly connected to the Internet, or those that form part of a subnet that is not firewalled, should never be considered secure. These kinds of configurations can be dangerous in some circumstances, even if they are convenient for remotely administering many different machines.

CAUTION   The most dangerous use of /etc/hosts.equiv occurs, for example, when the file contains the single line: +. This allows any users from any host that has equivalent usernames to remotely log in.

The *.rhosts* file is also considered dangerous in some situations. For example, it is common practice in some organizations to allow the root and privileged users to permit automatic logins by root users from other machines by creating an /*.rhosts* file. A more insidious problem can occur when users define their own *.rhosts* files, however, in their own home directories. These files are not directly controlled by the system administrator and may be exploited by malicious remote users. One way to remove this threat is to enforce a policy of disallowing user *.rhosts* files and activating a nightly cron job to search for and remove any files named *.rhosts* in the user directories. If cron entry for a root like this

```
0 2 * * * find /staff -name .rhosts -print -exec rm{} \;
```

should execute this simple `find` and `remove` command every morning at 2:00 A.M. for all user accounts whose home directories lie within the /*staff* partition.

Using Remote Access Tools

With the increased use of the Internet for business-to-business and consumer-to-business transactions, securing remote access has become a major issue in the provision of Solaris services. Fortunately, solutions based around the encryption of sessions and authentication of clients have improved the reliability of remote access facilities in a security-conscious operating environment.

Secure Shell (SSH)

Open Secure Shell, OpenSSH, or just plain SSH is a secure client and server solution that facilitates the symmetric and asymmetric encryption of identification and authentication sequences for remote access. It is designed to replace the telnet and rlogin applications on the client side, with clients available for Solaris, Windows, and many other operating systems. On the server side, it improves upon the nonsecure services supported by inetd, such as the r-commands. Figure 7-1 shows a typical SSH client session for **vpn.cassowary.net** from a Windows client.

SSH makes use of a generic transport layer encryption mechanism over TCP/IP, which uses the popular Blowfish or government-endorsed triple-DES (Data Encryption Standard) algorithms for the encryption engine. This is used to transmit encrypted packets, whose contents can still be sniffed like all traffic on the network, but by using public-key cryptography, implementing the Diffie-Hellman algorithm for key exchange, the contents of encrypted packets appear to be random without the appropriate "key" to decrypt them.

The use of encryption technology makes it extremely unlikely that the contents of the interactive session will ever be known to anyone except the client and the server. In addition to the encryption of session data, identification and authentication sequences are also encrypted using RSA encryption technology. This means that username and password combinations also cannot be sniffed by a third party. SSH also provides automatic forwarding for graphics applications, based around the X11 windowing system, which is a substantial improvement over the text-only telnet client.

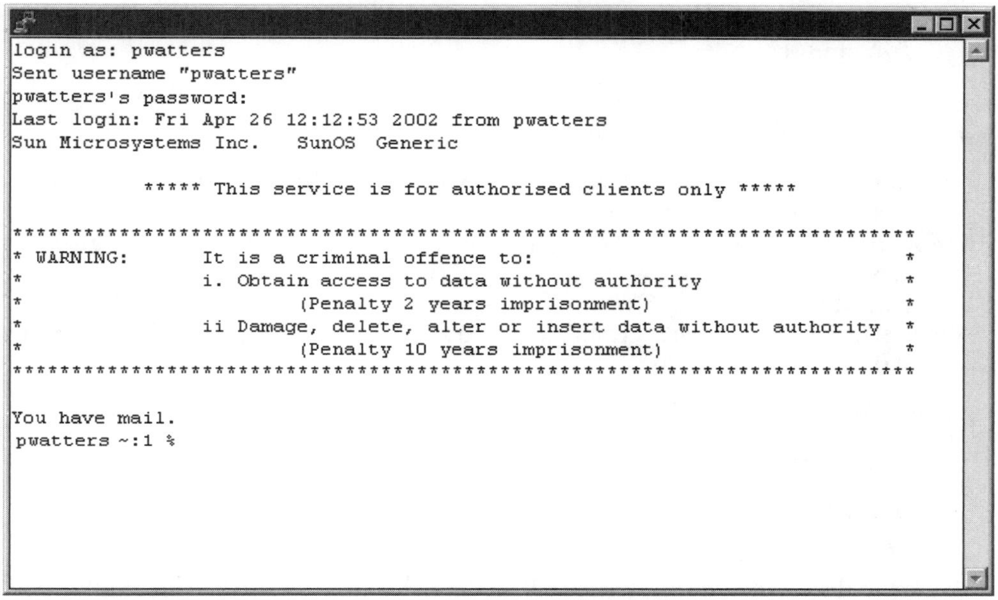

```
login as: pwatters
Sent username "pwatters"
pwatters's password:
Last login: Fri Apr 26 12:12:53 2002 from pwatters
Sun Microsystems Inc.   SunOS   Generic

            ***** This service is for authorised clients only *****

*********************************************************************************
* WARNING:      It is a criminal offence to:                                    *
*                i. Obtain access to data without authority                     *
*                     (Penalty 2 years imprisonment)                            *
*               ii Damage, delete, alter or insert data without authority       *
*                     (Penalty 10 years imprisonment)                           *
*********************************************************************************

You have mail.
pwatters ~:1 %
```

Figure 7-1   Typical SSH client session

The sequence of events for establishing an SSH client connection to a server is demonstrated in Figure 7-2, and proceeds as follows:

1. The client connects to a server port requesting a connection (usually port 22, but this can be adapted to suit local conditions).

2. The server replies with its standard public RSA host key (1024 bits), as well as another RSA server key (768 bits) that changes hourly. Since the server key changes hourly, even if the keys for the traffic of one session was cracked, historic data would still remain encrypted, limiting the utility of any such attack.

3. The server can be configured to reject connections from hosts that it doesn't know about, but by default it will accept connections from any client.

4. If the connection is accepted, the client generates a session key composed of a 256-bit random number and chooses an encryption algorithm that the server supports (triple-DES or Blowfish).

5. The client then encrypts the session key using RSA, using both the host and server key, and returns the encrypted key to the server.

6. The server decrypts the session key and encryption is enabled between the client and server.

7. If the default authentication mechanism is selected, the client passes the username and password for the server across the secure channel.

It is possible to disable the username/password authentication sequence by permitting logins to clients that have an appropriate private RSA key, as long as the server has a list of accepted public keys. However, if a client computer is stolen and the private key is retrieved by a rogue user, access to the server can be obtained without a valid username and password combination.

On the client side, a *knownhsts.txt* file is created and server keys are recorded there. Entries look like this:

```
server 1024 35 07448318855220650928863459182148090000874876031312
663202636556140699569229172676719815525201670198606754982042 3736
393736593998729350847306606972263971147429524250769197415119 5842
956063176626459842269220618785535980433268062460000169825137 5726
292755659298770421181014212617571545279674887150613189468540 1576
4183
```

In addition, a private key for the client is stored in *Identity*, and a public key for the client is stored in *Identity.pub*. Entries in this file are similar to the server key file:

```
1024 37 2590984202231997581736656902901504139087369478896425 6567
214642296672262274373983658165345290603280879390188028942276 4252
425961463654951899845052492381148100236043947385236354222335 9868
114619253961948185309446681933562979774158070860950587770774 2473
7311773531850692230437799694611176912728474735224921771041151
Paul Watters
```

TIP It is sensible in a commercial context to enforce a policy of SSH-only remote access for interactive logins. This can easily be enforced by enabling the SSH daemon on the server side and removing entries for the telnet and rlogin services in */etc/services* and */etc/inetd.conf*. Now that OpenSSH is supplied with Solaris, there is no excuse for not deploying SSH across all hosts in your local network.

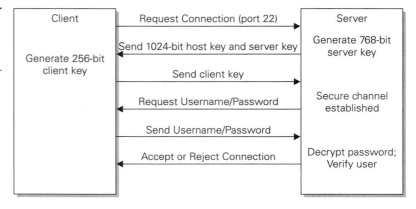

Figure 7-2
Authenticating a Secure Shell (SSH) connection

Client — Request Connection (port 22) → Server

Generate 256-bit client key

Send 1024-bit host key and server key — Generate 768-bit server key

Send client key — Secure channel established

Request Username/Password

Send Username/Password

Accept or Reject Connection — Decrypt password; Verify user

Monitoring User Activity

System access can be monitored interactively using a number of measures. For example, *syslog* entries can be automatically viewed in real time using this command:

```
$ tail -f /var/adm/messages
```

However, most administrators want to view interactively what remote users are doing on a system at any time. We will examine two methods here for viewing remote user activity. The command who displays who is currently logged into the system. The output of who displays the username, connecting line, date of login, idle time, process ID, and a comment. Here's an example output:

```
$ who
root        console     Nov 22 12:39
natashia    pts/0       Nov 19 21:05     (client.site.com)
```

This command can be automated to update the list of active users. An alternative to who is the w command, which displays a more detailed summary of the current activity on the system, including the current process name for each user. The header output from w shows the current time, the uptime of the current system, and the number of users actively logged into the system. The average system load is also displayed as a series of three numbers at the end of the w header, indicating the average number of jobs in the run queue for the previous 1, 5, and 15 minutes. In addition to the output generated by who, the w command displays the current foreground process for each user, which is usually a shell. For example, the following command shows that the root user has an active *shelltool* running under Open Windows, while the user natashia is running the Cornell shell:

```
7:15pm  up 1 day(s),  5:11,  2 users,  load average: 1.00, 1.00, 1.01
User     tty          login@  idle   JCPU   PCPU  what
root     console      Thu12pm 3days    6      6   shelltool
natashia pts/12       Thu11am 8:45     9          /usr/local/bin/tcsh
```

The w and who commands are useful tools for getting an overview of current usage patterns on any Solaris system. Another useful command is last, which displays historical usage patterns for the current system in a sequential format:

```
$ last
natashia  pts/4        hp             Wed Apr 11 19:00   still logged in
root      console      :0             Tue Apr 10 20:11   still logged in
natashia  pts/2        nec            Tue Apr 10 19:17 - 19:24  (00:06)
natashia  pts/6        austin         Tue Apr 10 15:53 - 15:53  (00:00)
root      console      :0             Tue Apr 10 14:24 - 16:25  (02:01)
reboot    system boot                 Tue Apr 10 14:04
natashia  pts/5        hp             Thu Apr  5 21:38 - 21:40  (00:01)
natashia  pts/5        hp             Thu Apr  5 21:22 - 21:37  (00:15)
natashia  pts/5        10.64.18.1     Thu Apr  5 19:30 - 20:00  (00:30)
natashia  pts/5        hp             Thu Apr  5 19:18 - 19:29  (00:11)
root      console      :0             Thu Apr  5 19:17 - 22:05  (4+02:48)
reboot    system boot                 Thu Apr  5 19:14
natashia  pts/5        hp             Tue Apr  3 16:14 - 18:26  (02:11)
natashia  pts/5        hp             Tue Apr  3 08:48 - 10:35  (01:47)
root      console      :0             Tue Apr  3 08:45 - 22:01  (13:15)
```

```
reboot      system boot                  Tue Apr   3 08:43
root        console       :0             Fri Mar 30 18:54 - 19:27  (00:32)
reboot      system boot                  Fri Mar 30 18:46
natashia    pts/6         hp             Tue Mar 27 20:46 - 21:51  (01:04)
root        console       :0             Tue Mar 27 19:50 - 21:51  (02:01)
reboot      system boot                  Tue Mar 27 19:48
root        console       :0             Mon Mar 26 17:43 - 17:47  (00:04)
```

An alternative view of system usage by application is provided by `lastcomm`. It shows the list of commands executed in reverse chronological order, as shown in this example:

```
$ lastcomm
man           pwatters pts/2            0.02 secs Mon Sep  2 20:24
sh            pwatters pts/2            0.01 secs Mon Sep  2 20:24
more          pwatters pts/2            0.03 secs Mon Sep  2 20:24
nsgmls        pwatters pts/2            0.84 secs Mon Sep  2 20:24
sh            pwatters pts/2            0.01 secs Mon Sep  2 20:24
mv            pwatters pts/2            0.01 secs Mon Sep  2 20:24
sh            pwatters pts/2            0.01 secs Mon Sep  2 20:24
col           pwatters pts/2            0.02 secs Mon Sep  2 20:24
nroff         pwatters pts/2            0.04 secs Mon Sep  2 20:24
eqn           pwatters pts/2            0.01 secs Mon Sep  2 20:24
tbl           pwatters pts/2            0.01 secs Mon Sep  2 20:24
cat           pwatters pts/2            0.01 secs Mon Sep  2 20:24
sh            pwatters pts/2            0.02 secs Mon Sep  2 20:24
sgml2rof      pwatters pts/2            0.01 secs Mon Sep  2 20:24
instant       pwatters pts/2            0.05 secs Mon Sep  2 20:24
sh            pwatters pts/2            0.01 secs Mon Sep  2 20:24
grep          pwatters pts/2            0.01 secs Mon Sep  2 20:24
lastcomm      pwatters pts/2            0.16 secs Mon Sep  2 20:24
```

Service Security

Since a port number can be specified on the command line, telnet clients can be used to connect to arbitrary ports on Solaris servers. This makes a telnet client a useful tool for testing whether services that should have been disconnected are actually active. For example, you can interactively issue commands to an FTP server on port 21, this way:

```
$ telnet server 21
Trying 172.16.1.1...
Connected to server.
Escape character is '^]'.
220 server FTP server (UNIX(r) System V Release 4.0) ready.
```

And on a sendmail server on port 25:

```
$ telnet server 25
Trying 172.16.1.1...
Connected to server.
Escape character is '^]'.
220 server ESMTP Sendmail 8.9.1a/8.9.1; Mon, 22 Nov 1999
    14:31:36 +1100 (EST)
```

Interactive testing of this kind has many uses. For example, if we telnet to port 80 on a server, we are usually connected to a web server where we can issue interactive commands using the Hypertext Transfer Protocol (HTTP). For example, to GET the default index page on a server, we could type **get index.html**:

```
Trying 172.16.1.1...
Connected to server.
Escape character is '^]'.
GET index.html
<!DOCTYPE HTML PUBLIC "-//IETF//DTD HTML 2.0//EN">
<HTML><HEAD>
<TITLE>Server</TITLE></HEAD>
<h1>Welcome to server!</h1>
```

This technique is useful when testing proxy server configurations for new kinds of HTTP clients (for example, a HotJava browser) or to be executed during a script to check whether the web server is active and serving expected content.

Security Architecture

So far, we have examined the essential features of Solaris security, including the need to protect individual files (as well as entire systems) from unauthorized access. In addition, we examined how both files and systems can be protected from remote access tools. However, we need to place these individual actions within a context that logically covers all aspects of security, typically known as levels. A level is an extra "step" that must be breached in order to obtain access to data.

In terms of physical security, a bank provides an excellent analogy. Breaking into a bank's front counter and teller area is as easy as walking through the door, because these doors are publicly accessible. However, providing this level of access sometimes opens doors deeper inside the building. For example, the private banking area, which may normally only be accessed by staff and identified private banking customers, may allow access using a smart card. If a smart card is stolen from a staff member, it could be used to enter the secure area, because the staff member's credentials would be authenticated. Entering this level would not necessarily provide access to the vault: superuser privileges would be required. However, a thorough physical search of the private banking area might yield the key required for entry. Alternatively, a brute force attack on the safe's combination might be used to guess the correct combination. Having accessed the vault, if readily negotiated currency or bullion is contained therein, then an intruder could easily steal them. However, if the vault contained checks that needed to be countersigned, the intruder may not be able to make use of the contents. The lesson here is simple: banks provide public services that open up pathways straight to the cash. Banks know that any or all of the physical security layers may be breached. That's why the storage of negotiable securities is always minimized, because any system designed by humans can be broken by humans, with enough time and patience. The only sensible strategy is to make sure that external layers are as difficult to breach as possible, and to ensure that security experts are immediately notified of breaches.

Similarly, public file areas, such as FTP and WWW servers, are publicly accessible areas on computer systems that sometimes provide entry to a different level in the system. An easily guessed or stolen password may provide user-level (but unprivileged) access to the system. A brute force attack against the local password database might even yield the superuser password. Accessing a local database might contain the target records of interest. However, instead of storing the data plaintext within tables, data may have been written using a stream cipher, making it potentially very difficult to obtain the data. And because 40-bit ciphers have been broken in the past, obtaining the encrypted data might eventually lead to its dissemination. Again, a key strategy is ensuring that data is secure by as many external layers as possible, and also that the data itself is difficult to negotiate.

Increasing the number of levels of security typically leads to a decrease in system ease of use—for example, setting a password for accessing a printer requires users to remember and enter a password when challenged. Whether or not printer access needs this level of security will depend on organizational requirements. For a printer that prints on plain paper, no password may be needed. However, for a printer that prints on bonded paper with an official company letterhead, a password should be used to protect the printer, and optionally, a copy of the file being sent to the printer may need to be stored securely for auditing purposes.

For government and military systems, there are a number of security specifications and policy documents available, which detail the steps necessary to secure Solaris systems in "top secret" installations. The U.S. Department of Defense, for example, publishes the Orange Book, formally known as the "Trusted Computer System Evaluation Criteria" specification. This book describes systems it has evaluated in terms of different protection levels, from weakest to strongest, including:

- Class D, which are systems that do not pass any tests and are therefore untrusted. No sensitive data should be stored on class D systems.

- Class C1, which are systems that require authentication based on a user model.

- Class C2, which are systems that provide auditing and logging on a per-user basis, ensuring that file accesses and related operations can always be traced to the initiating user.

- Class B1, which requires security labeling for all files. Labels range from "top secret" to "unclassified."

- Class B2, which separates normal system administration duties from security activities that are performed by a separate security officer. This level requires covert channels for data communications and verified testing of an installation's security procedures.

- Class B3, which requires that a stand-alone request monitor be available to authenticate all requests for file and resource access. In addition, the request monitor must be secured and all of its operations logged.

- Class A1, which is a formally tested and verified installation of a class B3 system.

All of the strategies that we discuss in this chapter are focused on increasing the number of layers through which a potential cracker (or disgruntled staff member) must pass
to obtain the data that they are illegally trying to access. Reducing the threat of remote
access exploits and protecting data are key components of this strategy.

Physical Security

It may seem obvious—if an intruder can physically access your system, then he or she may
be able to take control of your system without the root password, bypassing all of the software-based controls that normally limit such activity. How is this possible, you might ask?
If the intruder has access to a bootable CD-ROM drive, and a bootable CD-ROM (of Solaris,
Linux, or any other operating system that can mount UFS drives), it's trivial to enter the following command at the OpenBoot prompt and start the system without a password:

```
ok boot cdrom
```

Once the system has booted from the CD-ROM drive, a number of options are available
to the intruder:

- Do an ftp on any file on the system to a remote system.

- Copy any file on the system to a mass storage device (such as a DAT tape).

- Format all of the drives on the system.

- Launch a distributed denial of service attack against other networks, which
  you will be blamed for.

Of course, the possibilities are endless, but the result is the same. You may ask why it
is so easy to compromise a system in this way: one good reason is that if you forget your
root password, you can boot from the CD-ROM, mount the boot disk, and manually
edit the shadow password file.

This requirement doesn't really excuse poor security, and the OpenBoot monitor provides some options to secure the system. There are three security levels available:

- **None**   Surprisingly, this is the default. No password is required to execute
  any of the commands in OpenBoot. This is convenient but dangerous, for the
  reasons outlined earlier.

- **Command**   This level needs a password to be entered for all commands
  except `boot` and `go`. Thus, details of the SCSI bus and network traffic can't
  be observed by the casual browser, but an intruder could still boot from the
  CD-ROM.

- **Full**   This level requires a password for every command except `go`, including
  the boot command. Thus, even if the system is interrupted and rebooted
  using the boot command, only the default boot device will be available
  through `go`.

To set the security level, the `eeprom` command is used. To set the command level, use the following command:

```
# eeprom security-mode=command
```

Alternatively, to set the command level, use the following command:

```
# eeprom security-mode=full
```

The password for the command and full security levels must be set by using the `eeprom` command:

```
# eeprom security-password=
Changing PROM password:
New password:
Retype new password:
```

Note that if the root password and the full-level password are lost, there is no way to recover the system by software means: a new PROM will need to be ordered from Sun.

Disabling IP Ports

The first step in network security is to prevent unauthorized entry by disabling access to specific IP ports, as defined by individual entries in the services database. This action prevents specific services from operating, even if the inetd attempts to accept a connection for a service because it is still defined in */etc/inetd.conf*. In this section, we will examine how to disable specific services from inetd, in conjunction with the services database.

The following services are typically enabled in */etc/services* and configured in */etc/inetd.conf*. Most sites will want to disable them, and install more secure equivalents. For example, the ftp and telnet services may be replaced by the encrypted secure copy and secure shell programs, respectively. To disable the ftp, telnet, shell, login, exec, comsat, talk, uucp, and finger services, we would "comment out" their entries in */etc/inetd.conf* by inserting a hash character "#" at the first character position of the line that defines the service. The following configuration enables the ftp, telnet, shell, login, exec, comsat, talk, uucp, and finger services in */etc/inetd.conf*:

```
ftp     stream  tcp   nowait  root    /usr/sbin/in.ftpd      in.ftpd -l
telnet  stream  tcp   nowait  root    /usr/sbin/in.telnetd   in.telnetd
shell   stream  tcp   nowait  root    /usr/sbin/in.rshd      in.rshd
login   stream  tcp   nowait  root    /usr/sbin/in.rlogind   in.rlogind
exec    stream  tcp   nowait  root    /usr/sbin/in.rexecd    in.rexecd
comsat  dgram   udp   wait    root    /usr/sbin/in.comsat    in.comsat
talk    dgram   udp   wait    root    /usr/sbin/in.talkd     in.talkd
uucp    stream  tcp   nowait  root    /usr/sbin/in.uucpd     in.uucpd
finger  stream  tcp   nowait  nobody  /usr/sbin/in.fingerd   in.fingerd
```

The following configuration disables the ftp, telnet, shell, login, exec, comsat, talk, uucp, and finger services in */etc/inetd.conf*:

```
#ftp     stream  tcp    nowait  root    /usr/sbin/in.ftpd      in.ftpd -l
#telnet  stream  tcp    nowait  root    /usr/sbin/in.telnetd   in.telnetd
```

```
#shell    stream  tcp    nowait  root    /usr/sbin/in.rshd     in.rshd
#login    stream  tcp    nowait  root    /usr/sbin/in.rlogind  in.rlogind
#exec     stream  tcp    nowait  root    /usr/sbin/in.rexecd   in.rexecd
#comsat   dgram   udp    wait    root    /usr/sbin/in.comsat   in.comsat
#talk     dgram   udp    wait    root    /usr/sbin/in.talkd    in.talkd
#uucp     stream  tcp    nowait  root    /usr/sbin/in.uucpd    in.uucpd
#finger   stream  tcp    nowait  nobody  /usr/sbin/in.fingerd  in.fingerd
```

Similarly, the following configuration enables the ftp, telnet, shell, login, exec, comsat, talk, uucp, and finger services in */etc/services*:

```
ftp                21/tcp
telnet             23/tcp
shell              514/tcp         cmd
login              513/tcp
exec               512/tcp
biff               512/udp         comsat
talk               517/udp
uucp               540/tcp         uucpd
finger  stream  tcp    nowait  nobody  /usr/sbin/in.fingerd    in.fingerd
```

Similarly, the following configuration disables the ftp, telnet, shell, login, exec, comsat, talk, uucp, and finger services in */etc/services*:

```
#ftp               21/tcp
#telnet            23/tcp
#shell             514/tcp         cmd
#login             513/tcp
#exec              512/tcp
#biff              512/udp         comsat
#talk              517/udp
#uucp              540/tcp         uucpd
#finger  stream  tcp    nowait  nobody  /usr/sbin/in.fingerd   in.fingerd
```

Encryption

One of the potential weaknesses of Solaris and other UNIX systems is that the superuser is able to read the data of all users on the system. This means that if the system administrator account is breached, all data on the system can potentially be accessed by the intruder. In this context, it's important for individual users to ensure that they can protect the contents of their data, if not the representation of the data. This is where file encryption plays a major role: it is possible for users to store a form of their files on the file system that is readable by the superuser but whose contents cannot be easily discerned. This is because the file contents have been passed through a cipher that uses a mathematical function to scramble them, while ensuring that the contents can be successfully decrypted. The simplest encryption schemes are symmetric; that is, a key is used to encrypt the data, and the same key is used to decrypt the data.

TIP While most keys take the form of passwords, it's also possible to engage biometric devices, which perform iris scans and capture thumbprints, to extract and apply a key.

Symmetric Key Cryptography

The crypt command is a symmetric key encryption system: it accepts a key supplied on the command line, which is used to encrypt data supplied from standard input, and then pipes the data through a stream cipher to produce encrypted data on standard output. For example, if a set of medical records is stored in the file *medical.txt* and the encrypted records are to be stored in the file *medical.crypt* using the key 8rgbfde4f, then the following command could be used:

```
$ crypt 8rgbfde4f < medical.txt > medical.crypt
```

The contents of *medical.crypt* would then contain binary data that can be viewed on screen by using the following command:

```
$ strings medical.crypt
84jh$&;4-=+-45fsfg5HGhfdk
```

The original file *medical.txt* could then be deleted, and only a user who has both read access to the *medical.crypt* file and the key 8rgbfde4f would be able to decrypt the contents of the file, and obtain the original data. The crypt command is used to decrypt the data using the same format as encryption.

 CAUTION   Be aware that if you supply the key on the command line, and if the encryption takes a significant amount of time, the command string will be visible to all users by using the ps command. Thus, unless the command is being performed in a script, it's best to omit the key from the command line, in which case you will be prompted for it. In scripts, the key can be set as an environment variable prior to the use of the crypt command, and then unset after the command has completed.

It should be noted that the crypt algorithm is one of the least secure available—it is vulnerable to brute force cracking attacks, which is why it is not frequently used. A number of other symmetric key encryption programs can be used in place of crypt, such as the 56-bit Data Encryption Standard (DES), or its more secure variant, Triple DES, which uses three keys. No matter what symmetric key algorithm is used to encrypt the data, there is always the possibility that it may be decrypted by a cryptanalysis method. This typically involves matching known portions of the text to be decrypted to the encrypted text, and applying brute force methods to find a match. For example, if a letter sent on company letterhead contained the company name, that name could be successfully used as a starting point for cryptanalysis. However, if the target data cannot be easily guessed, cryptanalysis becomes much harder. One way of making cryptanalysis more difficult is to repeat the encryption process several times, each time substituting the encrypted file for the plaintext file. Thus, a triple encryption strategy (to some extent emulating Triple DES, which uses three 56-bit keys) would involve the following commands, assuming that the keys 8rgbfde4f, df454rfx, and 4gfdg56 were used:

```
$ crypt 8rgbfde4f < medical.txt > medical.crypt.3
$ crypt df454rfx < medical.crypt.3 > medical.crypt.2
$ crypt 4gfdg56< medical.crypt.2 > medical.crypt
$ rm medical.txt medical.crypt.3 medical.crypt.2
```

In each case, the contents of two previously encrypted files would need to be guessed before the original file could be decrypted. Given that encryption potentially takes a long time to perform, a faster method of scrambling the data can be used: a file compression program. In addition to reducing encryption time and file size, the contents of a compressed file are scrambled for all intents and purposes. Using several different compression algorithms on a file before encryption makes it very difficult to decrypt:

```
$ gzip medical.txt
$ compress medical.txt.gz
$ pack medical.txt.gz.Z
$ crypt 8rgbfde4f < medical.txt.gz.Z.z > medical.crypt
```

Security Auditing

After installing a new Solaris system, and applying the local security policy, a security audit must be undertaken to ensure that no known vulnerabilities exist in the system, particularly threats posed by remote access. As we have examined earlier, there are a number of strategies, such as switching off ports, that should be adopted prior to releasing a system into production and making it accessible through the Internet. A security audit should first examine what services are being offered, and determine an action plan based on services that should be disabled. In addition, monitoring and logging solutions should be installed for services that are sanctioned, so that it is possible at all times to determine what activity is occurring on any service. For example, a denial of service attack may involve hitting a specific port (such as port 80, the web server port) with a large number of packets, aimed at reducing overall performance of the web server and the host system. If you don't have logs of all this activity, it will be difficult to determine why your system performance is slow, and/or where any potential attacks have originated—that's why TCP wrappers are so important. The final phase of a security audit involves comparing the current list of services running on the system to the security bulletins that are released by the Computer Emergency Response Team (CERT) (**http://www.cert.org/**) and similar computer security groups.

 TIP   After determining the versions of software running on your system, you should determine which packages require patching and/or upgrading in order to eliminate the risks from known vulnerabilities.

SAINT

Running a security audit and implementing solutions based on the audit can be a time-consuming task. Fortunately, there are a number of tools available that can significantly reduce the amount of time required to conduct security audits, and cross-check existing applications with known security holes. One of these programs is called SAINT, which is freely available from World Wide Digital Security at **http://www.wwdsi.com/saint/**. SAINT, currently in version 3.0, is the Security Administrator's Integrated Network Tool, and is based in part on an earlier auditing tool known as SATAN. Both SATAN and SAINT have the ability to scan all of your system services and identify potential and/or known vulnerabilities. These are classified according to their risk: some items may be critical, requiring immediate attention, while other items may come in the form of suggestions rather than requirements. For example, while many local services are vulnerable to a buffer overflow, where the fixed boundaries on an array are deliberately overwritten by a remote client to "crash" the system, other issues, such as the use of "r" remote access commands, may be risky but acceptable in suitably protected local area networks. Thus, SAINT is not prescriptive in all cases, and suggested actions are always to be performed at the discretion of the local administrator.

Some administrators are concerned that using programs like SAINT actually contribute to cracking and system break-ins, because they provide a ready-made toolkit that can be used to identify system weaknesses in preparation for a break-in. However, if sites devote the necessary resources to monitoring system usage and identifying potential security threats, the risk posed by SAINT is minimal (particularly if its "suggestions" are acted upon). Indeed, World Wide Digital Security actually uses a web version of SAINT (called WebSAINT) as the basis for security consulting. For a fee, they will conduct a comprehensive security audit of your network, from the perspective of a remote (rather than a local) user. This can be very useful when attempting to identify potential weaknesses in your frontline systems, such as routers, gateways, and web servers.

In this section, we will examine how to install and configure the SAINT program, and run an audit on a newly installed Solaris 9 system. This will reveal many of the common issues that arise when Solaris is installed out of the box. Most of these issues are covered by CERT advisories. Sun often releases patches very soon after a CERT vulnerability that exists on shipped Solaris products is discovered. For example, a patch is available for a well-known vulnerability existing in the Berkeley Internet Daemon (BIND) package, which matches IP addresses with fully qualified domain names (**http://www.cert.org/advisories/CA-99-14-bind.html**). However, some CERT advisories are of a more general nature, since no specific code fix will solve the problem. One example is the identification of a distributed denial of service system known as "Stacheldraht," which combines the processing power and network resources of a group of systems (that are geographically distributed) and can prevent web servers from serving pages to clients (**http://www.cert.org/advisories/CA-2000-01.html**). CERT releases advisories on a regular basis, so it's advisable to keep up-to-date with all current security issues by reading their news.

One of the great strengths of the SAINT system is that it has an extensive catalog of CERT advisories and in-depth explanations of what each CERT advisory means for the local system. Every SAINT vulnerability is associated with a CVE number that matches descriptions of each security issue from the Common Vulnerabilities and Exposures database (**http://cve.mitre.org/**). Each identified vulnerability will contain a hyperlink back to the CVE database, so that information displayed about every issue is updated directly from the source. New patches and bug fixes are also listed.

PART I

SAINT has the ability to identify security issues for the following services:

- Domain name service (DNS), which is responsible for mapping the fully qualified domain name of Internet hosts to a machine-friendly IP address. In particular, the Berkeley Internet Daemon (BIND), commonly used for DNS resolution, is susceptible to vulnerabilities.

- File Transfer Protocol (FTP), which allows remote users to retrieve files from the local file system, has historically been associated with serious daemon buffer overflow problems.

- Internet Message Access Protocol (IMAP), which supports advanced e-mail exchange facilities between mail clients and mail servers, also has buffer overflow issues, which have previously allowed remote users to execute privileged commands arbitrarily on the mail server.

- Network File System (NFS) service, which shares disk partitions to remote client systems, is often misconfigured to provide world read access to all shared volumes, when this access should only be granted to specific users.

- Network Information Service (NIS), which is a distributed network service that shares maps of users, groups, and passwords between hosts to minimize administrative overheads, can be compromised if a rogue user can detect the NIS service operating.

- Sendmail Mail Transport Agent (MTA), which once allowed Solaris commands to be embedded within e-mails that were executed without authentication on the server side.

SAINT works by systematically scanning ports for services that have well-known exploits, and then reporting these exploits back to the user. In addition, it runs a large number of password checks for default passwords on system accounts, or accounts that often have no password. SAINT checks all of the services and exploits that it knows about, and the database of known exploits grows with each new release. SAINT also tests the susceptibility of your system to denial of service attacks, where a huge number of large-sized packets are directed to a specific port on your system. This tactic is typically used against web servers, where some high-profile cases in recent years have highlighted the inherent weakness of networked systems that allow traffic on specific ports without some kind of regulation. Many of the system daemons checked by SAINT will have a so-called "buffer overflow" problem, where a system may be crashed because memory is overwritten with arbitrary values outside the declared size of an array. Without appropriate bounds checking, passing a GET request to a web server of 1025 bytes when the array size is 1024 would clearly result in unpredictable behavior, as the C language does not prevent a program from doing this. Since Solaris daemons are typically written in C, a number have been fixed in recent years to prevent this problem from occurring (but you may be surprised at just how often new weaknesses are exposed).

The latest release of SAINT may be downloaded from **http://www.wwdsi.com/saint/**. To run SAINT, you will need to install the GNU C compiler or use the Sun C compiler. The Perl interpreter and Netscape web browser supplied with Solaris 8 or later are also required. After using `make` to build the SAINT binary, SAINT can be started by typing the command

```
# ./saint
```

This starts up the Netscape web browser, with the URL shown in Figure 7-3.

SAINT has several pages, including data management, target selection, data analysis, and configuration management. These pages can be visited sequentially in order to conduct your audit. The data management page, shown in Figure 7-4, allows you to create a

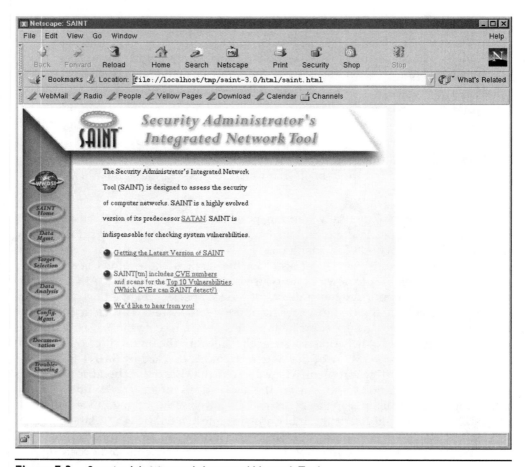

Figure 7-3   Security Administrator's Integrated Network Tool

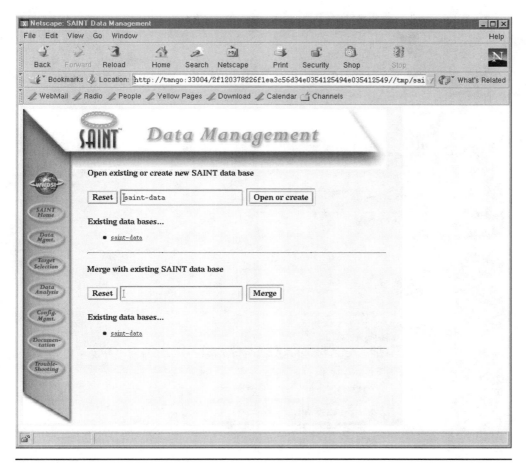

Figure 7-4   The Data Management page

new SAINT database in which to store the results of your current audit. Alternatively, you may open an existing SAINT database if you have created one previously, and/or merge data from other SAINT scans.

Next, you will need to use the target selection page to identify the host system that you wish to scan using SAINT, as shown in Figure 7-5. Here, you need to enter the fully quali-fied domain name of the host that you wish to scan. Alternatively, if you have a large number of hosts to scan, it may be more useful to create a file containing a list of hosts. This file could then be used by a system behind the firewall to identify locally visible weaknesses, and used by a system external to the firewall to reveal any threats visible to the outside world. You may also elect to scan all hosts in the local area network, which should only be performed after hours as it places a heavy load on network bandwidth.

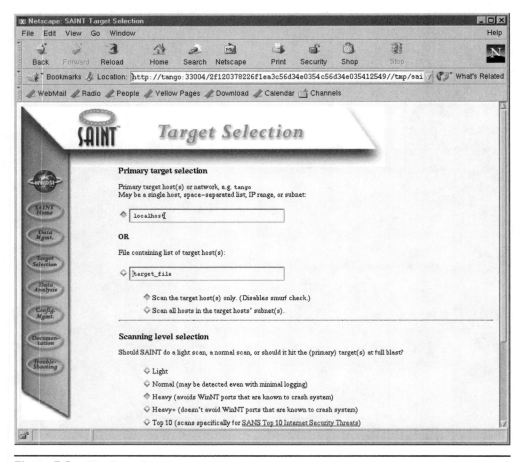

Figure 7-5   The Target Selection page

You also need to select a scanning level option, which includes the following:

- Light scanning, which is difficult to detect.
- Normal scanning, which is easy to detect.
- Heavy scanning, which won't crash Windows NT targets.
- Heavy+ scanning, which may well crash Windows NT targets.

There is a final option that just checks the "top ten" security flaws, as identified by the report at **http://www.sans.org/topten.htm**. These flaws include BIND weaknesses, vulnerable CGI programs, Remote Procedure Call (RPC) weaknesses, sendmail buffer overflow, mountd, UNIX NFS exports, User IDs (especially root/administrator with no passwords), IMAP and POP buffer overflow vulnerabilities, and SNMP community strings set to public and private.

Always remember that attempting to break in to a computer system is a criminal offense in many jurisdictions: you should obtain written authorization from the owner of your system before embarking on a security-related exercise of this kind; otherwise, it may be misconstrued as a real attack.

Once the target selection is complete, the data collection process begins by executing a number of scripts on the server, and reporting the results through the web browser. Data is collected by testing many different Solaris services, including ping, finger, RPC, login, rsh, sendmail, tooltalk, snmp, and rstatd.

SAINT uses several different modules to probe vulnerabilities in the system, including tcpscan, udpscan, and ddos, which scan for TCP, UDP, and denial of service issues, respectively. In addition, a number of well-known username and password combinations are also attempted, in order to break into an account—you would imagine that root/root would never be used as a username and password combination, but it does happen.

Once all of the data has been collected, the results of the scan are then displayed on the Data Analysis page, as shown in Figure 7-6. It is possible to list vulnerabilities by their danger level, by the type of vulnerability, or by the number of vulnerabilities in a specific category. Most administrators will want to deal with the most dangerous vulnerabilities, so the first option should be selected. In addition, it is possible to view information about the target system by class of service, type of system, domain name, subnet, and hostname.

Vulnerabilities are listed in terms of danger level: there are critical problems, areas of concern, and potential problems, as shown in Figure 7-7. For the local host okami, which was a standard Solaris install out of the box, two critical problems were identified, both associated with gaining root access via buffer overflow:

- The CDE-based Calendar Manager service may be vulnerable to a buffer overflow attack, as identified in CVE 1999-0320 and 1999-0696. The Calendar Manager is used to manage appointments and other date/time-based functions.

- The remote administration daemon (sadmind) may be vulnerable to a buffer overflow attack, as described in CVE 1999-0977. The remote administration daemon is used to manage system administration activities across a number of different hosts.

There were also two areas of concern identified, with information-gathering vulnerabilities exposed:

- The finger daemon returned personal information about users that could be used to stage an attack. For example, the home directory, full name, and project was displayed (CVE 1999-0612).

- The remote users list daemon was active, providing a list of users on the system to any remote user (CVE 1999-0626). Like the finger daemon, information gathered from the ruserd could be used to stage an attack.

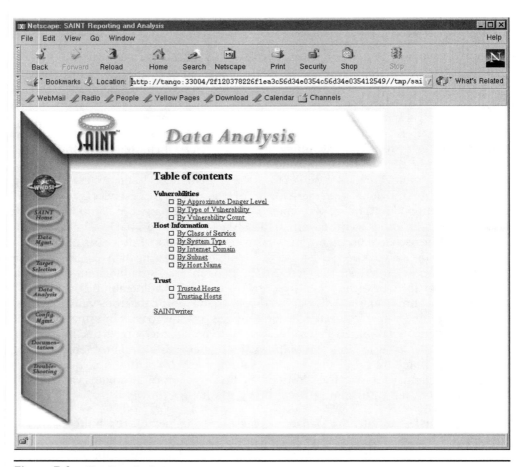

Figure 7-6   The Data Analysis page

Two possible vulnerabilities were identified:

- The chargen program is vulnerable to UDP flooding used in denial of service attacks, such as Fraggle (CVE 1999-0103).

- The sendmail server allows mail relaying, which may be used by remote users to forward mail using the server. This makes it easy for companies promoting SPAM to make it appear as if their mail originated from your server.

Six recommendations were made to limit Internet access, including stopping all of the "r" services: these make it easy for a remote user to execute commands on the local system, such as spawning a shell or obtaining information about system load, but have

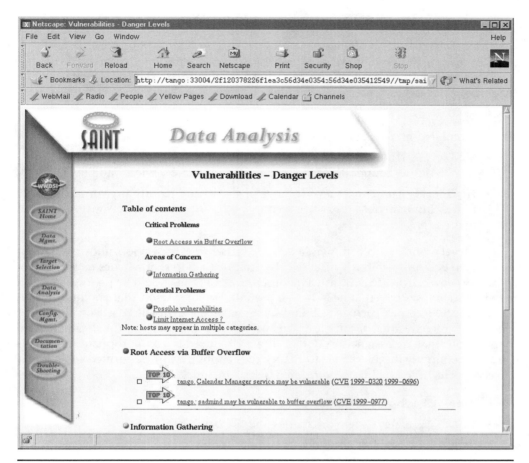

Figure 7-7 Identifying vulnerabilities

been used in the past to break into systems. In addition, some sendmail commands (such as EXPN and VRFY) are allowed by the sendmail configuration: this allows remote users to obtain a list of all users on the current system, which is often the first step to obtaining their passwords.

If you are concerned that a rogue user may be using SAINT against your network, you may download and run one of the many SAINT-detecting programs, such as Courtney (**http://ciac.llnl.gov/ciac/ToolsUnixNetMon.html#Courtney**). Courtney monitors TCP traffic to determine whether or not a single remote machine is systematically scanning the ports within a specified timeframe. Obviously, this program is useful for detecting all kinds of port scanning, and not just SAINT.

aset

The Automated Security Enhancement Tool (aset) is supplied by Sun as a multilevel system for investigating system weaknesses. In addition to reporting on potential vulnerabilities, aset can actually fix problems that are identified. There are three distinct operational levels (low, medium, and high) for aset:

- **Low level** Undertakes a number of checks, and reports any vulnerabilities found. No remedial action is performed.
- **Med level** Undertakes a moderate number of checks and reports any vulnerabilities found. Restricts system access to some services and files.
- **High level** Undertakes a wide range of checks and reports any vulnerabilities found. Implements a restrictive security policy by enforcing pessimistic access permissions.

Low-level reports are recommended to be run as a weekly cron job, allowing administrators to determine if newly installed applications, services, or patches have compromised system security. In contrast, a medium-level aset run should be performed on all newly installed systems that lie behind a firewall. For all systems that are directly connected to the Internet, such as web and proxy servers, a high-level aset run should be performed directly after installation. This will ensure that many of the default system permissions that are assigned to system files are reduced to an appropriate scope. It is possible to modify the *asetenv* file to change the actions that are performed when aset is executed. The individual tasks performed by aset include:

- **tune** Checks all file permissions.
- **cklist** Validates system directories and file permissions.
- **usrgrp** Checks user accounts and groups for integrity.
- **sysconf** Verifies the system files stored in /etc.
- **env** Parses environment variables stored in configuration files.
- **eeprom** Checks the security level of the OpenBoot PROM monitor.
- **firewall** Determines whether or not the system is secure enough to operate as a packet filter.

TCP Wrappers

Logging access information can reveal whether an organization's networks have an authentication problem. In addition, specific instances of unauthorized access to various resources can be collated and, using statistical methods, assessed for regular patterns of abuse. Monitoring of log files can also be used by applications to accept or reject connections, based on historical data contained in centralized logging mechanisms provided under Solaris, such as the syslogd system logging daemon.

One reason why access monitoring is not often discussed is that implementations of the standard UNIX network daemons that are spawned by the Internet superserver inetd (discussed earlier) do not have a provision to write directly to a syslog file. Later Internet service daemons, such as the Apache web server, run as stand-alone services not requiring inetd, but have enhanced logging facilities that are used to track web site usage.

Wietse Venema's TCP Wrappers are a popular method of enabling daemons launched from inetd to log their accepted and rejected connections, since the wrapper programs that are installed for each service do not require alterations to existing binary software distributions or to existing configuration files. TCP Wrappers can be downloaded in source form from **ftp://ftp.porcupine.org/pub/security/index.html**.

In their simplest form, TCP Wrappers are used for monitoring only, but they could be used to build better applications that can reject connections on the basis of failed connections. For example, a flood of requests to log in using rsh from an untrusted host could be terminated after three failed attempts from a single host. TCP Wrappers work by compiling a replacement daemon that points to the "real" daemon file, often located in a subdirectory below the daemon wrappers. The wrappers log the date and time of a service request, with a client hostname and whether the request was rejected or accepted. The current version of TCP Wrappers supports the SVR4 (System V Release 4) TLI network programming interface under Solaris, which has equivalent functionality to the Berkeley socket programming interface. In addition, the latest release supports access control and detection of host address or hostname spoofing. The latter is particularly important in the context of authentication services that provide access to services based on IP subnet ranges or specific hostnames in a local area network: if these are spoofed, and access is granted to a rogue client, the entire security infrastructure has failed. It is critical to detect and reject any unauthorized connections at an early stage, and TCP Wrappers are an integral part of this mechanism.

When writing access information to syslog, the output looks like this:

```
Nov 18 11:00:52 server in.telnetd[1493]: connect from client.site.com
Nov 18 11:25:03 server in.telnetd[1510]: connect from workstation.site.com
Nov 18 11:25:22 server in.telnetd[1511]: connect from client.site.com
Nov 18 12:16:30 server in.ftpd[1556]: connect from workstation.site.com
```

These entries indicate that between 11:00 A.M. and 1:00 P.M. on November 18th, clients connected using telnet from **client.site.com** and **workstation.site.com**. In addition, there was an FTP connection from **workstation.site.com**. Although we've only examined wrappers for in.ftpd and in.telnetd, wrappers can be compiled for most services launched from inetd, including finger, talk, tftp (trivial ftp) and rsh (remote shell).

Summary

Security is a central concern of the system administrator. In this chapter, you have learned the basic concepts and practices of system security. The tools introduced will be useful when attempting to secure a system connected to the Internet.

Questions

1. Which of the following files do not need to be owned by a user?

   A. Directories

   B. Device files

   C. Metadevices

   D. None of the above

2. Which of the following printouts represents a possible output from the id command?

   A. gid=1001(scott) uid=100(tiger)

   B. uid=1001(scott) gid=100(tiger)

   C. uid=1001(scott) gid=-100(tiger)

   D. None of the above

3. What is the UID of the superuser?

   A. 0

   B. 1

   C. 100

   D. 666

4. Name one restriction placed on the root account?

   A. The root user cannot read other users' e-mail.

   B. The root user cannot delete a user's account without their permission.

   C. The root user cannot rlogin to another system as root without a credential.

   D. The root user cannot modify disk partition sizes.

5. Name the default permissions mask set in the user's shell?

   A. mask

   B. omask

   C. chmod

   D. umask

6. How could read, write, and execute permissions be set on a file called */etc/passwd* for all users?

   A. chmod a+rwx /etc/passwd

   B. chmod o+rwx /etc/passwd

   C. chmod u+rwx /etc/passwd

   D. chmod u-rwx /etc/passwd

7. How could read, write, and execute permissions be removed from a file called */etc/passwd* for all users who do not belong to the owner's group?

   A. `chmod a+rwx /etc/passwd`

   B. `chmod o+rwx /etc/passwd`

   C. `chmod u+rwx /etc/passwd`

   D. `chmod o-rwx /etc/passwd`

8. Which command displays the username, connecting line, date of login, idle time, process ID, and a comment for all logged-in users?

   A. `who`

   B. `w`

   C. `which`

   D. `show`

Answers

1. **D.** All files need to be owned by someone.

2. **B.** All UIDs and GIDs must be positive and the UID precedes the GID.

3. **A.** The UID of the superuser is always 0, even if the name is changed from root to something else.

4. **C.** Credentials are required, unless blanket access is granted by use of hosts.equiv or .rhosts.

5. **D.** The umask is the default permissions mask.

6. **A.** All users are denoted by "a" in permissions strings.

7. **D.** Permissions are removed with "-".

8. **A.** The `who` command displays the username, connecting line, date of login, idle time, process ID, and a comment for all logged-in users.

Processes

In this chapter, you will

- Understand how the `ps` command can be used to monitor system processes
- Send signals to processes to modify their behavior using the `kill` command
- Configure the at daemon to schedule the execution of a job
- Configure the cron daemon to regularly schedule the execution of a job

Processes lie at the heart of modern multiuser operating systems, providing the ability to run multiple applications and services concurrently on top of the kernel. In user terms, process management is a central feature of using a single login shell to start and stop multiple jobs running concurrently, often suspending their execution while waiting for input. Solaris 9 provides many tools for process management, which have changed significantly during the transition from Solaris 1. This chapter highlights the new process management tools and command formats, and it discusses the innovative */proc* file systems and associated tools that allow administrators to deal with "zombie" processes. This chapter will also talk about automating tasks and using the scheduling facility.

Process Concepts

One of the appealing characteristics of Solaris and other UNIX-like systems is that applications can execute (or *spawn*) other applications: after all, user shells are nothing more than applications themselves. A shell can spawn another shell or application, which can spawn another shell or application, and so on. Instances of applications, such as the sendmail mail transport agent or the telnet remote access application, can be uniquely identified as individual processes and are associated with a unique process identifier (PID), which is an integer.

You may be wondering why process identifiers are not content addressable—that is, why the sendmail process cannot be identified as simply sendmail. Such a scheme would be quite sensible if it were impossible to execute multiple, independent instances of the same application (like early versions of the MacOS). However, Solaris allows the same user or different users to concurrently execute the same application independently, which means that an independent identifier is required for each process. This also means that each PID is related to a user identifier (UID) and to that user's group identifier (GID). The UID in this case can be either the *real* UID of the user who executed the process or the *effective* UID if the file executed is setUID. Similarly, the GID in this case can either be the *real* GID, which the user who executed the process belongs to, or the *effective* GID if the file executed is setGID.

TIP When an application can be executed as setUID and setGID, other users can execute such a program as the user who owns the file. This means that setting a file as setGID for root can be dangerous in some situations, although necessary in others.

An application, such as a shell, can spawn another application by using the system call `system()` in a C program. This is expensive performance-wise, however, because a new shell process is spawned in addition to the target application. An alternative is to use the `fork()` system call, which spawns child processes directly, with applications executed using `exec()`. Each child process is linked back to its parent process: if the parent process exits, the parent process automatically reverts to PID 1, which exits when the system is shut down or rebooted.

In this section, you'll look at ways to determine which processes are currently running on your system and how to examine process lists and tables to determine what system resources are being used by specific processes.

The main command used to list commands is `ps`, which is highly configurable and has many command-line options. These options, and the command format, changed substantially from Solaris 1.x to Solaris 2.x: the former used BSD-style options, like `ps aux`, while the latter uses System V–style parameters, like `ps -eaf`. The proctool monitoring application is also supplied with Solaris 9.

`ps` takes a snapshot of the current process list; many administrators find that they need to interactively monitor processes on systems that have a high load, so they kill processes that are consuming too much memory, or at least assign them a lower execution priority.

TIP One popular process monitoring tool is top, which is described later in this chapter in the section "Using the top Program."

As shown in Figure 8-1, the CDE (Common Desktop Environment) also has its own graphical "process finder," which lists currently active processes. It is possible to list processes here by PID, name, owner, percentage of CPU time consumed, physical memory used, virtual memory used, date started, parent PID, and the actual command executed. This does not provide as much information as top, but it is a useful tool within the CDE.

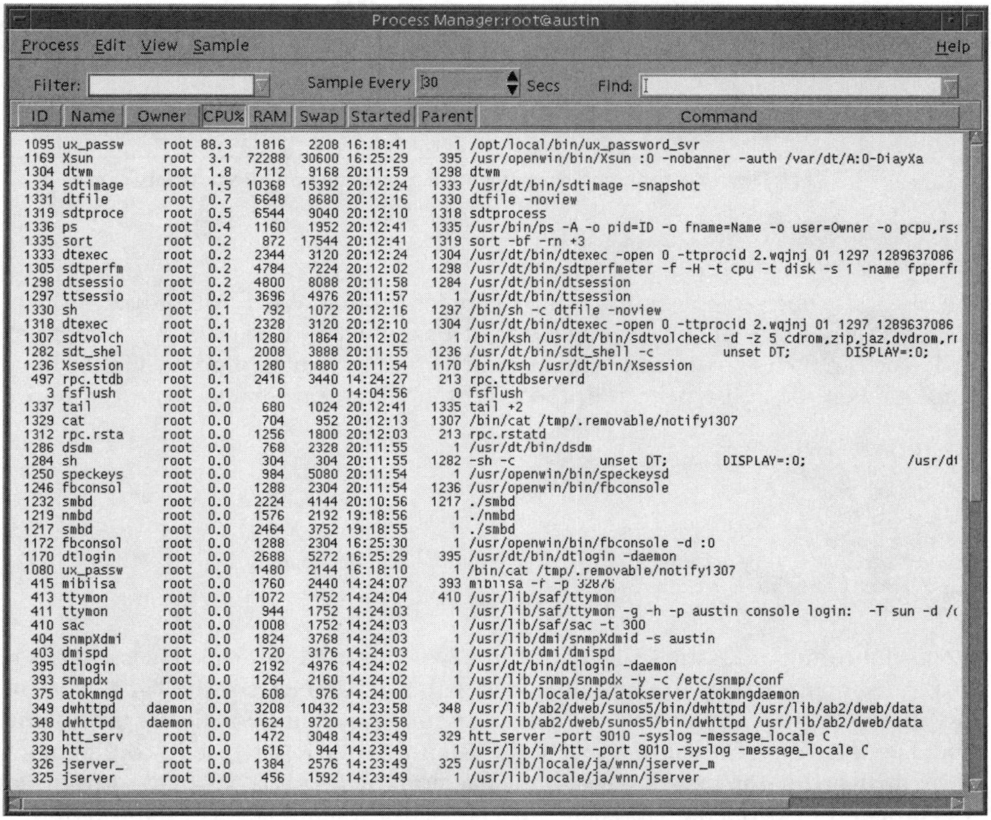

Figure 8-1 CDE's graphical process finder

Sending Signals

Because all processes are identifiable by a single PID, the PID can be used to manage that process by means of a *signal*. Signals can be sent to other processes in C programs using the `signal()` function, or they can be sent directly from within the shell. Solaris supports a number of standard signal types that can be used as a means of interprocess communication.

A common use for signals is to manage user applications that are launched from a shell. A "suspend" signal, for example, can be sent to an application running in the foreground by pressing CTRL-Z at any time. To run this application in the background in the C shell, for example, you would need to type **bg** at the command prompt. A unique background job number is then assigned to the job, and typing **fg *n***, where *n* is that job number, brings the process back to the foreground.

 EXAM TIP   You can run as many applications as you like in the background.

In the following example, httpd is run in the foreground. When you press CTRL-Z, the process is suspended, and when you type **bg**, it is assigned the background process number 1. You can then execute other commands, such as `ls`, while httpd runs in the background. When you then type **fg**, the process is brought once again into the foreground.

```
client 1% httpd
^z
Suspended
client 2% bg
[1] httpd&
client 3% ls
httpd.conf   access.conf   srm.conf
client 4% fg
```

A useful command is the `kill` command, which is used to send signals directly to any process on the system. It is usually called with two parameters—the signal type and the PID. For example, if you have made changes to the configuration file for the Internet superdaemon, you must send a signal to the daemon to tell it to reread its configuration file. Note that you don't need to restart the daemon itself: This is one of the advantages of a process-based operating system that facilitates interprocess communication. If inetd had the PID 167, typing

```
# kill -1 167
```

would force inetd to reread its configuration file and update its internal settings. The `-1` parameter stands for the *SIGHUP* signal, which means "hang up." However, imagine a situation in which you wanted to switch off inetd temporarily to perform a security check. You could send a `kill` signal to the process by using the `-9` parameter (the *SIGKILL* signal):

```
# kill -9 167
```

Although *SIGHUP* and *SIGKILL* are the most commonly used signals in the shell, several others are used by programmers and are defined in the *signal.h* header file. Another potential consequence of sending a signal to a process is that instead of "hanging up" or "being killed," the process could exit and dump a *core file*, which is a memory image of the process to which the message was sent. This result is useful for debugging, although too many core files will quickly fill up your file system! You can always obtain a list of available signals to the kill command by passing the -1 option:

```
$ kill -l
HUP INT QUIT ILL TRAP ABRT EMT FPE KILL BUS SEGV SYS PIPE
ALRM TERM USR1 USR2 CLD PWR WINCH URG POLL STOP TSTP CONT
TTIN TTOU VTALRM PROF XCPU XFSZ WAITING LWP FREEZE THAW
RTMIN RTMIN+1 RTMIN+2 RTMIN+3 RTMAX-3 RTMAX-2 RTMAX-1
RTMAX
```

Listing Processes

You can use the ps command to list all currently active processes on the local system. By default, ps prints the processes belonging to the user who issues the ps command:

```
$ ps
PID TTY        TIME CMD
 29081 pts/8    0:00 ksh
```

The columns in the default ps list are the process identifier (PID), the terminal from which the command was executed (TTY), the CPU time consumed by the process (TIME), and the actual command that was executed (CMD), including any command- line options passed to the program.

Alternatively, if you would like more information about the current user's processes, you can add the -f parameter:

```
$ ps -f
     UID      PID    PPID    C STIME     TTY        TIME CMD
    pwatters 29081  29079    0 10:40:30 pts/8       0:00 /bin/ksh
```

Again, the PID, TTY, CPU time, and command are displayed. However, the username is also displayed, as is the PID of the parent process (PPID), along with the starting time of the process (STIME). In addition, a deprecated column (C) is used to display processor utilization. To obtain the maximum detail possible, you can also use the -1 option, which means "long"—and long it certainly is, as shown in this example:

```
$ ps -l
 F S   UID    PID   PPID C PRI NI     ADDR   SZ     WCHAN TTY      TIME CMD
 8 S 6049 29081  29079 0  51 20 e11b4830 372 e11b489c pts/8    0:00 ksh
 8 O 6049 29085  29081 0  51 20 e101b0d0 512          pts/8    0:00 bash
```

Here, you can see the following:

- The flags (F) associated with the processes
- The state (S) of the processes (29081 is sleeping "S," 29085 is running "O")
- The process identifier (29081 and 29085)

- Parent process identifier (29079 and 29081)
- Processor utilization (deprecated)
- Process priority (PRI), which is 51
- Nice value (NI), which is 20
- Memory address (ADDR), which is expressed in hex (e11b4830 and e101b0d0)
- Size (SZ), in pages of memory, which is 372 and 512
- The memory address for sleeping process events (WCHAN), which is e11b489c for PID 29081
- CPU time used (TIME)
- The command executed (CMD)

If you're a system administrator, you're probably not interested in the status of just your own processes; you probably want details about all or some of the processes actively running on the system, and you can do this in many ways. You can generate a process list using the −A or the −e option, for example, and either of these lists information for all processes currently running on the machine:

```
# ps -A
   PID TTY         TIME CMD
     0 ?           0:00 sched
     1 ?           0:01 init
     2 ?           0:01 pageout
     3 ?           9:49 fsflush
   258 ?           0:00 ttymon
   108 ?           0:00 rpcbind
   255 ?           0:00 sac
    60 ?           0:00 devfseve
    62 ?           0:00 devfsadm
   157 ?           0:03 automount
   110 ?           0:01 keyserv
   112 ?           0:04 nis_cache
   165 ?           0:00 syslogd
```

Again, the default display of PID, TTY, CPU time, and command is generated. The processes listed relate to the scheduler, *init*, the system logging facility, the NIS cache, and several other standard applications and services.

 TIP It is good practice for you to become familiar with the main processes on your system and the relative CPU times they usually consume. This can be useful information when troubleshooting or when evaluating security.

One of the nice features of the ps command is the ability to combine multiple flags to print out a more elaborate process list. For example, we can combine the −A option (all processes) with the −f option (full details) to produce a process list with full details. Here are the full details for the same process list:

```
# ps -Af
     UID    PID   PPID   C     STIME  TTY     TIME  CMD
     root     0      0   0     Mar 20  ?      0:00  sched
     root     1      0   0     Mar 20  ?      0:01  /etc/init -
     root     2      0   0     Mar 20  ?      0:01  pageout
     root     3      0   0     Mar 20  ?      9:51  fsflush
     root   258    255   0     Mar 20  ?      0:00  /usr/lib/saf/ttymon
     root   108      1   0     Mar 20  ?      0:00  /usr/sbin/rpcbind
     root   255      1   0     Mar 20  ?      0:00  /usr/lib/saf/sac -t 300
     root    60      1   0     Mar 20  ?      0:00  /usr/lib/devfsadm/devfseventd
     root    62      1   0     Mar 20  ?      0:00  /usr/lib/devfsadm/devfsadmd
     root   157      1   0     Mar 20  ?      0:03  /usr/lib/autofs/automountd
     root   110      1   0     Mar 20  ?      0:01  /usr/sbin/keyserv
     root   112      1   0     Mar 20  ?      0:05  /usr/sbin/nis_cachemgr
     root   165      1   0     Mar 20  ?      0:00  /usr/sbin/syslogd
```

Another common use for ps is to print process information in a format that is suitable for the scheduler:

```
% ps -c
   PID   CLS PRI TTY       TIME CMD
 29081    TS  48 pts/8     0:00 ksh
 29085    TS  48 pts/8     0:00 bash
```

This can be useful when used in conjunction with the priocntl command, which displays the parameters used for process scheduling. This allows administrators, in particular, to determine the process classes currently available on the system, or to set the class of a specific process to interactive or time-sharing. You can obtain a list of all supported classes by passing the -l parameter to priocntl:

```
# priocntl -l
CONFIGURED CLASSES
==================
SYS (System Class)
TS (Time Sharing)
        Configured TS User Priority Range: -60 through 60
IA (Interactive)
        Configured IA User Priority Range: -60 through 60
```

You can combine this with a -f full display flag to ps -c to obtain more information:

```
$ ps -cf
     UID   PID  PPID  CLS PRI    STIME TTY       TIME CMD
    paul 29081 29079   TS  48 10:40:30 pts/8     0:00 /bin/ksh
    paul 29085 29081   TS  48 10:40:51 pts/8     0:00 /usr/local/bin/bash
```

If you want to obtain information about processes being executed by a particular group of users, this can be specified on the command line by using the -g option, followed by the GID of the target group. In this example, all processes from users in group 0 will be printed:

```
$ ps -g 0
   PID TTY       TIME CMD
     0 ?         0:00 sched
```

```
1 ?          0:01 init
2 ?          0:01 pageout
3 ?          9:51 fsflush
```

Another common configuration option used with ps is -j, which displays the session identifier (SID) and the process group identifier (PGID), as shown here:

```
$ ps -j
   PID  PGID   SID TTY       TIME CMD
 29081 29081 29081 pts/8     0:00 ksh
 29085 29085 29081 pts/8     0:00 bash
```

Finally, you can print out the status of lightweight processes (LWPs) in your system. These are virtual CPU or execution resources, which are designed to make the best use of available CPU resources based on their priority and scheduling class. Here is an example:

```
$ ps -L
   PID  LWP TTY       LTIME CMD
 29081    1 pts/8     0:00 ksh
 29085    1 pts/8     0:00 bash
```

Using the top Program

If you're an administrator, you probably want to keep an eye on all processes running on a system, particularly if the system is in production use. This is because buggy programs can consume large amounts of CPU time, preventing operational applications from carrying out their duties efficiently. Monitoring the process list almost constantly is necessary, especially if performance begins to suffer on a system. Although you could keep typing **ps –eaf** every 5 minutes or so, a much more efficient method is to use the top program to monitor the processes in your system interactively, and to use its "vital statistics," such as CPU activity states, real and virtual memory status, and the load average. In addition, top displays the details of the leading processes that consume the greatest amount of CPU time during each sampling period. An alternative to top is prstat, which has the advantage of being bundled with the operating system.

The display of top can be customized to include any number of these leading processes at any one time, but displaying the top 10 or 20 processes is usually sufficient to keep an eye on rogue processes.

 TIP   The latest version of top can always be downloaded from **ftp://ftp.groupsys.com/pub/top**.

---

top reads the */proc* file system to generate its process statistics. This usually means that top runs as a setUID process, unless you remove the read and execute permissions for nonroot users and run it only as root. Paradoxically, doing this may be just as dangerous, because any errors in top may impact the system at large if executed by the root user. Again, setUID processes are dangerous, and you should evaluate whether the tradeoff between accessibility and security is worthwhile in this case.

CAUTION One of the main problems with top running on Solaris is that top is very sensitive to changes in architecture and/or operating system versions. This is particularly the case if the GNU gcc 2.x compiler is used to build top, as it has its own set of include files. These must exactly match the version of the current operating system; otherwise, top will not work properly: the CPU state percentages may be wrong, indicating that processes are consuming all CPU time, when the system is actually idle. The solution is to rebuild gcc so that it generates header files that are appropriate for your current operating system version.

Let's examine a printout from top:

```
last PID: 16630;  load averages:  0.17,  0.08,  0.06      09:33:29
72 processes:  71 sleeping, 1 on cpu
CPU states: 87.6% idle, 4.8% user, 7.5% kernel, 0.1% iowait, 0.0% swap
Memory: 128M real, 3188K free, 72M swap in use, 172M swap free
```

This summary tells us that the system has 72 processes, with only 1 running actively and 71 sleeping. The system was 87.6 percent idle in the previous sampling epoch, and there was little swapping or iowait activity, ensuring fast performance. The load average for the previous 1, 5, and 15 minutes was 0.17, 0.08, and 0.06 respectively—this is not a machine that is taxed by its workload. The last PID to be issued to an application, 16630, is also displayed.

```
  PID USERNAME THR PRI NICE   SIZE   RES STATE    TIME    CPU COMMAND
  259 root       1  59    0    18M 4044K sleep  58:49   1.40% Xsun
16630 pwatters    1  59    0 1956K 1536K cpu     0:00   1.19% top
  345 pwatters 8  33    0 7704K 4372K sleep   0:21   0.83% dtwm
16580 pwatters    1  59    0 5984K 2608K sleep   0:00   0.24% dtterm
 9196 pwatters 1  48    0   17M 1164K sleep   0:28   0.01% netscape
13818 pwatters 1  59    0 5992K  872K sleep   0:01   0.00% dtterm
  338 pwatters 1  48    0 7508K    0K sleep   0:04   0.00% dtsession
  112 pwatters 3  59    0 1808K  732K sleep   0:03   0.00% nis_cachemgr
  157 pwatters 5  58    0 2576K  576K sleep   0:02   0.00% automountd
  422 pwatters 1  48    0 4096K  672K sleep   0:01   0.00% textedit
 2295 pwatters 1  48    0 7168K    0K sleep   0:01   0.00% dtfile
 8350 root      10  51    0 3000K 2028K sleep   0:01   0.00% nscd
 8757 pwatters 1  48   10 5992K 1340K sleep   0:01   0.00% dtterm
 4910 nobody     1   0    0 1916K    0K sleep   0:00   0.00% httpd
  366 pwatters 1  28    0 1500K    0K sleep   0:00   0.00% sdtvolcheck
```

This top listing shows a lot of information about each process running on the system, including the PID, the user who owns the process, the nice value (priority), the size of the application, the amount resident in memory, its current state (active or sleeping), the CPU time consumed, and the command name. For example, the Apache web server runs as the httpd process (PID=4910), by the user nobody, and is 1916KB in size.

Changing the nice value of a process ensures that it receives more or less priority from the process scheduler. Reducing the nice value ensures that the process priority is increased, while increasing the nice value decreases the process priority. Unfortunately, while ordinary users can increase their nice value, only the superuser can decrease the nice value for a process. In the preceding example for top, the dtterm process is running with a nice value of 10, which is low. If the root user wanted to increase the priority of the process to 20, he or she would issue the command

```
# nice --20 dtterm
```

Increasing the nice value can be performed by any user. To increase the nice value of the top process, the following command would be used:

```
$ nice -20 ps
```

Now, if you execute an application that requires a lot of CPU power, you will be able to monitor the impact on the system as a whole by examining the changes in the processes displayed by top. If you execute the command

```
$ find . -name apache -print
```

the impact on the process distribution is immediately apparent:

```
last PID: 16631;   load averages: 0.10, 0.07, 0.06    09:34:08
73 processes:  71 sleeping, 1 running, 1 on cpu
CPU states:   2.2% idle,   0.6% user, 11.6% kernel, 85.6% iowait, 0.0% swap
Memory: 128M real, 1896K free, 72M swap in use, 172M swap free
```

This summary tells you that the system now has 73 processes, with only 1 running actively, 1 on the CPU, and 71 sleeping. The new process is the find command, which is actively running. The system is now only 2.2 percent idle, a large increase on the previous sampling epoch. There is still no swapping activity, but iowait activity has risen to 85.6 percent, slowing system performance. The load average for the previous 1, 5, and 15 minutes was 0.10, 0.07, and 0.06, respectively—on the average, this machine is still not taxed by its workload and wouldn't be unless the load averages grew to greater than 1. The last PID to be issued to an application, 16631, is also displayed, and in this case it again refers to the find command.

```
  PID USERNAME THR PRI NICE  SIZE   RES STATE    TIME    CPU COMMAND
16631 pwatters 1  54    0  788K  668K run      0:00  1.10% find
  259 root        1  59    0  18M 4288K sleep  58:49  0.74% Xsun
16630 pwatters 1  59    0 1956K 1536K cpu      0:00  0.50% top
 9196 pwatters 1  48    0  17M 3584K sleep     0:28  0.13% netscape
 8456 pwatters 1  59    0 5984K   0K sleep     0:00  0.12% dtpad
  345 pwatters 8  59    0 7708K   0K sleep     0:21  0.11% dtwm
16580 pwatters 1  59    0 5992K 2748K sleep    0:00  0.11% dtterm
13838 pwatters 1  38    0 2056K  652K sleep    0:00  0.06% bash
13818 pwatters 1  59    0 5992K 1884K sleep    0:01  0.06% dtterm
  112 root        3  59    0 1808K  732K sleep   0:03  0.02% nis_cachemgr
  337 pwatters 4  59    0 4004K   0K sleep     0:00  0.01% ttsession
  338 pwatters 1  48    0 7508K   0K sleep     0:04  0.00% dtsession
  157 root        5  58    0 2576K  604K sleep   0:02  0.00% automountd
 2295 pwatters 1  48    0 7168K   0K sleep     0:01  0.00% dtfile
  422 pwatters 1  48    0 4096K   0K sleep     0:01  0.00% textedit
```

find now uses 1.1 percent of CPU power, which is the highest of any active process (that is, in the "run" state) on the system. It uses 788K of RAM, less than most other processes; however, most other processes are in the "sleep" state, and do not occupy much resident memory.

Using the truss Program

If you've identified a process that appears to be having problems, and you suspect it's an application bug, it's not just a matter of going back to the source to debug the program or making an educated guess about what's going wrong. In fact, one of the great features of Solaris is the ability to trace system calls for every process running on the system. This means that if a program is hanging—for example, because it can't find its initialization file—the failed system call revealed using truss would display this information. truss prints out each system call, line by line, as it is executed by the system. The syntax is rather like a C program, making it easy for C programmers to interpret the output. The arguments are displayed by retrieving information from the appropriate headers, and any file information is also displayed.

As an example, let's look at the output from the `cat` command, which we can use to display the contents of */etc/resolv.conf*, which is used by the Domain Name Service (DNS) to identify domains and name servers. Let's look at the operations involved in running this application:

```
# truss cat /etc/resolv.conf
execve("/usr/bin/cat", 0xEFFFF740, 0xEFFFF74C)  argc = 2
open("/dev/zero", O_RDONLY)                     = 3
mmap(0x00000000, 8192, PROT_READ|PROT_WRITE|PROT_EXEC, MAP_PRIVATE, 3, 0) =
 0xEF7B0000
open("/usr/lib/libc.so.1", O_RDONLY)            = 4
fstat(4, 0xEFFFF2DC)                            = 0
mmap(0x00000000, 8192, PROT_READ|PROT_EXEC, MAP_PRIVATE, 4, 0) = 0xEF7A0000
mmap(0x00000000, 704512, PROT_READ|PROT_EXEC, MAP_PRIVATE, 4, 0) =
 0xEF680000
munmap(0xEF714000, 57344)
            = 0
mmap(0xEF722000, 28368, PROT_READ|PROT_WRITE|PROT_EXEC, MAP_PRIVATE|
MAP_FIXED, 4, 598016) = 0xEF722000
mmap(0xEF72A000, 2528, PROT_READ|PROT_WRITE|PROT_EXEC, MAP_PRIVATE|
MAP_FIXED, 3, 0) = 0xEF72A000
close(4)                                        = 0
open("/usr/lib/libdl.so.1", O_RDONLY)           = 4
fstat(4, 0xEFFFF2DC)                            = 0
mmap(0xEF7A0000, 8192, PROT_READ|PROT_EXEC, MAP_PRIVATE|
MAP_FIXED, 4, 0) = 0xEF7A0000
close(4)                                        = 0
open("/usr/platform/SUNW,Ultra-2/lib/libc_psr.so.1", O_RDONLY) = 4
fstat(4, 0xEFFFF0BC)                            = 0
mmap(0x00000000, 8192, PROT_READ|PROT_EXEC, MAP_PRIVATE, 4, 0) = 0xEF790000
mmap(0x00000000, 16384, PROT_READ|PROT_EXEC, MAP_PRIVATE, 4, 0) =
 0xEF780000
close(4)                                        = 0
close(3)                                        = 0
munmap(0xEF790000, 8192)                        = 0
fstat64(1, 0xEFFFF648)                          = 0
open64("resolv.conf", O_RDONLY)                 = 3
fstat64(3, 0xEFFFF5B0)                          = 0
llseek(3, 0, SEEK_CUR)                          = 0
mmap64(0x00000000, 98, PROT_READ, MAP_SHARED, 3, 0) = 0xEF790000
read(3, " d", 1)                                = 1
memcntl(0xEF790000, 98, MC_ADVISE, 0x0002, 0, 0) = 0
domain paulwatters.com
nameserver 192.56.67.16
nameserver 192.56.67.32
nameserver 192.56.68.16
write(1, " d o m a i n   p a u l w a t t e r s .".., 98)    = 98
llseek(3, 98, SEEK_SET)                         = 98
munmap(0xEF790000, 98)                          = 0
llseek(3, 0, SEEK_CUR)                          = 98
```

```
close(3)                                          = 0
close(1)                                          = 0
llseek(0, 0, SEEK_CUR)                            = 57655
_exit(0)
```

Firstly, `cat` is called using `execve()`, with two arguments (that is, the application name, *cat*, and the file to be displayed, */etc/resolv.conf*). The arguments to `execve()` include the name of the application (*/usr/bin/cat*), a pointer to the argument list (0xEFFFF740), and a pointer to the environment (0xEFFFF74C). Next, library files such as */usr/lib/libc.so.1* are read. Memory operations (such as `mmap()`) are performed continuously. The *resolv.conf* file is opened as read-only, after which the contents are literally printed to standard output. Then the file is closed.

TIP truss can be used to trace the system calls for any process running on your system.

Automating Jobs

Many system administration tasks need to be performed on a regular basis. For example, log files for various applications need to be archived nightly and a new log file created. Often a short script is created to perform this, by following these steps:

1. Kill the daemon affected, using the `kill` command.
2. Compress the log file using the `gzip` or `compress` command.
3. Change the log filename to include a time stamp so that it can be distinguished from other log files by using the `time` command.
4. Move it to an archive directory, using the `mv` command.
5. Create a new log file by using the `touch` command.
6. Restart the daemon by calling the appropriate */etc/init.d* script.

Instead of the administrator having to execute these commands interactively at midnight, they can be scheduled to run daily using the cron scheduling command. Alternatively, if a job needs to be run only once at a particular time, like bringing a new web site online at 7:00 A.M. one particular morning, the `at` scheduler can be used. The next section looks at the advantages and disadvantages of each scheduling method.

Using at

You can schedule a single system event for execution at a specified time by using the `at` command. The jobs are specified by files in the */var/spool/cron/atjobs*, while configuration is managed by the file */etc/cron.d/at.deny*. The job can be a single command, or it can refer to a script that contains a set of commands.

Suppose, for example, that you want to start up sendmail at a particular time because some maintenance of the network infrastructure is scheduled to occur until 8:30 A.M. tomorrow morning, but you really don't feel like logging in early and starting up sendmail (you've switched it off completely during an outage to prevent users from filling the queue). You can add a job to the queue, which is scheduled to run at 8:40 A.M., giving the network crew a 10-minute window to do their work:

```
$ at 0840
at> /usr/lib/sendmail -bd
at> <EOT>
commands will be executed using /bin/ksh
job 954715200.a at Mon Apr  3 08:40:00 2000
```

After submitting a job using at, check that the job is properly scheduled by seeing whether an *atjob* has been created:

```
$ cd /var/spool/cron/atjobs
client% ls -l
total 8
-r-Sr--r--    1 paul      other         3701 Apr  3 08:35 954715200.a
```

The file exists, which is a good start. Now check that it contains the appropriate commands to run the job:

```
$ cat 954715200.a
: at job
: jobname: stdin
: notify by mail: no
export PWD; PWD='/home/paul'
export _; _='/usr/bin/at'
cd /home/paul
umask 22
ulimit unlimited
/usr/lib/sendmail -bd
```

This looks good. After 8:40 A.M. the next morning, the command should have executed at the appropriate time, and some output should have been generated and sent to you as an e-mail message.

Here's what the message contains:

```
From paul Sat Apr  1 08:40:00 2000
Date: Sat Apr  1 2000 08:40:00 +1000 (EST)
From: paul <paul>
To: paul
Subject: Output from "at" job
Your "at" job on austin
"/var/spool/cron/atjobs/954715200.a"
produced the following output:
/bin/ksh[5]: sendmail: 501 Permission denied
```

Oops! You forgot to submit the job as root: normal users don't have permission to start sendmail in the background daemon mode. You would need to submit this job as root to be successful.

Scheduling with cron

An at job executes only once at a particular time. However, cron is much more flexible because you can schedule system events to execute repetitively at regular intervals by using the crontab command.

Each user on the system can have a crontab file, which allows them to schedule multiple events at multiple times on multiple dates. The jobs are specified by files in the /var/spool/cron/cronjobs, while configuration information is managed by the files /etc/cron.d/cron.allow and /etc/cron.d/cron.deny.

To check root's crontab file, you can use the `crontab -l` command:

```
# crontab -l root
10 3 * * 0,4 /etc/cron.d/logchecker
10 3 * * 0   /usr/lib/newsyslog
15 3 * * 0 /usr/lib/fs/nfs/nfsfind
1 2 * * * [ -x /usr/sbin/rtc ] && /usr/sbin/rtc -c > /dev/null 2>&1
30 3 * * * [ -x /usr/lib/gss/gsscred_clean ] && /usr/lib/gss/gsscred_clean
```

This is the standard `crontab` command generated by Solaris for root, and it performs tasks like checking whether the cron log file is approaching the system limit at 3:10 A.M. on Sundays and Thursdays, creating a new system log at 3:10 A.M. only on Sundays, and reconciling time differences at 2:01 A.M every day of the year.

The six fields in the crontab file stand for the following:

- Minutes, in the range 0–59
- Hours, in the range 0–23
- Days of the month, in the range 1–31
- Months of the year, in the range 1–12
- Days of the week, in the range 0–6, starting with Sundays
- The command to execute

If you want to add or delete an entry from your crontab file, you can use the `crontab -e` command. This will start up your default editor (vi on the command line, textedit in CDE, or as defined by the *EDITOR* environment variable), and you can make changes interactively.

CAUTION   After saving your job, you need to run crontab by itself to make the changes.

Managing Processes

Now that you have examined what processes are, you will now look at some special features of processes as implemented in Solaris. One of the most innovative characteristics of processes under Solaris is the process file system (PROCFS), which is mounted as the /proc file system. Images of all currently active processes are stored in the /proc file system by their PID.

Here's an example. First, a process is identified—in this example, the current Korn shell for the user pwatters:

```
# ps -eaf | grep pwatters
pwatters 310    291  0   Mar 20 ?         0:04 /usr/openwin/bin/Xsun
pwatters 11959 11934  0 09:21:42 pts/1   0:00 grep pwatters
pwatters 11934 11932  1 09:20:50 pts/1   0:00 -ksh
```

Now that you have a target PID (11934), you can change to the */proc/11934* directory and you will be able to view the image of this process:

```
# cd /proc/11934
 # ls -l
total 3497
-rw-------   1 pwatters    other    1769472 Mar 30 09:20 as
-r--------   1 pwatters    other        152 Mar 30 09:20 auxv
-r--------   1 pwatters    other         32 Mar 30 09:20 cred
--w-------   1 pwatters    other          0 Mar 30 09:20 ctl
lr-x------   1 pwatters    other          0 Mar 30 09:20 cwd ->
dr-x------   2 pwatters    other       1184 Mar 30 09:20 fd
-r--r--r--   1 pwatters    other        120 Mar 30 09:20 lpsinfo
-r--------   1 pwatters    other        912 Mar 30 09:20 lstatus
-r--r--r--   1 pwatters    other        536 Mar 30 09:20 lusage
dr-xr-xr-x   3 pwatters    other         48 Mar 30 09:20 lwp
-r--------   1 pwatters    other       2016 Mar 30 09:20 map
dr-x------   2 pwatters    other        544 Mar 30 09:20 object
-r--------   1 pwatters    other       2552 Mar 30 09:20 pagedata
-r--r--r--   1 pwatters    other        336 Mar 30 09:20 psinfo
-r--------   1 pwatters    other       2016 Mar 30 09:20 rmap
lr-x------   1 pwatters    other          0 Mar 30 09:20 root ->
-r--------   1 pwatters    other       1440 Mar 30 09:20 sigact
-r--------   1 pwatters    other       1232 Mar 30 09:20 status
-r--r--r--   1 pwatters    other        256 Mar 30 09:20 usage
-r--------   1 pwatters    other          0 Mar 30 09:20 watch
-r--------   1 pwatters    other       3192 Mar 30 09:20 xmap
```

Each of the directories with the name associated with the PID contains additional subdirectories, which contain state information and related control functions. In addition, a watchpoint facility is provided, which is responsible for controlling memory access.

TIP   A series of proc tools are available to interpret the information contained in the */proc* subdirectories.

Using proc tools

The proc tools are designed to operate on data contained within the */proc* file system. Each utility takes a PID as its argument and performs operations associated with the PID. For example, the `pflags` command prints the flags and data model details for the PID in question.

For the preceding Korn shell example, you can easily print out this status information:

```
# /usr/proc/bin/pflags 29081
29081:  /bin/ksh
        data model = _ILP32   flags = PR_ORPHAN
   /1:  flags = PR_PCINVAL|PR_ASLEEP [ waitid(0x7,0x0,0x804714c,0x7) ]
```

You can also print the credential information for this process, including the effective and real UID and GID of the process owner, by using the `pcred` command:

```
$ /usr/proc/bin/pcred 29081
29081:  e/r/sUID=100  e/r/sGID=10
```

Here, both the effective and the real UID is 100 (user pwatters), and the effective and real GID is 10 (group staff).

To examine the address space map of the target process, you can use the pmap command and all of the libraries it requires to execute:

```
# /usr/proc/bin/pmap 29081
29081:   /bin/ksh
08046000       8K read/write/exec       [ stack ]
08048000     160K read/exec             /usr/bin/ksh
08070000       8K read/write/exec       /usr/bin/ksh
08072000      28K read/write/exec       [ heap ]
DFAB4000      16K read/exec             /usr/lib/locale/en_AU/en_AU.so.2
DFAB8000       8K read/write/exec       /usr/lib/locale/en_AU/en_AU.so.2
DFABB000       4K read/write/exec       [ anon ]
DFABD000      12K read/exec             /usr/lib/libmp.so.2
DFAC0000       4K read/write/exec       /usr/lib/libmp.so.2
DFAC4000     552K read/exec             /usr/lib/libc.so.1
DFB4E000      24K read/write/exec       /usr/lib/libc.so.1
DFB54000       8K read/write/exec       [ anon ]
DFB57000     444K read/exec             /usr/lib/libnsl.so.1
DFBC6000      20K read/write/exec       /usr/lib/libnsl.so.1
DFBCB000      32K read/write/exec       [ anon ]
DFBD4000      32K read/exec             /usr/lib/libsocket.so.1
DFBDC000       8K read/write/exec       /usr/lib/libsocket.so.1
DFBDF000       4K read/exec             /usr/lib/libdl.so.1
DFBE1000       4K read/write/exec       [ anon ]
DFBE3000     100K read/exec             /usr/lib/ld.so.1
DFBFC000      12K read/write/exec       /usr/lib/ld.so.1
 total      1488K
```

It's always surprising to see how many libraries are loaded when an application is executed, especially something as complicated as a shell, leading to a total of 1488KB memory used. You can obtain a list of the dynamic libraries linked to each process by using the pldd command:

```
# /usr/proc/bin/pldd 29081
29081:   /bin/ksh
/usr/lib/libsocket.so.1
/usr/lib/libnsl.so.1
/usr/lib/libc.so.1
/usr/lib/libdl.so.1
/usr/lib/libmp.so.2
/usr/lib/locale/en_AU/en_AU.so.2
```

As discussed in the previous section "Sending Signals," signals are the way in which processes communicate with each other, and they can also be used from shells to communicate with spawned processes (usually to suspend or kill them).

By using the psig command, it is possible to list the signals associated with each process:

```
$ /usr/proc/bin/psig 29081
29081:   /bin/ksh
HUP     caught  RESTART
INT     caught  RESTART
QUIT    ignored
```

```
ILL       caught   RESTART
TRAP      caught   RESTART
ABRT      caught   RESTART
EMT       caught   RESTART
FPE       caught   RESTART
KILL      default
BUS       caught   RESTART
SEGV      default
SYS       caught   RESTART
PIPE      caught   RESTART
ALRM      caught   RESTART
TERM      ignored
USR1      caught   RESTART
USR2      caught   RESTART
CLD       default  NOCLDSTOP
PWR       default
WINCH     default
URG       default
POLL      default
STOP      default
TSTP      ignored
CONT      default
TTIN      ignored
TTOU      ignored
VTALRM    default
PROF      default
XCPU      caught   RESTART
XFSZ      ignored
WAITING   default
LWP       default
FREEZE    default
THAW      default
CANCEL    default
LOST      default
RTMIN     default
RTMIN+1   default
RTMIN+2   default
RTMIN+3   default
RTMAX-3   default
RTMAX-2   default
RTMAX-1   default
RTMAX     default
```

It is also possible to print a hexadecimal format stack trace for the lightweight process (LWP) in each process by using the pstack command. This can be useful in the same way that the truss command was used:

```
$ /usr/proc/bin/pstack 29081
29081:   /bin/ksh
 dfaf5347 waitid    (7, 0, 804714c, 7)
 dfb0d9db _waitPID  (ffffffff, 8047224, 4) + 63
 dfb40617 waitPID   (ffffffff, 8047224, 4) + 1f
 0805b792 job_wait  (719d) + 1ae
 08064be8 sh_exec   (8077270, 14) + af0
 0805e3a1 ???????? ()
 0805decd main      (1, 8047624, 804762c) + 705
  0804fa78 ???????? ()
```

Perhaps the most commonly used proc tool is the `pfiles` command, which displays all of the open files for each process. This is useful for determining operational dependencies between data files and applications:

```
$ /usr/proc/bin/pfiles 29081
29081:  /bin/ksh
  Current rlimit: 64 file descriptors
    0: S_IFCHR mode:0620 dev:102,0 ino:319009 UID:6049 GID:7 rdev:24,8
       O_RDWR|O_LARGEFILE
    1: S_IFCHR mode:0620 dev:102,0 ino:319009 UID:6049 GID:7 rdev:24,8
       O_RDWR|O_LARGEFILE
    2: S_IFCHR mode:0620 dev:102,0 ino:319009 UID:6049 GID:7 rdev:24,8
       O_RDWR|O_LARGEFILE
   63: S_IFREG mode:0600 dev:174,2 ino:990890 UID:6049 GID:1 size:3210
       O_RDWR|O_APPEND|O_LARGEFILE FD_CLOEXEC
```

In addition, it is possible to obtain the current working directory of the target process by using the `pwdx` command:

```
$ /usr/proc/bin/pwdx 29081
29081:  /home/paul
```

If you need to examine the process tree for all parent and child processes containing the target PID, you can use the `ptree` command. This is useful for determining dependencies between processes that are not apparent by consulting the process list:

```
$ /usr/proc/bin/ptree 29081
247   /usr/dt/bin/dtlogin -daemon
  28950 /usr/dt/bin/dtlogin -daemon
    28972 /bin/ksh /usr/dt/bin/Xsession
      29012 /usr/dt/bin/sdt_shell -c        unset DT;      DISPLAY=lion:0;
        29015 ksh -c        unset DT;       DISPLAY=lion:0;
              /usr/dt/bin/dt
          29026 /usr/dt/bin/dtsession
            29032 dtwm
              29079 /usr/dt/bin/dtterm
                29081 /bin/ksh
                  29085 /usr/local/bin/bash
                    29230 /usr/proc/bin/ptree 29081
```

Here, `ptree` has been executed from the Bourne again shell (bash), which was started from the Korn shell (ksh), spawned from the dtterm terminal window, which was spawned from the dtwm window manager, and so on.

 TIP   Although many of these proc tools will seem obscure, they are often very useful when trying to debug process-related application errors, especially in large applications like database management systems.

Using the lsof Command

`lsof` stands for "list open files" and lists information about files that are currently opened by the active processes running on Solaris. It is not included in the Solaris distribution; however, the current version can always be downloaded from

ftp://vic.cc.purdue.edu/pub/tools/unix/lsof. Keep in mind that `lsof` is very sensitive to changes in OS releases, and recompilation may be necessary between Solaris 8 and 9.

What can you use `lsof` for? The answer largely depends on how many problems you encounter that relate to processes and files. Often, administrators are interested in knowing which processes are currently using a target file or files from a particular directory. This can occur when a file is locked by one application but is required by another application (again, a database system's data files are one example where this might happen, if two database instances attempt to write to the files at once). If you know the path to a file of interest, you can use `lsof` to determine which processes are using files in that directory.

To examine the processes that are using files in the */tmp* file system, use this:

```
$ lsof /tmp
COMMAND     PID USER      FD    TYPE DEVICE SIZE/OFF       NODE NAME
ssion       338 pwatters  txt   VREG    0,1   271596 471638794 /tmp (swap)
(unknown)   345 pwatters  txt   VREG    0,1   271596 471638794 /tmp (swap)
le         2295 pwatters  txt   VREG    0,1   271596 471638794 /tmp (swap)
le         2299 pwatters  txt   VREG    0,1   271596 471638794 /tmp (swap)
```

Obviously, there's a bug in the routines that obtain the command name (the first four characters are missing!), but since the PID is correct, this is enough information to identify the four applications that are currently using files in */tmp*. For example, dtsession (PID 338) manages the CDE session for the user pwatters, who is using a temporary text file in the */tmp* directory. Later versions of `lsof` have fixed this bug.

Another common problem that `lsof` is used for, with respect to the */tmp* file system, is the identification of processes that continue to write to unlinked files: thus space is being consumed, but it may appear that no files are growing any larger! This confusing activity can be traced back to a process by using `lsof`. However, rather than using `lsof` on the */tmp* directory directly, you would need to examine the root directory ("/") on which */tmp* is mounted. After finding the process that is writing to an open file, the process can be killed. If the size of a file is changing across several different sampling epochs (for example, by running the command once a minute), you've probably found the culprit:

```
# lsof /
COMMAND     PID  USER  FD   TYPE DEVICE SIZE/OFF    NODE NAME
(unknown)   1    root  txt  VREG  102,0   446144 118299 / (/dev/dsk/c0d0s0)
(unknown)   1    root  txt  VREG  102,0     4372 293504 / (/dev/dsk/c0d0s0)
(unknown)   1    root  txt  VREG  102,0   173272 293503 / (/dev/dsk/c0d0s0)
sadm        62   root  txt  VREG  102,0   954804 101535 / (/dev/dsk/c0d0s0)
sadm        62   root  txt  VREG  102,0   165948 101569 / (/dev/dsk/c0d0s0)
sadm        62   root  txt  VREG  102,0    16132 100766 / (/dev/dsk/c0d0s0)
sadm        62   root  txt  VREG  102,0     8772 100765 / (/dev/dsk/c0d0s0)
sadm        62   root  txt  VREG  102,0   142652 101571 / (/dev/dsk/c0d0s0)
```

One of the restrictions on mounting a file system is that you can't unmount that file system if files are open on it: if files are open on a file system and it is dismounted, any changes made to the files may not be saved, resulting in data loss. Looking at a process list may not always reveal which processes are opening which files, and this can be very frustrating if Solaris refuses to unmount a file system because some files are open. Again, lsof can be used to identify the processes that are opening files on a specific file system.

The first step is to consult the output of the df command to obtain the names of currently mounted file systems:

```
$ df -k
Filesystem        kbytes    used   avail capacity  Mounted on
/proc                  0       0       0     0%     /proc
/dev/dsk/c0d0s0  2510214  929292 1530718    38%     /
fd                     0       0       0     0%     /dev/fd
/dev/dsk/c0d0s3  5347552  183471 5110606     4%     /usr/local
swap              185524   12120  173404     7%     /tmp
```

If you wanted to unmount the */dev/dsk/c0d0s3* file system, but you were prevented from doing so because of open files, you can obtain a list of all open files under */usr/local* by using this command:

```
$ lsof /dev/dsk/c0d0s3
COMMAND PID   USER  FD TYPE DEVICE SIZE/OFF   NODE NAME
httpd   981   root txt VREG  102,3 1747168  457895 /usr/local
httpd   982   root txt VREG  102,3  333692   56455 /usr/local
httpd   983   root txt VREG  102,3  333692   56455 /usr/local
httpd   984   root txt VREG  102,3  333692   56455 /usr/local
javac   985   root txt VREG  102,3  333692   56455 /usr/local
httpd   986   root txt VREG  102,3  333692   56455 /usr/local
httpd   987   root txt VREG  102,3  333692   56455 /usr/local
httpd   988   root txt VREG  102,3  333692   56455 /usr/local
httpd   989   root txt VREG  102,3  333692   56455 /usr/local
httpd   990   root txt VREG  102,3  333692   56455 /usr/local
```

Obviously, all of these processes will need to stop using the open files before the file system can be unmounted. If you're not sure where a particular command is running from, or on which file system its data files are stored, you can also use lsof to check open files by passing the PID on the command line. First, you need to identify a PID by using the ps command:

```
$ ps -eaf | grep apache
  nobody 4911 4905 0  Mar 22 ?    0:00 /usr/local/apache/bin/httpd
  nobody 4910 4905 0  Mar 22 ?    0:00 /usr/local/apache/bin/httpd
  nobody 4912 4905 0  Mar 22 ?    0:00 /usr/local/apache/bin/httpd
  nobody 4905    1 0  Mar 22 ?    0:00 /usr/local/apache/bin/httpd
  nobody 4907 4905 0  Mar 22 ?    0:00 /usr/local/apache/bin/httpd
  nobody 4908 4905 0  Mar 22 ?    0:00 /usr/local/apache/bin/httpd
  nobody 4913 4905 0  Mar 22 ?    0:00 /usr/local/apache/bin/httpd
  nobody 4909 4905 0  Mar 22 ?    0:00 /usr/local/apache/bin/httpd
  nobody 4906 4905 0  Mar 22 ?    0:00 /usr/local/apache/bin/httpd
```

Now examine the process 4905 for Apache to see what files are currently being opened by it:

```
$ lsof -p 4905
COMMAND  PID  USER   FD   TYPE DEVICE  SIZE/OFF    NODE NAME
d       4905 nobody txt   VREG  102,3   333692    56455 /usr/local
(/dev/dsk/c0d0s3)
```

```
d         4905 nobody txt    VREG  102,0    17388 100789 / (/dev/dsk/c0d0s0)
d         4905 nobody txt    VREG  102,0   954804 101535 / (/dev/dsk/c0d0s0)
d         4905 nobody txt    VREG  102,0   693900 101573 / (/dev/dsk/c0d0s0)
d         4905 nobody txt    VREG  102,0    52988 100807 / (/dev/dsk/c0d0s0)
d         4905 nobody txt    VREG  102,0     4396 100752 / (/dev/dsk/c0d0s0)
d         4905 nobody txt    VREG  102,0   175736 100804 / (/dev/dsk/c0d0s0)
```

Apache obviously has a number of open files!

The ps Command

The following table summarizes the main options used with ps.

Option	Description
-a	Lists most frequently requested processes.
-A, -e	Lists all processes.
-c	List processes in scheduler format.
-d	List all processes.
-f	Prints comprehensive process information.
-g	Prints process information on a group basis for a single group.
-G	Prints process information on a group basis for a list of groups.
-j	Includes SID and PGID in printout.
-l	Prints complete process information.
-L	Displays LWP details.
-p	Lists process details for a list of specified processes.
-P	Lists the CPU ID to which a process is bound.
-s	Lists session leaders.
-t	Lists all processes associated with a specific terminal.
-u	Lists all processes for a specific user.

kill

The following table summarizes the main signals used to communicate with processes using kill.

Signal	Code	Action	Description
SIGHUP	1	Exit	Hang up
SIGINT	2	Exit	Interrupt
SIGQUIT	3	Core	Quit
SIGILL	4	Core	Illegal instruction
SIGTRAP	5	Core	Trace
SIGABRT	6	Core	Abort
SIGEMT	7	Core	Emulation trap
SIGFPE	8	Core	Arithmetic exception

Signal	Code	Action	Description
SIGKILL	9	Exit	Killed
SIGBUS	10	Core	Bus error
SIGSEGV	11	Core	Segmentation fault
SIGSYS	12	Core	Bad system call
SIGPIPE	13	Exit	Broken pipe
SIGALRM	14	Exit	Alarm clock
SIGTERM	15	Exit	Terminate

pgrep

The pgrep command is used to search for a list of processes whose names match a pattern specified on the command line. The command returns a list of corresponding PIDs. This list can then be piped to another command, such as kill, to perform some action on the processes or send them a signal.

For example, to kill all processes associated with the name "java," the following command would be used:

```
$ kill -9 `pgrep java`
```

pkill

The pkill command can be used to send signals to processes that have the same name. It is a more specific version of ?, since it can be used only to send signals, and the list of PIDs cannot be piped to another program.

To kill all processes associated with the name "java," the following command would be used:

```
$ pkill -9 java
```

killall

The killall command is used to kill all processes running on a system. It is called by shutdown when the system is being brought to run level 0. However, since a signal can be passed to the killall command, it is possible for a superuser to send a different signal (other than 15) to all processes. For example, to send a SIGHUP signal to all processes, the following command could be used:

```
# killall 1
```

Summary

In this chapter, we have examined how to manage and monitor processes. Since processes and threads are the entities that actually carry out the execution of applications, it's important that administrators understand how to send signals to manage their activity.

Questions

1. Which of the following statements is true?

   A. A shell can spawn another shell or application.

   B. A shell can spawn another shell, but not an application.

   C. A shell cannot spawn another shell, but can spawn an application.

   D. A shell can never spawn another shell or application.

2. What is a process ID?

   A. A string corresponding to the name of the application executed

   B. A randomly generated string that distinguishes one process from another

   C. A class associated with a process's allocated priority

   D. A sequentially allocated integer that distinguishes one process from another

3. A process that can have its effective ownership changed is known as what?

   A. A setGID process

   B. A magic number process

   C. A setUID process

   D. A process that has a magic cookie

4. What is the ultimate parent PID for all processes on a system?

   A. a

   B. 1

   C. 0

   D. init

5. What does the acronym PPID stand for?

   A. Processor PID

   B. Priority PID

   C. Personal PID

   D. Parent PID

6. What does the acronym STIME stand for?

   A. Process starting time

   B. Standard process execution time

   C. Single process execution time

   D. Time zone environment variable

7. What is the acronym for the memory address of sleeping processes?

   A. SLPADDR

   B. ADDR

    C. WCHAN

    D. CHANADDR

8. What command sequence is used to suspend a process?

    A. CTRL-C

    B. ESC-C

    C. CTRL-Z

    D. ESC-Z

9. How can the `kill` command be used to send a SIGHUP to pid 2192?

    A. `kill -1 2192`

    B. `kill -2 2192`

    C. `kill -3 2192`

    D. `kill -9 2192`

10. How can the kill command be used to send a SIGKILL to pid 2192?

    A. `kill -1 2192`

    B. `kill -2 2192`

    C. `kill -3 2192`

    D. `kill -9 2192`

Answers

1. **A.** A shell can spawn any type of application, or another shell.

2. **D.** A sequentially allocated integer that distinguishes one process from another. When the maximum PID is allocated, new PIDs are allocated from 1 again. However, PIDs associated with running processes are never duplicated.

3. **C.** Effective ownership changes are always associated with a setUID process.

4. **B.** All processes start with 1 and increase from there.

5. **D.** A process that spawns a child process is known as a parent.

6. **A.** STIME represents a process starting time.

7. **C.** WCHAN is the acronym.

8. **C.** Hold down the CTRL key and press Z on the keyboard.

9. **A.** A SIGHUP is represented by 1.

10. **D.** A SIGKILL is represented by 9.

Introduction to File Systems

In this chapter, you will
- Learn the structure of Solaris file systems
- Learn to create new file systems
- Learn to monitor disk space usage
- Discover how to repair file systems using fsck

File systems are the main data persistence mechanism employed by Solaris. Typically, file systems are built on hard disk slices (or partitions) to store system and user data. In this chapter, the layout of Solaris file systems is examined, along with instructions for creating and repairing file systems.

File System Structure

Solaris file systems are generally of the type UFS (UNIX File System), although other file system types can be defined in */etc/default/fs*. UFS file systems are found on hard disks that have both a raw and block device interface on Solaris, as found in the */dev/dsk* and */dev/rdsk* directories, respectively. Every partition created on a Solaris file system will have its own entry in */dev/dsk* and */dev/rdsk*. A UFS file system contains the following elements:

- A boot block, which contains booting data if the file system is bootable
- A superblock, which contains the location of inodes, file system size, number of blocks, and status
- Inodes, which store the details of files on the file system
- Data blocks, which actually store the files

In order to create a new UFS file system, a disk needs to be partitioned into different slices. These slices can then be used for creating new file systems by using the mkfs or newfs command. For example, the following two commands are equivalent for the purposes of creating a new file system on the partition c0t0d0s1:

```
# newfs /dev/rdsk/c0t0d0s1
# mkfs -F ufs /dev/rdsk/c0t0d0s1
```

Monitoring Disk Usage

The most commonly used command for monitoring disk space usage is /usr/bin/df, which, by default, displays the number of free blocks and files on all currently mounted volumes. Alternatively, many administrators create an alias for df in their shell initialization script (for example, ~/.cshrc for C shell) like df -k, which displays the amount of free disk space in kilobytes. The basic output for df for a SPARC system looks like this:

```
# df
Filesystem              kbytes     used    avail capacity  Mounted on
/dev/dsk/c0t0d0s0       245911    30754   190566    14%    /
/dev/dsk/c0t0d0s4      1015679   430787   523952    46%    /usr
/proc                        0        0        0     0%    /proc
fd                           0        0        0     0%    /dev/fd
/dev/dsk/c0t0d0s3       492871   226184   217400    51%    /var
/dev/md/dsk/d1         4119256  3599121   478943    89%    /opt
swap                    256000    43480   212520    17%    /tmp
/dev/dsk/c0t2d0s3      4119256  3684920   393144    91%    /disks/vol1
/dev/md/dsk/d0       17398449 12889927  4334538    75%    /disks/vol2
/dev/md/dsk/d3        6162349  5990984   109742    99%    /disks/vol3
/dev/dsk/c1t1d0s0     8574909  5868862  1848557    77%    /disks/vol4
/dev/dsk/c2t3d0s2     1820189  1551628   177552    90%    /disks/vol5
/dev/dsk/c1t2d0s0     4124422  3548988   575434    87%    /disks/vol6
/dev/dsk/c2t2d0s3     8737664  8281113   456551    95%    /disks/vol7
/dev/md/dsk/d2        8181953  6803556  1296578    84%    /disks/vol8
client:/disks/junior_developers
                      4124560  3469376   613944    85%    /disks/junior_developers
```

For an Intel system, the output is similar, although disk slices have a different naming convention:

```
# df
Filesystem              kbytes     used    avail capacity  Mounted on
/proc                        0        0        0     0%    /proc
/dev/dsk/c0d0s0          73684    22104    44212    34%    /
/dev/dsk/c0d0s6         618904   401877   161326    72%    /usr
fd                           0        0        0     0%    /dev/fd
/dev/dsk/c0d0s1          29905     4388    22527    17%    /var
/dev/dsk/c0d0s7        7111598        9  7040474     1%    /export/home
swap                    222516      272   222244     1%    /tmp
/vol/dev/diskette0/unnamed_floppy
                          1423      131     1292    10%    /floppy/unnamed_floppy
```

df has a number of command-line options that can used to customize the collection and display of information. For example,

```
# df -a
Filesystem            kbytes     used    avail capacity  Mounted on
/dev/dsk/c0t0d0s0     245911    30754   190566    14%    /
/dev/dsk/c0t0d0s4    1015679   430787   523952    46%    /usr
/proc                      0        0        0     0%    /proc
fd                         0        0        0     0%    /dev/fd
/dev/dsk/c0t0d0s3     492871   226185   217399    51%    /var
/dev/md/dsk/d1       4119256  3599121   478943    89%    /opt
swap                  256000    43480   212520    17%    /tmp
/dev/dsk/c0t2d0s3    4119256  3684920   393144    91%    /disks/vol1
/dev/md/dsk/d0      17398449 12889927  4334538    75%    /disks/vol2
/dev/md/dsk/d3       6162349  5990984   109742    99%    /disks/vol3
/dev/dsk/c1t1d0s0    8574909  5868862  1848557    77%    /disks/vol4
/dev/dsk/c2t3d0s2    1820189  1551628   177552    90%    /disks/vol5
/dev/dsk/c1t2d0s0    4124422  3548988   575434    87%    /disks/vol6
auto_direct          4124560  3469376   613944    85%    /disks/www
auto_direct                0        0        0     0%    /disks/ftp
server:vold(pid329)
                           0        0        0     0%    /vol
/dev/dsk/c2t2d0s3    8737664  8281113   456551    95%    /disks/vol7
/dev/md/dsk/d2       8181953  6803556  1296578    84%    /disks/vol8
client:/disks/junior_developers
                     4124560  3469376   613944    85%    /disks/junior_developers
```

prints usage data for all file systems, even those that have the "ignore" option set in their entries in */etc/mnttab*:

```
# cat /etc/mnttab
/dev/dsk/c0t0d0s0        /       ufs     rw,suid,dev=800000,largefiles    944543087
/dev/dsk/c0t0d0s4        /usr    ufs     rw,suid,dev=800004,largefiles    944543087
/proc   /proc   proc    rw,suid,dev=29c0000     944543087
fd      /dev/fd fd      rw,suid,dev=2a80000     944543087
/dev/dsk/c0t0d0s3        /var    ufs     rw,suid,dev=800003,largefiles    944543087
/dev/md/dsk/d1  /opt    ufs     suid,rw,largefiles,dev=1540001  944543105
swap    /tmp    tmpfs   ,dev=1 944543105
/dev/dsk/c0t2d0s3       /disks/vol1     ufs     suid,rw,largefiles,dev=800013    944543105
/dev/md/dsk/d0  /disks/vol2     ufs     nosuid,rw,largefiles,quota,dev=1540000 944543105
/dev/md/dsk/d3  /disks/vol3     ufs     nosuid,rw,largefiles,dev=1540003         944543106
/dev/dsk/c1t1d0s0       /disks/vol4 ufs     nosuid,rw,largefiles,dev=800080 944543105
/dev/dsk/c2t3d0s2       /disks/vol5 ufs     nosuid,rw,largefiles,dev=80010a 944543106
/dev/dsk/c1t2d0s0       /disks/vol6 ufs     suid,rw,largefiles,dev=800088    944543106
auto_direct     /disks/www      autofs  ignore,direct,nosuid,dev=2c00001         944543181
auto_direct     /disks/ftp autofs  ignore,direct,nosuid,dev=2c00002         944543181
server:vold(pid329)     /vol    nfs     ignore,noquota,dev=2bc0002      944543192
/dev/dsk/c2t2d0s3       /disks/vol7 ufs     nosuid,rw,largefiles,dev=800103 944548661
/dev/md/dsk/d2  /disks/vol8 ufs     nosuid,rw,largefiles,quota,dev=1540002  944553321
client:/disks/junior_developers /disks/junior_developers            nfs
nosuid,dev=2bc0040      944604066
```

To avoid delays in printing resource information on NFS-mounted volumes, it is also possible to just check local file systems with the following command:

```
# df -l
Filesystem             kbytes      used   avail capacity  Mounted on
/dev/dsk/c0t0d0s0      245911     30754  190566    14%    /
/dev/dsk/c0t0d0s4     1015679    430787  523952    46%    /usr
/proc                       0         0       0     0%    /proc
fd                          0         0       0     0%    /dev/fd
/dev/dsk/c0t0d0s3      492871    226184  217400    51%    /var
/dev/md/dsk/d1        4119256   3599121  478943    89%    /opt
swap                   256000     43488  212512    17%    /tmp
/dev/dsk/c0t2d0s3     4119256   3684920  393144    91%    /disks/vol1
/dev/md/dsk/d0       17398449  12889901 4334564    75%    /disks/vol2
/dev/md/dsk/d3        6162349   5990984  109742    99%    /disks/vol3
/dev/dsk/c1t1d0s0     8574909   5868862 1848557    77%    /disks/vol4
/dev/dsk/c2t3d0s2     1820189   1551628  177552    90%    /disks/vol5
/dev/dsk/c1t2d0s0     4124422   3548988  575434    87%    /disks/vol6
/dev/dsk/c2t2d0s3     8737664   8281113  456551    95%    /disks/vol7
/dev/md/dsk/d2        8181953   6803556 1296578    84%    /disks/vol8
```

A block device can be specified on the command line, and its individual usage measured—for example, a slice on controller 1:

```
# df /dev/dsk/c1d0d2
Filesystem             kbytes      used   avail capacity  Mounted on
/dev/dsk/c1t1d0s0     8574909   5868862 1848557    77%    /disks/vol4
```

Users can also check the status of the disks holding their individual user directories and files by using df. For example,

```
# df /staff/pwatters
Filesystem             kbytes      used   avail capacity  Mounted on
/dev/md/dsk/d0       17398449  12889146 4335319    75%    /disks/vol2
```

will display the disk space usage for the disk on which the home directory exists for user pwatters, while

```
# df /tmp/mbox.pwatters
Filesystem             kbytes      used   avail capacity  Mounted on
swap                   256000     45392  210608    18%    /tmp
```

checks the size of the partition on which the temporary mailbox for the user pwatters was created by the elm mail-reading program.

TIP   The size of the partition on which the temporary mailbox resides is a good thing to check if you intend sending a lot of mail messages!

Another way of obtaining disk space usage information with more directory-by-directory detail is by using the /usr/bin/du command. This command prints the sum of the sizes of every file in the current directory, and performs the same task recursively for any subdirectories. The size is calculated by adding together all of the file sizes in the directory, where the size for each file is rounded up to the nearest 512-byte block. For example, taking a du of the /etc directory looks like this:

```
# cd /etc
# du
14        ./default
7         ./cron.d
6         ./dfs
8         ./dhcp
201       ./fs/hsfs
681       ./fs/nfs
1         ./fs/proc
209       ./fs/ufs
1093      ./fs
26        ./inet
127       ./init.d
339       ./lib
37        ./mail
4         ./net/ticlts
2429      .
```

Thus, /etc and all its subdirectories contain a total of 2429 blocks of data. Of course, this kind of output is fairly verbose, and probably not much use in its current form. The size in kilobytes can be displayed by using df -k.

Fixing Problems with fsck

/usr/sbin/fsck is a file system checking and repair program commonly found on Solaris and other UNIX platforms. It is usually executed by the superuser while the system is in a single-user mode state (for example, after entering run level S), but can also be performed on individual volumes during multiuser run levels. However, there is one golden rule for using fsck: never, ever apply fsck to a mounted file system. To do so could leave the file system in an inconsistent state and cause a kernel panic, at which point it's best to head for the backup tape locker! Any fixes to potential problems on a mounted file system could end up creating more damage than the original problem. In this section, we will examine the output of fsck, as well as look at some examples of common problems, and investigate how fsck repairs corrupt and inconsistent disk data. Of course, you must enable logging for each file system in /etc/vfstab before being confident that data can be recovered accurately using journaling.

Although Solaris 7, 8, and 9, still retain fsck, it is really only necessary for Solaris 2.6 and prior releases. This is because logging is now provided for UNIX file systems. Thus, before any changes are made to a file system, details of the change are recorded in a log prior to their physical application. While this consumes some extra CPU and disk overhead (approximately 1 percent of disk space on each volume with logging enabled is required), it does ensure that the file system is never left in an inconsistent state.

TIP Boot time is reduced, because fsck does not need to be executed.

Why do inconsistencies occur in the first place? In theory, they shouldn't, but there are three common reasons:

- Switching off a Solaris server like an old MS-DOS machine, without powering down first

- Halting a system without synchronizing disk data (it is advisable to explicitly use `sync` before shutting down using `halt`)

- Defective hardware, including damage to disk blocks and heads, which can be caused by moving the system, and/or power surges.

These problems realize themselves in corruption to the internal set of tables that every UNIX file system keeps to manage free disk blocks and inodes, leading to blocks that are actually free and reported as already allocated, and conversely, some blocks occupied by a program, but that might be recorded as being free. This is obviously problematic for mission-critical data, which is a good advertisement for RAID storage (or at least, reliable backups).

 CAUTION Disk corruption is obviously problematic for mission-critical data, which is a good advertisement for RAID storage (or at least, reliable backups).

The Phases of fsck

The first step to running fsck is to enable file system checking to occur during boot. To do this, it is necessary to specify an integer value in the fsck field in the virtual file system configuration file/*etc/vfstab*. Entering a 1 in this field ensures sequential fsck checking, while entering 2 does not ensure sequential checking, as in the following example:

```
#device device mount FS fsck mount mount
#to mount to fsck point type pass at boot options
#
/dev/dsk/c1t2d1s3 /dev/rdsk/c1t2d1s3 /usr ufs 2 yes -/
-
```

After being enabled for a particular file system, fsck can be executed. fsck checks the integrity of several different features of the file system. Most significant is the superblock, which stores summary information for the volume. Since the superblock is the most modified item on the file system being written and rewritten when data is changed on a disk, it is the most commonly corrupted feature. Checks on the superblock include:

- A check of the file system size, which obviously must be greater than the size computed from the number of blocks identified in the superblock

- The total number of inodes, which must be less than the maximum number of inodes
- A tally of reported free blocks and inodes

If any of these values are identified as corrupt by fsck, the superuser can select one of the many superblock backups that were created during initial file system creation as a replacement for the current superblock. We will examine superblock corruption and how to fix it in the next section. In addition to superblock, the number and status of cylinder group blocks, inodes, indirect blocks, and data blocks are also checked. Since free blocks are located by maps stored in the cylinder group, fsck verifies that all the blocks marked as free are not actually being used by any files—if they are, files could be corrupted. If all blocks are correctly accounted for, fsck determines whether the number of free blocks plus the number of used blocks equals the total number of blocks in the file system. If fsck detects any incongruity, the maps of unallocated blocks are rebuilt, although there is obviously a risk of data loss whenever there is a disagreement over the actual state of the file system. fsck always uses the actual count of inodes and/or blocks if the superblock information is wrong, and replaces the incorrect value if this is verified by the superuser. We will revisit this issue in the next section.

When inodes are examined by fsck, the process is sequential in nature and aims to identify inconsistencies in format and type, link count, duplicate blocks, bad block numbers, and inode size. Inodes should always be in one of three states: allocated (being used by a file), unallocated (not being used by a file), and partially allocated, meaning that during an allocation or unallocation procedure, data has been left behind that should have been deleted or completed. Alternatively, partial allocation could result from a physical hardware failure. In both of these cases, fsck will attempt to clear the inode.

The link count is the number of directory entries that are linked to a particular inode. fsck always checks that the number of directory entries listed is correct, by examining the entire directory structure beginning with the root directory, and tallying the number of links for every inode. Clearly, the stored link count and the actual link count should agree, but the stored link count can occasionally be different than the actual link count. This could result from a disk not being synchronized before a shutdown, for example, and while changes to the file system have been saved, the link count has not been correctly updated. If the stored count is not zero, but the actual count is zero, then disconnected files are placed in the *lost+found* directory found in the top level of the file system concerned. In other cases, the actual count replaces the stored count.

An indirect block is a pointer to a list of every block claimed by an inode. fsck checks every block number against a list of allocated blocks: if two inodes claim the same block number, that block number is added to a list of duplicate block numbers. The administrator may be asked to choose which inode is correct—obviously a difficult decision, and usually time to verify files against backups. fsck additionally checks the integrity of the actual block numbers, which can also become corrupt—it should always lie in the interval between the first data block and the last data block. If a bad block number is detected, the inode is cleared.

Directories are also checked for integrity by fsck. Directory entries are equivalent to other files on the file system, except they have a different mode entry in the inode. fsck checks the validity of directory data blocks, checking for the following problems: unallocated nodes associated with inode numbers, inode numbers exceeding the maximum number of inodes for a particular file system, incorrect inode numbers for the standard directory entries "." and "..", and directories actually being accidentally disconnected from the file system. We will examine some of these errors and how they are rectified in the next section.

fsck examines each disk volume in five distinct stages, performing all of the checks discussed earlier: phase 1, in which blocks and sizes are checked; phase 2, where pathnames are verified; phase 3, where connectivity is examined; phase 4, where an investigation of reference counts is undertaken; and phase 5, where the actual cylinder groups are checked.

EXAM TIP   You should be able to identify the different phases of fsck and their purposes.

fsck Examples

In this section, we will examine a full run of fsck, outlining the most common problems and how they are rectified, as well as presenting some examples of less commonly encountered problems. On a SPARC 20 system, fsck for the / file system looks like this:

```
** /dev/rdsk/c0d0s0
** Currently Mounted on /
** Phase 1 - Check Blocks and Sizes
** Phase 2 - Check Pathnames
** Phase 3 - Check Connectivity
** Phase 4 - Check Reference Counts
** Phase 5 - Check Cyl groups
FREE BLK COUNT(S) WRONG IN SUPERBLK
SALVAGE?
```

Clearly, the actual block count and the block count recorded in the superblock are at odds with each other. At this point, fsck requires superuser permission to install the actual block count in the superblock, which the administrator indicates by pressing Y. The scan continues with the /usr partition:

```
1731 files, 22100 used, 51584 free (24 frags, 6445 blocks,  0.0% fragmentation)
** /dev/rdsk/c0d0s6
** Currently Mounted on /usr
** Phase 1 - Check Blocks and Sizes
** Phase 2 - Check Pathnames
** Phase 3 - Check Connectivity
** Phase 4 - Check Reference Counts
** Phase 5 - Check Cyl groups

FILE SYSTEM STATE IN SUPERBLOCK IS WRONG; FIX?
```

In this case, the file system state in the superblock records is incorrect, and again the administrator is required to give consent for it to be repaired. The scan then continues with the */var* and */export/home* partitions:

```
26266 files, 401877 used, 217027 free (283 frags, 27093 blocks,  0.0% fragmentation)
** /dev/rdsk/c0d0s1
** Currently Mounted on /var
** Phase 1 - Check Blocks and Sizes
** Phase 2 - Check Pathnames
** Phase 3 - Check Connectivity
** Phase 4 - Check Reference Counts
** Phase 5 - Check Cyl groups
1581 files, 4360 used, 25545 free (41 frags, 3188 blocks,  0.1% fragmentation)
** /dev/rdsk/c0d0s7
** Currently Mounted on /export/home
** Phase 1 - Check Blocks and Sizes
** Phase 2 - Check Pathnames
** Phase 3 - Check Connectivity
** Phase 4 - Check Reference Counts
** Phase 5 - Check Cyl groups
2 files, 9 used, 7111589 free (13 frags, 888947 blocks,  0.0% fragmentation)
```

Obviously, the */var* partition and */export/home* have passed examination by fsck, and are intact. However, the fact that the / and */usr* file systems were in an inconsistent state suggests that the file systems were not cleanly unmounted, perhaps during the last re-boot. Fortunately, the superblock itself was intact. However, this is not always the case. In this example, the superblock of */dev/dsk/c0t0d0s2* has a bad magic number, indicating that it is damaged beyond repair:

```
# fsck /dev/dsk/c0t0d0s2
 BAD SUPER BLOCK: MAGIC NUMBER WRONG
 USE ALTERNATE SUPER-BLOCK TO SUPPLY NEEDED INFORMATION
eg. fsck [-F ufs] -o b=# [special ...]
where # is the alternate super block. SEE fsck_ufs(1M).
```

In this case, you need to specify one of the alternative superblocks that were created by the `newfs` command. When a file system is created, there is a message printed about the creation of superblock backups:

```
super-block backups (for fsck -b #) at:
32, 5264, 10496, 15728, 20960, 26192, 31424, 36656, 41888,
47120, 52352, 57584, 62816, 68048, 73280, 78512, 82976, 88208,
93440, 98672, 103904, 109136, 114368, 119600, 124832, 130064,
135296, 140528, 145760, 150992, 156224, 161456.
```

In the previous example, you may need to specify one of these alternative superblocks, so that the disk contents are once again readable. If you didn't record the superblock backups during the creation of the file system, you can easily retrieve them by using `newfs` (and using -N to prevent the creation of a new file system):

```
# newfs -Nv /dev/dsk/c0t0d0s2
```

Once you have determined an appropriate superblock replacement number (for example, 32), use fsck again to replace the older superblock with the new one:

```
# fsck -o b=32 /dev/dsk/c0t0d0s2
```

Disks that have physical hardware errors often report being unable to read inodes beyond a particular point. For example, the error message

```
Error reading block 31821 (Attempt to read from filesystem
resulted in short read) while doing inode scan. Ignore error
<y> ?
```

stops the user from continuing with the fsck scan, and correcting the problem. This is probably a good time to replace a disk, rather than attempting any corrective action. Never be tempted to ignore these errors, and hope for the best—especially in commercial organizations, you will ultimately have to take responsibility for lost and damaged data.

 TIP Users will be particularly unforgiving if you had advance warning of a problem.

Here is an example of what can happen when there is a link count problem:

```
# fsck /
 ** /dev/rdsk/c0t1d0s0
 ** Currently Mounted on /
 ** Phase 1 - Check Blocks and Sizes
 ** Phase 2 - Check Pathnames
 ** Phase 3 - Check Connectivity
 ** Phase 4 - Check Reference Counts
LINK COUNT DIR I=4  OWNER=root MODE=40700
SIZE=4096 MTIME=Nov  1 11:56 1999  COUNT 2 SHOULD BE 4
ADJUST? y
```

If the adjustment does not fix the error, use the find command to track down the problem file, and delete it this way:

```
# find / -mount -inum 4 -ls
```

It should be in the *lost+found* directory for the partition in question (in this case, */lost+found*).

As previously outlined, duplicate inodes can also be a problem:

```
** Phase 1 - Check Blocks and Sizes
 314415 DUP I=5009
 345504 DUP I=12011
 345505 DUP I=12011
 854711 DUP I=91040
 856134 DUP I=93474
 856135 DUP I=93474
```

This problem is often found in Solaris 2.5 and 2.6, although not usually seen in Solaris 7, 8 or 9, and so an upgrade may correct the problem.

Summary

In this chapter, we examined methods for file system management and usage monitoring. In addition, we examined how to set up and configure UFS file systems which are standard for all Solaris releases.

Questions

1. Which file specifies the default file system type?

   A. */etc/defaultfs*

   B. */etc/defaultfstype*

   C. */etc/default/fs*

   D. */etc/default/fstype*

2. What does a superblock contain?

   A. The location of inodes, file system size, number of blocks, and status

   B. The location of files in a map

   C. A list of supported file system types

   D. The location of backup blocks, file system size, number of blocks, and status

3. What is the df command used for?

   A. Monitoring disk space usage

   B. Adding a disk to the system

   C. Creating default file systems

   D. Recovering deleted files

4. What does the du command do?

   A. Checks for duplicate inodes

   B. Checks for duplicate files in the same directory

   C. Prints number of blocks used in each directory

   D. Script for retrieving DNS data using dig (that is, "dig up" DNS data)

5. What operation should never be performed using fsck?

   A. Attempting to work on an unmounted file system

   B. Attempting to work on a mounted file system

   C. Checking UFS file systems

   D. Running fsck as root

6. Which of the following does not cause file system inconsistencies?

A. Switching off a Solaris server without powering down first

B. Halting a system without synchronizing disk data

C. Defective hardware, including damage to disk blocks and heads

D. Copying files between file systems

7. What does phase 1 of fsck involve?

A. Checks blocks and sizes

B. Pathname verification

C. Connectivity check

D. Reference count check

8. What does phase 2 of fsck involve?

A. Checks blocks and sizes

B. Pathname verification

C. Connectivity check

D. Reference count check

9. What does phase 3 of fsck involve?

A. Checks blocks and sizes

B. Pathname verification

C. Connectivity check

D. Reference count check

10. What does phase 4 of fsck involve?

A. Checks blocks and sizes

B. Pathname verification

C. Checking cylinder groups

D. Reference count check

11. What does phase 5 of fsck involve?

A. Checks blocks and sizes

B. Pathname verification

C. Checking cylinder groups

D. Reference count check

Answers

1. **C.** The file system default is stored in */etc/default/fs*.

2. **A.** The superblock stores the location of inodes, file system size, number of blocks, and status.

3. **A.** The df command monitors "disk free" space.

4. **C.** The du command displays a list of blocks used in directories.

5. **B.** Because fsck repairs file systems, it should never be used on a mounted file system.

6. **D.** Copying files does not normally cause corruption.

7. **A.** Phase 1 checks blocks and sizes.

8. **B.** Phase 2 verifies pathnames.

9. **C.** Phase 3 checks connectivity.

10. **D.** Phase 4 performs a reference count check.

11. **C.** Phase 5 checks cylinder groups.

Files, Directories and Scripts

In this chapter, you will

- Learn how to manage files and directories
- Learn how to work with the shell
- Understand how to write shell scripts
- Review commonly used shell commands

Although graphical user environments (GUIs) are an increasingly popular metaphor for interacting with computer systems, character user interfaces (CUIs) are a core feature of Solaris 9 because they provide a programmatic environment in which commands can be executed. Many operations on Solaris systems are performed in the context of a script, whether starting services at boot time or processing text to produce a report. Indeed, one of the key advantages of UNIX and UNIX-like environments over non-UNIX systems is the capability to combine large numbers of small commands in a CUI, in conjunction with pipes and filters, to create complex command sets that perform repetitive tasks.

Another key feature of Solaris 9 shells is the ability to write complex scripts that perform repetitive actions and can process various kinds of decision logic. There are many more commands available for the Bourne again shell than for MS-DOS batch files, which makes them quite powerful. However, Microsoft Windows Script is evolving to provide some of the advanced functionality featured by Solaris shell scripts. Script files are more dependent on understanding file permissions than just using the shell to enter commands, which makes them more complex. In this chapter, we review how to create executable scripts that can be used with the Bourne again shell. Finally, we focus on the advanced text processing features of the Solaris shell, and how these can be used when developing scripts.

The Shell

All shells have a command prompt—the prompt usually tells the user which shell is currently being used, the user who owns the shell, and/or the current working directory. For example, the following prompt

```
#
```

usually indicates that the current user has superuser privileges. Shell prompts are completely customizable—the default for bash is just the name of the shell:

```
bash-2.04$
```

When you start a new terminal window from within the CDE, a shell is automatically spawned for you. This will be the same shell that is specified in your */etc/passwd* entry:

```
apache:x:1003:10:apache user:/usr/local/apache:/usr/local/bin/bash
```

In this case, the apache user has the bash shell set as default. To be a valid login shell, */usr/local/bin/bash* must also be included in the shells database (stored in the file */etc/shells*).

If the default shell prompt is not to your liking, you can easily change its format by setting two environment variables—*PS1* and *PS2*. Environment variables are covered in the "Setting Environment Variables" section later in this chapter, but the Solaris environment is equivalent to that found in Linux and Windows NT. For example, to set the prompt to display the username and host, you would use the following command:

```
PS1='\u@\H> '; export PS1
```

The prompt displayed by the shell would then look like this:

```
oracle@db>
```

Many users like to display their current username, hostname, and working directory, which can be set using the following command:

```
PS1='\u@\H:\w> '; export PS1
```

When executed, this shell prompt is changed to the following

```
oracle@db:/usr/local>
```

where oracle is the current user, db is the hostname, and */usr/local* is the current working directory. A list of different customization options for shell prompts is given in Table 10-1.

At the shell prompt, you enter commands in the order in which you intend for them to be executed. For example, to execute the admintool from the command prompt, you would type this command:

```
oracle@db:/usr/sbin> ./admintool
```

Setting	Description	Output
\a	ASCII beep character	"beep"
\d	Date string	Wed Sep 6
\h	Short hostname	www
\H	Full hostname	www.paulwatters.com
\s	Shell name	bash
\t	Current time (12-hour format)	10:53:44
\T	Current time (24-hour format)	10:53:55
\@	Current time (A.M./P.M. format)	10:54 A.M.
\u	Username	root
\v	Shell version	2.03
\W	Shell version with revision	2.03.0
\!	Command history number	223
\$	Privilege indicator	#
\u\$	Username and privilege indicator	root#
\u:\!:\$	Username, command history number, and privilege indicator	root:173:#

Table 10-1   Environment Variable Setting for Different Command Prompts Under Bash

The ./ in this example indicates that the admintool application resides in the current directory—you could also execute the application with the following command, using its complete path:

```
oracle@db:/usr/sbin> /usr/sbin/admintool
```

The admintool window would then appear on the desktop, assuming that you're using a terminal window to execute a shell. Once the shell is executing a command in the foreground, like admintool, no other commands can be executed. However, by sending a command process into the background, you can execute more than one command in the shell. You can send a process into the background immediately by adding an ampersand (&) to the end of the command line:

```
oracle@db:/usr/sbin> ./admintool &
```

Or, once a command has been executed, you can suspend it by pressing CTRL-Z, and then send it into the background by using the command bg:

```
oracle@db:/usr/sbin> ./admintool
^Z[1] + Stopped (SIGTSTP)          admintool
oracle@db:/usr/sbin> bg
[1] admintool&
oracle@db:/usr/sbin>
```

The application name is displayed along with the job number. You can bring an application back into the foreground by using the following command:

```
oracle@db:/usr/sbin> fg
admintool
```

This will bring job number 1 back into the foreground by default. However, if you had multiple jobs suspended, you would need to specify a job number with the `fg` command:

```
oracle@db:/usr/local/bin> ./netscape
^Z[2] + Stopped (SIGTSTP)           netscape
oracle@db:/usr/sbin> bg
[2] netscape&
oracle@db:/usr/sbin> fg
netscape
```

 TIP   You can obtain a list of all running jobs in the current shell by typing the following command:

```
$ jobs
[2] +   Running                 ./netscape&
[1] -   Running                 admintool&
```

File Permissions

One of the most confusing issues for novice users of Solaris is understanding the Solaris file access permissions system. The basic approach to setting and interpreting relative file permissions is using a set of symbolic codes to represent users and permission types. However, even advanced users may find it difficult to understand the octal permissions codes that are used to set absolute permissions.

 TIP   When combined with a default permission mask set in the user's shell (the *umask*), octal permission codes are more powerful than symbolic permission codes.

Symbolic File Permissions

The Solaris file system permits three basic kinds of file access—the ability to read (r), to write (w), and to execute (x) a file or directory. These permissions can be granted exclusively or nonexclusively on individual files, or on a group of files specified by a wildcard (*). These permissions can be set by using the `chmod` command, in combination with a + operator. Permissions can be easily removed with the `chmod` command by using the - operator.

For example, to set read permissions (for the current user) on the file */usr/local/lib/ libproxy.a*, you would use this command:

```
$ chmod +r /usr/local/lib/libproxy.a
```

Or, to set read permissions for all users on the file */usr/local/lib/libproxy.a*, you would use this command:

```
$ chmod a+r /usr/local/lib/libproxy.a
```

To remove read permissions on the file */usr/local/lib/libproxy.a* for all users who are not members of the current user's default group, you would use this command:

```
$ chmod o-r /usr/local/lib/libproxy.a
```

This does not remove the group and user read permissions that were set previously. Similarly, you can set execute and write permissions. For example, to set execute permissions on the */usr/local/bin/gcc* files for each class of user (current user, group, and world), you would use the commands:

```
$ chmod u+x /usr/local/bin/gcc
$ chmod g+x /usr/local/bin/gcc
$ chmod o+x /usr/local/bin/gcc
```

To explicitly remove write permissions on the */usr/local/bin/gcc* files for each class of user (current user, group, and world), you would use the commands

```
$ chmod u-w /usr/local/bin/gcc
$ chmod g-w /usr/local/bin/gcc
$ chmod o-w /usr/local/bin/gcc
```

It makes sense to combine these settings into a single command:

```
$ chmod oug-w /usr/local/bin/gcc
```

The rationale behind using read and write permissions should be clear: permitting read access on a file allows an identified user to access the text of a file by reading it byte by byte; write access permits the user to modify or delete any file on which the write permission is granted, regardless of who originally created the file. Thus, individual users can create files that are readable and writable by any other user on the system.

The permission to execute a file must be granted on scripts (such as shell scripts or Perl scripts) in order for them to be executed. Compiled and linked applications must also have the execute bit set on a specific application.

 TIP The executable permission must also be granted on the special files that represent directories on the file system, if the directory's contents are to be accessed by a specific class of user.

The different options available for granting file access permissions can sometimes lead to interesting but confusing scenarios: For example, permissions can be set to allow a group to delete a file but not to execute it. More usefully, a group might be given execute

permission on an application but be unable to write over it. In addition, setting file permissions using relative permission strings (rather than absolute octal permission codes) means that permissions set by a previous change of permission command (chmod) are not revoked by any subsequent chmod commands.

However, the permissions themselves are only half the story. Unlike single-user file systems, permissions on Solaris are associated with different file owners (all files and processes on a Solaris system are "owned" by a specific user). In addition, groups of users can be granted read, write, and execute permissions on a file or set of files stored in a directory. Or, file permissions can be granted on a system-wide basis, effectively granting file access without respect to file ownership. Because file systems can be exported using NFS and/or Samba, it's bad practice to grant system-wide read, write, and execute permissions on any file unless every user needs access to that file. For example, all users need to read the password database (*/etc/passwd*), but only the root user should have read access to the shadow password database (*/etc/shadow*).

CAUTION Blindly exporting all files with world read, write, or execute permissions on an NFS-shared volume is inviting trouble.

The three file system categories of ownership are defined by three permission setting categories: the user (*u*), who owns the file; group members (*g*), who have access to the file; and all other users (*o*) on the system. The group specified by *g* can be the user's primary group (as defined in */etc/passwd*), or a secondary group to which the file has been assigned (defined in */etc/group*). Remember that there are ultimately few secrets on a Solaris file system: The root user has full access at all times (read, write, and execute) on all files on the file system, even if a user removes all permissions on a file, the rule of root is absolute. If the contents of a file really need to be hidden, encrypting a file's contents using PGP, crypt, or a similar product is best. A root user can also change the ownership of a file—thus, a user's files do not absolutely belong to a specific user. The chown command can be used only by the superuser for this purpose.

Policies regarding default file permissions need to be set selectively in different environments. For example, in a production web server system that processes credit card data, access should be denied by default to all users except those required to conduct online transactions (for example, the "apache" user for the Apache web server). On a system that supports team-based development, permissions will obviously need to be set that allow the exchange of data between team partners, but that prevent the access to development files by others.

TIP Very few Solaris systems would allow a default world-writable policy on any file system, except for the temporary swap (*/tmp*) file system.

Enforcing system-wide permissions is possible by using a default umask, which sets the read, write, and execute permissions on all new files created by a specific user. If a user wishes to use a umask other than the default system-wide setting, he or she can achieve this by setting it on the command line when required, or in the user's shell startup file (for example, .kshrc for Korn shell).

We start our examination of Solaris file permissions by examining how to create files, set permissions, and change ownerships and group memberships, and how to use the ls command to examine existing file permissions. All of these commands can be used by nonprivileged users, except for the chown command.

The ls command is the main directory and file permission listing program used in Solaris. When displaying a long listing, it prints file access permissions, user and group ownerships, file size and creation date, and the filename. For example, for the password file */etc/passwd*, the output from ls would look like this:

```
$ ls -l /etc/passwd
-r--r--r--   1 root     other         256 Sep  18 00:40 passwd
```

This directory entry can be read from left to right in the following way:

- The password file is not a directory, indicated by the first "-". This could also indicate a character or block special device
- The password file has read-only permissions for the owner *r--* (but not execute or write permissions).
- The password file has read-only permissions for group members *r--*.
- The password file has read-only permissions for other staff *r--*.
- The password file is owned by the root user.
- The password file has group other permissions.
- The password file size is 256 kilobytes.
- The password file was created on September 18th, at 00:40 A.M.
- The name of the password file is *passwd*.

The permissions string shown changes depending on the permissions that have been set by the owner. For example, if the password file had execute and write permissions for the root user, the permissions string would read *-rwxr--r--*, rather than just *-r--r--r--*. Each of the permissions can be set using symbolic or octal permissions codes, by using the chmod command.

Except the GID setting on a directory, which must be set using chmod g+s dirname, everything else can be set using octal codes.

You've seen how a normal file looks under ls, but let's compare this with a directory entry, which is a special kind of file that is usually created by the mkdir command:

```
# mkdir samples
```

You can check the permissions of the directory entry by using the ls command:

```
# ls -l
total 8
drwxrwxr-x   2 root      other          512 Sep  5 13:41 samples
```

The directory entry for the directory *samples* can be read from left to right in the following way:

- The directory entry is a special file denoted by a leading *d*.
- The directory entry has read, write, and execute permissions for the owner *rwx*.
- The directory entry has read, write, and execute permissions for group members *rwx*.
- The directory entry has read and execute permissions for other staff *r-x*.
- The directory entry is owned by the root user.
- The directory entry has other group permissions.
- The directory entry size is 512 kilobytes.
- The directory entry was created on September 5th of the current year, at 1:41 P.M.
- The name of the directory is *samples*.

For a directory to be accessible to a particular class of user, the executable bit must be set using the chmod command.

EXAM TIP   You must be able to identify every element of a file permissions string.

Octal File Permissions

Some expert users prefer not to separate user and permission information by using the user symbols (*o*, *u*, *g*) and the permission symbols (*r*, *w*, *x*). Instead, a numeric code can be used to combine both user and permission information. If you use a lot of common permissions settings, it may be easier for you to remember a single octal code than to work out the permissions string symbolically. The octal code consists of three numbers, which represent owner permissions, group permissions, and other user permissions, respectively (from left to right). The higher the number, the greater the permissions for each user. For example, to set a file to have read, write, and execute permissions for the file owner, you can use the octal code 700 with the chmod command:

```
$ chmod 700 *
```

You can now check to see if the correct permissions have been granted:

```
$ ls -l
total 4
drwx------    2 root     users            4096 Jun  8 20:10 test
-rwx------    1 root     users               0 Jun  8 20:10 test.txt
```

You can also grant read, write, and execute permissions to members of the group users by changing the middle number from 0 to 7:

```
$ chmod 770 *
```

Again, the changes are reflected in the symbolic permissions string displayed by `ls`:

```
$ ls -l
total 4
drwxrwx---    2 root     users            4096 Jun  8 20:10 test
-rwxrwx---    1 root     users               0 Jun  8 20:10 test.txt
```

If you want to grant read, write, and execute permissions to all users, simply change the third permissions number from 0 to 7:

```
$ chmod 777 *
```

Now, all users on the system have read, write, and execute permissions on all files in the directory:

```
$ ls -l
total 4
drwxrwxrwx    2 root     users            4096 Jun  8 20:10 test
-rwxrwxrwx    1 root     users               0 Jun  8 20:10 test.txt
```

Of course, the codes that can be used to specify permissions are usually not just 0 or 7. For example, the code 5 gives read and execute access, but not write access. So, if you wanted to grant read and execute access to members of the group, but deny write access, you could use the code 750:

```
$ chmod 750 *
```

This produces the following result:

```
$ ls -l
total 4
drwxr-x---    2 root     users            4096 Jun  8 20:10 test
-rwxr-x---    1 root     users               0 Jun  8 20:10 test.txt
```

If you wanted to remove all access permissions from the files in the current directory, you could use the code 000 (you should not normally need to do this):

```
$ chmod 000 *
```

Let's examine the result of the command:

```
$ ls -l
total 4
d---------   2 root      users       4096 Jun  8 20:10 test
----------   1 root      users          0 Jun  8 20:10 test.txt
```

All access permissions have been removed, except for the directory indicator on the special file *test*. Note the main difference between setting files using symbolic codes rather than octal codes: Symbolic codes are relative, numeric codes are absolute. This means that unless you explicitly revoke a file permission when setting another using symbolic codes, it will persist. Thus, if a file already has group write access, and you grant group execute access (or remove group execute access), the write access permission is not removed. However, if you specify only group execute access using an octal code, the group write access will automatically be removed if it has been previously set.

TIP You may well find that in startup scripts and situations where the permissions are unknown in advance, using octal codes is safer.

EXAM TIP You must be able to interpret every element of an octal permissions code.

Setting Default Permissions (umask)

You can enforce system-wide permissions by using a default "user mask" (umask), which sets the read, write, and execute permissions on all new files created by a specific user. If a user wants to use a umask other than the default system-wide setting, he or she can achieve this by setting it on the command line when required, or in the user's shell startup file (for example, *.kshrc* for Korn shell), or in the global system default file */etc/default/login*. In addition, the mask that is set for the current user can be displayed by using the umask command by itself.

Like file permissions, the umask is set using octal codes (symbolic codes cannot be used). There are two different strategies for computing umasks. For directories, you must subtract the octal value of the default permission you want to set from octal 777. For files, you must subtract the octal value of the default permission you want to set from octal 666. For example, to set the default permission to 444 (all read-only), you would subtract 444 from 666 for files, to derive the umask of 222. For the default per mission 600 (user read/write, no other access), you would subtract 600 from 666, leaving a umask of 066 (which will often be displayed as 66).

If you want all users to have full access permissions on all files that you create, you would set the umask to 000 (666-000=666):

```
$ umask 000
```

Let's examine the results, after creating a file called *data.txt* and after setting the umask to 000:

```
$ touch data.txt
 $ ls -l
total 4
-rw-rw-rw-   1 root       users          0 Jun  8 20:20 data.txt
```

Everyone now has full access permissions. However, you are more likely to set a umask like 022, which would give new files the permissions 755 (777 – 022=755). This would give the file owner read, write, and execute access, but only read permissions for group members and other users:

```
$ umask 022
```

If you now create a new file called *newdata.txt* with the new umask, you should see that the default permissions have changed:

```
$ touch newtest.txt
 $ ls -l
total 4
-rw-r--r--   1 root       root           0 Jun  8 20:21 newdata.txt
-rw-rw-rw-   1 root       users          0 Jun  8 20:20 data.txt
```

If you're more conservative, and you don't want to grant any access permissions to other users (including group members), you can set the umask to 077, which still gives the file owner full access permissions:

```
bash-2.03$ umask 077
```

Let's see what happens when you create a new file called *lastminute.txt*:

```
bash-2.03$ touch lastminute.txt
bash-2.03$ ls -l
total 4
-rw-r--r--   1 root       root           0 Jun  8 20:21 newdata.txt
-rw-------   1 root       root           0 Jun  8 20:22 lastminute.txt
-rw-rw-rw-   1 root       users          0 Jun  8 20:20 data.txt
```

The new file has full access permissions for the owner, but no access permissions for other users. Resetting the umask does not affect the permissions of other files that have already been created.

It is interesting that you can also get umask to print the symbolic codes using `umask -S`—this is the actual binary, not the shell built-in, though.

setuid and setgid Permissions

The file permissions we've covered so far are used by users in their day-to-day file management strategies. However, administrators can make use of a different set of file permissions, which allow files to be executed as a particular user (setuid), and/or as a member of a particular group (setgid). These facilities are very powerful, because they allow unprivileged users to gain access to limited superuser privileges in many cases, without requiring superuser authentication. For example, the volume daemon (vold) allows unprivileged users logged into the console to mount and unmount CD-ROMs and floppy disks, an operation which required superuser privileges in previous Solaris releases. Here, the effective user ID is set to 0, meaning that unprivileged users can effectively run processes as root.

The downside to this is obvious: setgid and setuid permissions open up a Pandora's box in terms of security, because normal authentication procedures are bypassed. For example, imagine a device management tool that needed to run as setuid 0 in order to read and write device files. If the tool had a standard feature of many UNIX programs (the ability to spawn a shell), the shell spawned would have full root privileges, rather than the privileges of the original user. For this reason, some administrators refuse to allow setgid and setuid permissions to be set.

TIP   The find command can be used to scan all file systems and automatically remove any files with setuid or setgid privileges.

You can determine whether a file is setuid by root by (a) checking for files that are owned by root and (b) checking whether these files have the *s* flag assigned to the user's permissions. For example, if a file management tool called filetool was setuid root, the following directory listing would clearly indicate this property:

```
-r-sr-sr-x 3 root sys 1220334 Jul 18 11:01 /usr/local/bin/filetool
```

The first *s* in the permissions table refers to setuid root. In addition, this file is also setgid for the sys group, which is indicated by the second *s* in the permissions table.

The setuid bit can be set by using a command like this

```
# chmod u+s file.txt
```

where *file.txt* is the file that requires setuid to be set. The setgid bit can be set by using a command like this

```
# chmod g+s file.txt
```

where *file.txt* is the file that requires setgid to be set.

Sticky Bit Permissions

A network administrator once explained to me that sticky bits were those bits that slowed down network transmission rates, because they were highly attracted to magnetic qualities of the Ethernet. This is not true! A sticky bit is a special permission that prevents files in common file areas from being deleted by other users. For example, a download area consisting of a large 10GB partition may be set aside for user downloads, which are not counted against individual user quotas. This means that users could download up to 10GB of data without infringing on their allocated directory space. However, although a shared public file area sounds like a great idea, it would be unwise to allow users to overwrite one another's files. In this case, the sticky bit can be set on the top-level directory of the public file area, allowing only users who created individual files to delete them.

You can set the sticky bit by using a command like this:

```
# chmod +t somedir
```

where *somedir* is the directory that requires the sticky bit to be set. You could also use the 1755 for octal.

Access Control Lists

One problem with assigning file access permissions is that users other than one's self fall into two categories: group members or nongroup members. Thus, if you want to make some files available to one group of users and not another, you will need to ask the system administrator to create a group for you. Of course, the main problem with the random group creation approach is group sprawl—administrators are generally unwilling to create groups at the request of users because of the overhead in administering potentially hundreds of different groups on each system, and the number of groups that one user can be in is limited.

The best solution to the problem is to leave group members to reflect organizational divisions, and to use access control lists (ACLs) to manage file access. While it may seem like creating more work to have two sets of file access permissions operating, in reality it's the simplest solution for users that doesn't require superuser permission.

To grant the user charles read-only access to the file *secret.doc*, which is owned by the user ainsley and has read-write permissions only for ainsley, the following command would be executed by ainsley:

```
$ setfacl -m user:charles:r-- secret.doc
```

Alternatively, to allow charles to have read-write access to the file, the following command can be used:

```
$ setfacl -m user:charles:rw- secret.doc
```

When an ACL has been set, the file listing shows a + symbol at the end of the permissions string:

```
# ls -l /home/charles/secret.doc
-rw-------+   1 charles    admin            105433  Jan 24 12:07
    /home/charles/secret.doc
```

 TIP The `getfacl` command can be used to display the ACLs for any file on the file system, displaying the real and effective access permissions on files as determined by file permissions and ACLs.

The output of `getfacl` for a file (*/etc/passwd* in this example) looks like this:

```
$ getfacl /etc/passwd
# file: /etc/passwd
# owner: root
# group: sys
user::rw-
group::r--                      #effective:r--
mask:r--
other:r--
```

Setting Environment Variables

Environment variables are used to store information in a form that is accessible to commands within the shell and other applications that are spawned from the shell. You can obtain a list of all environment variables that have been set in a shell by using the following command:

```
bash-2.03$ set
BASH=/usr/local/bin/bash
BASH_VERSINFO=([0]="2" [1]="03" [2]="0" [3]="1" [4]="release" \
   [5]="i386-pc-solaris2.9")
BASH_VERSION='2.03.0(1)-release'
COLUMNS=80
DIRSTACK=()
DISPLAY=cassowary:0.0
EDITOR=/usr/bin/vi
ENV=/.kshrc
EUID=0
GROUPS=()
HELPPATH=/usr/openwin/lib/locale:/usr/openwin/lib/help
HISTFILE=/.sh_history
HISTFILESIZE=500
HISTSIZE=500
HOME=/
HOSTNAME=cassowary
HOSTTYPE=i386
IFS=' '
LANG=en_AU
LC_COLLATE=en_AU
LC_CTYPE=en_AU
LC_MESSAGES=C
LC_MONETARY=en_AU
LC_NUMERIC=en_AU
LC_TIME=en_AU
LD_LIBRARY_PATH=/usr/local/lib:/usr/openwin/lib:/usr/dt/lib
LINES=24
LOGNAME=root
MACHTYPE=i386-pc-solaris2.9
MAIL=/var/mail/root
MAILCHECK=60
```

```
MANPATH=/usr/dt/man:/usr/man:/usr/openwin/share/man
OPENWINHOME=/usr/openwin
OPTERR=1
OPTIND=1
OSTYPE=solaris2.9
PATH=/usr/sbin:/usr/bin:/bin:/usr/ucb:/usr/local/bin:/usr/ccs/bin
PIPESTATUS=([0]="1")
PPID=1584
PS1='\s-\v\$ '
PS2='> '
PS4='+ '
PWD=/etc
SESSION_SVR=tango
SHELL=/bin/ksh
SHLVL=1
TERM=dtterm
TERMINAL_EMULATOR=dtterm
TZ=Australia/NSW
UID=0
USER=root
WINDOWID=58720265
```

Although this seems to be a lot of shell variables, the most significant ones include the following:

BASH	The path to the shell on the file system
COLUMNS	The column's width for the terminal
DISPLAY	The display variable that is used for X11 graphics
HOME	The default home directory for the user
HOSTNAME	The hostname of the current system
LD_LIBRARY_PATH	The path to system and user libraries
LOGNAME	The username of the shell owner
MANPATH	The path to the system manuals
NNTPSERVER	The hostname of the NNTP server
PATH	The path that is searched to find applications where no absolute path is specified on the command line
PPID	The parent process ID
TERM	The terminal type (usually VT100)
UID	The user ID
WINDOWMANAGER	The name of the X11 window manager

The values of all shell variables can be set on the command line by using the `export` command. For example, if you wanted to set the terminal type to VT220, you would use this command:

```
$ TERM=vt220; export TERM
```

Shell Commands

The following commands are commonly used to get the most from the shell. Help for each of these commands is usually available through the man facility or the GNU `info` command.

Source (.)

The `source` command reads in and executes the lines of a shell script. The format of this command is

```
. file
```

where *file* is a valid filename that contains a Bourne shell script. The first line should contain a directive that points to the absolute location of the shell:

```
#!/bin/sh
```

Or, you can execute Bourne shell scripts by calling them with a new shell invocation, or calling them directly if the executable bit is set for the executing user. For example, the following three commands would each execute the script file *myscript.sh*:

```
$ . myscript.sh
$ sh myscript.sh
$ ./myscript.sh
```

However, only the source command (.) preserves any environment variable settings made in the script.

basename

The basename command strips a filename of its extension. The format of this command is

```
basename filename.ext
```

where *filename.ext* is a valid filename like *mydata.dat*. The basename command parses *mydata.dat*, and extracts *mydata*. Because file extensions are not mandatory in Solaris, this command is very useful for processing files copied from Windows or MS-DOS.

cat

The cat command prints out the contents of the file, without any special screen control features like scrolling backwards or forwards in a file. The format of this command is as follows:

```
cat filename
```

To display the groups database, for example, you could run this command:

```
$ cat /etc/group
root::0:root
other::1:
bin::2:root,bin,daemon
sys::3:root,bin,sys,adm
adm::4:root,adm,daemon
uucp::5:root,uucp
mail::6:root
tty::7:root,tty,adm
lp::8:root,lp,adm
nuucp::9:root,nuucp
staff::10:
```

cd

The `cd` command changes the current working directory to a new directory location, which you can specify in both absolute or relative terms. The format of this command is as follows:

```
cd directory
```

For example, if the current working directory is */usr/local*, and you type the command

```
cd bin
```

the new working directory would be */usr/local/bin*. However, if you type the command

```
cd /bin
```

the new working directory would be */bin*. For interactive use, relative directory names are often used; however, scripts should always contain absolute directory references.

chgrp

The `chgrp` command modifies the default group membership of a file. The format of this command is

```
chgrp group file
```

where group is a valid group name, defined in the groups database (*/etc/groups*), and *file* is a valid filename. Because permissions can be assigned to individual users or groups of users, assigning a nondefault group membership can be useful for users who need to exchange data with members of different organizational units (for example, the web master who swaps configuration files with the database administrator, and also exchanges HTML files with web developers).

TIP   Only the file owner or the superuser can modify the group membership of a file.

date

This command prints the current system date and time. The format of this command is as follows:

```
date
```

The default output for the command output is of this form:

```
Tuesday February  12 13:43:23 EST 2002
```

You can also modify the output format by using a number of parameters corresponding to days, months, hours, minutes, and so on. For example, the command

```
date '+Current Date: %d/%m/%y%nCurrent Time:%H:%M:%S'
```

produces the following output:

```
Current Date: 06/09/00
Current Time:13:45:43
```

grep

The grep command searches a file for a string (specified by string) and prints the line wherever a match is found. The format of this command is as follows:

```
grep string file
```

The grep command is very useful for interpreting log files, where you just want to display a line that contains a particular code (for example, a web server log file can be grepped for the string 404, which indicates a page not found).

head

The head command displays the first page of a file. The format of this command is as follows:

```
head filename
```

The head command is very useful for examining the first few lines of a very long file. For example, to display the first page of the name service switch configuration file (*/etc/nsswitch.conf*), you could use this command:

```
$ head /etc/nsswitch.conf
# /etc/nsswitch.nisplus:
# An example file that could be copied over to /etc/nsswitch.conf; it
# uses NIS+ (NIS Version 3) in conjunction with files.
# "hosts:" and "services:" in this file are used only if the
# /etc/netconfig file has a "-" for nametoaddr_libs of "inet" transports.
# the following two lines obviate the "+" entry in /etc/passwd and /etc/group.
```

less

The less command prints a file "file" on the screen, and it allows searching backwards and forwards through the file. The format of this command is as follows:

```
less filename
```

To scroll through the contents of the system log configuration file (*/etc/syslog.conf*), you would use the following command:

```
less /etc/syslog.conf
#ident    "@(#)syslog.conf       1.4     96/10/11 SMI"   /* SunOS 5.0 */
# Copyright (c) 1991-1993, by Sun Microsystems, Inc.
# syslog configuration file.
# This file is processed by m4 so be careful to quote (`') names
# that match m4 reserved words.  Also, within ifdef's, arguments
# containing commas must be quoted.
*.notice                                        @loghost
*.err;kern.notice;auth.notice                   /dev/console
*.err;kern.debug;daemon.notice;mail.crit;daemon.info    /var/adm/messages
*.alert;kern.err;daemon.err                     operator
*.alert                                         root
```

The less command has a number of commands that can be issued interactively. For example, to move forward one window, just type **F**, or to move back one window just type **B**. less also supports searching with the /pattern command.

ls

The ls command prints the names of files contained in the directory *dir* (by default, the contents of the current working directory are displayed). The format of the command is

```
ls directory
```

where *directory* is the name of the directory whose contents you wish to list. For example, to list the contents of the */var/adm* directory, which contains a number of system logs, you could use this command:

```
$ ls /var/adm
aculog       log          messages.1   passwd      utmp      wtmp
ftpmessages  messages     messages.2   spellhist   utmpx     wtmpx
lastlog      messages.0   messages.3   sulog       vold.log
```

mkdir

The mkdir command makes new directory entries. The format of this command is as follows:

```
mkdir directory
```

For example, if the current working directory is */sbin*, and you type the command

```
mkdir oracle
```

the new directory would be */sbin/oracle*. However, if you type the command

```
mkdir /oracle
```

the new directory would be */oracle*. For interactive use, relative directory names are often used; however, scripts should always contain absolute directory references.

more

The more command prints the contents of a file, like the less command, but just permits scrolling forward through a file. The format of this command is as follows:

```
more filename
```

To scroll through the contents of the disk device configuration file (*/etc/format.dat*), you would use the following command:

```
more /etc/format.dat
#pragma ident    "@(#)format.dat 1.21    98/01/24 SMI"
# Copyright (c) 1991,1998 by Sun Microsystems, Inc.
# All rights reserved.
# Data file for the 'format' program.  This file defines the known
# disks, disk types, and partition maps.
# This is the list of supported disks for the Emulex MD21 controller.
disk_type = "Micropolis 1355" \
        : ctlr = MD21 \
        : ncyl = 1018 : acyl = 2 : pcyl = 1024 : nhead = 8 : nsect = 34 \
        : rpm = 3600 : bpt = 20832
```

The more command has a number of commands that can be issued interactively. For example, to move forward one window, just press the SPACEBAR, or to move forward one line, just press ENTER. more also supports searching with the /pattern command.

pwd

The pwd command prints the current working directory in absolute terms. The format of the command is as follows:

```
pwd
```

For example, if you change the directory to */etc* and issue the pwd command, you would see the following result:

```
$ cd /etc
 $ pwd
/etc
```

rmdir

The rmdir command deletes a directory. However, the directory concerned must be empty for the rmdir command to be successful. The format of this command is as follows:

```
rmdir directory
```

For example, if the current working directory is */usr/local*, and you want to remove the directory *oldstuff*, you would use this command:

```
rmdir oldstuff
```

However, you could use the command

```
rmdir /usr/local/oldstuff
```

to remove the directory as well. For interactive use, relative directory names are often used; however, scripts should always contain absolute directory references.

tail

The `tail` command displays the last page of a file. The format of this command is as follows:

```
tail filename
```

The `tail` command is very useful for examining the last few lines of a very long file. For example, to display the first page of a web log file (*/usr/local/apache/logs/access_log*), you could use this command:

```
$ tail /usr/local/apache/logs/access_log
192.168.205.238 - - [12/Feb/2002:09:35:59 +1000]
  "GET /images/picture10.gif HTTP/1.1" 200 53
192.168.205.238 - - [12/Feb/2002:09:35:59 +1000]

  "GET /images/ picture1.gif HTTP/1.1" 200 712
192.168.205.238 - - [12/Feb/2002:09:35:59 +1000]

  "GET /images/ picture5.gif HTTP/1.1" 200 7090
192.168.205.238 - - [12/Feb/2002:09:35:59 +1000]

  "GET /images/ picture66.gif HTTP/1.1" 200 997
192.168.205.238 - - [12/Feb/2002:09:35:59 +1000]

  "GET /images/ picture49.gif HTTP/1.1" 200 2386
192.168.205.238 - - [12/Feb/2002:09:36:09 +1000]

  "GET /servlet/SimpleServlet HTTP/1.1" 200 10497
```

The `tail` command also has an option that allows you to continuously monitor all new entries made to a file. This is very useful for monitoring a live service such as Apache, where you need to observe any error made in real time. The format for this command is as follows:

```
tail -f filename
```

Summary

In this chapter, we have examined how to manage files and directories, and how to work with the shell. In addition, we have examined the commands used to write shell scripts, and other commonly used shell commands. Since the shell is the administrator's interface to the operating system, it's important that administrator's become familiar with shell commands and procedures.

Questions

1. What command would be used to set read permissions (for the current user) on the file */usr/local/lib/libproxy.a*?

   A. chmod +r /usr/local/lib/libproxy.a

   B. chmod a+r /usr/local/lib/libproxy.a

   C. chmod g+r /usr/local/lib/libproxy.a

   D. chmod u+r /usr/local/lib/libproxy.a

2. What command would be used to set read permissions for all users on the file */usr/local/lib/libproxy.a*?

   A. chmod +r /usr/local/lib/libproxy.a

   B. chmod a+r /usr/local/lib/libproxy.a

   C. chmod g+r /usr/local/lib/libproxy.a

   D. chmod u+r /usr/local/lib/libproxy.a

3. What command would be used to set write permissions for the current user's group on the file */usr/local/lib/libproxy.a*?

   A. chgrp +w /usr/local/lib/libproxy.a

   B. chmod a+w /usr/local/lib/libproxy.a

   C. chmod g+w /usr/local/lib/libproxy.a

   D. chmod u+w /usr/local/lib/libproxy.a

4. What command would be used to remove write permissions for the current user's group on the file */usr/local/lib/libproxy.a*?

   A. chgrp -w /usr/local/lib/libproxy.a

   B. chmod a-w /usr/local/lib/libproxy.a

   C. chmod g-w /usr/local/lib/libproxy.a

   D. chmod u-w /usr/local/lib/libproxy.a

5. What command would be used to set the sticky bit on */public*?

   A. `chmod +t /public`

   B. `chmod +s /public`

   C. `chmod +S /public`

   D. `chmod t+s /public`

6. What command would be used to remove the sticky bit on */public*?

   A. `chmod -t /public`

   B. `chmod -s /public`

   C. `chmod -S /public`

   D. `chmod t-s /public`

7. What command would be used to set setuid on */public/shell*?

   A. `chmod +t /public/shell`

   B. `chmod +s /public/shell`

   C. `chmod +S /public/shell`

   D. `chmod t+s /public/shell`

8. What command would be used to remove the setuid bit on */public/shell*?

   A. `chmod -t /public/shell`

   B. `chmod -s /public/shell`

   C. `chmod -S /public/shell`

   D. `chmod t-s /public/shell`

Answers

1. **A.** Read permissions can be set with the *r* permissions flag.

2. **B.** Read permissions for all users can be set with the *r* flag in combination with the *a* (all) flag.

3. **C.** Write permissions for the group can be set with the *w* flag in combination with the *g* (group) flag.

4. **C.** Write permissions for the group can be removed with the *w* flag in combination with the *g* (group) flag, but using the - rather than the + operator.

5. **A.** The sticky bit is always set with the *t* operator.

6. **A.** The sticky bit is removed with the *t* operator, but with the - rather than the + operator.

7. **B.** setuid is always removed with the *s* operator.

8. **B.** setuid is always removed with the *s* operator, but with the - rather than the + operator.

Booting and Initialization

In this chapter, you will

- Understand default shell variables set in *.profile*
- Learn to modify system-wide templates for *.profile* in */etc/skel/profile.local*
- Review commonly used commands for use in *.profile*
- Cover basic shell scripting
- Add packages to the system

This chapter covers the customization of the initialization and booting process, including writing shell scripts and startup files.

The Shell

Using the command line (or "shell") has the following advantages over GUI environments:

- The shell is essential for programming repetitive tasks, which can only be performed laboriously through a GUI—for example, searching a file system for all document files that have changed each day, and making a copy of all these files (with the extension *.doc*) to a backup directory (with the extension *.bak*).

- The shell can be used to search for, modify, edit, and replace Solaris configuration files, which are typically stored in text format. This is much like the approach taken with Windows *.ini* configuration files, which were text-based. However, versions of Windows after Windows 95 used the Registry to store configuration information in a binary format, making it impossible to manually edit. All Solaris configuration files are text-based.

- The shell has a number of built-in commands that typically mirror those provided in the C programming language. This means it is possible to write small programs as shell statements that are executed as sequential steps, without having to use a compiler (just like MS-DOS batch files are interpreted without requiring a compiler).

- The shell can be used to launch applications that use a character user interface (CUI), which is especially useful for logging in to a remote system and being able to use all the commands that the administrator can use on the console. In the era of global information systems, this is very useful. While Windows applications like Symantec's pcAnywhere can be used for remote access to the Windows desktop, they don't easily support multiuser access (or multiuser access where one user requires a CUI and another a graphical user interface, GUI).

- The shell can be used to execute commands for which there is no equivalent GUI application. Although many operations could conceivably be performed using a GUI, it is usually easier to write a shell script than create a completely new GUI application.

Every time a user logs into a system, a shell is spawned. The type of shell spawned is determined by the default shell entry in */etc/passwd* for the user concerned:

```
apache:x:1003:10:apache user:/usr/local/apache:/bin/sh
```

In this case, the apache user has the Bourne shell (*/bin/sh*) set as default. To be a valid login shell, */bin/sh* must also be included in the shells database (stored in the file */etc/shells*). The default system shell is the Bourne shell (*/bin/sh*). When a login shell is spawned, an initialization script is executed by the shell, which contains a series of commands that are executed sequentially—in addition to a number of environment variables being set. Each shell has its own initialization script; in the case of the Bourne shell, the initialization script is called *.profile*.

TIP The *.profile* is typically located in the user's home directory, although a system-wide */etc/profile* script is also executed.

The .profile **Script**

The *.profile* file can contain any commands and environment settings that a normal shell script can.

The values of all shell variables can be set in *.profile*. For example, if we wanted to set the current terminal type to VT220, we would insert the following environment variable definition into the *.profile* file:

```
TERM=vt220; export TERM
```

In this example, the *TERM* variable is created and the value vt220 assigned to it. At this point, the scope of the variable is just the *.profile* script itself. In order to ensure that the value is exported to shell proper, the `export` command should be used as shown.

Since many environment variables are set system-wide (such as the location of database files), each user will expect to have variables consistently set. One way to ensure that users are using the correct variables is to define the */etc/skel/profile.local* file. This skeleton file contains variable definitions that will be copied to new users' accounts when they are created with admintool or useradd.

Exercise 11-1

Check the environment variables that are set in your current shell.

Writing Startup Scripts

Shell scripts are combinations of shell and user commands that are executed in noninteractive mode for a wide variety of purposes. Whether you require a script that converts a set of filename extensions or need to alert the system administrator by e-mail that disk space is running low, shell scripts can be used. The commands that you place inside a shell script should normally execute in the interactive shell mode as well, making it easy it to take apart large scripts and debug them line by line in your normal login shell. In this section, we will only examine shell scripts that run under the Bourne shell—although many of the scripts will work without modification using other shells, it is always best to check the syntax chart of your own shell before attempting to run the scripts on another shell.

Processing Shell Arguments

A common goal of writing shell scripts is to make them as general as possible, so that they can be used with many different kinds of input. For example, in the cat examples presented earlier, we wouldn't want to have to create an entirely new script for every file that we wanted to insert data into. Fortunately, shell scripts are able to make use of command-line parameters, which are numerically ordered arguments that are accessible from within a shell script. For example, a shell script to move files from one computer to another computer might require parameters for the source host, the destination host, and the name of the file to be moved. Obviously, we want to be able to pass these arguments to the script, rather than "hardwiring" them into the code. This is one advantage of shell scripts (and Perl programs) over compiled languages like C: scripts are easy to modify, and their operation is completely transparent to the user.

Arguments to shell scripts can be identified by a simple scheme: the command executed is referred to with the argument $0, with the first parameter identified as $1, the second parameter identified by $2, and so on, up to a maximum of nine parameters.

Thus, a script executed with the parameters

```
display_hardware.sh cdrom scsi ide
```

would refer internally to "cdrom" as $1, "scsi" as $2, and "ide" as $3. This approach would be particularly useful when calling smaller scripts from the main .*profile* script.

Let's see how arguments can be used effectively within a script to process input parameters. The first script we will create simply counts the number of lines in a file (using the wc command), specified by a single command-line argument ($1). To begin with, we create an empty script file:

```
touch count_lines.sh
```

Next, we set the permissions on the file to be executable:

```
chmod +x count_lines.sh
```

Next, we edit the file

```
vi count_lines.sh
```

and add the appropriate code:

```
#!/bin/sh
echo "Number of lines in file " $1
wc -l $1
```

The script will take the first command-line argument, then print the number of lines, and then exit. We run the script with this command

```
./count_lines.sh /etc/group
```

which gives the following output:

```
Number of lines in file /etc/group
43
```

Although the individual activity of scripts is quite variable, the procedure of creating the script file, setting its permissions, editing its contents, and executing it on the command line remains the same across scripts. Of course, you may wish to make the script only available to certain users or groups for execution—this can be enabled by using the `chmod` command, and explicitly adding or removing permissions when necessary.

Testing File Properties

One of the assumptions that we made in the previous script was that the file specified by $1 actually existed; if it didn't exist, we obviously would not be able to count the number of lines it contained. If the script is running from the command line, we can safely debug it and interpret any error conditions that arise (such as a file not existing, or having incorrect permissions). However, if a script is intended to run as a scheduled job (using the cron or at facility), it is impossible to debug in real time. Thus, it is often useful to write scripts that can handle error conditions gracefully and intelligently, rather than leaving administrators wondering why a job didn't produce any output when it was scheduled to run.

The number one cause of runtime execution errors is the incorrect setting of file permissions. Although most users remember to set the executable bit on the script file itself, they often neglect to include error checking for the existence of data files that are used by the script. For example, if we want to write a script that checked the syntax of a configuration file (like the Apache configuration file, *httpd.conf*), we need to make sure the file actually exists before performing the check; otherwise, the script may not return an error message, and we may erroneously assume that the script file is correctly configured.

Fortunately, Bourne shell makes it easy to test for the existence of files by using the (conveniently named) test facility. In addition to testing for file existence, files that exist can also be tested for read, write, and execute permissions prior to any read, write, or execute file access being attempted by the script. Let's revise our previous script that counted the number of lines in a file by first verifying that the target file (specified by $1) exists, and then printing the result; otherwise, an error message will be displayed:

```
#!/bin/sh
if test -a $1
then
echo "Number of lines in file " $1
wc -l $1
else
        echo "The file" $1 "does not exist"
fi
```

When we run this command, if a file exists, it should count the number of lines in the target file as before; otherwise, an error message will be printed. If the */etc/group* file did not exist, for example, we'd really want to know about it:

```
./count_lines.sh /etc/group
The file /etc/group does not exist
```

There may be some situations where we want to test another file property. For example, the */etc/shadow* password database must only be readable by the superuser. Thus, if we execute a script to check whether or not the */etc/shadow* file is readable by a nonprivileged user, it should not return a positive result. We can check file readability by using the −r option rather than the −a option. Here's the revised script:

```
#!/bin/sh
if test -r $1 then
echo "I can read the file " $1
else
        echo "I can't read the file" $1
fi
```

The following file permissions can also be tested using the test facility:

- −b File is a special block file.
- −c File is a special character file.
- −d File is a directory.
- −f File is a normal file.
- −h File is a symbolic link.
- −p File is a named pipe.
- −s File has nonzero size.
- −w File is writable by the current user.
- −x File is executable by the current user.

Looping

All programming languages have the ability to repeat blocks of code for a specified number of iterations. This makes performing repetitive actions very easy for a well-written program. The Bourne shell is no exception. It features a for loop, which repeats the actions of a code block for a specified number of iterations as defined by a set of consecutive arguments to the `for` command. In addition, an iterator is available within the code block to indicate which of the sequence of iterations that will be performed is currently being performed. If that sounds a little complicated, let's have a look at a concrete example, which uses a for loop to generate a set of filenames. These filenames are then tested using the test facility to determine whether or not they exist:

```
#!/bin/sh
for i in apple orange lemon kiwi guava
do
        DATAFILE=$i".dat"
        echo "Checking" $DATAFILE
        if test -s $DATAFILE
        then
            echo $DATAFILE "is OK"

        else
                echo $DATAFILE "has zero-length"

        fi
done
```

The for loop is repeated five times, with the variable $i taking on the values apple, orange, lemon, kiwi, and guava. Thus, when on the first iteration, when $i=apple, the shell interprets the for loop in the following way:

```
FILENAME="apple.dat"
echo "Checking apple.dat"
if test -s apple.dat
then
echo "apple.dat has zero-length"
else
echo "apple.dat is OK"
fi
```

If we run this script in a directory with files of zero length, we would expect to see the following output:

```
./zero_length_check.sh
Checking apple.dat
apple.dat is zero-length
Checking orange.dat
orange.dat is zero-length
```

```
Checking lemon.dat
lemon.dat is zero-length
Checking kiwi.dat
kiwi.dat is zero-length
Checking guava.dat
guava.dat is zero-length
```

However, if we entered data into each of the files, we should see them receive the "OK" message:

```
./zero_length_check.sh
Checking apple.dat
apple.dat is OK
Checking orange.dat
orange.dat is OK
Checking lemon.dat
lemon.dat is OK
Checking kiwi.dat
kiwi.dat is OK
Checking guava.dat
guava.dat is OK
```

Using Shell Variables

In the previous example, we assigned different values to a shell variable, which was used to generate filenames for checking. It is common to modify variables within scripts by using export, and to attach error codes to instances where variables are not defined within a script. This is particularly useful if a variable that is available within a user's interactive shell is not available in their noninteractive shell. For example, we can create a script called *show_errors.sh* that returns an error message if the *PATH* variable is not set:

```
#!/bin/sh
echo ${PATH:?PATH_NOT_SET}
```

Of course, since the *PATH* variable is usually set, we should see output similar to the following:

```
# ./path_set.sh
/sbin:/bin:/usr/games/bin:/usr/sbin:/root/bin:/usr/local/bin:/usr/local/sbin/
:/usr/bin:
/usr/X11R6/bin: /usr/games:/opt/gnome/bin:/opt/kde/bin
```

However, if the *PATH* was not set, we would see the following error message:

```
./show_errors.sh: PATH_NOT_SET
```

It is also possible to use system-supplied error messages, by not specifying the optional error string:

```
#!/bin/sh
echo ${PATH:?}
```

Thus, if the *PATH* variable is not set, we would see the following error message:

```
# ./path_set.sh
./showargs: PATH: parameter null or not set
```

We can also use the numbered shell variables ($1, $2, $3, and so forth) to capture the space-delimited output of certain commands, and perform actions based on the value of these variables using the `set` command. For example, the command

```
# set `ls`
```

will sequentially assign each of the fields within the returned directory listing to a numbered shell variable. So, if our directory listing contained the entries

```
apple.dat   guava.dat   kiwi.dat   lemon.dat   orange.dat
```

We could retrieve the values of these filenames by using the `echo` command:

```
# echo $1
apple.dat
# echo $2
guava.dat
# echo $3
kiwi.dat
# echo $4
lemon.dat
# echo $5
orange.dat
```

This approach is very useful if your script needs to perform some action based on only one component of the date. For example, if you wanted to create a unique filename to assign to a compressed file, you could combine the values of each variable with a *.Z* extension to produce a set of strings like *orange.dat.Z*.

Package Management

All Solaris software installed as part of the operating environment is included in an archive known as a *package*. Solaris packages provide an easy way to bring together application binaries, configuration files, and documentation for distribution to other systems. In addition to the Solaris packaging system, Solaris also supports standard UNIX archiving and compression tools, such as *tar* (tape archive) and *compress*. In this chapter, we examine how you can manage packages using the standard Solaris packaging tools, CLI (Command Line Interface) and admintool. Operations reviewed include installing packages, displaying information about packages, and removing packages using both the CLI tools and the admintool GUI utility.

Packages are text files that contain archives of binary applications, configuration files, documentation, and even source code. All files in the Solaris operating environment are supplied as part of a package, making it easy for you to group files associated with different applications. If files are installed without packaging, it can become difficult over the years for administrators to remember which files were installed with particular applications. Packaging makes it easy to recognize application dependencies, because all files required by a specific application can be included within the archive.

Getting Information About Packages

Administrators can use the `pkgchk` command to examine the package properties of a file that has already been installed:

```
# pkgchk -l -p /usr/bin/mkdir
Pathname: /usr/bin/mkdir
Type: regular file
Expected mode: 0555
Expected owner: bin
Expected group: bin
Expected file size (bytes): 9876
Expected sum(1) of contents: 38188
Expected last modification: Oct 06 05:47:55 PM 1998
Referenced by the following packages:
        SUNWcsu
Current status: installed
```

Another advantage of using packages is that they make use of the standard installation interface provided to install Solaris packages. This means that all Solaris applications are installed using one of two standard installation applications (pkgadd or the admintool), rather than each application having its own installation program. This reduces coding time and makes it easier for administrators to install software, because only a single interface with standard options, such as overwriting existing files, needs to be learned. Using packages reduces the administrative overhead of software management on Solaris 9.

In this chapter, we examine how to install new packages, display information about downloaded packages, and remove packages that have been previously installed on the system, by using both admintool and the command-line package tools.

Viewing Package Information with pkginfo

At any time, you can examine which packages have been installed on a system using the pkginfo command:

```
# pkginfo
application GNUlstdc       libstdc++
application GNUmake        make
system      NCRos86r       NCR Platform Support,
                           OS Functionality (Root)
system      SFWaalib       ASCII Art Library
system      SFWaconf       GNU autoconf
system      SFWamake       GNU automake
system      SFWbison       GNU bison
system      SFWemacs       GNU Emacs
system      SFWflex        GNU flex
system      SFWfvwm        fvwm virtual window manager
system      SFWgcc         GNU compilers
system      SFWgdb         GNU source-level debugger
system      SFWgimp        GNU Image Manipulation Program
system      SFWglib        GLIB - Library of useful routines
                           for C programming
system      SFWgm4         GNU m4
system      SFWgmake       GNU make
system      SFWgs          GNU Ghostscript
system      SFWgsfot       GNU Ghostscript Other Fonts
system      SFWgsfst       GNU Ghostscript Standard Fonts
system      SFWgtk         GTK - The GIMP Toolkit
system      SFWjpg         The Independent JPEG Groups JPEG software
system      SFWlxrun       lxrun
system      SFWmpage       mpage - print multiple pages per sheet
system      SFWmpeg        The MPEG Library
system      SFWncur        ncurses library
system      SFWolvwm       OPEN LOOK Virtual Window Manager
system      SFWpng         PNG reference library
```

As you can see, this system has quite a few packages installed in both the system and application categories, including lxrun, the application that allows Linux binaries to be executed on Solaris Intel, and the Gimp, a graphics manipulation program. There are no restrictions on the kinds of files and applications that can be installed with packages.

Viewing Package Information with admintool

Viewing information about installed packages is easy using the admintool utility's graphical user interface (GUI). You execute admintool by using the command /usr/bin/admintool. After choosing Browse | Software from admintool's menu bar, you can view all the installed software packages, as shown in Figure 11-1. In the figure, you can see that many packages have already been installed on the system, including PC File Viewer Help in Swedish, Italian, French, and German, as well as support files for the ShowTV multimedia software suite.

Figure 11-1   Browsing installed packages on a Solaris system

Using admintool, you can also display only files that have been installed as packages in the system category by deselecting All Software from the software selection drop-down menu, and selecting System Software, as shown in Figure 11-2. Here you can see that several key system packages have been installed, including operating system

Figure 11-2   Browsing all installed system packages on a Solaris system

(OS), Common Desktop Environment (CDE), Open Windows (OW), and 64-bit architecture support for Eastern European, Central European, Southern European, and German locales.

It is also possible to display only files that have been installed as application packages by
deselecting System Software from the software selection drop-down menu and selecting
Application Software, as shown in Figure 11-3. You can see that several key application

Figure 11-3   Browsing all installed application packages on a Solaris system

packages have been installed, including many support packages for the ShowTV multimedia software suite.

Installing a Solaris Package Using the CLI

The best way to learn about adding packages is to use an example. In this section, you'll download a package from **http://www.sunfreeware.com** called gpw-6.94-sol8-intel-local

.gz, which is Tom Van Vleck's random password creation application. Let's look more closely at the package name to determine what software this package contains:

- The .gz extension indicates that the package file has been compressed using gzip after it was created. Other possible extensions include .Z, which indicates compression with the compress program, while a .z extension suggests compression by the pack program.

- The *local* string indicates that the package contents will be installed under the directory /usr/local. Other typical installation targets include the /opt directory, where optional packages from the Solaris distribution are installed.

- The *intel* string states that the package is intended for use on Solaris Intel and not Solaris Sparc.

- The *6.94* string indicates the current software revision level.

- The *gpw* string states the application's name.

To use the package file, you first need to decompress it using the `gzip` command:

```
# gzip -d gpw-6.94-sol8-intel-local
```

You can then examine the contents of the file by using the `head` command:

```
# head gpw-6.94-sol8-intel-local
# PaCkAgE DaTaStReAm
TVVgpw 1 150
# end of header
NAME=gwp
ARCH=intel
VERSION=6.94
CATEGORY=application
VENDOR=Tom Van Vleck
EMAIL=steve@smc.vnet.net
```

This kind of header exists for all Solaris packages and makes it easy to understand what platform a package is designed for, who the vendor was, and who to contact for more information.

Now that the package is decompressed and ready, you can begin the installation process by using the `pkgadd` command. To install the gpw-6.94-sol8-intel-local package, use the following command:

```
# pkgadd -d gpw-6.94-sol8-intel-local
```

You'll see the following output:

```
The following packages are available:
  1  TVVgpw     gwp
                (sparc) 6.94

Select package(s) you wish to process (or 'all' to process
all packages). (default: all) [?,??,q]:  all
```

Press ENTER at this point to proceed with the installation:

```
Processing package instance <TVVgpw> from </tmp/gpw-6.94-sol8-intel-local>

gwp
(sparc) 6.94
Tom Van Vleck
Using </usr/local> as the package base directory.
## Processing package information.
## Processing system information.
   2 package pathnames are already properly installed.
## Verifying disk space requirements.
## Checking for conflicts with packages already installed.
## Checking for setuid/setgid programs.

Installing gwp as <TVVgpw>

## Installing part 1 of 1.
/usr/local/bin/gpw
/usr/local/doc/gpw/README.gpw
[ verifying class <none> ]

Installation of <TVVgpw> was successful.
```

After processing package and system information and checking that the required amount of disk space is available, the `pkgadd` command copies only two files from the archive to the local file system: /usr/local/bin/gpwand/usr/local/doc/ gpw/ README.gpw.

Uninstalling a Solaris Package Using the CLI

After a package has been installed on the system, it can easily be removed by using the `pkgrm` command. For example, if you wanted to remove the gpw program after it was installed in the /usr/local directory, you would use this command

```
# pkgrm TVVgpw
```

and respond to the following information:

```
The following package is currently installed:
   TVVgpw          gwp
                   (sparc) 6.94

Do you want to remove this package? y

## Removing installed package instance <TVVgpw>
## Verifying package dependencies.
## Processing package information.
## Removing pathnames in class <none>
/usr/local/doc/gpw/README.gpw
/usr/local/doc/gpw
/usr/local/doc <shared pathname not removed>
/usr/local/bin/gpw
/usr/local/bin <shared pathname not removed>
## Updating system information.

Removal of <TVVgpw> was successful.
```

The `pkgrm` command also operates in an interactive mode, in which multiple packages can be removed using the same interface:

```
# pkgrm

The following packages are available:
  1  GNUlstdc      libstdc++
                   (i86pc) 2.8.1.1
  2  GNUmake       make
                   (i86pc) 3.77
  3  NCRos86r      NCR Platform Support, OS Functionality (Root)
                   (i386) 1.1.0,REV=1998.08.07.12.41
  4  SFWaalib      ASCII Art Library
                   (i386) 1.2,REV=1999.11.25.13.32
  5  SFWaconf      GNU autoconf
                   (i386) 2.13,REV=1999.11.25.13.32
  6  SFWamake      GNU automake
                   (i386) 1.4,REV=1999.11.25.13.32
  7  SFWbison      GNU bison
                   (i386) 1.28,REV=1999.11.25.13.32
  8  SFWemacs      GNU Emacs
                   (i386) 20.4,REV=1999.11.25.13.32
  9  SFWflex       GNU flex
                   (i386) 2.5.4,REV=1999.11.25.13.32
 10  SFWfvwm       fvwm virtual window manager
                   (i386) 2.2.2,REV=1999.11.25.13.32

... 288 more menu choices to follow;
<RETURN> for more choices, <CTRL-D> to stop display:
```

At this point, you can enter the number of the package that you wish to remove.

Installing a Solaris Package with admintool

As shown in Figure 11-4, admintool provides an easy-to-use interface for installing packages, in which the following options may be selected from drop-down boxes:

- Check for existing files.
- Check for existing packages.
- Check for existing partial installations.
- Allow setuid/setgid files to be installed.
- Allow setuid/setgid scripts to be run.
- Check that installation dependencies have been met.
- Check that removal dependencies have been met.
- Check for correct run level.
- Check for sufficient space.
- Display copyrights.
- Run the installation interactively.

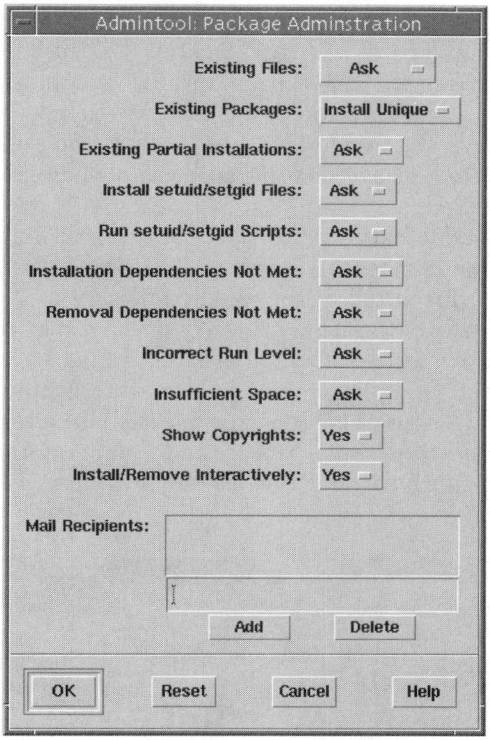

Figure 11-4   The admintool GUI for adding packages

The admintool also allows the administrator to specify an installation source, so that packages may be installed directly from a CD-ROM, as shown in Figure 11-5.

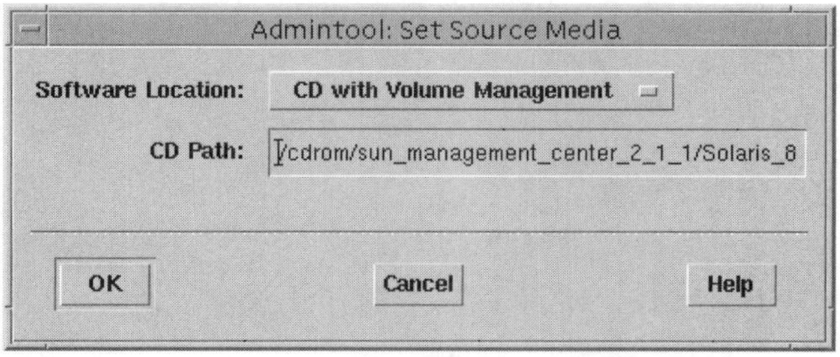

Figure 11-5   The admintool interface for selecting the package installation source

Once a valid CD-ROM directory containing packages has been selected, the Add Software interface is displayed, as shown in Figure 11-6. The left-hand pane shows the full titles for the packages that have been located in the specified directory. The right-hand pane shows the description of the last selected software package. For example, the package SUNWcesh, shown in Figure 11-6, is the Sun Management Center Simplified Chinese Help package distributed by Sun Microsystems and is less than 1MB in size when installed.

You should always verify that sufficient space is available in the indicated partitions by checking the Space Meter shown in Figure 11-7. Here you can see that more than sufficient space is available for installing the required files for the SUNWcesh package.

After checking the boxes associated with every package that you wish to install, you can proceed with installation by clicking the Add button. A separate installation window then appears, as shown in Figure 11-8. In this example, the SUNWescon software package (the Sun Management Center console package) is being installed. After setting the installation target directory (/opt), package and system information is processed. After disk space requirements have been verified, any conflicts with existing packages are

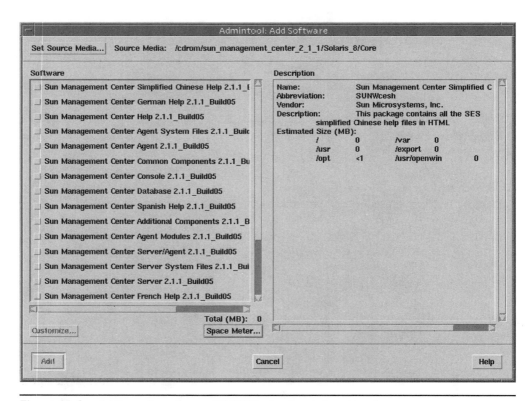

Figure 11-6   Adding packages from a CD-ROM using the admintool interface

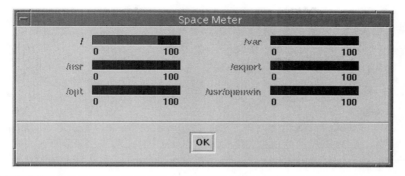

Figure 11-7 Checking available disk space using the Space Meter

identified. Next, all setuid and setgid applications are identified, and assent must be granted to install any setuid or setgid files that are found in the package. Finally, the files are installed into their appropriate target directories.

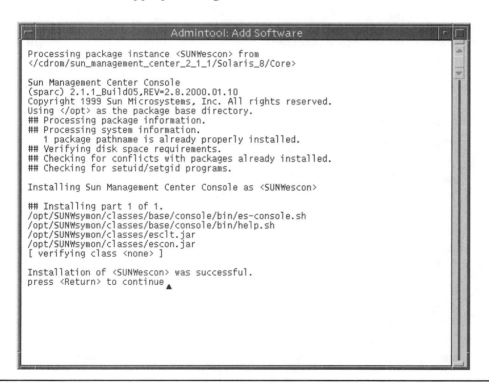

Figure 11-8 Package installation phase during admintool installation

Figure 11-9   The admintool interface for selecting the package installation source

Packages may also be installed from a special package spooling directory, at */var/spool/pkg*, using the admintool utility, or from any directory that contains a valid package file, as shown in Figure 11-9. The */var/spool/pkg* folder has an important role in upgrading machines in an automated fashion, since it can be mounted automatically using the Network File System (NFS) and the automounter from another server. It is possible to use a script or a cron job to then noninteractively install or upgrade new software.

After a valid spooling directory containing packages has been selected, the Add Software interface is displayed, as shown in Figure 11-10. The left-hand pane shows all the full titles for the packages that have been located in the specified directory. The right-hand pane shows the description of the last selected software package. The only

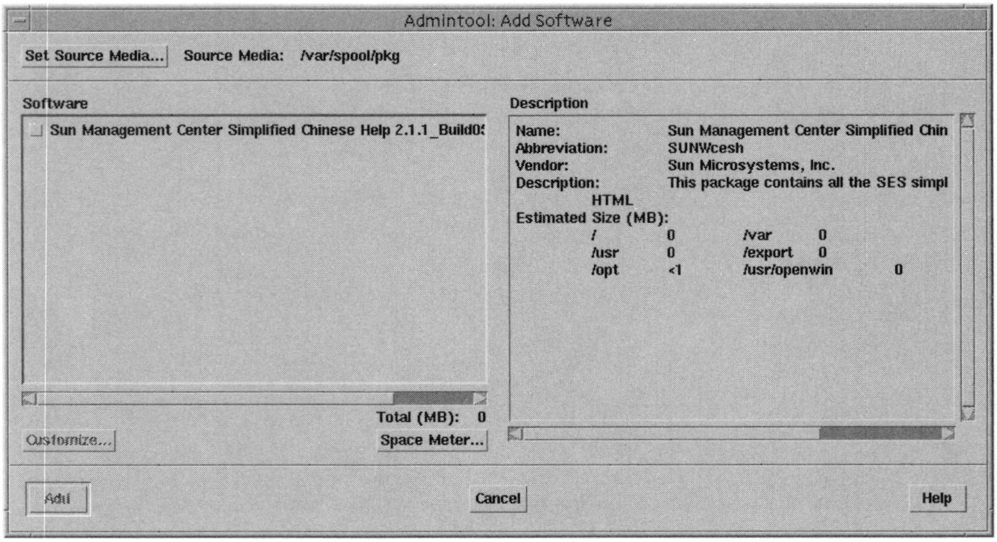

Figure 11-10   Adding packages from the spooling directory using the admintool interface

Figure 11-11   Removing packages using the admintool interface

package shown is SUNWcesh. After checking the boxes associate with the SUNWcesh package, you can proceed with installation by clicking the Add button. A separate installation window appears, and the software is installed.

Uninstalling a Solaris Package Using admintool

After a package has been installed on the system, it can easily be removed by using admintool. Choose Browse | Software, highlight the package that you wish to remove, and then choose Edit | Delete. A popup window then appears, as shown in Figure 11-11, asking for confirmation of the deletion instruction.

After you click OK, a separate window will show the output of the package removal:

```
The following package is currently installed:
   SUNWdesmt        ShowMe TV German Localization Files
                    (sparc) 1.1,REV=1999.04.30

Do you want to remove this package? y

## Removing installed package instance <SUNWdesmt>
## Verifying package dependencies.
## Processing package information.
## Removing pathnames in class <none>
/opt/SUNWsmtv/lib/locale/de/share/showmetv-defaults
/opt/SUNWsmtv/lib/locale/de/share
/opt/SUNWsmtv/lib/locale/de/help/xdh_saveFile.html
/opt/SUNWsmtv/lib/locale/de/help/xdh_printItem.html
/opt/SUNWsmtv/lib/locale/de/help/xdh_openFile.html
/opt/SUNWsmtv/lib/locale/de/help/xdh_historyDialog.html
/opt/SUNWsmtv/lib/locale/de/help/xdh_findText.html
/opt/SUNWsmtv/lib/locale/de/help/xdh_entry.html
/opt/SUNWsmtv/lib/locale/de/help/watchtimer.html
/opt/SUNWsmtv/lib/locale/de/help/videosettings.html
/opt/SUNWsmtv/lib/locale/de/help/undelete.html
/opt/SUNWsmtv/lib/locale/de/help/transmitterproperties.html
/opt/SUNWsmtv/lib/locale/de/help/transmitter.html
/opt/SUNWsmtv/lib/locale/de/help/statistics.html
/opt/SUNWsmtv/lib/locale/de/help/showcards.html
/opt/SUNWsmtv/lib/locale/de/help/recordtimer.html
/opt/SUNWsmtv/lib/locale/de/help/record.html
/opt/SUNWsmtv/lib/locale/de/help/receiver.html
/opt/SUNWsmtv/lib/locale/de/help/properties.html
```

```
/opt/SUNWsmtv/lib/locale/de/help/programinfo.html
/opt/SUNWsmtv/lib/locale/de/help/printsnap.html
/opt/SUNWsmtv/lib/locale/de/help/printformat.html
/opt/SUNWsmtv/lib/locale/de/help/print.html
/opt/SUNWsmtv/lib/locale/de/help/preview.html
/opt/SUNWsmtv/lib/locale/de/help/preferences.html
/opt/SUNWsmtv/lib/locale/de/help/open.html
/opt/SUNWsmtv/lib/locale/de/help/new.html
/opt/SUNWsmtv/lib/locale/de/help/mail.html
/opt/SUNWsmtv/lib/locale/de/help/import.html
/opt/SUNWsmtv/lib/locale/de/help/group.html
/opt/SUNWsmtv/lib/locale/de/help/findres.html
/opt/SUNWsmtv/lib/locale/de/help/filewindow.html
/opt/SUNWsmtv/lib/locale/de/help/exportcards.html
/opt/SUNWsmtv/lib/locale/de/help/broadcast.html
/opt/SUNWsmtv/lib/locale/de/help/addrbook.html
/opt/SUNWsmtv/lib/locale/de/help/addfields.html
/opt/SUNWsmtv/lib/locale/de/help
...
## Updating system information.

Removal of <SUNWdesmt> was successful.
press <Return> to continue
```

Solstice Launcher

The Solstice Launcher is part of an integrated suite of system administration tools which are an alternative to admintool and the command-line toolset. Solstice maintains a separate application registry that determines which applications are displayed in the Launcher, in addition to Sun's own tools. Thus, it is possible to customize the interface to suit local requirements. Note that the application package must have been already installed prior to registry addition.

To add an application to the registry, the /usr/snadm/bin/soladdapp command is used. For example, to add an application called Database Query, the following command could be used:

```
# soladdapp -r /opt/SUNWadm/etc/.solstice_registry \
  -n "Database Query" \
  -i /usr/local/CSWdbquery/dbquery.xpm \
  -e /usr/local/CSWdbquery/bin/dbquery
```

This would add an item for Database Query with the path to the application set to */usr/local/CSWdbquery/bin/dbquery*, an icon located in */usr/local/CSWdbquery/* dbquery.xpm, and the default registry path of */opt/SUNWadm/etc/.solstice_registry*.

In a similar fashion, an application can be removed from the registry by using the /usr/snadm/bin/soldelapp command. In this case, the name of the package must be supplied, along with the registry path:

```
# /usr/snadm/bin/soldelapp \
  -r /opt/SUNWadm/etc/.solstice_registry \
  -n "Database Query"
```

Note that this does not delete the application package from the system.

Command	Description
pkgproto	Creates a prototype file that specifies the files contained in a package
pkgmk	Creates a package directory
pkgadd	Installs a package from a package file
pkgtrans	Converts a package directory into a file
pkgrm	Uninstalls a package
pkgchk	Verifies that a package is valid
pkginfo	Prints the contents of a package

Table 11-1   Solaris Packaging Commands

Package Commands

Table 11-1 summarizes the various commands used to create, install, and remove packages.

install

The install command is not part of the standard package tools, but is often used in scripts to copy files from a source to destination directory, as part of an installation process. It does not require super-user privileges to execute, and will not overwrite files unless the effective user has permission. However, if the super-user is executing the command, then files can be written with a specific username, group membership, and octal permissions code. This allows a super-user to install multiple files with different permissions, and ownership different to root.

The three ownership and permission options are specified by:

- -m   Octal permissions code
- -u   File owner
- -g   Group membership

There are four options that indicate which operations are to be performed:

- -c   Copies a source file to a target directory
- -f   Overwrite the target file with a source file if the former exists
- -n   Copies a source file to a target directory if and only if it does not exist in any of a specified set of directories
- -d   Create a directory

To install the file */tmp/setup_server.sh* to the directory */opt/scripts*, as the user bin and group sysadmin, the following command would be used:

```
# install -c /opt/scripts -m 0755 -u bin -g sysadmin /tmp/setup_scripts
```

Summary

In this chapter, we examined how to create shell initialization scripts, by examining how to set environment variables and execute commonly used script commands. In addition, we reviewed some basic shell script patterns, which can be used within *.profile* (and other shell scripts) to perform a wide variety of repetitive actions.

Questions

1. What is the name of the Bourne shell initialization script?

   A. *.cshrc*

   B. *.login*

   C. *.profile*

   D. *.init*

2. What is the name of the site-wide skeleton file for the Bourne shell initialization file?

   A. */etc/skel/local.cshrc*

   B. */etc/skel/local.login*

   C. */etc/skel/local.profile*

   D. */etc/skel/local.init*

3. What command would be used to set the value of the environment variable *TERM* to be vt220?"

   A. `TERM=vt220`

   B. `TERM='vt220'`

   C. `TERM=vt220`

   D. `setenv TERM='vt220'`

4. What escape string is used to print an ASCII beep character in a shell prompt?

   A. `\a`

   B. `\d`

   C. `\h`

   D. `\H`

5. What escape string is used to print a date string in a shell prompt?

   A. `\a`

   B. `\d`

   C. `\h`

   D. `\H`

6. What escape string is used to print the full hostname in a shell prompt?

   A. \a

   B. \d

   C. \h

   D. \H

7. What escape string is used to print a short hostname in a shell prompt?

   A. \a

   B. \d

   C. \h

   D. \H

8. What command is used to source another shell script while maintaining all environment settings?

   A. source

   B. sh

   C. .

   D. ./

9. What command would be used to display the string "Status OK" while *.profile* was being executed during shell initialization?

   A. println "Status OK"

   B. printf "Status OK"

   C. echo "Status OK"

   D. cat "Status OK" > /dev/null

10. What parameter is used with the test command to determine whether a file is a special block file?

    A. -b

    B. -block

    C. -blockfile

    D. -bf

Answers

1. C. The name of the Bourne shell initialization script is *.profile*.

2. C. The name of the site-wide skeleton file for the Bourne shell initialization file is */etc/skel/local.profile*.

3. **A.** TERM=vt220 will set the environment variable for the terminal type to vt220.

4. **A.** The ASCII beep character is \a.

5. **B.** The date string is represented by \d.

6. **D.** The shell prompt is set by \H.

7. **C.** The short hostname is represented by \h.

8. **C.** The source command is ".".

9. **C.** The command echo "Status OK" will display the "Status OK" string.

10. **A.** The −b option is used to test for special block files.

Disk Configuration and Naming

In this chapter, you will
- Gain an understanding of Solaris physical device names
- Gain an understanding of Solaris logical device names
- Learn how to use the `format` and `dmesg` commands to review system hardware
- Learn to display the system configuration with the `prtconf` command

Configuring and naming disks is a key administrative task. Solaris provides a number of complementary schemes for naming disks, file systems, slices, and partitions, which we examine in this chapter.

Physical and Logical Device Names

One of the most challenging aspects of understanding Solaris hardware is the device names and references used by Solaris to manage devices. Solaris uses a very specific set of naming conventions to associate physical devices with instance names on the operating system. For administrators who are new to Solaris, this can be incredibly confusing. In addition, devices can also be referred to by their device name, which is associated with a device file created in the */dev* directory after configuration. For example, a hard disk may have the physical device name /pci@1f,0/pci@1,1/ide@3/dad@0,0, which is associated with the device file */dev/dsk/c0t0d0*. In Microsoft Windows, disks are simply labeled by their drive letter (C:, D:, E: and so forth), while in Linux, device files are much simplified (for example, */dev/hda* for an IDE hard disk, or */dev/sda* for a SCSI hard disk). The benefit of the more complex Solaris logical device names and physical device references is that it is easy to interpret the characteristics of each device by simply looking at its name. For the disk example given above, we can see that the IDE hard drive is located on a PCI bus at target 0. When we view the amount of free disk space on the system, for example, it is easy to identify slices on the same disk by looking at the device name:

```
# df -k
Filesystem             kbytes    used   avail capacity  Mounted on
/proc                       0       0       0     0%    /proc
/dev/dsk/c0t0d0s0     1982988  615991 1307508    33%    /
```

```
fd                            0        0        0    0%   /dev/fd
/dev/dsk/c0t0d0s3       1487119   357511  1070124   26%   /usr
swap                     182040      416   181624    1%   /tmp
```

Here, we can see that */dev/dsk/c0t0d0s0* and */dev/dsk/c0t0d0s3* are slice 0 and slice 3 of the disk */dev/dsk/c0t0d0*.

The format Command

If you're ever unsure of which physical disk is associated with a specific disk device name, the `format` command will tell you:

```
# format
Searching for disks...done
AVAILABLE DISK SELECTIONS:
0. c1t3d0 <SUN2.1G cyl 2733 alt 2 hd 19 sec 80>
 /pci@1f,0/pci@1/scsi@1/sd@3,0
```

Here, we can see that physical device /pci@1f,0/pci@1/scsi@1/sd@3,0 is matched with the disk device */dev/dsk/c1t3d0* from the `df` output shown above.

TIP You can use the `format` command for this purpose without actually formatting a disk.

The /etc/path_to_inst File

A list of mappings between physical devices to instance names is always kept in the */etc/path_to_inst* file. In the following example, we review the device to instance name mapping for an SBUS-based SPARC system:

```
"/sbus@1f,0" 0 "sbus"
"/sbus@1f,0/sbusmem@2,0" 2 "sbusmem"
"/sbus@1f,0/sbusmem@3,0" 3 "sbusmem"
"/sbus@1f,0/sbusmem@0,0" 0 "sbusmem"
"/sbus@1f,0/sbusmem@1,0" 1 "sbusmem"
"/sbus@1f,0/SUNW,fas@2,8800000" 1 "fas"
"/sbus@1f,0/SUNW,fas@2,8800000/ses@f,0" 1 "ses"
"/sbus@1f,0/SUNW,fas@2,8800000/sd@1,0" 16 "sd"
"/sbus@1f,0/SUNW,fas@2,8800000/sd@0,0" 15 "sd"
"/sbus@1f,0/SUNW,fas@2,8800000/sd@3,0" 18 "sd"
"/sbus@1f,0/SUNW,fas@2,8800000/sd@2,0" 17 "sd"
"/sbus@1f,0/SUNW,fas@2,8800000/sd@5,0" 20 "sd"
"/sbus@1f,0/SUNW,fas@2,8800000/sd@4,0" 19 "sd"
"/sbus@1f,0/SUNW,fas@2,8800000/sd@6,0" 21 "sd"
"/sbus@1f,0/SUNW,fas@2,8800000/sd@9,0" 23 "sd"
"/sbus@1f,0/SUNW,fas@2,8800000/sd@8,0" 22 "sd"
"/sbus@1f,0/SUNW,fas@2,8800000/sd@a,0" 24 "sd"
"/sbus@1f,0/SUNW,fas@2,8800000/st@1,0" 8 "st"
"/sbus@1f,0/SUNW,fas@2,8800000/st@0,0" 7 "st"
"/sbus@1f,0/SUNW,fas@2,8800000/sd@c,0" 26 "sd"
"/sbus@1f,0/SUNW,fas@2,8800000/st@3,0" 10 "st"
```

```
"/sbus@1f,0/SUNW,fas@2,8800000/sd@b,0" 25 "sd"
"/sbus@1f,0/SUNW,fas@2,8800000/st@2,0" 9 "st"
"/sbus@1f,0/SUNW,fas@2,8800000/sd@e,0" 28 "sd"
"/sbus@1f,0/SUNW,fas@2,8800000/st@5,0" 12 "st"
"/sbus@1f,0/SUNW,fas@2,8800000/sd@d,0" 27 "sd"
"/sbus@1f,0/SUNW,fas@2,8800000/st@4,0" 11 "st"
"/sbus@1f,0/SUNW,fas@2,8800000/sd@f,0" 29 "sd"
"/sbus@1f,0/SUNW,fas@2,8800000/st@6,0" 13 "st"
"/sbus@1f,0/SUNW,CS4231@d,c000000" 0 "audiocs"
"/sbus@1f,0/dma@0,81000" 0 "dma"
"/sbus@1f,0/dma@0,81000/esp@0,80000" 0 "esp"
"/sbus@1f,0/dma@0,81000/esp@0,80000/sd@0,0" 30 "sd"
"/sbus@1f,0/dma@0,81000/esp@0,80000/sd@1,0" 31 "sd"
"/sbus@1f,0/dma@0,81000/esp@0,80000/sd@2,0" 32 "sd"
"/sbus@1f,0/dma@0,81000/esp@0,80000/sd@3,0" 33 "sd"
"/sbus@1f,0/dma@0,81000/esp@0,80000/sd@4,0" 34 "sd"
"/sbus@1f,0/dma@0,81000/esp@0,80000/sd@5,0" 35 "sd"
"/sbus@1f,0/dma@0,81000/esp@0,80000/sd@6,0" 36 "sd"
"/sbus@1f,0/dma@0,81000/esp@0,80000/st@0,0" 14 "st"
"/sbus@1f,0/dma@0,81000/esp@0,80000/st@1,0" 15 "st"
"/sbus@1f,0/dma@0,81000/esp@0,80000/st@2,0" 16 "st"
"/sbus@1f,0/dma@0,81000/esp@0,80000/st@3,0" 17 "st"
"/sbus@1f,0/dma@0,81000/esp@0,80000/st@4,0" 18 "st"
"/sbus@1f,0/dma@0,81000/esp@0,80000/st@5,0" 19 "st"
"/sbus@1f,0/dma@0,81000/esp@0,80000/st@6,0" 20 "st"
"/sbus@1f,0/sbusmem@f,0" 15 "sbusmem"
"/sbus@1f,0/sbusmem@d,0" 13 "sbusmem"
"/sbus@1f,0/sbusmem@e,0" 14 "sbusmem"
"/sbus@1f,0/cgthree@1,0" 0 "cgthree"
"/sbus@1f,0/SUNW,hme@e,8c00000" 0 "hme"
"/sbus@1f,0/zs@f,1000000" 1 "zs"
"/sbus@1f,0/zs@f,1100000" 0 "zs"
"/sbus@1f,0/SUNW,bpp@e,c800000" 0 "bpp"
"/sbus@1f,0/lebuffer@0,40000" 0 "lebuffer"
"/sbus@1f,0/lebuffer@0,40000/le@0,60000" 0 "le"
"/sbus@1f,0/SUNW,hme@2,8c00000" 1 "hme"
"/sbus@1f,0/SUNW,fdtwo@f,1400000" 0 "fd"
"/options" 0 "options"
"/pseudo" 0 "pseudo"
```

Here, we can see entries for the network interface /sbus@1f,0/SUNW,hme@2,8c00000, as well as the floppy disk /sbus@1f,0/SUNW,fdtwo@f,1400000 and the SBUS sbus@1f,0. For a PCI-based system, like a Sun Blade 100, the output would look like this:

```
"/pci@1f,0" 0 "pcipsy"
"/pci@1f,0/isa@7" 0 "ebus"
"/pci@1f,0/isa@7/power@0,800" 0 "power"
"/pci@1f,0/isa@7/dma@0,0" 0 "isadma"
"/pci@1f,0/isa@7/dma@0,0/parallel@0,378" 0 "ecpp"
"/pci@1f,0/isa@7/dma@0,0/floppy@0,3f0" 0 "fd"
"/pci@1f,0/isa@7/serial@0,2e8" 1 "su"
"/pci@1f,0/isa@7/serial@0,3f8" 0 "su"
"/pci@1f,0/pmu@3" 0 "pmubus"
"/pci@1f,0/pmu@3/i2c@0" 0 "smbus"
"/pci@1f,0/pmu@3/i2c@0/temperature@30" 0 "max1617"
"/pci@1f,0/pmu@3/i2c@0/card-reader@40" 0 "scmi2c"
"/pci@1f,0/pmu@3/i2c@0/dimm@a0" 0 "seeprom"
```

```
"/pci@1f,0/pmu@3/fan-control@0" 0 "grfans"
"/pci@1f,0/pmu@3/ppm@0" 0 "grppm"
"/pci@1f,0/pmu@3/beep@0" 0 "grbeep"
"/pci@1f,0/ebus@c" 1 "ebus"
"/pci@1f,0/usb@c,3" 0 "ohci"
"/pci@1f,0/usb@c,3/mouse@2" 0 "hid"
"/pci@1f,0/usb@c,3/keyboard@4" 1 "hid"
"/pci@1f,0/firewire@c,2" 0 "hci1394"
"/pci@1f,0/ide@d" 0 "uata"
"/pci@1f,0/ide@d/dad@0,0" 0 "dad"
"/pci@1f,0/ide@d/sd@1,0" 0 "sd"
"/pci@1f,0/sound@8" 0 "audiots"
"/pci@1f,0/SUNW,m64B@13" 0 "m64"
"/pci@1f,0/network@c,1" 0 "eri"
"/pci@1f,0/pci@5" 0 "pci_pci"
"/options" 0 "options"
"/SUNW,UltraSPARC-IIe@0,0" 0 "us"
"/pseudo" 0 "pseudo"
```

Here, we can see that all of the "sbus" entries have been replaced by the "pci" entries, and that the network interface is no longer an hme, but an eri ("/pci@1f,0/network@c,1" 0 "eri"). In addition, some completely new types of hardware, such as a smart card reader ("/pci@1f,0/pmu@3/i2c@0/card-reader@40" 0 "scmi2c") are also available.

The dmesg Command

The dmesg command is often used to determine whether specific device drivers, for network interfaces and mass storage devices, have been correctly loaded at boot time.

 TIP While its functions have largely been taken over by the syslog daemon (syslogd), dmesg provides a useful record of error and status messages printed by the kernel.

When the system boots, several status messages of log level *kern.notice* will be recorded, and can be subsequently retrieved by using dmesg:

```
May 15 14:23:16 austin genunix: [ID 540533 kern.notice]
   SunOS Release 5.9 Version Generic_112233-01 64-bit
May 15 14:23:16 austin genunix: [ID 784649 kern.notice]
   Copyright 1983-2000 Sun Microsystems, Inc.  All rights reserved.
May 15 14:23:16 austin genunix: [ID 678236 kern.info]
   Ethernet address = 0:3:ba:4:a4:e8
May 15 14:23:16 austin unix: [ID 389951 kern.info]
   mem = 131072K (0x8000000)
May 15 14:23:16 austin unix: [ID 930857 kern.info]
   avail mem = 121085952
```

Here, we can see that a 64-bit kernel has been loaded successfully, for SunOS 5.9 (Solaris 9). Sun's copyright banner is also recorded, along with the Ethernet address of the primary network interface card (0:3:ba:4:a4:e8), the amount of installed RAM, and the amount of currently available RAM after the kernel has been loaded.

Before the kernel begins loading device drivers, it performs an integrity check to determine if any naming conflicts exist. If a conflict is found, it is logged for future reference and action:

```
May 15 14:23:16 austin genunix: [ID 723599 kern.warning] WARNING: Driver
alias "cal" conflicts with an existing driver name or alias.
```

Here, we can see that the device driver alias "cal" has been used more than once, giving rise to a naming conflict. Next, details about the system architecture and its main bus type are displayed:

```
May 15 14:23:16 austin rootnex: [ID 466748 kern.info]
  root nexus = Sun Blade 100 (UltraSPARC-IIe)
May 15 14:23:16 austin rootnex: [ID 349649 kern.info]
  pcipsy0 at root: UPA 0x1f 0x0
May 15 14:23:16 austin genunix: [ID 936769 kern.info]
  pcipsy0 is /pci@1f,0
May 15 14:23:16 austin pcipsy: [ID 370704 kern.info]
  PCI-device: pmu@3, pmubus0
May 15 14:23:16 austin pcipsy: [ID 370704 kern.info]
  PCI-device: ppm@0, grppm0
May 15 14:23:16 austin genunix: [ID 936769 kern.info]
  grppm0 is /pci@1f,0/pmu@3/ppm@0
```

Here, we can see that the system is a Sun Blade 100, and that its PCI bus architecture has been correctly identified. The next stage involves identifying the hard drives attached to the system, as follows:

```
May 15 14:23:27 austin pcipsy: [ID 370704 kern.info] PCI-device: ide@d, uata0
May 15 14:23:27 austin genunix: [ID 936769 kern.info] uata0 is /pci@1f,0/ide@d
May 15 14:23:28 austin uata: [ID 114370 kern.info] dad0 at pci10b9,52290
May 15 14:23:28 austin uata: [ID 347839 kern.info]  target 0 lun 0
May 15 14:23:28 austin genunix: [ID 936769 kern.info]
  dad0 is /pci@1f,0/ide@d/dad@0,0
May 15 14:23:28 austin dada: [ID 365881 kern.info]
  <ST315320A cyl 29649 alt 2 hd 16 sec 63>
May 15 14:23:29 austin swapgeneric: [ID 308332 kern.info]
  root on /pci@1f,0/ide@d/disk@0,0:a fstype ufs
```

The IDE hard drive installed on the system has been correctly detected (/pci@1f,0/ide@d/dad@0,0), and has the label "ST315320A cyl 29649 alt 2 hd 16 sec 63." In addition, the file system type has been identified as native UFS.

The status of every device on the system is logged during device driver loading, so it's possible to use the dmesg command to determine whether drivers have been correctly loaded. In the following entry, the FDDI interface cannot be activated because it is not correctly installed:

```
May 15 14:26:38 austin smt: [ID 272566 kern.notice] smt0: nf FDDI driver is
not active.  Initialization of this driver cannot be completed.
```

The prtconf Command

If you're ever confused about the devices that have been detected on a system and are currently active, you can use the prtconf command to display their configuration details:

```
# prtconf
System Configuration:  Sun Microsystems   sun4u
Memory size: 128 Megabytes
```

Initially, the system architecture is displayed (sun4u in the case of an Ultra 5 workstation), along with the amount of physical RAM. What follows is a hierarchical list of all system peripherals and attached drivers (where appropriate), arranged in logical order—for example, all PCI devices listed under the pci node being associated with either pci instance #0 or pci instance #1:

```
System Peripherals (Software Nodes):
SUNW,Ultra-5_10
    packages (driver not attached)
        terminal-emulator (driver not attached)
        deblocker (driver not attached)
        obp-tftp (driver not attached)
        disk-label (driver not attached)
        SUNW,builtin-drivers (driver not attached)
        sun-keyboard (driver not attached)
        ufs-file-system (driver not attached)
    chosen (driver not attached)
    openprom (driver not attached)
        client-services (driver not attached)
    options, instance #0
    aliases (driver not attached)
    memory (driver not attached)
    virtual-memory (driver not attached)
    pci, instance #0
        pci, instance #0
            ebus, instance #0
                auxio (driver not attached)
                power, instance #0
                SUNW,pll (driver not attached)
                se, instance #0
                su, instance #0
                su, instance #1
                ecpp (driver not attached)
                fdthree, instance #0
                eeprom (driver not attached)
                flashprom (driver not attached)
                SUNW,CS4231 (driver not attached)
            network, instance #0
            SUNW,m64B (driver not attached)
            ide, instance #0
                disk (driver not attached)
                cdrom (driver not attached)
                dad, instance #0
                sd, instance #30
        pci, instance #1
            scsi, instance #0
                disk (driver not attached)
```

```
        tape (driver not attached)
        sd, instance #0 (driver not attached)
        sd, instance #1 (driver not attached)
        sd, instance #2 (driver not attached)
        sd, instance #3
        sd, instance #4 (driver not attached)
        sd, instance #5 (driver not attached)
        sd, instance #6 (driver not attached)
        sd, instance #7 (driver not attached)
        sd, instance #8 (driver not attached)
        sd, instance #9 (driver not attached)
        sd, instance #10 (driver not attached)
        sd, instance #11 (driver not attached)
        sd, instance #12 (driver not attached)
        sd, instance #13 (driver not attached)
        sd, instance #14 (driver not attached)
    scsi, instance #1
        disk (driver not attached)
        tape (driver not attached)
        sd, instance #15 (driver not attached)
        sd, instance #16 (driver not attached)
        sd, instance #17 (driver not attached)
        sd, instance #18 (driver not attached)
        sd, instance #19 (driver not attached)
        sd, instance #20 (driver not attached)
        sd, instance #21 (driver not attached)
        sd, instance #22 (driver not attached)
        sd, instance #23 (driver not attached)
        sd, instance #24 (driver not attached)
        sd, instance #25 (driver not attached)
        sd, instance #26 (driver not attached)
        sd, instance #27 (driver not attached)
        sd, instance #28 (driver not attached)
        sd, instance #29 (driver not attached)
SUNW,UltraSPARC-IIi (driver not attached)
SUNW,ffb, instance #0
pseudo, instance #0
```

mkfile

The mkfile command creates a file of a specified size that is padded with zeros. File sizes can be specified in gigabytes "g," megabytes "m," bytes "b," or kilobytes "k." For example, to create a 1-gigabyte file in */tmp/newfile*, the following command would be used:

```
# mkfile 1g /tmp/newfile
```

If disk blocks should not be allocated until a request from an application, then the -n option should be passed on the command line. This conserves disk space while ensuring that the file created does not exceed its maximum flagged size.

mkfs

The mkfs command creates a new file system on the raw disk device specified on the command line. The file system type is determined by the contents of the file */etc/*

default/fs. In most Solaris systems, the contents of this file are "LOCAL=ufs," indicating that UFS file systems are the default. If a different file system type is to be created, the -F option can be passed on to the command line, followed by the file system type. For example, to create a file system of type pcfs, which uses a standard FAT type on a floppy disk, the following command would be used:

```
# mkfs -F pcfs /dev/rdiskette
```

A number of aliases to the mkfs command are also available, which can be used to create file systems of different types directly. These commands include:

- mkfs_udfs Creates a Universal Disk File System (UDFS) format file system.
- mkfs_pcfs Creates a FAT format file system.
- mkfs_udfs Creates a UFS format file system.

In addition, passing the -m option displays the complete command string that was used to create the file system. This is useful for extracting and storing in a script to re-create the file system on another disk.

newfs

The newfs command uses the mkfs command to create UFS file systems. The main difference is the number of parameters that can be passed to newfs to tune the file system during creation. The following parameters can be used to specify file system parameters:

- -a *n*   Specifies *n* blocks to be held in reserve to replace bad blocks.
- -b *n*   Sets the block size on the file system to be *n* bytes.
- -c *n*   Indicates that *n* cylinders should be allocated to each cylinder group.
- -C *n*   Specifies *n* as the maximum number of contiguous disk blocks per file.
- -d *n*   Sets the rotational delay to *n* milliseconds.
- -f *n*   Sets the smallest disk fragment for a single file to *n* bytes.
- -i *n*   Specifies that *n* bytes should be allocated to each inode.
- -m *n*   Specifies that *n* percent of the physical file system should be reserved as free.
- -n *n*   Sets the number of different group cylinder rotations to *n*.
- -r *n*   Sets the disk speed to *n* revolutions per minute.
- -s *n*   Sets the disk size to *n* sectors.
- -t *n*   Specifies that *n* tracks be allocated to each cylinder.

For most applications, the defaults selected by newfs will provide adequate performance. However, some specialized applications do require smaller or larger disk minimum fragments or block sizes for their file systems, and these can easily be set during file system creation. Since most modern disks are greater than 1G in capacity, most capacities will be specified in gigabytes.

lofiadm

The `lofiadm` command is used to initialize a file on an existing partition that is labeled as a raw device, by making use of the loopback file device driver. A new file system can then be created on the device by using `newfs` or `mkfs` as if it was a separate partition. This can be useful if a new partition needs to be created, but the disk cannot be easily reformatted—particularly if it's only required temporarily.

To create a file system on a file, the `mkfile` command should be used to create a file to be a specific size. Next, the association between the file and the loopback file device driver needs to be made. For example, if the file */tmp/datafile* was created with `mkfile`, the following command would create the association:

```
# lofiadm -a /tmp/datafile /dev/lofi/2
```

Finally, a new file system can be created by using the `newfs` command:

```
# newfs /dev/rlofi/2
newfs: construct a new file system /dev/rlofi/2: (y/n)? y
```

The file system can then be mounted on a mount point (such as */testdata*) as required:

```
# mount /dev/lofi/2 /testdata
```

When the file system is no longer required, the `umount` command can be used to remove the file system from operation, while the `lofiadm` command can be used to remove the association between the file and the loopback file device driver:

```
# umount /testdata
# lofiadm -d /tmp/datafile
```

sync

The `sync` command is generally executed prior to a shutdown or halt, to flush all disk buffers and write the superblock. This ensures data integrity is preserved when the system is either rebooted or where the run level is modified. It is simply executed without options as shown next:

```
# sync
```

tunefs

The `tunefs` command allows a file system's performance to be tuned to specific requirements. The key setting that can be modified is optimization for speed of execution or amount of disk space required. Generally, unless a system is critically low on disk space, it is best to optimize for speed. The following options are supported:

- -a *n* Specifies *n* blocks be written before a pause in rotation.
- -e *n* Specifies *n* as the maximum number of contiguous disk blocks per file.
- -d *n* Sets the rotational delay to *n* milliseconds.
- -m *n* Specifies that *n* percent of the physical file system should be reserved as free.
- -o *key* Optimizes the file system for a *key*, which is either "time" or "space."

Summary

In this chapter, we've examined how to use various commands to determine the status of devices (particularly disk devices) that are attached to the system. In addition, we looked at how to match up Solaris logical device names to physical device references, which can be difficult for newcomers.

Questions

1. Which of the following is a valid device name for an IDE hard drive?

   A. /pci@1f,0/pci@1,1/ide@3/dad@0,0

   B. /sbus@1f,0/SUNW,fas@2,8800000/sd@c,0

   C. /sbus@1f,0/SUNW,fas@2,8800000/ide@c,0

   D. /pci@1f,0/pci@1,1/ide@3/dad@x,x

2. Which of the following is a valid "available device" selection for the `format` command?

   A. c1t3d0 <SUN2.1G cyl 2733 alt 2 hd 19 sec 80>

   B. /pci@1f,0/pci@1/scsi@1/sd@3,0

   C. /pci@1f,0/pci@1/scsi@1/sd@3,0 <SUN2.1G cyl 2733 alt 2 hd 19 sec 80>

   D. c1t3d0 </pci@1f,0/pci@1/scsi@1/sd@3,0>

3. The /etc/path_to_inst file contains what?

   A. A list of all physical device names

   B. A list of all installed device drivers

   C. A list of mappings between device drivers and their filenames

   D. A list of mappings between physical devices and instance names

4. What error message might be displayed if a hardware device was not installed, but the kernel loaded its device driver?

  A. May 15 14:23:16 hostname genunix: [ID 723599 kern.warning] WARNING: Driver alias "name" conflicts with an existing driver name or alias.

  B. May 15 14:26:38 hostname smt: [ID 272566 kern.notice] device is not active (conflicts with an existing driver name or alias). Initialization of this driver cannot be completed.

  C. May 15 14:26:38 hostname smt: [ID 272566 kern.notice] device is not active. Initialization of this driver cannot be completed.

  D. May 15 14:26:38 hostname smt: [ID 272566 kern.info] device is not active. Initialization of this driver cannot be completed.

5. What does `prtconf` *not* display?

  A. System peripherals (software nodes)

  B. System architecture type

  C. Physical memory installed

  D. Virtual memory installed

6. What command would be used to create a loopback file system on */dev/rlofi/2*?

  A. `newfs /dev/rlofi/2`

  B. `createfs /dev/rlofi/2`

  C. `format /dev/rlofi/2`

  D. `lofiadm /dev/rlofi/2`

7. What command would be used to create a MS-DOS file system on a floppy disk?

  A. `mkfs -F dos /dev/rdiskette`

  B. `mkfs -F pcfs /dev/rdiskette`

  C. `mkfs -F pcfs /dev/dsk/floppy`

  D. `mkfs -F dos /dev/dsk/floppy`

8. What command would be used to create a new file */tmp/newfile* with a 2G capacity?

  A. `newfile 2g /tmp/newfile`

  B. `mkfile 2g /tmp/newfile`

  C. `makefile 2g /tmp/newfile`

  D. `newfs 2g /tmp/newfile`

9. What command creates a new FAT file system?

   A. mkfs_dos

   B. mkfs_fat

   C. mkfs_pcfs

   D. mkfs_cifs

10. Which of the following statements is true?

   A. tunefs tunes for both "time" and "space"

   B. tunefs tunes for "time" only

   C. tunefs tunes for "space" only

   D. tunefs tunes for "space" or "time"

Answers

1. **A.** Only /pci@1f,0/pci@1,1/ide@3/dad@0,0 is a valid IDE drive name.

2. **A.** Available device descriptions contain the disk name and label (c1t3d0 <SUN2.1G cyl 2733 alt 2 hd 19 sec 80).

3. **D.** The *path_to_inst* file contains a list of mappings between physical devices and instance names.

4. **C.** Only "hostname smt: [ID 272566 kern.notice] device is not active. Initialization of this driver cannot be completed." is valid.

5. **D.** prtconf does not query virtual memory.

6. **A.** newfs is always used to create file systems in this context.

7. **B.** pcfs is the file system type and */dev/rdiskette* is the floppy device.

8. **B.** The mkfile command is used to make files of a specified capacity.

9. **C.** The mkfs_pcfs command is valid in this context.

10. **D.** The tunefs command must optimize for either speed or time.

Disk Partitions and Format

In this chapter, you will

- Gain an understanding of hard disk layouts
- Learn about formatting disks
- Learn to create new file systems

Before disks can be used to host file systems, they must be formatted using the Solaris format program. When assigning file systems to slices, the administrators can generally choose their own slices. However, there are a number of standard conventions that should be obeyed. In this chapter, formatting and file system creation are covered in depth.

Hard Disk Layout

When formatted for operation with the Solaris operating system, hard disks are logically divided into one or more "slices" (or partitions) on which a single file system resides. File systems contain sets of files, which are hierarchically organized around a number of directories. The Solaris system contains a number of predefined directories that often form the top level of a file system hierarchy. Many of these directories lie one level below the root directory, often denoted by "/", which exists on the primary system disk of any Solaris system. In addition to a primary disk, many Solaris systems will have additional disks that provide storage space for user and daemon files. Each file system has a mount point, which is usually created in the top level of the root file system. For example, the */export* file system is obviously mounted in the top level of "/". The mount point is created by using the mkdir command:

```
# mkdir /export
```

In contrast, the */export/home* file system, which usually holds the home directories of users, and user files, is mounted in the top level of the */export* file system. Thus, the mount point is created by using this command:

```
# mkdir /export/home
```

A single logical file system can be created on a single slice, but cannot exist on more than one slice unless there is an extra level of abstraction between the logical and physical file systems (for example, a metadevice can be created using DiskSuite, providing striping across many physical disks). A physical disk can also contain more than one slice. On SPARC architecture systems, there are eight slices that can be used, numbered 0–7. On Intel architecture systems, however, there are ten available slices, numbered 0–9.

The actual assignment of logical file systems to physical slices is a matter of discretion for the individual administrator, and while there are customary assignments recommended by Sun and other hardware vendors, it is possible that a specific site policy (or an application's requirements) necessitates the development of a local policy. For example, database servers often make quite specific requirements about the allocation of disk slices to improve performance. However, with modern high-performance RAID systems, these recommendations are often redundant.

TIP Since many organizations will have many different kinds of systems deployed, it is useful to maintain compatibility between systems as much as possible.

Figure 13-1 shows the typical file system layout for a SPARC architecture system following customary disk slice allocations. Slice 0 holds the root partition, while slice 1 is allocated to swap space. For systems with changing virtual memory requirements, it might be better to use a swap file on the file system rather than allocating an entire slice for swap. Slice 2 often refers to the entire disk, while /export on slice 3 traditionally holds older versions of the operating system, which are used by client systems with lower performance (for example, Classic or LX systems that use the trivial FTP daemon, tftpd, to download their operating system upon boot). These systems may also use slice 4 as exported swap space. Export may also be used for file sharing using the networked file system, NFS. Slice 5 holds the /opt file system, which is the default location under Solaris 9 for local packages installed using the pkgadd command. Under earlier versions of Solaris, the /usr/local file system held local packages, and this convention is still used by many sites. The system package file system /usr is usually located on slice 6, while /export/home usually contains user home directories on slice 7. Again, earlier systems located user home directories under /home, but since this is used by the automounter program in Solaris 9, some contention can be expected.

Figure 13-2 shows the typical file system layout for an Intel architecture system following customary disk slice allocations. Slice 0 again holds the root partition, while slice 1 is also allocated to swap space. Slice 2 continues to refer to the entire disk, while /export on slice 3 again holds older versions of the operating system, which are used by client systems, and slice 4 contains exported swap space for these clients. The local package file system /opt is still located on slice 5, and the system package file system /usr is again located on slice 6. Slice 7 contains the user home directories on /export/home. However, the two extra slices serve very different purposes: boot information for Solaris is located on slice 8, and is known as the "boot slice," while slice 9 provides space for alternative disk blocks, and is known as the "alternative slice."

Figure 13-1
Typical file
system layout
for a SPARC
architecture
system

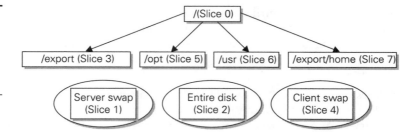

Formatting

Hard disk installation and configuration on Solaris is often more complicated than other UNIX systems. However, this complexity is required to support the sophisticated hardware operations typically undertaken by Solaris systems. For example, Linux refers to hard disks using a simple BSD-style scheme: */dev/hd*n are the IDE hard disks on a system, and */dev/sd*n are the SCSI hard disks on a system, where *n* refers to the hard disk number. A system with two IDE hard disks and two SCSI hard disks will therefore have the following device files configured:

```
/dev/had
/dev/hdb
/dev/sda
/dev/sdb
```

Partitions created on each drive are also sequentially numbered: if */dev/hda* is the boot disk, it may contain several partitions on the disk, reflecting the basic UNIX system directories:

```
/dev/hda1 (/ partition)
/dev/hda2 (/usr)
/dev/hda3 (/var)
/dev/hda4 (swap)
```

Figure 13-2
Typical file
system layout
for an Intel
architecture
system

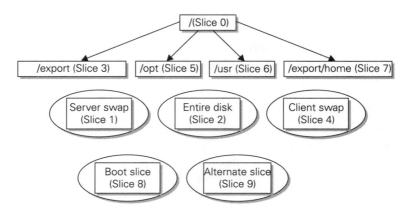

Instead of simply referring to the disk type, disk number, and partition number, the device filename for each partition ("slice") on a Solaris disk contains four identifiers: controller (c), target (t), disk (d), and slice (s). Thus, the device file

```
/dev/dsk/c0t3d0s0
```

identifies slice 0 of disk 0, controller 0 at SCSI target ID 3. To complicate matters further, disk device files exist in both the */dev/dsk* and */dev/rdsk* directories, which correspond to block device and raw device entries, respectively. Raw and block devices refer to the same physical partition, but are used in different contexts: using raw devices only allows operations of small amounts of data, whereas a buffer can be used with a block device to increase the data read size. It is not always clear whether to use a block or raw device interface, but low-level system commands (like the `fsck` command, which performs disk maintenance) typically use raw device interfaces.

Commands that operate on the entire disk (such as `df`, which reports disk usage) will most likely use block devices.

To install a new hard drive on a Solaris system, just follow these steps:

1. Prepare the system for a reconfiguration boot, by issuing this command:

   ```
   # touch /reconfigure
   ```

2. Synchronize disk data, and power down the system using this command:

   ```
   # sync; init 0
   ```

3. Switch off power to the system and attach the new hard disk to the external SCSI chain, or install it internally into an appropriate disk bay.

4. Check that the SCSI device ID does not conflict with any existing SCSI devices. If a conflict exists, simply change the ID using the switch;

5. Power on the system, and use the `boot` command to load the kernel, if the OpenBoot monitor appears:

   ```
   ok boot
   ```

The next step, assuming that you have decided which partitions you wish to create on your drive, using the information supplied above, is to run the format program. In addition to creating slices, format also displays information about existing disks and slices, and can be used to repair a faulty disk. When format is invoked without a command-line argument:

```
# format
```

it displays a list of the current disks, and asks the administrator to enter the number of the disk to format. Selecting a disk for formatting at this point is nondestructive, so even if you make a mistake you can always exit the format program without damaging data. For example, on a SPARC-20 system with three 1.05G SCSI disks, format opens with the screen:

```
Searching for disks...done
AVAILABLE DISK SELECTIONS:
0. c0t1d0 <SUN1.05 cyl 2036 alt 2 hd 14 sec 72>
```

```
/iommu@f,e0000000/sbus@f,e0001000/espdma@f,400000/esp@f,800000/
sd@1,0
1. c0t2d0 <SUN1.05 cyl 2036 alt 2 hd 14 sec 72>
/iommu@f,e0000000/sbus@f,e0001000/espdma@f,400000/esp@f,800000/
sd@2,0
2. c0t3d0 <SUN1.05 cyl 2036 alt 2 hd 14 sec 72>
/iommu@f,e0000000/sbus@f,e0001000/espdma@f,400000/esp@f,800000/
sd@3,0
Specify disk (enter its number):
```

It is also possible to pass a command-line option to format, comprising the disk (or disks) to be formatted—for example:

```
# format /dev/rdsk/c0t2d0
```

After selecting the appropriate disk, the message

```
[disk formatted]
```

will appear if the disk has previously been formatted. This is an important message, as it is a common mistake to misidentify a target disk from the available selection of both formatted and unformatted disks. The menu looks like this:

```
FORMAT MENU:
        disk       - select a disk
        type       - select (define) a disk type
        partition  - select (define) a partition table
        current    - describe the current disk
        format     - format and analyze the disk
        fdisk      - run the fdisk program
        repair     - repair a defective sector
        show       - translate a disk address
        label      - write label to the disk
        analyze    - surface analysis
        defect     - defect list management
        backup     - search for backup labels
        verify     - read and display labels
        save       - save new disk/partition definitions
        volname    - set 8-character volume name
        !<cmd>     - execute <cmd>, then return
        quit
format>
```

If the disk has not been formatted, the first step is to prepare the disk to contain slices and file systems by formatting the disk, by issuing the command format:

```
format> format
Ready to format. Formatting cannot be interrupted
and takes 15 minutes (estimated). Continue? yes
```

The purpose of formatting is to identify defective blocks, and mark them as bad, and generally to verify that the disk is operational from a hardware perspective. Once this has been completed, new slices can be created and sized by using the "partition" option at the main menu:

```
format> partition
```

In this case, we want to create a new slice 5 on disk 0 at target 3, which will be used to store user files when mounted as */export/home*, and corresponding to block device */dev/dsk/c0t2d0s5*. After determining the maximum amount of space available, enter that size in gigabytes (in this case, 1.05g) when requested to do so by the format program for slice 5 (enter 0 for the other slices). If the disk is not labeled, you will also be prompted to enter a label that contains details of the disk's current slices, which is useful for recovering data. This is an important step, as the operating system will not be able to find any newly created slices unless the volume is labeled. To view the disk label, use the prtvtoc command. Here's the output from the primary drive in an x86 system:

```
# prtvtoc /dev/dsk/c0d0s2
* /dev/dsk/c0d0s2 partition map
*
* Dimensions:
*       512 bytes/sector
*        63 sectors/track
*       255 tracks/cylinder
*     16065 sectors/cylinder
*      1020 cylinders
*      1018 accessible cylinders
*
* Flags:
*     1: unmountable
*    10: read-only
*
*                          First     Sector    Last
* Partition  Tag  Flags    Sector    Count     Sector   Mount Directory
       0      2    00       48195     160650    208844   /
       1      7    00      208845      64260    273104   /var
       2      5    00           0    16354170 16354169
       3      3    01      273105     321300    594404
       6      4    00      594405     1317330  1911734   /usr
       7      8    00     1911735    14442435 16354169   /export/home
       8      1    01           0       16065     16064
       9      9    01       16065       32130     48194
```

The disk label contains a full partition table, which can be printed for each disk using the print command:

```
format> print
```

For our 1.05g disk, the partition table will look like this:

```
Part Tag Flag Cylinders Size Blocks
0 root wm 0 0 (0/0/0) 0
1 swap wu 0 0 (0/0/0) 0
2 backup wm 0 - 3732 (3732/0/0) 2089920
3 unassigned wm 0 0 (0/0/0) 0
4 unassigned wm 0 0 (0/0/0) 0
5 home wm 0 - 3732 1075MB (3732/0/0) 2089920
6 usr wm 0 0 (0/0/0) 0
7 unassigned wm 0 0 (0/0/0) 0
```

After saving the changes to the disk's partition table, exit the format program and create a new UFS file system on the target slice using the newfs command:

```
# newfs /dev/rdsk/c0t2d0s5
```

For large disks, the −m flag should be used. After a new file system is constructed, it is ready to be mounted. First, a mount point is created

```
# mkdir /export/home
```

followed by the appropriate mount command:

```
# mount /dev/dsk/c0t2d0s5 /export/home
```

At this point, the disk is available to the system for the current session. However, if you want the disk to be available after reboot, it is necessary to create an entry in the virtual file systems table, which is created from *etc/vfstab* file. An entry like

```
/dev/dsk/c0t2d0s5 /dev/rdsk/c0t2d0s5 /export/home ufs 2 yes −
```

contains details of the slice's block and raw devices, the mount point, the file system type, instructions for fsck, and most importantly, a flag to force mount at boot. If you require a journaling file system, then you would need to include the logging flag here.

For an x86 system, the output of format looks slightly different, given the differences in the way that devices are denoted:

```
AVAILABLE DISK SELECTIONS:
       0. c0d0 <DEFAULT cyl 1018 alt 2 hd 255 sec 63>
          /pci@0,0/pci-ide@7,1/ata@0/cmdk@0,0
Specify disk (enter its number):
```

The partition table is similar to that for the SPARC architecture systems:

```
partition> print
Current partition table (original):
Total disk cylinders available: 1018 + 2 (reserved cylinders)
```

Part	Tag	Flag	Cylinders	Size	Blocks	
0	root	wm	3 - 12	78.44MB	(10/0/0)	160650
1	var	wm	13 - 16	31.38MB	(4/0/0)	64260
2	backup	wm	0 - 1017	7.80GB	(1018/0/0)	16354170
3	swap	wu	17 - 36	156.88MB	(20/0/0)	321300
4	unassigned	wm	0	0	(0/0/0)	0
5	unassigned	wm	0	0	(0/0/0)	0
6	usr	wm	37 - 118	643.23MB	(82/0/0)	1317330
7	home	wm	119 - 1017	6.89GB	(899/0/0)	14442435
8	boot	wu	0 - 0	7.84MB	(1/0/0)	16065
9	alternates	wu	1 - 2	15.69MB	(2/0/0)	32130

Mounting Local File Systems

Solaris (UNIX File System, or UFS) file systems are mapped in a one-to-one relationship to physical slices, which makes it easy for you to associate file systems with partitions, even if the physical and logical device references are complex. For example, the slice */dev/dsk/c0t2d0s5* may be mounted on the mount point */export/home*.

Mount points are simply empty directories that have been created using the `mkdir` command. One of the nice features of the UFS is that it has a one-to-many mapping to potential mount points: this means that a file system can be mounted, and its files and directories can be manipulated, unmounted, and then remounted on a different mount point. All of the data that was modified when the file system was mounted using a different mount point are retained. For example, if you mount */dev/dsk/c0t2d0s5* on */export/home*, create a directory called *pwatters* (that is, */export/home/pwatters*), unmount the file system, and then remount it on */usr/local*, the content of the folder *pwatters* will still be available, albeit with a new absolute path (*/usr/local/pwatters*).

The following procedure can be used to mount a local file system:

```
# mkdir /export/home
# mount  /dev/dsk/c0t2d0s5 /export/home
# cd /export/home
# mkdir pwatters
# ls
pwatters
```

There is also nothing stopping you from mounting the file system on a different mount point, preserving all data:

```
# umount /export/home
# mkdir /usr/local
# mount  /dev/dsk/c0t2d0s5 /usr/local
# cd /usr/local
# ls
pwatters
```

The `mkdir` command is used to create mount points, which are equivalent to directories. If you wish to make a mount point one level below an existing directory, you can use the `mkdir` command with no options. However, if you want to make a mount point several directory levels below an existing directory, you will need to pass the option –p to the `mkdir` command. For example, the following command will create the mount point /staff, since the parent / directory already exists:

```
# mkdir /staff
```

However, to create the mount point */staff/nfs/pwatters*, you would use the –p option, if the directory */staff/nfs* did not already exist:

```
# mkdir -p /staff/nfs/pwatters
```

Once a mount point has been created, the `mount` command is used to attach the file system to the mount point. For example, to mount the file system */dev/dsk/c0t3d0s5* on the mount point */export/home*, you would use the following command:

```
# mount  /dev/dsk/c0t2d0s5 /export/home
```

The `mount` command assumes a UFS will be mounted. If the target file system is non-UFS, an option specifying the file system type will need to be passed on the command line using the –F options. Supported file system types include:

- *nfs* Network File System (NFS)
- *pcfs* MS-DOS formatted file system
- *s5fs* System V compliant file system

Details of all currently mounted files are kept in the */etc/mnttab* file. This file should never be directly edited, even by the superuser. The */etc/mnttab* file will contain entries similar to the following:

```
# cat /etc/mnttab
/dev/dsk/c0t0d0s0 / ufs rw,intr,largefiles,suid,dev=1100000 921334412
/proc /proc proc dev=2280000 922234443
fd /dev/fd fd rw,suid,dev=2240000 922234448
mnttab /etc/mnttab mntfs dev=2340000 922234442
swap /tmp tmpfs dev=1 922234451
/dev/dsk/c0t0d0s5 /usr ufs rw,intr,onerror=panic,suid,dev=1100005 922234441
```

Unmounting Local File Systems

In normal operations, a file system is mounted at boot time if its mount point and options are specified in the virtual file systems table (*/etc/vfstab*). The file system is unmounted before the system is shut down. However, at times, you may find it necessary to unmount a file system manually. For example, if the file system's integrity needs to be checked using the `fsck` command, the target file system must be unmounted. Alternatively, if the mount point of a file system is going to be modified, the file system needs to be unmounted from its current mount point and remounted on the new mount point.

CAUTION You cannot mount a file system on two different mount points.

Configuring /etc/vfstab

If you want a disk to be available after reboot, you must create an entry in the virtual file systems table (*/etc/vfstab*). An entry like this

```
/dev/dsk/c0t2d0s5 /dev/rdsk/c0t2d0s5 /export/home ufs 2 yes -
```

contains details of the slice's block and raw devices, the mount point, the file system type, instructions for fsck, and most importantly a flag to force the mount at boot.

TIP These options are largely equivalent to those used with the `mount` command.

All file systems, including floppy disks, can be listed in the virtual file systems table. The mount point configuration for the floppy drive is typically similar to the following:

```
fd  -  /dev/fd  fd  -  no  -
```

Instead of mounting file systems individually using the mount command, all file systems defined in */etc/vfstab* can be mounted by using the mountall command:

```
# mountall
mount: /tmp already mounted
mount: /dev/dsk/c0t0d0s5 is already mounted
```

This attempts to mount all listed file systems, and reports file systems that have previously been mounted. Obviously, file systems that are currently mounted cannot be mounted twice.

mount

The mount command, executed without any options, provides a list of all mounted file systems:

```
# mount
/ on /dev/dsk/c0t0d0s0 read/write/setuid/intr/largefiles/onerror=
    panic on Tue Jul 10 09:10:01 2001
/usr on /dev/dsk/c0t0d0s6 read/write/setuid/intr/largefiles/
    onerror=panic on Tue Jul 10 09:10:02 2001
/proc on /proc read/write/setuid on Tue Jul 10 09:10:03 2001
/etc/mnttab on mnttab read/write/setuid on Tue Jul 10 09:10:04 2001
/tmp on swap read/write/setuid on Tue Jul 10 09:10:05 2001
/export/home on /dev/dsk/c0t0d0s7 read/write/setuid/intr/largefiles
    /onerror=panic on Tue Jul 10 09:10:06 2001
```

The mount command has several options, which are described below. These can also be used to specify mounting options in */etc/vfstab*:

bg	If mounting initially fails, continue to attempt mounting in the background. Useful for mounting NFS volumes where the server is temporarily unavailable. The default is fg, which attempts to mount in the foreground.
hard	Specifies that hard mounting is attempted, where requests to mount are continually sent. The alternative is soft, which just returns an error message.
intr	Allows keyboard commands to be used during mounting. To switch this off, use nointr.
largefiles	Enables support for large file systems (those greater than 2GB in size). To remove support for large file systems, the nolargefiles option is used.
logging	Allows a log of all UFS transactions to be maintained. In the event of a system crash, the log can be consulted and all transactions verified. This virtually eliminates the need to run lengthy fsck passes on file systems at boot. The default option is nologging since logs occupy around 1 percent of file system space.
noatime	Prevents access timestamps from being touched on files. This significantly speeds up access times on large file systems with many small files.
remount	Permits a file system's properties to be modified while it is still mounted, reducing downtime.

retry	Specifies the number of attempts to remount a file system.
rw	Specifies that the file system is to be mounted as read-write. Some file systems, however, are read-only (such as CD-ROMs). In this case, the `ro` option should be specified. Note that it is not physically possible to write to a read-only file system.
suid	Permits set user ID applications to be executed from the file system, while `nosuid` prevents set user ID applications from executing.

umount

Unmounting local file systems is easy using the `umount` command. The file system to be unmounted is specified on the command line. For example, to unmount the file system mounted on *export/home*, the following command would be used:

```
# umount /export/home
```

However, if there are open files on the file system, or users logging into their home directories on the target file system, it's obviously a bad idea to unmount the file system without giving users some kind of notice. It's also important to determine whether other processes are using files on the file system. In fact, `umount` requires that no processes have files open on the target file system. The `fuser` command can be used to determine which users are accessing a particular file system. For example, to determine whether any processes have open files on the *export/home* partition, the following command could be used:

```
# fuser -c /export/home
```

To give a listing of the UIDs associated with each process, the following command could be used:

```
# fuser -c -u /export/home
```

To warn users about the impending unmounting of the file system, the `wall` command can be used to send a message to all logged in users. For example, the following message could be sent:

```
# wall
Attention all users
/export/home is going down for maintenance at 6:00 p.m.
Please kill all processes accessing this file system (or I will)
```

At 6 P.M., a `fuser` check should show that no processes are accessing the file system. However, if some users did not heed the warning, the `fuser` command can be used to kill all processes that are still active:

```
# fuser -c -k /export/home
```

Alternatively, `umount -f` might be used. This is obviously a drastic step, but it may be necessary in emergency or urgent repair situations.

To save time, if you wish to unmount all user file systems (excluding /, /proc, /usr, and /var), you could use the `umountall` command:

```
# umountall
```

This command unmounts only file systems that are listed in the virtual file system table, except the aforementioned exclusions.

Summary

In this chapter, we've examined the physical and logical layout of Solaris file systems, and how file systems can be created and configured. We also reviewed the differences between Solaris SPARC and Solaris Intel file systems, and examined how to mount file systems once they've been formatted.

Questions

1. What command would be used to create the mount point /work?

   A. `mkpoint /work`

   B. `mkmountpoint /work`

   C. `touch /work`

   D. `mkdir /work`

2. On a SPARC system, which partition is traditionally located on slice 0?

   A. /

   B. swap

   C. /export

   D. /opt

3. On a SPARC system, which partition is traditionally located on slice 1?

   A. /

   B. swap

   C. /export

   D. /opt

4. On a SPARC system, which partition is traditionally located on slice 3?

   A. /

   B. swap

   C. /export

   D. /opt

5. On a SPARC system, which partition is traditionally located on slice 5?

   A. /

   B. swap

   C. /export

   D. /opt

6. What device file identifies slice 0 of disk 0, controller 0 at SCSI target ID 3?

   A. */dev/dsk/c0t3d0s0*

   B. */dev/dsk/c3t0d0s0*

   C. */dev/dsk/c0t0d0s3*

   D. */dev/dsk/c0t3d0s3*

7. Which of the following is not a valid option under the format menu?

   A. disk

   B. slice

   C. partition

   D. format

8. What command could be used to determine whether any processes have open files on the */export/home* partition?

   A. `fuser -c /export/home`

   B. `lofiam -c /export/home`

   C. `stat -c /export/home`

   D. `openfile -c /export/home`

9. What command unmounts all user file systems (excluding /, */proc*, */usr*, and */var*)?

   A. `unmount`

   B. `unmountall`

   C. `umountall`

   D. `mount -f`

10. What command mounts all file systems defined in */etc/vfstab*?

    A. `mount`

    B. `mount -all`

    C. `mountall`

    D. `umountall`

Answers

1. **D.** The `mkdir` command creates mount points.

2. **A.** Slice 0 contains the / file system.

3. **B.** Slice 1 contains the *swap* file system.

4. **C.** Slice 3 contains the */export* file system.

5. **D.** Slice 5 contains the */opt* file system.

6. **A.** */dev/dsk/c0t3d0s0* identifies slice 0 of disk 0, controller 0 at SCSI target ID 3.

7. **B.** Slice is not a valid option for format.

8. **A.** The `fuser` command determines whether any processes have open files on the */export/home* partition.

9. **C.** The `umountall` command unmounts all user file systems (excluding /, */proc, /usr,* and */var*).

10. **C.** The `mountall` command mounts all file systems defined in */etc/vfstab.*

## CHAPTER 14

Backups

In this chapter, you will

- Gain a better understanding of backups
- Determining appropriate backup strategies
- Select a suitable backup medium
- Use ufsdump and ufsrestore
- Use tar, dd, and cpio

Software and hardware failures are an unfortunate fact of life in the IT industry. These incidents often cause a sense of panic in organizations when missing or corrupt data is revealed during a peak service period. However, a system crash or a disk failure should not be a cause for alarm: it should be the signal to a well-armed and well-prepared administrator to determine the cause of the problem, rectify any hardware faults, and restore any lost data by using a recovery procedure. This general procedure can be followed regardless of whether user files or database tables have been lost or corrupted. Fortunately, Solaris provides a wide variety of backup and restore software that can be used in conjunction with any number of media—for example, magnetic and digital audio tapes, writable CD-ROMs, Zip drives, and redundant hard drives. In this chapter, we will examine the development and implementation of backup and recovery procedures with Solaris.

Understanding Backups

In many companies, valuable data is stored on Solaris server systems, in user files and database tables. The variety of information stored is endless—personnel files, supplier invoices, receipts, and all kinds of intellectual property. In addition, many organizations provide some kind of service that relies on server uptime and information availability to generate income or maintain prestige. For example, if a major business-to-consumer web site or business-to-business hub experiences any downtime, every minute that the system is unavailable costs money in lost sales, frustrated consumers, and reduced customer confidence. Alternatively, a government site like the Government Accounting Office (**http://www.gao.gov/**) provides valuable advice to government, business, and consumers, and is expected to be available continuously.

CAUTION The reputation of online service providers suffers greatly if servers go down.

On a smaller scale, but just as significant, is the departmental server, which might provide file serving, authentication services, and print access for several hundred PC systems or Sun Rays. If the server hard disk crashes, the affected users who can't read their mail or retrieve their files are going to be very angry at 9:00 A.M. if system data cannot be restored in a timely fashion. In this section, we will examine the background and rationale for providing a reliable backup and restore service, which will in turn ensure a high level of service provision, even in the event of hardware failure.

Why Do You Need Backups?

The first requirement of a backup service is the ability to rapidly restore a dysfunctional system to a functional state. The relationship between time of restoration and user satisfaction is inverse, as shown in Figure 14-1—the longer a restore takes, the faster users will become angry, while the rapid restoration of service will give users confidence in the service they are using. For this reason, many sites will take incremental backups of their complete file systems each night, but may take a weekly "full dump" snapshot that can be used to rapidly rebuild an entire system from a single tape or disk.

The second requirement for a backup service is data integrity: it is not sufficient just to restore some data and hope that it's close enough to the original. It is essential that all restored data can actually be used by applications, as if no break in service had occurred. This is particularly important for database applications, which may have several different kinds of files associated with them. Table indices, data files, and rollback segments must all be synchronized if the database is to operate correctly, and user data must be consistent with the internal structure and table ownership rights. If files are simply backed up onto disk while the database is open, these files can be restored, but the database system may not be able to use the files. It is essential to understand the restoration and data integrity requirements for all key applications on your system, and identify any risks to service provision associated with data corruption.

 TIP A comprehensive backup and restore plan should include provision for regular cold and warm dumps of databases to a file system that is regularly backed up.

Figure 14-1
The relationship between time to restore and user satisfaction is inverse.

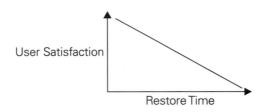

A third requirement for a backup and restore service is flexibility: data should be recorded and compressed on media that can potentially be read on a different machine, using a different operating system. In addition, using alternative media concurrently for concurrent backups is also useful for ensuring availability in case of hardware failure of a backup device. For example, you may use a DDS-3 DAT tape drive as your main backup device for nightly incremental backups, but you may also decide to burn a weekly CD-R containing a full dump of the database. If your server was affected by a power surge, and the DAT drive was damaged, and a replacement would take one week to arrive, then the CD-R dump can be used as a fallback even though it may not be completely up-to-date.

Determining a Backup Strategy

Typical backup and restore strategies employ two related methods for recording data to any medium: incremental and full dumps. A full dump involves taking a copy of an entire file system or set of file systems and copying it to a backup medium. Historically, large file systems have taken a long time to back up because of slow tape speeds and poor I/O performance, leading to the development of the incremental method. An incremental dump is an iterative method that involves taking a baseline dump on a regular basis (usually once every week), and then taking a further dump every day, of files that have changed since the previous full dump. Although this approach can require the maintenance of complex lists of files and file sizes, it reduces the overall time to back up a file system because on most file systems only a small proportion of the total number of files changes from week to week. This reduces the overall load on the backup server, and improves tape performance by minimizing friction on drive heads. However, using incremental backups can increase the time to restore a system, as up to seven backup tapes must be processed in order to restore data files fully. Therefore, a balance must be struck between convenience and the requirement for a speedy restore in the event of an emergency.

TIP Many sites use a combination of incremental and full daily dumps on multiple media to ensure that full restores can be performed rapidly, and to ensure redundant recording of key data.

After deciding on an incremental or full dump backup strategy, it is important to then plan how backups can be integrated into an existing network. There are four possible configurations that can be considered. The simplest approach is to attach a single backup device to each server, so that it acts as its own backup host. A possible configuration is shown in Figure 14-2.

Figure 14-2
Single server
and single
backup device
configuration

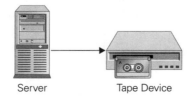

Server   Tape Device

Figure 14-3

Single server
and multiple
backup device
configuration

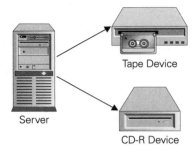

Tape Device

Server

CD-R Device

This approach is appealing because it allows data to be backed up and restored using the same device, without any requirement for network connectivity. However, it does not provide for redundancy through the use of multiple backup devices. This can be rectified by including multiple backup devices for a single host. This configuration is shown in Figure 14-3.

The cost of maintaining single or multiple backup devices for each server in an organization can be very expensive. In order to reduce cost, many organizations have moved to centralize the management and storage of data for entire departments or sites on a single server. This approach is detailed in Figure 14-4. Multiple client machines can have their local hard drives backed up to a central Solaris server, whether or not those clients are PCs running windows or other Solaris servers. The central backup server can also be attached to multiple backup devices, providing different levels of redundancy for more or less significant data. For example, data from user PCs may not require double or triple redundancy, which financial records might well deserve.

There is also an increasing trend towards developing "storage area networks" (SANs), where backup management and data storage are distributed across multiple backup hosts and multiple devices. Thus, a client's data could potentially be stored on many different backup servers, and management of that data could be performed from a remote manager running on the client. This configuration is shown in Figure 14-5. For example, there is a Veritas client for Windows called Backup Exec, which can connect to many different

Figure 14-4

Centralized
backup server
with multiple
storage devices

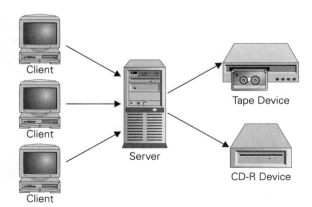

Client

Client

Server

Tape Device

Client

CD-R Device

Figure 14-5
Distributed
storage and
management of
backup services

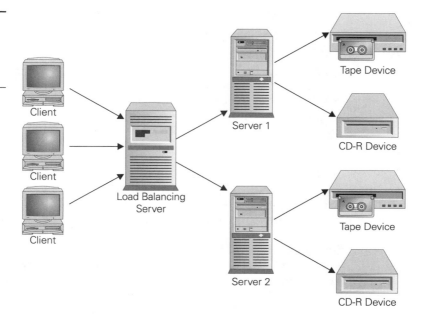

Solaris servers through an SMB service, backing up data to multiple mediums. Other server-side packages, such as Legato Networker, offer distributed management of all backup services. New to the game is Sun's own Java-based Jiro technology, which implements the proposed Federated Management Architecture (FMA) standard. FMA is one proposal for implementing distributed storage across networks in a standard way, and is receiving support from major hardware manufacturers like Hitachi, Quantum, Veritas, and Fujitsu for future integration with their products.

 TIP   More information on Jiro and FMA can be found at **http://www.jiro.com/**.

 EXAM TIP   You should be able to identify the different backup and restore strategies, and their strengths and weaknesses.

Selecting Backup Media

Selecting a backup medium should always attempt to best meet the requirements of rapid restoration, data integrity and flexibility. The four main media currently in use include tapes, disk drives, Zip and Jaz drives, and CD writing and CD rewriting technologies. Capacity and reliability criteria must also be considered—for example, while tapes are generally considered very reliable for bulk storage, tape drives are much slower than a hard drive. However, a 20G tape is much cheaper than an equivalent capacity hard drive, so the cost of any backup solutions must be weighed against the value of the data being stored.

 TIP For more information on choosing a bulk storage device, see the FAQ for the USENET forum **comp.arch.storage** at **http://alumni.caltech.edu/~rdv/comp-arch-storage/FAQ-1.html**.

Tape

Solaris supports tape drives from the old Archive "Quarter Inch Cartridge" QIC 150 1/4" tape drives (with a maximum 250M capacity), up to modern digital audio tape (DAT) and DLT systems. The QIC is a low-end drive that takes a two-reel cassette, which was widely in many early Sun workstations. DAT tapes for DDS-2 drives have a capacity of 4–8GB, while tapes for the newer DDS-3 standard have 12–24GB capacity, depending on compression ratios. DDS-2 drives can typically record between 400K and 800K per second, again depending on compression ratios. The transition from analog to digital encoding methods has increased the performance and reliability of tape-based backup methods, and they are still the most commonly used methods today. On the other hand, digital linear tape (DLT) drives are becoming more popular in the enterprise because of their very large storage capacities—for example, a Compaq 1624 DLT drive can store 35–70GB, depending on compression, which is much more than the DAT drives. They also feature much higher transfer rates of 1.25–2.5 megabytes per second. Of course, DLT drives are more expensive than DAT drives, and DAT drives have always been more costly than a QIC, although a QIC is generally much too small to be useful for most systems today.

Hard Drives

Since hard drives have the fastest seek times of all backup media, they are often used to store archives of user files, copied from client drives using an SMB service. In addition, hard drives form the basis of so-called RAID systems, or redundant array of inexpensive disks. Thus, an array of RAID drives can work together as a single, logical storage device, and collectively act as a single storage system that can withstand the loss of one or more of its constituent devices. For example, if a single drive is damaged by a power surge, then depending on the "level" of RAID protection, your system may be able to continue its functions with a minimum of administrator interference, with no impact on functionality, until the drive is replaced. Many systems now support hot-swapping of drives, so that the faulty drive can be removed and replaced, with the new drive coming seamlessly online. You may be wondering why, in the days of RAID, anybody would consider still using backups: the answer is that entire RAID arrays are just as vulnerable to power surges as a single drive, and so in the event of a full hardware failure, all your

PART I

data could still be lost unless it is stored safely offsite in a tape or CD-ROM. To circumvent concurrent drive corruption at the end of a disk's life, many administrators use drives of equivalent capacities from different manufacturers, some new and some used, in a RAID array. This ensures that drives are least likely to fail concurrently.

RAID has six levels that are numbered 0–5, although RAID levels 0 and 1 are most commonly used. RAID level 0 involves parallelizing data transfer between disks—spreading data across multiple drives, thereby improving overall data transmission rates. This technique is known as "striping." However, while RAID level 0 has the ability to write multiple disks concurrently, it does not support redundancy, which is provided with RAID level 1. This level makes an identical copy of a primary disk onto a secondary disk. This kind of "mirroring" provides complete redundancy: if the primary disk fails, the secondary disk is then able to provide all data contained on the primary disk until the primary disk is replaced. Because striping and mirroring consume large amounts of disk space, they are costly to maintain per megabyte of actual data. Thus, higher RAID levels attempt to use heuristic techniques to provide similar functionality to the lower RAID levels, while reducing the overall cost.

TIP   RAID level 4 stores parity information on a single drive, which reduces the overall amount of disk space required but is more risky than RAID level 1.

Software RAID solutions typically support both striping and mirroring. This speeds up data writing, and makes provisions for automating the transfer of control from the primary disk to the secondary disk in the event of a primary disk failure. In addition, many software solutions support different RAID levels on different partitions on a disk, which may also be useful in reducing the overall amount of disk space required to safely store data. For example, while users might require access to a fast partition using RAID level 0, there may be another partition that is dedicated to a financial database, which requires mirroring (thus RAID level 1). Sun's DiskSuite product is currently one of the most popular software RAID solutions.

TIP   Solaris 9 provides integrated RAID support.

Alternatively, custom hardware RAID solutions are also proving popular, because of the minimal administrative overhead involved with installing and configuring such systems. While not exactly "plug and play," external RAID arrays such as the StorEdge A1000 have many individual disks that can be used to support both mirroring and striping, with data transfer rates of up to 40 megabytes per second. In addition, banks of fast caching memory (up to 80MB) speeds up disk writes by temporarily storing them in RAM before writing them to one or more disks in the array. This makes the RAID solution not only safe, but significantly faster than a normal disk drive.

Zip/Jaz Disks

Zip and Jaz drives are portable, magnetic storage media that are ideal as a backup medium. Only SCSI interfaces are fully supported under Solaris, although it may be possible to use ATAPI interfaces on Solaris x86. USB and parallel port interfaces are presently unsupported under Solaris. Zip drives come in two storage capacities: the standard 100M drive, and the expanded 250M drive, which is backward compatible with the 100M drive. The 100M and 250M drives are not going to get you very far with backups, but Zip drives do have relatively fast write speeds compared with tape drives. Zip drives are most useful for dumps of database tables, and/or user files that need to be interchanged with PCs and other client systems.

Jaz drives offer several improvements over Zip technology, the most distinguishing characteristic being increased storage capacity. Jaz drives also come in two flavors: the standard 1G drive, and a newer 2G version, which is backward compatible with the standard drive. The Jaz drive is also much faster than the Zip drive, with reported average seek times of around 10ms. This makes Jaz drives comparable in speed to many IDE hard drives, and provides the flexibility of easily sharing data between server and client systems.

Further discussion of Zip and Jaz drives can be found on the **alt.iomega.zip.jazz** USENET forum.

 CAUTION   Zip drive technology has improved in recent years, but early versions of the 100M drive suffered from a problem known as the "click of death," where a drive would fail to read or write, and a number of repetitive clicks were heard from inside the drive. This problem has now completely disappeared with new models, and users should feel confident in using Zip as a storage medium. For historical information on the "click of death" problem, see Steve Gibson's page at **http://grc.com/clickdeath.htm**.

CD-Rs and CD-RWs

CD writing and CD rewriting devices are rapidly gaining momentum as desktop backup systems, which are cheap, fast, and in the case of CD-RW, reusable. CD-R and CD-RW devices serve two distinct purposes in backup systems: while CD-RW disks are very useful for day-to-day backup operations, because they can be reused, CD-R technology is more useful for archiving and auditing purposes. For example, many organizations outsource their development projects to third-party contractors—in this case, it is useful for both the contractor and the client to have an archival copy of what has been developed in case there is some later disagreement concerning developmental goals and milestones. Alternatively, contracts involved with government organizations may require regular snapshots to satisfy auditing requirements. Since CD-R is a write-once, read-only technology, it is best suited to this purpose. CD-R is wasteful as a normal backup medium, because writable CDs can only be used once. CD-RWs can be rewritten hundreds of times, and with over 600 megabytes of storage, they are competitive with Zip drives for storage, and much cheaper per unit than Jaz drives.

Backup and Restore

Backup and restore software falls into three different categories:

- Standard Solaris tools like tar, dd, cpio, ufsdump and ufsrestore. These tools are quite adequate for backing up single machines, with multiple backup devices.

- Centralized backup tools like AMANDA and Legato Networker, which are useful for backing up multiple machines through a single backup server.

- Distributed backup tools like Veritas NetBackup, which are capable of remotely managing storage for multiple machines.

In this section, we will examine the standard Solaris backup and restore tools that are generally used for single machines with one or two backup devices. In addition, these tools are often useful for normal users to manage their own accounts on the server. For example, users can create "tape archives" using the `tar` command, whose output can be written to a single disk file. This is a standard way of distributing source trees in the Solaris and broader UNIX community. Users can also make copies of disks and tapes using the `dd` command. It is also possible to back up database files in combination with standard Solaris tools. For example, Oracle server is supplied with an exp utility, which can be used to take a dump of the database while it is still running

```
exp system/manager FULL=Y
```

where system is the username for an administrator with DBA privileges, and manager is the password. This will create a file called *expat.dmp*, which can then be scheduled to be backed up every night using a cron job like the following:

```
0 3 * * * exp system/manager FULL=Y
```

Some sites prefer to take full dumps every night. This involves transferring an entire file to a backup medium, which is a small system overhead if the file is only a few megabytes. But for a database with a tablespace of 50 gigabytes, this would place a great strain on a backup server, especially if it was used for other purposes. Thus, it might be more appropriate to take an incremental dump, which only records data that has changed. Incremental dumps will be discussed in the section on ufsdump.

Using tar

The `tar` command is used to create a "tape archive," or to extract the files contained in a tape archive. Although tar was originally conceived with a tape device in mind, in fact, any device can hold a tar file, including a normal disk file system. This is why users have adopted tar as their standard archiving utility, even though it does not perform compression like the Zip tools for PCs. Tape archives are easy to transport between systems using FTP or secure copy in binary transfer mode, and are the standard means of exchanging data between Solaris systems.

As an example, let's create a tar file of the */opt/totalnet* package. Firstly, check the potential size of the tape archive by using the du command:

```
server% cd /opt/totalnet
server% du
4395    ./bin
367     ./lib/charset
744     ./lib/drv
434     ./lib/pcbin
777     ./lib/tds
5731    ./lib
5373    ./sbin
145     ./man/man1
135     ./man/man1m
281     ./man
53      ./docs/images
56      ./docs
15837   .
```

The estimated size of the archive is therefore 15387 blocks. To create a tape archive in the */tmp* directory for the whole package, including subdirectories, execute the following command:

```
server# tar cvf /tmp/totalnet.tar *
a bin/ 0K
a bin/atattr 54K
a bin/atconvert 58K
a bin/atkprobe 27K
a bin/csr.tn 6K
a bin/ddpinfo 10K
a bin/desk 17K
a bin/ipxprobe 35K
a bin/m2u 4K
a bin/maccp 3K
a bin/macfsck 3K
a bin/macmd 3K
a bin/macmv 3K
a bin/macrd 3K
a bin/macrm 3K
a bin/nbmessage 141K
a bin/nbq 33K
a bin/nbucheck 8K
a bin/ncget 65K
a bin/ncprint 66K
a bin/ncput 65K
a bin/nctime 32K
a bin/nwmessage 239K
a bin/nwq 26K
a bin/pfinfo 70K
a bin/ruattr 122K
a bin/rucopy 129K
a bin/rudel 121K
a bin/rudir 121K
a bin/ruhelp 9K
a bin/u2m 4K
a bin/rumd 120K
a bin/rumessage 192K
```

```
a bin/ruprint 124K
a bin/rurd 120K
a bin/ruren 121K
```

To extract the tar file's contents to disks, execute the following command:

```
server# cd /tmp
server# tar xvf totalnet.tar
x bin, 0 bytes, 0 tape blocks
x bin/atattr, 54676 bytes, 107 tape blocks
x bin/atconvert, 58972 bytes, 116 tape blocks
x bin/atkprobe, 27524 bytes, 54 tape blocks
x bin/csr.tn, 5422 bytes, 11 tape blocks
x bin/ddpinfo, 9800 bytes, 20 tape blocks
x bin/desk, 16456 bytes, 33 tape blocks
x bin/ipxprobe, 35284 bytes, 69 tape blocks
x bin/m2u, 3125 bytes, 7 tape blocks
x bin/maccp, 2882 bytes, 6 tape blocks
x bin/macfsck, 2592 bytes, 6 tape blocks
x bin/macmd, 2255 bytes, 5 tape blocks
x bin/macmv, 2866 bytes, 6 tape blocks
x bin/macrd, 2633 bytes, 6 tape blocks
x bin/macrm, 2509 bytes, 5 tape blocks
x bin/nbmessage, 143796 bytes, 281 tape blocks
x bin/nbq, 33068 bytes, 65 tape blocks
x bin/nbucheck, 7572 bytes, 15 tape blocks
x bin/ncget, 66532 bytes, 130 tape blocks
x bin/ncprint, 67204 bytes, 132 tape blocks
x bin/ncput, 65868 bytes, 129 tape blocks
x bin/nctime, 32596 bytes, 64 tape blocks
x bin/nwmessage, 244076 bytes, 477 tape blocks
x bin/nwq, 26076 bytes, 51 tape blocks
x bin/pfinfo, 71192 bytes, 140 tape blocks
x bin/ruattr, 123988 bytes, 243 tape blocks
x bin/rucopy, 131636 bytes, 258 tape blocks
x bin/rudel, 122940 bytes, 241 tape blocks
x bin/rudir, 123220 bytes, 241 tape blocks
x bin/ruhelp, 8356 bytes, 17 tape blocks
x bin/u2m, 3140 bytes, 7 tape blocks
x bin/rumd, 122572 bytes, 240 tape blocks
x bin/rumessage, 195772 bytes, 383 tape blocks
x bin/ruprint, 126532 bytes, 248 tape blocks
x bin/rurd, 122572 bytes, 240 tape blocks
x bin/ruren, 123484 bytes, 242 tape blocks
```

Tape archives are not compressed by default in Solaris. This means that they should be compressed with normal Solaris compression:

```
server% compress file.tar
```

This will create a compressed file called *file.tar.Z*. Alternatively, the GNU gzip utility often achieves better compression ratios than the standard `compress` command, so it should be downloaded and installed. When executed, it creates a file called *file.tar.gz*:

```
server% gzip file.tar
```

Although Solaris does come with tar installed, it is advisable to download, compile, and install GNU tar, because of the increased functionality that it includes with respect to compression. For example, to create a compressed tape archive *file.tar.gz*, use the z flag in addition to the normal cvf flags:

```
server% tar zcvf file.tar *
```

Using cpio

cpio is used for copying file archives, and is much more flexible than tar, because a cpio archive can span multiple volumes. cpio can be used in three different modes:

- Copy in mode, executed with cpio -i, extracts files from standard input, from a stream created by cat or a similar utility.
- Copy out mode, denoted by cpio -o, obtains a list of files from standard input, and creates an archive from these files, including their path name.
- Copy pass mode, performed by cpio -p, is equivalent to copy out mode, except that no archive is actually created.

The basic idea behind cpio for archiving is to generate a list of files to be archived, print it to standard output, and then pipe it through cpio in copy out mode. For example, to archive all of the text files in one's home directory and store them in an archive called *myarchive* in the */staff/pwatters* directory, use this command:

```
server% find . -name '*.txt' -print | cpio -oc > /staff/pwatters/myarchive
```

When the command completes, the number of blocks required to store the files is reported:

```
8048 blocks
```

The files themselves are stored in text format, with an identifying header, which we can examine with cat or head:

```
server% head myarchive
0707010009298a00008180000011fc0000005400000001380bb9b600001e9b0000005500000
0000000000000000000000000001f00000003Directory/file.txtThe quick brown fox ju
mps over the lazy dog.
```

Recording headers in ASCII is portable, and is achieved by using the -c option. This means that files can be extracted from the archive by using the cat command:

```
server% cat myarchive | cpio -icd "*"
```

This extracts all files and directories as required (specified by using the -d option). It is just as easy to extract a single file: to extract *Directory/file.txt*, we use this command:

```
server% cat myarchive | cpio -ic "Directory/file.txt"
```

If you are copying files directly to tape, it is important to use the same blocking factor when you retrieve or copy files from the tape to the hard disk as you did when you copied files from the hard disk to the tape. If you use the defaults, there should be no problems, although you can specify a particular blocking factor by using the −B directive.

Using dd

dd is a program that copies raw disk or tape slices block by block to other disk or tape slices: it is like cp for slices. It is often used for backing up disk slices to other disk slices and/or to a tape drive, and for copying tapes. To use dd, it is necessary to specify an input file "if" and an output file "of," and a block size. For example, to copy the root partition "/" on */dev/rdsk/c1t0d0s0* to */dev/rdsk/c1t4d0s0*, you can use this command:

```
server# dd if=/dev/rdsk/c1t0d0s0 of=/dev/rdsk/c1t4d0s0 bs=128k
```

To actually make the new partition bootable, you will also need to use the installboot command after dd. Another use for dd is backing up tape data from one tape to another tape. This is particularly useful for re-creating archival backup tapes that may be aging. For example, to copy from tape drive 0 (*/dev/rmt/0*) to tape drive 2 (*/dev/rmt/2*), use this command:

```
server# dd if=/dev/rmt/0h  of=/dev/rmt/1h
```

It is also possible to copy the contents of a floppy drive, by redirecting the contents of the floppy disk and piping it through dd:

```
server# dd < /floppy/floppy0 > /tmp/floppy.disk
```

Using ufsdump and ufsrestore

ufsdump and ufsrestore are standard backup and restore applications for UNIX file systems. ufsdump is often set to run from cron jobs late at night to minimize the load on server systems. ufsrestore is normally run in single-user mode after a system crash (that is, when restoring a complete file system). ufsdump can be run on a mounted file system, but it may be wise to unmount it first, perform a file system check (using fsck), re-mount it, and then perform the backup.

The key concept in planning ufsdumps is the "dump level" of any particular backup. The dump level determines whether or not ufsdump performs a full or incremental dump. A full dump is represented by a dump level of zero, while the numbers 1–9 can be arbitrarily assigned to incremental dump levels. The only restriction on the assignment of dump-level numbers for incremental backups is their numerical relationship to each other: a high number should be used for normal daily incremental dumps, followed once a week by a lower number that specifies that the process should be restarted. This approach uses the same set of tapes for all files, regardless of which day they were recorded on. For example, Monday through Saturday would have a dump level of 9, while Sunday would have a dump level of 1. After cycling through incremental backups during the weekdays and Saturday, the process starts again on Sunday.

Some organizations like to keep a day's work separate from other days in a single tape. This makes it easier to recover work from an incremental dump where speed is important, and/or whether or not backups from a particular day wish to be retrieved. For example, someone may wish to retrieve a version of a file that was edited on a Wednesday and the following Thursday, but they want the version just prior to the latest (that is, Wednesday). The Wednesday tape can then be used in conjunction with ufsdump to retrieve the file. A weekly full dump is scheduled to occur on Sunday, when there are few people using the system. Thus, Sunday would have a dump level of 0, followed by Monday, Tuesday, Wednesday, Thursday, and Friday with dump levels of 5, 6, 7, 8, and 9, respectively. To signal the end of a backup cycle, Saturday then has a lower dump level than Monday, which could be one of 1, 2, 3, or 4.

Prior to beginning a ufsdump, it is often useful to estimate the size of a dump to determine how many tapes will be required. This estimate can be obtained by dividing the size of the partition by the capacity of the tape. For example, to determine how many tapes would be required to back up the */dev/rdsk/c0t0d0s4* file system use:

```
server# ufsdump S /dev/rdsk/c0t0d0s4
50765536
```

The approximately 49MB on the drive will therefore easily fit onto a QIC, DAT, or DLT tape. To perform a full dump of an x86 partition (*/dev/rdsk/c0d0s0*) at level 0, we can use the following approach:

```
# ufsdump 0cu /dev/rmt/0 /dev/rdsk/c0d0s0
  DUMP: Writing 63 Kilobyte records
  DUMP: Date of this level 0 dump: Mon Feb 03 13:26:33 1997
  DUMP: Date of last level 0 dump: the epoch
  DUMP: Dumping /dev/rdsk/c0d0s0 (solaris:/) to /dev/rmt/0.
  DUMP: Mapping (Pass I) [regular files]
  DUMP: Mapping (Pass II) [directories]
  DUMP: Estimated 46998 blocks (22.95MB).
  DUMP: Dumping (Pass III) [directories]
  DUMP: Dumping (Pass IV) [regular files]
  DUMP: 46996 blocks (22.95MB) on 1 volume at 1167 KB/sec
  DUMP: DUMP IS DONE
  DUMP: Level 0 dump on Mon Feb 03 13:26:33 1997
```

The parameters passed to ufsdump include 0 (dump level), c (cartridge: blocking factor 126), and u (updates the dump record */etc/dumpdates*). The dump record is used by ufsdump and ufsrestore to track the last dump of each individual file system:

```
server# cat /etc/dumpdates
/dev/rdsk/c0t0d0s0           0 Wed Feb  2 20:23:31 2000
/dev/md/rdsk/d0             0 Tue Feb  1 20:23:31 2000
/dev/md/rdsk/d2             0 Tue Feb  1 22:19:19 2000
/dev/md/rdsk/d3             0 Wed Feb  2 22:55:16 2000
/dev/rdsk/c0t0d0s3           0 Wed Feb  2 20:29:21 2000
/dev/md/rdsk/d1             0 Wed Feb  2 21:20:04 2000
/dev/rdsk/c0t0d0s4           0 Wed Feb  2 20:24:56 2000
/dev/rdsk/c2t3d0s2           0 Wed Feb  2 20:57:34 2000
/dev/rdsk/c0t2d0s3           0 Wed Feb  2 20:32:00 2000
```

```
/dev/rdsk/c1t1d0s0          0 Wed Feb  2 21:46:23 2000
/dev/rdsk/c0t0d0s0          3 Fri Feb  4 01:10:03 2000
/dev/rdsk/c0t0d0s3          3 Fri Feb  4 01:10:12 2000
```

ufsdump is very flexible, because it can be used in conjunction with rsh (remote shell) and remote access authorization files (*.rhosts* and */etc/hosts.equiv*) to remotely log in to another server and dump the files to one of the remote server's backup devices. However, the problem with this approach is that using *.rhosts* leaves the host system vulnerable to attack: if an intruder gains access to the client, he or she can then remotely log in to a remote backup server without a username and password. The severity of the issue is compounded by the fact that a backup server that serves many clients has access to most of that client's information in the form of tape archives.

 CAUTION A concerted attack on a single client, leading to an unchallenged remote login to a backup server, can greatly expose an organization's data.

A handy trick often used by administrators is to use ufsdump to move directories across file systems. A ufsdump is taken of a particular file system, which is then piped through ufsrestore to a different destination directory. For example, to move existing staff files to a larger file system, use these commands:

```
server# mkdir /newstaff
server# cd /staff
server# ufsdump 0f - /dev/rdsk/c0t0d0s2 | (cd /newstaff; ufsrestore xf -)
```

The larger file system can then be backed up, thus closing the security loophole.

After backing up data using ufsdump, it's easy to restore the same data using the ufsrestore program. To extract data from a tape volume on */dev/rmt/0*, use this command:

```
# ufsrestore xf /dev/rmt/0
You have not read any volumes yet.
Unless you know which volume your file(s) are on you should start
with the last volume and work towards the first.
Specify next volume #: 1
set owner/mode for '.'? [yn] y
```

ufsrestore then extracts all of the files on that volume. However, you can also list the table of contents of the volume to standard output, if you are not sure of the contents of a particular tape:

```
# ufsrestore tf /dev/rmt/0
1        ./openwin/devdata/profiles
2        ./openwin/devdata
3        ./openwin
9        ./lp/alerts
1        ./lp/classes
15       ./lp/fd
1        ./lp/forms
1        ./lp/interfaces
1        ./lp/printers
```

```
1          ./lp/pwheels
36         ./lp
2          ./dmi/ciagent
3          ./dmi/conf
6          ./dmi
42         ./snmp/conf
```

ufsrestore also supports an interactive mode, which has online help to assist you in finding the correct volume to restore from:

```
# ufsrestore I
ufsrestore > help
Available commands are:
        ls [arg] - list directory
        cd arg - change directory
        pwd - print current directory
        add [arg] - add `arg' to list of files to be extracted
        delete [arg] - delete `arg' from list of files to be extracted
        extract - extract requested files
        setmodes - set modes of requested directories
        quit - immediately exit program
        what - list dump header information
        verbose - toggle verbose flag (useful with ``ls'')
        help or `?' - print this list
If no `arg' is supplied, the current directory is used
ufsrestore >
```

Since Veritas and Legato are software packages in their own right, coverage is beyond the scope of the current volume.

Summary

In this chapter, you learned the basic concepts behind backup and restore, which are two crucial elements of a high availability and data protection strategy. Solaris provides a number of tools, such as ufsdump and ufsrestore, to implement these tasks. Alternatively, a third-party package may be used to increase functionality.

Questions

1. What is a full dump?

   A. A file system or set of file systems that is fully copied to a backup medium

   B. An uncompressed tape archive

   C. A compressed tape archive

   D. A selective backup strategy based on only recently modified files being backed up

2. What is an incremental dump?

   A. A file system or set of file systems that is copied to a backup medium

   B. An uncompressed tape archive

   C. A compressed tape archive

   D. A selective backup strategy based on only recently modified files being backed up

3. What media can be used for a backup?

   A. Hard disk, Zip drive, DAT tape, or CD-RW

   B. Zip drive, DAT tape, CD-RW only

   C. DAT tape or QIC tape only

   D. Hard disk, Zip drive, DAT tape, or EPROM

4. What is a RAID level 0?

   A. Mirroring

   B. Striping

   C. Mirroring + striping

   D. Blocking

5. What is a RAID level 1?

   A. Mirroring

   B. Striping

   C. Mirroring + striping

   D. Blocking

6. What command would be used to extract a tar file called *backup.tar* using verbose output?

   A. `tar zvf backup.tar`

   B. `tar xvf backup.tar`

   C. `tar evf backup.tar`

   D. `tar zevf backup.tar`

7. What does cpio "copy in" mode do?

   A. Inserts files into an archive, with data sourced from a stream created by cat or a similar utility.

   B. Inserts files into an archive by extracting them directly from the file system (using the `-f` option).

      C. Acts like cp for slices.

      D. Extracts files from standard input, from a stream created by cat or a similar utility.

8. What does dd do?

      A. Inserts files into an archive, with data sourced from a stream created by cat or a similar utility.

      B. Inserts files into an archive by extracting them directly from the file system (using the -f option).

      C. Acts like tar for disk slices.

      D. Extracts files from standard input, from a stream created by cat or a similar utility.

Answers

1. **A.** A full dump makes a copy of everything on a specified file system.

2. **D.** An incremental dump saves time by only backing up modified files.

3. **A.** Anything that stores data can be used for backups.

4. **B.** Striping logically extends the space available on disk volumes.

5. **A.** Mirroring ensures data integrity by copying blocks concurrently to multiple disks.

6. **B.** xvf means e(x)tract, (v)erbose, (f)ile.

7. **D.** "copy in" literally means what it says.

8. **C.** dd can be used to copy slices as if they were files.

Basic Command Syntax

In this chapter, you will
- Gain an understanding of text processing utilities
- Learn about sed and awk
- Learn how to write shell scripts

A key feature of Solaris 9 shells is the ability to write complex scripts that perform repetitive actions and can process various kinds of decision logic. There are many more commands available for the Bourne again shell than for MS-DOS batch files, which makes them very powerful. However, script files are more dependent on understanding file permissions than just using the shell to enter commands, which makes them more complex. In this chapter, we review how to create executable scripts that can be used with the Bourne again shell. In addition, we examine how to schedule shell scripts to run at regular intervals using the cron and at facilities. Finally, we focus on the advanced text processing features of the Solaris shell and how these can be used when developing scripts.

Text Processing Utilities

Solaris has many user commands available to perform tasks ranging from text processing, to file manipulation, to terminal management. In this section, we will look at some standard UNIX utilities that are the core of using a shell in Solaris. However, readers are urged to obtain an up-to-date list of the utilities supplied with Solaris by typing the command:

```
$ man intro
```

The cat command displays the contents of a file to standard output, without any kind of pagination or screen control. It is most useful for viewing small files, or for passing the contents of a text file through another filter or utility (for example, the grep command, which searches for strings). To examine the contents of the groups database, for example, we would use this command:

```
# cat /etc/group
root::0:root
other::1:
bin::2:root,bin,daemon
sys::3:root,bin,sys,adm
adm::4:root,adm,daemon
```

```
uucp::5:root,uucp
mail::6:root
tty::7:root,tty,adm
lp::8:root,lp,adm
nuucp::9:root,nuucp
staff::10:
postgres::100:
daemon::12:root,daemon
sysadmin::14:
nobody::60001:
noaccess::60002:
nogroup::65534:
```

The cat command is not very useful for examining specific sections of a file. For example, if you need to examine the first few lines of a web server's log files, using cat would display them but they would quickly scroll off the screen out of sight. However, you can use the head command to display only the first few lines of a file. In this example, we extract the lines from the log file of the Inprise application server:

```
bart:/usr/local/inprise/ias41/logs/bart/webpageservice > head access_log
203.16.206.43 - - [31/Aug/2000:14:32:52 +1000] "GET /index.jsp HTTP/1.0" 200 24077
203.16.206.43 - - [31/Aug/2000:14:32:52 +1000] "GET /index.jsp HTTP/1.0" 200 24077
203.16.206.43 - - [31/Aug/2000:14:32:52 +1000] "GET /index.jsp HTTP/1.0" 200 24077
203.16.206.43 - - [31/Aug/2000:14:32:52 +1000] "GET /index.jsp HTTP/1.0" 200 24077
203.16.206.43 - - [31/Aug/2000:14:32:52 +1000] "GET /index.jsp HTTP/1.0" 200 24077
203.16.206.43 - - [31/Aug/2000:14:32:52 +1000] "GET /index.jsp HTTP/1.0" 200 24077
203.16.206.43 - - [31/Aug/2000:14:32:52 +1000] "GET /index.jsp HTTP/1.0" 200 24077
203.16.206.43 - - [31/Aug/2000:14:32:53 +1000] "GET /index.jsp HTTP/1.0" 200 24077
203.16.206.43 - - [31/Aug/2000:14:32:53 +1000] "GET /index.jsp HTTP/1.0" 200 24077
203.16.206.43 - - [31/Aug/2000:14:32:53 +1000] "GET /index.jsp HTTP/1.0" 200 24077
```

Alternatively, if you just want examine the last few lines of a file, you could use the cat command to display the entire file ending with the last few lines, or you could use the tail command to specifically display these lines. If the file is large (for example, an Inprise application server log file of 2MB), it would be a large waste of system resources to display the whole file using cat, whereas tail is very efficient. Here's an example of using tail to display the last few lines of a file:

```
bart:/usr/local/inprise/ias41/logs/bart/webpageservice > tail access_log
203.16.206.43 - - [31/Aug/2000:14:32:52 +1000]
"GET /index.jsp HTTP/1.0" 200 24077
203.16.206.43 - - [31/Aug/2000:14:32:52 +1000]
"GET /index.jsp HTTP/1.0" 200 24077
203.16.206.43 - - [31/Aug/2000:14:32:52 +1000]
"GET /index.jsp HTTP/1.0" 200 24077
203.16.206.43 - - [31/Aug/2000:14:32:52 +1000]
"GET /index.jsp HTTP/1.0" 200 24077
203.16.206.43 - - [31/Aug/2000:14:32:52 +1000]
"GET /index.jsp HTTP/1.0" 200 24077
203.16.206.43 - - [31/Aug/2000:14:32:52 +1000]
"GET /index.jsp HTTP/1.0" 200 24077
203.16.206.43 - - [31/Aug/2000:14:32:52 +1000]
"GET /index.jsp HTTP/1.0" 200 24077
203.16.206.43 - - [31/Aug/2000:14:32:53 +1000]
"GET /index.jsp HTTP/1.0" 200 24077
203.16.206.43 - - [31/Aug/2000:14:32:53 +1000]
"GET /index.jsp HTTP/1.0" 200 24077
```

```
203.16.206.43 - - [31/Aug/2000:14:32:53 +1000]
"GET /index.jsp HTTP/1.0" 200 24077
```

Now, imagine that you were searching for a particular string within the *access_log* file, such as a 404 error code, which indicates that a page has been requested that does not exist. Webmasters regularly check log files for this error code, to create a list of links that need to be checked. To view this list, we can use the grep command to search the file for a specific string (in this case, "404"), and the more command can be use to display the results page by page:

```
bart:/usr/local/inprise/ias41/logs/bart/webpageservice > grep 404 access_log | more
203.16.206.56 - - [31/Aug/2000:15:42:54 +1000] "GET
/servlet/LibraryCatalog?command=mainmenu HTTP/1.1" 200 21404
203.16.206.56 - - [01/Sep/2000:08:32:12 +1000] "GET
/servlet/LibraryCatalog?command=searchbyname HTTP/1.1" 200 14041
203.16.206.237 - - [01/Sep/2000:09:20:35 +1000] "GET /images/L
INE.gif HTTP/1.1" 404 1204
203.16.206.236 - - [01/Sep/2000:10:10:35 +1000] "GET /images/L
INE.gif HTTP/1.1" 404 1204
203.16.206.236 - - [01/Sep/2000:10:10:40 +1000] "GET /images/L
INE.gif HTTP/1.1" 404 1204
203.16.206.236 - - [01/Sep/2000:10:10:47 +1000] "GET /images/L
INE.gif HTTP/1.1" 404 1204
203.16.206.236 - - [01/Sep/2000:10:11:09 +1000] "GET /images/L
INE.gif HTTP/1.1" 404 1204
203.16.206.236 - - [01/Sep/2000:10:11:40 +1000] "GET /images/L
INE.gif HTTP/1.1" 404 1204
203.16.206.236 - - [01/Sep/2000:10:11:44 +1000] "GET /images/L
INE.gif HTTP/1.1" 404 1204
203.16.206.236 - - [01/Sep/2000:10:12:03 +1000] "GET /images/L
INE.gif HTTP/1.1" 404 1204
203.16.206.41 - - [01/Sep/2000:12:04:22 +1000] "GET /data/books/576586955.pdf H
TTP/1.0" 404 1204
--More--
```

These log files contain a line for each access to the web server, with entries relating to the source IP address, date and time of access, the HTTP request string sent, the protocol used, and the success/error code. When you see the --More-- prompt, the SPACEBAR can be pressed to advance to the next screen, or the ENTER key can be pressed to advance by a single line in the results. As you have probably guessed, the pipeline operator | was used to pass the results of the grep command through to the more command.

In addition to the pipeline, there are four other operators that can be used on the command line to direct or append input streams to standard output, or output streams to standard input. Although that sounds convoluted, it can be very useful when working with files to direct the output of a command into a new file (or append it to an existing file). Alternatively, the input to a command can be generated from the output of another command. These operations are performed by the following operators:

- > Redirect standard output to a file.
- >> Append standard output to a file.
- < Redirect file contents to standard input.
- << Append file contents to standard input.

Bash also has logical operators, including the "less than" (lt) operator, which uses the test facility to make numerical comparisons between two operands. Other commonly used operators include

- a –eq b   a equals b.
- a –ne b   a not equal to b.
- a –gt b   a greater than b.
- a –ge b   a greater than or equal to b.
- a –le b   a less than or equal to b.

Let's look at an example with the `cat` command, which displays the contents of files, and the `echo` command, which echoes the contents of a string or an environment variable that has been previously specified. For example, imagine if we wanted to maintain a database of endangered species in a text file called *animals.txt*. If we wanted to add the first animal "zebra" to an empty file, we could use this command:

```
# echo "zebra" > animals.txt
```

We could then check the contents of the file *animals.txt* with the following command:

```
# cat animals.txt
zebra
```

Thus, the insertion was successful. Now, imagine that we want to add a second entry (the animal "emu") to the *animals.txt* file. We could try using the command

```
# echo "emu" > animals.txt
```

but the result may not be what we expected:

```
# cat animals.txt
emu
```

This is because the > operator always overwrites the contents of an existing file, while the >> operator always appends to the contents of an existing file. Let's run that command again with the correct operators:

```
# echo "zebra" > animals.txt
# echo "emu" >> animals.txt
```

Luckily, the output is just what we expected:

```
# cat animals.txt
zebra
emu
```

Once we have a file containing a list of all the animals, we would probably want to sort it alphabetically, making searching for specific entries easy. To do this, we can use the `sort` command:

```
# sort animals.txt
emu
zebra
```

The sorted entries are then displayed on the screen in alphabetical order. It is also possible to redirect the sorted list into another file (called *sorted_animals.txt*) by using this command:

```
# sort animals.txt > animals_sorted.txt
```

If you wanted to check that the sorting process actually worked, you could compare the contents of the *animals.txt* file line by line with the *sorted_animals.txt* file by using the diff command:

```
# diff animals.txt sorted_animals.txt
1d0
< zebra
2a2
> zebra
```

This result indicates that the first and second lines of the *animals.txt* and *sorted_animals.txt* files are different, as expected. If the sorting process had failed, the two files would have been identical, and no differences would have been reported by diff.

A related facility is the basename facility, which is designed to remove file extensions from a filename specified as an argument. This is commonly used to convert files with one extension to another extension. For example, let's imagine that we had a graphic file conversion program that took as its first argument the name of a source JPEG file and took the name of a target bitmap file. Somehow, we'd need to convert a filename of the form *filename.jpg* to a file of the form *filename.bmp*. We can do this with the basename command. In order to strip a file extension from an argument, we need to pass the filename and the extension as separate arguments to basename. For example, the command

```
# basename maya.gif .gif
```

will produce the following output:

```
maya
```

If we want the *.gif* extension to be replaced by a *.bmp* extension, we could use

```
# echo `basename maya.gif .gif`.bmp
```

which will produce the following output:

```
maya.bmp
```

Of course, we are not limited to extensions like *.gif* and *.bmp*. Also, keep mind that the basename technique is entirely general—and since Solaris does not have mandatory filename extensions, the basename technique can be used for other purposes, such as generating a set of strings based on filenames.

sed and awk

So far, we've looked at some fairly simple examples of text processing. However, the power of Solaris-style text processing lies with advanced tools like sed and awk. `sed` is a command-line editing program, which can be used to perform search and replace operations on very large files, as well as other kinds of noninteractive editing. awk, on the other hand, is a complete text processing programming language and has a C-like syntax, and can be used in conjunction with sed to program repetitive text processing and editing operations on large files. These combined operations include double and triple spacing files, printing line numbers, left- and right-justifying text, performing field extraction and field substitution, and filtering on specific strings and pattern specifications. We'll examine some of these applications below.

To start this example, we'll create a set of customer address records stored in a flat text, tab-delimited database file called *test.dat*:

```
$ cat test.dat
Bloggs  Joe      24 City Rd       Richmond         VA      23227
Lee     Yat Sen  72 King St       Amherst MA       01002
Rowe    Sarah    3454 Capitol St  Los Angeles      CA      90074
Sakura  Akira    1 Madison Ave    New York         NY      10017
```

This is a fairly common type of record, storing a customer's surname, first name, street address, city, state, and ZIP code. For presentation, we can double space the records in this file by redirecting the contents of the *test.dat* file through the `sed` command, with the G option:

```
$ sed G < test.dat
Bloggs  Joe      24 City Rd       Richmond         VA      23227

Lee     Yat Sen  72 King St       Amherst MA       01002

Rowe    Sarah    3454 Capitol St  Los Angeles      CA      90074

Sakura  Akira    1 Madison Ave    New York         NY      10017
```

The power of `sed` lies in its ability to be used in pipelines; thus, an action can literally be performed in conjunction with many other operations. For example, to insert double spacing and then remove it, we simply invoke `sed` twice with the appropriate commands:

```
$ sed G < test.dat | sed 'n;d'
Bloggs  Joe      24 City Rd       Richmond         VA      23227
Lee     Yat Sen  72 King St       Amherst MA       01002
Rowe    Sarah    3454 Capitol St  Los Angeles      CA      90074
Sakura  Akira    1 Madison Ave    New York         NY      10017
```

When printing reports, you'll probably be using line numbering at some point to uniquely identify records. You can generate line numbers dynamically for display by using `sed`:

```
$ sed '/./=' test.dat | sed '/./N; s/\n/ /'
1 Bloggs        Joe      24 City Rd       Richmond      VA       23227
```

```
2 Lee    Yat Sen 72 King St      Amherst MA      01002
3 Rowe   Sarah   3454 Capitol St Los Angeles     CA      90074
4 Sakura         Akira  1 Madison Ave  New York        NY      10017
```

For large files, it's often useful to be able to count the number of lines. While the wc command can be used for this purpose, sed can also be used in situations where wc is not available:

```
$ cat test.dat | sed -n '$='
4
```

When you're printing databases for display, you might want comments and titles left-justified, but all records being displayed with two blank spaces before each line. This can be achieved by using sed:

```
$ cat test.dat | sed 's/^/  /'
  Bloggs        Joe     24 City Rd      Richmond        VA      23227
  Lee    Yat Sen 72 King St      Amherst         MA      01002
  Rowe   Sarah   3454 Capitol St Los Angeles     CA      90074
  Sakura         Akira  1 Madison Ave  New York   NY      10017
```

Imagine that due to some municipal reorganization, all cities currently located in CT were being reassigned to MA. sed would be the perfect tool to identify all instances of CT in the data file and replace them with MA:

```
$ cat test.dat | sed 's/MA/CT/g'
Bloggs   Joe     24 City Rd      Richmond        VA      23227
Lee      Yat Sen 72 King St      Amherst         CT      01002
Rowe     Sarah   3454 Capitol St Los Angeles     CA      90074
Sakura   Akira   1 Madison Ave   New York        NY      10017
```

If a data file has been entered as a first in last out (FILO) stack, then you'll generally be reading records from the file from top to bottom. However, if the data file is to be treated as a last in first out (LIFO) stack, then it would be useful to be able to reorder the records from the last to the first:

```
$ cat test.dat | sed '1\!G;h;$\!d'
Sakura   Akira   1 Madison Ave   New York        NY      10017
Rowe     Sarah   3454 Capitol St Los Angeles     CA      90074
Lee      Yat Sen 72 King St      Amherst MA      01002
Bloggs   Joe     24 City Rd      Richmond        VA      23227
```

Some data hiding applications require that data be encoded in some way that is nontrivial for another application to detect a file's contents. One way to foil such programs is to reverse the character strings that comprise each record, which can be achieved by using sed:

```
$ cat test.dat | sed '/\n/\!G;s/\(.\)\(.*\n\)/&\2\1/;//D;s/.//'
72232    AV      dnomhciR        dR ytiC 42      eoJ     sggolB
20010    AM      tsrehmA tS gniK 27      neS taY eeL
47009    AC      selegnA soL     tS lotipaC 4543 haraS   ewoR
71001    YN      kroY weN        evA nosidaM 1   arikA   arukaS
```

Some reporting applications might require that the first line of a file be processed before deletion. Although the head command can be used for this purpose, sed can also be used:

```
$ sed q < test.dat
Bloggs  Joe     24 City Rd      Richmond        VA      23227
```

Alternatively, if a certain number of lines are to be printed, sed can be used to extract the first *q* lines:

```
$ sed 2q < test.dat
Bloggs  Joe     24 City Rd      Richmond        VA      23227
Lee     Yat Sen 72 King St      Amherst MA      01002
```

The grep command is often used to detect strings within files. However, sed can also be used for this purpose, as shown in the following example where the string CA (representing California) is searched for:

```
$ cat test.dat | sed '/CA/\!d'
Rowe    Sarah   3454 Capitol St Los Angeles     CA      90074
```

However, this is a fairly gross and inaccurate method, because CA might match a street address like "1 CALGARY Rd," or "23 Green CAPE." Thus, it's necessary to use the field extraction features of awk. In the following example, we use awk to extract and print the fifth column in the data file, representing the state:

```
$ cat test.dat | awk 'BEGIN {FS = "\t"}{print $5}'
VA
MA
CA
NY
```

Note that the tab character "\t" is specified as the field delimiter. Now, if we combine the field extraction capability of awk with the string searching facility of sed, we should be able to print out a list of all occurrences of the state CA:

```
$ cat test.dat | awk 'BEGIN {FS = "\t"}{print $5}' | sed '/CA/\!d'
CA
```

Alternatively, we could simply count the number of records that contained CA in the State field:

```
$ cat test.dat | awk 'BEGIN {FS = "\t"}{print $5}' | sed '/CA/\!d' | sed -n '$='
1
```

When producing reports, it's useful to be able to selectively display fields in a different order. For example, while surname is typically used as a primary key, and is generally the first field, most reports would display the first name before the surname, which can be achieved by using awk:

```
$ cat test.dat | awk 'BEGIN {FS = "\t"}{print $2,$1}'
Joe Bloggs
```

```
Yat Sen Lee
Sarah Rowe
Akira Sakura
```

It's also possible to split such reordered fields across different lines and use different format specifiers. For example, the following script prints the first name and surname on one line and the state on the following line. Such code is the basis of many mail merge and bulk printing programs:

```
$ cat test.dat | awk 'BEGIN {FS = "\t"}{print $2,$1,"\n"$5}'
Joe Bloggs
VA
Yat Sen Lee
MA
Sarah Rowe
CA
Akira Sakura
NY
```

Since awk is a complete programming language, it contains many common constructs, like if/then/else evaluations of logical states. These states can be used to test business logic cases. For example, in a mailing program, the bounds of valid ZIP codes could be checked by determining whether the ZIP code lay within a valid range. For example, the following routine checks to see whether a ZIP code is less than 9999 and rejects it as invalid if it is greater than 9999:

```
$ cat test.dat | awk 'BEGIN {FS = "\t"}{print $2,$1}{if($6<9999) {print
 "Valid zipcode"} else {print "Invalid zipcode"}}'
Joe Bloggs
Invalid zipcode
Yat Sen Lee
Valid zipcode
Sarah Rowe
Invalid zipcode
Akira Sakura
Invalid zipcode
```

sed

The standard options for sed are shown here:

- -n   Prevents display of pattern space.
- -e *filename*   Executes the script contained in the file *filename*.
- -V   Displays the version number.

awk

The standard POSIX options for awk are shown here:

- -f *filename*   Where *filename* is the name of the awk file to process.
- -F *field*   where *field* is the field separator.

- `-v x=y` Where x is a variable and y is a value.

- `-W lint` turns on lint checking.

- `-W lint-old` Uses old-style lint checking.

- `-W traditional` enforces traditional usage.

- `-W version` Displays the version number.

Installing Patches

Patches are binary code modifications that affect the way Sun-supplied software operates. They can be released by Sun because of previously identified bugs which have been fixed, or because a security exploit has been discovered in a piece of software, and a simple workaround is inadequate to prevent intrusion or disruption of normal system activity. For example, many of the older Solaris daemons suffered from buffer overflow vulnerabilities until recently, where the fixed boundaries on an array are deliberately over-written by a rogue client to crash the system. Many of the system daemons, such as web servers, may be crashed because memory is overwritten with arbitrary values outside the declared size of an array. Without appropriate bounds checking, passing a GET request to a web server of 1025 bytes when the array size is 1024 would clearly result in unpredictable behavior, as the C language does not prevent a program from doing this. Since Solaris daemons are typically written in C, a number have been fixed in recent years to prevent this problem occurring (but you may be surprised at just how often new weaknesses are exposed). Sendmail, IMAP, and POP daemons for Solaris have all experienced buffer overflow vulnerabilities in the past which have required an urgent installation of security patches.

For early Solaris 9 installations out-of-the-box, two critical problems were typically identified, both associated with gaining root access via buffer overflow:

- The CDE-based Calendar Manager service may be vulnerable to a buffer overflow attack, as identified in CVE 1999-0320 and 1999-0696. The Calendar Manager is used to manage appointments and other date/time based functions.

- The remote administration daemon (sadmind) may be vulnerable to a buffer overflow attack, as described in CVE 1999-0977. The remote administration daemon is used to manage system administration activities across a number of different hosts.

The CVE number matches descriptions of each security issue from the Common Vulnerabilities and Exposures database (**http://cve.mitre.org/**). Each identified vulnerability will contain a hyperlink back to the CVE database, so that information displayed about every issue is updated directly from the source. New patches and bug fixes are also listed.

To find out information about current patches, sysadmins are directed to the **http://www.sunsolve.com/** site. Here, details about current patches for each operating system release can be found. There are two basic types of patches available from SunSolve: single patches and jumbo patches. Single patches have a single patch number associated with them; are generally aimed at resolving a single outstanding issue; and usually insert, delete, or update data in a small number of files. Single patches are also targeted at resolving specific security issues. Each patch is associated with an internal bug number from Sun's bug database. For example, patch number 108435-01 aims to fix BugId 4318566, involving a shared library issue with the 64-bit C++ compiler.

In contrast, a jumbo patch consists of many single patches that have been bundled together, on the basis of operating system release levels, to ensure that the most common issues for a particular platform are resolved by the installation of the jumbo patch. It's standard practice to install the current jumbo patch for Solaris 9 once it's been installed from scratch, or if the system has been upgraded from Solaris 7.

Some of the latest patches released for Solaris 9 include the following:

- 110322-01: Patch for /usr/lib/netsvc/yp/ypbind
- 110853-01: Patch for Sun-Fire-880
- 110856-01: Patch for /etc/inet/services
- 110888-01 : Patch for figgs
- 110894-01: Patch for country name
- 110927-01: Patch for SUNW_PKGLIST
- 111078-01: Patch Solaris Resource Manager
- 111295-01: Patch for /usr/bin/sparcv7/pstack and /usr/bin/sparcv9/pstack
- 111297-01: Patch for /usr/lib/libsendfile.so.1
- 111337-01: Patch for /usr/sbin/ocfserv
- 111400-01: Patch for KCMS configure tool
- 111402-01: Patch for crontab
- 111431-01: Patch for /usr/lib/libldap.so.4
- 111439-01: Patch for /kernel/fs/tmpfs
- 111473-01: Patch for PCI Host Adapter
- 111562-01: Patch for /usr/lib/librt.so.1
- 111564-01 Patch for SunPCi 2.2.1
- 111570-01: Patch for uucp
- 111588-01: Patch for /kernel/drv/wc
- 111606-01: Patch for /usr/sbin/in.ftpd
- 111624-01: Patch for /usr/sbin/inetd
- 111648-01 Patch for env3test, cpupmtest, ifbtest, and rsctest
- 111656-01: Patch for socal and sf drivers
- 111762-01 Patch for Expert3D and SunVTS

One of the most useful guides to the currently available patches for Solaris 9 is the SunSolve Patch Report (**ftp://sunsolve.sun.com/pub/patches/Solaris8.PatchReport**). This report provides a quick reference to all newly released patches for the platform, as well as updates on previous patches that have now been modified. A list of suggested patches for the platform is also contained in the Report, while recommended security patches are listed separately. Finally, a list of obsolete patches is provided. Some of the currently listed security patches available include the following:

- 108528-09: Patch for kernel update
- 108869-06: Patch for snmpdx/mibiisa/libssasnmp/snmplib
- 108875-09: Patch for c2audit
- 108968-05: Patch for vol/vold/rmmount
- 108975-04: Patch for /usr/bin/rmformat and /usr/sbin/format
- 108985-03: Patch for /usr/sbin/in.rshd
- 108991-13: Patch for /usr/lib/libc.so.1
- 109091-04: Patch for /usr/lib/fs/ufs/ufsrestore
- 109134-19: Patch for WBEM
- 109234-04: Patch for Apache and NCA
- 109279-13: Patch for /kernel/drv/ip
- 109320-03: Patch for LP
- 109322-07: Patch for libnsl
- 109326-05: Patch for libresolv.so.2 and in.named
- 109354-09: Patch for dtsession
- 109783-01: Patch for /usr/lib/nfs/nfsd
- 109805-03: Patch for pam_krb5.so.1
- 109887-08: Patch for smartcard
- 109888-05: Patch for platform drivers
- 109892-03: Patch for /kernel/drv/ecpp driver
- 109894-01: Patch for /kernel/drv/sparcv9/bpp driver
- 109896-04: Patch for USB driver
- 109951-01: Patch for jserver buffer overflow

Figure 15-1 shows the main screen on SunSolve that lists all of the available jumbo patches and recommended clusters for Solaris 9.

Figure 15-1
Retrieving
patches from
SunSolve.

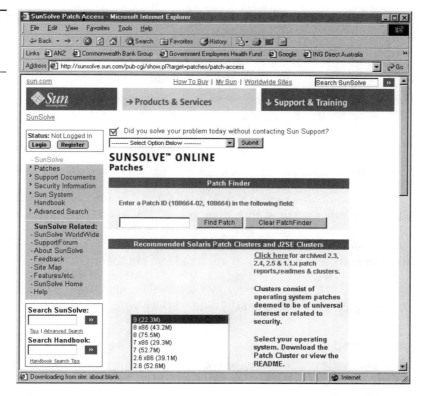

Patch Example

To determine which patches are currently installed on your system, you need to use the showrev command as follows:

```
# showrev -p
Patch: 107430-01 Obsoletes:  Requires:  Incompatibles:  Packages: SUNWwsr
Patch: 108029-01 Obsoletes:  Requires:  Incompatibles:  Packages: SUNWwsr
Patch: 107437-03 Obsoletes:  Requires:  Incompatibles:  Packages: SUNWtiu8
Patch: 107316-01 Obsoletes:  Requires:  Incompatibles:  Packages: SUNWploc
Patch: 107453-01 Obsoletes:  Requires:  Incompatibles:  Packages: SUNWkvm, SUNWc
ar
Patch: 106541-06 Obsoletes: 106976-01, 107029-01, 107030-01, 107334-01 Requires:
  Incompatibles:  Packages:  SUNWkvm, SUNWcsu, SUNWcsr, SUNWcsl, SUNWcar, SUNWesu
, SUNWarc, SUNWatfsr, SUNWcpr, SUNWdpl, SUNWhea, SUNWtoo, SUNWpcmci, SUNWtnfc, S
UNWvolr
Patch: 106541-10 Obsoletes: 106832-03, 106976-01, 107029-01, 107030-01, 107334-0
1, 107031-01, 107117-05, 107899-01 Requires: 107544-02 Incompatibles:  Packages:
 SUNWkvm, SUNWcsu, SUNWcsr, SUNWcsl, SUNWcar, SUNWesu, SUNWarc, SUNWatfsr, SUNWs
cpu, SUNWcpr, SUNWdpl, SUNWhea, SUNWipc, SUNWtoo, SUNWpcmci, SUNWpcmcu, SUNWtnfc
, SUNWvolr
Patch: 106541-15 Obsoletes: 106832-03, 106976-01, 107029-01, 107030-01, 107334-0
1, 107031-01, 107117-05, 107899-01, 108752-01, 107147-08, 109104-04 Requires: 10
7544-02 Incompatibles:  Packages: SUNWkvm, SUNWcsu, SUNWcsr, SUNWcsl, SUNWcar, S
UNWesu, SUNWarc, SUNWatfsr, SUNWscpu, SUNWcpr, SUNWdpl, SUNWhea, SUNWipc, SUNWto
o, SUNWnisu, SUNWpcmci, SUNWpcmcu, SUNWtnfc, SUNWvolu, SUNWvolr
```

From the example shown here, we can see that showrev reports several different properties of each patch installed:

- The patch number.
- Whether the patch obsoletes a previously released patch (or patches) and which version numbers.
- Whether there are any prerequisite patches (and their version numbers) on which the current patch depends.
- Whether the patch is incompatible with any other patches.
- What standard Solaris packages are affected by installation of the patch.

From one of these examples (106541-15), we can see that it obsoletes a large number of other patches, including 106832-03, 106976-01, 107029-01, 107030-01, 107334-01, 107031-01, 107117-05, 107899-01, 108752-01, 107147-08, and 109104-04. In addition, it depends on patch 107544-02, and is compatible with all other known patches. Finally, it affects a large number of different packages, including SUNWkvm, SUNWcsu, SUNWcsr, SUNWcsl, SUNWcar, SUNWesu, SUNWarc, SUNWatfsr, SUNWscpu, SUNWcpr, SUNWdpl, SUNWhea, SUNWipc, SUNWtoo, SUNWnisu, SUNWpcmci, SUNWpcmcu, SUNWtnfc, SUNWvolu, and SUNWvolr.

patchadd

To install single patches, you simple need to use the patchadd command

```
# patchadd /patches/106541-15
```

where */patches* is the directory where your patches are downloaded to, and 106541-15 is the name of the patch filename (it should be the same as the patch number).

To add a large number of patches from the same directory, the following command can be used

```
# patchadd /patches/106541-15 106541-10 107453-01
```

where 106541-15, 106541-10, and 107453-01 are the patches to be installed. Once the patches have been successfully installed, they can be verified by using the showrev command. For example, to check that patch 106541-15 has been successfully installed, the following command could be used:

```
# showrev -p | grep 106541-15
```

patchrm

Patches can be easily removed by using the patchrm command. For example, to remove the patch 106541-15, the following command would be used:

```
# patchrm 106541-15
```

If the patch was previously installed, it would now be removed. However, if the patch was not previously installed, the following errors message would be displayed:

```
Checking installed packages and patches...
Patch 106541-15 has not been applied to this system.
patchrm is terminating.
```

Summary

In this chapter, we examined basic command syntax and text processing using the sed and awk utilities. While many administrators use perl for automating tasks and performing pattern matching, many sed and awk scripts are still in use and administrators should ensure they can edit and modify them where necessary.

Questions

1. What is the logical result of the test "-n str"?

   A. Is true if and only if the string str has zero length.

   B. Is true if and only if the characters comprising the string str1 are not identical and in the same order as the characters comprising the string str2.

   C. Is true if and only if the string str is non-null.

   D. Is true if and only if the string str has nonzero length.

2. What is the logical result of the test "str"?

   A. Is true if and only if the string str has zero length.

   B. Is true if and only if the characters comprising the string str1 are not identical and in the same order as the characters comprising the string str2.

   C. Is true if and only if the string str is non-null.

   D. Is true if and only if the string str has nonzero length.

3. What is the logical result of the test "str1 != str2"?

   A. Is true if and only if the string str has zero length.

   B. Is true if and only if the characters comprising the string str1 are not identical and in the same order as the characters comprising the string str2.

   C. Is true if and only if the string str is non-null.

   D. Is true if and only if the string str has nonzero length.

4. What is the logical result of the test "-z str"?

   A. Is true if and only if the string str has zero length.

   B. Is true if and only if the characters comprising the string str1 are not identical and in the same order as the characters comprising the string str2.

C. Is true if and only if the string str is non-null.

D. Is true if and only if the string str has nonzero length.

5. What is the logical result of the test "a –eq b"?

   A. Is true if and only if a is less than or equal to b.

   B. Is true if and only if a is greater than b.

   C. Is true if and only if a is greater than or equal to b.

   D. Is true if and only if a is equal to b.

6. What is the logical result of the test "a –ge b"?

   A. Is true if and only if a is less than or equal to b.

   B. Is true if and only if a is greater than b.

   C. Is true if and only if a is greater than or equal to b.

   D. Is true if and only if a is equal to b.

7. What is the logical result of the test "a –gt b"?

   A. Is true if and only if a is less than or equal to b.

   B. Is true if and only if a is greater than b.

   C. Is true if and only if a is greater than or equal to b.

   D. Is true if and only if a is equal to b.

8. What is the logical result of the test "a –le b"?

   A. Is true if and only if a is less than or equal to b.

   B. Is true if and only if a is greater than b.

   C. Is true if and only if a is greater than or equal to b.

   D. Is true if and only if a is equal to b.

9. What is the logical result of the test "-b file"?

   A. Is true if and only if file is a special block file.

   B. Is true if and only if file is a special character file.

   C. Is true if and only if file is a directory.

   D. Is true if and only if file is a normal file.

10. What is the logical result of the test "-c file"?

   A. Is true if and only if file is a special block file.

   B. Is true if and only if file is a special character file.

   C. Is true if and only if file is a directory.

   D. Is true if and only if file is a normal file.

11. What is the logical result of the test "-d file"?

    A. Is true if and only if file is a special block file.

    B. Is true if and only if file is a special character file.

    C. Is true if and only if file is a directory.

    D. Is true if and only if file is a normal file.

12. What is the logical result of the test "-f file"?

    A. Is true if and only if file is a special block file.

    B. Is true if and only if file is a special character file.

    C. Is true if and only if file is a directory.

    D. Is true if and only if file is a normal file.

13. What is the logical result of the test "-p file"?

    A. Is true if and only if file is a named pipe.

    B. Is true if and only if file has nonzero size.

    C. Is true if and only if file is writable by the current user.

    D. Is true if and only if file is executable by the current user.

14. What is the logical result of the test "-s file"?

    A. Is true if and only if file is a named pipe.

    B. Is true if and only if file has nonzero size.

    C. Is true if and only if file is writable by the current user.

    D. Is true if and only if file is executable by the current user.

15. What is the logical result of the test "-w file"?

    A. Is true if and only if file is a named pipe.

    B. Is true if and only if file has nonzero size.

    C. Is true if and only if file is writable by the current user.

    D. Is true if and only if file is executable by the current user.

Answers

1. **D.** The logical result of the test "-n str" is true if and only if the string str has nonzero length.

2. **C.** The logical result of the test "str" is true if and only if the string str is non-null.

3. **B.** The logical result of the test "str1 != str2 is true if and only if the characters comprising the string str1 are not identical and in the same order as the characters comprising the string str2.

4. **A.** The logical result of the test "-z str" is true if and only if the string str has zero length.

5. **D.** The logical result of the test "a –eq b" is true if and only if a is equal to b.

6. **C.** The logical result of the test "a –ge b" is true if and only if a is greater than or equal to b.

7. **B.** The logical result of the test "a –gt b" is true if and only if a is greater than b.

8. **A.** The logical result of the test "a –le b" is true if and only if a is less than or equal to b.

9. **A.** The logical result of the test "-b file" is true if and only if file is a special block file.

10. **B.** The logical result of the test "-c file" is true if and only if file is a special character file.

11. **C.** The logical result of the test "-d file" is true if and only if file is a directory.

12. **D.** The logical result of the test "-f file" is true if and only if file is a normal file.

13. **A.** The logical result of the test "-p file" is true if and only if file is a named pipe.

14. **B.** The logical result of the test "-s file" is true if and only if file has nonzero size.

15. **C.** The logical result of the test "-w file" is true if and only if file is writable by the current user.

Editor

In this chapter, you will
- Learn how to use the vi editor
- Create new text files
- Edit existing text files

An editor is used primarily to create new text files or edit existing text files. Few UNIX users would have escaped learning about the visual editor ("vi") when first learning how to use a Solaris shell. In this chapter, the aim is to review some of the more esoteric vi usages, and to review commonly used command-mode and ex-mode commands.

Visual Editor (vi)

vi is a text processing tool that carries out the following tasks on Solaris and other UNIX systems:

- Creates new text files
- Modifies existing files
- Searches for a text string in a file
- Replaces one string with another in a file
- Moves or copies a string within a file
- Removes a string from a file

To run vi from the command line and create a new file, the following command can be used:

```
$ vi
```

To run vi from the command line and edit an existing file, the following command can be used:

```
$ vi file.txt
```

where *file.txt* is the filename of the file to be edited. The result of editing a file (such as */etc/passwd.txt*) is shown in Figure 16-1.

Figure 16-1

Editing the
/etc/passwd file

```
[x] xterm                                                      _ [] [X]
root:x:0:1:Super-User:/:/sbin/sh
daemon:x:1:1::/:
bin:x:2:2::/usr/bin:
sys:x:3:3::/:
adm:x:4:4:Admin:/var/adm:
lp:x:71:8:Line Printer Admin:/usr/spool/lp:
uucp:x:5:5:uucp Admin:/usr/lib/uucp:
nuucp:x:9:9:uucp Admin:/var/spool/uucppublic:/usr/lib/uucp/uucico
listen:x:37:4:Network Admin:/usr/net/nls:
nobody:x:60001:60001:Nobody:/:
noaccess:x:60002:60002:No Access User:/:
nobody4:x:65534:65534:SunOS 4.x Nobody:/:
natashia:x:1001:10:Natashia Herewane:/export/home/natashia:/bin/csh
pwatters:x:1002:10:Paul Watters:/export/home/pwatters:/bin/bash
~
~
~
~
~
~
~
~
"/etc/passwd" 14 lines, 546 characters
```

When editing an existing file, the visual editor copies the bytes from disk into a member buffer, which is then operated on according to user commands. Text can be inserted during edit mode, while commands are executed during command mode. Changes are not written to disk until the appropriate save command is executed. During edit mode, special keys like the arrow keys will not operate as commands to move the cursor around the screen; instead, the actual code will be inserted into the file. These keys can only be used when the editor is in command mode. During edit mode, you can switch to command mode by pressing the ESCAPE key. When in command mode, you can switch to edit mode by pressing the I key.

The following commands can be executed in command mode:

- / Performs a forward search for a text string.
- ? Performs a backward search for a text string.
- : Runs an ex editor command on the current line.
- ! Executes a shell within vi.
- ZZ Saves a file and exits.
- h Moves the cursor left.
- j Moves the cursor down.
- k Moves the cursor up.
- l Moves the cursor right.

- *n*G   Moves cursor to line *n*.
- w   Moves to next word.
- b   Moves back one word.
- dw   Deletes words.
- *n*dw   Deletes *n* words.
- d^   Deletes all words to the beginning of the line.
- dd   Deletes the current line.
- dG   Deletes all lines to the end of the file.
- D   Deletes all words to the end of the line.
- x   Deletes the current character.
- *n*x   Deletes *n* characters to the right.
- *n*Y   Yanks *n* lines into the buffer.
- p   Pastes to the right of the cursor.
- P   Pastes to the left of the cursor.

EXAM TIP   You should be able to identify the functions of each of these commands for the exam.

A separate set of commands, called the ex commands, can be run by using the colon in conjunction with one of these commands:

- :*n*   Moves cursor to line *n*.
- :$ Moves cursor to the end of the file.
- :%s/*a*/*b*/g   Replaces all occurrences of string *a* with string *b*.
- :wq   Saves modified file and quits.
- :q!   Quits without saving any changes.
- :set   Sets a number of different options.

Let's examine the result of using the ex command :%s/*a*/*b*/g. Figure 16-2 shows the /etc/passwd with an ex command that will search for all occurrences of "export" and replace them with "staff".

Figure 16-3 shows the result output. The string /export/home now changes to /staff/home.

Figure 16-2
Using an ex
command

Figure 16-3
Performing text
substitutions

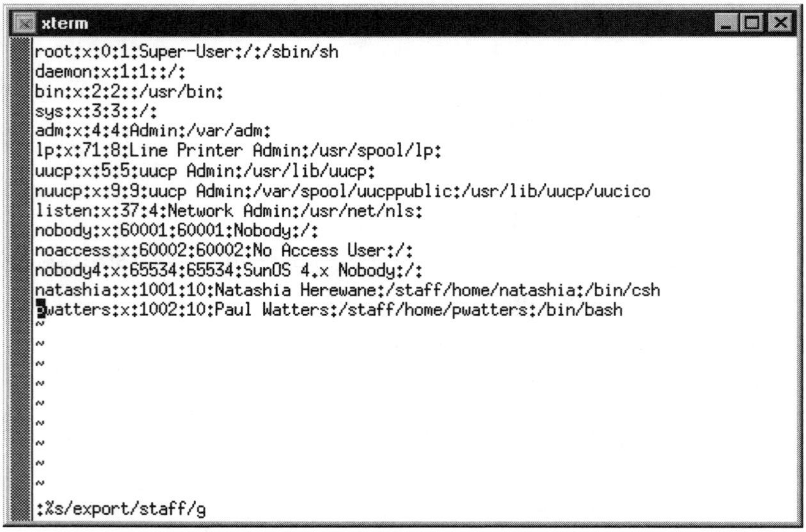

```
root:x:0:1:Super-User:/:/sbin/sh
daemon:x:1:1::/:
bin:x:2:2::/usr/bin:
sys:x:3:3::/:
adm:x:4:4:Admin:/var/adm:
lp:x:71:8:Line Printer Admin:/usr/spool/lp:
uucp:x:5:5:uucp Admin:/usr/lib/uucp:
nuucp:x:9:9:uucp Admin:/var/spool/uucppublic:/usr/lib/uucp/uucico
listen:x:37:4:Network Admin:/usr/net/nls:
nobody:x:60001:60001:Nobody:/:
noaccess:x:60002:60002:No Access User:/:
nobody4:x:65534:65534:SunOS 4.x Nobody:/:
natashia:x:1001:10:Natashia Herewane:/staff/home/natashia:/bin/csh
pwatters:x:1002:10:Paul Watters:/staff/home/pwatters:/bin/bash
~
~
~
~
~
~
~
~
~
:%s/export/staff/g
```

Summary

Using a text editor is such a fundamental skill that it should be mastered as a UNIX user before attempting to become a Solaris administrator, so we've only examined the basic operation of vi in this chapter. For more information, read the vi man page.

Questions

1. What command is used to perform a forward search for a text string?

   A. /

   B. ?

   C. :

   D. !

2. What command is used to perform a backward search for a text string?

   A. /

   B. ?

   C. :

   D. !

3. What command is used to run an ex editor command on the current line?

   A. /

   B. ?

   C. :

   D. !

4. What command is used to execute a shell within vi?

   A. /

   B. ?

   C. :

   D. !

5. What command is used to save a file and exit vi?

   A. ZZ

   B. h

   C. j

   D. k

6. What command is used to move the cursor left?

   A. ZZ

   B. h

   C. j

   D. k

7. What command is used to move the cursor down?

   A. ZZ

   B. h

   C. j

   D. k

8. What command is used to move the cursor up?

   A. ZZ

   B. h

   C. j

   D. k

9. What command is used to move the cursor to line *n*?

   A. :n

   B. :$

   C. :%s/a/b/g

   D. :wq

10. What command is used to move the cursor to the end of the file?

   A. :n

   B. :$

   C. :%s/a/b/g

   D. :wq

11. What command is used to replace all occurrences of string *a* with string *b*?

   A. :n

   B. :$

   C. :%s/a/b/g

   D. :wq

12. What command is used to save a modified file and quit?

   A. :n

   B. :$

   C. :%s/a/b/g

   D. :wq

Answers

   1. A. / performs a forward search for a text string.

   2. B. ? performs a backward search for a text string.

   3. C. : runs an ex editor command on the current line.

   4. D. ! executes a shell within vi.

   5. A. ZZ saves a file.

   6. B. h moves the cursor left.

   7. C. j moves the cursor down.

   8. D. k moves the cursor up.

   9. A. :n moves the cursor to line n.

   10. B. :$ moves the cursor to the end of the file.

   11. C. :%s/a/b/g replaces all occurrences of string *a* with string *b*.

   12. D. :wq saves a modified file and quits.

## CHAPTER 17

Remote Access

In this chapter, you will

- Learn how to remotely access a Solaris system
- Review methods for securing remote access
- Discover the benefits of Kerberos authentication

In this chapter, we examine the most commonly used methods to remotely access Solaris systems with a focus on setting up Internet access.

Internet Access

Most users access a Solaris system by means of a remote terminal, across a secure or insecure communications channel, and with or without X11 graphics support. This variety of access methods makes Solaris an ideal multiuser system, since different users can interact with a server using a number of different techniques, based on local conditions. For example, clients on a local network not connected to the Internet may use telnet and X11 graphics to run an application on a server, while a remote user in a foreign country with just VT100 terminal access would be able to use OpenSSH.

Telnet

Telnet is the standard remote access tool for logging into a Solaris machine from a client using the original DARPA TELNET protocol. A client can be executed on most operating systems that support TCP/IP. Alternatively, a Java telnet client is available (**http://srp.stanford.edu/~tjw/telnet.html**), which is supported on any operating system that has a browser that runs Java natively or as a plug-in. Telnet is a terminal-like program that gives users interactive access to a login shell of their choice (for example, the C shell, or csh). Most telnet clients support VT100 or VT220 terminal emulations. The login shell can be used to execute scripts, develop applications, and read e-mail and news—in short, everything a Solaris environment should provide to its users, with the exception of X11 graphics and OpenWindows, or more recently the common desktop environment (CDE). A common arrangement in many organizations is for a Solaris server to be located in a secure area of a building with telnet-only access allowed.

The sequence of events that occur during a telnet session begins with a request for a connection from the client to the server. The server responds (or times out) with a connection being explicitly accepted or rejected. A rejection may occur because the port that normally accepts telnet client connections on the server has been blocked by a packet filter or firewall. If the connection is accepted, the client is asked to enter a username followed by a password. If the username and password combination is valid, a shell is spawned and the user is logged in. The sequence of events in shown in Figure 17-1.

The standard port for telnet connections is 23. Thus, a command like,

```
$ telnet server
```

is expanded to give the effective command:

```
$ telnet server 23
```

This means that telnet can be used as a tool to access a service on virtually any port. Telnet is controlled by the super Internet daemon (inetd), which invokes the in.telnetd server. An entry is made in */etc/services* that defines the port number for the telnet service, which looks like this:

```
telnet      23/tcp
```

The configuration file */etc/inetd.conf* also contains important details of the services provided by inetd. The telnet daemon's location and properties are identified here:

```
telnet stream tcp nowait root /pkgs/tcpwrapper/bin/tcpd in.telnetd
```

In this case, we can see that in.telnetd is protected by the use of TCP *wrappers*, which facilitate the logging of telnet accesses through the Solaris syslog facility. In addition, inetd has some significant historical security holes and performance issues that, although mostly fixed in recent years, have caused administrators to shy away from servers invoked by inetd. The Apache web server (**http://www.apache.org**), for example, runs as a stand-alone daemon process and does not use inetd.

The Solaris telnet client has an extensive help facility available, which can be viewed by keying the escape sequence (usually ^]), and typing the command **help**. The main telnet commands are shown in Table 17-1.

Figure 17-1

Telnet access
event sequence

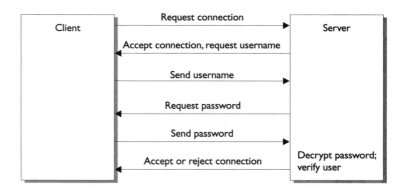

	Command	Description
Table 17-1 Telnet Client Commands	close	Quit telnet session.
	logout	Close connection.
	display	Print connection characteristics.
	mode	Change mode.
	open	Open connection.
	quit	Quite telnet session.
	send	Send special characters.
	set	Set connection characteristics.
	unset	Unset connection characteristics.
	status	Display connection status.
	toggle	Change connection characteristics.
	slc	Toggle special character mode.
	z	Suspend connection.
	!	Spawn shell.
	environ	Update environment variables.
	?	Display help.
	ENTER	Return to session.

As an example of how these commands work, the `display` command will print all of the current settings being used by your terminal:

```
telnet> display
will flush output when sending interrupt characters.
won't send interrupt characters in urgent mode.
won't skip reading of ~/.telnetrc file.
won't map carriage return on output.
will recognize certain control characters.
won't turn on socket level debugging.
won't print hexadecimal representation of network traffic.
won't print user readable output for "netdata".
won't show option processing.
won't print hexadecimal representation of terminal traffic.
echo            [^E]
escape          [^]]
rlogin          [off]
tracefile       "(standard output)"
flushoutput     [^O]
interrupt       [^C]
quit            [^\]
eof             [^D]
erase           [^?]
kill            [^U]
lnext           [^V]
susp            [^Z]
```

```
reprint        [^R]
worderase      [^W]
start          [^Q]
stop           [^S]
forw1          [off]
forw2          [off]
ayt            [^T]
```

Alternatively, the `status` command reveals the characteristics of the current telnet connection:

```
telnet> status
Connected to currawong.cassowary.net.
Operating in single character mode
Catching signals locally
Remote character echo
Escape character is '^]'.
```

To resume the telnet session, simply hit the ENTER key at the telnet> prompt.

inetd also controls many other standard remote access clients, including the so-called r-commands, including the remote login (rlogin) and remote shell (rsh) applications. The rlogin application is similar to telnet in that it establishes a remote connection through TCP/IP to a server, spawning an interactive login shell. For example, the command

```
$ rlogin server
```

by default produces the response,

```
password:
```

after which the password is entered, authenticated by the server, and access denied or granted. If the target user account has a different name than your current user account, you can try this:

```
$ rlogin server -l user
```

However, there are two main differences between telnet and rlogin that are significant. The first is that rlogin attempts to use the username on your current system as the account name to connect to on the remote service, whereas telnet always prompts for a separate username. This makes remotely logging into machines on a single logical network with rlogin much faster than with telnet. Second, on a trusted, secure network, it is possible to set up a remote authentication mechanism by which the remote host allows a direct, no-username/no-password login from authorized clients. This automated authentication can be performed on a system-wide level by defining an "equivalent" host for authentication purposes on the server in */etc/hosts.equiv*, or on a user-by-user basis with the file *.rhosts*. If the file */etc/hosts.equiv* contains the client machine name and your username, you will be permitted to automatically execute a remote login. For example, if the */etc/hosts.equiv* file on the server contains the line

```
client
```

any user from the machine client may log into a corresponding account on the server without entering a username and password. Similarly, if your username and client machine name appear in the *.rhosts* file in the home directory of the user with the same name on the server, you will also be permitted to remotely log in without an identification/authentication challenge. This means that a user on the remote system may log in with all the privileges of the user on the local system, without being asked to enter a username or password—clearly a dangerous security risk.

Remote-shell (rsh) connects to a specified hostname and executes a command. rsh is equivalent to rlogin when no command arguments are specified. rsh copies its standard input to the remote command, the standard output of the remote command to its standard output, and the standard error of the remote command to its standard error. Interrupt, quit, and terminate signals are propagated to the remote command. In contrast to commands issued interactively through rlogin, rsh normally terminates when the remote command does.

As an example, the following executes the command df –k on the server, returning information about disk slices and creating the local file server.*df.txt* that contains the output of the command:

```
$ rsh server df -k > server.df.txt
```

Clearly, rsh has the potential to be useful in scripts and automated command processing.

Testing Service Connectivity

Because a port number can be specified on the command line, telnet clients can be used to connect to arbitrary ports on Solaris servers. This makes a telnet client a useful tool for testing whether services that should have been disconnected are actually active. For example, you can interactively issue commands to an FTP server on port 21

```
$ telnet server 21
Trying 172.16.1.1...
Connected to server.
Escape character is '^]'.
220 server FTP server (UNIX(r) System V Release 4.0) ready.
```

and on a sendmail server on port 25:

```
$ telnet server 25
Trying 172.16.1.1...
Connected to server.
Escape character is '^]'.
220 server ESMTP Sendmail 8.9.1a/8.9.1; Mon, 22 Nov 1999
    14:31:36 +1100 (EST)
```

Interactive testing of this kind has many uses. For example, if we telnet to port 80 on a server, we are usually connected to a web server, where we can issue interactive commands using the Hypertext Transfer Protocol (HTTP). For example, to GET the default index page on a server, we could type **get index.html**:

```
Trying 172.16.1.1...
Connected to server.
Escape character is '^]'.
GET index.html
<!DOCTYPE HTML PUBLIC "-//IETF//DTD HTML 2.0//EN">
<HTML><HEAD>
<TITLE>Server</TITLE></HEAD>
<h1>Welcome to server!</h1>
```

This technique is useful when testing proxy server configurations for new kinds of HTTP clients (for example, a HotJava browser), or the technique can be executed during a script to check whether the web server is active and serving expected content.

Using Remote Access Tools

With the increased use of the Internet for business-to-business and consumer-to-business transactions, securing remote access has become a major issue in the provision of Solaris services. Fortunately, solutions based around the encryption of sessions and authentication of clients have improved the reliability of remote access facilities in a security-conscious operating environment.

Secure Shell (SSH)

Open Secure Shell, OpenSSH, or just plain SSH, is a secure client and server solution that facilitates the symmetric and asymmetric encryption of identification and authentication sequences for remote access. It is designed to replace the telnet and rlogin applications on the client side, with clients available for Solaris, Windows, and many other operating systems. On the server side, it improves upon the nonsecure services supported by inetd, such as the r-commands.

SSH makes use of a generic transport layer encryption mechanism over TCP/IP, which uses the popular Blowfish or government-endorsed Triple-DES (Data Encryption Standard) algorithms for the encryption engine. This is used to transmit encrypted packets whose contents can still be sniffed like all traffic on the network by using public-key cryptography, implementing the Diffie-Hellman algorithm for key exchange. Thus, the contents of encrypted packets appear to be random without the appropriate "key" to decrypt them.

The use of encryption technology makes it extremely unlikely that the contents of the interactive session will ever be known to anyone except the client and the server. In addition to the encryption of session data, identification and authentication sequences are also encrypted using RSA encryption technology. This means that username and password combinations also cannot be sniffed by a third party. SSH also provides automatic forwarding for graphics applications, based around the X11 windowing system, which is a substantial improvement over the text-only telnet client.

The sequence of events for establishing an SSH client connection to a server is as follows:

1. The client connects to a server port requesting a connection (usually port 22, but this can be adapted to suit local conditions).

2. The server replies with its standard public RSA host key (1024 bits), as well as another RSA server key (768 bits) that changes hourly. Since the server key changes hourly, even if the keys for the traffic of one session were cracked, historic data would still remain encrypted, limiting the utility of any such attack.

3. The server can be configured to reject connections from hosts that it doesn't know about, but by default it will accept connections from any client.

4. If the connection is accepted, the client generates a session key composed of a 256-bit random number and chooses an encryption algorithm that the server supports (Triple-DES or Blowfish).

5. The client then encrypts the session key using RSA, using both the host and server key, and returns the encrypted key to the server.

6. The server decrypts the session key and encryption is enabled between the client and server.

7. If the default authentication mechanism is selected, the client passes the username and password for the server across the secure channel.

It is possible to disable the username/password authentication sequence by permitting logins to clients that have an appropriate private RSA key, as long as the server has a list of accepted public keys. However, if a client computer is stolen and the private key is retrieved by a rogue user, access to the server can be obtained without a valid username and password combination.

On the client side, a *knownhsts.txt* file is created, and server keys are recorded there. Entries look like this:

```
server 1024 35 07448318855220650928863459182148090000874876031312
663202636556140699569229172676719815525201670198606754982042373 6
393736593998729350847306606972263971147429524250769197415119584 2
956063176626459842269220618785535980433268062460000169825137572 6
292755659298770421181014212617571545279674887150613189468540157 6
4183
```

In addition, a private key for the client is stored in *Identity*, and a public key for the client is stored in *Identity.pub*. Entries in this file are similar to the server key file:

```
1024 37 25909842022319975817366569029015041390873694788964256567
21464229667226227437398365816534529060328087939018802894227642 52
42596146365495189984505249238114810023604394738523635422233598 68
11461925396194818530944668193356297977415807086095058777077424 73
73117735318506922304377996946111769127284747352249217710411 51
Paul Watters
```

It is sensible in a commercial context to enforce a policy of SSH-only remote access for interactive logins. This can easily be enforced by enabling the SSH daemon on the server side and removing entries for the telnet and rlogin services in */etc/services* and */etc/inetd.conf*. Now that OpenSSH is supplied with Solaris, there is no excuse for not deploying SSH across all hosts in your local network.

Kerberos

While SSH is an excellent tool for remote access between a single client and multiple servers, maintaining local databases of keys on every client machine is costly in terms of disk space and network traffic. Although some argue that such information should always be distributed across the network, the level of redundancy that SSH requires for installations of 1,000 or more clients is inefficient.

One alternative to using SSH servers as the primary means of authentication across a network is to use a centralized authentication system such as Kerberos, which grew out of the Athena Project at the Massachusetts Institute of Technology (MIT). Kerberos is a network authentication protocol that is designed to provide strong authentication for client/server applications by using secret-key cryptography, which is similar to that provided by SSH. However, the main difference between the two systems is that while authentication is performed by the target server when using SSH, a Kerberos authentication server can provide services to many different servers for a large number of clients. Thus, the many-to-many relationships realized in the Kerberos authentication database make the network authentication process more streamlined and efficient.

Kerberos is also designed to provide authentication to hosts inside and outside a firewall, since many attacks may originate in internal networks that are normally considered trusted. In addition, Release 5 introduced the notion of *realms*, which are external but trusted networks with authentication being extended beyond the firewall. Another advantage of the Kerberos system is that the protocol has been published and widely publicized. Of course, the greatest advantage for Solaris users is that it's no longer necessary to download the free implementation from MIT. While Solaris 8 supplied client tools for Kerberos, Solaris 9 now supports Kerberos servers and clients that are compliant with Kerberos Release 5 v1.1. The Kerberos daemon in Solaris is kadmind, which is responsible for running the primary key distribution center (KDC).

Kerberos is based on a certificate granting and validation system called *tickets*. If a client machine wants to make a connection to a target server, it requests a ticket from a centralized authentication server, which can be physically the same machine as the target server but is logically quite separate. An encrypted ticket is produced by the authentication server that authorizes the client to request a specific service from a specific host, generally for a specific time period. This is similar to a parking ticket machine that grants the drivers of motor vehicles permission to park on a specific street for one or two hours only. Release 5 of Kerberos supports tickets that can be renewed.

When authentication is requested from the authentication server, a session key is created by that server that is based on your password, which it retrieves from your username—a random value that represents the requested service. The session key is like a voucher that the client then sends to a ticket-granting server, which then returns a ticket that can be used to access the target server. Clearly, some overhead is involved in making a request to an authentication server, a ticket-granting server, and a target server. However, the overhead is well worth the effort if important data is at risk of interception.

A significant limitation of Kerberos is that all applications that make use of its authentication services must be "kerberized"—that is, significant changes must be made to the application's source code for it to make use of Kerberos services.

Kerberos configuration is reasonably straightforward given appropriate network resources. A configuration file (*/etc/krb5/krb5.conf*) contains entries like this:

```
[libdefaults]
        default_realm = site.com

[realms]
        site.com = {
                kdc = kerberos1.site.com
                kdc = kerberos2.site.com
                admin_server = kerberos1.site.com
        }
```

This configuration is for a domain called **site.com**, which has a primary KDC called **kerberos1.site.com** and a backup server called **kerberos2.site.com**. In addition to *krb5.conf*, several other configuration files are maintained by Kerberos:

- */var/krb5/principal.db*   Database of principals
- */var/krb5/principal.kadm5*   Principal management database
- */etc/krb5/kadm5.acl*   Access control list for principals
- */etc/krb5/kadm5.keytab*   Local key tab

kadmin

The `kadmin` command is used to manage local Kerberos services, by administering key tabs, principals, and policies. There are two versions of kadmin available: kadmin.local is used only on the master KDC, and does not require authentication, while kadmin, when executed on any other server, requires Kerberos authentication across a secure link. Once logged in, the following prompt is displayed, ready for commands to be entered:

```
kadmin:
```

When kadmin starts up, it checks the value of the *USER* environment variable to determine the principal name. For example, if *USER*=pwatters, the principal name would be pwatters/admin. Alternatively, the -p option can be passed to kadmin when starting up, followed by the principal name. In addition, if a realm other than the default is to be administered, the realm name must be supplied on the command line after the -r option is passed. The user will be prompted for a password, unless one has been passed on the command line with the -w option. Thus, to start kadmin for the realm **site.com** with the principal pwatters/admin and the password 6fgj4gsd, the following command would be used:

```
# kadmin -p pwatters/admin -r site.com -w 6fgj4gsd
```

The following commands are supported by kadmin:

- `list_requests` Displays all kadmin commands.
- `add_principal` Adds a new principal.
- `get_privs` Displays the Access Control Lists (ACLs) for the current principal.
- `-expire` Sets the principal's effective end date.
- `-pwexpire` Sets the principal's password effective end date.
- `-maxlife` Specifies an upper time limit for tickets.
- `-maxrenewlife` Specifies an upper time limit for ticket renewal.
- `-policy` Sets the policy name.
- `-pw` Sets the principal's password.
- `delete_principal` Completely removes a principal.
- `modify_principal` Updates the principal's characteristics.
- `get_principal` Displays the principal's characteristics.
- `list_principals` Prints all known principal names.
- `add_policy` Attaches a new policy.
- `delete_policy` Completely removes a policy.
- `get_policy` Displays the characteristics of a policy.
- `list_policy` Displays policy names.
- `ktadd` Attaches a principal to a key tab.
- `ktadd` Removes a principal from a key tab.

kdb5_util

The kdb5_util program is used to manage the Kerberos database files. It accepts the database name as an argument on the command line after the `-d` option has been passed. One of the following options must also be included to perform a specific action:

- `create` Creates a new database.
- `destroy` Deletes an existing database.
- `stash` Initializes a stash file to store the master key for the database.
- `dump` Exports the database to ASCII format.
- `load` Imports the database from ASCII format.

Modem Access

The service access facility (SAF) is a port management system that manages requests and responses for access to system ports. In this case, a port is defined as the physical connection between a peripheral device and the system. For example, most systems have one or more serial ports that allow for sequential data transmission, effectively down a single line. In contrast, a parallel port allows for several lines of data to be transmitted bidirectionally. The SAF system is designed to allow requests to be made to the system from peripheral devices through ports and ensure that these requests are appropriately serviced by the relevant port monitor.

Modems, which allow Solaris 9 systems to connect to the Internet over a phone line, require SAF to operate through system serial ports. Thus, it's important to understand how to configure ports, port monitors, and listeners in preparation for making an Internet connection using a modem. Note that most Solaris systems are never accessed through a modem; however, if a system's only network card has died and the console is physically inaccessible, a modem can be a lifesaver.

The Point-to-Point Protocol (PPP) daemon is commonly used to set up modem access to an Internet service provider (ISP). PPP supports TCP/IP and provides the Challenge Handshake Authentication Protocol (CHAP), providing a higher level of security than usually found on modem links. The PPP daemon relies on the chat program to perform the dial-up and handle connections. In this section, we'll examine how to set up port monitors and PPP for Internet connections.

Port Monitors

Central to the idea of providing services through serial ports is the port monitor, which continuously monitors the serial ports for requests to log in. The port monitor doesn't process the communication parameters directly, but accepts requests and passes them to the operating system. Solaris 9 uses the ttymon port monitor, which allows multiple concurrent getty requests from serial devices.

To configure the port for a terminal, start up admintool and enter the user mode, which can be either Basic, More, or Expert. In most cases, Basic setup will be sufficient . admintool allows the configuration of most parameters for the port, including the baud rate for communications, default terminal type, flow control, and carrier detection. The values entered here should match those on the matching VT-100 terminal. Once the settings have been saved, it is possible to check the validity of the settings by using the pmadm command:

```
# pmadm -l -s ttyb
```

The Service Access Facility (SAF)

The process that initiates the service access facility is known as the service access controller (/usr/lib/saf/sac). It is started when the system enters run level 2, 3, or 4, as shown in this /etc/inittab entry:

```
sc:234:respawn:/usr/lib/saf/sac -t 300
```

Here, the respawn entry indicates that if a process is not running when it should be, it should be respawned. For example, if a system changes from run level 2 to run level 3, sac should be running. If it is not present, it will be restarted.

When sac is started, it reads the script */etc/saf/_sysconfig*, which contains any local configurations tailored for the system. Next, the standard configuration file */etc/saf/_sactab* is read, and sac spawns a separate child process for each of the port monitors it supports (ttymon and listen). A sample _sactab is shown here:

```
# VERSION=1
zsmon:ttymon::0:/usr/lib/saf/ttymon #
```

Port monitors also read a configuration file (*/etc/saf/zsmon/_pmtab*) that is used to configure the ttymon and listen port monitors. A sample _pmtab file is shown here:

```
# VERSION=1
ttya:u:root:reserved:reserved:reserved:/dev/term/a:I::
/usr/bin/login::9600:ldterm,ttcompat:ttya login\: ::tvi925:y:#
ttyb:u:root:reserved:reserved:reserved:/dev/term/b:I::
/usr/bin/login::9600:ldterm,ttcompat:ttyb login\: ::tvi925:y:#
```

The point of this hierarchical configuration file structure is that values read from */etc/saf/_sysconfig* and */etc/saf/_sactab* by sac are inherited by the spawned port monitor processes, which then have the ability to configure their own operations.

The SAF has two types of port monitors: the terminal port monitor (ttymon) and the network port monitor (listen). For example, the ttymon port monitor for the console is started in run levels 2, 3, and 4, through an */etc/inittab* entry like the following:

```
co:234:respawn:/usr/lib/saf/ttymon -g -h -p
    "`uname -n` console login: " -T vt100 -d
    /dev/console -l console -m ldterm,ttcompat
```

The ttymon process is active when a monitor is connected to a server, such as a dumb terminal, rather than a graphics monitor.

Point-to-Point Protocol (PPP)

PPP is the most commonly used protocol for connecting modems over a phone line (or, uncommonly, over a normal serial line) to support TCP/IP. It replaces the earlier Serial Line Interface Protocol (SLIP), which did not provide any level of security or authentication for serial line services. The Solaris 9 implementation of PPP is based on the ANU version (**ftp://cs.anu.edu.au/pub/software/ppp**). PPP provides reliable access to the Internet because it includes error correction and the ability to autodetect some network parameters. All of the parameters for the PPP daemon (pppd) are stored in */etc/ppp/options*. Alternatively, for options that are specific to each serial port, a new configuration file can be created (such as */etc/ppp/options.cua.a* for the serial port */dev/cua/a*). This is useful where two modems are connected to the two standard serial interfaces on a SPARC system that are connected to two separate modems, which in turn dial completely different ISPs—the lesson for high availability is to "be prepared" for the worst-case scenario. Supporting network operations through a 56K modem is going to be challenging, but not impossible, in an emergency. Figure 17-2 shows a PPP configuration with high availability in mind.

Setting Up Port Listeners

The listen port monitor is managed by the `listen` and `nlsadmin` commands. In contrast to ttymon, the listen port monitor manages network ports and connections by listening for requests to access services and daemons. The listen monitor uses the Transport Layer Interface (TLI) and STREAMS to implement OSI-compliant network service layers. Specific networks ports are assigned to the listen monitor, and child processes are spawned to handle each client request. One of the key features of listen is that it can provide services that are not managed by inetd—since all daemons can be accessed through a listen service. This is an important feature for the different users accessing services on a Solaris system. For example, a network connection could serve web traffic, while a dial-in connection could cater to telnet or SSH access.

The `nlsadmin` command is used to set up transport providers for STREAMS-compatible network services. In order to configure a TLI listener database, the `nlsadmin` command can be used to configure the listener. First, the TCP/IP database is created:

```
# nlsadmin -i tcp
```

Next, set the local hexadecimal address:

```
# nlsadmin -l \x11331223a11a58310000000000000000 tcp
```

All services that need to be run will then need to be entered into the TLI listener database.

Adding a Serial Port

Like any modern server system, Solaris 9 supports the connection of simple external devices through both a serial (RS-232-C or RS-423) and a parallel port. The two most common uses for serial devices on a SPARC system are connecting a VT-100 terminal or

Figure 17-2
PPP configuration
with high
availability

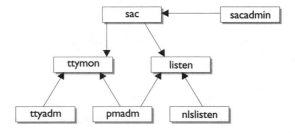

equivalent, to operate as the system console if no graphics device is installed, and as a modem, enabling dial-up Internet access using the Point-to-Point Protocol (PPP). The former is a common practice in many server rooms, where the expense of a monitor and video card can be eliminated by using a VT-100 terminal as the console, because many SPARC machines require a display device to boot at all. On *x*86 systems, there are many more devices available that often only have drivers available for other operating systems. Sun and other third-party hardware vendors are slowly making releases available for these devices through the Solaris Developer Connection. If you need to obtain an updated copy of the Solaris Device Configuration Assistant, and any updated device drivers for supported external devices, these are currently available for download at **http://soldc.sun.com/support/drivers/boot.html**.

Solaris 9 has a graphical user interface (GUI) for serial device configuration, provided through the admintool program. admintool is generally used for system administration tasks, like adding users and groups, but it also has facilities for configuring parallel devices (like printers) and serial devices (like modems). It contains templates for configuring standard modem and terminal devices, and supports multiple ports. It's important to note that SMC is slated to replace admintool in future releases of Solaris.

Adding a Modem

Solaris 9 works best with external Hayes-compatible modems, which are also supported by other operating systems such as Microsoft Windows. However, modems that require specific operating system support (such as so-called "WinModems"), will not work with Solaris 9. In addition, internal modem cards are generally not supported by Solaris 9. While older modems tend to use external (but sometimes internal!) DIP switches, modern modems can be configured using software to set most of their key operational parameters.

Modem access can be configured to allow inbound-only, outbound-only, and bidirectional access, which allows traffic in both directions, using a similar scheme. In the following example, we'll consider the scenario of dial-out-only access. The modem should be connected to one of the system's serial ports (A or B) and switched on. The A and B serial ports map to the devices */dev/cua/a* and */dev/cua/b*, respectively.

To test the modem, use the `tip` command

```
# tip hardwire
```

where hardwire should be defined in */etc/remote*. The hardwire entry should be similar to this entry

```
hardwire:\
        :dv=/dev/cua/a:br#19200:el=^C^S^Q^U^D:ie=%$:oe=^D:
```

where 19,200 bps is the connection speed between the modem and the serial port. In addition, */etc/remote* should have a connection string associated with each modem that's connected to the system. For example, the string

```
cua1:dv=/dev/cua/a:p8:br#19200
```

specifies that 19,200 bps is the connection speed between the modem and the serial port, with 8-bit transmission and with no parity enabled. To use this entry specifically, you would use the command

```
# tip cua1
```

If the message

```
connected
```

appears on your terminal, the system is able to communicate successfully with the modem. For Hayes-compatible modems, command strings can be entered directly like this:

```
ATE1V1
```

If you see "ok", the modem is communicating as expected and can be configured to run PPP.

Setting Up PPP

The first step in configuring PPP is to insert appropriate configuration information in */etc/ppp/options*. The following options are the most commonly used:

- `<tty_name>` Name of the terminal device to use for communication.
- `<speed>` Speed at which to transmit data.
- `auth` Specifies that authentication is required (`noauth` specifies that no authentication is required).
- `callback` Requests a callback from the remote server. Useful for saving on long distance charges!
- `connect` or `init` Specifies the chat script to configure line communications.
- `mru` Sets a maximum receive unit (MRU) value that specifies a limit on the packet size transmitted by the server.
- `mtu` Sets a maximum transmit unit (MTU) value that specifies a limit on the packet size transmitted by the client.

Other options may be required, especially for authentication, but using these options is generally sufficient to make a connection. For further information, you should consult Celeste Stokely's PPP guide: **http://www.stokely.com/unix.serial.port. resources/ppp.slip.html**.

Using ttymon

The ttymon port monitor is managed by the `ttyadm` command. ttymon is designed to monitor requests from ports to allow remote access to the system. The ttymon operates continually, spawning child processes when appropriate in order to service requests, which are sequentially numbered (for example, ttymon1, ttymon2, and so forth). The most common request for terminals is probably for an interactive login; thus, */usr/bin/ login* is requested. The `sacadm` command can be used to list all current ttymon processes:

```
# sacadm -l
PMTAG    PMTYPE   FLGS   RCNT   STATUS    COMMAND
ttymon1  ttymon   -      2      ENABLED   /usr/lib/saf/ttymon #ttymon1
ttymon2  ttymon   -      2      ENABLED   /usr/lib/saf/ttymon #ttymon2
ttymon3  ttymon   -      2      ENABLED   /usr/lib/saf/ttymon #ttymon3
```

In order to view the services currently being provided through a particular monitor, you can use the `pmadm` command for each monitor process:

```
# pmadm -l -p ttymon2
PMTAG      PMTYPE    SVCTAG      FLGS      ID        <PMSPECIFIC>
ttymon2    ttymon    11          u         root      /dev/term/11
   -    -  /usr/bin/login - 9600 - login:   -tvi925
ttymon2    ttymon    12          u         root      /dev/term/12
   -    -  /usr/bin/login - 9600 - login:   -tvi925
ttymon2    ttymon    13          u         root      /dev/term/13
   -    -  /usr/bin/login - 9600 - login:   -tvi925
ttymon2    ttymon    14          u         root      /dev/term/14
   -    -  /usr/bin/login - 9600 - login:   -tvi925
```

Here, we can see that ports */dev/term/11* through */dev/term/14* are being serviced using the login service.

Connecting to an ISP

Once the */etc/ppp/options* file has been set up, a connection can then be made from the command line. For example, to connect using a 56K modem using the chat script *emergency1.chat*, the following command will establish a connection without authentication:

```
# pppd connect 'chat -f emergency1.chat' /dev/cua/a 57600 noauth
```

pmadm

The port monitors are managed by the `pmadm` command. Port services can be managed by using the following commands:

pmadm -a	Adds a port monitor service.
pmadm -d	Disarms a port monitor service.
pmadm -e	Enables a port monitor service.
pmadm -r	Removes a port monitor service.

sacadm

The `sacadm` command is used to manage port monitors. The following functions are available:

`sacadm -a`	Attaches a new port monitor
`sacadm -e`	Arms a port monitor
`sacadm -d`	Disarms a port monitor
`sacadm -s`	Initializes a port monitor
`sacadm -k`	Kills a port monitor
`sacadm -l`	Lists port monitor details
`sacadm -r`	Deletes a port monitor

tip

`tip` is a command that acts like a terminal. It can be used, for example, to access remote systems directly through a serial port, where one system acts as the console for the other. Next, we'll use the `tip` command to connect a Solaris 9 system to a modem. Before proceeding, however, we'll examine some of the key features of `tip` in its own right.

`tip` uses the */etc/remote* file to enable it to make connections through the serial port. For example, if you have a profile set up in */etc/remote*, it's possible to fire up a terminal session immediately by using the command

```
# tip profile
```

where *profile* is the name of the profile that you've set up with all the settings that the port requires to operate. `tip` also uses initialization settings in the *.tiprc* file to specify its operational parameters.

The following table shows the most commonly used `tip` commands:

Command	Description
`~.`	Exits the session.
`~c`	Changes directory.
`~!`	Spawns a shell.
`~>`	Sends a local file.
`~<`	Receives a remote file.
`~p`	Sends a local file.
`~t`	Receives a remote file.
`~C`	Allows a local application to connect to a remote system.
`~#`	Issues a `break` command.
`~s`	Defines a variable.
`~^z`	Suspends `tip`.

Summary

In this chapter, we have examined how to remotely access a Solaris system using traditional and the newer, more secure tools. In addition, we examined how to perform distributed authentication using Kerberos and how to practically connect Solaris systems to the Internet.

Questions

1. What is the function of the telnet `close` command?

   A. Quit telnet session

   B. Close connection

   C. Print connection characteristics

   D. Change mode

2. What is the function of the telnet `logout` command?

   A. Quit telnet session

   B. Close connection

   C. Print connection characteristics

   D. Change mode

3. What is the function of the telnet `display` command?

   A. Quit telnet session

   B. Close connection

   C. Print connection characteristics

   D. Change mode

4. What is the function of the telnet `mode` command?

   A. Quit telnet session

   B. Close connection

   C. Print connection characteristics

   D. Change mode

5. What is the function of the telnet `open` command?

   A. Open connection

   B. Quit telnet session

   C. Send special characters

   D. Set connection characteristics

6. What is the function of the telnet `quit` command?

   A. Open connection

   B. Quit telnet session

   C. Send special characters

   D. Set connection characteristics

7. What is the function of the telnet `send` command?

   A. Open connection

   B. Quit telnet session

   C. Send special characters

   D. Set connection characteristics

8. What is the function of the telnet `set` command?

   A. Open connection

   B. Quit telnet session

   C. Send special characters

   D. Set connection characteristics

9. What is the function of the telnet `unset` command?

   A. Unset connection characteristics

   B. Display connection status

   C. Change connection characteristics

   D. Toggle special character mode

10. What is the function of the telnet `status` command?

    A. Unset connection characteristics

    B. Display connection status

    C. Change connection characteristics

    D. Toggle special character mode

11. What is the function of the telnet `toggle` command?

    A. Unset connection characteristics

    B. Display connection status

    C. Change connection characteristics

    D. Toggle special character mode

12. What is the function of the telnet `slc` command?

    A. Unset connection characteristics

    B. Display connection status

    C. Change connection characteristics

    D. Toggle special character mode

13. What is the function of the telnet z command?

    A. Unset connection characteristics

    B. Suspend connection

    C. Spawn shell

    D. Update environment variables

14. What is the function of the telnet ! command?

    A. Unset connection characteristics

    B. Suspend connection

    C. Spawn shell

    D. Update environment variables

15. What is the function of the telnet environ command?

    A. Unset connection characteristics

    B. Suspend connection

    C. Spawn shell

    D. Update environment variables

Answers

1. **A.** The function of the telnet close command is to quit the telnet session.

2. **B.** The function of the telnet logout command is to close the telnet session.

3. **C.** The function of the telnet display command is to print the session characteristics.

4. **D.** The function of the telnet mode command is to change the telnet mode.

5. **A.** The function of the telnet open command is to open a connection.

6. **B.** The function of the telnet quit command is to quit the telnet session.

7. **C.** The function of the telnet send command is to send special characters.

8. **D.** The function of the telnet set command is to set connection characteristics.

9. **A.** The function of the telnet unset command is to unset connection characteristics.

10. **B.** The function of the telnet status command is to display the session status.

11. **D.** The function of the telnet `toggle` command is to toggle the special character mode.

12. **D.** The function of the telnet `slc` command is to toggle the special character mode.

13. **B.** The function of the telnet `Z` command is to suspend a connection.

14. **C.** The function of the telnet `!` command is to spawn a shell.

15. **A.** The function of the telnet `environ` command is to update environment variables.

PART II

Exam Objectives

Device Management

In this chapter, you will
- Be introduced to physical hardware devices
- Review logical device references
- Learn how to view configured system devices

One of the most important but most challenging roles of a system administrator is device management. Devices, in this context, can be defined as both physical and logical entities that together constitute a hardware system. Although some operating systems hide device configuration details from all users (even administrators!) in proprietary binary formats, Solaris device configuration is easy to use, with configuration information stored in special files known as *device files*. In addition to providing the technical background on how device files operate, and how device drivers can be installed, this chapter provides practical advice on installing standard devices, such as new hard drives, as well as more modern media like CD-Rs and Zip drives.

Solaris 9 now supports the dynamic reconfiguration of many system devices on some SPARC platforms, particularly in the medium-level server range (for example, E450) and above. This allows administrators to remove faulty hardware components and replace them without having to power down a system and perform a reconfiguration boot, which is necessary for older systems. This is particularly significant for systems that have a high redundancy of system components to guarantee uptime under all but the most critical of circumstances.

Device Files

Device files are special files that represent devices in Solaris 9. Device files reside in the */dev* directory, and its subdirectories (such as */dev/dsk*), while the */devices* directory is a tree that completely characterizes the hardware layout of the system in the file system namespace. Although it may seem initially confusing that separate directories exist for devices and for system hardware, the difference between the two systems will become apparent in the discussion that follows. Solaris refers to both physical and logical devices in three separate ways, with physical device names, physical device files, and logical device names. Physical device names are easily identified because they are long strings that provide all details relevant to the physical installation of the device. Every physical device has a physical name.

For example, an SBUS could have the name */sbus@1f,0*, while a disk device might have the name */sbus@1f,0/SUNW,fas@2,8800000/sd@1,0*. Physical device names are usually displayed at boot time and when using selected applications that access hardware directly, such as format. On the other hand, physical device files, which are located in the */devices* directory, comprise an instance name that is an abbreviation for a physical device name, which can be interpreted by the kernel. For example, the SBUS */sbus@1f,0* might be referred to as *sbus*, and a device disk */sbus@1f,0/SUNW,fas@2,8800000/sd@1,0* might be referred to as *sd1*. The mapping of instance names to physical devices is not hardwired: the */etc/path_to_inst* file always contains these details, keeping them consistent between boots. For an Ultra 2, this file looks like this:

```
"/sbus@1f,0" 0 "sbus"
"/sbus@1f,0/sbusmem@2,0" 2 "sbusmem"
"/sbus@1f,0/sbusmem@3,0" 3 "sbusmem"
"/sbus@1f,0/sbusmem@0,0" 0 "sbusmem"
"/sbus@1f,0/sbusmem@1,0" 1 "sbusmem"
"/sbus@1f,0/SUNW,fas@2,8800000" 1 "fas"
"/sbus@1f,0/SUNW,fas@2,8800000/ses@f,0" 1 "ses"
"/sbus@1f,0/SUNW,fas@2,8800000/sd@1,0" 16 "sd"
"/sbus@1f,0/SUNW,fas@2,8800000/sd@0,0" 15 "sd"
"/sbus@1f,0/SUNW,fas@2,8800000/sd@3,0" 18 "sd"
"/sbus@1f,0/SUNW,fas@2,8800000/sd@2,0" 17 "sd"
"/sbus@1f,0/SUNW,fas@2,8800000/sd@5,0" 20 "sd"
"/sbus@1f,0/SUNW,fas@2,8800000/sd@4,0" 19 "sd"
"/sbus@1f,0/SUNW,fas@2,8800000/sd@6,0" 21 "sd"
"/sbus@1f,0/SUNW,fas@2,8800000/sd@9,0" 23 "sd"
"/sbus@1f,0/SUNW,fas@2,8800000/sd@8,0" 22 "sd"
"/sbus@1f,0/SUNW,fas@2,8800000/sd@a,0" 24 "sd"
"/sbus@1f,0/sbusmem@f,0" 15 "sbusmem"
"/sbus@1f,0/sbusmem@d,0" 13 "sbusmem"
"/sbus@1f,0/sbusmem@e,0" 14 "sbusmem"
"/sbus@1f,0/cgthree@1,0" 0 "cgthree"
"/sbus@1f,0/SUNW,hme@e,8c00000" 0 "hme"
"/sbus@1f,0/zs@f,1000000" 1 "zs"
"/sbus@1f,0/zs@f,1100000" 0 "zs"
"/sbus@1f,0/SUNW,bpp@e,c800000" 0 "bpp"
"/sbus@1f,0/lebuffer@0,40000" 0 "lebuffer"
"/sbus@1f,0/lebuffer@0,40000/le@0,60000" 0 "le"
"/sbus@1f,0/SUNW,hme@2,8c00000" 1 "hme"
"/sbus@1f,0/SUNW,fdtwo@f,1400000" 0 "fd"
"/options" 0 "options"
"/pseudo" 0 "pseudo"
```

/dev and /devices Directories

In addition to physical devices, Solaris also needs to refer to logical devices. For example, physical disks may be divided into many different slices, so the physical disk device will need to be referred to using a logical name. Logical device files in the */dev* directory are symbolically linked to physical device names in the */devices* directory. Most user applications will refer to logical device names. A typical listing of the */dev* directory has numerous entries that look like the following:

arp	ptys0	ptyyb	rsd3a	sd3e	ttyu2
audio	ptys1	ptyyc	rsd3b	sd3f	ttyu3
audioctl	ptys2	ptyyd	rsd3c	sd3g	ttyu4
bd.off	ptys3	ptyye	rsd3d	sd3h	ttyu5
be	ptys4	ptyyf	rsd3e	skip_key	ttyu6
bpp0	ptys5	ptyz0	rsd3f	sound/	ttyu7

...

Many of these device filenames are self-explanatory:

- */dev/console* represents the console device—error and status messages are usually written to the console by daemons and applications using the syslog service (described in Chapter 20). */dev/console* typically corresponds to the monitor in text mode; however, the console is also represented logically in windowing systems, such as OpenWindows, where the command `server% cmdtool -C` brings up a console window.

- */dev/hme* is the network interface device file.

- */dev/dsk* contains device files for disk slices.

- */dev/tty*n and */dev/pty*n are the *n* terminal and *n* pseudoterminal devices attached to the system.

- */dev/null* is the endpoint of discarded output to which many applications pipe their output.

The `drvconfig` command creates the */devices* directory tree, which is a logical representation of the physical layout of devices attached to the system, and pseudodrivers. `drvconfig` is executed automatically after a reconfiguration boot. It reads file permission information for new nodes in the tree form */etc/minor_perm*, which contains entries like this:

```
sd:* 0666 httpd staff
```

where *sd* is the node name for a disk device, 0666 is the default file permission, *httpd* is the owner, and *staff* is the group.

Storage Devices

Solaris 9 supports many different kinds of mass-storage devices, including SCSI hard drives (and IDE drives on the x86 platform), reading and writing standard and rewritable CD-ROMs, Iomega Zip and Jaz drives, tape drives, DVD-ROM, and floppy disks. Hard drives are the most common kinds of storage devices found on a Solaris 9 system, ranging from individual drives used to create system and user file systems to highly redundant, server-based RAID systems. These RAID configurations can comprise a set of internal disks, managed through software (such as DiskSuite), or high-speed external arrays like the A1000, which include dedicated RAM for write caching. Because disk writing is one of the slowest operations in any modern server system, this greatly increases overall operational speed.

Hard drives have faced stiff competition in recent years, with new media such as Iomega's Zip and Jaz drives providing removable media for both random and sequential file access. This makes them ideal media for archival backups, competing with the traditional magnetic tape drives. The latter have largely been replaced in modern systems by the digital DAT tape system, which has high reliability and data throughput rates (especially the DDS-3 standard).

In this section, we look at the issues surrounding the installation and configuration of storage devices for Solaris 9, providing practical advice for installing a wide range of hardware.

CD-ROMs

A popular format of read-only mass storage on many servers is the compact disc read-only memory (CD-ROM). Although earlier releases of Solaris worked best with Sun-branded CD-ROM drives, as of Solaris 2.6, Solaris fully supports all SCSI-2 CD-ROMs. For systems running older versions of Solaris, it may still be possible to use a third-party drive, but the drive must support 512-byte sectors (the Sun standard). A second Sun default to be aware of is that CD-ROMs must usually have the SCSI target ID of 6, although this limitation has again been overcome in later releases of the kernel. However, a number of third-party applications with "autodetect" functions may still expect to see the CD-ROM drive at SCSI ID 6.

A number of different CD formats are also supported with the `mount` command, which is used to attach CDs to the file system. It is common to use the mount point */cdrom* for the primary CD-ROM device in Solaris 9 systems, although it is possible to use a different mount point for mounting the device by using a command-line argument to `mount`.

Zip and Jaz Drives

There are two ways to install Zip and Jaz drives: by treating the drive as a SCSI disk, in which case format data needs to be added to the system to recognize it, or to use Andy Polyakov's ziptool, which will format and manage protection modes supported by Zip 100 and Jaz 1GB/2GB drives. Both of these techniques only support SCSI and not parallel port drives.

Treating the Zip 100 SCSI drive or the Jaz 1GB drive as a normal SCSI device is the easiest approach, because there is built-in Solaris 9 support for these SCSI devices. However, only standard, non-write-protected disks can be used.

Tape Drives

Solaris 9 supports a wide variety of magnetic tapes using the "remote magtape" (rmt) protocol. Tapes are generally used as backup devices, rather than as interactive storage devices. What they lack in availability, they definitely make up for in storage capacity—many digital audio tape (DAT) drives have capacities of 24GB, making it easy to perform a complete backup of many server systems on a single tape. This removes the need for late-night monitoring by operations staff to insert new tapes when full (as many administrators will have experienced in the past).

Device files for tape drives are found in the */dev/rmt* directory. They are numbered sequentially from 0, so default drives will generally be available as */dev/rmt/0*.

To back up to a remote drive, use the command ufsdump, which is an incremental file system dumping program. For example, to create a full backup of the */dev/ rdsk/ c0t1d0s1* file system to the tape system */dev/rmt/0*, simply use the following command:

```
# ufsdump 0 /dev/rmt/0 /dev/rdsk/c0t1d0s1
```

This command specifies a level 0 (that is, complete) dump of the file system, specifying the target drive and data source as */dev/rmt/0* and */dev/rdsk/c0t1d0s1*, respectively. Other devices like 0c and 0cb may also be used.

Floppy Disks

Floppy disk drives (1.44MB capacity) are standard on both SPARC and Intel architecture systems. In addition, by using the Volume Manager, detecting and mounting floppy disks is straightforward. Insert the target disk into the drive, and use this command:

```
# volcheck
```

This will check all volumes that are managed by volume management and will mount any valid file system that is found. The mount point for the floppy drive is determined by the settings in */etc/vfstab*:

```
fd    -    /dev/fd    fd    -    no    -
```

Refer to the section on entering disk information into the virtual file system database for more details on configuring the */etc/vfstab* file. A very useful feature of the volcheck command is to automatically check for new volumes; for example,

```
# volcheck -i 60 -t 3600 /dev/diskette0 &
```

works in the background to check every minute if a floppy is in the drive. However, this polling takes place only for one hour unless renewed.

CD-ROMs and DVD-ROMs

CD-ROMs are supported directly by the operating system in SPARC architectures and do not require any special configuration, other than the usual process of initializing the system for a reconfiguration reboot: powering down the system, attaching the CD-ROM device to the SCSI bus, and powering on the system. It is not necessary to use format or newfs to read the files on the CD-ROM, nor is it usually necessary to manually mount the file system, because the volume manager (vold) is usually enabled on server systems.

A common problem for Solaris x86 users is that there are few tested and supported CD-ROM brands for installing the operating system (although most fully compliant ATA/ATAPI CD-ROMs should work). The older Sound Blaster IDE interface for CD-ROMs does not appear to be suitable, although support may be included in a later release (the Alternate Status register is apparently not implemented on the main integrated circuit for the controller board). It is always best to check the current Hardware Compatibility List (HCL) on the Sun developer site.

Many recent SPARC and Intel systems come installed with a DVD-ROM drive. Although the drive cannot be yet used to play movies, it can be effectively used as a mass storage device, with a capacity equal to several individual CD-ROMs. Future releases of Solaris may include a DVD player and support for the newer DVD-RAM technology.

CD-Rs and CD-RWs

Solaris 9 supports both reading and writing CD-ROMs. In addition to the CD-R (CD-Readable) format, Solaris 9 also supports CD-RW (CD-ReWritable), previously known as CD-Erasable. It is a new optical disc specification created by the industry organization OSTA (**www.osta.org**). You can hook up many different SCSI CD-R and CD-RW devices to a SPARC system on SCSI device ID 6, and they will function as normal CD-ROM drives. Although the technical ability to support any SCSI-based device is a given for the operating system, a potentially limiting factor for nonstandard hardware is usually finding software to adequately support it. Luckily, many different open source and commercial editions of CD-recording software are available for the Solaris platform. To obtain support for both Solaris 1.*x* and 2.*x*, the best application is cdrecord, by Jörg Schilling, which you can download from **ftp://ftp.fokus.gmd.de /pub/ unix/ cdrecord/**. It is freeware, and it makes use of the real-time scheduler in Solaris. It also compiles on the Solaris x86 platform, and can create both music and data discs. It has a rather clunky command-line interface, but it has more features than some of the commercial systems, including the capability to simulate a recording for test purposes (-dummy option); using a single CD for multiple recording sessions (-multi option); manually fixing the disk, if you want to view data from an open session on a normal CD-ROM (-fix option); and setting the recording speed factor (-speed option). If you prefer a commercial system, GEAR for UNIX is also available (**http://www .gearcdr .com/ html/products/gear/unix/index.html**), as well as Creative Digital Research's CDR Publisher (**http://www.cdr1.com/**), which is available through Sun's Catalyst program. For more general information about the CD recording process, see Andy McFadden's very comprehensive FAQs at **http://www.fadden.com/cdrfaq/**.

Adding Devices

In many cases, adding new devices to a Solaris system is straightforward because most devices connect to the SCSI bus, which is a standard interface. The steps involved are usually: preparing the system for a reconfiguration boot, powering down the system, connecting the hardware device, noting the SCSI device number, powering on the system, and using the format command (if necessary) to create a file system. In this section, we examine the procedure for adding disks to both SPARC and Intel architecture machines and highlight potential problems that may occur.

Hard Drives

Hard disk installation and configuration on Solaris 9 is often more complicated than other UNIX systems. However, this complexity is required to support the sophisticated hardware operations typically undertaken by Solaris systems. For example, Linux refers to hard disks using a simple BSD-style scheme: */dev/hdn* are the IDE hard disks on a system, and */dev/sdn* are the SCSI hard disks on a system, where *n* refers to the hard disk number. On Linux, a system with two IDE hard disks and two SCSI hard disks will therefore have the following device files configured:

```
/dev/hda
/dev/hdb
/dev/sda
/dev/sdb
```

Partitions created on each drive are also sequentially numbered: if */dev/hda* is the boot disk, it may contain several partitions on the disk, reflecting the basic UNIX system directories:

```
/dev/hda1 (/ partition)
/dev/hda2 (/usr)
/dev/hda3 (/var)
/dev/hda4 (swap)
```

Instead of simply referring to the disk type, disk number, and partition number, the device filename for each partition ("slice") on a Solaris disk contains four identifiers: controller (*c*), target (*t*), disk (*d*), and slice (*s*). Thus, the device file,

```
/dev/dsk/c0t3d0s0
```

identifies slice 0 of disk 0, controller 0 at SCSI target ID 3. To complicate matters further, disk device files exist in both the */dev/dsk* and */dev/rdsk* directories, which correspond to block device and raw device entries, respectively. Raw and block devices refer to the same physical partition, but are used in different contexts: using raw devices allows only operations of small amounts of data, whereas a buffer can be used with a block device to increase the data read size. It is not always clear whether to use a block or raw device interface, but low-level system commands (like the `fsck` command, which performs disk maintenance) typically use raw device interfaces, whereas commands that operate on the entire disk (such as `df`, which reports disk usage) will most likely use block devices.

To install a new hard drive on a Solaris system, just follow these steps:

1. Prepare the system for a reconfiguration boot by issuing the following command:
   ```
   server# touch /reconfigure
   ```

2. Synchronize disk data and power down the system using these commands:
   ```
   server# sync; sync; sync; shutdown
   ```

PART II

3. Switch off power to the system and attach the new hard disk to the external SCSI chain, or install it internally into an appropriate disk bay.

4. Check that the SCSI device ID does not conflict with any existing SCSI devices. If a conflict exists, simply change the ID using the switch.

5. Power on the system and use the `boot` command in this manner to load the kernel if the OpenBoot monitor appears:

```
ok boot
```

The next step (assuming that you have decided which partitions you want to create on your drive), using the information supplied earlier, is to run the format program. In addition to creating slices, format also displays information about existing disks and slices and can be used to repair a faulty disk. When format is invoked without a command-line argument,

```
# format
```

it displays the current disks and asks the administrator to enter the number of the disk to format. Selecting a disk for formatting at this point is nondestructive, so even if you make a mistake, you can always exit the format program without damaging data. For example, on a SPARC-20 system with three 1.05G SCSI disks, format opens with this screen:

```
Searching for disks...done
AVAILABLE DISK SELECTIONS:
0. c0t1d0 <SUN1.05 cyl 2036 alt 2 hd 14 sec 72>
/iommu@f,e0000000/sbus@f,e0001000/espdma@f,400000/esp@f,800000/
sd@1,0
1. c0t2d0 <SUN1.05 cyl 2036 alt 2 hd 14 sec 72>
/iommu@f,e0000000/sbus@f,e0001000/espdma@f,400000/esp@f,800000/
sd@2,0
2. c0t3d0 <SUN1.05 cyl 2036 alt 2 hd 14 sec 72>
/iommu@f,e0000000/sbus@f,e0001000/espdma@f,400000/esp@f,800000/
sd@3,0
Specify disk (enter its number):
```

It is also possible to pass a command-line option to format, comprising the disk (or disks) to be formatted—for example:

```
# format /dev/rdsk/c0t2d0
```

After selecting the appropriate disk, the message

```
[disk formatted]
```

will appear if the disk has previously been formatted. This is an important message, because it is a common mistake to misidentify a target disk from the available selection of both formatted and unformatted disks. The menu looks like this:

```
FORMAT MENU:
        disk       - select a disk
        type       - select (define) a disk type
        partition  - select (define) a partition table
        current    - describe the current disk
        format     - format and analyze the disk
        fdisk      - run the fdisk program
        repair     - repair a defective sector
```

```
show       - translate a disk address
label      - write label to the disk
analyze    - surface analysis
defect     - defect list management
backup     - search for backup labels
verify     - read and display labels
save       - save new disk/partition definitions
volname    - set 8-character volume name
!<cmd>     - execute <cmd>, then return
quit
```

If the disk has not been formatted, the first step is to prepare the disk to contain slices and file systems by formatting the disk by issuing the command format:

```
format> format
Ready to format. Formatting cannot be interrupted
and takes 15 minutes (estimated). Continue? yes
```

The purpose of formatting is to identify defective blocks and mark them as bad, and generally to verify that the disk is operational from a hardware perspective. Once this has been completed, new slices can be created and sized by using the partition option at the main menu:

```
format> partition
```

In this case, we want to create a new slice 5 on disk 0 at target 3, which will be used to store user files when mounted as */export/home*, and corresponding to block device */dev/dsk/c0t3d0s5*. After determining the maximum amount of space available, enter that size in gigabytes (in this case, 1.05GB) when requested to do so by the format program for slice 5 (enter 0 for the other slices). If the disk is not labeled, you will also be prompted to enter a label, which contains details of the disk's current slices (useful for recovering data). This is an important step, because the operating system will not be able to find any newly created slices unless the volume is labeled. To view the disk label, use the prtvtoc command. Here's the output from the primary drive in an x86 system:

```
# prtvtoc /dev/dsk/c0d0s2
* /dev/dsk/c0d0s2 partition map
*
* Dimensions:
*     512 bytes/sector
*      63 sectors/track
*     255 tracks/cylinder
*   16065 sectors/cylinder
*    1020 cylinders
*    1018 accessible cylinders
*
* Flags:
*    1: unmountable
*   10: read-only
*
*                         First     Sector      Last
* Partition  Tag  Flags   Sector     Count     Sector   Mount Directory
         0     2    00     48195    160650     208844   /
         1     7    00    208845     64260     273104   /var
         2     5    00         0  16354170   16354169
         3     3    01    273105    321300     594404
         6     4    00    594405   1317330    1911734   /usr
```

```
7       8    00     1911735  14442435  16354169    /export/home
8       1    01           0     16065     16064
9       9    01       16065     32130     48194
```

The disk label contains a full partition table, which can be printed for each disk by using the `print` command:

```
format> print
```

For the 1.05GB disk, the partition table will look like this:

```
Part Tag Flag Cylinders Size Blocks
0 root wm 0 0 (0/0/0) 0
1 swap wu 0 0 (0/0/0) 0
2 backup wm 0 - 3732 (3732/0/0) 2089920
3 unassigned wm 0 0 (0/0/0) 0
4 unassigned wm 0 0 (0/0/0) 0
5 home wm 0 - 3732 1075MB (3732/0/0) 2089920
6 usr wm 0 0 (0/0/0) 0
7 unassigned wm 0 0 (0/0/0) 0
```

After saving the changes to the disk's partition table, using label, exit the format program and create a new UFS file system on the target slice by using the `newfs` command:

```
# newfs /dev/rdsk/c0t3d0s5
```

After a new file system is constructed, it is ready to be mounted. First, a mount point is created

```
# mkdir /export/home
```

followed by the appropriate `mount` command:

```
# mount /dev/dsk/c0t3d0s5 /export/home
```

At this point, the disk is available to the system for the current session. However, if you want the disk to be available after reboot, you need to create an entry in the virtual file systems table, which is created from */etc/vfstab* file. An entry like this,

```
/dev/dsk/c0t3d0s5 /dev/rdsk/c0t3d0s5 /export/home ufs 2 yes -
```

contains details of the slice's block and raw devices, the mount point, the file system type, instructions for fsck, and most importantly, a flag to force mount at boot.

For an x86 system, the output of format looks slightly different, given the differences in the way that devices are denoted:

```
AVAILABLE DISK SELECTIONS:
       0. c0d0 <DEFAULT cyl 1018 alt 2 hd 255 sec 63>
          /pci@0,0/pci-ide@7,1/ata@0/cmdk@0,0
   Specify disk (enter its number):
```

The partition table is similar to that for the SPARC architecture systems:

```
partition> print
Current partition table (original):
Total disk cylinders available: 1018 + 2 (reserved cylinders)
```

Part	Tag	Flag	Cylinders	Size	Blocks	
0	root	wm	3 - 12	78.44MB	(10/0/0)	160650
1	var	wm	13 - 16	31.38MB	(4/0/0)	64260

```
2      backup    wm       0  - 1017      7.80GB    (1018/0/0)  16354170
3        swap    wu      17  -   36    156.88MB      (20/0/0)    321300
4  unassigned    wm       0               0          (0/0/0)         0
5  unassigned    wm       0               0          (0/0/0)         0
6         usr    wm      37  -  118    643.23MB      (82/0/0)   1317330
7        home    wm     119  - 1017      6.89GB     (899/0/0)  14442435
8        boot    wu       0  -    0      7.84MB       (1/0/0)     16065
9  alternates    wu       1  -    2     15.69MB       (2/0/0)     32130
```

Installing a Zip/Jaz Drive

The steps for installation are similar for both the Zip and Jaz drives:

1. Set the SCSI ID switch to any ID that is not reserved.

2. Attach the Zip or Jaz drive to your SCSI adapter or chain and ensure that it has power.

3. Create a device entry in */etc/format.dat* by editing the file and inserting the following for a Zip drive:

```
disk_type="Zip 100"\
                    :ctlr=SCSI\
                    :ncyl=2406:acyl=2:pcyl=2408:nhead=2\
                    :nsect=40:rpm=3600:bpt=20480
        partition="Zip 100"\
                    :disk="Zip 100":ctlr=SCSI\
                    :2=0,192480
                    :2=0,1159168
```

For a Jaz drive, enter the following information in */etc/format.dat*:

```
disk_type="Jaz 1GB"\
                    :ctlr=SCSI\
                    :ncyl=1018:acyl=2:pcyl=1020:nhead=64\
                    :nsect=32:rpm=3600:bpt=16384
        partition="Jaz 1GB"\
                    :disk="Jaz 1GB":ctlr=SCSI\
                    :2=0,2084864
```

4. Perform a reconfiguration boot by typing
   `ok boot -r`
   at the OpenBoot prompt, or by using these commands from a superuser shell:
   `server# touch /reconfigure`
   `server# sync; sync; init 6`

The drive should now be visible to the system. To actually use the drive to mount a volume, insert a Zip or Jaz disk into the drive prior to booting the system. After booting, run the format program:

```
# format
```

5. Assuming that the *sd* number for your drive is 3, select this *sd* as the disk to be formatted. Create the appropriate partition using the `partition` option, then create an appropriate label for the volume and quit the format program.

Next, create a new file system on the drive by using the `newfs` command—for example:

```
# newfs -v /dev/sd3c
```

6. After creating the file system, you can mount it by typing

```
# mount /dev/sd3c /mount_point
```

where /*mount_point* is something self documenting (such as /*zip* or /*jaz*). You need to create this before mounting by typing the following:

```
# mkdir /zip
```

or

```
# mkdir /jaz
```

An alternate and more flexible approach is to use the ziptool program, which is available at **http://fy.chalmers.se/~appro/ziptool.html**. Ziptool supports all Zip and Jaz drive protection modes, permits unconditional low-level formatting of protected disks, disk labeling, and volume management for Solaris 2.6 and later. The program has to be executed with root privileges regardless of the access permissions set on SCSI disk device driver's entries in /*devices*. Consequently, if you want to let all users use it, you must install it as set-root-uid:

```
# /usr/ucb/install -m 04755 -o root ziptool /usr/local/bin
```

However, you should note that running setuid programs has security implications.

After downloading and unpacking the sources, you can compile the program by using this:

```
# gcc -o ziptool ziptool.c -lvolmgt
```

Of course, you will need to ensure that the path to *libvolmgt.a* is in your *LD_LIBRARY_PATH* (usually /*lib*)

```
ziptool device command
```

where *device* must be the full name of a raw SCSI disk file, such as /*dev/rsdk/c0t5d0s2*, and *command* is one or more of the following:

rw	Unlocks the Zip disk temporarily.
RW	Unlocks the Zip disk permanently.
ro	Puts the Zip disk into read-only mode.
RO	Puts the Zip disk into a read-only mode that is password protected.
WR(*)	Protects the disk by restricting reading and writing unless a password is entered.
eject	Ejects the current Zip disk.
noeject	Stops the Zip disk being ejected.

You can find further information on installing Jaz and Zip drives on the Iomega support web site:

```
http://www.iomega.com/support/documents/4019.html
http://www.iomega.com/support/documents/2019.html
```

Checking for Devices

Obtaining a listing of devices attached to a Solaris system is the best way to begin examining this important issue. In Solaris, you can easily obtain system configuration information, including device information, by using the print configuration command,

```
# prtconf
```

on any SPARC or Intel architecture system. On an Ultra 5 workstation, the system configuration looks like this:

```
SUNW,Ultra-5_10
    packages (driver not attached)
        terminal-emulator (driver not attached)
        deblocker (driver not attached)
        obp-tftp (driver not attached)
        disk-label (driver not attached)
        SUNW,builtin-drivers (driver not attached)
        sun-keyboard (driver not attached)
        ufs-file-system (driver not attached)
    chosen (driver not attached)
    openprom (driver not attached)
        client-services (driver not attached)
    options, instance #0
    aliases (driver not attached)
    memory (driver not attached)
    virtual-memory (driver not attached)
    pci, instance #0
        pci, instance #0
            ebus, instance #0
                auxio (driver not attached)
                power (driver not attached)
                SUNW,pll (driver not attached)
                se, instance #0
                su, instance #0
                su, instance #1
                ecpp (driver not attached)
                fdthree (driver not attached)
                eeprom (driver not attached)
                flashprom (driver not attached)
                SUNW,CS4231, instance #0
            network, instance #0
            SUNW,m64B, instance #0
            ide, instance #0
                disk (driver not attached)
                cdrom (driver not attached)
                dad, instance #0
                atapicd, instance #2
        pci, instance #1
            pci, instance #0
                pci108e,1000 (driver not attached)
                SUNW,hme, instance #1
                SUNW,isptwo, instance #0
                    sd (driver not attached)
                    st (driver not attached)
    SUNW,UltraSPARC-IIi (driver not attached)
    pseudo, instance #0
```

Never panic about the message that a driver is "not attached" to a particular device. Because device drivers are loaded only on demand in Solaris 9, only those devices that are actively being used will have their drivers loaded. When a device is no longer being used, the device driver is unloaded from memory. This is a very efficient memory management strategy that optimizes the use of physical RAM by deallocating memory for devices when they are no longer required. In the case of the Ultra 5, we can see that devices like the PCI bus and the IDE disk drives have attached device drivers, and they were being used while prtconf was running.

For an x86 system, the devices found are quite different:

```
System Configuration:  Sun Microsystems  i86pc
Memory size: 128 Megabytes
System Peripherals (Software Nodes):
i86pc
    +boot (driver not attached)
        memory (driver not attached)
    aliases (driver not attached)
    chosen (driver not attached)
    i86pc-memory (driver not attached)
    i86pc-mmu (driver not attached)
    openprom (driver not attached)
    options, instance #0
    packages (driver not attached)
    delayed-writes (driver not attached)
    itu-props (driver not attached)
    isa, instance #0
        motherboard (driver not attached)
        asy, instance #0
        lp (driver not attached)
        asy, instance #1
        fdc, instance #0
            fd, instance #0
            fd, instance #1 (driver not attached)
        kd (driver not attached)
        bios (driver not attached)
        bios (driver not attached)
        pnpCTL,0041 (driver not attached)
        pnpCTL,7002 (driver not attached)
        kd, instance #0
        chanmux, instance #0
    pci, instance #0
        pci8086,1237 (driver not attached)
        pci8086,7000 (driver not attached)
        pci-ide, instance #0
            ata, instance #0
                cmdk, instance #0
                sd, instance #1
        pci10ec,8029 (driver not attached)
        pci5333,8901 (driver not attached)
    used-resources (driver not attached)
    objmgr, instance #0
    pseudo, instance #0
```

At Boot Time

The OpenBoot monitor has the ability to diagnose hardware errors on system devices before booting the kernel. This can be particularly useful for identifying bus connectivity issues, such as unterminated SCSI chains, but also for basic functional issues such as whether devices are responding. Issuing the command,

```
ok reset
```

will also force a self-test of the system.

Just after booting, it is useful to review the system boot messages, which you can retrieve by using the dmesg command or by examining the */var/log/messages* file. This displays a list of all devices that were successfully attached at boot time, and it also displays any error messages that were detected. Let's look at the dmesg output for a SPARC Ultra architecture system:

```
# dmesg
Jan 17 13:06
cpu0: SUNW,UltraSPARC-IIi (upaid 0 impl 0x12 ver 0x12 clock 270 MHz)
SunOS Release 5.9 Version Generic_103640-19
[UNIX(R) System V Release 4.0]
Copyright (c) 1983-2002, Sun Microsystems, Inc.
mem = 131072K (0x8000000)
avail mem = 127852544
Ethernet address = 8:0:20:90:b3:23
root nexus = Sun Ultra 5/10 UPA/PCI (UltraSPARC-IIi 270MHz)
pci0 at root: UPA 0x1f 0x0
PCI-device: pci@1,1, simba #0
PCI-device: pci@1, simba #1
dad0 at pci1095,6460 target 0 lun 0
dad0 is /pci@1f,0/pci@1,1/ide@3/dad@0,0
         <Seagate Medalist 34342A cyl 8892 alt 2 hd 15 sec 63>
root on /pci@1f,0/pci@1,1/ide@3/disk@0,0:a fstype ufs
su0 at ebus0: offset 14,3083f8
su0 is /pci@1f,0/pci@1,1/ebus@1/su@14,3083f8
su1 at ebus0: offset 14,3062f8
su1 is /pci@1f,0/pci@1,1/ebus@1/su@14,3062f8
keyboard is </pci@1f,0/pci@1,1/ebus@1/su@14,3083f8>
  major <37> minor <0>
mouse is </pci@1f,0/pci@1,1/ebus@1/su@14,3062f8>
  major <37> minor <1>
stdin is </pci@1f,0/pci@1,1/ebus@1/su@14,3083f8>
  major <37> minor <0>
SUNW,m64B0 is /pci@1f,0/pci@1,1/SUNW,m64B@2
m64#0: 1280x1024, 2M mappable, rev 4754.9a
stdout is </pci@1f,0/pci@1,1/SUNW,m64B@2> major <8> minor <0>
boot cpu (0) initialization complete - online
se0 at ebus0: offset 14,400000
se0 is /pci@1f,0/pci@1,1/ebus@1/se@14,400000
SUNW,hme0: CheerIO 2.0 (Rev Id = c1) Found
SUNW,hme0 is /pci@1f,0/pci@1,1/network@1,1
SUNW,hme1: Local Ethernet address = 8:0:20:93:b0:65
pci1011,240: SUNW,hme1
SUNW,hme1 is /pci@1f,0/pci@1/pci@1/SUNW,hme@0,1
```

```
dump on /dev/dsk/c0t0d0s1 size 131328K
SUNW,hme0: Using Internal Transceiver
SUNW,hme0: 10 Mbps half-duplex Link Up
pcmcia: no PCMCIA adapters found
```

Output from dmesg shows that the system first performs a memory test, sets the Ethernet address for the network interface, and then initializes the PCI bus. Setting the Ethernet address is critical on SPARC systems, because the Ethernet interfaces will have the same address stored in PROM. An IDE disk is then recognized and mapped into a physical device, and the appropriate partitions are activated. The standard input devices (keyboard and mouse) are then activated, and the boot sequence is largely complete. However, the output is slightly different for the x86 system:

```
Jan 17 08:32
SunOS Release 5.9 Version Generic [UNIX(R) System V Release 4.0]
Copyright (c) 1983-2002, Sun Microsystems, Inc.
mem = 130688K (0x7fa0000)
avail mem = 114434048
root nexus = i86pc
isa0 at root
pci0 at root: space 0 offset 0
        IDE device at targ 0, lun 0 lastlun 0x0
        model ST310230A, stat 50, err 0
                cfg 0xc5a, cyl 16383, hd 16, sec/trk 63
                mult1 0x8010, mult2 0x110, dwcap 0x0, cap 0x2f00
                piomode 0x200, dmamode 0x200, advpiomode 0x3
                minpio 240, minpioflow 120
                valid 0x7, dwdma 0x407, majver 0x1e
ata_set_feature: (0x66,0x0) failed
        ATAPI device at targ 1, lun 0 lastlun 0x0
        model CD-912E/ATK, stat 50, err 0
                cfg 0x85a0, cyl 0, hd 0, sec/trk 0
                mult1 0x0, mult2 0x0, dwcap 0x0, cap 0xb00
                piomode 0x200, dmamode 0x200, advpiomode 0x1
                minpio 209, minpioflow 180
                valid 0x2, dwdma 0x203, majver 0x0
PCI-device: ata@0, ata0
ata0 is /pci@0,0/pci-ide@7,1/ata@0
Disk0:  <Vendor 'Gen-ATA ' Product 'ST310230A         '>
cmdk0 at ata0 target 0 lun 0
cmdk0 is /pci@0,0/pci-ide@7,1/ata@0/cmdk@0,0
root on /pci@0,0/pci-ide@7,1/ide@0/cmdk@0,0:a fstype ufs
ISA-device: asy0
asy0 is /isa/asy@1,3f8
ISA-device: asy1
asy1 is /isa/asy@1,2f8
Number of console virtual screens = 13
cpu 0 initialization complete - online
dump on /dev/dsk/c0d0s3 size 156 MB
```

While the System Is Up

If you are working remotely on a server system, and you are unsure of the system architecture, the command

```
# arch -k
```

returns *sun4u* on the Ultra 5 system, but *sun4m* on a SPARC 10 system. For a complete view of a system's device configuration, you may also want to try the `sysdef` command, which displays more detailed information concerning pseudodevices, kernel loadable modules, and parameters. Here's the sysdef output for an x86 server:

```
# sysdef
# sysdef
*
* Hostid
*
  0ae61183
*
* i86pc Configuration
*
*
* Devices
*
+boot (driver not attached)
        memory (driver not attached)
aliases (driver not attached)
chosen (driver not attached)
i86pc-memory (driver not attached)
i86pc-mmu (driver not attached)
openprom (driver not attached)
options, instance #0
packages (driver not attached)
delayed-writes (driver not attached)
itu-props (driver not attached)
...
*
* System Configuration
*
  swap files
swapfile            dev  swaplo blocks    free
/dev/dsk/c0d0s3     102,3      8 321288 321288
```

The key sections in the sysdef output are details of all devices, such as the PCI bus and pseudodevices for each loadable object path (including */kernel* and */usr/kernel*). Loadable objects are also identified, along with swap and virtual memory settings. Although the output may seem verbose, the information provided for each device can prove to be very useful in tracking down hardware errors or missing loadable objects.

Summary

In this chapter, we have examined how to configure hardware devices on a Solaris system. In addition to standard disks, RAM modules, and CPUs, many other devices are supported by Solaris system and peripheral buses. Administrators should be aware of common techniques used to manage and configure devices such as disks.

Questions

1. What command is used to format disks in Solaris?

   A. mkdir

   B. format

   C. fmat

   D. chkdsk

2. What command is used to print a disk's label?

   A. print

   B. label

   C. prtvtoc

   D. prtlabel

3. What command can be used to create only UFS file systems?

   A. newfs

   B. ufs_fs

   C. newfs_ufs

   D. mknewfs

4. What command is used to display the number of disk blocks used by each directory?

   A. blocks

   B. df

   C. free

   D. du

5. In what directory are physical device names stored?

   A. /devices

   B. /dev

   C. /etc

   D. /usr

6. In what directory are logical device names stored?

   A. /devices

   B. /dev

   C. /etc

   D. /usr

7. What are /dev/tty1 and /dev/pty1?

    A. Terminal and pseudoterminal devices

    B. Terminal and pseudoterminal device drivers

    C. Login windows

    D. Terminal types

8. What form do physical device arguments always take?

    A. address@driver:arguments

    B. driver@address:arguments

    C. address:arguments@driver

    D. driver:arguments@address

9. What command is used to display a system's configuration?

    A. `displayconf`

    B. `writeconf`

    C. `prtconf`

    D. `confprint`

10. What command creates a new file system?

    A. `createfs`

    B. `createfilesystem`

    C. `newfilesystem`

    D. `newfs`

11. What command is used to create a mount point?

    A. `mkdir`

    B. `mkfile`

    C. `mkmount`

    D. `mkpoint`

12. What command prints the volume table of contents?

    A. `toc`

    B. `vtoc`

    C. `prtvtoc`

    D. `dispvtoc`

13. What slice should hold the root partition?

    A. 0

    B. 1

    C. 2

    D. 3

14. What slice should hold the export partition?

    A. 0

    B. 1

    C. 2

    D. 3

15. What slice should hold the virtual memory partition?

    A. 0

    B. 1

    C. 2

    D. 3

Answers

1. **B.** The command used to format disks in Solaris is `format`.

2. **C.** The command used to print a disk's label is `prtvtoc`.

3. **A.** The command used to create only UFS file systems is `newfs`.

4. **D.** The `du` command is used to display the number of disk blocks used by each directory.

5. **A.** The /*devices* directory stores physical device names.

6. **B.** The /*dev* directory stores logical device names.

7. **A.** /*dev/tty1* and /*dev/pty1* are terminal and pseudoterminal devices.

8. **B.** Physical device arguments always take the form driver@address:arguments.

9. **C.** The `prtconf` command is used to display a system's configuration.

10. **D.** The `newfs` command creates a new file system.

11. **A.** The `mkdir` command is used to create a mount point.

12. **C.** The `prtvtoc` command prints the volume table of contents.

13. **A.** Slice 0 should hold the root partition.

14. **D.** Slice 3 should hold the export partition.

15. **B.** Slice 1 should hold the virtual memory partition.

The Solaris 9 Network Environment

In this chapter, you will
- Gain an understanding of Solaris networking functions
- Review networking capabilities
- Investigate routing concepts

Solaris networks are comprised of Class A, B, and C subnets interconnected by routers. The simplest Solaris network consists of two hosts connected using a hub or crossover cable, to form a single Class C subnet. However, many larger Solaris networks are comprised of many Class C subnets that are connected to each other, perhaps as part of a large Class B network. In this chapter, we'll examine some networking basics that are essential for understanding more complex topics, such as routing. We'll also look at a typical network service—the File Transfer Protocol (FTP) daemon—to examine how low-level networking is used to implement high-level system services.

Hostnames and Interfaces

A Solaris network consists of a number of different hosts that are interconnected using a switch or a hub. Solaris networks connect through to each other by using routers, which can be dedicated hardware systems or Solaris systems that have more than one network interface. Each host on a Solaris network is identified by a unique hostname: these hostnames often reflect the function of the host in question. For example, a set of four web servers may have the hostnames www1, www2, www3, and www4, respectively.

Every host and network that is connected to the Internet uses the Internet Protocol (IP) to support higher-level protocols such as TCP and UDP. Every interface of every host on the Internet has a unique IP address, which is based on the network IP address block assigned to the local network. Networks are addressable by using an appropriate netmask, which corresponds to a Class A (255.0.0.0), Class B (255.255.0.0), or Class C (255.255.255.0) network.

Solaris supports multiple Ethernet interfaces, which can be installed on a single machine. These are usually designated by files like

```
/etc/hostname.hmen
```

or, for older machines,

`/etc/hostname.1e`*n*

where *n* is the interface number, and le and hme are interface types. Interface files contain a single hostname or IP address, with the primary network interface being designated with an interface number of zero. Thus, the primary interface of a machine called server would be defined by the file */etc/server.hme0*, which might contain the IP address 203.17.64.28. A secondary network interface, connected to a different subnet, might be defined in the file */etc/server.hme1*. In this case, the file might contain the IP address 10.17.65.28. This setup is commonly used in organizations that have a provision for a failure of the primary network interface, or to enable load balancing of server requests across multiple subnets (for example, for an intranet web server processing HTTP requests).

A system with a second network interface can either act as a router or as a multihomed host. Hostnames and IP addresses are locally administered through a naming service, which is usually the Domain Name Service (DNS) for companies connected to the Internet and the Network Information Service (NIS/NIS+) for companies with large internal networks that require administrative functions beyond what DNS provides, including centralized authentication.

It is also worth mentioning at this point that it is quite possible to assign different IP addresses to the same network interface, which can be useful for hosting "virtual" domains that require their own IP address, rather than relying on application-level support for multihoming (for example, when using the Apache web server). Simply create a new */etc/hostname.hmeX:Y* file for each IP address required, where *X* represents the physical device interface, and *Y* represents the virtual interface number.

The subnet mask used by each of these interfaces must also be defined in */etc/netmasks*. This is particularly important if the interfaces lie on different subnets or if they serve different network classes. In addition, it might also be appropriate to assign a fully qualified domain name to each of the interfaces, although this will depend on the purpose to which each interface is assigned.

Subnets are visible to each other by means of a mask. Class A subnets use the mask 255.0.0.0. Class B networks use the mask 255.255.0.0. Class C networks use the mask 255.255.255.0. These masks are used when broadcasts are made to specific subnets. A Class C subnet 134.132.23.0, for example, can have 255 hosts associated with it, starting with 134.132.23.1 and ending with 134.132.23.255. Class A and B subnets have their own distinctive enumeration schemes.

Internet daemon

inetd is the "super" Internet daemon that is responsible for centrally managing many of the standard Internet services provided by Solaris through the application layer. For example, telnet, ftp, finger, talk, and uucp are all run from the inetd. Even third-party web servers can often be run through inetd. Both UDP and TCP transport layers are supported with inetd. The main benefit of managing all services centrally through inetd is reduced administrative overhead, because all services use a standard configuration format from a single file. Just like Microsoft Internet Information Server (IIS), inetd is able to manage many network services with a single application.

There are also several drawbacks with using inetd to run all of your services. For example, doing so means there is now a single point of failure, meaning that if inetd crashes because of one service that fails, all of the other inetd services may be affected. In addition, connection pooling for services like the Apache web server is not supported under inetd. A general rule is that high-performance applications, where there are many concurrent client requests, should use a stand-alone daemon.

The Internet daemon relies on two files for configuration. The */etc/inetd.conf* file is the primary configuration file, consisting of a list of all services currently supported and their runtime parameters, such as the file system path to the daemon that is executed. In addition, the */etc/services* file maintains a list of mappings between service names and port numbers, which is used to ensure that services are activated on the correct port.

FTP Administration

FTP is one of the oldest and most commonly used protocols for transferring files between hosts on the Internet. Although it has been avoided in recent years for security reasons, anonymous FTP is still the most popular method for organizing and serving publicly available data. In this section, we will examine the FTP protocol and demonstrate how to set up an FTP site with the tools that are supplied with Solaris. We will also cover the popular topic of anonymous ftp and GUI FTP clients and explain some of the alternative ftp servers designed to handle large amounts of anonymous ftp traffic.

With the UNIX-to-UNIX Copy Program (UUCP) beginning to show its age, in the era of Fast Ethernet and the globalization of the Internet, the File Transfer Protocol (FTP) was destined to become the de facto standard for transferring files between computers connected to each other using a TCP/IP network. FTP is simple, transparent, and has a rich number of client commands and server features that are very powerful in the hands of an experienced user. In addition, there are a variety of clients available on all platforms with a TCP/IP stack, which assists with transferring entire directory trees, for example, rather than performing transfers file by file.

Although originally designed to provide remote file access for users with an account on the target system, the practice of providing "anonymous FTP" file areas has become very common in recent years, allowing remote users without an account to download (and in some cases upload) data to and from their favorite servers. This allowed the easy dissemination of data and applications before the widespread adoption of more sophisticated systems for locating and identifying networked information sources (such as gopher and HTTP, the Hypertext Transfer Protocol). Anonymous FTP servers typically contain archives of application software, device drivers, and configuration files. In addition, many electronic mailing lists keep their archives on anonymous FTP sites so that an entire year's worth of discussion can be retrieved rapidly. However, relying on anonymous FTP can be precarious because sites are subject to change, and there is no guarantee that what is available today will still be there tomorrow.

FTP is a TCP/IP protocol specified in RFC 959. On Solaris, it is invoked as a daemon through the Internet super daemon (inetd); thus, many of the options that are used to configure an FTP server can be entered directly into the configuration file for inetd (*/etc/inetd.conf*). For example, *in.ftpd* can be invoked with a debugging option (-d) or a logging option (-l), in which case all transactions will be logged to the */var/adm/messages* file by default.

The objectives of providing a FTP server are to permit the sharing of files between hosts across a TCP/IP network reliably and without concern for the underlying exchanges that must take place to facilitate the transfer of data. A user need only be concerned with identifying which files he or she wishes to download or upload and whether or not binary or ASCII transfer is required. The most common file types, and the recommended transfer mode, are shown in Table 19-1. A general rule of thumb is that text-only files should be transferred using ASCII, but applications and binary files should be transferred using binary mode. Many clients have a simple interface that makes it very easy for users to learn to send and retrieve data using FTP.

FTP has evolved through the years, although many of its basic characteristics remain unchanged. The first RFC for FTP was published in 1971, with a targeted implementation on hosts at MIT (RFC 114), by A.K. Bhushan. Since that time, enhancements to the original RFC have been suggested, including

- RFC 2640: Internationalization of the File Transfer Protocol
- RFC 2389: Feature Negotiation Mechanism for the File Transfer Protocol
- RFC 1986: Experiments with a Simple File Transfer Protocol for Radio Links Using Enhanced Trivial File Transfer Protocol (ETFTP)
- RFC 1440: SIFT/UFT: Sender-Initiated/Unsolicited File Transfer

Extension	Transfer Type	Description
.arc	Binary	ARChive compression
.arj	Binary	Arj compression
.gif	Binary	Image file
.gz	Binary	GNU Zip compression
.hqx	ASCII	HQX (MacOS version of uuencode)
.jpg	Binary	Image file
.lzh	Binary	LH compression
.shar	ASCII	Bourne shell archive
.sit	Binary	Stuff-It compression
.tar	Binary	Tape archive
.tgz	Binary	Gzip compressed tape archive
.txt	ASCII	Plaintext file
.uu	ASCII	Uuencoded file
.Z	Binary	Standard UNIX compression
.zip	Binary	Standard zip compression
.zoo	Binary	Zoo compression

Table 19-1   Common File Types for Binary vs. ASCII Transfer Mode

- RFC 1068: Background File Transfer Program (BFTP)
- RFC 2585: Internet X.509 Public Key Infrastructure Operational Protocols: FTP and HTTP
- RFC 2428: FTP Extensions for IPv6 and NATs
- RFC 2228: FTP Security Extensions
- RFC 1639: FTP Operation Over Big Address Records (FOOBAR)

Some of these RFCs are informational only, but many suggest concrete improvements to FTP that have been implemented as standards. For example, many changes will be required to fully implement IPv6 at the network level, including support for IP addresses that are much longer than standard. Despite these changes and enhancements, however, the basic procedures for initiating, conducting, and terminating an FTP session have remained unchanged for many years. FTP is a client/server process—a client attempts to make a connection to a server, by using a command like

```
client% ftp server
```

If there is an FTP server active on the host server, the FTP process proper can begin. After a user initiates the FTP session through the user interface or client program, the client program requests a session through the client protocol interpreter (client PI), such as "DIR" for a directory listing. The client PI then issues the appropriate command to the server PI, which replies with the appropriate response number (for example, "200 Command OK," if the command is accepted by the server PI). FTP commands must reflect the desired nature of the transaction (for example, port number and data transfer mode, whether binary or ASCII) and the type of operating to be performed (for example, file retrieval with GET, file deletion with DELE, and so forth). The actual data transfer process (DTP) is conducted by the server DTP agent, which connects to the client DTP agent, transferring the data packet by packet. After transmitting the data, both the client and server DTP agents then communicate the end of a transaction, successful or otherwise, to their respective PIs. A message is then sent back to the user interface, and ultimately the user finds out whether or not their request has been processed. This process is shown in Figure 19-1.

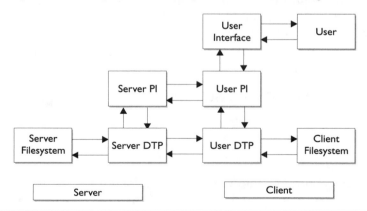

Figure 19-1 The FTP model

Anonymous FTP allows an arbitrary remote user to make an FTP connection to a remote host. The permissible usernames for anonymous FTP are usually "anonymous" or "ftp." Not all servers offer FTP—often, it is only possible to determine if anonymous FTP is supported by trying to login as "ftp" or "anonymous." Sites that support anonymous FTP usually allow the downloading of files from an archive of publicly available files. However, some servers also support an upload facility, where remote, unauthenticated, and unidentified users can upload files of arbitrary size. If this sounds dangerous, it is: if you don't apply quotas to the ftp users' directories on each file system that the ftp user has write access to, it is possible for a malicious user to completely fill up the disk with large files. This is a kind of "denial of service" attack, since a completely filled file system cannot be written to by other user or system processes. If a remote user really does need to upload files, it is best to give them a temporary account by which they can be authenticated and identified at login time.

Solaris 9 provides the `ftpconfig` command to install anonymous FTP.

Network Configuration Files

The */etc/hostname* file contains the fully qualified domain name of the local host. Thus, the system emu, in the DNS domain **cassowary.net**, has the fully qualified domain name **emu.cassowary.net**. Independent of DNS is the local hosts file (*/etc/hosts*), which is used to list local hostnames and IP addresses. For a network with large numbers of hosts, using the */etc/hosts* file is problematic because its values must be updated on every host on the network each time a change is made. This is why DNS (or NIS/NIS+) is a better solution for managing distributed host data.

However, the */etc/hosts* file contains entries for some key services, such as logging, so it usually contains at least the following entries:

- The loopback address, 127.0.0.1, which is associated with the generic hostname "localhost." This allows applications to be tested locally using the IP address 127.0.0.1 or the hostname localhost.

- The IP address, hostname, and fully qualified domain name of the localhost, because it requires this data before establishing a connection to a DNS server or NIS/NIS server when booting.

- An entry for a log host, so that syslog data can be redirected to the appropriate host on the local network.

A sample */etc/hosts* file is shown here:

```
127.0.0.1      localhost
192.68.16.1      emu    emu.cassowary.net
192.68.16.2      hawk   hawk.cassowary.net      loghost
192.68.16.3      eagle  eagle.cassowary.net
```

In this configuration, the localhost entry is defined, followed by the name and IP address of the localhost (hostname emu, with an IP address 192.68.16.1). In this case, emu redirects all of its syslog logging data to the host hawk (192.68.16.2), while another host eagle (192.68.16.3) is also defined.

Configuring Network Interfaces

The ifconfig command is responsible for configuring each network interface at boot time. ifconfig can also be used to check the status of active network interfaces by passing the –a parameter:

```
router# ifconfig -a
lo0: flags=849<UP,LOOPBACK,RUNNING,MULTICAST> mtu 8232
        inet 127.0.0.1 netmask ff000000
hme0: flags=863<UP,BROADCAST,NOTRAILERS,RUNNING,MULTICAST> mtu 1500
        inet 10.17.65.16 netmask ffffff00 broadcast 10.17.65.255
hme1: flags=863<UP,BROADCAST,NOTRAILERS,RUNNING,MULTICAST> mtu 1500
        inet 204.17.65.16 netmask ffffff00 broadcast 204.17.65.255
```

In this case, the primary interface hme0 is running on the internal network, while the secondary interface hme1 is visible to the external network. The netmask for a Class C network is used on both interfaces, while both have a distinct broadcast address. This ensures that information broadcast on the internal network is not visible to the external network. There are several parameters shown with ifconfig –a, including whether or not the interface is UP or DOWN (that is, active or inactive). In the following example, the interface has not been enabled at boot time:

```
server# ifconfig hme1
hme1: flags=863<DOWN,BROADCAST,NOTRAILERS,RUNNING,MULTICAST> mtu 1500
        inet 204.17.64.16 netmask ffffff00 broadcast 204.17.64.255
```

If the /etc/ethers database has been updated by the administrator to include details of the Ethernet addresses of hosts on the local network, there is also an entry displayed about the corresponding interface when using ifconfig:

```
server# cat /etc/ethers
8:0:19:7:f2:a1 server
server# ifconfig hme1
hme1: flags=863<UP,BROADCAST,NOTRAILERS,RUNNING,MULTICAST> mtu 1500
        inet 204.17.128.16 netmask ffffff00 broadcast 204.17.128.255
ether 8:0:19:7:f2:a1
```

It can also be useful in detecting problems with a routing network interface to examine the Address Resolution Protocol (ARP) results for the local area network. This will determine whether or not the interface is visible to its clients:

```
server# arp -a
Net to Media Table
Device   IP Address             Mask            Flags   Phys Addr
------   --------------------   ---------------  -----   ---------------
hme0     server1.cassowary.net  255.255.255.255          00:c0:ff:19:48:d8
hme0     server2.cassowary.net  255.255.255.255          c2:d4:78:00:15:56
hme0     server3.cassowary.net  255.255.255.255          87:b3:9a:c2:e9:ea
```

Modifying Interface Parameters

There are two methods for modifying network interface parameters. First, the `ifconfig` command can be used to modify operational parameters and bring an interface online (up) or shut it down (down). Second, one can use `ndd` to set parameters for TCP/IP transmission, which will affect all network interfaces. In this section, we will examine both of these methods and how they may be used to manage interfaces and improve performance.

It is sometimes necessary to shut down and start up a network interface in order to upgrade drivers or install patches affecting network service. To shut down a network interface, for example, one can use this command:

```
server# ifconfig hme1 down
server# ifconfig hme1
hme1: flags=863<DOWN,BROADCAST,NOTRAILERS,RUNNING,MULTICAST> mtu 1500
        inet 204.17.64.16 netmask ffffff00 broadcast 204.17.64.255
```

It also possible to bring this interface back up by using the `ifconfig` command:

```
server# ifconfig hme1 up
server# ifconfig hme1
hme1: flags=863<UP,BROADCAST,NOTRAILERS,RUNNING,MULTICAST> mtu 1500
        inet 204.17.64.16 netmask ffffff00 broadcast 204.17.64.255
```

To ensure that this configuration is preserved from boot to boot, it is possible to edit the networking startup file *etc/rc2.d/S69inet* and add this line to any others that configure the network interfaces.

It may be necessary to set several of these parameters in a production environment to ensure optimal performance, especially when application servers and web servers are in use. For example, when a web server makes a request to port 80 using TCP, a connection is opened and closed. However, the connection is kept open for a default time of two minutes to ensure that all packets are correctly received. For a system with a large number of clients, this can lead to a bottleneck of stale TCP connections, which can significantly impact the performance of the web server. Fortunately, the parameter that controls this behavior (`tcp_close_wait_interval`) can be set using the `ndd` command to something more sensible (like 30 seconds):

```
server# ndd -set /dev/tcp tcp_close_wait_interval 30000
```

However, administrators should be aware that altering this parameter will affect all TCP services, so while a web server might perform optimally with `tcp_close_wait_interval` equal to 30 seconds, a database listener that handles large datasets may require a much wider time window. The best way to determine optimal values is to perform experiments with low, moderate, and peak levels of traffic for both the web server and the database listener to determine a value that will provide reasonable performance for both applications. It is also important to check SunSolve for the latest patches and updates for recently discovered kernel bugs.

Configuring inetd

Services for inetd are defined in */etc/inetd.conf*. Every time you make a change to *inetd.conf*, you will need to send a HUP signal to the inetd process. You can identify the process ID (PID) of inetd by using the `ps` command, and then sending a kill SIGHUP signal to that PID from the shell. In addition, commenting an entry in the */etc/services* file will not necessarily prevent a service from running: strictly speaking, only services that make the `getprotobyname()` call to retrieve their port number require the */etc/services* file. So, for applications like sendmail, removing their entry in */etc/services* has no effect. To prevent sendmail from running, you would need to comment out its entry in */etc/inetd.conf*, and send a SIGHUP to the inetd process.

A service definition in */etc/inetd.conf* has the following format

```
service    socket    protocol    flags    user    server_name    arguments
```

where the service uses either datagrams or streams and uses UDP or TCP on the transport layer, with the server_name being executed by the user. An example entry is the UDP talk service:

```
talk    dgram    udp    wait    root    /usr/sbin/in.talkd    in.talkd
```

The talk service uses datagrams over UDP and is executed by the root user, with the talk daemon being physically located in */usr/sbin/in.talkd*. Once the talk daemon is running through inetd, it is used for interactive screen-based communication between two users (with at least one user "talking" on the local system).

In order to prevent users from using (or abusing) the talk facility, you would need to comment out the definition for the talk daemon in the */etc/inetd.conf* file. Thus, the line shown earlier would be changed to

```
#talk    dgram    udp    wait    root    /usr/sbin/in.talkd    in.talkd
```

In order for inetd to register the change, it needs to be restarted by using the `kill` command. To identify the PID for inetd, the following command may be used:

```
bash-2.03# ps -eaf | grep inetd
    root    206    1    0    May 16 ?        30:19 /usr/sbin/inetd -s
```

To restart the process, the following command would be used:

```
kill -1 206
```

The daemon would then restart after reading in the modified *inetd.conf* file.

/etc/inetd.conf

A sample *inetd.conf* file is shown here. It contains entries for the most commonly used Internet services:

```
ftp       stream  tcp     nowait  root    /usr/sbin/in.ftpd
   in.ftpd -l
telnet    stream  tcp     nowait  root    /usr/sbin/in.telnetd
   in.telnetd
name      dgram   udp     wait    root    /usr/sbin/in.tnamed
   in.tnamed
shell     stream  tcp     nowait  root    /usr/sbin/in.rshd
   in.rshd
login     stream  tcp     nowait  root    /usr/sbin/in.rlogind
   in.rlogind
exec      stream  tcp     nowait  root    /usr/sbin/in.rexecd
   in.rexecd
comsat    dgram   udp     wait    root    /usr/sbin/in.comsat
   in.comsat
talk      dgram   udp     wait    root    /usr/sbin/in.talkd
   in.talkd
uucp      stream  tcp     nowait  root    /usr/sbin/in.uucpd
   in.uucpd
tftp      dgram   udp     wait    root    /usr/sbin/in.tftpd
   in.tftpd -s /tftpboot
finger    stream  tcp     nowait  nobody  /usr/sbin/in.fingerd
   in.fingerd
systat    stream  tcp     nowait  root    /usr/bin/ps
   ps -ef
netstat           stream  tcp     nowait  root    /usr/bin/netstat
   netstat -f inet
time      stream  tcp     nowait  root    internal
time      dgram   udp     wait    root    internal
echo      stream  tcp     nowait  root    internal
echo      dgram   udp     wait    root    internal
discard   stream  tcp     nowait  root    internal
discard   dgram   udp     wait    root    internal
daytime   stream  tcp     nowait  root    internal
daytime   dgram   udp     wait    root    internal
chargen   stream  tcp     nowait  root    internal
chargen   dgram   udp     wait    root    internal
100232/10         tli     rpc/udp wait root /usr/sbin/sadmind      sadmind
rquotad/1         tli     rpc/datagram_v  wait root
   /usr/lib/nfs/rquotad  rquotad
rusersd/2-3       tli     rpc/datagram_v,circuit_v        wait root
   /usr/lib/netsvc/rusers/rpc.rusersd   rpc.rusersd
sprayd/1          tli     rpc/datagram_v  wait root
   /usr/lib/netsvc/spray/rpc.sprayd     rpc.sprayd
walld/1           tli     rpc/datagram_v  wait root
   /usr/lib/netsvc/rwall/rpc.rwalld     rpc.rwalld
rstatd/2-4        tli     rpc/datagram_v wait root
   /usr/lib/netsvc/rstat/rpc.rstatd rpc.rstatd
rexd/1            tli     rpc/tcp wait root /usr/sbin/rpc.rexd
   rpc.rexd
100083/1          tli     rpc/tcp wait root
   /usr/dt/bin/rpc.ttdbserverd rpc.ttdbserverd
ufsd/1 tli     rpc/*   wait    root    /usr/lib/fs/ufs/ufsd
   ufsd -p
```

```
100221/1        tli     rpc/tcp wait root
  /usr/openwin/bin/kcms_server  kcms_server
fs              stream  tcp     wait nobody /usr/openwin/lib/fs.auto
  fs
100235/1 tli rpc/tcp wait root /usr/lib/fs/cachefs/cachefsd
  cachefsd
kerbd/4         tli     rpc/ticlts      wait    root
  /usr/sbin/kerbd  kerbd
printer         stream  tcp     nowait  root
  /usr/lib/print/in.lpd   in.lpd
100234/1        tli     rpc/ticotsord   wait    root
  /usr/lib/gss/gssd gssd
dtspc stream tcp nowait root /usr/dt/bin/dtspcd
  /usr/dt/bin/dtspcd
100068/2-5 dgram rpc/udp wait root /usr/dt/bin/rpc.cmsd
  rpc.cmsd
```

/etc/services

Many inetd services must be mapped to a specific port number. A sample */etc/services* file, shown below, defines port numbers for most of the commonly used services:

```
tcpmux          1/tcp
echo            7/tcp
echo            7/udp
discard         9/tcp           sink null
discard         9/udp           sink null
systat          11/tcp          users
daytime         13/tcp
daytime         13/udp
netstat         15/tcp
chargen         19/tcp          ttytst source
chargen         19/udp          ttytst source
ftp-data        20/tcp
ftp             21/tcp
telnet          23/tcp
smtp            25/tcp          mail
time            37/tcp          timserver
time            37/udp          timserver
name            42/udp          nameserver
whois           43/tcp          nickname
domain          53/udp
domain          53/tcp
bootps          67/udp
bootpc          68/udp
hostnames       101/tcp         hostname
pop2            109/tcp         pop-2
pop3            110/tcp
sunrpc          111/udp         rpcbind
sunrpc          111/tcp         rpcbind
imap            143/tcp         imap2
ldap            389/tcp
ldap            389/udp
ldaps           636/tcp
ldaps           636/udp
tftp            69/udp
rje             77/tcp
finger          79/tcp
```

```
link            87/tcp          ttylink
supdup          95/tcp
iso-tsap        102/tcp
x400            103/tcp
x400-snd        104/tcp
csnet-ns        105/tcp
pop-2           109/tcp
uucp-path       117/tcp
nntp            119/tcp         usenet
ntp             123/tcp
ntp             123/udp
NeWS            144/tcp         news
cvc_hostd       442/tcp
exec            512/tcp
login           513/tcp
shell           514/tcp         cmd
printer         515/tcp         spooler
courier         530/tcp         rpc
uucp            540/tcp         uucpd
biff            512/udp         comsat
who             513/udp         whod
syslog          514/udp
talk            517/udp
route           520/udp         router routed
klogin          543/tcp

new-rwho        550/udp         new-who
rmonitor        560/udp         rmonitord
monitor         561/udp
pcserver        600/tcp
kerberos-adm    749/tcp
kerberos-adm    749/udp
kerberos        750/udp         kdc

kerberos        750/tcp         kdc
krb5_prop       754/tcp
ufsd            1008/tcp        ufsd
ufsd            1008/udp        ufsd
cvc             1495/tcp

www-ldap-gw     1760/tcp
www-ldap-gw     1760/udp
listen          2766/tcp
nfsd            2049/udp        nfs
nfsd            2049/tcp        nfs
eklogin         2105/tcp
lockd           4045/udp
lockd           4045/tcp
dtspc           6112/tcp
fs              7100/tcp
```

An Example FTP Transaction

After examining the possible client FTP commands and server response codes, let's see how this transactional system actually works in practice on Solaris. The first step is to make a connection to a remote host from the local system by using the standard client:

```
client% ftp server
Connected to server.
220 server FTP server (SunOS 5.9) ready.
Name (server:pwatters): pwatters
331 Password required for pwatters.
Password:
230 User pwatters logged in.
ftp>
```

In this simple transaction, a user logs in and enters their password, and a session is established. This involves the client program sending a session request, receiving a 220 response, sending a USER command ("USER pwatters"), receiving back a 331 response requesting a password, and sending the password ("PASS password"). If the username and password combination is correct, the session is established and a 230 response is generated by the server. Let's look at what happens when the incorrect password is typed:

```
client% ftp server
Connected to server.
220 server FTP server (SunOS 5.9) ready.
Name (server:pwatters): pwatters
331 Password required for pwatters.
Password:
530 Login incorrect.
Login failed.
ftp>
```

In this transaction, the user logs in as before, entering their password and establishing a session. This client program then sends a session request, receiving a 220 response, then sends a USER command ("USER pwatters") and receives back a 331 response requesting a password. The client then sends the password ("PASS password"), which in this example is incorrect: a 530 response is then sent back from the server to the client, and the user is left in their local client without establishing a session. However, the connect is still open, so mistyping your password can be remedied by using the following combination:

```
ftp> user pwatters
331 Password required for pwatters.
Password:
230 User pwatters logged in.
ftp>
```

Thus, the session is established, and we can proceed with retrieving or uploading files. Let's look at an example:

```
ftp> dir
200 PORT command successful.
150 ASCII data connection for /bin/ls (192.58.64.22,34754) (0 bytes).
total 72573
drwxr-xr-x  13 pwatters staff 2048 Mar 27 08:43 .
dr-xr-xr-x   2 root     root     2 Mar 21 18:55 ..
-rw-r--r--   1 pwatters staff    0 Jan 27 15:42 .addressbook
-rw-r--r--   1 pwatters staff 2285 Jan 27 15:42 .addressbook.lu
```

```
-rw-r--r--    1 pwatters staff 5989 Mar 27 08:42 .bash_history
lrwxrwxrwx    1 pwatters staff 8 Mar 27 08:43 .bash_profile -> .profile
drwxr-xr-x   16 pwatters staff 512 Mar 21 10:10 .dt
-rwxr-xr-x    1 pwatters staff 5113 Jan 27 15:59 .dtprofile
-rw-------    1 pwatters staff 10 Feb 23 13:18 .hist10161
-rw-------    1 pwatters staff 28 Feb 23 16:17 .hist11931
-rw-------    1 pwatters staff 20 Mar  7 15:30 .hist12717
-rw-------    1 pwatters staff 30 Feb 21 08:11 .hist1298
-rw-------    1 pwatters staff 24 Mar  7 16:05 .hist13069
-rw-------    1 pwatters staff 18 Feb 21 15:16 .hist1370
-rw-------    1 pwatters staff 8 Feb 21 15:21 .hist1395
-rw-------    1 pwatters staff 8 Feb 22 08:43 .hist15962
-rw-------    1 pwatters staff 100 Feb 28 11:15 .hist17367
-rw-------    1 pwatters staff 24 Feb 28 11:16 .hist17371
-rw-------    1 pwatters staff 16 Feb 22 11:14 .hist19318
-rw-------    1 paul staff 68 Mar  7 14:38 .hist1954
226 ASCII Transfer complete.
6162 bytes received in 0.092 seconds (65.34 Kbytes/s)
ftp>
```

This is the contents of the current directory. Let's say we wanted to examine the contents of the subdirectory *packages*:

```
cd packages
250 CWD command successful.
ftp> dir
200 PORT command successful.
150 ASCII data connection for /bin/ls (192.58.64.22,34755) (0 bytes).
total 224056
drwxr-xr-x    3 pwatters staff 1024 Mar 27 08:37 .
drwxr-xr-x   13 pwatters staff 2048 Mar 27 08:43 ..
-rw-r--r--    1 pwatters staff 2457088 Mar 17 14:37 apache-1.3.6-sol7
-rw-r--r--    1 pwatters staff 3912704 Mar 17 14:38 bash-2.03-sol7
-rw-r--r--    1 pwatters staff 12154880 Mar 27 08:18 communicator-v472
    -export.sparc-sun-solaris2.5.1.tar
drwxr-xr-x    2 pwatters staff 512 Feb  1 07:11 communicator-v472.
    sparc-sun-solaris2.5.1
-rw-r--r--    1 pwatters staff 597504 Mar 17 16:18 flex-2.5.4a-sol7-
    intel-local
-rw-r--r--    1 pwatters staff 59280384 Mar 17 14:42 gcc-2.95.2-sol7-
    intel-local
226 ASCII Transfer complete.
1389 bytes received in 0.051 seconds (26.51 Kbytes/s)
ftp>
```

Now, let's look at the situation in which we want to retrieve a binary and an ASCII file. An example would be a Java source file (with a *.java* extension), which must be transferred in ASCII mode, and a Java class file (with a *.class* extension), which must be transferred in binary mode:

```
ftp> ascii
200 Type set to A.
ftp> get test.java
200 PORT command successful.
150 ASCII data connection for test.java (192.168.205.48,34759) (117 bytes).
226 ASCII Transfer complete.
local: test.java remote: test.java
```

```
127 bytes received in 0.02 seconds (6.25 Kbytes/s)
ftp> bin
200 Type set to I.
ftp> get test.class
200 PORT command successful.
150 Binary data connection for test.class (192.168.205.48,34760) (431 bytes).
226 Binary Transfer complete.
local: test.class remote: test.class
431 bytes received in 0.0031 seconds (137.10 Kbytes/s)
ftp>
```

Although there are many more commands available in FTP, as previously discussed, these are the most commonly used commands and the responses associated with each kind of transfer.

Troubleshooting FTP

The most common mistake in configuring FTP is not to have a valid shells database (/etc/shells) on your system. Although you can insert any shell you like into the /etc/passwd file, if the shell is not registered in the database, users will not be able to log in. This is a security measure and prevents arbitrary shells with hidden features being used on the system.

One of the nice features of FTP is that you can test it by telnetting to the FTP port. This will allow you to issue FTP commands interactively and examine the results. It is possible to determine, using this method, whether there is a problem with the remote server or a problem with your local client. For example, if you receive a 421 response, you know that the remote FTP server is not running, in which case you can advise the administrator of the remote machine to check the status of inetd.

If your client attempts to connect to a host for a long time without receiving an acknowledgement, it's often worthwhile to check that the host is actually known through DNS. You can use the `nslookup` command to achieve this: if a host is not registered using DNS, you won't be able to make a connection.

If the host has a resolvable hostname, then you can use any one the network troubleshooting tools like ping or traceroute to determine whether a path exists between your local client and the remote server. If no valid path exists, you can contact the administrator of the intermediate site where the connection fails.

Checking If a Host Is Up

The easiest way to check if a remote host is accessible is to use the `ping` command. The following example checks whether the host emu is accessible from the host dingo:

```
dingo% ping emu
```

If emu is accessible, the following output will be generated:

```
emu is alive
```

However, if emu is not accessible, an error message similar to the following will be seen:

```
Request timed out
```

If you need to determine at what point in the network the connection is failing, the `traceroute` command can be used to display the path taken by packets between the two hosts as they travel across the network. For example, to observe the route of the path taken by packets from AT&T to Sun's web server, we would use the following command:

```
client% traceroute www.sun.com
Tracing route to wwwwseast.usec.sun.com [192.9.49.30]
over a maximum of 30 hops:
 1    184 ms    142 ms    138 ms   202.10.4.131
 2    147 ms    144 ms    138 ms   202.10.4.129
 3    150 ms    142 ms    144 ms   202.10.1.73
 4    150 ms    144 ms    141 ms   atm11-0-0-11.ia4.optus.net.au [202.139.32.17]
 5    148 ms    143 ms    139 ms   202.139.1.197
 6    490 ms    489 ms    474 ms   hssi9-0-0.sf1.optus.net.au [192.65.89.246]
 7    526 ms    480 ms    485 ms   g-sfd-br-02-f12-0.gn.cwix.net
[207.124.109.57]
 8    494 ms    482 ms    485 ms   core7-hssi6-0-0.SanFrancisco.cw.net
[204.70.10.9]
 9    483 ms    489 ms    484 ms   corerouter2.SanFrancisco.cw.net
[204.70.9.132]
10    557 ms    552 ms    561 ms   xcore3.Boston.cw.net [204.70.150.81]
11    566 ms    572 ms    554 ms   sun-micro-system.Boston.cw.net
[204.70.179.102]
12    577 ms    574 ms    558 ms   wwwwseast.usec.sun.com [192.9.49.30]
Trace complete.
```

If the connection was broken at any point, then "*" or "!" would be displayed in place of the average connection times displayed.

Enabling FTP Access

Now that we have examined the most common uses for FTP, we will now investigate how to configure the FTP daemon. The FTP server in Solaris is installed by default during configuration and package copying, during the initial installation or upgrade process. By default, the FTP server and protocol will also be active after installation. You can check the status of the FTP server on the local system by checking whether the FTP service is enabled in the *services* database, and in the configuration file for the inetd superdaemon:

```
server# grep ftp /etc/services
ftp-data        20/tcp
ftp             21/tcp
tftp            69/udp

server# grep ftp /etc/inetd.conf
ftp      stream  tcp    nowait  root    /usr/sbin/in.ftpd       in.ftpd
# Tftp service is provided primarily for booting.  Most sites run this
#tftp    dgram   udp    wait    root    /usr/sbin/in.tftpd      in.tftpd
 -s /tftpboot
```

We can see that FTP is both defined as a service (ftp 21/tcp) and as a daemon that runs from within the Internet superdaemon (*/usr/sbin/in.ftpd*). As long as the Internet superdaemon is started up during one of the single or multiple user init states, the FTP service will start. If you ever want to disable the FTP service, you need to comment out the appropriate line in both */etc/services* and */etc/inetd.conf*. You can do this by entering a hash character (#) in front of the appropriate line:

```
#ftp                21/tcp
#ftp       stream  tcp     nowait  root    /usr/sbin/in.ftpd          in.ftpd
```

You can also check the process list by using the command `ps -eaf | grep inetd` to verify that the Internet superdaemon is running at any point in time.

Using ndd

ndd is used to set parameters for network protocols, including TCP, IP, UDP, and ARP. It can be used to modify the parameters associated with IP forwarding and routing. For example, let's look at the set of configurable parameters for TCP transmission:

```
server# ndd /dev/tcp \?
?                              (read only)
tcp_close_wait_interval        (read and write)
tcp_conn_req_max_q             (read and write)
tcp_conn_req_max_q0            (read and write)
tcp_conn_req_min               (read and write)
tcp_conn_grace_period          (read and write)
tcp_cwnd_max                   (read and write)
tcp_debug                      (read and write)
tcp_smallest_nonpriv_port      (read and write)
tcp_ip_abort_cinterval         (read and write)
tcp_ip_abort_linterval         (read and write)
tcp_ip_abort_interval          (read and write)
tcp_ip_notify_cinterval        (read and write)
tcp_ip_notify_interval         (read and write)
tcp_ip_ttl                     (read and write)
tcp_keepalive_interval         (read and write)
tcp_maxpsz_multiplier          (read and write)
tcp_mss_def                    (read and write)
tcp_mss_max                    (read and write)
tcp_mss_min                    (read and write)
tcp_naglim_def                 (read and write)
tcp_rexmit_interval_initial    (read and write)
tcp_rexmit_interval_max        (read and write)
tcp_rexmit_interval_min        (read and write)
tcp_wroff_xtra                 (read and write)
tcp_deferred_ack_interval      (read and write)
tcp_snd_lowat_fraction         (read and write)
tcp_sth_rcv_hiwat              (read and write)
tcp_sth_rcv_lowat              (read and write)
tcp_dupack_fast_retransmit     (read and write)
tcp_ignore_path_mtu            (read and write)
tcp_rcv_push_wait              (read and write)
tcp_smallest_anon_port         (read and write)
tcp_largest_anon_port          (read and write)
tcp_xmit_hiwat                 (read and write)
tcp_xmit_lowat                 (read and write)
```

PART II

```
tcp_recv_hiwat                   (read and write)
tcp_recv_hiwat_minmss            (read and write)
tcp_fin_wait_2_flush_interval    (read and write)
tcp_co_min                       (read and write)
tcp_max_buf                      (read and write)
tcp_zero_win_probesize           (read and write)
tcp_strong_iss                   (read and write)
tcp_rtt_updates                  (read and write)
tcp_wscale_always                (read and write)
tcp_tstamp_always                (read and write)
tcp_tstamp_if_wscale             (read and write)
tcp_rexmit_interval_extra        (read and write)
tcp_deferred_acks_max            (read and write)
tcp_slow_start_after_idle        (read and write)
tcp_slow_start_initial           (read and write)
tcp_co_timer_interval            (read and write)
tcp_extra_priv_ports             (read only)
tcp_extra_priv_ports_add         (write only)
tcp_extra_priv_ports_del         (write only)
tcp_status                       (read only)
tcp_bind_hash                    (read only)
tcp_listen_hash                  (read only)
tcp_conn_hash                    (read only)
tcp_queue_hash                   (read only)
tcp_host_param                   (read and write)
tcp_1948_phrase                  (write only)
```

Parameters can also be set for IP, as well as TCP. For example, if the parameter `ip_forwarding` has a value of 2 (the default), it will only perform routing when two or more interfaces are active. However, if this parameter is set to zero, then `ip_forwarding` will never be performed (that is, to ensure that multihoming is enabled rather than routing). This can be set by using the following command:

```
server# ndd -set /dev/ip ip_forwarding 0
```

in.ftpd

As we mentioned in the previous section, FTP commands are associated with specific operations that are to be performed on the server. Most FTP clients and the Solaris FTP server support the following case-insensitive commands:

- **!** Escape to the default shell.
- **$** Execute a predefined macro.
- **account** Send account information to the remote server.
- **append** Append server output to a file.
- **ascii** Set ASCII transfer type. ASCII mode is the default transfer mode and is used for transferring text files.
- **bell** Beep when the specified command is completed.
- **binary** Set binary transfer type. Typically used for transferring binary files like .*ZIP* files, .*gif* giles, and .*Z* files.

- **bye**   Terminate the ftp session and exit from the client.
- **case**   Toggle get uppercase/lowercase mapping.
- **cd**   Change remote working directory. Changes the directory to the one named. If the directory named is not a subdirectory of the current directory, the path (for example, cd /pub/library) must be specified.
- **cdup**   Change remote working directory to parent directory.
- **close**   Terminate ftp session, but do not exit from the client.
- **cd**   Change remote working directory.
- **delete**   Delete the remote file specified.
- **debug**   Toggle/set debugging mode on server.
- **dir**   List the contents of a remote directory.
- **disconnect**   Terminate the current ftp session.
- **form**   Set file transfer format to be binary or ASCII.
- **get**   Download file from the server to the local client.
- **glob**   Toggle metacharacter expansion of local filenames.
- **hash**   Toggle printing "#" for each buffer transferred. Prints a hash "#" on the screen for every 1024 bytes transferred. This is useful for keeping track of a FTP transfer interactively.
- **help**   Gives local help on the use of commands within the ftp client.
- **lcd**   Change local working directory to that specified.
- **ls**   List contents of current remote directory.
- **macdef**   Define a macro interactively.
- **mdelete**   Delete multiple files as determined by a file specification (for example, MDELETE *.txt).
- **mdir**   List contents of multiple remote directories in one request.
- **mget**   Download multiple files, as specified by using a wildcard character * in the file specification.
- **mkdir**   Create a directory on the remote machine as a subdirectory relative to the current directory.
- **mls**   List contents of multiple remote directories in a single request.
- **mode**   Set file transfer mode to be ASCII or binary.
- **mput**   Upload multiple files from your local file system to the remote server.
- **nmap**   Set templates for default filename mapping.
- **ntrans**   Set translation table for default filename mapping.
- **open**   Connect to remote server.

PART II

- **prompt**   Force interactive prompting on multiple commands.
- **proxy**   Issue command on alternate connection.
- **sendport**   Toggle use of PORT cmd for each data connection.
- **put**   Upload one file at a time.
- **pwd**   Print working directory on remote machine.
- **quit**   Terminate ftp session and exit.
- **quote**   Send arbitrary ftp command.
- **recv**   Receive file.
- **remotehelp**   Get help from remote server.
- **rename**   Rename file.
- **reset**   Clear queued command replies.
- **rmdir**   Remove directory on the remote machine.
- **runique**   Toggle store unique for local files.
- **send**   Upload a single file.
- **status**   Show current status.
- **struct**   Set file transfer structure.
- **sunique**   Toggle store unique on remote machine.
- **tenex**   Set tenex file transfer type.
- **trace**   Toggle packet tracing.
- **type**   Set file transfer type.
- **user**   Send new user information.
- **verbose**   Toggle verbose mode.
- **?**   Print local help information.

The following is a list of possible response codes, which the server generates in response to each command issued from the client:

- **110**   Restart marker reply.
- **120**   Service ready in *nnn* minutes.
- **125**   Data connection already open; transfer starting.
- **150**   File status okay; about to open data connection.
- **200**   Command okay.
- **202**   Command not implemented, superfluous at this site.
- **211**   System status, or system help reply.
- **212**   Directory status.

- 213   File status.
- 214   Help message.
- 215   NAME system type.
- 220   Service ready for new user.
- 221   Service closing control connection.
- 225   Data connection open; no transfer in progress.
- 226   Closing data connection.
- 227   Entering passive mode (h1,h2,h3,h4,p1,p2).
- 230   User logged in, proceed.
- 250   Requested file action okay, completed.
- 257   "PATHNAME" created.
- 331   Username okay, need password.
- 332   Need account for login.
- 350   Requested file action pending further information.
- 421   Service not available, closing control connection.
- 425   Can't open data connection.
- 426   Connection closed; transfer aborted.
- 450   Requested file action not taken.
- 451   Requested action aborted: local error in processing.
- 452   Requested action not taken.
- 500   Syntax error, command unrecognized.
- 501   Syntax error in parameters or arguments.
- 502   Command not implemented.
- 503   Bad sequence of commands.
- 504   Command not implemented for that parameter.
- 530   Not logged in.
- 532   Need account for storing files.
- 550   Requested action not taken.
- 551   Requested action aborted: page type unknown.
- 552   Requested file action aborted.
- 553   Requested action not taken.

PART II

Summary

In this chapter, we have examined the basic configuration of network interfaces and simple application layer services like the File Transfer Protocol (FTP). In addition, we examined some basic methods for tuning interfaces and for configuring individual daemons through the Internet super daemin (inetd).

Questions

1. Name the three major types of subnet supported by Solaris.

   A. Class 1, Class 2, Class 3

   B. Class A, Class B, Class C

   C. T1, broadband, cable

   D. None of the above

2. What is the purpose of a router?

   A. To pass information from one network to another

   B. To pass information between two hosts only

   C. To provide two independent network interfaces on a single host

   D. None of the above

3. What is the main requirement of a router?

   A. To be connected to the Internet

   B. To run Solaris 9

   C. To have multiple network interfaces

   D. None of the above

4. What should *not* be contained in the file */etc/hostname.hme0*?

   A. A hostname

   B. A fully qualified domain name

   C. An IP address

   D. The default router's hostname

5. What is contained in the file */etc/defaultrouter*?

   A. The local router's hostname

   B. The local router's IP address

   C. The local router's hostname or IP address

   D. The local router's netmask

6. What file should be created for a nonrouting, multihomed host?

    A. */etc/noroute*

    B. */etc/notrouter*

    C. */etc/notroute*

    D. */etc/!route*

7. What command is used to set parameters for network protocols?

    A. `tcp`

    B. `ip`

    C. `tip`

    D. `ndd`

8. What command is used to display the kernel routing table?

    A. `kern`

    B. `route`

    C. `netstat -r`

    D. `route -r`

9. What command is used to start the network routing daemon?

    A. */usr/sbin/in.routed* `-q`

    B. */usr/sbin/in.RDISC* `-q`

    C. */usr/sbin/in.routed* `-s`

    D. */etc/init.d/routed.exe*

10. What command is used to set a default route to 204.54.56.1?

    A. `route -add default 204.54.56.1`

    B. `route add -default 204.54.56.1`

    C. `route -add -default 204.54.56.1`

    D. `route add default 204.54.56.1`

11. What command is used to disable IP forwarding?

    A. `ndd -forwarding 0`

    B. `ndd -set /dev/ip ip_forwarding 0`

    C. `ndd -set /dev/ip ip_-forwarding +0`

    D. `ndd -noforward`

12. What command is used to verify the status of a network interface?

  A. `netview`

  B. `netlook`

  C. `ifconfig`

  D. `hmelook`

13. What command is used to check the table of IP address to MAC address mappings?

  A. `arp`

  B. `ar`

  C. `ndd`

  D. `netstat`

14. Which of the following is a valid network topology?

  A. Star

  B. Box

  C. Square

  D. Circle

15. Which of the following is a valid network topology?

  A. Cube

  B. Angle

  C. Cross

  D. Ring

Answers

  1. **B.** Class A, Class B, and Class C subnets are all supported by Solaris.

  2. **A.** The purpose of a router is to pass information from one network to another.

  3. **C.** The main requirement of a router is to have multiple network interfaces.

  4. **D.** The default router's hostname should *not* be contained in the file */etc/hostname.hme0*.

  5. **C.** The local router's hostname or IP address is contained in the file */etc/defaultrouter*.

  6. **B.** The */etc/notrouter* file should be created for a nonrouting, multihomed host.

  7. **D.** The `ndd` command is used to set parameters for network protocols.

  8. **C.** The `netstat -r` command is used to display the kernel routing table.

9. **A.** The */usr/sbin/in.routed* –q command is used to start the network routing daemon.

10. **D.** The route add default 204.54.56.1 command is used to set a default route to 204.54.56.1.

11. **B.** The ndd -set /dev/ip ip_forwarding 0 command is used to disable IP forwarding.

12. **C.** The ifconfig command is used to verify the status of a network interface.

13. **A.** The arp command is used to check the table of IP address to MAC address mappings.

14. **A.** Star is a valid network topology. Actually, a star and a circle, or ring, are valid, but neither are discussed in the chapter.

15. **D.** Ring is a valid network topology.

PART II

System Logging, Accounting, and Tuning

In this chapter, you will

- Understand the role of system logging
- Learn how to implement syslog
- Discover accounting procedures
- Review system performance procedures

A well-managed system needs to be continuously monitored for security, accounting, and performance purposes. Solaris provides several built-in mechanisms to use in accounting for resource usage, which you can then use with an automated billing procedure. This is very useful for Internet service providers and shared-use systems that must account for the resources utilized by users or groups. In addition, you can easily detect inappropriate use of resources by unauthorized individuals, and you can limit utilization by enforcing quotas.

System Logging

Syslog is a centralized logging facility that provides different classes of events that are logged to a log file, as well as providing an alerting service for certain events. Because syslogd is configurable by root, it is very flexible in its operations. Multiple log files can exist for each daemon whose activity is being logged, or a single log file can be created. The syslog service is controlled by the configuration file */etc/syslog.conf*, which is read at boot time or whenever the syslog daemon receives a HUP signal. This file defines the facility levels or system source of logged messages and conditions. Priority levels are also assigned to system events recorded in the system log, while an action field defines what action is taken when a particular class of event is encountered. These events can range from normal system usage, such as FTP connections and remote shells, to system crashes.

The source facilities defined by Solaris are for the kernel (kern), authentication (auth), daemons (daemon), mail system (mail), print spooling (lp), and user processes (user). Priority levels are classified as system emergencies (emerg), errors requiring immediate attention (attn), critical errors (crit), messages (info), debugging output (debug), and other errors (err). These priority levels are defined for individual systems and architectures in *<sys/syslog.h>*.

 TIP It is easy to see how logging applications, such as TCP wrappers, can take advantage of the different error levels and source facilities provided by syslogd.

On the Solaris platform, the syslog daemon depends on the m4 macro processor being present. m4 is typically installed with the software developer packages, and it is usually located in */usr/ccs/bin/m4*. This version has been installed by default since Solaris 2.4. Users should note that the syslogd supplied by Sun has been error-prone in previous releases. With early Solaris 2.*x* versions, the syslog daemon left behind zombie processes when alerting logged-in users (for example, notifying root of an emerg).

 TIP If syslogd does not work, check that m4 exists and is in the path for root, and/or run the syslogd program interactively by invoking it with a −d parameter.

Examining Log Files

Log files are fairly straightforward in their contents, and you can stipulate what events are recorded by instructions in the *syslog.conf* file. Records of mail messages can be useful for billing purposes and for detecting the bulk sending of unsolicited commercial e-mail (spam). The system log will record the details supplied by sendmail: a message ID, when a message is sent or received, a destination, and a delivery result, which is typically "delivered" or "deferred." Connections are usually deferred when a connection to a site is down.

 TIP sendmail will usually try to redeliver failed deliveries in 4-hour intervals.

When using TCP wrappers, connections to supported Internet daemons are also logged. For example, an FTP connection to a server will result in the connection time and date being recorded, along with the hostname of the client. A similar result is achieved for telnet connections.

A delivered mail message is recorded as

```
Feb 20 14:07:05 server sendmail[238]: AA00238: message-id=<bulk.11403.19990219175554@sun.com>
Feb 20 14:07:05 server sendmail[238]: AA00238: from=<sun-developers-l@sun.com>,
size=1551, class=0, received from gateway.site.com (172.16.1.1)
Feb 20 14:07:06 server sendmail[243]: AA00238: to=<pwatters@mail.site.com>,
 delay=00:00:01, stat=Sent, mailer=local
```

whereas a deferred mail message is recorded differently:

```
Feb 21 07:11:10 server sendmail[855]: AA00855: message
-id=<Pine.SOL.3.96.990220200723.5291A-100000@oracle.com>
Feb 21 07:11:10 server sendmail[855]: AA00855: from=<support@oracle.com>,
 size=1290, class=0, received from gateway.site.com (172.16.1.1)
Feb 21 07:12:25 server sendmail[857]: AA00855: to=pwatters@mail.site.com,
 delay=00:01:16, stat=Deferred: Connection timed out during user open with
 mail.site.com, mailer=TCP
```

An FTP connection is recorded in a single line,

```
Feb 20 14:35:00 server in.ftpd[277]: connect from workstation.site.com
```

in the same way that a telnet connection is recorded:

```
Feb 20 14:35:31 server in.telnetd[279]: connect from workstation.site.com
```

Logging Disk Usage

For auditing purposes, many sites generate a df report at midnight or during a change of administrator shifts, to record a snapshot of the system. In addition, if disk space is becoming an issue, and extra volumes need to be justified in a systems budget, it is useful to be able to estimate how rapidly disk space is being consumed by users. Using the cron utility, you can set up and schedule a script using crontab to check disk space at different time periods and to mail this information to the administrator (or even post it to a web site, if system administration is centrally managed).

A simple script to monitor disk space usage and mail the results to the system administrator (*root@server*) looks like this:

```
#!/bin/csh -f
df | mailx -s "Disk Space Usage" root@localhost
```

As an example, if this script were named */usr/local/bin/monitor_usage.csh*, and executable permissions were set for the nobody user, you could create the following crontab entry for the nobody user to run at midnight every night of the week:

```
0 0 * * * /usr/local/bin/monitor_usage.csh
```

Or, you could make the script more general, so that users could specify another user who would be mailed:

```
#!/bin/csh -f
df | mailx -s "Disk Space Usage" $1
```

The crontab entry would then look like this:

```
0 0 * * * /usr/local/bin/monitor_usage.csh remote_user@client
```

The results of the disk usage report would now be sent to the user *remote_user@client* instead of *root@localhost*.

You can find further information on the cron utility and submitting cron jobs in Chapter 8.

Another way of obtaining disk space usage information with more directory-by-directory detail is by using the `/usr/bin/du` command. This command prints the sum of the sizes of every file in the current directory and performs the same task recursively for any subdirectories. The size is calculated by adding together all of the file sizes in the directory, where the size for each file is rounded up to the next 512-byte block. For example, taking a du of the */etc* directory looks like this:

```
# du /etc

14        ./default
7         ./cron.d
6         ./dfs
8         ./dhcp
201       ./fs/hsfs
681       ./fs/nfs
1         ./fs/proc
209       ./fs/ufs
1093      ./fs

...
2429      .
```

Thus, */etc* and all its subdirectories contain a total of 2,429KB of data. Of course, this kind of output is fairly verbose and probably not much use in its current form. If you were only interested in *recording* the directory sizes, in order to collect data for auditing and usage analysis, you could write a short Perl script to collect the data, as follows:

```
#!/usr/local/bin/perl
# directorysize.pl: reads in directory size for current directory
# and prints results to standard output
@du = `du`;
for (@du)
{
($sizes,$directories)=split /\s+/, $_;
print "$sizes\n";
}
```

If you saved this script as *directorysize.pl* in the */usr/local/bin/directory* and set the executable permissions, it would produce a list of directory sizes as output, like the following:

```
# cd /etc
 # /usr/local/bin/directorysize.pl

28
14
12
16
402
1362
2
418
2186
...
```

Because you are interested in usage management, you might want to modify the script to display the total amount of space occupied by a directory and its subdirectories, as well as the average amount of space occupied. The latter is very important when evaluating caching or investigating load-balancing issues:

```
#!/usr/local/bin/perl
# directorysize.pl: reads in directory size for current directory
# and prints the sum and average disk space used to standard output
$sum=0;
$count=0;
@ps = `du -o`;
for (@ps)
{
  ($sizes,$directories)=split /\s+/, $_;
  $sum=$sum+$sizes;
  $count=$count+1;
}
print "Total Space: $sum K\n";
print "Average Space: $count K\n";
```

Note that du –o was used as the command, so that the space occupied by subdirectories is not added to the total for the top-level directory. The output from the command for /etc now looks like this:

```
# cd /etc
 # /usr/local/bin/directorysize.pl
Total Space: 4832 K
Average Space: 70 K
```

Again, you could set up a cron job to mail this information to an administrator at midnight every night. To do this, first create a new shell script to call the Perl script, which is made more flexible by passing the directory to be measured, and the user to which the mail will be sent as arguments:

```
#!/bin/csh -f
cd $1
/usr/local/bin/directorysize.pl | mailx -s "Directory Space Usage" $2
```

If you save this script to /usr/local/bin/checkdirectoryusage.csh and set the executable permission, you could then schedule a disk space check of a cache file system. You could include a second command that sends a report for the /disks/junior_developers file system, which is remotely mounted from client, to the team leader on server:

```
0 0 * * * /usr/local/bin/checkdirectoryusage.csh /cache squid@server
1 0 * * * /usr/local/bin/checkdirectoryusage.csh /disks/junior_developers
team_leader@server
```

 TIP Tools may already be available on Solaris to perform some of these tasks more directly. For example, the du –s command will return the sum of directory sizes automatically. However, the purpose of this section has been to demonstrate how to customize and develop your own scripts for file system management.

EXAM TIP You will be required to interpret scripts in the exam.

The syslog.conf File

The file */etc/syslog.conf* contains information used by the system log daemon, syslogd, to forward a system message to appropriate log files and/or users. syslogd preprocesses this file through m4 to obtain the correct information for certain log files, defining LOGHOST if the address of "loghost" is the same as one of the addresses of the host that is running syslogd.

The default syslogd configuration is not optimal for all installations. Many configuration decisions depend on the degree to which the system administrator wishes to be alerted immediately should an alert or emergency occur, or whether it is sufficient for all auth notices to be logged and a cron job run every night to filter the results for a review in the morning. For noncommercial installations, the latter is probably a reasonable approach. A crontab entry like this,

```
0 1 * * * cat /var/adm/messages | grep auth | mail root
```

will send the root user a mail message at 1:00 A.M. every morning with all authentication messages.

A basic *syslog.conf* should contain provision for sending emergency notices to all users, as well as altering to the root user and other nonprivileged administrator accounts. Errors, kernel notices, and authentication notices probably need to be displayed on the system console. It is generally sufficient to log daemon notices, alerts, and all other authentication information to the system log file, unless the administrator is watching for cracking attempts, as shown here:

```
*.alert                                         root,pwatters
*.emerg                                         *
*.err;kern.notice;auth.notice                   /dev/console
daemon.notice                      /var/adm/messages
auth.none;kern.err;daemon.err;mail.crit;*.alert /var/adm/messages
auth.info                                       /var/adm/authlog
```

Quotas

Resource management is one of the administrator's key responsibilities, particularly where the availability of a service is the organization's primary source of income (or recognition). For example, if an application server requires 10MB of free disk space for internal caching of objects retrieved from a database, performance on the client side will suffer if this space is not available because a user decided to dump his or her collection of MP3 music files onto the system hard drive. If external users cannot access a service because of internal resource allocation problems, they are unlikely to continue using your service. There is also a possibility that a rogue user (or competitor) may attempt to disrupt your service by attempting any number of well-known exploits to reduce your providing service to clients. In this section, we examine resource management strategies that are flexible enough to meet the needs of casual users, but which limit the potential for accidental or malicious resource misuse.

Implementing Quotas

Solaris provides a number of tools to enforce policies on disk and resource usage, based around the idea of quotas, or a prespecified allocation of disk space for each user and file system. Thus, a single user can have disk space allocated on different slices, and file systems can have quotas either enabled or disabled (they are disabled by default). Although many organizations disable disk quotas for fear of reducing productivity by placing unnecessary restrictions on the development staff, there are often some very good reasons for implementing quotas on specific slices. For example, if an open file area, like an anonymous FTP "incoming" directory, is located on the same partition as normal user data, a denial-of-service attack could be initiated by a rogue user who decides to fill the incoming directory with large files until all free space is consumed. Or, a CGI application that writes data to a user's home directory (for example, a guestbook) can also fall victim to a denial-of-service attack: a malicious script could be written to enter a million fake entries into the address book, thereby filling the partition to capacity. The result in both of these cases is loss of service and loss of system control. It is therefore important that networked systems have appropriate checks and balances in place to ensure that such situations are avoided.

CAUTION   Quotas are also critical to ensure fair resource sharing among developers. Otherwise, a developer who decides to back up his PC drive to his home directory on a server, completely filling the partition, could prevent other users from writing valuable data.

In addition to security concerns, enforcing quotas is also optimal from an administrative point of view—it forces users to rationalize their own storage requirements, so that material that is not being used can be moved offline or deleted. This saves administrators from having to make such decisions for users (who may be dismayed at the results if the administrator has to move things in a hurry!).

One simple policy is to enforce disk quotas on all public file systems that have network access. Increasing quotas for all users is easy, so the policy can be flexible. In addition, quotas can be hard or soft: *hard* quotas strictly enforce incursions into unallocated territory, whereas *soft* quotas provide a buffer for temporary violations of a quota, and the users are given warning before enforcement begins.

TIP   Depending on the security level at which your organization operates (for example, C2 standards for military organizations), a quota policy may already be available for you to implement.

A total limit on the amount of disk space available to users can be specified using quotas for each user individually. Let's take the user pwatters on server as an example. You may allot this user, a Java developer, a quota of 10MB for development work on the */staff* file system. To set up this quota, you need to undertake the following steps:

1. Edit the */etc/vfstab* file as root and add the rq flag to the mount options field for the */staff* file system. This enables quotas for the file system.

2. Change directory to */staff* and create a file called *quotas*.

3. Set permissions on */staff/quotas* to be read and write for root only.

4. Edit user quotas for user pwatters on file system */staff* by using the edquota command and entering the number of inodes and 1KB blocks that will be available to user pwatters—for example, enter the following:

    fs /staff blocks (soft = 10000, hard = 11000) inodes (soft = 0, hard = 0)

5. Check the settings that you have created by using the quota command.

6. Enable the quota for user pwatters by using the quotaon command.

You can implement these steps by entering the following:

```
# vi /etc/vfstab
# cd /staff
# touch quotas
# chmod u+rw quotas
# edquota pwatters
# quota -v pwatters
# quotaon /staff
```

When you verify the quotas using quota -v,

```
# quota -v pwatters
```

the output should look like the following:

```
Disk quotas for pwatters (uid 1001):
Filesystem      usage  quota  limit      timeleft  files  quota
/staff              0  10000  11000             0      0      0
```

You can see that a soft limit of 10MB and a hard limit of 11MB was entered for user pwatters. If halfway through the development project this user requests more space, you could adjust the quota by using the edquota command again. To check quotas for all users, use the repquota command:

```
# repquota /staff

Block limits
User            used    soft    hard
jsmith     --   2048    4096    8192
pwatters   --    131   10000   20000
qjones     --  65536   90000  100000
llee       --   4096    8192   10000
```

If a user attempts to exceed his or her quota during an interactive session, unless you've set up a warning to be issued under those circumstances, the first indication that the user will have will often come in the form of a "file system full" or "write failed" message. After checking the amount of free space on the partition where their home disk is located, many users are at a loss to explain why they can no longer edit files or send e-mail!

System Accounting

Solaris provides a centralized auditing service known as *system accounting*. This service is very useful for accounting for the various tasks that your system may be involved in—you can use it to monitor resource usage, troubleshoot system failures, isolate bottlenecks in the system, and assist in system security. In addition, system accounting acts as a real accounting service, and you can use it for billing in the commercial world. In this section, we review the major components of system accounting, including several applications and scripts that are responsible for preparing daily reports on connections, process, and disk load and usage statements for users.

TIP Once you enable the appropriate script in */etc/init.d*, system accounting does not typically involve administrator intervention.

Collecting Accounting Data

Collecting data for accounting is simple: Create a startup script (*/etc/rc2.d/S22acct*) in order to begin collecting data soon after the system enters multiuser mode and optionally create a kill script (*/etc/rc0.d/K22acct*) to turn off data collection cleanly before the system shuts down. As per standard System V practice, you should create a single script in */etc/init.d* (for example, */etc/init.d/accounting*) and link it symbolically to both of those filenames, thus ensuring that both a start and a stop parameter can be interpreted by the script. When accounting is enabled, details of processes, storage, and user activity are recorded in specially created log files, which are then processed daily by the */usr/lib/acct/runacct* program. The output from *runacct* is also processed by */usr/lib/acct/prdaily* (which generates the reports described in the next section). There is also a separate monthly billing program called */usr/lib/acct/monacct*, which is executed monthly and generates accounts for individual users.

The accounting file startup and shutdown script should look like this:

```
parameter=$1
case $parameter in
'start')
     echo "Initializing process accounting"
        /usr/lib/acct/startup
        ;;
'stop')
        echo "Halting process accounting"
        /usr/lib/acct/shutacct
        ;;
esac
```

When called with the `start` parameter, this script executes another script, */usr/lib/acct/startup*, which is responsible for executing the */usr/lib/acct/acctwtmp* program—which sets up record-writing utilities in the */var/adm/wtmp* file. It then starts a script called turnacct, which is called with the name of the file in which the kernel records the process accounting details (usually named */var/adm/pacct*). Finally, the startup section of the script removes all the temporary files associated with previous accounting activities.

Generating Accounting Reports

Once you have enabled data collection, generating reports is a simple matter of setting up a cron job for a nonprivileged user (usually adm), typically at a time of low system load. In the following example, accounting runs are performed at 6:00 A.M.:

```
0 6 * * * /usr/lib/acct/runacct 2> /var/adm/acct/nite/fd2log
```

Accounting runs involve several discrete stages, which are executed in the following order:

SETUP	Prepares accounting files for running the report.
WTMPFIX	Checks the soundness of the *wtmpx* file and repairs it, if necessary.
CONNECT	Gathers data for user connect time.
PROCESS	Gathers data for process usage.
MERGE	Integrates the connection and process data.
FEES	Gathers fee information and applies to connection and process data.
DISK	Gathers data on disk usage and integrates with fee, connection, and process data.
MERGETACCT	Integrates accounting data for the past 24 hours (*daytacct*) with the total accounting data (*/var/adm/acct/sum/tacct*).
CMS	Generates command summaries.
CLEANUP	Removes transient data and cleans up before terminating.

After each stage of *runacct* has been successfully completed, the *statefile* (*/var/adm/acct/nite/statefile*) is overwritten with the name of that stage. Thus, if the accounting is disrupted for any reason, it can be easily resumed by rereading the *statefile*. On January 23rd, if the *statefile* contained *FEES* but terminated during *DISK*, you could restart the accounting run for the day by using the following command:

```
# runacct 2301 DISK >> /var/adm/acct/nite/fd2log
```

Once the daily run has been completed, the *lastdate* file is updated with the current date in *ddmm* format, where *dd* is the day and *mm* is the month of the last run. In addition, you can review a number of files manually to obtain usage summaries. For example, the daily report is stored in a file called *rprtddmm*, where *dd* is the day and *mm* is the month of the run. This contains the cms and lastlogin data, as well as a connection usage summary:

```
Jan 26 02:05 2002  DAILY REPORT FOR johnson Page 1
from Fri Jan 25 02:05:23 2002
to   Sat Jan 26 02:05:54 2002

TOTAL DURATION IS 46 MINUTES
LINE          MINUTES   PERCENT   # SESS   # ON   # OFF
/dev/pts/1    0         0         0        0      0
pts/1         46        0         8        8      8
TOTALS        46        --        8        8      8
```

Here you can see that the total connection time for the previous day was 46 minutes.

Login Logging

The *loginlog* file contains a list of the last login dates for all local users. Some system accounts appear as never having logged in, which is expected:

```
00-00-00   adm
00-00-00   bin
00-00-00   daemon
00-00-00   listen
00-00-00   lp
00-00-00   noaccess
00-00-00   nobody
00-00-00   nuucp
00-00-00   smtp
00-00-00   sys
02-01-20   root
02-01-26   pwatters
```

You should check the *loginlog* file for access to system accounts, which should never be accessed, and for unexpected usage of user accounts.

Command Summaries

A typical command summary (cms) statement generated by the *runacct* program is shown in Table 20-1.

Once you know what each column in this report represents, it becomes obvious that in this example, reading, sending, and receiving mail are the main uses of this server, on a daily basis at least, while the `runacct` command, which actually performs the accounting, was one of the least-used programs. Here is an explanation of the columns in the preceding report:

- **COMMAND NAME** Shows the command as executed. This can lead to some ambiguity, because different commands could have the same filename. In addition, any shell or Perl scripts executed would be displayed under the shell and Perl interpreter, respectively, rather than showing up as a process on their own.

PART II

Command Name	Number Cmds	Total kcoremin	Total CPU Min	Total Realmin	Mean Size-K	Mean CPU-Min	Hog Factor	Chars Trnsfrd	Blocks read
totals	1034	1843.03	0.46	546.88	4049.14	0.00	0.00	107141376	982
pine	5	1426.41	0.11	177.47	13477.87	0.02	0.00	72782400	237
sendmail	171	176.44	0.09	4.73	1873.71	0.00	0.02	14895311	306
sh	107	31.15	0.04	0.29	881.70	0.00	0.12	58380	0
uudemon	114	27.91	0.02	0.10	1154.92	0.00	0.24	67765	8
in.ftpd	1	23.20	0.02	0.69	1435.05	0.02	0.02	6422528	7
mail.loc	13	19.69	0.02	0.06	1193.21	0.00	0.27	11973498	57
tcsh	4	13.61	0.01	179.98	1361.33	0.00	0.00	153040	1
uuxqt	48	11.01	0.01	0.08	1159.30	0.00	0.13	35568	0
uusched	48	10.99	0.01	0.09	1014.52	0.00	0.13	36096	180
popper	9	7.84	0.01	1.55	1205.74	0.00	0.00	155107	32
sed	58	7.63	0.01	0.02	618.38	0.00	0.58	44907	2
date	34	7.26	0.01	0.01	821.74	0.00	0.72	26348	1
rm	36	5.68	0.01	0.02	681.44	0.00	0.45	0	8
acctcms	4	4.92	0.01	0.01	953.03	0.00	0.97	125984	1
in.telne	4	4.85	0.00	180.03	1076.74	0.00	0.00	55744	0
cp	42	4.47	0.01	0.02	525.65	0.00	0.36	14434	60
ckpacct	24	4.23	0.00	0.09	907.14	0.00	0.05	49200	0
awk	26	4.01	0.01	0.02	616.82	0.00	0.36	950	0
chmod	37	3.69	0.01	0.01	553.60	0.00	0.55	0	0
cat	22	3.58	0.00	0.01	825.54	0.00	0.55	1540	2
acctprc	1	2.98	0.00	0.00	744.00	0.00	0.96	46152	0

Table 20-1   A Typical Command Summary (cms) Statement

- **NUMBER CMNDS**   Displays the number of times that the command named under COMMAND NAME was executed during the accounting period.
- **TOTAL KCOREMIN**   Shows the cumulative sum of memory segments (in kilobytes) used by the process identified under COMMAND NAME per minute of execution time.
- **TOTAL CPU-MIN**   Prints the accumulated processing time for the program named under COMMAND NAME.
- **TOTAL REAL-MIN**   Shows the actual time in minutes that the program named in COMMAND NAME consumed during the accounting period.
- **MEAN SIZE-K**   Indicates the average of the cumulative sum of consumed memory segments (TOTAL KCOREMIN) over the set of invocations denoted by NUMBER CMDS.
- **MEAN CPU-MIN**   The average CPU time computed from the quotient of NUMBER CMDS divided by TOTAL CPU-MIN.
- **HOG FACTOR**   The amount of CPU time divided by actual elapsed time. This ratio indicates the degree to which a system is available compared to its use. The hog factor is often used as a metric to determine overall load levels for a system, and it is useful for planning upgrades and expansion.

- **CHARS TRNSFRD** Displays the sum of the characters transferred by system calls.
- **BLOCKS READ** Shows the number of physical block reads and writes that the program named under COMMAND NAME accounted for.

Often, the values of these parameters are confusing. For example, let's compare the characteristics of pine, which is a mail client, and sendmail, which is a mail transport agent. pine was executed only five times, but accounted for 1426.41 KCOREMIN, while sendmail was executed 171 times with a KCOREMIN of 176.44. The explanation for this apparent anomaly is that users probably log in once in the morning and leave their pine mail client running all day. The users sent an average of 34.2 messages during this day, many of which contained attachments—thus accounting for the high CPU overhead.

monacct

When examined over a number of days, accounting figures provide a useful means of understanding how processes are making use of the system's resources. When examined in isolation, however, they can sometimes misrepresent the dominant processes that the machine is used for. This is a well-known aspect of statistical sampling: Before you can make any valid generalizations about a phenomenon, your observations must be repeated and sampled randomly. Thus, it is useful to compare the day-to-day variation of a system's resource use with the monthly figures that are generated by */usr/lib/acct/ monacct*. Compare these daily values with the previous month's values generated by monacct in Table 20-2.

As you can see in Table 20-2, the individual day's figures were misleading. In fact, spread over a whole month, the Netscape program tended to use more resources than the pine mail client, being invoked 1,538 times, and using 163985.79 KCOREMIN, compared to 165 invocations and 43839.27 KCOREMIN for pine.

Command name	Number CMDS	Total KCORE MIN	Total CPU MIN	Total REALMIN	Mean Size-K	Mean CPU-MIN	HOG factor	CHARS trnsfrd	Blocks read
totals	513833	52911.94	262.83	632612.94	2013.17	0.00	0.00	8959614208	138299
nscp	1538	163985.79	6.77	59865.58	24233.18	0.00	0.00	4744854	720
installp	110508	58676.62	33.65	197.77	1743.57	0.00	0.17	27303024	139
sed	122726	45704.45	40.87	98.07	1118.16	0.00	0.42	20044188	171
pine	165	43839.27	3.88	1594.97	11304.12	0.02	0.00	1578316160	4675
project	13	37654.92	22.76	22.79	1654.41	1.75	1.00	6187332	106
ll-ar	4	24347.44	26.49	50.37	919.24	6.62	0.53	201642	5
nawk	75544	21678.96	24.46	40.21	886.40	0.00	0.61	61351684	135
predict	289	16808.70	13.59	13.74	1236.66	0.05	0.99	38996306	293
sqpe	17	15078.86	4.15	10.30	3636.67	0.24	0.40	90547712	889
grep	71963	13042.15	18.69	26.47	697.69	0.00	0.71	377825714	3
pkgparam	24578	11360.71	9.11	9.68	1246.38	0.00	0.94	102325648	0
false_ne	7	10399.85	2.12	2.13	4899.81	0.30	1.00	212530	5
pkgremov	89	10073.67	8.95	22.70	1125.88	0.10	0.39	1129787392	18845
pkginsta	125	7163.67	4.75	38.21	1508.46	0.04	0.12	1912983552	4077
tee	8622	3237.38	2.03	2.30	1592.24	0.00	0.88	2134692	0
ls	8825	3133.31	2.59	3.31	1209.06	0.00	0.78	2038136	215

Table 20-2 Monthly Account Summary

TIP It is very useful to examine monthly averages for a more reliable, strategic overview of system activity, while daily summaries are useful for making tactical decisions about active processes.

Charging Fees Using Accounting

In the previous section, we looked at the output for monacct, which is the monthly accounting program. To enable monacct, you need to create a cron job for the adm account, which is similar to the entry for the `runacct` command in the previous section:

```
0 5 1 * * /usr/lib/acct/monacct
```

In addition to computing per-process statistics, monacct also computes usage information on a per-user basis, which you can use to bill customers according to the number of CPU minutes they used. Examine the user reports in Table 20-3 for the same month that was reviewed in the previous section.

Of the nonsystem users, obviously pwatters is going to have a large bill this month, with 65 prime CPU minutes consumed. Billing could also proceed on the basis of KCOREMINS utilized; pwatters, in this case, used 104572 KCOREMINS. How an organization bills its users is probably already well established, but even if users are not billed for cash payment, examining how the system is used is very valuable for planning expansion and for identifying rogue processes that reduce the availability of a system for legitimate processes.

	Login	CPU (MINS)	KCORE-MINS	Connect (MINS)	Disk	# Of	# Of	# Disk	Fee			
UID	NAME	PRIME	NPRIME	PRIME	NPRIME	PRIME E	NPRIME	BLOCKS	PROCS	SESS	SAMPLES	0
TOTAL	233	30	363969	158762	1061	1005	11830502	513833	134	45	0	
0	root	157	4	180984	3881	546	0	1858608	444602	3	3	0
1	daemon	0	0	0	0	0	0	6	0	0	3	0
2	bin	0	0	0	0	0	0	5759280	0	0	3	0
3	sys	0	0	114	89	0	0	18	51	0	3	0
4	adm	1	7	618	4856	0	0	15136	20005	0	3	0
5	uucp	1	4	1371	3557	0	0	5088	22036	0	3	0
10	pwatters	65	6	104572	15758	197	88	2026666	1842	68	3	0
12	llee	0	0	0	0	0	0	12	0	0	3	0
71	lp	0	0	0	26	0	0	13822	134	0	3	0
108	jsmith	0	0	0	0	0	0	318	0	0	3	0
436	dbrown	0	0	0	0	0	0	48	0	0	3	0
1001	bjones	0	0	16	9	0	2	78	21	2	3	0
1002	ledwards	0	0	130	21	0	0	34	102	0	3	0
1003	tgonzale	0	0	0	0	0	0	40896	0	0	3	0
1012	ljung	5	10	74282	130564	318	915	2110492	3521	61	3	0
60001	nobody	3	0	1883	0	0	0	0	21519	0	0	0

Table 20-3   Charging Fees Using Accounting

Performance

Measuring performance is a necessary task to determine whether current utilization levels require a system to be upgraded and/or whether user applications and system services are executing as quickly and efficiently as possible. Solaris provides a wide variety of tools to tune and monitor the operation of individual devices and core system elements, and other tools that can be applied to improve performance. These tools work with the kernel, disk, memory, network, compilers, applications, and system services. An alternative to the tools provided with Solaris is to use the SymbEL tools developed by Adrian Cockroft and Richard Pettit (**www.sun.com/sun-on-net/performance/se3**), which are fully described in their book, *Sun Performance and Tuning*, published by Sun Microsystems Press (1998). In this chapter, we examine how to use some of the standard Solaris tools to monitor performance, identify performance issues and bottlenecks, and implement new settings.

Collecting Performance Data

The following applications are commonly used to measure system performance:

`iostat`	Collects data about input/output operations for CPUs, disks, terminals, and tapes from the command line.
`vmstat`	Collects data on virtual memory performance from the command line and prints a summary.
`mpstat`	Breaks down CPU usage per operation type.
`sar`	Runs through cron or the command line to collect statistics on disk, tape, CPU, buffering, input/output, system calls, interprocess communication, and many other variables.

The following sections examine how each of these commands is used.

iostat

The kernel maintains low-level counters to measure various operations, which you can access by using `iostat`. When you first execute it, `iostat` reports statistics gathered since booting. Subsequently, the difference between the first report and the current state is reported for all statistics. Thus, when you run it at regular intervals (such as each minute), you can obtain high-resolution samples for establishing system performance within a specific epoch by using `iostat`. This can be very useful for gaining an accurate picture of how system resources are allocated.

To display disk usage statistics, the following command produces 10 reports over epochs of 60 seconds:

```
# iostat -x 60 10
device r/s w/s kr/s kw/s wait actv svc_ t %w %b
sd0    0.2 0.4 12.2 9.0  1.0  2.0  38.6   0  1
```

```
...
device r/s w/s kr/s kw/s wait actv svc_t %w %b
sd0    0.3 0.3 12.5 8.0  2.0  1.0  33.2   0  1
...
```

Let's review what each column indicates for the disk device:

`device`	Shows the device name (*sd1* indicates a disk).
`r/s`	Displays the number of disk reads per second.
`w/s`	Prints the number of disk writes per second.
`kr/s`	Shows the total amount of data read per second (in kilobytes).
`kw/s`	Displays the total amount of data written per second (in kilobytes).
`wait`	Prints the mean number of waiting transactions.
`actv`	Shows the mean number of transactions being processed.
`svc_t`	Displays the mean period for service in milliseconds.
`%w`	Prints the percentage of time spent waiting.
`%b`	Shows the percentage of time that the disk is working.

To display statistics for the CPU at second intervals 20 times, you could use the following command:

```
# iostat -c 1 20
```

The output would display four columns, showing user time, system time, I/O wait, and idle time, respectively, in percentage terms.

vmstat

One of the greatest performance issues in system tuning is virtual memory capacity and performance. Obviously, if your server is using large amounts of swap, running off a slow disk, the time to perform various operations will increase. One application that reports on the current state of virtual memory is the vmstat command, which displays a large collection of statistics concerning virtual memory performance. As you can see from the following display, the virtual memory report on the server is not encouraging: 1,346,736,431 total address translation faults were recorded, as well as 38,736,546 major faults, 1,346,736,431 minor faults, and 332,163,181 copy-on-write faults. This suggests that more virtual memory is required to support operations, or at least, the disk on which the swap partition is placed should be upgraded to 10,000 rpm:

```
# vmstat -s
        253 swap ins
      237 swap outs
      253 pages swapped in
   705684 pages swapped out
1346736431 total address trans. faults taken
 56389345 page ins
 23909231 page outs
152308597 pages paged in
 83982504 pages paged out
```

```
  26682276 total reclaims
  26199677 reclaims from free list
         0 micro (hat) faults
1346736431 minor (as) faults
  38736546 major faults
 332163181 copy-on-write faults
 316702360 zero fill page faults
  99616426 pages examined by the clock daemon
       782 revolutions of the clock hand
 126834545 pages freed by the clock daemon
  14771875 forks
   3824010 vforks
  29303326 execs
 160142153 cpu context switches
2072002374 device interrupts
3735561061 traps
2081699655 system calls
1167634213 total name lookups (cache hits 70%)
  46612294 toolong
 964665958 user    cpu
 399229996 system cpu
1343911025 idle    cpu
 227505892 wait    cpu
```

mpstat

Another factor influencing performance is the system load—obviously, on a system that runs a large number of processes and consistently has a load of greater than 1.0 cannot be relied upon to give adequate performance in times of need. You can use the `mpstat` command to examine a number of system parameters, including the system load, over a number of regular intervals. Many administrators take several hundred samples using mpstat and compute an average system load for specific times of the day when a peak load is expected (for example, at 9:00 A.M.). This can greatly assist in capacity planning of CPUs to support expanding operations.

 TIP SPARC hardware architectures support large numbers of CPUs, so it's not difficult to scale up to meet demand.

The output from `mpstat` contains several columns, which measure the following parameters:

- Context switches
- Cross-calls between CPUs
- Idle percentage of CPU time
- Interrupts
- Minor and major faults
- Sys percentage of CPU time
- Thread migrations
- User percentage of CPU time

For the server output shown next, the proportion of system time consumed is well below 100 percent—the peak value is 57 percent for only one of the CPUs in this dual-processor system. Sustained values of sys at or near the 100-percent level indicate that you should add more CPUs to the system:

```
# mpstat 5
CPU minf mjf xcal intr ithr  csw icsw migr smtx  srw syscl  usr sys  wt idl
  0   46   1  250   39  260  162   94   35  104    0    75   31  14   8  47
  1   45   1   84  100  139  140   92   35  102    0    14   35  13   7  45
CPU minf mjf xcal intr ithr  csw icsw migr smtx  srw syscl  usr sys  wt idl
  0  141   3  397  591  448  539  233   38  111    0 26914   64  35   1   0
  1  119   0 1136  426  136  390  165   40  132    0 21371   67  33   0   0
CPU minf mjf xcal intr ithr  csw icsw migr smtx  srw syscl  usr sys  wt idl
  0    0   0  317  303  183  367  163   28   63    0  1110   94   6   0   0
  1    0   0    4  371  100  340  148   27   86    0 56271   43  57   0   0
```

sar

The sar command is the most versatile method for collecting system performance data. From the command line, it produces a number of snapshots of current system activity over a specified number of time intervals. Or, if you don't specify an interval, the current day's data extracted from sar's regular execution by cron is used. For example, to display a summary of disk activity for the current day, you can use the following command:

```
# sar -d
SunOS 5.9 sun4u    01/25/02
09:54:33    device   %busy   avque   r+w/s   blk/s   avwait   avserv
             sd01      27     5.8      6       8      21.6     28.6
             sd03      17     2.4      4       7      14.2     21.2
             sd05      13     1.7      3       6       9.3     18.3
             sd06      35     6.9      8      10      25.7     31.8
```

In this example, you can see that several disk devices are shown with varying percentages of busy time, mean number of transaction requests in the queue, mean number of disk reads and writes per second, mean number of disk blocks written per second, mean time for waiting in the queue, and mean time for service in the queue.

When a new disk, memory, or CPU is added to the system, you should take a baseline sar report to determine the effect on performance. For example, after adding an 128MB of RAM on the system, you should be able to quantify the effect on mean system performance by comparing sar output before and after the event during a typical day's workload.

Performance Tuning

In previous sections, we've examined how to use tools such as sar, vmstat, and iostat to measure system performance before and after key events such as adding new RAM or CPUs or upgrading disks to faster speeds. In addition to these hardware changes, it is possible to increase the performance of an existing system by tuning the kernel. This could involve switching from a 32-bit to a 64-bit kernel, if supported by hardware, and setting appropriate parameters for shared memory, semaphores, and message queues in */etc/system*. However, note that the Solaris 9 kernel is self-tuning to some extent for normal operations. Once database servers with special requirements are installed, or many users must be supported on a single system, it may be necessary to tweak some parameters and reboot.

If a system is slow, the process list is the first place to look, as described in Chapter 8. One of the reasons that so much space is devoted to process management in this book is that it is often user processes, rather than system CPU time, that adversely impact system performance. The only time that kernel tuning will really assist is where shared memory and other parameters need to be adjusted for database applications, other large applications, or where system time for processes far exceeds the user time. This can generally be established by using the `time` command. We examine some commonly modified parameters in the */etc/system* file shortly, which you can use to improve system performance. After you make changes to */etc/system*, you need to reboot the system.

 NOTE If a syntax error is detected in */etc/system*, the system may not be able to booted except with the `boot -as` command.

The first step in tuning the kernel is generally to set the maximum number of processes permitted per user to a sensible value. This is a hard limit that prevents individual users from circumventing limits imposed by quotas and nice values set by the superuser. To insert a maximum of 100 processes per user, you need to make the following entry in */etc/system*:

```
set maxuprc=100
```

If you are running a database server, your manual will no doubt supply minimum requirements for shared memory for the server. Shared memory is memory that can be locked but can be shared between processes, thereby reducing overhead for memory allocation. You can set the following parameters to determine how shared memory is allocated:

shmmax	The peak shared memory amount.
shmmin	The smallest shared memory amount.
shmmni	The largest number of concurrent identifiers permitted.
shmseg	The quantity of segments permitted for each process.
semmap	The initial quantity of entries in the semaphore map.
semmni	The largest number of semaphore sets permitted.
semmns	The total number of semaphores permitted.
semmsl	The largest number of semaphores in each semaphore set.

The following example entry for */etc/system* allocates 128MB of shared memory and sets other parameters appropriately:

```
set shmsys:shminfo_shmmax=134217728
set shmsys:shminfo_shmmin=100
set shmsys:shminfo_shmmni=100
set shmsys:shminfo_shmseg=100
set semsys:seminfo_semmap=125
set semsys:seminfo_semmni=250
set semsys:seminfo_semmns=250
```

Summary

In this chapter, we have examined how to manage and monitor the system using accounting and the system logs. In addition, we examined how to profile and tune the kernel's performance. Production systemsin particular require careful monitoring of resource usage to ensure optimal performance.

Questions

1. Which file contains loghost definitions?

   A. */etc/loghost*

   B. */etc/syslog.conf*

   C. */etc/hosts*

   D. */etc/system*

2. What is the name of the syslog configuration file?

   A. */etc/loghost*

   B. */etc/syslog.conf*

   C. */etc/hosts*

   D. */etc/system*

3. Which of the following is *not* a source facility defined in the syslog configuration file?

   A. kern

   B. auth

   C. default

   D. mail

4. What is the name of the macro processor used to process syslog data?

    A. perl

    B. sed

    C. awk

    D. m4

5. Name the default syslog file?

    A. */var/log/syslog*

    B. */var/adm/messages*

    C. */etc/syslog*

    D. */var/adm/messages/syslog*

6. The w command displays the system load for what time intervals?

    A. 1, 2, and 3 minutes

    B. 1, 5, and 10 minutes

    C. 1, 10, and 15 minutes

    D. 1, 5, and 15 minutes

7. What command would display statistics for the CPU at second intervals 20 times?

    A. `iostat -c 1 20`

    B. `vmstat -c 1 20`

    C. `iostat -c 20`

    D. `vmstat -c 20`

8. What does the */etc/system* parameter *shmmax* represent?

    A. The peak shared memory amount

    B. The smallest shared memory amount

    C. The largest number of concurrent identifiers permitted

    D. The quantity of segments permitted for each process

9. What does the */etc/system* parameter *shmmin* represent?

    A. The peak shared memory amount

    B. The smallest shared memory amount

    C. The largest number of concurrent identifiers permitted

    D. The quantity of segments permitted for each process

10. What does the */etc/system* parameter *shmmni* represent?

   A. The peak shared memory amount

   B. The smallest shared memory amount

   C. The largest number of concurrent identifiers permitted

   D. The quantity of segments permitted for each process

11. What does the */etc/system* parameter *shmseg* represent?

   A. The peak shared memory amount

   B. The smallest shared memory amount

   C. The largest number of concurrent identifiers permitted

   D. The quantity of segments permitted for each process

Answers

1. **C.** The *hosts* database contains definitions for the loghost, as well as other hostnames.

2. **B.** The *syslog.conf* file defines all parameters for running syslog.

3. **C.** There is no default source facility defined in the syslog configuration file.

4. **D.** The m4 macro processor is used for syslog data.

5. **B.** The default syslog file is */var/adm/messages*, but others can be defined if required.

6. **D.** The 1, 5, and 15 minute figures give you an indication if a system is consistently overloaded.

7. **A.** The `iostat` command must have two parameters (1 and 20) in this scenario.

8. **A.** *shmmax* represents the peak shared memory amount.

9. **B.** *shmmin* represents the smallest shared memory amount.

10. **C.** *shmmni* represents largest number of concurrent identifiers permitted.

11. **D.** *shmseg* represents the quantity of segments permitted for each process.

Disk Management

In this chapter, you will
- Learn how to mount and unmount local file systems
- Repair disks using fsck
- Discover how to configure RAID systems

Solaris servers are often set up to be "highly available," meaning that the databases, application servers, and distributed applications that they host must be accessible to clients at all times. Such applications and services are often deployed on Solaris because of the failover technologies provided by Sun's hardware offerings: for example, many high-end SPARC systems feature dual power supplies, and allow for the installation of many hard disks in a single cabinet. The E-450, for example, can house up to 20 high-speed, high-capacity disks (for example, 18GB @ 10,000 rpm).

RAID

Production systems of this kind invariably experience two kinds of capacity problems. First, even though the E-450 system discussed here may have a total capacity of 360GB, the largest file size that can be supported by the system is the size of an individual hard drive. This means that database servers, for example, would require multiple mount points to be located on a single file system for storing extremely large data files. Having 20 hard disks in this context is only as useful as having one. One solution is to wait until hard disks with higher capacities are manufactured, but relying on future hardware updates is not feasible for systems that have immediate deployment requirements. What is required is some way of splitting physical data storage across several physical disk volumes, while providing a single logical interface for access.

The second problem that arises is that hard disks and other physical media inevitably fail after periods of heavy use. Even if quality hard drives have mean time between failures (MTBFs) of several years, this is an average figure: some drives last ten years, others only last one. Again, superior Sun hardware provides some relief here: it is possible to "hot swap" hard drives in an E-450, for example, without having to shut down the system and reboot. The faulty drive is simply removed, and the new drive replaced. Once backups have been loaded, the system will be available once again.

However, the length of time it takes to restore disk contents from backups might take several hours: customers often complain of downtime counted in minutes. So, while restoring from backups is an excellent strategy for countering catastrophic failure, it is simply not an option for production systems experiencing single-disk failures. What is required is some level of content redundancy that retains more than one copy of a system's data across different disks.

To solve the capacity and redundancy problem, Solaris provides support for the redundant array of inexpensive disks (RAID) standard. RAID defines a number of different "levels," which provide various types of "striping" and "mirroring." In this context, "striping" means the process of spreading data across different physical disks while presenting a single logical interface for the logical volume. Thus, a striped disk set containing four 18GB drives would have a total logical capacity of 72GB. This configuration is shown in Figure 21-1.

A different approach is offered by mirroring: here, a logical volume's contents are copied in real time to more than one physical device. Thus, four 18GB drives could be mirrored to provide two completely redundant 18GB volumes. This means that if one disk failed, its mirror would automatically be used to continue create, read, update, and delete operations on the file system while the disk was physically replaced (again, with no reboot required). This kind of seamless operation requires no downtime. This configuration is shown in Figure 21-2.

Alternatively, the four disks could be configured so that a 36GB striped volume could be created, combining the capacities of two disks, while the remaining two disks could be used to mirror this striped volume. Thus, the system is provided with a logical 36GB volume that also features complete redundancy. This configuration is shown in Figure 21-3.

There are six major RAID levels supported by DiskSuite, the tool that is used to set up mirrored and striped virtual file systems on Solaris. RAID level 0 is the primary striping level, which allows a virtual file system to be constructed of several physical disks. Their capacities are effectively combined to produce a single disk with a large capacity. In contrast, RAID level 1 is the primary mirroring level: all data that is written to the virtual file system is also copied in real time to a separate physical disk that has the same capacity as

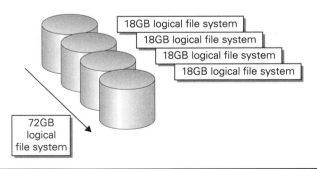

Figure 21-1   Striped disk configuration

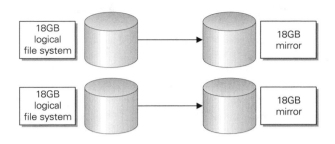

Figure 21-2   Mirrored disk configuration

the original. This level has the slowest performance because all data must be written twice to two different disks, and costs the most because each drive to be mirrored makes use of a second drive, which cannot be used for any other purpose. However, full redundancy can be achieved using RAID level 1.

The remaining RAID levels are variations on these two themes. RAID level 2 is a secondary mirroring level, which uses Hamming codes for error correction. RAID levels 3 and 4 are secondary striping levels, writing parity information to a single drive but writing all other data to multiple physical disks.

In contrast, RAID level 5 is a striping and mirroring level that allows data to be written to different disks, including parity information. RAID 5 offers the best solution for systems that require both mirroring and striping. These levels are summarized in Table 21-1.

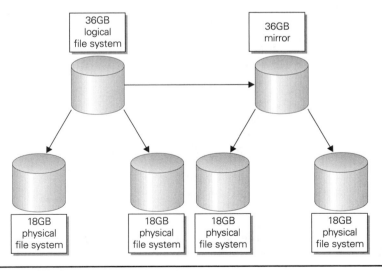

Figure 21-3   Striped and mirrored disk configuration

Level	Description
0	Primary striping level, allowing a single virtual file system to be constructed of multiple physical disks.
1	Primary mirroring level, where all data written to a virtual file system is copied in real time to a separate mirroring disk.
2	A secondary mirroring level, which uses Hamming codes for error correction.
3	A secondary striping level, which writes parity information to a single drive, but writes all other data to multiple drives.
4	A secondary striping level, which writes parity information to a single drive but writes all other data to multiple drives.
5	A striping and mirroring level which allows data to be written to different disks, including parity information.

Table 21-1   Commonly Used RAID Levels

Setting Up RAID

The first step in setting up any kind of RAID system is to ensure that the DiskSuite packages are installed and then prepare the disks for mirroring or striping by formatting them. Primary disks and their mirrors must be set up with exactly the same partition structure to ensure that virtual file systems can be created that are compatible with both primary and mirror.

Once the DiskSuite packages have been installed, it is necessary to prepare disks that will be used with DiskSuite. This preparation includes creating state database replicas for virtual file systems used on the system. Ideally, these state database replicas will be distributed across each controller and/or disk so that maximum redundancy can be achieved. A small partition must be created on each disk that will contain the state database (typically around 5MB). For example, to create a state database replica on the file system /dev/dsk/c1t0d0s7, we would use the following command:

```
# metadb -c 3 -a -f /dev/dsk/c1t0d0s7 /dev/dsk/c0t0d0s7
```

This creates three replicas on each of the two disks specified (/dev/dsk/c1t0d0s7 and /dev/dsk/c0t0d0s7). Note that there are two controllers used rather than one.

If there are no existing state database replicas, the following message will be displayed:

```
metadb: There are no existing databases
```

Striping

Next, we need to create configurations for the virtual file systems that we wish to use. These can be permanently recorded in the DiskSuite configuration file (md.tab). For example, the striping configuration we mentioned previously, involving four 18GB disks, could have its configuration recorded with the following entry, if the virtual file system (s5) had the path /dev/md/dsk/d5:

```
d5 4 1 c1t1d0s5 1 c1t2d0s5 1 c2t1d0s5 1 c2t2d0s5
```

Here, the four physical disks involved are */dev/dsk/c1t1d0s5*, */dev/dsk/c1t2d0s5*, */dev/dsk/c2t1d0s5*, and */dev/dsk/c2t2d0s5*. To ensure that the virtual file system is mounted at boot time, it could be included in the */etc/vfstab* file, just like a normal file system. Indeed, there should only be an entry for */dev/md/dsk/d5* in */etc/vfstab* after striping is complete, and the entries for */dev/dsk/c1t1d0s5*, */dev/dsk/c1t2d0s5*, */dev/dsk/c2t1d0s5*, and */dev/dsk/c2t2d0s5* should be commented out.

To initialize the *d5* metadevice, we would use the following command:

```
# metainit d5
```

If this command succeeds, we simply treat the new metadevice as if it were a new file system and initialize a UFS file system on it:

```
# newfs /dev/md/rdsk/d5
```

Next, we need to create an appropriate mount point for the device (such as */staff*) and mount the metadevice:

```
# mkdir /staff
# mount /dev/md/dsk/d5 /staff
```

The striped volume *d5* is now ready for use.

Mirroring

In order to create a mirror between two file systems, we follow a similar procedure of creating an entry in the *md.tab* file. For example, if we want to create a mirror of */dev/dsk/c1t1d0s5* with */dev/dsk/c0t1d0s5* (note the different controller), we would need to create a virtual file system (*d50*) that mirrored the primary file system (*d52*) to its mirror (*d53*). The following entries would need to be made in *md.tab*:

```
d50 -m /dev/md/dsk/d52 /dev/md/dsk/d53
d52 1 1 /dev/dsk/c1t1d0s5
d53 1 1 /dev/dsk/c0t1d0s5
```

To initialize the *d5* metadevice, we would use this command:

```
# metainit d50
# metainit d52
# metainit d53
```

If this command succeeds, we simply treat the new metadevice as if it were a new file system and initialize a UFS file system on it:

```
# newfs /dev/md/rdsk/d50
# newfs /dev/md/rdsk/d52
# newfs /dev/md/rdsk/d53
```

PART II

Next, we need to create an appropriate mount point for the device (such as /work) and mount the metadevice:

```
# mkdir /work
# mount /dev/md/dsk/d50 /work
```

The mirrored volume *d50* is now ready for use.

Summary

In this chapter, we have examined how to set up and manage disk volumes using the Redundant Array of Inexpensive Disks (RAID) technology. This technology is used in all production systems to ensure reliability and high availability.

Questions

1. What is the primary striping level, allowing a single virtual file system to be constructed of multiple physical disks?

   A. 0

   B. 1

   C. 2

   D. 3

2. What is the primary mirroring level, where all data written to a virtual file system is copied in real time to a separate mirroring disk?

   A. 0

   B. 1

   C. 2

   D. 3

3. What is the process of spreading data across different physical disks while presenting a single logical interface for the logical volume?

   A. Backups

   B. Mirroring

   C. Striping

   D. Parity

4. What is the level of content redundancy that retains more than one copy of a system's data across different disks?

   A. Backups

   B. Mirroring

C. Striping

D. Parity

5. What is the command that creates state database replicas for virtual file systems?

   A. metastat

   B. metaclear

   C. metainit

   D. metadb

6. What is the command that initializes metadevices?

   A. metastat

   B. metaclear

   C. metainit

   D. initmeta

7. Which of the following is a possible cause of disk failure?

   A. Switching off a Solaris server without first powering down

   B. Halting a system without synchronizing disk data

   C. Defective hardware, including damage to disk blocks and heads

   D. All of the above

8. Which of the following checks is not performed on inodes during fsck?

   A. A check of the file system size

   B. A check of the total number of inodes

   C. Making a tally of reported free blocks and inodes

   D. Checking that all file systems are mounted

9. What happens if a bad block number is detected by fsck?

   A. The superblock is backed up

   B. The superblock is cleared

   C. The inode is cleared

   D. The disk needs to be reformatted at a low level

10. Which of the following is not a valid fsck phase?

    A. Check Blocks and Sizes

    B. Check Filenames

    C. Check Pathnames

    D. Check Connectivity

Answers

1. **A.** 0 is the primary striping level.

2. **B.** 1 is the primary mirroring level.

3. **C.** Striping is the process of spreading data across different physical disks while presenting a single logical interface for the logical volume.

4. **B.** Mirroring retains more than one copy of a system's data across different disks.

5. **D.** The `metadb` command creates state database replicas for virtual file systems.

6. **C.** The command that initializes metadevices is `metainit`.

7. **D.** Disk failures can be caused by all of the issues listed.

8. **D.** No check is made during fsck to see if all file systems are mounted.

9. **C.** The inode is cleared if a bad block number is detected by fsck.

10. **B.** Filenames are not checked during an fsck phase.

Pseudo File Systems and Swap Space

In this chapter, you will
- Learn the basic concepts of file systems
- Examine the tools used to work with pseudo file systems
- Discover how to manage virtual memory

A pseudo file system is a file system that has a different purpose than just storing files. One of the core pseudo file systems used in Solaris is the process file system.

Pseudo File Systems

In Chapter 8, you examined the characteristics of processes and how to work with them. Most modern operating systems have a process model. However, you will now look at some special features of processes as implemented in Solaris. One of the most innovative characteristics of processes under Solaris is the process file system (PROCFS), which is mounted on /proc. The state of all normal threads and processes is stored on the PROCFS. Each entry in the top-level file system corresponds to a specific process ID, under which a number of subdirectories contain all state details. Applications and system services can communicate with the PROCFS as if it were a normal file system. Thus, state persistence can be provided using the same mechanism as normal file storage.

 TIP   Images of all currently active processes are stored in the /proc file system by their PID.

The internals of the PROCFS can seem a little complicated, but luckily Solaris provides a number of tools to work with the /proc file system. Here's an example of how process state is persisted on the PROCFS: first, a process is identified—in this example, the current Korn shell for the user pwatters:

```
# ps -eaf | grep pwatters
pwatters  310   291   0   Mar 20 ?         0:04 /usr/openwin/bin/Xsun
 pwatters 11959 11934   0 09:21:42 pts/1    0:00 grep pwatters
 pwatters 11934 11932   1 09:20:50 pts/1    0:00 ksh
```

Now that you have a target PID (11934), you can change to the */proc/11934* directory and you will be able to view the image of this process:

```
# cd /proc/11934
# ls -l
total 3497
-rw-------   1 pwatters    other      1769472 Mar 30 09:20 as
-r--------   1 pwatters    other          152 Mar 30 09:20 auxv
-r--------   1 pwatters    other           32 Mar 30 09:20 cred
--w-------   1 pwatters    other            0 Mar 30 09:20 ctl
lr-x------   1 pwatters    other            0 Mar 30 09:20 cwd ->
dr-x------   2 pwatters    other         1184 Mar 30 09:20 fd
-r--r--r--   1 pwatters    other          120 Mar 30 09:20 lpsinfo
-r--------   1 pwatters    other          912 Mar 30 09:20 lstatus
-r--r--r--   1 pwatters    other          536 Mar 30 09:20 lusage
dr-xr-xr-x   3 pwatters    other           48 Mar 30 09:20 lwp
-r--------   1 pwatters    other         2016 Mar 30 09:20 map
dr-x------   2 pwatters    other          544 Mar 30 09:20 object
-r--------   1 pwatters    other         2552 Mar 30 09:20 pagedata
-r--r--r--   1 pwatters    other          336 Mar 30 09:20 psinfo
-r--------   1 pwatters    other         2016 Mar 30 09:20 rmap
lr-x------   1 pwatters    other            0 Mar 30 09:20 root ->
-r--------   1 pwatters    other         1440 Mar 30 09:20 sigact
-r--------   1 pwatters    other         1232 Mar 30 09:20 status
-r--r--r--   1 pwatters    other          256 Mar 30 09:20 usage
-r--------   1 pwatters    other            0 Mar 30 09:20 watch
-r--------   1 pwatters    other         3192 Mar 30 09:20 xmap
```

Each of the directories with the name associated with the PID contains additional subdirectories, which contain state information and related control functions. For example, the status file contains entries that contain a structure that defines state elements including the following:

- Process flags
- Process ID
- Parent process ID
- Process group ID
- Session ID
- Thread ID
- Process pending signal set
- Process heap virtual address
- Process stack size
- User and system CPU time
- Total child process user and system CPU time
- Fault traces

The process flags contained in the structure define specific process state characteristics, including the following:

- **PR_ISSYS**   System process flag
- **PR_VFORKP**   vforked child parent flag
- **PR_FORK**   Inherit-on-fork flag
- **PR_RLC**   Run-on-last-close flag
- **PR_KLC**   Kill-on-last-close flag
- **PR_ASYNC**   Asynchronous-stop flag
- **PR_MSACCT**   Microstate accounting on flag
- **PR_MSFORK**   Post-fork microstate accounting inheritance flag
- **PR_BPTADJ**   Breakpoint on flag
- **PR_PTRACE**   ptrace-compatibility on flag

 EXAM TIP   Read the materials on **docs.sun.com** for more information about the proc file system.

In addition, a watchpoint facility is provided, which is responsible for controlling memory access. A series of proc tools interpret the information contained in the /proc subdirectories, which display the characteristics of each process.

The proc tools are designed to operate on data contained within the /proc file system. Each utility takes a PID as its argument and performs operations associated with the PID. For example, the pflags command prints the flags and data model details for the PID in question. For the Korn shell example, we can easily print out this status information:

```
# /usr/proc/bin/pflags 29081
29081:  /bin/ksh
        data model = _ILP32  flags = PR_ORPHAN
  /1:    flags = PR_PCINVAL|PR_ASLEEP [ waitid(0x7,0x0,0x804714c,0x7) ]
```

We can also print the credential information for this process, including the effective and real UID and GID of the process owner, by using the pcred command:

```
# /usr/proc/bin/pcred 29081
29081:  e/r/suid=100  e/r/sgid=10
```

Here, both the effective and the real UID is 100 (user pwatters), and the effective and real GID is 10 (group staff). To examine the address space map of the target process, and all of the libraries it requires to execute it, we can use the pmap command:

```
# /usr/proc/bin/pmap 29081
29081:  /bin/ksh
08046000      8K read/write/exec     [ stack ]
08048000    160K read/exec           /usr/bin/ksh
08070000      8K read/write/exec     /usr/bin/ksh
```

```
08072000      28K   read/write/exec      [ heap ]
DFAB4000      16K   read/exec            /usr/lib/locale/en_AU/en_AU.so.2
DFAB8000       8K   read/write/exec      /usr/lib/locale/en_AU/en_AU.so.2
DFABB000       4K   read/write/exec      [ anon ]
DFABD000      12K   read/exec            /usr/lib/libmp.so.2
DFAC0000       4K   read/write/exec      /usr/lib/libmp.so.2
DFAC4000     552K   read/exec            /usr/lib/libc.so.1
DFB4E000      24K   read/write/exec      /usr/lib/libc.so.1
DFB54000       8K   read/write/exec      [ anon ]
DFB57000     444K   read/exec            /usr/lib/libnsl.so.1
DFBC6000      20K   read/write/exec      /usr/lib/libnsl.so.1
DFBCB000      32K   read/write/exec      [ anon ]
DFBD4000      32K   read/exec            /usr/lib/libsocket.so.1
DFBDC000       8K   read/write/exec      /usr/lib/libsocket.so.1
DFBDF000       4K   read/exec            /usr/lib/libdl.so.1
DFBE1000       4K   read/write/exec      [ anon ]
DFBE3000     100K   read/exec            /usr/lib/ld.so.1
DFBFC000      12K   read/write/exec      /usr/lib/ld.so.1
 total      1488K
```

It's always surprising to see how many libraries are loaded when an application is executed, especially something as complicated as a shell—in the example here, leading to a total of 1488KB memory used. You can obtain a list of the dynamic libraries linked to each process by using the `pldd` command:

```
# /usr/proc/bin/pldd 29081
29081:   /bin/ksh
/usr/lib/libsocket.so.1
/usr/lib/libnsl.so.1
/usr/lib/libc.so.1
/usr/lib/libdl.so.1
/usr/lib/libmp.so.2
/usr/lib/locale/en_AU/en_AU.so.2
```

Signals are the way in which processes communicate with each other, and can also be used from shells to communicate with spawned processes (usually to suspend or kill them). We examine signals in detail in Chapter 8. However, by using the `psig` command, it is possible to list the signals associated with each process:

```
# /usr/proc/bin/psig 29081
29081:   /bin/ksh
HUP     caught   RESTART
INT     caught   RESTART
QUIT    ignored
ILL     caught   RESTART
TRAP    caught   RESTART
ABRT    caught   RESTART
EMT     caught   RESTART
FPE     caught   RESTART
KILL    default
BUS     caught   RESTART
SEGV    default
SYS     caught   RESTART
PIPE    caught   RESTART
ALRM    caught   RESTART
TERM    ignored
```

```
USR1      caught   RESTART
USR2      caught   RESTART
CLD       default  NOCLDSTOP
PWR       default
WINCH     default
URG       default
POLL      default
STOP      default
TSTP      ignored
CONT      default
TTIN      ignored
TTOU      ignored
VTALRM    default
PROF      default
XCPU      caught   RESTART
XFSZ      ignored
WAITING   default
LWP       default
FREEZE    default
THAW      default
CANCEL    default
LOST      default
RTMIN     default
RTMIN+1   default
RTMIN+2   default
RTMIN+3   default
RTMAX-3   default
RTMAX-2   default
RTMAX-1   default
RTMAX     default
```

It is also possible to print a hexadecimal format stack trace for the LWP in each process by using the `pstack` command. This can be useful in the same way that the `truss` command was used:

```
# /usr/proc/bin/pstack 29081
29081:  /bin/ksh
 dfaf5347 waitid    (7, 0, 804714c, 7)
 dfb0d9db _waitpid  (ffffffff, 8047224, 4) + 63
 dfb40617 waitpid   (ffffffff, 8047224, 4) + 1f
 0805b792 job_wait  (719d) + 1ae
 08064be8 sh_exec   (8077270, 14) + af0
 0805e3a1 ???????? ()
 0805decd main      (1, 8047624, 804762c) + 705
  0804fa78 ???????? ()
```

Perhaps the most commonly used proc tool is the `pfiles` command, which displays all of the open files for each process. This is very useful for determining operational dependencies between data files and applications:

```
# /usr/proc/bin/pfiles 29081
29081:  /bin/ksh
  Current rlimit: 64 file descriptors
    0: S_IFCHR mode:0620 dev:102,0 ino:319009 uid:6049 gid:7 rdev:24,8
       O_RDWR|O_LARGEFILE
    1: S_IFCHR mode:0620 dev:102,0 ino:319009 uid:6049 gid:7 rdev:24,8
       O_RDWR|O_LARGEFILE
```

```
  2: S_IFCHR mode:0620 dev:102,0 ino:319009 uid:6049 gid:7 rdev:24,8
     O_RDWR|O_LARGEFILE
 63: S_IFREG mode:0600 dev:174,2 ino:990890 uid:6049 gid:1 size:3210
     O_RDWR|O_APPEND|O_LARGEFILE FD_CLOEXEC
```

In addition, it is possible to obtain the current working directory of the target process by using the pwdx command:

```
# /usr/proc/bin/pwdx 29081
29081:  /home/paul
```

If you need to examine the process tree for all parent and child processes containing the target PID, this can be achieved by using the ptree command. This is useful for determining dependencies between processes that are not apparent by consulting the process list:

```
# /usr/proc/bin/ptree 29081
247   /usr/dt/bin/dtlogin -daemon
  28950 /usr/dt/bin/dtlogin -daemon
    28972 /bin/ksh /usr/dt/bin/Xsession
      29012 /usr/dt/bin/sdt_shell -c     unset DT;      DISPLAY=lion:0;
        29015 ksh -c      unset DT;      DISPLAY=lion:0;
/usr/dt/bin/dt
          29026 /usr/dt/bin/dtsession
            29032 dtwm
              29079 /usr/dt/bin/dtterm
                29081 /bin/ksh
                  29085 /usr/local/bin/bash
                    29230 /usr/proc/bin/ptree 29081
```

Here, ptree has been executed from the Bourne again shell (bash), which was started from the Korn shell (ksh), spawned from the dtterm terminal window, which was spawned from the dtwm window manager, and so on.

TIP   Although many of these proc tools will seem obscure, they are often very useful when trying to debug process-related application errors, especially in large applications like database management systems.

Virtual Memory

The swap command is used to add virtual RAM to a system. Virtual RAM is typically used to provide memory for process execution when physical memory has been exhausted. Disk blocks are used to simulate physical memory locations using an interface that is invisible to the user. Thus, users never need to be concerned about the type of RAM that their process is addressing. While virtual memory allows a system's effective capacity to be increased to many times its physical capacity, it is much slower than physical RAM. When a system experiences peak demands for memory, causing virtual memory to be used, the CPU must work harder to support virtual memory operations. Coupled with the relatively slow speed of disk writing, this has a significant impact on performance.

When virtual memory is being utilized, and many new memory access calls are made along with normal file reading and writing, so-called "disk thrashing" can occur because the number of disk operations requested far exceeds the capacity of the disk to read and write.

 TIP If disk thrashing is a common occurrence, extra physical RAM should be installed into the system, and/or the file system may need to be tuned with tunefs.

Virtual memory should generally be added to the system at twice the physical RAM installed. Thus, for a 256MB system, 512MB of virtual memory should be initialized. In order to add virtual memory, an empty file of the required size should be created with the mkfile command. For example, to create two swap files with 4097072KB each, the following commands would be used:

```
# mkfile 4097072k /u1/swap
# mkfile 4097072k /u2/swap
```

Next, the swap command must be used to add the file into the pool of available disk space. For example, if two swap files are created on different file systems for redundancy (such as /u1/swap and /u2/swap), they can be added to the swap space pool by using the following commands:

```
# swap -a /u1/swap
# swap -a /u2/swap
```

To verify that the swap has been correctly added to the pool, the following command can be used:

```
# swap -l
swapfile            dev   swaplo blocks    free
/dev/dsk/c0t0d0s1   118,17     16 8194144 6240336
/dev/dsk/c3t4d0s1   118,1      16 8194144 6236384
```

In this example, you can see that the partitions c0t0d0s1 and c3t4d0s1 have 8194144 blocks each allocated for swap, and have 6240336 and 6236384 free blocks, respectively.

A summary of the swap space can also be printed by using the swap -s command:

```
# /usr/sbin/swap -s
total: 2360832k bytes allocated + 130312k reserved = 2491144k used, 7238792k available
```

In this example, you can see that 2360832K has been allocated, while 130312k has been reserved.

If you have a dedicated slice set aside for swap, the block device name can simply be passed on the command line:

```
# swap -a /dev/dsk/c1t1d2s1
```

To ensure that this partition is added as swap during boot, the following entry can be entered into the */etc/vfstab* file:

```
#device             device          mount       FS    fsck   mount    mount
#to mount           to fsck         point       type  pass   atboot      ops
/dev/dsk/c1t1d2s1                   swap               no            -
```

To remove a file (or device) from the swap pool, the −d option needs to be passed on the command line. Thus, to remove */u1/swap* and */dev/dsk/c1t1d2s1* from the swap pool, the following commands would be used:

```
# swap -d /u1/swap
# swap -d /dev/dsk/c1t1d2s1
```

The file */u1/swap* can now be safely deleted, and the slice */dev/dsk/c1t1d2s1* can be safely used for other purposes, as long as the */etc/vfstab* entries have been deleted.

An issue that commonly arises when swap partitions are enabled on production systems is whether or not swap space should be created on a mirrored partition (that is, RAID level 1). Mirroring ensures that when data is written to a partition on one disk it is also copied in full to a sister partition on another drive. This ensures that if data on the first drive is destroyed, it can be recovered automatically from the mirrored volume.

Creating swap files on mirrored partitions ensures that virtual memory cannot be corrupted by a disk failure. Thus, if a disk containing virtual memory for a production system is corrupt while executing a critical application, such as a database server, then the correct data will automatically be read from the mirrored volume if corruption is detected. However, since RAID mirroring requires that all data written to the source volume also be written immediately afterwards to the mirrored volume, this can significantly slow down effective write speeds for the entire system—because data must be written twice.

Summary

In this chapter, we have examined advanced topics in process and memory management, especially in the area of pseudo file systems. Configuration of pseudo file systems and swap files can be tricky, so administrators should always select their parameters carefully.

Questions

1. What is the mount point for the process file system?

   A. */process*

   B. */proc*

   C. */dev/process*

   D. */dev/proc*

2. What is the meaning of the process flag PR_ISSYS?

   A. System process flag

   B. Vforked child parent flag

   C. Inherit-on-fork flag

   D. Run-on-last-close flag

3. What is the meaning of the process flag PR_VFORKP?

   A. System process flag

   B. Vforked child parent flag

   C. Inherit-on-fork flag

   D. Run-on-last-close flag

4. What is the meaning of the process flag PR_FORK?

   A. System process flag

   B. Vforked child parent flag

   C. Inherit-on-fork flag

   D. Run-on-last-close flag

5. What is the meaning of the process flag PR_RLC?

   A. System process flag

   B. Vforked child parent flag

   C. Inherit-on-fork flag

   D. Run-on-last-close flag

6. What is the meaning of the process flag PR_KLC?

   A. Kill-on-last-close flag

   B. Asynchronous-stop flag

   C. Microstate accounting on flag

   D. Post-fork microstate accounting inheritance flag

7. What is the meaning of the process flag PR_ASYNC?

   A. Kill-on-last-close flag

   B. Asynchronous-stop flag

   C. Microstate accounting on flag

   D. Post-fork microstate accounting inheritance flag

8. What is the meaning of the process flag PR_MSACCT?

   A. Kill-on-last-close flag

   B. Asynchronous-stop flag

    C. Microstate accounting on flag

    D. Post-fork microstate accounting inheritance flag

9. What is the meaning of the process flag PR_MSFORK?

    A. Kill-on-last-close flag

    B. Asynchronous-stop flag

    C. Microstate accounting on flag

    D. Post-fork microstate accounting inheritance flag

10. What is the purpose of the `swap -a` command?

    A. Add swap space

    B. Summarize swap space usage

    C. List details of swap space usage

    D. Delete swap space

11. What is the purpose of the `swap -s` command?

    A. Add swap space

    B. Summarize swap space usage

    C. List details of swap space usage

    D. Delete swap space

12. What is the purpose of the `swap -l` command?

    A. Add swap space

    B. Summarize swap space usage

    C. List details of swap space usage

    D. Delete swap space

13. What is the purpose of the `swap -d` command?

    A. Add swap space

    B. Summarize swap space usage

    C. List details of swap space usage

    D. Delete swap space

14. What entities can be used for swap space?

    A. Files

    B. Partitions

    C. Both files and partitions

    D. Neither files nor partitions

15. To ensure that a swap partition is added as swap during boot, in what file should an entry be made?

    A. /etc/swaptab

    B. /etc/sharetab

    C. /etc/vfstab

    D. /etc/dhcptab

Answers

1. **B.** The mount point for the process file system is /proc.

2. **A.** The process flag PR_ISSYS is a system process flag.

3. **B.** The process flag PR_VFORKP is a vforked child parent flag.

4. **C.** The process flag PR_FORK is an inherit-on-fork flag.

5. **D.** The process flag PR_RLC is a run-on-last-close flag.

6. **A.** The process flag PR_KLC is a kill-on-last-close flag.

7. **B.** The process flag PR_ASYNC is an asynchronous-stop flag.

8. **C.** The process flag PR_MSACCT is a microstate accounting on flag.

9. **D.** The process flag PR_MSFORK is a post-fork microstate accounting inheritance flag.

10. **A.** The purpose of the swap -a command is to add swap space.

11. **B.** The purpose of the swap -s command is to summarize swap space usage.

12. **C.** The purpose of the swap -l command is to list details of swap space usage.

13. **D.** The purpose of the swap -d command is to delete swap space.

14. **C.** Both files and partitions can be used for swap space.

15. **C.** An entry should be made in /etc/vfstab to ensure that a swap partition is added as swap during boot.

Network File System (NFS)

23

In this chapter, you will
- Gain an understanding of NFS client/server architecture
- Configure a NFS server
- Configure a NFS client
- Share file systems
- Mount remote file systems

In this chapter we examine Sun's Network File System (NFS), which is a distributed file system architecture based on the remote procedure call (RPC) protocol. RPC is a standard method of allocating and managing shared resources between Solaris systems. Although NFS is similar to Samba in concept, supporting transparent file system sharing between systems, NFS features high data throughput because of dedicated support in the Solaris kernel, and support for both NFS 2 and 3 clients.

NFS was one of the first distributed network applications to ever be successfully deployed on local area networks. It allows users to mount volumes of other systems connected to the network, with the same ability to change permissions, delete and create files, and apply security measures as any other locally mounted file system. One of the great advantages of NFS is its efficient use of network bandwidth, achieved by using RPCs (remote procedure calls). In Solaris 9, the NFS concept has been extended to the Internet, with the new WebNFS providing file system access through a URL similar to that used for web pages. In this section, we will examine the theory behind distributed file systems and examine how they can best be established in practice.

Prior to Solaris 2.5, NFS 2 was deployed, which used the unreliable UDP protocol for data transfer—hence NFS 2's poor reputation for data integrity. However, the more modern NFS 3 protocol, based around TCP, is now implemented in all new Solaris releases. NFS 3 allows an NFS server to cache NFS client requests in RAM, speeding up disk writing operations and the overall speed of NFS transactions. In addition, Solaris 2.6 and onwards provide support for a new type of NFS called WebNFS. The WebNFS protocol allows file systems to be shared across the Internet, as an alternative to traditional Internet file-sharing techniques like FTP. In addition, initial testing has shown that

Sun's WebNFS server has greater bandwidth than a traditional web server, meaning that it might one day replace the Hypertext Transfer Protocol (HTTP) as the web standard for transferring data.

NFS Architectures

A Solaris system can share any of its file systems with other systems, making them available for remote mounting. NFS considers the system that shares the file system to be a server, and the system that remotely mounts the file system to be a client. When an NFS client mounts a remote file system, it is connected to a mount point on the local file system, which means it appears to local users as just another file system. For example, a system called carolina may make its mail directory */var/mail* available for remote mounting by NFS clients. This would allow users on machines like georgia, virginia, and fairfax to read their mail—stored actually on carolina—locally from their own machines, without having to explicitly log in to carolina. This means that a single mail server, which acts as an NFS server, can serve all NFS clients on a local area network with mail. Figure 23-1 shows this configuration.

However, one important aspect of NFS is the ability to export file systems and mount them on a remote mount point that is different from the original shared directory. For example, the NFS server carolina may also export its Sun *Answerbook* files (from the directory */opt/answerbook*) to the clients virginia, georgia, and fairfax. However, virginia mounts these files in the */usr/local/www/htdocs* directory, as it publishes them via the world wide web, while georgia mounts them in */opt/doc/answerbook*. The client fairfax mounts them in */opt/answerbook*, just like they are exported from carolina. The point is that the remote mount point can be completely different from the actual directory exported by an NFS server. This configuration is shown in Figure 23-2.

Remote Procedure Calls (RPC)

NFS makes use of RPC technology, which makes it easy for systems to make requests for the remote execution of procedures on server systems. RPC is currently supported across a number of different operating systems, including Solaris, Linux, and Microsoft's

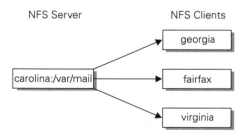

Figure 23-1   The NFS server carolina exports its mail directory to NFS clients georgia, fairfax, and virginia, using the same mount point as the exported file system.

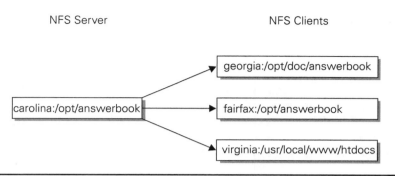

NFS Server   NFS Clients

Figure 23-2   The NFS server carolina exports its mail directory to NFS clients georgia, fairfax, and virginia using their own mount points.

Windows. The purpose of RPC is to abstract the connection details and methods required to access procedures across networks—that is, the client and server programs do not need to implement separate networking code, because a simple API is provided for finding services through a service called the portmapper (or rpcbind). The portmapper should be running on at least the server for NFS to operate correctly.

TIP   The portmapper is registered with both UDP and TCP 111, because requests may be generated for, or received using, NFS 2 or NFS 3, respectively.

Configuring an NFS Server

If you installed the NFS server during installation, a startup script will have been created in */etc/init.d*, called *nfs.server*. Thus, the NFS server can be started manually by typing the following command:

```
# /etc/init.d/nfs.server start
```

This command will start at least two daemons: the NFS server (*/usr/lib/nfs/nfsd*) and the mount daemon (*/usr/lib/nfs/mountd*). nfsd is responsible for answering access requests from clients for shared volumes on the server, while mountd is responsible for providing information about mounted file systems.

To check whether or not the NFS server has started correctly, it is possible to examine the process list for nfsd and mountd by using the following commands:

```
# ps -eaf | grep nfsd
   root 19961    1  0   Aug 31 ?       0:09 /usr/lib/nfs/nfsd -a 16
# ps -eaf | grep mountd
   root   370    1  0   May 16 ?       2:49 /usr/lib/nfs/mountd
```

Or, to save space:

```
   # ps -aef | egrep 'mountd|nfsd'
```

In this case, both nfsd and mountd are operating correctly. In order to stop the NFS server, the following command may be used:

```
# /etc/init.d/nfs.server stop
```

There are some optional services started by the NFS server startup script, including daemons that support diskless booting (the Reverse Address Resolution Protocol daemon, */usr/sbin/in.rarpd*, and the boot parameter server, */usr/sbin/rpc.bootparamd*). In addition, a separate daemon for x86 boot support (*/usr/sbin/rpld*), using the Network Booting RPL (Remote Program Load) protocol, may also be started.

 TIP   You only need to configure these services if you wish to provide diskless booting for local clients; otherwise, they can be safely commented from the */etc/init.d/nfs.server* script.

Sharing File Systems

To actually share file systems and directories, you can use the share command. For example, if you want to share the */var/mail* directory from carolina to georgia, you could use the following command:

```
# share -F nfs -o rw=georgia /var/mail
```

In this example, "-F nfs" stands for "a file system of type NFS." Of course, we really want to share to virginia and fairfax as well, so we would probably use this command:

```
# share -F nfs -o rw=georgia,virginia,fairfax /var/mail
```

The */var/mail* volume is shared to these clients because users on these systems need to read and write their e-mail. However, if we need to share a CD-ROM volume, we obviously need to share it read-only:

```
# share -F nfs -o ro /cdrom
```

Normally, the volumes to be shared are identified in the */etc/dfs/dfstab* file. One of the really innovative features of NFS is that a system that shares volumes to other systems can actually remotely mount shared volumes from its own clients. For example, while carolina might share the volume */cdrom* to georgia, fairfax, and virginia, virginia might share the */staff* directory, which contains home directories, to carolina, georgia, and fairfax using the following command:

```
# share -F nfs -o rw=georgia,carolina,fairfax /staff
```

File systems can be unshared using the unshare command. For example, if we are going to change a CD-ROM on carolina that is shared to clients using NFS, it might be wise to unmount it first:

```
# unshare -F nfs /cdrom
```

To unshare all volumes that are currently being shared from a NFS server, the following command can be used:

```
# unshareall
```

The command `dfmounts` shows the local resources shared through the networked file system that are currently mounted by specific clients:

```
# dfmounts
RESOURCE   SERVER PATHNAME                CLIENTS
   -          carolina /cdrom               virginia,Georgia
   -          carolina /var/mail            fairfax,virginia,Georgia
   -        carolina /opt/answerbook      fairfax
```

However, dfmounts does not provide information about the permissions by which directories and file systems are shared, nor does it show those shared resources that have no clients currently using them. To display this information, we need to use the `share` command with no arguments. On virginia, this looks like this:

```
# share
/staff rw=georgia,fairfax,carolina   "staff"
```

while on carolina, the volumes are different:

```
# share
-                   /cdrom  ro=georgia,fairfax,carolina "cdrom"
-                 /var/mail  rw=georgia,fairfax,carolina "mail"
```

Conversely, as a client, you want to determine which volumes are available for you to mount from NFS servers. This can be achieved by using the `dfshares` command. For example, to view the mounts available from the server virginia, executed on carolina, the dfshares would be entered as shown, and the following output would be displayed:

```
# dfshares -F nfs virginia
RESOURCE                 SERVER          ACCESS         TRANSPORT
virginia:/staff          virginia        -              -
```

Table 23-1 shows the most common options for the `share` command.

Parameter	Description
anon=username	Sets the username of unknown users to username.
log	Starts NFS logging.
nosuid	Prevents applications from executing as setuid.
nosub	Prevents client access to subdirectories of exported server volumes.
ro	Prevents writing to an exported file system.
root	Allows remote access by remote root users as the local root user.
rw	Permits reading and writing to an exported file system.
sec	Specifies the authentication level (sys, dh, or krb4).

Table 23-1   NFS Server Options

Installing an NFS Client

In order to access file systems being shared from an NFS server, a separate NFS client must be operating on the client system. There are two main daemon processes that must be running in order to use the `mount` command to access shared volumes: the NFS lock daemon (*/usr/lib/nfs/lockd*), and the NFS stat daemon (*/usr/lib/nfs/statd*). lockd manages file sharing and locking at the user level, while the statd is used for file recovery after connection outage.

If NFS was installed during the initial system setup, a file called *nfs.client* should have been created in */etc/init.d*. In order to run the NFS client, the following command needs to be executed:

```
# /etc/init.d/nfs.client start
```

Just like the NFS server, you can verify that the NFS daemons have started correctly by using the following commands:

```
# ps -eaf | grep statd
   daemon  211    1  0   May 16 ?         0:04 /usr/lib/nfs/statd
# ps -eaf | grep lockd
     root  213    1  0   May 16 ?         0:03 /usr/lib/nfs/lockd
```

These commands can be combined as follows:

```
# ps -aef | egrep 'statd|lockd'
```

If these two daemons are not active, the NFS client will not run. The next step is for the client to consult the */etc/vfstab* file, which lists both the UFS and NFS file systems that need to be mounted, and attempts to mount the latter if they are available by using the `mountall` command.

To stop the NFS client once it is operating, the following command may be used:

```
# /etc/init.d/nfs.client stop
```

The NFS server is usually started automatically during run level 3.

Checking portmapper Status

If you're having trouble starting the NFS daemon, it's often an rpc problem. In order to determine whether an rpc portmapper is running, you may use the `rpcinfo` command:

```
# rpcinfo -p
   program vers proto   port  service
    100000    4   tcp    111  rpcbind
    100000    3   tcp    111  rpcbind
    100000    2   tcp    111  rpcbind
    100000    4   udp    111  rpcbind
    100000    3   udp    111  rpcbind
    100000    2   udp    111  rpcbind
    100007    3   udp  32774  ypbind
    100007    2   udp  32774  ypbind
```

```
100007     1     udp    32774    ypbind
100007     3     tcp    32771    ypbind
100007     2     tcp    32771    ypbind
100007     1     tcp    32771    ypbind
100011     1     udp    32785    rquotad
100024     1     udp    32789    status
100024     1     tcp    32775    status
100021     1     udp     4045    nlockmgr
100021     2     udp     4045    nlockmgr
100021     3     udp     4045    nlockmgr
100021     4     udp     4045    nlockmgr
100068     2     udp    32809
100068     3     udp    32809
100068     4     udp    32809
100068     5     udp    32809
100083     1     tcp    32795
100021     1     tcp     4045    nlockmgr
100021     2     tcp     4045    nlockmgr
100021     3     tcp     4045    nlockmgr
100021     4     tcp     4045    nlockmgr
100005     1     udp    32859    mountd
100005     2     udp    32859    mountd
100005     3     udp    32859    mountd
100005     1     tcp    32813    mountd
100005     2     tcp    32813    mountd
100005     3     tcp    32813    mountd
100026     1     udp    32866    bootparam
100026     1     tcp    32815    bootparam
```

In this example, both mountd and nfsd are running, along with several other services, so the NFS daemon should have no problems executing. However, the RPL service is not active, so x86 clients would not be able to use the local server as a boot server.

Mounting Remote File Systems

On the client side, if we want to mount a volume that has been shared from an NFS server, we use the mount command. For example, if we want to mount the exported CD-ROM from carolina on the NFS client virginia, we would use this command:

```
# mount -F nfs -o ro carolina:/cdrom /cdrom
```

Like the */etc/dfs/dfstab* files, which record a list of volumes to be exported, the */etc/vfstab* file can contain entries for NFS volumes to be mounted from remote servers. For example, on the machine fairfax, if we wanted the */var/mail* volume on carolina to be mounted locally as */var/mail*, we would enter the following line in */etc/vfstab*:

```
carolina:/var/mail      -      /var/mail      nfs      -      yes      rw
```

This line can be interpreted as a request to mount */var/mail* from carolina read/write on the local mount point */var/mail* as an NFS volume that should be mounted at boot time. If you made the appropriate changes to the */etc/vfstab* file on virginia, and you want to mount the */var/mail* partition, you can use the following command:

```
# mount /var/mail
```

This will attempt to mount the remote */var/mail* directory from the server carolina. Alternatively, you can use the command,

```
# mountall
```

which will mount all partitions that are listed in */etc/vfstab*, but which have not yet been mounted.

File systems can be unmounted by using the umount command. For example, if the */cdrom* file system on carolina is mounted on virginia as */cdrom*, then the command,

```
# umount /cdrom
```

will unmount the mounted NFS volume. Alternatively, the unmountall command can be used, which unmounts all currently mounted NFS volumes. For example, the command,

```
# umountall -F nfs
```

unmounts all volumes that are currently mounted through NFS. The umount -f command forcibly unmounts a file system:

```
# umount -f /cdrom
```

When a remote volume is mounted on a local client, it should be visible to the system just like a normal disk, and so commands like df, which displays disk slice information, can be readily used:

```
# df -k
carolina:/cdrom        412456 341700  70756     83%    /cdrom
carolina:/var/mail      4194304 343234  3851070    8%    /var/mail
carolina:/opt/answerbook  2097152  1345634   750618 64%
/opt/answerbook
```

The main options available for mounting NFS file systems are shown in Table 23-2.

Enhancing Security

So far, we've examined NFS without considering the security implications of sharing a file system to clients. In a local intranet environment, with protection from a firewall, some administrators implement open NFS sharing, where client lists are not supplied to

Option	Description
ro	Mounts a file system's read-only permissions.
rw	Mounts a file system's read/write permissions.
hard	No timeouts permitted—the client will repeatedly attempt to make a connection.
soft	Timeouts permitted—the client will attempt a connection, and give an error message if connection fails.
bg	Attempts to mount a remote file system in the background if connection fails.

Table 23-2   NFS Client Options

share commands to limit access to server volumes. The problem with this approach is spoofing: an external system may be able to "pretend" to be part of your local network, thereby gaining access to globally shared NFS volumes. Given that NFS authentication is usually based on mappings of usernames on the client to the server, if a spoofed system contains equivalent user accounts to those found on the server, unauthorized clients will be able to read and write data at will. This is why it's critical to only share volumes to specific client systems, using the appropriate "read-write" or "read-only" designation.

The other key parameter for the `share` command, `sec`, specifies the type of authentication required to access server volumes. By default, the sys level is used, whereby usernames and groups are mapped between client and server. Thus, the user lynda on the client will have the same access permissions as lynda on the server. However, other alternatives are available, depending on the relative risks involved in data loss. If sensitive data is being shared by a NFS server, it may be wise to implement a more sophisticated authentication method, including one based on DES public-key cryptography (the dh level, standing for Diffie-Hellman), or the Kerberos 4 authentication method (the krb4 level). If a volume is exported with the dh or krb4 authentication levels, then all clients must use the method specified to access data on the volume specified. To support the dh or krb4 authentication levels, secure RPC must be running.

TIP   User keys can be updated by using the `chkey` command.

Performance

NFS performance is determined by a number of factors, including:

- Server CPU speed, and number of server CPUs
- Server physical RAM and virtual RAM
- Server disk speed
- Server system load
- Server CacheFS capacity
- Server network interfaces
- Number of clients
- Speed of local network
- Domain Name Lookup Cache (DNLC) speed

Many sites develop NFS services incrementally—as the number of users grows, so does the number of CPUs, memory, and network interfaces, along with faster disks allocated to improving NFS performance.

TIP   A number of software methods, including the CacheFS and DNLC settings, can be modified to improve data throughput.

One of the best methods for determining how NFS is performing, from both a client and server perspective, is to use the `nfsstat` command to gather performance statistics over a period of weeks or months. In particular, counting the number of calls and bad calls can show the proportion of successful to unsuccessful requests, respectively, to the server. To run nfsstat on the server, the following command is used:

```
# nfsstat -s
...
Server nfs:
calls badcalls
575637455 3433
...
```

Here, we can see that the proportion of bad calls to the total number of calls is 3433 ÷ 575637455, which is much less than 1 percent. After gathering statistics for each interval, the counters can be reset to zero by using the following command:

```
# nfsstat -z
```

Summary

In this chapter, we have examined the basic operation of the Network File System (NFS). This system is widely used to share volumes from servers to multiple clients, and is flexible enough to support systems that are both clients and servers. Since NFS is ubiquitous in the Solaris environment, administrators should be very familiar with the many configuration options available.

Questions

1. An NFS volume shared from a server to a client can be accessed by which of the following?

   A. Mount point

   B. URL

   C. URI

   D. SMB client

2. Which daemons must be run to support a NFS server?

   A. inetd, sendmail

   B. nfsd, mountd

   C. pc.nfsd, in.rpld

   D. mountd, syslogd

3. Which of the following commands would share the volume */staff* to the hosts georgia, carolina, and fairfax read-only using NFS?

   A. `share -F NFS -o rw=georgia,carolina,fairfax /staff`

   B. `share -protocol NFS -o rw=georgia,carolina,fairfax /staff`

   C. `share /staff -protocol nfs -o rw=georgia,carolina,fairfax`

   D. `share -F nfs -o ro=georgia,carolina,fairfax /staff`

4. Which of the following commands would stop sharing the volume */data* using NFS?

   A. `shareoff /data`

   B. `umount /data`

   C. `unshare -F nfs /data`

   D. `unshare -protocol NFS /data`

5. Which of the following commands would mount the shared volume */data* using NFS from the server zemindar (read-write) on the mount point */zemindar*?

   A. `mount -protocol nfs -w ro zemindar:/data /data`

   B. `mount zemindar:/data -F NFS -rw zemindar:/data /data`

   C. `mount /zemindar -F nfs -rw zemindar:/data`

   D. `mount -F nfs -o rw zemindar:/data /zemindar`

6. Which of the following commands would mount all partitions listed in */etc/vfstab* that are not currently mounted?

   A. `mount /etc/vfstab`

   B. `mountall -F nfs /etc/vfstab`

   C. `mountall`

   D. `vfsmount`

7. Which of the following commands shows the local resources shared through the networked file systems that are currently mounted by specific clients?

   A. `dfmounts`

   B. `share`

   C. `showmounts`

   D. `nfsmounts`

8. What command resets nfsstat counters to zero?

    A. `nfsstat -z`

    B. `nfsstat -r`

    C. `nfsreset`

    D. `nfsrst`

9. Which of the following factors does *not* influence NFS server performance?

    A. Server CPU speed and number of server CPUs

    B. Server physical RAM and virtual RAM

    C. Server disk speed

    D. Server kernel size

Answers

1. **A.** Any disk volume is always accessed through a mount point.

2. **B.** Both nfsd and mountd must be running to support NFS services.

3. **D.** Read-only is specified by using the `ro` option.

4. **C.** Volumes can be unshared by using the `unshare` command.

5. **D.** Read-write is specified by using the `rw` option.

6. **C.** To mount all volumes, use `mountall`.

7. **A.** The `dfmounts` command shows the local resources shared through NFS that are mounted.

8. **A.** The `nfsstat` command counters must be reset with the `-z` option.

9. **D.** The size of the kernel does not directly affect NFS performance.

## CHAPTER 24

Automount

In this chapter, you will

- Gain an understanding of the role of the automounter
- Use automounter maps
- Create direct, indirect, and master maps

The automounter is a program that automatically mounts NFS file systems when they are accessed and then unmounts them when they are no longer needed. It requires you to use special files, known as automounter maps, which contain information about the servers, the pathname to the NFS file system on the server, the local pathname, and the mount options. By using the automounter, you don't have to update the entries in */etc/vfstab* on every client by hand every time you make a change to the NFS servers.

Normally, only root can mount file systems, so when users need to mount an NFS file system, they need to find the system administrator. The main problem is that once users are finished with a file system, they rarely tell the system administrator. If the NFS server containing that file system ever crashed, you would be left with one or more hanging processes. This can easily increase your workload if you are responsible for maintaining an NFS server. The automounter can solve both of these problems, because it automatically mounts an NFS file system when a user references a file in that file system and it will automatically unmount the NFS file system if it is not referenced for more than five minutes.

The automounter is a RPC daemon that services requests from clients to mount and unmount remote volumes using NFS. During installation, a set of server-side maps are created that list the file systems to be automatically mounted. Typically, these file systems include shared user home directories (under */home*), and network-wide mail directories (*/var/mail*).

Enabling the Automounter

The `automount` command installs autofs mount points, and associates an automount map with each mount point. This requires that the automount daemon be running (automountd). When the automount daemon is initialized on the client, no exported directories are mounted by the clients—these are only mounted when a remote user attempts to access a file on the directory from a client. The connection eventually times out, in which case the exported directory is unmounted by the client.

Automounter maps usually use a network information service, like NIS+, to manage shared volumes, meaning that a single home directory for individual users can be provided on request from a single server, no matter which client machine they log in to. Connection and reconnection is handled by the automount daemon. If automount starts up and has nothing to mount or unmount, this is reported (and is quite normal):

```
burbank# automount
automount: no mounts
automount: no unmounts
```

Automounter Maps

The behavior of the automounter is determined by a set of files called automounter maps. There are two main types of maps: indirect and direct. An indirect map is useful when you are mounting several file systems that will share a common pathname prefix. As we will see shortly, an indirect map can be used to manage the directory tree in */home*. A direct map is used to mount file systems where each mount point does not share a common prefix with other mount points in the map. In this section, we will look at examples of each of these types of maps.

 TIP   An additional map, called the master map, is used by the automounter to determine the names of the files corresponding to the direct and indirect maps.

Indirect Maps

The most common type of automounter maps are indirect maps, which correspond to "regularly" named file systems like */home*, or */usr* directory trees. Regularly named file systems share the same directory prefix. For example, the directories */home/jdoe* and */home/sdoe* are regularly named directories in the */home* directory tree.

Normally, indirect maps are stored in the */etc* directory, and are named with the convention auto_directory, where "directory" is the name of the directory prefix (without slashes) which the indirect map is responsible for. As an example, the indirect map responsible for the */home* directory is usually named auto_home. An indirect map is made up of a series of entries in the following format:

```
directory      options      host:filesystem
```

Here "directory" is the relative pathname of a directory that will be appended to the name of the directory that is corresponding to this indirect map as specified in the master map file. (The master map is covered later in this section.) For "options," you can use any of the mount options covered earlier in Chapter 23. To specify options, you will need to prefix the first option with a dash (–). If you do not need any extra options, you can omit the options entirely.

TIP The final entry in the map contains the location of the NFS file system.

Here is an example of the indirect map that is responsible for the directories in */home*:

```
# /etc/auto_home - home directory map for automounter
jdoe          orem:/store/home/jdoe
sdoe          orem:/store/home/sdoe
kdoe -bg srv-ss10:/home/kdoe
```

Here the entries for jdoe, sdoe, and kdoe correspond to the directories */home/jdoe*, */home/sdoe*, and */home/kdoe*, respectively. The first two entries indicate that the automounter should mount the directories */home/jdoe* and */home/sdoe* from the NFS server orem, while the last one specifies that the directory */home/kdoe* should be mounted from the NFS server srv-ss10. The last entry also demonstrates the use of options.

Now that we have taken a look at an indirect map, let's walk through what happens when you access a file on an NFS file system that is handled by the automounter. For example, consider the following command that accesses the file */home/jdoe/docs/book/ch17.doc*:

```
$ more /home/jdoe/docs/book/ch17.doc
```

Since the directory */home/jdoe* is automounted, the following steps are used by the automounter to allow you to access the file:

1. The automounter looks at the pathname and determines that the directory */home* is controlled by the indirect map auto_home.

2. The automounter looks at the rest of the pathname for a corresponding entry in the auto_home map. In this case, it finds the matching entry jdoe.

3. Once a matching entry has been found, the automounter checks to see if the directory */home/jdoe* is already mounted. If the directory is already mounted, you can directly access the file; otherwise, the automounter mounts this directory and then allows you to access the file.

Direct Maps

When you use an indirect map, the automounter takes complete control of the directory corresponding to the indirect map. This means that no user, not even root, can create entries in a directory corresponding to an indirect map. For this reason, directories specified in an indirect map cannot be automounted on top of an existing directory. In this case, you need a special type of map known as a direct map. A direct map allows you to mix automounter mount points and normal directories in the same directory tree. The directories specified in a direct map have "non-regular" mount points, which simply mean that they do not share a common prefix.

 TIP A common use for direct maps is to allow for directories in the */usr* directory tree to be automounted.

The direct map is normally stored in the file */etc/auto_direct*. The format of this file is similar to the format of the indirect maps:

```
directory      options      host:filesystem
```

Here "directory" is the absolute pathname of a directory. For "options," you can use any of the mount options covered earlier in this chapter. To specify options, you will need to prefix the first option with a dash (–). If you do not need any extra options, you can omit the options entirely. The final entry in the map contains the location of the NFS file system. Here is an example of the direct map that is responsible for some of the directories in */usr*:

```
# /etc/auto_direct - Direct Automount map
/usr/pubsw/man  orem:/internal/opt/man
/usr/doc        orem:/internal/httpd/htdocs
```

When any files in the directories */usr/pubsw/man* or */usr/doc* are accessed, the automounter will automatically handle the mounting of these directories.

Master Maps

When the automounter first starts, it reads the file */etc/auto_master* to determine where to find the direct and indirect map files. The *auto_master* file is known as the master map. Its contents consists of lines whose format is as follows:

```
directory    map
```

Here, "directory" is the name of the directory that corresponds to the indirect map. For a direct map, this entry is /–. The "map" is the name of the map file in the */etc* directory corresponding to the "directory" given in the first column. The following example shows a master map file for the direct and indirect maps given earlier in this section:

```
# Master map for automounter
/home        auto_home
/-           auto_direct
```

Other entries can also be made in the master map. For example, to share a common directory for mail between a number of clients and a mail server, we would enter the definition:

```
/-               /etc/auto_mail
```

This creates a share called "auto_mail," which makes mail on a single server accessible to all client machines upon request. Automounter permits two kinds of shares that can be defined by direct and indirect maps: a direct map is a set of arbitrary mount points that are listed together, while an indirect map mounts everything under a specific directory. For example, auto_home mounts user directories and all subdirectories underneath them.

If an automounted share is available on the server, then you should see its details being displayed in the */etc/mnttab* file:

```
burbank:/var/mail    /var/mail nfs      nosuid,dev=2bc0012    951071258
```

Continuing with the example of auto_mail, as defined in the master map, a file */etc/auto_mail* would have to contain the following entry:

```
denver# cat /etc/auto_mail
  /var/mail burbank:/var/mail
```

This ensures that the burbank server knows where to find the */var/mail* directory physically, and that automount can mount the shared volume at will. Sometimes, the network load caused by mounting and unmounting home directories can lead to an increase in I/O load, and reduce the effective bandwidth of a network. For this reason, only volumes that need to be shared should be shared.

 TIP The timeout parameter for automount can be modified to extend its latency for mounting and unmounting directories.

 EXAM TIP You should be able to explain the differences between direct, indirect, and master maps for the exam.

Automount and NIS+

A common problem with auto_home is that systems in a NIS+ environment may create user accounts on a file system mounted as */home*. This means that if auto_home is active, as defined by */etc/auto_master*, then after rebooting, the shared home directories are mounted on */home*, and when the local */home* attempts to mount the same point, it fails. This is one of the most frequently asked questions about Solaris, as the convention was different for earlier Solaris systems, which used local */home* directories. The recommended practice is now to create home directories under */export/home*, on the local file system if required, or to use auto_home in a NIS+ environment. However, if you wish to disable this feature altogether, and stick with a local */home*, then simply remove "+auto_master" from the master map (*/etc/auto_master*).

Starting and Stopping the Automounter

Starting and stopping the automounter is normally handled by your system at boot and shutdown time, and you will not have to start and stop the automounter manually if you make changes to any of its map files.

The automount daemon is typically started from */etc/init.d/autofs* during the multiuser startup, with a command like the following:

```
# /etc/init.d/autofs start
```

This should start the automounter. You can confirm that it started correctly by using the following command:

```
# /bin/ps -ef | grep automountd
```

The output should look like the following:

```
root 21642     1  0 11:27:29 ?          0:00 /usr/lib/autofs/automountd
```

If you receive no output, the automounter has not started correctly. In that case, you should run the startup script again.

Stopping the NFS client is similar to starting it:

```
# /etc/init.d/autofs stop
```

The stop script usually stops the automounter, but you can confirm this using the following command:

```
# /bin/ps -ef | grep automountd
```

This is the same command that is used to check to see if the automounter is running, except that once you stop it, this command should not produce any output. If you do see some output and it contains a `grep` command, you can ignore those lines. Any other output indicates that the automounter has not stopped, in which case you should execute the NFS client `stop` command again.

If you receive a message similar to the following

```
/home: busy
```

then you will need to determine if anyone is logged on to the system and is using files from /home. If you cannot determine this, you can use the following command to get a list of all of the mounted directories in the directory that caused the error message (in this case /home):

```
$ df -k -F nfs
/home/jdoe
```

Just replace /home with the name of the directory that produced the error message. In this case, only one directory, /home/jdoe, was automounted. Once you have a list of these directories, try unmounting each one with the umount command. When you receive an error message, you will know which directory contains the files that are in use. You can ask the user to finish with those files, and then proceed to stop the automounter.

Summary

In this chapter, we have examined how to use the automounter to automatically mount commonly used remote drives, such as */home*, to provide centralized file-sharing services on Solaris. We explored the uses of master, direct, and indirect maps, and reviewed some issues between NIS+ and the automounter.

Questions

1. Which of the following programs must be running to support automount?

   A. automountd, in.rpld

   B. automountd, rpcbind

   C. nfsd, rpcbind

   D. rpcbind, in.rpld

2. Which of the following is an example of the indirect map that is responsible for the directories in */home* for the use pwatters on server toga?

   A. `pwatters    auto    toga:/home/pwatters`

   B. `toga:/ home/pwatters    pwatters    auto`

   C. `ALL    toga:/home/pwatters`

   D. `pwatters    toga:/home/pwatters`

3. Which of the following is an example of the direct map that is responsible for mapping the directory */games/adventure/misc* on toga to */usr/local/games*?

   A. `/usr/local/games toga:/games/adventure/misc`

   B. `/usr/local/* ALL toga:/games/adventure/misc`

   C. `/usr/local/games ALL toga:/games/*`

   D. `/usr/local/games -rw toga:/games/adventure/misc`

4. What command is used to check whether the automount daemon is running?

   A. `/bin/ps -ef | grep automountd`

   B. `automountchk`

   C. `chkautomount`

   D. `autofsstat`

5. What command is used to start the automounter?

   A. `/etc/init.d/automount start`

   B. `/etc/init.d/autofs start`

   C. `/etc/init.d/automounter start`

   D. `/sbin/autofs`

Answers

1. **B.** The automountd requires RPC support (rpcbind) to run.

2. **D.** Home directories are automounted under /home in this configuration.

3. **A.** The local mount point is always specified first.

4. **A.** The `ps` command must be used—there is no special checking command.

5. **B.** /etc/init.d/autofs is the default startup file.

## CHAPTER 25

The CacheFS File System

In this chapter, you will

- Understand the role of caches
- Configure a CacheFS file system

Caching is an important strategy in distributed computing, which aims to effectively speed up client access to servers. In NFS terms, caching can significantly reduce latencies across wide area networks, improving the performance of distributed file systems. This chapter examines how to install and configure caching file systems.

Configuring a CacheFS File System

In general terms, a cache is a place where important material can be placed so that it can be quickly retrieved. The location of the cache may be quite different from the normal storage location for the specified material. For example, field commanders in the army may store ammunitions in local caches so that their forces can obtain their required materials quickly in case of war. These ammunitions would normally be stored securely well away from the battlefield, but must be "highly available" when required. The state of the battlefield may make it difficult to access outside sources of ammunition during live fire, so a sizable cache of arms is always wise.

This analogy can be easily extended to client/server scenarios, where an unreliable or slow data link may give rise to performance issues. A cache, in this case, can be created to locally store commonly used files, rather than retrieving them each time they are requested from a server. The cache approach has the advantage of speeding up client access to data. However, it has the disadvantage of data asynchronization, where a file is modified on the server after it has been stored in the cache. Thus, if a local file retrieved from the cache is modified before being sent back to the server, any modifications performed on the server's copy of the file would be overwritten.

 CAUTION   Cached data may be out-of-date by the time it is retrieved by the local client, meaning that important decisions could be made based on inaccurate information.

Many Internet client/server systems, involved in the exchange of data across an HTTP link, use a cache to store data. This data is never modified and sent back to the server, so overwriting server-side data is never an issue. Small ISPs with limited bandwidth often use caches to store files that are commonly retrieved from a server. For example, if the ISP has 1,000 customers who routinely download the front page of the *Sydney Morning Herald* each morning, it makes sense to download the file once from the *Sydney Morning Herald* web site, and store it locally for the other 999 users to retrieve. Since the front page only changes from day to day, the page will always be current as long as the cache purges the front page file at the end of each day. The daily amount of data to be downloaded from the *Sydney Morning Herald* web site has been reduced by 99.9 percent, which can significantly boost the ISPs performance in downloading other noncached files from the Internet and reduce the overall cost of data throughput.

Solaris provides a cache file system (CacheFS) that is designed to improve NFS client/server performance across slow or unreliable networks. The principles underlying CacheFS are exactly the same as the two examples listed previously: locally stored files that are frequently requested can be retrieved by users on the client system without having to download them again from the server. This approach minimizes the number of connections required between an NFS client and server to retrieve the same amount of data, in a manner that is invisible to users on the client system. Users will notice that their files are retrieved more quickly than before the cache was introduced.

 TIP   Improving speed of access and retrieval is critical for many users.

CacheFS seamlessly integrates with existing NFS installations, with only simple modifications to `mount` command parameters and */etc/vfstab* entries required to make use of the facility. The first task in configuring a cache is to create a mount point and a cache on a client system. If a number of NFS servers are to be used with the cache, it makes sense to create individual caches underneath the same top-level mount point. Many sites use the mount point */cache* to store individual caches. In this example, we'll assume that a file system from the NFS server yorktown will be cached on the local client system midway, so the commands to create a cache on midway are

```
midway# mkdir /cache
midway # cfsadmin -c /cache/yorktown
```

Here, we've used the `cfsadmin` command to create the cache once the mount point */cache* has been created. Now, let's examine how we would force the cache to be used for all accesses from midway to yorktown for the remote filesystem */staff*, which is also mounted locally on */staff*:

```
midway# mount -F cachefs -o backfstype=nfs,cachedir=/cache/Yorktown
 yorktown:/staff /staff
```

Once the *yorktown:/staff* file system has been mounted in this way, users on midway will not notice any difference in operation, except that file access to */staff* will be much quicker.

It is possible to check the status of the cache by using the `cachefsstat` command. In order to verify that */cache/yorktown* is operating correctly, the following command would be used:

```
midway# cachefsstat /cache/yorktown
```

Alternatively, the `cfsadmin` command can be used:

```
# cfsadmin -l /cache/Yorktown
cfsadmin: list cache FS information
maxblocks 80%
minblocks 0%
threshblocks 75%
maxfiles 80%
minfiles 0%
threshfiles 75%
maxfilesize 12MB
yorktown:_staff:_staff
```

Note the last line, which is the current cache ID. You will need to remember the cache ID if you ever want to delete the cache. If a cache needs to be deleted, the `cfsadmin` command can be used with the `-d` option:

```
midway# umount /staff
midway# cfsadmin -d yorktown:_staff:_staff /cache/yorktown
```

Here, we've unmounted the */staff* volume on midway locally, before attempting to remove the cache by providing its ID along with its mount point.

Summary

In this chapter, we've examined how to configure and install a NFS cache, which can be used to significantly increase the speed of access to files on a remote NFS server. In addition, we examined how to review the performance of a cache, and delete it if necessary.

Questions

1. What is the command used to create a cache?

   A. `cfscreate`

   B. `cfsadmin`

   C. `cfsmake`

   D. `newfs`

2. What is the command used to delete a cache?

   A. cfscreate

   B. cfsadmin

   C. cfsmake

   D. newfs

3. What is the command used to check cache status?

   A. cfscreate

   B. cfsadmin

   C. cfsmake

   D. newfs

4. What is the command used to check cache statistics?

   A. cachestat

   B. cachecheck

   C. checkcache

   D. cachefsstat

5. Which of the following commands can be used to monitor the performance of a caching file system?

   A. cachefsstat

   B. cachestat

   C. statcache

   D. cfsstats

Answers

1. **B.** The cfsadmin command can create new caches.

2. **B.** The cfsadmin command can delete existing caches.

3. **B.** The cfsadmin command can check cache status.

4. **D.** Cache statistics are not checked by cfsadmin—cachefsstat is required.

5. **A.** The cachefsstat command can be used to monitor cache performance.

DNS

In this chapter, you will

- Learn about the Domain Name Service (DNS)
- Discover how to configure a DNS server
- Review the configuration of DNS clients

Although Solaris 9 has its own naming service, known as the Network Information Service (NIS), support is also provided for DNS, which maps IP addresses to hostnames. Every computer that is connected to the Internet must have an IP address, which identifies it uniquely within the network. For example, 192.18.97.241 is the IP address of the web server at Sun. IP addresses are hard for humans to remember, and don't adequately describe the network on which a host resides. Thus, by examining the Fully Qualified Domain Name (FQDN) of 192.18.97.241—**www.sun.com**—it's immediately obvious that the host "www" lies within the "sun.com" domain. The mapping between human-friendly domain names and machine-friendly IP addresses is performed by a distributed naming service, known as the Domain Name Service (DNS). In this chapter, we examine how DNS servers manage records of network addresses, and how this information can be accessed by Solaris applications. In addition, we examine how to build and configure the latest version of the Berkeley Internet Daemon (BIND) from source, just in case security issues leave your existing Berkeley Internet Daemon (BIND) service vulnerable to attack.

Overview of DNS

The Domain Name Service (DNS) is a distributed database that maps human friendly fully qualified hostnames, like **paulwatters.com**, to a numeric IP address like 209.67.50.203. In the early days of the Internet, a single file was distributed to various hosts (called the *HOSTS.TXT* file), which contained an address to hostname mapping for known hosts. Administrators would periodically upload a list of any new hosts added to their networks, after which they would download the latest version of the file. However, as the Internet grew, maintaining this text database became impossible. A new system for mapping addresses to names was proposed in RFCs 882 and 883, based around information about local networks being sourced from designated servers for each network. It should be noted that Solaris retains a variant of the *HOSTS.TXT* file in the form of the */etc/hosts* file, which is typically used to map IP addresses to domain names for the localhost, as well as key network servers such as the local domain name server. This is very useful in situations where the DNS server is not responding, or while the system is being booted. The */etc/hosts* file is consulted by some applications, such as the syslog daemon (syslogd) to determine which host (the "loghost") should be used for system logging. A typical */etc/hosts* file looks like this:

```
127.0.0.1           localhost
204.168.14.23       bryce        bryce.paulwatters.com       loghost
204.168.14.24       wasatch      wasatch.paulwatters.com
```

Of course, only key servers and the localhost should be defined in the */etc/hosts* file; otherwise, any change in IP address for that server will not be reflected in the value resolved from */etc/hosts*.

Exercise 26-1 Checking Hosts Entries

Check the entries in your */etc/hosts*. Are there entries for localhost and loghost?

DNS works on a simple client/server principle: if you know the name of a DNS server for a particular network, you will be able to retrieve the IP address of any host within that network. For example, if I know that the name server for the domain *paulwatters.com* is **dns20.register.com**, I can contact **dns20.register.com** to retrieve the address for any host within the **paulwatters.com** domain (including **www.paulwatters.com**, or 209.67.50.203). Of course, this leads us to a classic "chicken and egg" problem—how would we know in the first instance that the DNS server **dns20.register.com** was authoritative for **paulwatters.com**? The answer is that, in the same way that the addresses of all hosts under **paulwatters.com** are managed by its DNS server, the address of the DNS server is managed by the next server along the chain—in this case, the DNS server for the ".com" domain.

There are many such top-level domains now in existence, including the traditional **.edu** (educational organizations), **.com** (commercial organizations), and **.net** (network) top-level domains. Most countries now have their own top-level domains, including **.au** (Australia), **.ck** (Cook Islands), and **.ph** (Philippines). Underneath each top-level domain are a number of second-level domains: for example, Australia has **.com.au** (Australian commercial organizations), **.edu.au** (Australian educational organizations), and **.asn.au** (Australian nonprofit associations).

TIP The organizations that manage each top-level and second-level domain can also be quite different.

As an example, let's look at how the hostname **www.finance.saltlake.com** is resolved: the client resolver needs to determine which DNS server is authoritative for **.com** domains, followed by the DNS server that is authoritative for **saltlake.com** domains, potentially followed by the DNS server that is authoritative for the **finance.saltlake.com** domain, if all mappings for **saltlake.com** are not stored on a single server. The **.com** resolution is taken care of by the list of root servers provided by the Whois database (**ftp://ftp.rs.internic.net/domain/named.root**):

```
>>> Last update of whois database: Mon, 9 Oct 2000 09:43:11 EDT <<<
The Registry database contains ONLY .COM, .NET, .ORG, .EDU domains and
Registrars.
ftp://ftp.rs.internic.net/domain/named.root
;          This file holds the information on root name servers needed to
;          initialize cache of Internet domain name servers
;          (e.g. reference this file in the "cache  .  <file>"
;          configuration file of BIND domain name servers).
;
;          This file is made available by InterNIC registration services
;          under anonymous FTP as
;              file                /domain/named.root
;              on server           FTP.RS.INTERNIC.NET
;          -OR- under Gopher at    RS.INTERNIC.NET
;              under menu          InterNIC Registration Services (NSI)
;                  submenu         InterNIC Registration Archives
;              file                named.root
;
;          last update:    Aug 22, 1997
;          related version of root zone:    1997082200
.                              3600000  IN  NS   A.ROOT-SERVERS.NET.
A.ROOT-SERVERS.NET.            3600000      A    198.41.0.4
.                              3600000      NS   B.ROOT-SERVERS.NET.
B.ROOT-SERVERS.NET.            3600000      A    128.9.0.107
.                              3600000      NS   C.ROOT-SERVERS.NET.
C.ROOT-SERVERS.NET.            3600000      A    192.33.4.12
.                              3600000      NS   D.ROOT-SERVERS.NET.
D.ROOT-SERVERS.NET.            3600000      A    128.8.10.90
.                              3600000      NS   E.ROOT-SERVERS.NET.
E.ROOT-SERVERS.NET.            3600000      A    192.203.230.10
.                              3600000      NS   F.ROOT-SERVERS.NET.
F.ROOT-SERVERS.NET.            3600000      A    192.5.5.241
.                              3600000      NS   G.ROOT-SERVERS.NET.
G.ROOT-SERVERS.NET.            3600000      A    192.112.36.4
.                              3600000      NS   H.ROOT-SERVERS.NET.
H.ROOT-SERVERS.NET.            3600000      A    128.63.2.53
.                              3600000      NS   I.ROOT-SERVERS.NET.
I.ROOT-SERVERS.NET.            3600000      A    192.36.148.17
.                              3600000      NS   J.ROOT-SERVERS.NET.
J.ROOT-SERVERS.NET.            3600000      A    198.41.0.10
.                              3600000      NS   K.ROOT-SERVERS.NET.
K.ROOT-SERVERS.NET.            3600000      A    193.0.14.129
.                              3600000      NS   L.ROOT-SERVERS.NET.
L.ROOT-SERVERS.NET.            3600000      A    198.32.64.12
.                              3600000      NS   M.ROOT-SERVERS.NET.
M.ROOT-SERVERS.NET.            3600000      A    202.12.27.33
```

The *named.root* file shown previously can be used by systems to resolve IP addresses for root DNS servers. After obtaining an IP address for a root server for the **.com** domain, a query is then made to the DNS server authoritative for **saltlake.com** for the address **www.finance.saltlake.com**. Two possible scenarios can occur at this point: either the DNS server that is authoritative for the entire **saltlake.com** domain can resolve the address, or the query is passed to a DNS server for the **finance.saltlake.com** domain if the root server has delegated authority to another server. In the latter situation, the **saltlake.com** DNS server does not know the IP address for any hosts within the finance.saltlake.com domain, except for the address of the DNS server. DNS is therefore a very flexible system for managing the mapping of domain names to IP addresses.

The software that carries out the client request for, and server resolution of, IP addresses is typically the Berkeley Internet Daemon (BIND).

 TIP Although most vendors, including Sun, ship their own customized version of BIND, it is possible to download, compile, configure, and install your own version of BIND (available for download from **http://www.isc.org/**).

DNS Client Tools

Configuring a DNS client in Solaris is very easy, and can be accomplished in a few easy steps. First, you must have installed the Berkeley Internet Daemon (BIND) package during system installation to use the DNS client tools. Secondly, you must configure the name service switch (*/etc/nsswitch.conf*) to consult DNS for domain name resolution, in addition to checking the */etc/hosts* file and/or NIS/NIS+ maps or tables for hostnames. The following line must appear in */etc/nsswitch.conf* for DNS to work correctly:

```
/etc/nsswitch.conf hosts:  dns [NOTFOUND=return] files
```

If you have NIS+ running, the line would look like this:

```
/etc/nsswitch.conf hosts:  dns nisplus nis [NOTFOUND=return] files
```

Next, the name of the local domain should be entered into the file */etc/defaultdomain*. For example, the */etc/defaultdomain* file for the host **www.paulwatters.com** should have the following entry:

```
paulwatters.com
```

Finally, the */etc/resolv.conf* file needs to contain the name of the local domain, as well as the IP addresses of the local primary DNS server, as well as a secondary (off-site) DNS server. This means that even if your local DNS server goes down you can rely on the secondary to provide up-to-date information about external hosts, instead of relying on data within the */etc/hosts* file to resolve local addresses. In the following example, we demonstrate how the */etc/resolv.conf* file might look for the host **www.finance .saltlake.com**:

```
domain finance.saltlake.com
domain saltlake.com
nameserver 204.168.12.1
nameserver 204.168.12.16
nameserver 64.58.24.1
```

Here, there are two domains to which the host belongs: the subdomain **finance .saltlake.com**, as well as the domain **saltlake.com**. Thus, there are two primary DNS servers listed within the local domain (204.168.12.1 and 204.168.12.16). In addition, an external secondary is also listed, corresponding to **ns.utahisp.com**, or 64.58.24.1.

Once the client resolver is configured in this way, we can use a number of tools to test whether DNS is working, and also to further examine how IP addresses are resolved. The most important tool for performing DNS resolutions is nslookup, which can be used in a simple command-line mode to look up fully-qualified domain names from IP addresses, and vice versa. However, nslookup also features an interactive mode that is very useful for retrieving name server characteristics for a particular domain, and to determine which DNS servers are authoritative for a specific host or network.

Let's look at a simple example—if we wanted to determine the IP address of the host **www.paulwatters.com**, using a client on the host **provo.cassowary.net**, we would use the following command:

```
$ nslookup www.paulwatters.com
```

The following response would be returned:

```
Server:   provo.cassowary.net
Address:  206.68.216.16

Name:     paulwatters.com
Address:  209.67.50.203
Aliases:  www.paulwatters.com
```

This means that the primary DNS server for the local (**cassowary.net**) domain is **provo.cassowary.net** (206.68.216.16). This server then makes a connection through to the DNS server, which is authoritative for the domain **paulwatters.com** (**dns19.hostsave.com**). This server then returns the canonical (actual) name for the host (**paulwatters.com**), the alias name (**www.paulwatters.com**), and the desired IP address. If we reversed the process, and instead supplied the IP address 209.67.50.203 on the command line, we would be able to perform a reverse lookup on that address, which would resolve to the domain name **paulwatters.com**.

Exercise 26-2 Using nslookup

Use nslookup to determine the IP address of **www.sun.com**.

If you want to verify that your DNS server is returning the correct IP address, or if you want to verify an address directly yourself, then running nslookup in interactive mode allows you to set the name of the DNS server to use for all lookups. For example, if we wanted to resolve the domain name for the web server of the University of Sydney, we could use the following command:

```
$ nslookup www.usyd.edu.au
```

The following response would then be returned:

```
Server:   provo.cassowary.net
Address:  206.68.216.16

Name: solo.ucc.usyd.edu.au
Address:  129.78.64.2
Aliases:  www.usyd.edu.au
```

However, we could verify that this IP address was indeed correct by setting our DNS server to be the DNS server that was authoritative for the **ucc.usyd.edu.au** domain:

```
$ nslookup
Default Server:  provo.cassowary.net
Address:  206.68.216.16
```

Here, we enter the name of the DNS server that is authoritative for the target domain:

```
> server metro.ucc.su.oz.au
Default Server:  metro.ucc.su.oz.au
Address:  129.78.64.2
```

Next, we enter the name of the host to resolve:

```
> www.usyd.edu.au
Server:  metro.ucc.su.oz.au
Address:  129.78.64.2
```

And the IP address is returned correctly:

```
Name:     solo.ucc.usyd.edu.au
Address:  129.78.64.24
Aliases:  www.usyd.edu.au
```

If you wanted to determine some of the key characteristics of the DNS entry for **www.usyd.edu.au**, such as the DNS server that is authoritative for the host and the mail address of the administrator who is responsible for the host, it is possible to retrieve the Start of Authority (SOA) record through nslookup:

```
$ nslookup
Default Server:  provo.cassowary.net
Address:  206.68.216.16

> server metro.ucc.su.oz.au
Default Server:  metro.ucc.su.oz.au
Address:  129.78.64.2
> set q=soa
> www.usyd.edu.au
Server:  metro.ucc.su.oz.au
Address:  129.78.64.2

www.usyd.edu.au canonical name = solo.ucc.usyd.edu.au
ucc.usyd.edu.au
        origin = metro.ucc.usyd.edu.au
        mail addr = root.metro.ucc.usyd.edu.au
        serial = 316
        refresh = 3600 (1 hour)
        retry   = 1800 (30 mins)
        expire  = 36000 (10 hours)
        minimum ttl = 43200 (12 hours)
```

This SOA record indicates the following:

- The canonical name of **www.usyd.edu.au** is **solo.ucc.usyd.edu.au**.

- The origin of the DNS record is **metro.ucc.usyd.edu.au** (and this server is authoritative for the host **solo.ucc.usyd.edu.au**).

- The serial number for the current record is 316. Next time a change is made to the record, the serial number should be incremented.

- The refresh rate is 1 hour.

- The retry rate is 30 minutes.

- The expiry rate is 10 hours.

- The TTL is 12 hours.

 EXAM TIP You should be able to identify the different fields in a SOA record for the exam.

We further examine the meaning of each field, when we discuss how to create DNS records for the server. The use of nslookup to determine which servers are authoritative for a particular query is not limited to individual hosts—in fact, the authoritative servers for entire networks can be determined by using nslookup. For example, if we wanted to determine which servers were authoritative for the Cook Islands top-level domain (**.ck**), we would use the following command:

```
$ nslookup
> set type=ns
> ck.
Server:  provo.cassowary.net
Address:  206.68.216.16

Non-authoritative answer:
ck        nameserver = DOWNSTAGE.MCS.VUW.AC.NZ
ck        nameserver = NS1.WAIKATO.AC.NZ
ck        nameserver = PARAU.OYSTER.NET.ck
ck        nameserver = POIPARAU.OYSTER.NET.ck
ck        nameserver = CIRCA.MCS.VUW.AC.NZ

Authoritative answers can be found from:
DOWNSTAGE.MCS.VUW.AC.NZ internet address = 130.195.6.10
NS1.WAIKATO.AC.NZ       internet address = 140.200.128.13
PARAU.OYSTER.NET.ck     internet address = 202.65.32.128
POIPARAU.OYSTER.NET.ck  internet address = 202.65.32.127
CIRCA.MCS.VUW.AC.NZ     internet address = 130.195.5.12
```

Some servers that are authoritative for the top-level domains of the Cook Islands are located in New Zealand. This geographic separation may seem strange, but it makes sense if you've ever lived through a tropical storm in Rarotonga—if the power to the **OYSTER.NET.ck** network was disrupted, hostnames could still be resolved through the backup servers at **WAIKATO.AC.NZ**.

It's also possible to obtain a list of all the networks and hosts within a particular top-level domain by using the `ls` command—but be warned, the output can be verbose:

```
$ nslookup
> set type=ns
```

```
> ls ck.
[DOWNSTAGE.MCS.VUW.AC.NZ]
 ck.                                 server = parau.oyster.net.ck
 parau.oyster.net                    202.65.32.128
 ck.                                 server = poiparau.oyster.net.ck
 poiparau.oyster.net                 202.65.32.127
 ck.                                 server = downstage.mcs.vuw.ac.nz
 ck.                                 server = circa.mcs.vuw.ac.nz
 sda.org                             server = parau.oyster.net.ck
 parau.oyster.net                    202.65.32.128
 sda.org                             server = poiparau.oyster.net.ck
```

The final tool that is often useful for resolving hostnames is the whois command. This uses InterNIC servers to perform all of the resolutions for you, and includes useful information like the registrar of the domain name (useful when making complaints about SPAM or harassment on the net!). Here's the whois entry for **paulwatters.com**:

```
$ whois paulwatters

Whois Server Version 1.3

Domain names in the .com, .net, and .org domains can now be
registered with many different competing registrars. Go to
http://www.internic.net for detailed information.

   Domain Name: PAULWATTERS.COM
   Registrar: REGISTER.COM, INC.
   Whois Server: whois.register.com
   Referral URL: www.register.com
   Name Server: DNS19.REGISTER.COM
   Name Server: DNS20.REGISTER.COM
   Updated Date: 30-may-2000
```

Configuring a DNS Server

Now that we've examined DNS from a client viewpoint, and explored concepts like SOAs, IP-to-address mapping, and address-to-IP mapping, it should be obvious what kind of services a DNS server needs to provide to clients. In addition, DNS servers need to be able to support both primary and secondary services as described earlier.

The Berkeley Internet Daemon (BIND) is the most commonly used DNS server for Solaris. It is supplied in a package that is generally installed during the initial system configuration. Its main configuration file is */etc/named.conf* for BIND 8 supplied with Solaris 9.

CAUTION   BIND 4 and earlier used a configuration file called */etc/named.boot*; however, these versions are no longer supported by the ISC, and administrators running BIND 4 should upgrade to BIND 8 or 9.

The */etc/named.conf* file is responsible for controlling the behavior of the DNS servers and provides the following keywords, which are used to define operational statements:

acl	Defines an access control list that determines which clients can use the server.
include	Reads an external file that contains statements in the same format as *letc/named.conf*. This is very useful when your configuration file becomes very large, as different sections can be divided into logically related files.
logging	Determines which activities of the server are logged in the log file specified by the statement.
options	Defines local server operational characteristics.
server	Defines operational characteristics of other servers.
zone	Creates local DNS zones.

Let's examine a sample statement involving each of these keywords.

acl

If we want to define an access control list for all hosts on the local network (10.24.58.*), we would insert this statement:

```
acl local_network {
10.24.58/24
};
```

Here, 24 indicates the netmask 255.255.255.0 in prefix notation. Now, if our router was the host 10.24.58.32, and we wanted to prevent any access to the DNS server from that address, we would amend the previous statement to the following:

```
acl local_network {
!10.24.58.32; 10.24.58/24
};
```

Note that the negation of a specific address from a subnet that is also permitted must precede the definition of that subnet in the statement.

include

A little later, we'll examine how to configure DNS zones. Since these definitions can be very long for large networks, administrators often place them in a separate file so that they can be managed separately from ACL definitions and system options. Thus, to include all of the zone definitions from the file */var/named/zones.conf*, we would insert the following statement into the */etc/named.conf* file:

```
include "/var/named/zones.conf"
```

options

The options section sets key parameters that affect the runtime behavior of the BIND server. Typically, these are the directories in which the zone databases are stored, and the file in which the process ID of the named process is stored. The following example gives the standard options for BIND 8:

```
options {
directory "/var/named";
pid-file "/var/named/pid";
}
```

server

The server statement defines characteristics of remote name servers. There are two main options that can be set with a server statement: whether or not a remote server is known to transmit incorrect information, and whether or not the remote server can answer multiple queries during a single request. A sample server statement would look like this:

```
server 10.24.58.32
{
    bogus yes;
    transfer-format many-answers;
}
```

zone

A zone must be created for each network or subdomain that your DNS server manages. Zones can either be created as primary or secondary, depending on which server is authoritative for a particular domain. Entries for IP-to-name and name-to-IP mappings must also be included to correctly resolve both IP address and domain names. For the domain **cassowary.net**, the following zone entries would need to be created:

```
zone "cassowary.net"
{
    type master;
    file "cassowary.net.db";
}
zone "58.24.10.in-addr.arpa"
{
    type master;
    file "cassowary.net.rev";
}
```

In this case, the two zone files */var/named/cassowary.net.db* and */var/named/cassowary .net.rev* need to be populated with host information. A sample */var/named/cassowary.net .db* file would contain SOA entries like this:

```
@    IN    SOA    cassowary.net.    root.cassowary.net.    (
        2000011103    ;serial number
        10800         ;refresh every three hours
        1800          ;retry every 30 mins
        1209600       ;Two week expiry
        604800)       ;Minimum one week expiry
        IN    NS     ns.cassowary.net.
        IN    MX     10    firewall.cassowary.net.
```

```
firewall    IN    A      10.24.58.1    ;firewall
natalie          IN    A      10.24.58.2    ;webserver
catherine        IN    A      10.24.58.3    ;webserver
tazdevil    IN    A      10.24.58.4    ;kerberos
security    IN    CNAME      tazdevil
```

A sample */var/named/cassowary.net.rev* file would contain SOA entries like this:

```
@    IN    SOA    58.24.10.in-addr.arpa.    root.cassowary.net.    (
          2000011103    ;serial number
          10800         ;refresh every three hours
          1800          ;retry every 30 mins
          1209600       ;Two week expiry
          604800)       ;Minimum one week expiry
          IN    NS     ns.cassowary.net.
1         IN    PTR    firewall.cassowary.net.
2         IN    PTR    natalie.cassowary.net.
3         IN    PTR    catherine.cassowary.net.
4         IN    PTR    tazdevil.cassowary.net.
```

Each host within the domain must have an IP-to-domain mapping as well as a domain-to-IP mapping. Once a change is made to the zone file, the serial number should be incremented as appropriate. Note that in addition to address (A) and pointer (PTR) records for IP address and domain names, it is also possible to identify hosts as mail exchangers (MX) and by canonical names (CNAME). The former is required to define which host is responsible for handling mail within a domain, while the latter is used to create aliases for specific machines (thus, the tazdevil Kerberos server is also known as **security.cassowary.net**).

Summary

In this chapter, we have examined how to install and configure a DNS server. Since DNS is a complex topic, you should read the man pages for the daemons utilized for DNS services.

Questions

1. Which of the following is a fully qualified domain name?

   A. savannah

   B. 255.0.0.0

   C. **savannah.georgia.com**

   D. 192.23.34.255

2. Which of the following is a valid */etc/hosts* entry?

   A. 204.168.14.23   leura   10.168.14.23

   B. 204.168.14.23   leura   leura.paulwatters.com   loghost

    C. leura   204.168.14.23 leura.paulwatters.com   loghost

    D. leura   leura.paulwatters.com   204.168.14.23

3. Which of the following is defined in *named.root*?

    A. Root name server data required to initialize the DNS server cache

    B. Authorization for the root user to set up DNS services

    C. Access permissions for nonroot users to access DNS data installed by root

    D. Zone data for hosts within the local root NIS+ domain

4. Which of the following is defined in */etc/defaultdomain*?

    A. The fully qualified domain name of the localhost

    B. The default web site domain to connect through using Netscape

    C. The name of the local NIS+ domain

    D. The name of the local DNS domain

5. What is the purpose of `nslookup`?

    A. To resolve IP addresses using hostnames only

    B. To resolve hostnames using IP addresses only

    C. To resolve both hostnames or IP addresses given an IP address or hostname

    D. To look up a list of users who can edit zone files

6. What fields can be found in the SOA record?

    A. origin, mail addr, serial, refresh, retry, expire, minimum ttl

    B. original serial, mail refresh, ttl retry, expiry date

    C. original serial, mail addr, ttl retry, ttl expire, minimum refresh

    D. origin, serial date, refresh time, retry, expire, minimum ttl

7. What command can be used to resolve IP addresses on the command line?

    A. `zip`

    B. `resolve`

    C. `list`

    D. `nslookup`

8. What is the purpose of the server statement in an SOA record?

    A. Defines characteristics of remote name servers

    B. Defines characteristics of local name servers

    C. Defines characteristics of NIS servers

    D. Defines characteristics of NIS+ servers only

9. What is the main requirement of the zone record?

   A. One must be created for each network or subdomain that your DNS server manages.

   B. Two must be created for each network or subdomain that your DNS server manages.

   C. Three must be created for each network or subdomain that your DNS server manages.

   D. Four must be created for each network or subdomain that your DNS server manages.

10. What is the role of the options statement?

   A. Optional parameters for clients

   B. Sets key parameters that affect the runtime behavior of the BIND server

   C. Sets key parameters that affect the shutdown behavior of the BIND server

   D. Sets key parameters that affect the clustering and high availability of the BIND server

Answers

1. **C.** Qualified domain names must have a hostname and a domain name.

2. **B.** IP addresses must map to hostnames.

3. **A.** The *named.root* file always contains the root name server data.

4. **D.** The *defaultdomain* defines the local domain.

5. **C.** The `nslookup` command can resolve IP addresses and hostnames.

6. **A.** The origin, mail addr, serial, refresh, retry, expire, and minimum ttl fields can all be contained within an SOA record.

7. **D.** The `nslookup` command can resolve IP addresses as well as hostnames.

8. **A.** The server statement only defines the characteristics of remote name servers.

9. **A.** One zone record must be created for each network or subdomain that your DNS server manages.

10. **B.** The options statement sets key parameters that affect the runtime behavior of the BIND server.

## CHAPTER 27

Network Information Service (NIS/NIS+)

In this chapter, you will

- Learn how to configure NIS/NIS+ servers
- Discover the role of NIS/NIS+ in enterprise networks
- Find a reference for commonly used NIS/NIS+ commands

In Chapter 26, we introduced the notion of a naming service. Solaris 9 supports NIS+, which is an improved version of the NIS, the Network Information Service, which was popular with Solaris 1. However, NIS/NIS+ will eventually be deprecated in favor of the Lightweight Directory Access Protocol (LDAP), which is an industry standard. NIS+ is comprised of a centralized repository of information about hosts, networks, services, and protocols on a local area network. This information is physically stored in a set of maps that are intended to replace the network configuration files usually stored in a server's /etc directory. The set of all maps on a NIS+ network is known as a namespace, supporting large networks of up to 10,000 hosts where responsibilities can be delegated to local servers. NIS+ improves on standard NIS by allowing enhancements to authentication processes, combined with sophisticated resource authorization. This allows NIS+ namespaces to exist over public networks like the Internet without risk of data loss or interception, with the caveat that NIS+ relies on the relatively weak DES encryption algorithm.

In this chapter, we will examine the processing of setting up a NIS+ server and highlight the differences between NIS+ and NIS, and between NIS+ and other naming services like DNS. In fact, many sites will choose to run DNS alongside NIS+, which is also possible. In addition, we will review the role and configuration of primary and slave servers, and walk through the installation of NIS+ using the script method.

Basic NIS Concepts

NIS+ is a Solaris network information service whose primary focus is the management of users, hosts, networks, services, and protocols. NIS+ does not replace DNS, however. DNS is still required for host addressing and identification. However, NIS+ namespaces can be constructed to parallel the host designations assigned through DNS, to simplify operations, and to make the integration of both services more seamless. NIS+ gives networks more than just DNS: namespaces are used as centralized repositories of shared network information that can be used to more effectively manage large networks. However, many organizations choose not to use NIS+ because it has some overlap with DNS, and because of the extra administrative burden involved in installing and configuring NIS+ primary and slave servers. However, if you use the NIS+ scripts to install and configure namespaces, instead of using NIS+ commands direct, NIS+ can be much easier to configure.

NIS revolves around the idea of maps: a map is generally a database with two columns, of which one is a primary key that is used to retrieve an associated value. This associative nature makes the storage and retrieval of group, mail, passwords, and Ethernet information fast for small networks, but can rapidly become difficult to manage (not to mention slow) for large networks. NIS+, in contrast, uses tables, of which 16 are defined by the system. Tables store information like server addresses, time zones, and networks services. In this section, we review the most commonly used types of NIS maps and NIS+ tables.

First, however, we present a conceptual overview of how NIS+ could be used to better manage an organization's network data. Let's imagine that we're setting up a Solaris network for an imaginary college called Panther College, which has a DNS domain of **panther.edu**. Panther has two teaching divisions: an undergraduate school (**undergrad.panther.edu**) and a graduate school (**graduate.panther.edu**). **panther.edu** has a Class C network (192.12.1.0), as do each of the undergraduate (192.12.2.0) and graduate schools (192.12.3.0). Each of these networks can have up to 254 hosts each, which more than adequately covers the staff members in both teaching divisions. To support DNS, there may be a campus-wide DNS server **ns.panther.edu** at 192.12.10, while the **undergrad.panther.edu** network has its own DNS server at **ns.undergrad.panther.edu** (192.12.2.0), and **ns.graduate.panther.edu** (192.12.3.0). This is a fairly standard setup for a medium-sized network like a college campus, and is demonstrated in Figure 27-1.

The NIS+ domains for Panther College can exactly mirror the DNS configuration, as shown in Figure 27-2. However, some differences in naming are immediately apparent: while DNS uses lowercase names by convention, which do not terminate in a period, the NIS+ convention is to name write elements in a domain beginning with capital letters, and terminating with a period.

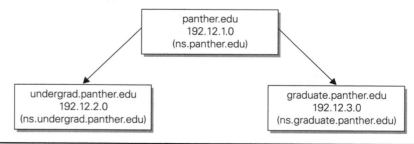

Figure 27-1　DNS configuration for a fictional college with two divisions: graduate and undergraduate, both of which have their own name server

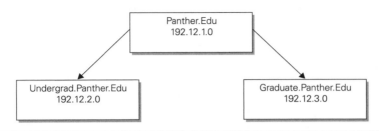

Figure 27-2 NIS+ domains for Panther College

In addition, the second-level domain identified in DNS as **panther.edu** would be the "root domain" in a NIS+ network, and the third-level domains **undergrad.panther.edu** and **graduate.panther.edu** would be described as "nonroot domains." Each of these domains would be associated with a server, in which case the existing DNS servers would double up as NIS+ servers. In fact, in normal NIS+ usage, each of the three domains at Panther College would require two servers: a master server and at least one replica or slave server. This ensures that if the master server is disrupted or experiences hardware failure, the replica server holds copies of network service information. The expanded NIS+ domains for Panther College, with a master and slave server each (called Master and Replica), are shown in Figure 27-3.

In addition to domains and servers, NIS+ also caters to clients. Each client is associated with a specific server and domain. For example, a client in the chemistry lab in the graduate school (**Curie.Graduate.Panther.Edu.**) would be served by **Master.Graduate.Panther.Edu.**, and would be part of the **Graduate.Panther.Edu.** domain. Alternatively, a history professor in the undergraduate school with a computer named **FDR.Undergrad.Panther.Edu** would be served by **Master.Undergrad.Panther.Edu.**, and would be part of the **Undergrad.Panther.Edu.** domain. Figure 27-4 shows the

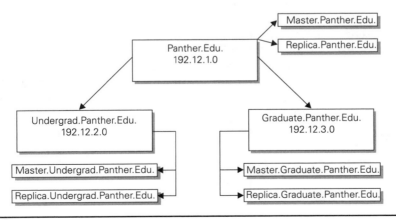

Figure 27-3 NIS+ domains with a master and a slave server each

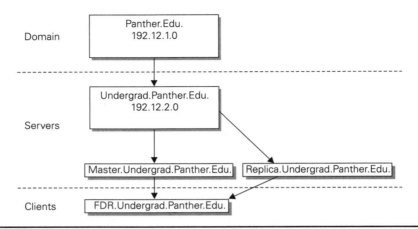

Figure 27-4   Hierarchy of control for a specific domain client (FDR.Undergrad.Panther.Edu.)

hierarchy of control for the **FDR.Undergrad.Panther.Edu.** client. When each client is installed, a directory cache is created, which enables the client to locate other hosts and services via the appropriate server.

So far, we have mentioned only one of the many kinds of namespace components: the domain. However, there are many other components that exist in the namespace, including group objects, directory objects, and table objects. We will examine these important features of the namespace in the following sections. In addition, we'll review the specific configuration of NIS maps and NIS+ tables.

It is worth mentioning at this point that one of the main reasons that organizations choose to implement NIS+ is the improved security that accompanies the system. For example, NIS+ tables are not directly editable, unlike their normal Solaris counterparts in the */etc* directory. Requests to change or even access information in the namespace can only take place once a user has been authenticated. In addition to authentication, each user must be authorized to access a particular resource. This doubly protects sensitive and organizational data in a networked environment. The main authentication exchange takes place when either a user presents their credentials or a host presents its credentials, in an unencrypted LOCAL form or a more secure DES-encrypted exchange. The former is used for testing, while the latter is always used for deployment. After authentication, authorization for the requested resource is checked.

TIP   Access rights can always be examined by using the `niscat` command, which is discussed later in this chapter in the section "niscat".

NIS Maps

As we mentioned previously, NIS used a series of maps to encode data about the network structure. Many of these are in a form that can be accessed through an address key (having a "byaddr" suffix), or through a name (with a "byname" suffix). Whenever a client needs to find information about a particular host, service, group, network, or netgroup, it can be retrieved by consulting the appropriate map as defined in the namespace. The main system maps are

- **bootparams**   Contains a list of diskless clients for a domain.
- **ethers.byaddr**   Contains a list of the Ethernet addresses of all hosts in the domain, and their hostnames.
- **ethers.byname**   Contains a list of the hostnames of all hosts in the domain, and their Ethernet addresses.
- **group.bygid**   Contains a list of groups that are indexed by group ID (gid).
- **group.byname**   Contains a list of groups that are indexed by group name.
- **hosts.byaddr**   Contains a list of the addresses of all hosts in the domain, and their hostnames.
- **hosts.byname**   Contains a list of the hostnames of all hosts in the domain, and their addresses.
- **mail.aliases**   Contains a list of mail aliases within the namespace, indexed by name.
- **mail.byaddr**   Contains a list of mail aliases within the namespace, indexed by address.
- **netgroup**   Contains netgroup information, indexed by group name.
- **netgroup.byhost**   Contains netgroup information, indexed by hostname.
- **netgroup.byuser**   Contains netgroup information, indexed by username.
- **netid.byname**   Contains the netname of hosts and users.
- **netmasks.byaddr**   Defines the netmasks defined in the domain namespace.
- **networks.byaddr**   Defines the networks in the domain namespace, sorted by address.
- **networks:byname**   Defines the networks in the domain namespace, sorted by name.
- **passwd.byname**   Defines the password database, sorted by username.
- **passwd.byuid**   Defines the password database, sorted by user ID.
- **protocols.byname**   Defines the network protocols used in the domain, sorted by name.

- **protocols.bynumber**   Defines the network protocols used in the domain, sorted by number.

- **publickey.byname**   Contains public keys for RPC.

- **rpc.bynumber**   Contains RPC details indexed by number.

- **services.byname**   Defines all available Internet services by name.

- **ypservers**   Contains a list of all NIS servers available.

As we can see, there are many similarities in name and function between the NIS maps and the */etc* system files they are intended to replace. However, both the */etc* files and NIS maps perform poorly under heavy loads when the number of hosts defined in a specific namespace exceeds the hundreds. In this case, it is much more appropriate to bypass NIS and */etc*, and move directly to an NIS+ installation where a single table (such as Ethers) replaces the dual lookup system used by NIS (such as ethers.byname and ethers.byaddr).

NIS+ Tables

Namespace information in NIS+ is stored in tables that are based around a centralized administration model, even though particular functions can be delegated to specific servers. NIS+ is similar to DNS because it arranges hosts and resources hierarchically into domains, it has built-in redundancy with master and slave servers, and it can store much more information about a network than just its hosts. However, since each host in a domain has many different characteristics and user details that must be recorded and stored centrally, updating these details can be time-consuming. In addition, issues like contention in the recording of user and host data often arise. However, NIS+ namespaces can be updated incrementally as changes occur, so that the entire database does not need to be updated immediately. Changes are entered into a master domain server and are then propagated through time to the rest of the domain. This process is governed by a time-to-live setting similar to that used for DNS. Commonly used tables include:

- **Hosts**   The Hosts table lists all of the hosts in a particular domain, matching their IP address with a hostname and an optional nickname. For example, if the host maria had an alias called bruny and had the IP address 192.34.54.3, the entry in the Hosts table would look like this:
  ```
  192.34.54.3  maria  bruny
  ```

- **Bootparams**   The Bootparams tables contains the necessary information to boot and configure any diskless clients in the domain, or provide JumpStart services. In addition to installation information, it can also contain entries for server-based dump and swap, as well as a root directory, for each client. For example, if there is a diskless client called pembroke and it is configured by the server downing, the Bootparams table would contain the following entry:

```
pembroke   root=downing:/export/root/pembroke \
swap=downing:/export/swap/pembroke \
dump=downing:/export/dump/Pembroke
```
Thus, each diskless client will have its own Bootparams entry and resources available on the server.

- **Passwd** The passwd table stores all the standard user information expected on Solaris hosts, including username, encrypted password, user ID, group ID, user's real name, their home directory, and their login shell. A typical entry may look like this:
```
pwatters:8dfjh4h.rj:101:10:Paul A.
Watters:/home/pwatters:/bin/tcsh:10905:-1:-1:-1:-1::0
```
In addition to the standard details, there is extra information that specifies how often a password must be changed, or how many days until it must next be changed. This significantly increases the functionality of NIS+ over standard Solaris password authorization.

- **Group** The Group table consists of a group name, group password, group ID number, and member list, and stores information about the three kinds of groups accessible by NIS+ clients: Solaris groups (such as "staff"), NIS+ groups, and netgroups.

- **Netgroups** The Netgroup table defines a group of hosts and users that are authorized to perform specific operations on one or more other hosts within a group. The table format contains entries that identify the name of the group as well as its members. For small organizations, everyone belongs to a single group, perhaps called everyone:
```
everyone   paulwatters.com
```

- **Mail Aliases** The Mail Aliases table replicates the functionality of the old */etc/aliases* file for the local mail transport agent (MTA), which is typically sendmail. An aliases table can store an alias for a specific user, or it can be used to construct a mailing list. For example, if the user bounty wanted to receive mail as endeavour, the Mail Aliases entry would look like this:
```
endeavour:bounty
```
However, if an advertising company had a local mailing list for newclients, these messages could be distributed nationally to local offices by using an alias like this:
```
newclients:layton,miami,oakton,sanfran
```

- **Timezone** Defines the local time zone, which will affect all system settings and applications, such as sendmail. For example, the entry,
```
hartog Australia/NSW
```
allows the host hartog to be identified as belonging to the New South Wales time zone in Australia. In addition, time zones can be specified on a host-by-host basis.

This allows systems that exist in different time zones to belong to the same domain. For example, a SPARC 20 system in Sydney can belong to the same domain as an Ultra 5 in San Francisco. The Timezone table consists of entries that relate a time zone to a specific host.

- **Networks**   Contains details of the local networks and their IP addresses. For example, if a Class B network 192.12.0.0 was known on the Internet as brunswick but had an alias essendon, it would be entered into the Networks table as
  ```
  brunswick    192.12.0.0 essendon
  ```

- **Netmasks**   The Netmasks table specifies the netmasks for all local Class A, Class B, and Class C networks. For example, if the network 192.12.34.0 has a netmask of 255.255.255.0, the entry would look like this:
  ```
  192.12.34.0   255.255.255.0
  ```

- **Ethers**   The ethers table contains entries that associate a hostname with a specific hardware address. For example, if the host freycinet has an Ethernet address of 00:ff:a1:b3:c4:6c, the ethers table entry would look like this:
  ```
  00:ff:a1:b3:c4:6c   freycinet
  ```

- **Services**   Contains a list of the IP services that are available, through both TCP and UDP. For example, the HTTP service provided by many web servers, such as Apache, is usually available through TCP port 80. This would be defined in the services table as
  ```
  http    80/tcp
  ```

- **Protocols**   Defines the protocols available to the network. A necessary entry for Internet use would be the internet protocol (IP),
  ```
  ip   0   IP
  ```
  which identifies ip as protocol number zero, which also has the alias IP.

- **RPC**   Defines the RPC programs available to the network. An entry consists of a name, a program number, and an alias. For example, rpcbind is also known as portmap, sunrpc, and the portmapper. The entry for rpcbind looks like this:
  ```
  rpcbind 100000   portmap   sunrpc   portmapper
  ```

- **Auto_Home**   This table is an automounter map that facilitates the mounting of a home directory for any user in the local domain. It is typically used to share a common home directory for a user who has accounts on multiple machines. It is also the cause of some consternation among administrators who attempt to create their user's home directories under */home*, but who don't use the automounter! The Auto_Home table has two columns: a common username that is consistent across all machines in a domain, and a physical location for the user's shared home directory. For example, the home directory of user pwatters might be located physically on the server winston, in the directory */u1/export/pwatters*. In this case, the entry in Auto_Home would be
  ```
  pwatters   winston:/u1/export/pwatters
  ```

- **Auto_Master** The auto_master maps the physical mount points of all of the NFS automounter maps in a particular domain to a name. For example, it can be used to map user home directories to */home* or */staff* using auto_home, with either of the following mount points, respectively:

```
/home  auto_home
/staff auto_home
```

NIS+ Configuration

In this section, we will walk through a configuration session with NIS+, focusing on using a script-based installation, which makes using NIS+ much easier. The main tasks involved in setting up NIS+ involve domain, master server, slave server, and user configuration. These tasks can only be performed once a network has been designed along the lines discussed in previous sections.

Whether or not you are setting up a root or a nonroot domain, the basic process is the same: after initializing a master server and creating the appropriate administrative groups, the NIS+ tables are populated, and clients and servers can then be installed. In the case of a root domain, these servers can then act as master servers for lower-level domains. In this section, we review the process of setting up a master server, populating the NIS+ tables, configuring clients and servers, and setting up other domains.

Setting Up a Root Domain

The first step in creating an NIS+ namespace is to create the root master server for the new domain. Continuing with the example for the **Panther.Edu.** domain, we create the root master server for **Panther.Edu** by using the `nisserver` command. The server will be known in DNS as **ns.panther.edu**. This command is used for most server configuration operations. In this case, we use the following command:

```
ns.panther.edu# nisserver -r -d Panther.Edu.
```

This creates a root domain master server without backward compatibility with NIS. In order to enable NIS support, you need to use this command:

```
ns.panther.edu# nisserver -Y -r -d Panther.Edu.
```

Populating Tables

After creating the master root server for the **Panther.Edu.** domain on **ns.panther.edu**, the next step is to populate the NIS+ tables. To achieve this, we need to use the `nispopulate` command:

```
ns.panther.edu# nispopulate -F -p /nis+files -d Panther.Edu.
```

This populates all the tables for the **Panther.Edu.** domain and stores the information on the master server. Again, if you need to support NIS, you need to include the -Y option:

```
ns.panther.edu# nispopulate -Y -F -p /nis+files -d Panther.Edu.
```

In order to administer the NIS+ namespace, we need to add administrators to the admin group. We can achieve this by using the `nisgrpadmin` command. In the **Panther.Edu.** example, imagine we have two administrators, michael and adonis. In order to add these administrators, use the following command:

```
ns.panther.edu# nisgrpadm -a admin.Panther.Edu. michael.Panther.Edu. adonis.Panther.Edu.
```

If you are satisfied with the configuration, it is best to checkpoint the configuration and transfer the domain configuration information to disk copies of the tables. This can be achieved by using the `nisping` command:

```
ns.panther.edu# nisping -C Panther.Edu.
```

Now that we have successfully created the root domain, we can create clients that will act as master and slave servers for the two subdomains in the **Panther.Edu.** root domain: **Graduate.Panther.Edu.** and **Undergrad.Panther.Edu.**

Setting Up Clients

To create master servers for the nonroot domain **Undergrad.Panther.Edu.**, we first need to set up the client within a domain by using the `nisclient` command. For the host **client1.panther.edu**, which will become the master server for the nonroot domain, the command is

```
client1.panther.edu# nisclient -i -d Panther.Edu. -h Ns.Panther.Edu
```

In order to actually set up clients within the domain, we can use also use the command `nisclient`, when executed from a nonprivileged user's shell:

```
client1.panther.edu% nisclient -u
```

If this was for the user maya, maya would now be able to access the namespace. Next, we need to turn the client host we have initialized into a nonroot domain master server.

Setting Up Servers

After the root server is created, most organizations will want to create new master servers for each of the subdomains that form the domain. For example, in **the Panther.Edu.** domain, there are two subdomains (**Undergrad.Panther.Edu.** and **Graduate.Panther.Edu.**). In this case, two clients must be created from the root master server and then converted to be servers. Initially, these are root server replicas, but their designation then changes to a nonroot master server for each of the subdomains. Replica servers for the subdomain master servers can also be enabled.

In the following example, we designate two client machines whose DNS names are **client1.panther.edu** and **client2.panther.edu** (recall that the master server for the root domain is **ns.panther.edu**). These two clients will actually become the master and slave servers for the subdomain **Undergrad.Panther.Edu.** To begin the server creation process, a similar approach is followed for the root domain as for the creation of the master server. First, we need to start the rpc daemon on the client machine that will become the master server for the nonroot domain:

```
client1.panther.edu# rpc.nisd
```

Next, we need to convert the client1 server to a root replica server in the first instance. This ensures that the subdomain inherits the appropriate settings from the top-level domain:

```
ns.panther.edu# nisserver -R -d Panther.Edu. -h client1.panther.edu
```

After replicating the settings from the root master server, the new nonroot master server is ready to begin serving the new subdomain. In this case, the root master server (**ns.panther.edu**) must delegate this authority explicitly to the master of **Undergrad.Panther.Edu.**, which is **client1.panther.edu**:

```
ns.panther.edu# nisserver -M -d Undergrad.Panther.Edu. -h client1.panther.edu
```

Following the same routine we outlined for the root master server, we must now populate the tables of the new subdomain server **client1.panther.edu**:

```
client1.panther.edu# nispopulate -F -p /nis+files -d Undergrad.Panther.Edu.
```

Finally, having created a new master server for the new subdomain, we have to create a replica server to ensure service reliability in the event of failure:

```
client1.panther.edu# nisclient -R -d Undergrad.Panther.Edu. -h client2.panther.edu
```

The process of installing a server for the **Undergrad.Panther.Edu.** subdomain would need to be adapted to create the other subdomain (**Graduate.Panther.Edu.**), but the general process of setting up a client, converting it to a replicate server, and populating the tables would be very similar to this domain. Now that we have investigated how to create subdomains, the next section covers the day-to-day usage of NIS+, and the most commonly used commands that access tables, groups, and objects in the namespace.

Using NIS+

The following examples provide some real-world cases for installing and running NIS/NIS+, using the name service switch. You might be wondering, in a mixed network information service environment comprising NIS maps, NIS+ tables, and DNS servers, how name services are selected to resolve particular requests. The answer provided in Solaris 2.x is the name service switch, whose configuration is specified in the file */etc/nsswitch.conf*. Non-NIS+ users who performed Solaris 1 to Solaris 9 upgrades know this as the pesky file that appeared to prevent DNS from working; however, the name service switch is very useful because it enables the administrator to configure which name service handles specific kinds of requests. It is also possible to specify more than one kind of service for every kind of request; thus, if a request fails on the default service, it can be applied to a different service. For example, to resolve hostnames, many sites will have at least some local hostnames statically hardwired into the */etc/hosts* database. In addition, many sites connected to the Internet will use the DNS for resolving hostnames. Where does this leave the relative sophistication of NIS+ namespaces, or the legacy of NIS maps? The answer is that files, DNS, NIS, and NIS+ can be configured to be selected as the first, second, third, and fourth choices as the default name service for resolving hosts in */etc/nsswitch.conf*. For example, the line

```
hosts: files dns nisplus nis
```

indicates that the */etc/hosts* file should be consulted first, and if a match cannot be found for a hostname, try DNS second. If DNS fails to resolve, then NIS+ should be tried. As a last resort, NIS map resolution can be attempted. This is a useful setup for a network that makes great use of the Internet, and relies less on NIS+ and NIS. Of course, many NIS+ advocates would suggest using the line

```
hosts: nisplus nis files dns
```

because this ensures that NIS+ is always selected over the */etc/hosts* database or DNS.

In addition to host resolution, *nsswitch.conf* also allows the configuration of 14 other options, which roughly correspond to the contents of the NIS+ tables and/or the NIS maps. A NIS+ oriented *nsswitch.conf* file would look like this:

```
passwd:       files nisplus
group:        files nisplus
hosts:        nisplus dns [NOTFOUND=return] files
services:     nisplus [NOTFOUND=return] files
networks:     nisplus [NOTFOUND=return] files
protocols:    nisplus [NOTFOUND=return] files
rpc:          nisplus [NOTFOUND=return] files
ethers:       nisplus [NOTFOUND=return] files
netmasks:     nisplus [NOTFOUND=return] files
bootparams:   nisplus [NOTFOUND=return] files
publickey:    nisplus
netgroup:     nisplus
automount: nisplus files
aliases: nisplus files
sendmailvars: nisplus files
```

In most of these situations NIS+ is consulted before the files, except for the password and group information. In addition, DNS is listed as a host resolution method after NIS+. However, it would also be possible to implement a bare-bones system that only relied on files for most resource information and DNS for name resolution:

```
passwd:       files
group:        files
hosts:        dns [NOTFOUND=return] files
networks:     files
protocols:    files
```

```
rpc:          files
ethers:       files
netmasks:     files
bootparams:   files
publickey:    files
netgroup:     files
automount:    files
aliases:      files
services:     files
sendmailvars:    files
```

Before any other services may be installed, NIS+ requires that the master server for the root domain be created. The master server will primarily be responsible for the management of the NIS+ namespace. For example, for the **Panther.Edu.** domain, the DNS server (**ns.panther.edu**) will also be used for NIS+. This means that the nisserver script can be executed on the DNS server system (**ns.panther.edu**) in order to initialize the master server for the root domain:

```
ns.panther.edu# nisserver -r -d Panther.Edu.
This script sets up this machine "ns" as an NIS+
root master server for domain Panther.Edu..

Domain name             : Panther.Edu.
NIS+ group              : admin.Panther.Edu.
NIS (YP) compatibility  : OFF
Security level          : 2=DES

Is this information correct? (type 'y' to accept, 'n' to change) y
This script will set up your machine as a root master server for
domain Panther.Edu. without NIS compatibility at security level 2.

Use "nisclient -r" to restore your current network service environment.

Do you want to continue? (type 'y' to continue, 'n' to exit this script)

setting up domain information "Panther.Edu." ...

setting up switch information ...

running nisinit ...
This machine is in the "Panther.Edu." NIS+ domain.
Setting up root server .

starting root server at security level 0 to create credentials...

running nissetup to create standard directories and tables ...

running nissetup to create standard directories and tables ...
org_dir.Panther.Edu. created
groups_dir.Panther.Edu. created
passwd.org_dir.Panther.Edu. created
group.org_dir.Panther.Edu. created
auto_master.org_dir.Panther.Edu. created
auto_home.org_dir.Panther.Edu. created
bootparams.org_dir.Panther.Edu. created
cred.org_dir.Panther.Edu. created
ethers.org_dir.Panther.Edu. created
```

```
hosts.org_dir.Panther.Edu. created
ipnodes.org_dir.Panther.Edu. created
mail_aliases.org_dir.Panther.Edu. created
sendmailvars.org_dir.Panther.Edu. created
netmasks.org_dir.Panther.Edu. created
netgroup.org_dir.Panther.Edu. created
networks.org_dir.Panther.Edu. created
protocols.org_dir.Panther.Edu. created
rpc.org_dir.Panther.Edu. created
services.org_dir.Panther.Edu. created
timezone.org_dir.Panther.Edu. created
client_info.org_dir.Panther.Edu. created
auth_attr.org_dir.Panther.Edu. created
exec_attr.org_dir.Panther.Edu. created
prof_attr.org_dir.Panther.Edu. created
user_attr.org_dir.Panther.Edu. created
audit_user.org_dir.Panther.Edu. created

adding credential for ns.Panther.Edu...
Enter login password:
creating NIS+ administration group: admin.Panther.Edu. ...
adding principal ns.Panther.Edu. to admin.Panther.Edu. ...

restarting NIS+ root master server at security level 2 ...
starting NIS+ password daemon ...
starting NIS+ cache manager ...

This system is now configured as a root server for domain Panther.Edu.
You can now populate the standard NIS+ tables by using the
nispopulate script or /usr/lib/nis/nisaddent command.
```

That's all that's required for NIS+ support. However, in order to enable support for NIS clients within the domain, you would need to use the following command instead:

```
ns.panther.edu# nisserver -Y -r -d Panther.Edu.
```

NIS+ Commands

Having reviewed the configuration of NIS+ and the main tables that are used to define a NIS+ domain, we now examine how to use NIS+ effectively to manage hosts and resources within a domain. As we have seen, many different objects can be managed and identified within a NIS+ domain, and there are several commands that are used to access them. In this section, we examine commands such as `nisdefault`, which displays the NIS+ settings for the local client system, and `nischmod`, which is used to set access rights on NIS+ objects. In addition, the `nisls` command is reviewed, which can be used for object lookups and queries. Finally, we will examine the `niscat` command, which displays the contents of table entries and can be used to examine NIS+ objects in detail.

nisdefaults

The current settings for a local client system and the active user can be displayed by using the `nisdefaults` command. The `nisdefaults` command is commonly used when attempting to troubleshoot an error, such as a user's credentials not being correctly authenticated from the passwd table. As an example, let's examine the nisdefaults for the host comorin when executed by the user walter:

```
comorin$ nisdefaults
Principal Name : walter.develop.panther.edu.
Domain Name    : develop.panther.edu.
Host Name      : comorin.develop.panther.edu.
Group Name     : develop
Access Rights  : ----rmcdr---r---
Time to live   : 11:00:00
Search Path    : develop.panther.edu. panther.edu.
```

The output of the `nisdefaults` command can be interpreted in the following way:

- The principal user is walter, who belongs to the NIS+ domain **develop.panther.edu**.
- The primary domain name is **develop.panther.edu**.
- The hostname of the local system is **comorin.develop.panther.edu**.
- The user walter's primary group is develop.
- The time-to-live setting is 11 hours.
- The client's access rights within the domain are stated.
- The search path starts with the current nonroot domain (**develop.panther.edu**), followed by the root domain (**panther.edu**).

The access rights stated for the user in this example are outlined in more detail in the following section.

nischmod

Every user has a set of access rights for accessing objects within the network. The notation for setting and accessing object permissions is very similar to that used for Solaris file systems. The following permissions may be set on any object, or may be defined as the default settings for a particular client:

- **c**   Sets create permission
- **d**   Sets delete permission
- **m**   Sets modify permission
- **r**   Sets read permission

This `nischmod` command is used to set permissions on objects within the domain. The following operands are used to specify access rights for specific classes of users:

- **a** All (all authenticated and unauthenticated users)
- **g** Group
- **n** Nobody (all unauthenticated users)
- **o** Object owner
- **w** World (all authenticated users)

There are two operators that can be used to set and remove permissions:

- **+** Sets a permission
- **-** Removes a permission

Some examples of how permissions strings are constructed will clarify how these operators and operands are combined for use with the `nichmod` command. The following command removes all modify (`m`) and create (`c`) access rights on the password table for all unauthenticated (`n`) users:

```
moorea# nischmod n-cm passwd.org_dir
```

Even unauthenticated users require read (`r`) access to the password table for authentication, which can be granted with the following command:

```
moorea# nischmod n+r passwd.org_dir
```

To grant modify and create access rights to the current user (in this case, root) and his or her primary group on the same table, we would use the following command:

```
moorea# nischmod og+cm passwd.org_dir
```

NIS+ permission strings are easy to remember, but hard to combine into single commands where some permissions are granted while others are removed—unlike the octal codes used to specify absolute permissions on Solaris file systems. However, it is possible to combine permissions strings by using a comma to separate individual strings. The following complex string is an example of how it is possible to set permissions within a single string, but equally shows how challenging it is to interpret:

```
moorea# nischmod o=rmcd,g=rmc,w=rm,n=r hosts.org_dir
```

This command grants the following permissions to four different categories of users:

- **owner** Read, modify, create, and delete
- **group** Read, modify, and create

- **world**   Read and modify

- **nobody**   Read only

nisls

The nisls command is used as a lookup and query command which can provide views on NIS+ directories and tables. For example, to view all of the NIS+ directories that have been populated within the local namespace, we can use the nisls command:

```
moorea# nisls
develop.panther.edu.:
org_dir
groups_dir
```

There are two directory object types listed here: the *org_dir*, which lists all of the tables that have been set up within the namespace, and the *groups_dir*, which stores details of all NIS+ groups. We can view a list of tables by using the nisls command once again on the *org_dir* directory:

```
moorea# nisls org_dir
org_dir.sales.panther.edu.:
auto_home
auto_master
bootparams
client_info
cred
ethers
group
hosts
mail_aliases
netgroup
netmasks
networks
passwd
protocols
rpc
sendmailvars
services
timezone
```

A large number of tables have been populated for this domain. The groups directory contains the admin group we created earlier, which lists all of the administrators, as well as several other groups that are based on distinct organizational units within the current domain:

```
moorea# nisls groups_dir
groups_dir.sales.panther.edu.:
admin
adverts
legal
media
```

niscat

The `niscat` command is used to retrieve the contents of objects within the domain, primarily the data contained within NIS+ tables. For example, all hosts listed within the domain can be listed by using the following command:

```
moorea$ niscat -h hosts.org_dir
moorea.panther.edu moorea 10.58.64.16
borabora.panther.edu borabora 10.58.64.17
tahiti.panther.edu tahiti 10.58.64.18
orana.panther.edu orana 10.58.64.19
```

Alternatively, we can use the `niscat` command to examine the contents of the passwd table:

```
moorea$ niscat passwd.org_dir
moppet:*LK*:1001:1:moppet:/staff/moppet:/bin/tcsh:10910:-1:-1:-1:-1::0
miki:*LK*:1002:1:miki:/staff/miki:/bin/bash:10920:-1:-1:-1:-1::0
maya:*LK*:1003:1:maya:/staff/maya:/bin/sh:10930:-1:-1:-1:-1::0
paul:*LK*:1004:1:paul:/staff/paul:/bin/csh:10940:-1:-1:-1:-1::0
```

Next, we can examine which groups these users belong to by using the `niscat` command once again:

```
moorea$ niscat group.org_dir
root::0:root
staff::1:moppet,miki,maya,paul
bin::2:root,bin,daemon
sys:*:3:root,bin,sys,adm
adm::4:root,adm,daemon
uucp::5:root,uucp
mail::6:root
```

All of the hosts that form part of the local domain can be examined based on their Ethernet address, which is extracted from the ethers table, as shown in the following example:

```
moorea$ niscat ethers.org_dir
1:4a:16:2f:13:b2 moorea.panther.edu.
1:02:1e:f4:61:2e borabora.panther.edu.
f4:61:2e:1:4a:16 tahiti.panther.edu.
2f:13:b2:1:02:1e orana.panther.edu.
```

In order to determine which services are offered within the local domain, we can also examine the services table:

```
moorea$ niscat services.org_dir
tcpmux tcpmux tcp 1
echo echo tcp 7
echo echo udp 7
discard discard tcp 9
discard sink tcp 9
discard null tcp 9
discard discard udp 9
discard sink udp 9
```

```
discard null udp 9
systat systat tcp 11
systat users tcp 11
daytime daytime tcp 13
daytime daytime udp 13
```

Every other table that is defined within the domain may be viewed by using the niscat command in this way.

EXAM TIP Read the man page for the niscat command and ensure that you can memorize all of the available options.

PART II

Summary

In this chapter, we have examined the installation and configuration of the Network Information Service. Using NIS is necessary in large network environments where changes must be made. Although NIS is a difficult and complex package to master, it is very flexible and can reduce administrator burden greatly in many situations.

Questions

1. What does the nisserver command do?

   A. Sets up a root NIS+ domain

   B. Sets up a nonroot NIS+ domain

   C. Starts the NIS+ daemon

   D. None of the above

2. What does the nispopulate command do?

   A. Adds clients to a NIS+ table

   B. Adds clients to a NIS map

   C. Extracts data from existing /etc files and inserts it into NIS+ tables

   D. None of the above

3. What does the nisgrpadm command do?

   A. Adds users to a NIS+ group

   B. Adds users to a NIS map

   C. Extracts data from existing /etc files and inserts it into NIS+ tables

   D. None of the above

4. What does the nisclient command do?

   A. Adds clients to a NIS+ table

   B. Adds clients to a NIS map

    C. Extracts data from existing /*etc* files and inserts it into NIS+ tables

    D. Assigns the role of replica server

5. What command would you use to create a NIS+ configuration checkpoint?

    A. `nisclient`

    B. `nisping`

    C. `nischeck`

    D. `nisgrpadm`

6. What does the Auto_Home table do?

    A. Enables some groups within a domain to access a single home directory.

    B. Enables all groups within a domain to access multiple home directories.

    C. Enables all users within a domain to access a single home directory.

    D. Enables all users to have an account on each system in the domain.

7. What does the Netgroups table do?

    A. Enables some groups within a domain to access a single home directory.

    B. Enables all groups within a domain to access multiple home directories.

    C. Enables all users within a domain to access a single home directory.

    D. Contains authorization lists that can be used to govern access to resources within a network.

8. Which are valid object permissions?

    A. c, d, m, r

    B. x, d, m r

    C. r, w, x, S

    D. r, w, x, C

9. What operands are used to specify access rights for specific classes of users?

    A. a, d, S, x

    B. S, g, m, x

    C. A, g, x, S

    D. a, g, n, o, w

10. What does the `niscat` command do?

    A. It's used to retrieve the contents of objects within the domain

    B. It's used to display user lists

    C. It's used to grant/deny access to network resources

    D. It's used to display lists of current access permissions

Answers

1. **A.** The `nisserver` command sets up a root NIS+ domain.

2. **C.** The `nispopulate` command extracts data from existing /*etc* files and inserts it into NIS+ tables.

3. **A.** The `nisgrpadm` command adds users to a NIS+ group.

4. **D.** The `nisclient` command assigns the role of replica server.

5. **B.** The `nisping` command is used to create a NIS+ configuration checkpoint.

6. **C.** The Auto-Home table enables all users within a domain to access a single home directory.

7. **D.** The Netgroups table contains authorization lists that can be used to govern access to resources.

8. **A.** Valid object permissions are c, d, m, and r.

9. **D.** The operands a, g, n, o, and w are used to specify access rights for specific classes of users.

10. **A.** The `niscat` command is used to retrieve the contents of objects within the domain.

Role-Based Access Control

In this chapter, you will

- Learn how to configure Role-Based Access Control (RBAC)
- Discover the benefits of using RBAC over sudo
- Learn how to use commands like smexec to set up roles and profiles

One of the most frustrating aspects of setting a strict security policy is that some actions require a form of access privilege that must occasionally be undertaken by nonprivileged users. Although you don't want normal users to have all of root's privileges for obvious reasons, there are occasions when normal users could conveniently and securely perform certain actions without jeopardizing system integrity. In other words, a number of specific roles require superuser privileges, which you may need to grant to users who should not have complete root access.

In Solaris 1.x, the solution to this problem was to prevent normal users from having any kind of privileged access. Normal users, for example, could not eject a floppy disk or CD-ROM drive without root access! However, this draconian solution just led to the root password being shared around to every user who needed to eject a floppy (not very security conscious!). Alternatively, applications can be compiled as setuid root, allowing an unprivileged user to execute specific commands as the root user, without requiring a password. This approach is fine, as long as the scope of the application is restricted. For example, any application that allows the effective user to spawn a shell is not suited to be setuid root, because an unprivileged user could then spawn a root shell without a password. Relying on a single superuser to protect a system's resources is one of the great strengths and weaknesses of UNIX and UNIX-like systems.

More often than not, operations on a system can be classified as being associated with a specific role. For example, a network administrator who is responsible for backups really needs only have write access to tape devices, but not to any local file systems—other than for spooling. Thus, a backup "role" can have its scope limited in a way that doesn't overlap with a printer administrator, who needs to be able to manage print jobs and write to spooling areas, while the print administrator must also be denied write access to tape drives. Identifying tasks and roles is the first step in ensuring that privileges are granted only to those who need them.

Three approaches are commonly used to provide "role-based" access to Solaris systems: installing Trusted Solaris, installing sudo, or using the Role-Based Access Control

(RBAC) features built into Solaris. Trusted Solaris requires a new operating system in stallation to take advantage of its role-based features, which build on top of RBAC by introducing security labels ranging from "top secret" to "unclassified." In contrast, sudo is a small utility that you can download and install, providing a simple role-based access system. However, RBAC provides a system for role-based access that is integrated into the operating system, providing a superior solution to sudo.

 EXAM TIP The sudo command will not be directly examined, but it has much in common with RBAC, which will be discussed.

sudo

sudo allows privileged roles to be assigned to various users by maintaining a database of privileges mapped to usernames. These privileges are identified by sets of different commands listed in the database. In order to access a privileged item, qualified users simply need to reenter their own passwords (not the root password) after the command name has been entered on the command line. The sudo command permits a user to format disks, for instance, but have no other root privileges.

One of the most useful features of sudo is its logging. By maintaining a log file of all operations performed using the sudo facility, system administrators can audit the log file and trace any actions that may have had unintended consequences. This is something that the normal su facility does not provide. Alternatively, patterns of malicious behavior can also be identified: sudo logs all successful and unsuccessful attempts to perform privileged actions. This can be very important in a security context, because brute force attacks against weak passwords of unprivileged accounts might now be able to access some superuser functions through sudo. Thus, if the user nobody is given access via sudo to format disks, and the password for the user nobody is guessed, an intruder would be able to format disks on the system without requiring the root password. In addition, because the effective user ID of a user executing a privileged application through sudo is set to zero (that is, the superuser), then such applications should not allow shells to be spawned.

All of the roles in sudo are independent. Thus, granting one or more roles to one user and one or more roles to another is possible. User roles can be shared, or they may be completely separate. For example, the user harry may have the privilege to format disks, and the user butler may have the privilege to both format disks and write to tape drives. To access these privileges, harry and butler do not need to know the root password.

The sudo facility is configured by the file */etc/sudoers*. This file contains a list of all users who have access to the sudo facility and defines their privileges. A typical entry in */etc/sudoers* looks like this:

```
jdoe    ALL=(ALL) ALL
```

This entry gives the user jdoe access to all applications as the superuser. For the user jdoe to run commands as the superuser, he or she simply needs to prefix the command string with sudo. Thus, to execute the `format` command as root, jdoe would enter the following command string:

```
$ sudo format
```

The following output will be displayed:

```
We trust you have received the usual lecture from the local System
Administrator. It usually boils down to these two things:

        #1) Respect the privacy of others.
        #2) Think before you type.

Password:
```

If jdoe correctly types in his or her normal password, the `format` command will execute with root privileges. If jdoe incorrectly types the password up to three times, the following messages appear after each prompt:

```
Take a stress pill and think things over.
Password:
You silly, twisted boy you.
Password:
He has fallen in the water!
Password not entered correctly
```

At this point, an alert is e-mailed to the superuser, informing him or her of the potential security breach—repeated login attempts of this kind may signal a password-guessing attack by a rogue user. Equally, it could indicate that someone is incorrectly typing his or her password (perhaps the CAPS LOCK key is on) or that he or she is entering the root password rather than his or her own.

In order to list all of the privileges currently allowed for a user, that user simply needs to run sudo with the -1 option:

```
$ sudo -1
You may run the following commands on this host:
    (ALL) ALL
```

In addition to granting full superuser access, sudo can more usefully delegate authority to specific individuals. For example, you can create command aliases that correspond to the limited set of commands that sudo-ers can execute:

```
Cmnd_Alias  TCPD=/usr/sbin/tcpd
```

In this case, you are giving users control over the TCP daemon. You can also specify a group of users other than ALL, which share the ability to execute different classes of commands:

```
User_Alias  DEVELOPERS=pwatters,tgibbs
User_Alias  ADMINS=maya,natashia
```

Thus, the DEVELOPERS group can be assigned access to specific facilities that are not available to ADMINS. Putting it all together, you can create complex user specifications like this:

```
ADMINS ALL=(ALL) NOPASSWD: ALL
DEVELOPERS     ALL=TCPD
```

This specification allows admins to perform operations without a password, while giving developers privileges to operate on the TCP daemon. Notice that we've included administrators in the user specification, even though these users probably know the root password. This is because sudo leaves an audit trail for every command executed, meaning that you can trace actions to a specific user account. This makes it easy to find out which individual is responsible for system problems. Of course, these administrators can just use the su facility to bypass the sudo facility, if they know the root password. This is the main drawback of using sudo on Solaris—it is not integrated into the operating system; rather, it is just an application.

RBAC

Role-Based Access Control (RBAC) was first introduced in Solaris 8 as a means of defining roles for managing a specific task or set of tasks, based on a set of administrator-defined profiles. Although the RBAC implementation supplied with Solaris is a Sun-specific product, it is based on a standard developed by NIST (see **http://csrc.nist.gov/rbac/** for more information). Broadly defined, access control extends beyond the notion of administrative access. It can be defined as the ability to create, read, update, and delete data from a system. Standard file system permissions are based on this principle: various users and groups have access permissions to data stored in files based on a permission string that is associated with every file on the file system. However, although file access can be easily demarcated along organizational lines, deciding who should and who should not have administrative access to execute applications can be a more complex issue. What if a secretary needs to have root access to a system to add or delete users as they join an organization? Data entry of this kind seems like a reasonable task for a secretary, but it is usually assigned to system administrators because it requires root access. RBAC allows tasks like these to be separated from other tasks that do require a high level of technical knowledge, such as managing metadevices.

Roles

The first stage of implementing RBAC is to define roles, which are then assigned to individual users. Access rights to various resources can then be associated with a specific role name. As with any organization, the change to roles and the users associated with roles is inevitable, so the process for reflecting these changes in the list of roles and users needs to be as easy to implement as possible. In addition, individual tasks are not always easy to associate with a single role: indeed, in a large organization, some tasks will be performed by a number of different employees.

CAUTION It's also possible to assign specific authorizations to specific users—bypassing roles—but this defeats the whole "role-based" purpose of RBAC and is not recommended.

One way of dealing with task overlap is to introduce the notion of hierarchies. Profiles and authorizations at the bottom of a conceptual hierarchy are "inherited" by the assignment of a role at a higher level. For example, a role defined as "backup maintainer" involves running ufsdump, which in turn requires write access to the tape device. Thus, the backup role inherently requires access to lower level profiles for which new roles do not need to be separately defined. Another role, such as "device manager," may also require write access to the tape device, through the `tapes` command. Again, no separate role is required to be created for those tasks that form part of the role by inference. However, although Solaris RBAC does support hierarchies of profiles and authorizations, it does not support hierarchies of roles. When a user assumes a role, the effect is all or nothing: No inheritance of roles is allowed.

By default, Solaris 9 supports three different system management roles:

- **A Primary Administrator (PA)** Assigns rights to other users and is responsible for security.
- **A System Administrator (SA)** Responsible for day-to-day administration that is not security-related.
- **An Operator** Performs backups and device maintenance.

Figure 28-1 shows the hierarchy of rights associated with the different roles. The distinction between PA and SA will depend on the local security policy. For example, whereas the default PA role permits both adding users and changing passwords, the default SA role does not permit password modifications. However, for many sites, denying an SA access to passwords would be impractical. One of the great benefits of RBAC is that the rights granted to different profiles can be easily modified and customized to suit local requirements. Parallels can be drawn with Trusted Solaris and the assignment of tasks with different levels of authority to completely different roles.

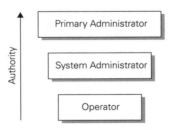

Figure 28-1 Hierarchy of rights associated with the different roles

Profiles

Associated with the concept of overlapping roles are the notions of authority and operational responsibility. Two individuals may carry out operations using similar roles, but for entirely different purposes. For example, a clerk in a supermarket may be allowed to enter cash transactions into the cash register, but only a supervisor can void transactions already entered. Conversely, a supervisor cannot enter cash transactions because the organizational requirements mandate a separation of supervisory and procedural roles, even though both operate on the same set of data and devices. Clearly, these roles and their associated operations must be defined "offline" before being implemented using the Solaris RBAC facility.

A profile is a specific command or set of commands for which an authorization can be granted. These authorizations are linked together to form a role, which is in turn associated with a single user or a number of different users, as shown in Figure 28-2. Profiles can be executed several ways:

- The new `pfexec` command can be used to execute a single command contained in a profile.

- Commands in profiles can be executed through new, restricted versions of the standard shells, such as pfsh (profile Bourne shell) and pfcsh (profile C shell).

A new user account for each role can be created, with its own home directory and password. To execute commands contained in a profile, users who have access to the role can just su to the new account—they are not allowed to log in directly. Note that if two users su to the same role account, they will both be operating on the same files and could potentially overwrite each other's data. The same is true for the normal root account. However, one difference between using su to access a role and using su to access a normal account is auditing—all of the operations carried out when using su to access a role are logged with the user's original UID. Thus, the operations of individual users who access roles can be logged (and audited) distinctively.

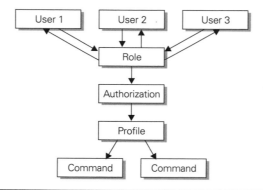

Figure 28-2   Profiles and authorizations are associated with roles that are granted to individual users.

Authorizations

Let's look more closely at authorizations before examining how they are assigned to different roles. An authorization is a privilege that is granted to a role to allow operations to be performed, and that is defined in the file */etc/security/auth_attr*. Some applications allow RBAC authorizations to be checked before allowing an action to be performed, including the device management commands (for example, `allocate` and `deallocate`), as well as the batch processing commands (for example, `at`, `crontab`). Authorizations have a form similar to Internet domain names: reading from left to right, the company name is followed by more specific package and function information. For example, *net.cassowary.** is an authorization that pertains to any function supplied by the vendor *cassowary.net*. By default, all Solaris packages are identified by the prefix "solaris." Thus, the authorization for changing passwords is identified as *solaris.admin.usermgr.pswd* rather than the longer *com.sun.solaris.admin.usermgr.pswd*. Many authorizations are fine-grained, allowing read access but not write access, and vice versa. For example, a Primary Administrator may have the *solaris.admin.usermgr.read* and *solaris.admin.usermgr.write* authorizations that allow read and write access to user configuration files respectively. However, an SA may only be granted the *solaris.admin .usermgr.read* authorization but not the *solaris.admin.usermgr.write* authorization, effectively preventing him or her from changing the contents of user configuration files even if they have read access to the same files. The following examples show some of the common *solaris.admin* authorizations currently defined:

```
solaris.admin.fsmgr.::::Mounts and Shares::
solaris.admin.fsmgr.read:::View Mounts and Shares::help=AuthFsmgrRead.html
solaris.admin.fsmgr.write:::Mount and Share Files::help=AuthFsmgrWrite.html
solaris.admin.logsvc.::::Log Viewer::
solaris.admin.logsvc.purge:::Remove Log Files::help=AuthLogsvcPurge.html
solaris.admin.logsvc.read:::View Log Files::help=AuthLogsvcRead.html
solaris.admin.logsvc.write:::Manage Log Settings::help=AuthLogsvcWrite.html
solaris.admin.serialmgr.::::Serial Port Manager::
solaris.admin.usermgr.::::User Accounts::
solaris.admin.usermgr.pswd:::Change Password::help=AuthUserMgrPswd.html
solaris.admin.usermgr.read:::View Users and Roles::
  help=AuthUsermgrRead.html
solaris.admin.usermgr.write:::Manage Users::help=AuthUsermgrWrite.html
```

We can see that several authorizations have been defined for *solaris.admin*, including file system management (fsmgr), logging system management (logsvc), port management (serialmgr), and user management (userxmgr). The corresponding help files are also listed.

An important aspect of authorizations is the capability to transfer permissions to other users by using the `grant` keyword. Once `grant` is attached to the end of an authorization string, it enables the delegation of authorizations to other users. For example, the *solaris.admin.usermgr.grant* authorization, in conjunction with *solaris.admin.usermgr.pswd*, allows password changing to be performed by a delegated user.

How do roles, profiles, and authorizations fit together? Figure 28-3 attempts to show the flow of data from the definition of authorizations and command definition through to the association of authorizations to specific profiles, which are in turn utilized by users

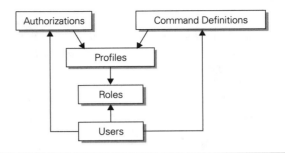

Figure 28-3   Integrating roles, profiles, and authorizations

who have been assigned various roles. The sense in which RBAC abstracts users from directly using commands and authorizations is shown by the dotted lines in the diagram. In this diagram, it is easy to see how central roles are in systems where profiles for different tasks are well defined.

RBAC Operations

Common operations performed in the context of RBAC include setting up profiles and defining roles. The following commands are commonly used.

- **smexec**   Creates, reads, updates, and deletes rows in the *exec_attr* database.
- **smmultiuser**   Performs batch functions.
- **smuser**   Performs operations on user accounts.
- **smprofile**   Creates, reads, updates, and deletes profiles in the *prof_attr* database.
- **smrole**   Creates, reads, updates, and deletes role accounts.
- **rolemod**   Modifies roles.
- **roledel**   Deletes roles.
- **roleadd**   Adds roles.

The *prof_attr* database contains all of the profile definitions for the system. For example, profiles might be created for the Primary Administrator, System Administrator, Operator, Basic Solaris User, and Printer Manager. A special profile is the All Rights profile, which is associated with all commands that have no security restrictions enforced on their use. This is the default profile, which covers all commands not designated as requiring specific authorization. In contrast, the Primary Administrator is granted explicit rights over all security-related commands and operations, as defined by the *solaris.** authorization. The Primary Administrator can then delegate tasks to other users where appropriate if the *solaris.grant* authorization is granted. The scope of the Primary Administrator can be limited if this role is considered too close in power to the superuser.

The System Administrator, in contrast, has a much more limited role. Specific authorizations are granted to the System Administrator, rather than using wildcards to allow complete access. Typical commands defined in this profile allow auditing and accounting, printer administration, batch processing, device installation and configuration, file system repairs, e-mail administration, name and directory service configuration, process administration, and setting up new software. The Operator profile has very few privileges at all: Only printer and backup administration are permitted. Note that the Operator is not allowed to restore data; this privilege is reserved for the System Administrator or Primary Administrator. As an alternative to the Operator, the Printer Manager profile allows only printer administration tasks to be performed. Typical authorizations that are permitted include *solaris.admin.printer.delete*, *solaris.admin.printer.modify*, and *solaris.admin.printer.read*, encompassing commands like `lpsched`, `lpstat`, and `lpq`.

A slightly different approach is taken for the definition of the Basic Solaris User: This policy is contained within the *policy.conf* file. Typical authorizations permitted for the Basic Solaris User include the following:

solaris.admin.dcmgr.read	Solaris.admin.diskmgr.read	solaris.admin.fsmgr.read
solaris.admin.logsvc.read	Solaris.admin.printer.read	solaris.admin.procmgr.user
solaris.admin.prodreg.read	Solaris.admin.serialmgr.read	solaris.admin.usermgr.read
solaris.compsys.read	Solaris.jobs.user	solaris.profmgr.read

The following databases play a key role in RBAC's operations.

user_attr

The *user_attr* file is the RBAC user database. It contains a single entry by default, which defines the security information for every user that has access to RBAC. The following entry gives the root user permission to do everything on the system:

```
root::::type=normal;auths=solaris.*,solaris.grant;profiles=All
```

Clearly, if the power of root was to be reduced, *solaris.** would need to be replaced with something more restricted in scope, such as *solaris.admin.**.

auth_attr

The *auth_attr* file is the RBAC authorization database. It contains lists of all authorizations defined on the system. Some sample entries are shown here:

```
solaris.admin.fsmgr.::::Mounts and Shares::
solaris.admin.fsmgr.read:::View Mounts and Shares::help=AuthFsmgrRead.html
solaris.admin.fsmgr.write:::Mount and Share Files::help=AuthFsmgrWrite.html
solaris.admin.logsvc.::::Log Viewer::
solaris.admin.logsvc.purge:::Remove Log Files::help=AuthLogsvcPurge.html
solaris.admin.logsvc.read:::View Log Files::help=AuthLogsvcRead.html
solaris.admin.logsvc.write:::Manage Log Settings::help=AuthLogsvcWrite.html
solaris.admin.serialmgr.::::Serial Port Manager::
```

```
solaris.admin.usermgr.:::User Accounts::
solaris.admin.usermgr.pswd:::Change Password::help=AuthUserMgrPswd.html
solaris.admin.usermgr.read:::View Users and Roles::
help=AuthUsermgrRead.html
solaris.admin.usermgr.write:::Manage Users::help=AuthUsermgrWrite.html
```

prof_attr

The *prof_attr* file is the RBAC profile database. Sample *prof_attr* entries for the Basic Solaris User, User Management, and User Security are shown here:

```
Basic Solaris User:::Automatically assigned rights:
auths=solaris.profmgr.read,solaris.jobs.users,
solaris.admin.usermgr.read,solaris.admin.logsvc.read,
solaris.admin.fsmgr.read,solaris.admin.serialmgr.read,
solaris.admin.diskmgr.read,solaris.admin.procmgr.user,
solaris.compsys.read,solaris.admin.printer.read,
solaris.admin.prodreg.read,solaris.admin.dcmgr.read;
profiles=All;help=RtDefault.html
User Management:::Manage users, groups, home directory:
auths=profmgr.read,solaris.admin.usermgr.write,
solaris.admin.usermgr.read;help=RtUserMngmnt.html
User Security:::Manage passwords, clearances:
auths=solaris.role.*,solaris.profmgr.*,solaris.admin.usermgr.*;
help=RtUserSecurity.html
```

exec_attr

The *exec_attr* file is the RBAC command database. It contains lists of commands associated with a specific profile. For example, a set of entries for the User Manager profile would look like this:

```
User Management:suser:cmd:::/etc/init.d/utmpd:uid=0;gid=sys
User Management:suser:cmd:::/usr/sbin/grpck:euid=0
User Management:suser:cmd:::/usr/sbin/pwck:euid=0
```

RBAC Commands

The following RBAC commands allow operations to be performed on the different databases that are used with RBAC.

smexec

The smexec command is used to create, update, and delete rows in the *exec_attr* database. One of three options must be passed to the command upon execution: add, which adds an entry; delete, which deletes an entry; or modify, which updates an entry. In order to use smexec, the user must have the *solaris.profmgr.execattr.write* authorization. There are two sets of parameters that can be passed to smexec (depending on which option has been selected): authorization parameters and specific parameters for each option.

The authorization parameters are common to each option, and they specify the following characteristics:

-domain	The domain to be administered
-hostname:port	The hostname and port on which operations are to be performed (default port is 898)
-rolepassword	The password for role authentication
-password	The password for the user rather than the role
-rolename	The name of the role
-username	The name of the user

For adding entries using smexec add, the following parameters can be passed on the command line:

-c	Specifies the full path to the new command name to be added
-g	Specifies the effective GID for executing the new command
-G	Specifies the actual GID for executing the new command
-n	Specifies the profile name with which the command is associated
-t cmd	Specifies that the operation is a command
-u	Specifies the effective UID for executing the new command
-U	Specifies the actual UID for executing the new command

An example smexec add operation looks like this:

```
# smexec add -hostname localhost -password xyz123 -username root -- -n
"Print Manager" -t cmd -c /usr/sbin/lpsched -u 0 -g 0
```

This entry adds the capability to start the printing service to the Printer Manager profile, with the effective UID and GID of 0 (that is, root).

For removing entries using smexec delete, the following parameters can be passed on the command line:

-c	Specifies the full path to the command name to be deleted
-n	Specifies the profile name with which the command is currently associated
-t cmd	Specifies that the operation is a command

To remove the entry for lpsched, you would use the following command:

```
# smexec delete -hostname localhost -password xyz123 -username root -- -n
"Print Manager" -t cmd -c /usr/sbin/lpsched
```

For changing entries using smexec modify, the following parameters can be passed on the command line:

-c	Specifies the full path to the command name to be modified.
-g	Specifies the modified effective GID for executing the new command.
-G	Specifies the modified actual GID for executing the new command.

`-n`	Specifies the modified profile name with which the command is associated.
`-t cmd`	Specifies that the operation is a command.
`-u`	Specifies the modified effective UID for executing the new command.
`-U`	Specifies the modified actual UID for executing the new command.

An example `smexec modify` operation looks like this:

```
# smexec modify -hostname localhost -password xyz123 -username root -- -n
"Print Manager" -t cmd -c /usr/some/new/path/lpsched -u 0 -g 0
```

This entry modifies the command to start the printing service for the Printer Manager profile, from the path */usr/sbin/lpsched* to */usr/some/new/path/lpsched*.

smmultiuser

The `smmultiuser` command is used to perform batch functions, such as adding or deleting a large number of users. This is particularly useful when a file already exists that specifies all of the required user data. For instance, a backup system may need a setup that is similar to a current production system. Rather than just copying the file systems directly, all of the operations associated with new account creation can be performed, such as creating home directories. In addition, the file that specifies the user data can be updated to include pathname changes. For example, if the original system's home directories were exported using NFS, they could be mounted under the */export* mount point on the new system, and the data in the user specification file could be updated accordingly before being processed. Or, if mount points changed at a later time, user data on the system could be modified by using the `smmultiuser` command as well.

Like `smexec`, `smmultiuser` has three options that must be passed to the command upon execution: `add`, which adds multiple user entries; `delete`, which deletes one or more user entries; and `modify`, which modifies a set of existing entries. In order to use `smmultiuser` to change passwords, the user must have the *solaris.admin.usermgr.pswd authorization*. Two sets of parameters—authorization parameters and operation parameters—can be passed to `smmultiuser`, depending on which option has been selected.

The authorization parameters are common to each option, and they specify the following characteristics:

`-domain`	The domain to be administered
`-hostname:port`	The hostname and port on which operations are to be performed (default port is 898)
`-password`	The password for the user rather than the role
`-rolename`	The name of the role
`-rolepassword`	The password for role authentication
`-trust`	Required when operating in batch mode
`-username`	The name of the user

For add, delete, and modify operations using `smmultiuser`, the following parameters can be passed on the command line:

-i	Specifies the input file to be read. This contains data for all entries to be added, modified, or deleted.
-L	Specifies the name of the log file that records whether individual operations in the batch job were a success or failure.

In the following example, a set of records is read in from */home/paul/newaccounts.txt* and added to the system:

```
# smmultiuser add -hostname localhost -p xyz123 -username root -- -I
/home/paul/newaccounts.txt
```

smuser

The `smuser` command is used to perform operations on user accounts, whether the data is retrieved from the local user databases or from NIS/NIS+. It is similar to `smmultiuser`; however, it is generally used only to add single users, rather than a set of users in batch mode. In addition to adding, deleting, and modifying user records, existing user data can be retrieved and listed. One of four options must be passed to the command upon execution: `add`, which adds an entry; `delete`, which deletes an entry; `list`, which lists all existing entries; or `modify`, which updates an entry. In order to use `smuser add`, `delete`, or `modify`, the user must have the *solaris.profmgr.execattr.write* authorization. However, only the *solaris.admin.usermgr.write* authorization is required to list entries.

There are two sets of parameters that can be passed to `smuser` (depending on which option has been selected): authorization parameters and specific parameters for each option. The authorization parameters are common to each option, and they specify the following characteristics:

-domain	The domain to be administered. This can be the local databases (file), NIS (nis), NIS+ (nisplus), DNS (dns), or LDAP (ldap). To administer the host *foxtrot.cassowary.net* using LDAP, you would specify the domain as *ldap://foxtrot/cassowary.net*.
-hostname:port	The hostname and port on which operations are to be performed. The default port is **898**.
-password	The password for the user rather than the role.
-rolename	The name of the role.
-rolepassword	The password for role authentication.
-username	The name of the user.

For adding entries using `smuser add`, the parameters are similar to those discussed for adding users using `useradd`. The following parameters can be passed on the command line:

-c	Specifies an account description, such as "Joe Bloggs."
-d	Specifies the user's home directory.
-e	Specifies the account expiration date.

−f	Specifies a limit on the number of inactive days before an account is expired.
−F	Specifies a full name for the account, which must not be used by another account within the domain.
−g	Specifies the account GID.
−n	Specifies the account name.
−p	Specifies the account password.
−s	Specifies the default shell.
−u	Specifies the account UID.

An example `smuser add` command is shown here:

```
# smuser add -H localhost -p xyz123 -u root -- -F "Paul Watters"
-n walrus -c "Paul A Watters Director" -P jimmy123 -g 10 -u 1025
```

This command adds an account called walrus to the system for Paul Watters, with the password jimmy123. The UID for the account is 1025, and the GID is 10.

For removing entries using `smuser delete`, only the –n parameter (specifying the account name) needs to be passed on the command line. The following command would remove the account for walrus on the localhost:

```
# smuser delete -H localhost -p xyz123 -u root -- -n walrus
```

The `smuser list` command can display a list of users without any parameters, by using a command like this:

```
# smuser list -H localhost -p xyz123 -u root --
```

For modifying entries using `smuser modify`, the same parameters can be passed on the command line as for `smuser add`, with any new supplied values resulting in the appropriate fields being updated. For example, to modify the default shell for a user to the Korn shell, the following command would be used:

```
# smuser update -H localhost -p xyz123 -u root -- -n walrus -s /bin/ksh
```

smprofile

The `smprofile` command is used to create, list, update, and delete profiles in the *prof_attr* database, using `smprofile add`, `smprofile list`, `smprofile modify`, and `smprofile delete`, respectively. The authorization arguments are similar to those used for `smuser` and `smexec`. For adding entries using `smprofile add`, the following parameters can be passed on the command line:

−a	Adds a single authorization or a set of authorizations.
−d	Adds a description for the new profile.
−m	Specifies the path to the HTML help file associated with the profile.
−n	Specifies a name for the profile.

An example `smprofile add` command is shown here:

```
# smprofile add -H localhost -p xyz123 -u root -- -n "Password Manager" \
  -d "Change user passwords" -a solaris.admin.usermgr.pswd \
  -m PasswordManager.html
```

This command adds a profile for the Password Manager who has the authorization *solaris.admin.usermgr.pswd* to change passwords.

For listing entries using `smprofile list`, only the –n parameter cannot be passed on the command line, which optionally specifies the name of the profile to list. An example `smprofile list` command is shown here:

```
# smprofile list -H localhost -p xyz123 -u root --
```

For modifying entries using `smprofile modify`, the same parameters can be passed on the command line as for `smprofile add`. Any parameters specified will result in the corresponding field being updated. An example `smprofile modify` command is shown here:

```
# smprofile modify -H localhost -p xyz123 -u root -- \
  -n "Password Manager" -d "Modify user passwords"
```

This example changes the description for the profile Password Manager.

For deleting entries using `smprofile delete`, only the –n parameter can be passed on the command line, which specifies the name of the profile to delete. An example `smprofile delete` command is shown here:

```
# smprofile delete -H localhost -p xyz123 -u root -- \
  -n "Password Manager"
```

smrole

The `smrole` command is used to perform operations on role accounts. It is generally used to add single roles rather than a set of roles in batch mode. In addition to adding, deleting, and modifying role account records, existing role data can be retrieved and listed. One of four options must be passed to the command upon execution: `add`, which adds an entry; `delete`, which deletes an entry; `list`, which lists all existing entries; or `modify`, which updates an entry. In order to use `smrole add`, `delete`, or `modify`, the user must have the *solaris.role.write* authorization. However, only the *solaris.admin.usermgr.read* authorization is required to list entries. There are two sets of parameters that can be passed to `smrole` (depending on which option has been selected): authorization parameters and specific parameters for each option. The authorization parameters are similar to those used for `smuser`.

For adding entries using `smrole add`, the following parameters can be passed on the command line:

-c	Specifies a role account description, such as "System Manager."
-d	Specifies the role account's home directory.

−G	Specifies any secondary GIDs for the role account, because the primary GID is always *sysadmin*.
−n	Specifies the role name.
−P	Specifies the account password.
−s	Specifies the default shell.
−u	Specifies the account UID.

An example `smrole add` command is shown here:

```
# smrole add -H localhost -p xyz123 -u root -- -F "System Manager" \
  -n bofh -P abc123 -G 10 -u 666
```

This command adds an account called bofh to the system for System Manager, with the password jimmy123. The UID for the account is 666, and the secondary GID is 10.

For removing entries using `smrole delete`, only the −n parameter, specifying the role account name, needs to be passed on the command line. The following command would remove the account for bofh on the localhost:

```
# smrole delete -H localhost -p xyz123 -u root -- -n bofh
```

The `smrole list` command can display a list of roles without any parameters, by using a command like this:

```
# smrole list -H localhost -p xyz123 -u root --
```

For modifying entries using `smrole modify`, the same parameters can be passed on the command line as for `smrole add`, with any new supplied values resulting in the appropriate fields being updated. For example, to modify the default shell for a role to the Bourne shell, the following command would be used:

```
# smrole update -H localhost -p xyz123 -u root -- -n walrus -s /bin/sh
```

Summary

Role-Based Access Control is slowly changing Solaris away from a monolithic administrative model where power is concentrated around a single superuser, to a more distributed set of delegated authorities to execute discrete tasks. While this removes the risk inherent in a centralized model, it also makes effectively managing multiple administrators difficult.

Questions

1. What is the purpose of sudo?

   A. Upgrade the su command.

   B. Revert the effects of su.

    C. Allow privileged roles to be assigned to users.

    D. Allow RBAC databases to be updated.

2. What is the main configuration file for sudo?

    A. */etc/sudo*

    B. */etc/sudoers*

    C. */var/sudo*

    D. */etc/susers*

3. Which of the following is *not* an RBAC role?

    A. Primary Administrator

    B. System Administrator

    C. Operator

    D. Security Administrator

4. What is an RBAC profile?

    A. Definitions stored in each user's *.profile* file

    B. A command for which an authorization can be granted

    C. A role for which an authorization can be granted

    D. A user who is allowed to execute RBAC commands

5. What is an RBAC authorization?

    A. A privilege granted to a role

    B. A privilege granted to a profile

    C. A privilege granted to a user

    D. A Kerberos security level

6. What is the purpose of the `smexec` command?

    A. Execute commands using the su facility.

    B. Execute commands using the sudo facility.

    C. Execute commands symmetrically.

    D. Create, read, update, and delete rows in the *exec_attr* database.

7. What is the purpose of the `smmultiuser` command?

    A. Allocate one role to multiple users.

    B. Execute commands symmetrically for multiple users.

    C. To perform batch functions.

    D. Create, read, update, and delete rows in the *exec_attr* database.

8. What is the purpose of the `smuser` command?

   A. Allocate multiple roles to single users.

   B. Execute commands symmetrically for multiple users.

   C. To perform user account operations.

   D. Create, read, update, and delete rows in the *exec_attr* database.

Answers

1. **C.** The purpose of sudo is to allow privileged roles to be assigned to users.

2. **B.** */etc/sudoers* is the main configuration file for sudo.

3. **D.** Security Administrator is *not* an RBAC role.

4. **C.** An RBAC profile is a role for which an authorization can be granted.

5. **A.** An RBAC authorization is a privilege granted to a role.

6. **D.** The purpose of the `smexec` command is to create, read, update, and delete rows in the *exec_attr* database.

7. **C.** The purpose of the `smmultiuser` command is to perform batch functions.

8. **C.** The purpose of the `smuser` command is to perform user account operations.

## CHAPTER 29

Solaris Management Console

In this chapter, you will

- Be introduced to the SMC
- Get a description of the services that can be performed with the SMC
- Cover the steps involved in configuring the SMC
- Learn how to add new tasks and hosts to the SMC

In the past, several attempts have been made to develop an extensible, easy-to-use GUI for managing individual Solaris systems and groups of Solaris systems. Until recently, the admintool was the main GUI administration tool supplied with the Solaris distribution. However, since the Solaris 8 Admin Pack release, a new tool has been made available—the Solaris Management Console (SMC). In this chapter, we will examine all of the functionality available through the SMC to manage individual servers and groups of servers.

Introduction to SMC

The Solaris Management Console (SMC) is designed as a replacement for the admintool, which provided a limited and nonextensible set of tools for GUI system management. The motivation for providing GUI tools to seasoned command-line hackers may seem unclear; however, SMC provides methods for managing a large number of servers from a single interface, and it provides easy methods for extending the functionality of the core interface. This means that customized applications can be added to the toolbox, or the collection of administration applications for a specific system, by using the appropriate commands. It should be noted that SMC may not be of great benefit to administrators who manage a single system—it is an advanced tool that suits sites that deal with large numbers of systems.

 TIP If you run NIS+ or JumpStart, you'll more than likely find SMC to be useful.

SMC allows system and application packages to be managed, along with users and groups. Multiple systems can be managed from a single system and user interface based on Java. SMC allows managed systems to be rebooted or shut down, for their root passwords to be set, for Point-to-Point Protocol (PPP) support to be enabled, and for naming services like the Domain Name Service (DNS) to be administered. Processes can be reviewed in real time, along with system resources such as virtual and physical memory.

The following administrative tasks can be performed by software contained within SMC toolboxes:

- Assign rights and roles to users
- Configure and format new disks for the system, including laying out partitions and copying configurations from one disk to another in preparation for RAID
- Create a single user account or generate multiple accounts using a consistent specification
- Create new groups or modify existing groups
- Create user policies and apply them
- Execute jobs in real time or schedule them for regular, repeated execution
- Install support for serial ports, modems, and related physical layer technologies such as PPP
- Monitor processes and search for resumed, deleted, or suspended processes
- Review system logs and search for anomalous or suspicious entries
- Set up mailing lists
- View mounted file systems

These management operations and applications are not provided intrinsically by SMC, but SMC provides an interface to access them.

TIP   All of the administrative operations utilized by SMC have been covered in previous chapters, along with their related tools

.

EXAM TIP   You should be able to identify the various components of the SMC and their functions.

Starting the SMC

The SMC operates by collecting data from systems, providing an interface for viewing that data, and allowing administrative tasks to be executed on the basis of that data. Different servers can store localized toolboxes. Alternatively, if a high-resolution graphics card and/or monitor is not available, SMC can be started with a command-line interface.

The command that starts the SMC is `/usr/sadm/bin/smc`. This assumes that SMC is to be opened for operations. An alternative mode of operation is provided by the smc edit mode, where toolboxes can be modified or updated. The following options are available to the `smc` command when starting up:

- **-auth-data**   Allows authentication data to be read from a file.

- **-toolbox**   Stipulates the name of a toolbox to read in from a file. Alternatively, a URL can be specified that points to the location of a toolbox.

- **-domain**   Designates the domain name for the systems that are being managed. LDAP, DNS, NIS, and NIS+ domains are supported. The form of the URL for a DNS domain **cassowary.net** and the host midnight would be **dns:/midnight/ cassowary.net**.

- **-hostname:port**   Nominates the hostname and port number of the server to manage. The default port number is 898.

- **-J**   Passes any command-line options to the Java Virtual Machine, such as the initial and maximum heap sizes.

- **-rolepassword**   Specifies a password for the role rolename.

- **-password**   Specifies a password for username.

- **-rolename**   Specifies a role to execute SMC.

- **-t**   Executes SMC in terminal mode.

- **-trust**   Allows all downloaded code to be trusted.

- **-tool**   Specifies a tool to be executed.

- **-username**   Specifies a username with which SMC is to be executed.

- **-yes**   By default, answers yes to all interactive questions.

The format of data in an *auth-data* file is as follows:

```
hostname=ivana
username=root
password=my1asswd
rolename=su
rolepassword=su1asswd
```

Of course, any *auth-data* file should be read-only by root, or by the user who is assigned the role of SMC management. However, there is always an inherent risk in storing passwords plaintext in a file on any file system, because it could be removed and mounted on another system and its contents read directly. Alternatively, gaining unauthorized access to the *auth-data* file may allow a cracker to obtain administrative access to a large number of servers whose authentication tokens are stored in the file.

TIP   One file is normally created for every server whose credentials must be locally stored.

Exercise 29-1 Using SMC   Start SMC using a set of credentials stored in an *auth-data* file. Can you identify any security weaknesses with this approach?

There are a number of different Java options that may be useful for the initialization of the SMC that can be passed using the −J option. These options include the following:

- **-Xmixed**   Runs in mixed mode execution.
- **-Xint**   Runs in interpreted mode.
- **-Xbootclasspath**   Lists directories in which to search for classes for bootstrapping.
- **-Xbootclasspath/a**   Appends directories in which to search for classes for bootstrapping.
- **-Xbootclasspath/p**   Prepends directories in which to search for classes for bootstrapping.
- **-Xnoclassgc**   Switches off garbage collection.
- **-Xincgc**   Switches on progressive garbage collection.
- **-Xbatch**   Switches off compilation in the background.
- **-Xms**   Sets an initial size for the Java heap.
- **-Xmx**   Sets a maximum size for the Java heap.
- **-Xss**   Sets a size for the Java thread stack.
- **-Xprof**   Displays CPU profiling output.
- **-Xrunhprof**   Displays heap or monitor profiling output.
- **-Xdebug**   Allows debugging remotely.
- **-Xfuture**   Enforces strict checking.
- **-Xrs**   Minimizes native calls.

Exercise 29-2 SMC and Java   Start SMC using a set of Java options that minimize the amount of memory utilized initially, but allow for a maximum of 64MB of RAM to be utilized. Monitor the performance of the application using prstat. Does it ever come close to consuming the maximum amount of RAM allocated to the JVM?

Working with the SMC

When you start the SMC, you are presented with a login screen, as shown in Figure 29-1. This screen allows you to connect through to the server specified on the command line, or in the text box, and authenticate yourself as the administrator. Generally, the username will be root, but it could be any nonprivileged user who has been assigned administrative roles.

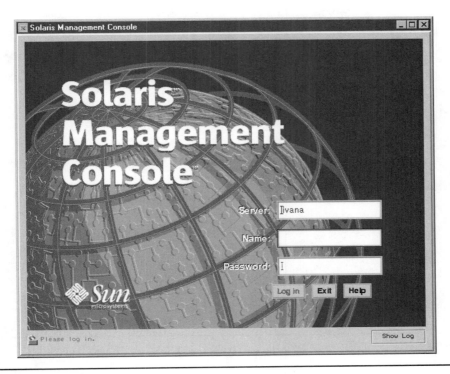

Figure 29-1   The SMC login screen

The main screen for the SMC is shown in Figure 29-2. There are three menus: Console, View, and Help; two tabs (Applications View, and SMC Server View); a navigation pane on the left-hand side; and a view pane on the right-hand side, below which there is a status and information pane. By default, the Applications view is enabled. To switch to the SMC Server view, you simply need to click the SMC Server View tab.

In the Applications view, shown in Figure 29-3, there are a number of broad headings used to differentiate the applications used to manage the system. Each of these headings can be activated by clicking the appropriate text or folder icon, after which a list of applications and application types appears in the view pane. The classes of applications supported by SMC include Connectivity, Documentation, Infrastructure, Jobs, Security, Software, and User & Group.

There are several different connectivity applications supported by SMC. These are shown in the view pane after selecting the Connectivity heading or folder icon, as shown in Figure 29-3. Supported applications include DNS Client, Default Routing, Network Interface, PPP Configuration, and Point-to-Point Protocol. In the Documentation class of applications, as shown in Figure 29-4, only the Answerbook is supported.

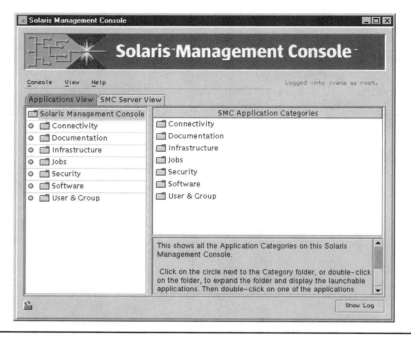

Figure 29-2 The SMC main screen

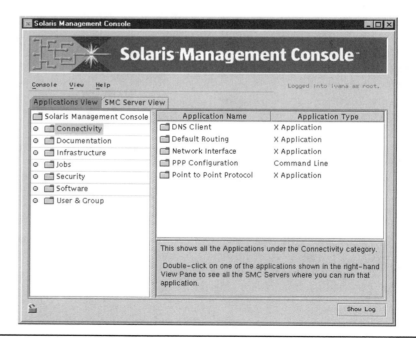

Figure 29-3 SMC Applications view

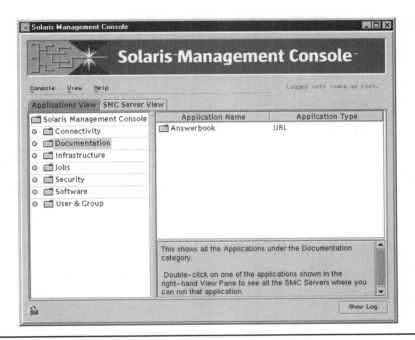

Figure 29-4   SMC documentation applications

In the Infrastructure class of applications, shown in Figure 29-5, a number of different applications are supported. These include AdminSuite, Admintool, Performance Meter, Shutdown / Restart the Computer, Terminal, and Workstation Information.

In the Jobs class of applications, shown in Figure 29-6, only the Process Manager is supported by default.

In the Security class of applications, shown in Figure 29-7, only the Kerberos v5 server (SEAM) is supported by default.

In the Software class of applications, shown in Figure 29-8, a number of different applications are supported. These include DNS Server, Software Manager, and Solaris Product Registry.

In the User & Group class of applications, shown in Figure 29-9, only the Change Root Password operation is supported by default.

Every application listed underneath each main application class heading can be configured by the administrator by double-clicking the appropriate heading and selecting the software product to be configured. This operation is shown in Figure 29-10 for the DNS Server software package underneath the Software applications heading. The parameters that can be modified include the application name, the server name on which it is to be executed, and the user who will run the application.

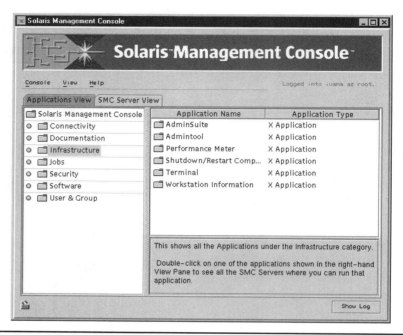

Figure 29-5 SMC Infrastructure applications

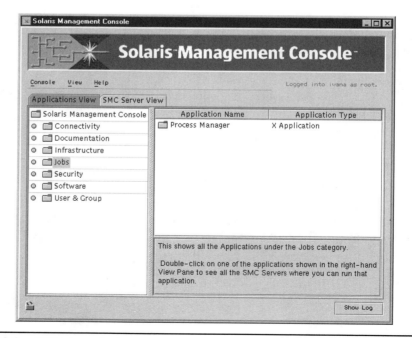

Figure 29-6 SMC Jobs applications

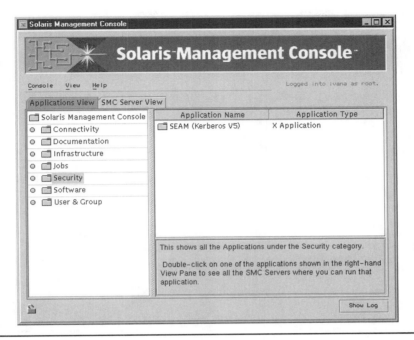

Figure 29-7   SMC Security applications

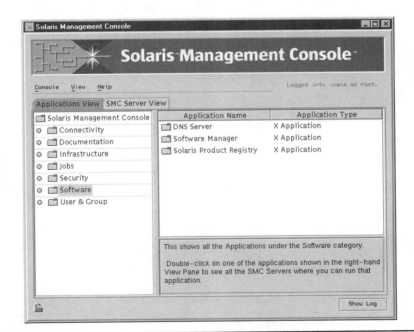

Figure 29-8   SMC Software applications

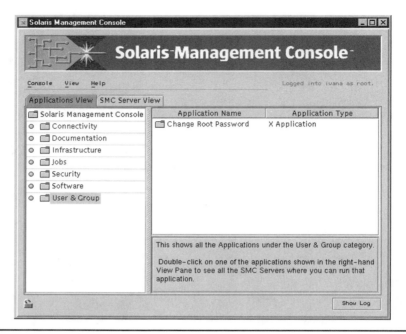

Figure 29-9   SMC User & Group applications

Figure 29-10   SMC application configuration

The list of applications in each category is limited to those installed by default in the Solaris installation. However, SMC only becomes really useful when a number of new applications are included in the toolbox. These can be configured on a per-system basis rather than having a "one size fits all" toolbox configuration. For example, a backup server might have Legato administration options added to SMC, while a database server might have the Oracle administration options integrated into SMC. To add new applications to an existing category, you select Add Application from the Console menu, as shown in Figure 29-11. Alternatively, if you want to remove an existing application from an existing SMC category, you need to select it in the view pane and then select Remove Application from the Console menu. Finally, if you just want to modify the configuration of an existing application in an existing application category, you can select Modify Application from the Console menu.

When you choose to add an application, the Add Application screen appears, as shown in Figure 29-12. Here, you can choose the application type, application category, user to run the application as, and the application name. In addition, you can specify the executable path, any optional command-line arguments, and whether or not to use the default icon or a customized icon.

When removing an application, the Remove Application screen is displayed. Here, you must choose whether to remove the application's SMC entry or whether to cancel the application, as shown in Figure 29-13.

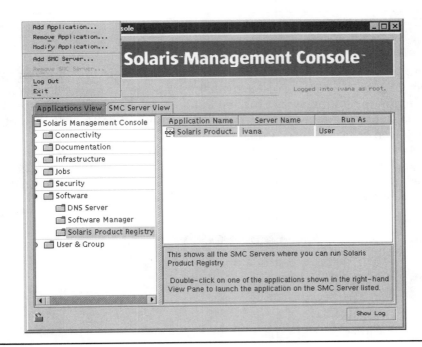

Figure 29-11   The SMC Console menu

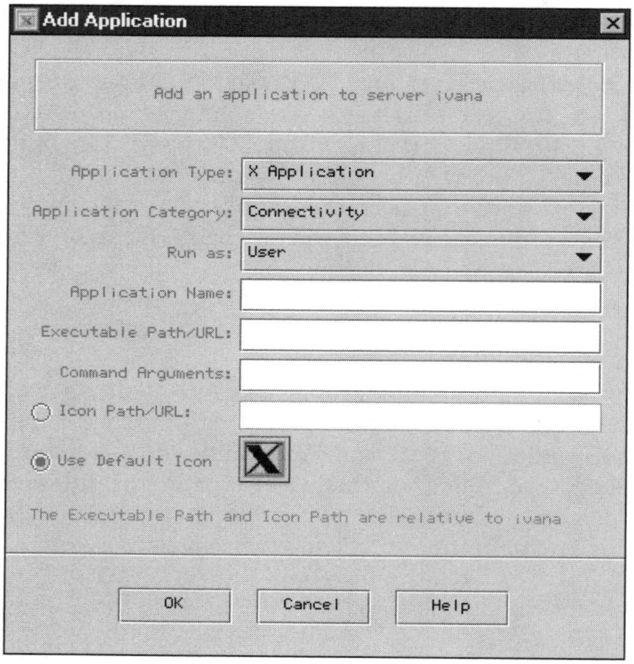

Figure 29-12   The SMC Add Application screen

When you choose to modify an application, the Modify Application screen appears, as shown in Figure 29-14. Here, you can modify the application type, application category, user to run the application as, and the application name. In addition, you can modify the executable path, any optional command-line arguments, and whether or not to use the default icon or a customized icon.

One of the main benefits of the SMC application is that multiple servers can be added into the pool of servers managed from a single interface, as shown in Figure 29-15. This reduces administrative overhead, especially in large installations where literally hundreds of servers may need to be managed by a single administrator or team of administrators.

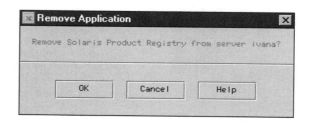

Figure 29-13   The SMC Remove Application screen

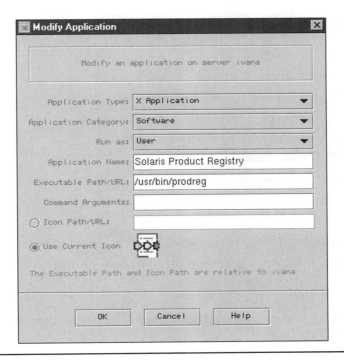

Figure 29-14   The SMC Modify Application screen

Summary

SMC is a powerful and versatile tool for managing multiple systems from a single interface where different systems can be customized to administer their own local applications, as well as a set of common applications. This flexibility gives SMC a number of advantages over the admintool or command-line administration. For more information on SMC, read the administrator's guide on **docs.sun.com**.

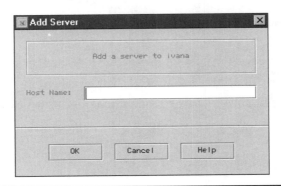

Figure 29-15   The SMC Add Server screen

Questions

1. What is the optimal use for SMC?

    A. Managing single systems with no customization

    B. Managing single systems with customization

    C. Managing multiple systems with no customization

    D. Managing multiple systems with customization

2. How is SMC customized?

    A. By compiling new applications

    B. By the creation of toolboxes that define applications for each system

    C. By the creation of a toolbox that defines applications for all systems

    D. By leveraging the object-oriented patterns in Java (SMC is built on Java)

3. Which of the following is not performed by SMC by default?

    A. Assign rights and roles to users.

    B. Configure and format new disks for the system, including laying out partitions, and copying configurations from one disk to another in preparation for RAID.

    C. Create a single user account or generate multiple accounts using a consistent specification.

    D. Optimize parallel execution of intermediate source bytecode.

4. Which of the following is not performed by SMC by default?

    A. Manage RMI services through a distributed interface.

    B. Create new groups or modify existing groups.

    C. Create user policies and apply them.

    D. Execute jobs in real time or schedule them for regular, repeated execution.

5. Which of the following is not performed by SMC by default?

    A. Install support for serial ports, modems, and related physical layer technologies such as PPP.

    B. Monitor processes and search for resumed, deleted, or suspended processes.

    C. Support developers through profiling and disassembly.

    D. Review system logs and search for anomalous or suspicious entries.

6. Which of the following is not performed by SMC by default?

    A. Set up mailing lists.

    B. View mounted file systems.

C. Authenticate administrative users

D. Authenticate nonadministrative users

7. What does the SMC option `-auth-data` allow?

    A. Allows authentication data to be read from a file

    B. Stipulates the name of a toolbox to read in from a file

    C. Designates the domain name for the systems that are being managed

    D. Nominates the hostname and port number of the server to manage

8. What does the SMC option `-toolbox` allow?

    A. Allows authentication data to be read from a file

    B. Stipulates the name of a toolbox to read in from a file

    C. Designates the domain name for the systems that are being managed

    D. Nominates the hostname and port number of the server to manage

9. What does the SMC option `-domain` designate?

    A. Allows authentication data to be read from a file

    B. Stipulates the name of a toolbox to read in from a file

    C. Designates the domain name for the systems that are being managed

    D. Nominates the hostname and port number of the server to manage

10. What does the SMC option `-hostname:port` nominate?

    A. Allows authentication data to be read from a file

    B. Stipulates the name of a toolbox to read in from a file

    C. Designates the domain name for the systems that are being managed

    D. Nominates the hostname and port number of the server to manage

11. What does the SMC option `-J` specify?

    A. Passes any command-line options to the Java Virtual Machine, such as the initial and maximum heap sizes

    B. Specifies a password for the role rolename

    C. Specifies a password for username

    D. Specifies a role to execute SMC

12. What does the SMC option `-rolepassword` specify?

    A. Passes any command-line options to the Java Virtual Machine, such as the initial and maximum heap sizes

    B. Specifies a password for the role rolename

    C. Specifies a password for username

    D. Specifies a role to execute SMC

13. What does the SMC option -password specify?

  A. Passes any command-line options to the Java Virtual Machine, such as the initial and maximum heap sizes

  B. Specifies a password for the role rolename

  C. Specifies a password for username

  D. Specifies a role to execute SMC

14. What does the SMC option -rolename specify?

  A. Passes any command-line options to the Java Virtual Machine, such as the initial and maximum heap sizes

  B. Specifies a password for the role rolename

  C. Specifies a password for username

  D. Specifies a role to execute SMC

15. Which of the following is not a valid entry in the *auth-data* file?

  A. hostname=ivana

  B. username=root

  C. password=my1asswd

  D. clash=su

Answers

1. **D.** The optimal use for SMC is to manage multiple systems with customization.

2. **B.** SMC is customized by the creation of toolboxes that define applications for each system.

3. **D.** SMC does not perform, by default, optimized parallel execution of intermediate source bytecode.

4. **A.** SMC does not perform, by default, management of RMI services through a distributed interface.

5. **C.** SMC does not support, by default, developers through profiling and disassembly.

6. **D.** SMC does not perform, by default, authentication of nonadministrative users.

7. **A.** The SMC option -auth-data allows authentication data to be read from a file.

8. **B.** The SMC option -toolbox stipulates the name of a toolbox to read in from a file.

9. **C.** The SMC option –`domain` designates the domain name for the systems that are being managed.

10. **D.** The SMC option –`hostname:port` nominates the hostname and port number of the server to manage.

11. **A.** The SMC option –`J` passes any command-line options to the Java Virtual Machine, such as the initial and maximum heap sizes.

12. **B.** The SMC option –`rolepassword` specifies a password for the role rolename.

13. **C.** The SMC option –`password` specifies a password for username.

14. **D.** The SMC option –`rolename` specifies a role to execute SMC.

15. **D.** `clash=su` is not a valid entry in the *auth-data* file.

Advanced Installation and Management

In this chapter, you will

- Learn how to install systems using JumpStart
- Learn how to upgrade systems using Live Upgrade
- Review key security architecture issues
- State how to allocate resources effectively in Solaris

JumpStart is a client/server system for installing Solaris systems on a local area network using a Standard Operating Environment (SOE). This removes the need to individually configure each installation on every host on a subnet. This greatly reduces the administrative burden on sysadmins, as most client systems use exactly the same settings, particularly within the same organizational unit.

JumpStart

JumpStart has three roles that are filled by different systems on the network:

- An install server, which provides all of the data and services required to install the system.
- A boot server, which allows the RARP daemon to boot client systems that have not been installed.
- An install client, which is the target system for installation.

Boot Servers

A boot server provides a copy of the operating system to be installed on a target host. Once the target host has been booted using the network and install options (see the following), a kernel is downloaded to the target host from an install server and booted locally. Once the system has been loaded, the operating system is then downloaded from the boot server. The rules for downloading and installing specific files are located in the *rules.ok* file.

Individual systems can have their own entries in the rules file, or generic rules can be inserted. After loading the system from the boot server, the install client then executes a post installation script, and will then be ready for use.

Installing Servers

The install server uses RARP to listen for requests to install the system from target hosts. Once such a request is received, a miniroot system is downloaded from the install server to the target host.

To set up an install server, you need to perform the following tasks:

```
# mkdir -p /export/install /export/config
# cp -r /cdrom/sol_9_sparc/s0/Solaris_2.9/Misc/jumpstart_sample/ /export/config
# /cdrom/sol_9_sparc/s0/Solaris_2.9/Tools ./setup_install_server /export/install
```

This assumes that */export/install* has sufficient space to store the installation files, and that the JumpStart configuration data, such as the rules file, will be stored in */export/config*. Here is a sample *host_class* file, which is referred to in rules, that specifies the UFS disk layout for all boot clients:

```
install_type initial_install
system_type standalone
partitioning explicit
filesys c1t2d0s0 512 /
filesys c1t2d0s3 2048 /usr
filesys c1t2d0s4 256 /var
filesys c0t3d1s0 1024 swap
filesys c0t3d1s1 free /export
cluster SUNWCall
```

Here, we can see that the standard layout allocated 512MB to /, 2048MB to */usr*, 256MB to */var*, 1024MB to swap, and all free space to */export*. In addition, the cluster SUNWCall is to be installed.

This is a very specific setup, so you might want to use something more general like:

```
#
install_type     initial_install
# This machine is standalone
system_type      standalone
# Disk partitioning
partitioning     explicit
filesys          rootdisk.s0     2000    /
filesys          rootdisk.s1     1000    swap
filesys          rootdisk.s4     1000    /tmp
filesys          rootdisk.s5     free    /var
# Start with the entire OS...
cluster          SUNWCall
```

Once the rules file has been customized, its contents must be verified by using the check command. Once the check command parses the rules file and validates its contents, a *rules.ok* file is created.

Boot Clients

In order to set up a boot client, the target system must be shut down to init level 0, by using the `init 0` command or equivalent. Next, the system needs to be booted by using the following command from the "ok" prompt:

```
boot net - install
```

At this point, a broadcast is made on the local subnet to locate an install server. Once an install server is located, a miniroot system is downloaded to the target system. Once the kernel is loaded from the miniroot system, the operating system is then downloaded from the boot server:

```
Resetting ...
SPARCstation 20 MP (2 X SuperSPARC-II)
ROM Rev. 2.28, 256 MB memory installed, Serial #345665.
Ethernet address 8:0:19:6b:22:a2, Host ID: 49348a3.
Initializing Memory |
Boot device: /iommu/sbus/ledma@f,400010/le@f,c00000 File and args: -
hostname: paul.cassowary.net
domainname: cassowary.net
root server: installserv
root directory: /solaris_2.9/export/exec/kvm/sparc.sun
Copyright (c) 1983-2001, Sun Microsystems, Inc.
The system is coming up. Please wait.
```

Once the system has started, you'll see individual clusters being installed:

```
Selecting cluster: SUNWCXall

Total software size: 324.55 MB

Preparing system to install Solaris. Please wait.

Setting up disk c1t2d0:

Creating Solaris disk label (VTOC)

Creating and checking UFS file systems:

- Creating / (c1t2d0)
- Creating /var (c1t2d0)
- Creating /scratch (c1t2d0)
- Creating /opt (c1t2d0)
- Creating /usr (c1t2d0)
- Creating /staff (c1t2d0)
Beginning Solaris package installation...
SUNWcsu.....done. 321.23 MB remaining.
SUNWcsr.....done. 277.34 MB remaining.
SUNWcsd.....done. 312.23 MB remaining.
```

sysidcfg

When installing JumpStart on a large number of clients, installation can be expedited by using a *sysidcfg* file, which defines a number of standard parameters for installation. The sysidcfg file can contain configuration entries for the properties shown in Table 30-1.

Property	sysidcfg Parameter
Date and time	Timeserver
DHCP	dhcp
Domain name	domain_name
Graphics card	display
Hostname	hostname
IP address	ip_address
IPv6	protocol_ipv6
Keyboard language	keyboard
Monitor type	monitor
DNS, LDAP or NIS/NIS+ name server	name_server
DNS, LDAP or NIS/NIS+ name service	name_service
DNS domains to search	search
LDAP profile	profile
Netmask	netmask
Network interface	network_interface
Pointing device	pointer
Root password	root_password
Security policy	security_policy
Kerberos administration server	admin_server
Kerberos KDC	kdc
Kerberos realm	default_realm
Terminal type	terminal
Timezone	timezone

Table 30-1   Configurable *sysidcfg* Properties

The following is a sample sysidcfg file:

```
system_locale=en_US
timezone=US/Eastern
timeserver=localhost
network_interface=le0 {netmask=255.255.255.0 protocol_ipv6=yes}
security_policy=NONE
terminal=dtterm
name_service=NONE
root_password=f7438:;H2ef
```

Resource Manager

For workstations, resource allocation is usually not an issue because only a small number of applications are generally running at any one time. Of these applications, CDE and X11 may consume the largest amount of CPU time, particularly if the workspace is fully utilized. However, servers have very diverse needs with respect to resource management, particularly in a shared hosting environment, where time and process priority are billable items. Being able to specify which processes have priority over others is a key requirement for servers running hundreds of different processes for potentially hundreds of different customers.

EXAM TIP   You should be able to identify the different priority classes and values utilized by the kernel.

The concept of process priority is built in to the kernel: if processes belong to the time sharing (TS) priority class, a priority value (PRI) may be assigned to them that determines the order in which their operations are executed on the CPU. The scheduler is responsible for allocating resources to different processes according to priority values.

TIP   Nonprivileged users can only decrease the priority associated with their processes, while the superuser can actually increase the priority associated with any user's processes.

One way to appreciate this is to use the ps command to display the process list in the scheduler format. This includes two extra columns in the ps output: the priority class memberships, and the process priority values:

```
$ ps -c
  PID   CLS PRI TTY       TIME CMD
 6667    TS   45 pts/8    0:00 sh

 6675    TS   35 pts/8    0:00 httpd
```

In this example, the httpd command and the Bourne shell (sh) are both members of the Time Sharing class, meaning that a priority value may be assigned to their respective processes. In this example, the sh process has a higher priority value than the httpd process, and thus has greater access to the system's resources.

An unprivileged user can reduce any of the processes they own by reducing the priority granted to the ps process—this is done by using the nice command for a new process, or the renice command for an existing process. The following example reduces the priority for sh by increasing the nice value, potentially increasing the amount of CPU available for the httpd process:

```
$ renice -30 sh
```

This would reduce the priority for the sh process to 15, well below the priority for httpd at 35. Alternatively, the superuser may directly increase the priority of a process by specifying a negative increment, which when subtracted from the process priority actually increases it (that is, subtracting a negative integer is equivalent to addition). The following example would increase the process priority for the httpd command from 35 to 55:

```
# renice --20 ps
```

Keep in mind that the C shell has a built-in nice function that differs from the /usr/bin/nice command. The nice command only solves part of the problem of resource allocation, because normal users still have unbounded access to execute as many applications as they wish unless the superuser continually monitors their activity, reducing priority values when necessary. In a multiprocessor system, it may be possible to run an "honor system," where individuals or groups agree only to use a specific CPU for their work by using the pbind command. pbind forces a process and its children to only use a specific CPU. For example, if an httpd process was started, and it had a PID of 2234, it could be bound to CPU 1 by using the following command:

```
$ pbind -b 1 2234
process id 2234: was 1, now 1
```

Again, a superuser can bind (or unbind) any process from a specific CPU if resources are being drained by using the pbind command. But this still requires monitoring and oversight from a system administrator. Another alternative is to create a processor set by using the psrset command, which binds a process to a single CPU or to a group of CPUs. This limits the maximum CPU usage by a specific process to whatever it can obtain from the CPU (or CPUs) it is bound to. The problem here is that a system has limited resources, so if a process does not use all of the CPU allocated to it, resources are being wasted as the CPU sits idling.

What is really required is a policy-based mechanism for ensuring that individual users and applications never exceed a preallocated quota of CPU resource, much like how disk quotas specify exactly how much disk space a user can utilize. The Resource Manager provides this functionality by implementing a fine-grained resource access policy, which limits the resources that can be utilized by different users. It allows CPU usage to be allocated on a per-user basis, and virtual memory consumption to be limited on both a user and process basis. In addition, the total number of processes spawned by a user, the number of concurrent logins, and their total connection time can be limited. This allows complete control over an individual user's access to the system, as well as to their individual processes. For example, a numerical scientist might have free access to the system except when running the Matlab (**www.mathworks.com**) application, where the matlab process might be limited to how much CPU and virtual memory can be consumed.

The simplest method of allocating CPU resources is to divide up the available CPU resources among the existing users according to organizational priorities. For example, a web server for an online catalogue may have three main accounts whose access to resources needs to be limited: the oracle account, responsible for running the Oracle database; the apache user, responsible for running the Apache web server; and the jdk user, responsible for executing the Java Virtual Machine (JVM) for the Apache Tomcat servlet runner. In order to prevent large numbers of httpd clients from causing a resource drain on the database, or from thread lock in the JVM causing the same problem, it is necessary to limit the maximum CPU usage of the httpd and java processes by setting limits on the amount of CPU that the apache and jdk users can utilize.

Since the Resource Manager allows for the hierarchical allocation of resources to groups of users and processes (known as sgroups), all allocations must descend from the root sgroup. In our example, only the root sgroup will be used, so we first associate the oracle, apache, and jdk users as descendants of the root sgroup by using the `limadm` command:

```
# limadm set sgroup=root oracle
# limadm set sgroup=root apache
# limadm set sgroup=root jdk
```

If the allocation of CPU to the oracle, apache, and jdk was 50 percent, 25 percent, and 25 percent, respectively, the following commands would set the share of each user appropriately:

```
# limadm set cpu.shares=50 oracle
# limadm set cpu.shares=25 apache
# limadm set cpu.shares=25 jdk
```

To check the status of the resources being used by the oracle user, we could use the `liminfo` command:

```
# liminfo -c oracle
Login name:    oracle              Uid (Real,Eff):   1024 (-,-)
Sgroup (uid)       root(0)          Gid (Real,Eff):   10(-,-)

Shares:             50         Myshares:        1
Share:              50 %       E-share:         0 %
Usage:              0          Accrued usage:   0

Mem usage:   0 B        Term usage:      0s
Mem limit:   0 B        Term accrue:     0s
Proc mem limit: 0 B         Term limit:           0s
Mem accrue: 0 B.s

Processes:   2          Current logins:     1
Process limit:      0
```

More complex sgroups can be created for a system, based on organizational units. For example, the sales division may require 25 percent of the CPU in a system while the finance division may be entitled to 75 percent. Individual sgroups must be created for each of these divisions underneath root, and then individual users who are members of the divisions must be associated with the correct sgroup.

Trusted Solaris

Trusted Solaris implements much stricter controls over UNIX than the standard releases, and is capable of meeting B1 level security by default. It is designed for organizations that handle military grade or commercially sensitive data. In addition to the mandatory use of Role-Based Access Control (as reviewed in Chapter 28), Trusted Solaris actually has no superuser at all: no single user is permitted to have control over every aspect of system service. This decentralization of authority is necessary in situations where consensus and/or authorization are required to carry out specific activities. For example, a system administrator installing a new web server might inadvertently interfere with the operations of an existing service. For a server that's handling sensitive production data, the results could be catastrophic. Once a system has been installed in production, it's crucial to define a set of roles that specify what operations need to be performed by a particular individual. For example, the role of managing a firewall is unrelated to the database administration role, so the two roles should be separated rather than being run from a single superuser account. In addition, access to files is restricted by special access control lists, which define file contents as "unclassified" up to "top secret."

 TIP Access to data that is labeled as more secret requires a higher level of authentication and authorization than unclassified data.

There are four roles defined by default under Trusted Solaris for system management purposes: the security officer manages all aspects of security on the system, such as auditing, logging, and password management; the system manager performs all system management tasks that are not related to security, except for installing new software; the root account is used for installing new software; and the oper account is used for performing backups. New roles can be created for other tasks, such as database and web server administration, where necessary.

Some aspects of a Trusted Solaris installation already form part of a standard Solaris installation. For example, Trusted Solaris requires that centralized authentication be performed across an encrypted channel using NIS+—this feature is also available on Solaris, although many sites are now moving to LDAP-based authentication.

Asymmetric Key Cryptography

One major limitation of symmetric key cryptography is that the same key is required to encrypt and decrypt data. This is fine for protecting individual files from unauthorized users, but many data protection scenarios require multiple users, and in many cases parties amongst which trust has never been established, to be involved. For example, if a manager in New York needed to exchange sales data with a manager in Buffalo, and this data required encryption, then both managers could simply share the key required to decrypt the data. However, this approach has two problems: first, users tend to apply the same password and key to multiple purposes, meaning that one manager might be able to access the other manager's files; second, what if more than two managers were involved? Clearly, passing a password around a user group of 1,000 users is tantamount to having no security at all! A system is required that allows individual users to encrypt data using one key, and for the file to be decrypted using a separate key for each user.

Asymmetric encryption allows separate keys to be used for encrypting and decrypting data. How is this possible? Basically, every user is assigned a private key, which they never release to anyone else, and a public key, which is supplied to other users who need to send the user encrypted data. For example, the New York manager would have a private key stored on a floppy disk, locked in a safe, as would the Buffalo manager. Both would also exchange their public keys via e-mail, or another offline method such as floppy disk, verifying that the keys were genuine by using a key "fingerprints" check over the telephone. To encrypt a file for the Buffalo manager, the New York manager would need to use both the Buffalo manager's public key and his own private key. Conversely, the Buffalo manager would need to use her private key and the New York manager's public key to encrypt a file for him. Remember that if you exchange public keys via e-mail, and have no other method of verifying who is on the other end of the line, then you're ripe for a "man in the middle attack," because the person you think you are exchanging data with could be an intermediary. For example, imagine if Joe substitutes his key in place of his manager's, and manages to place his machine between the manager's machine and an external router. Now Joe is able to pretend to be his manager, issuing his own public key with his manager's name for which he actually has the corresponding private key.

The most important feature (or limitation, depending on your requirements) of asymmetric key cryptography is that obtaining the private key used to encrypt data is not sufficient to decrypt that data: only the private key of the individual whose public key was used for signing can be used for this purpose. This can be very important in situations where data may be compromised in a specific location. For example, an embassy in a foreign country under threat of attack may decide to encrypt all data using the public key of an officer in the State Department in Washington, send it via e-mail, and then delete the on-site originals. Even if the encrypted data and the embassy's private key were obtained by force, they could not be used to decrypt the data.

Of course, asymmetry implies that if you lose your original data accidentally, you must rely on the public-key holder's private key to decrypt the data. However, at least there is one avenue of recourse available, unlike symmetric key cryptography, where a lost key almost certainly means lost data.

Public-Key Cryptography

One of the most commonly used "public key" systems that uses asymmetric keys is the Pretty Good Privacy (PGP) application (**http://www.pgp.com/**). PGP is available for a wide variety of operating systems, making it very popular among PC and UNIX users because data can be exchanged without conversion. PGP works both on the command line, to facilitate secure storage of files, and as a plug-in to e-mail programs, allowing messages to be exchanged securely. This ensures that intermediate mail servers and routers cannot intercept the decrypted contents of transmitted messages, even if they can intercept packets containing the encrypted data.

In order to use PGP, each user needs to generate their own public/private key pair. This can be performed by using the following command:

```
$ pgp -kg
```

The following prompt will be displayed:

```
Choose the type of your public key:
  1)  DSS/Diffie-Hellman - New algorithm for 5.0 (default)
  2)  RSA
Choose 1 or 2:
```

The public key format that you choose will determine what types of block ciphers can be used to encrypt your data. The DSS/Diffie-Hellman algorithm allows Triple DES, CAST, or IDEA, while RSA keys will only work with IDEA, so most users will want to select the DSS/Diffie-Hellman algorithm.

Next, you will need to select the key size:

```
Pick your public/private keypair key size:
(Sizes are Diffie-Hellman/DSS; Read the user's guide for more information)
  1)    768/768  bits- Commercial grade, probably not currently breakable
  2)   1024/1024 bits- High commercial grade, secure for many years
  3)   2048/1024 bits- "Military" grade, secure for foreseeable future(default)
  4)   3072/1024 bits- Archival grade, slow, highest security
Choose 1, 2, 3 or 4, or enter desired number of Diffie-Hellman bits
(768 - 4096):
```

Keep in mind that while a large key provides greater security, it also slows down operations significantly since it is CPU-intensive. Thus, if your needs are really commercial rather than military, you should use the 768- or 1,024-bit key. Military users should certainly select the largest key size available (currently 4,096 bits).

Next, you will need to enter a user ID. This should be recognizable by your intended recipients. For example, a programmer called Yayoi Rei from Rei Corporation would have a user ID of Yayoi Rei <yayoi@rei.com>. Even in countries where the family name is usually written first, the expectation for the key server is that the family name will appear last, followed by an e-mail address:

```
You need a user ID for your public key.  The desired form for this
user ID is your FULL name, followed by your E-mail address enclosed in
<angle brackets>, if you have an E-mail address.  For example:
  Joe Smith <user@domain.com>
Enter a user ID for your public key:
```

If you wish your key to be valid for a specific time period, you can enter its validity in days next. Alternatively, if the key is intended to be permanent, you can enter zero days:

```
Enter the validity period of your key in days from 0 - 999
0 is forever (and the default):
```

A password will need to be associated with the private key for future use, and will need to be entered twice for verification:

```
You need a pass phrase to protect your private key(s).
Your pass phrase can be any sentence or phrase and may have many
words, spaces, punctuation, or any other printable characters.
Enter pass phrase:
Enter again, for confirmation:
```

Finally, a number of random numbers needs to be generated from the intervals between random key presses on your keyboard. Try to insert some variation in the key press latency to ensure security:

```
We need to generate 595 random bits.  This is done by measuring the
time intervals between your keystrokes.  Please enter some random text
on your keyboard until you hear the beep:
```

Once the key pair has been created, it is possible to list all of the keys on your local key ring by using the following command:

```
$ pgp -kl
Type Bits KeyID        Created     Expires     Algorithm         Use
sec+  768 0x71849810 2002-01-07 ---------- DSS               Sign & Encrypt
sub   768 0x78697B9D 2002-01-07 ---------- Diffie-Hellman
uid  Yayoi Rei <yayoi@rei.com>
1 matching key found
```

The key pair is now available for use. In order to generate a copy of your public key for your correspondents and colleagues to use, you will need to extract this from your key ring as follows:

```
$pgp -x Yayoi
-----BEGIN PGP PUBLIC KEY BLOCK-----
mQFCBDw5+oURAwDBKeBtW+0PdDvCC7KO1/gUAF9X//uGRhbPkg6m83QzaA7pr6T+
QAVQE4q74NXFCakX8GzmhzHtA2/Hoe/yfpfHGHMhJRZHZIWQWTS6W+r5wHYRSObm
NNNTeJ4C+3/k1bEAoP/Mjlim4eMkfvYwNmifTUvak5zRAv48SrXOHmVI+5Mukx8Z
1T7txut60VeYd34QvidwtUbbL7p2IVVa3fGW/gsuo7whb1aW//+5Z/+4wxbaqnu6
WxT5vFObm1sJ7E20OW3SDLxdVjeTlYbzTUfNwbN/KHoUzMsC/2EZ3aDB6mGZuDPL
0SMT8sOoxlbpPouuBxnF/sbcxgOVKkGZDS5XrhodUbp2RUflwFSMyqjbmoqITnNq
xzpSXEhT0odwjjq3YeHj1icBaiy9xB/j0CBXe3QQKAXk5bXMEbQZWWF5b2kgUmVp
IDx5YXlvaUByZWkuY29tPokASwQQEQIACwUCPDn6hQQLAwECAAoJEHCOVqNxhJgQ
riMAn18a5kKYaepNk8BEksMJOTbRgDQmAKC0JD6wvYfo5zmziGr7TAv+uFWN5LkA
zQQ8OfqHEAMA6zd3dxeMkyKJmust3S3IrKvQzMLlMoRuQdb+N2momBYDF1+slo8k
EMK8F/Vrun+HdhJW+hWivgZRhTMe9fm6OL7PDYESkwuQsMizqAJJ1JF0yhbfTwE5
GjdVPcUMyPyTAAICAwCgdBO1XyiPbwdQtjxq+8CZ7uchASvJXsU28OFqbLzNcAW2
Q641WSs6qr2HNfgf+ikG8S8eVWVKEBgm6md9trr6CK25SYEu4oB3o1f45X4daa/n
iNytKUg1PPOJMK/rhJOJAD8DBRg8OfqHcI5Wo3GEmBARAs3mAJ0ZPQjmlYyNsMDY
ZVbR9/q2xQl8gACgkqVCNYR40mPIaxrd5Cw9ZrHqlkQ=
=Gsmt
-----END PGP PUBLIC KEY BLOCK-----
```

To encrypt a file using standard, symmetric encryption, you simply pass the −c option on the command line along with the name of the file that you want to encrypt. This provides Solaris users with an alternative to crypt, where a more secure encryption algorithm is desired:

```
$ pgp -c secret.doc
You need a passphrase to encrypt the file
Enter pass phrase:
Enter same passphrase again
Enter pass phrase:
Creating output file secret.pgp
```

After entering a password to protect the data in *secret.doc*, the encrypted file *secret.pgp* is created. In order to sign the file for another user, the −e option needs to be passed, along with the name of the user from your key ring who will have the power to decrypt your data:

```
$ pgp -e Henry secret.doc
   4096 bits, Key ID 76857743, Created 2002-01-07
   "Henry Bolingbroke <henry@bolingbroke.co.uk>"
Creating output file secret.pgp
```

The file can then be transmitted to Henry by UUencoding it, sending it as an e-mail attachment, or by directly generating the file in ASCII format:

```
$ pgp -ea Henry secret.doc
```

Summary

In this chapter, we have examined several advanced administration and installation issues that typically arise in an enterprise systems context. These issues are not important for single system management; however, when a network of systems must be managed, they can be very useful.

Questions

1. Which system provides all of the data and services required to install the system using JumpStart?

    A. Install server

    B. Boot server

    C. Install client

    D. Boot client

2. Which system provides the RARP daemon to boot client systems that have not been installed?

    A. Install server

    B. Boot server

    C. Install client

    D. Boot client

3. Which system is the target system for installation?

    A. Install server

    B. Boot server

    C. Install client

    D. Boot client

4. Which does a boot server provide?

    A. A PROM image downloaded to clients

    B. Internet access for ARP resolution

    C. Internet access for RARP resolution

    D. A copy of the operating system to be installed on a target host

5. What protocol does the install server use to listen for requests to install the system from target hosts?

    A. ARP

    B. RARP

    C. ICMP

    D. HTTP

6. What sort of distribution is downloaded from the install server to the target host?

    A. Minix

    B. Mini root

    C. Maxi root

    D. Full

7. What command would be used to install a system using JumpStart?

    A. `boot net - install`

    B. `boot net - jumpstart`

    C. `boot jumpstart`

    D. `boot net - js`

8. What file defines a number of standard parameters for installation?

    A. *sysid*

    B. *sysidcfg*

    C. *jscfg*

    D. *sysidjs*

Answers

1. **A.** The install server provides all of the data and services required to install the system using JumpStart.

2. **B.** The boot server provides the RARP daemon to boot client systems that have not been installed.

3. **C.** The target system for installation is the install client.

4. **D.** A boot server provides a copy of the operating system to be installed on a target host.

5. **B.** The install server uses RARP to listen for requests to install the system from target hosts.

6. **B.** A mini root distribution is downloaded from the install server to the target host.

7. **A.** The `boot net - install` command would be used to install a system using JumpStart.

8. **B.** The *sysidcfg* file defines a number of standard parameters for installation.

PART III

Solaris 9 Operating Environment Objectives

Lightweight Directory Access Protocol (LDAP)

In this chapter, you will

- Gain an understanding of white pages, DAP, and LDAP services
- Review the installation and configuration of the LDAP server
- Learn how to support LDAP clients
- Discover how to use directory services effectively in an organization

LDAP is a "white pages" type of service, which is similar to the older X.500 standard for managing organization-wide directory information, for which it originally acted as a front end. X.500 was based on the "heavyweight" Directory Access Protocol (DAP), while LDAP, as a "lightweight" protocol, sits directly on top of TCP/IP. Operations on LDAP servers like iDS are of two kinds: data management operations, where records are inserted, updated, or deleted, and queries, where authentication and identification tokens are retrieved from the organization's database. In theory, the LDAP protocol allows for a lot of different types of data about individuals and groups to be stored, including sounds, images, and text.

In Solaris 8, only an LDAP client was supplied with the operating environment release, making it less attractive to use than NIS/NIS+ because a separate LDAP server had to be purchased and installed. However, Solaris 9 has integrated the iPlanet Directory Server (iDS) into the core architecture, meaning that LDAP servers and clients can be installed and configured directly after and during installation, respectively. iDS, a key component of the iPlanet software suite, provides centralized authentication and authorization services for other iPlanet applications and for third-party applications. For example, access to the Internet mediated through the iPlanet Proxy Server can only be gained by being an attribute of a group defined within the local iDS database, demonstrating the key role that iDS plays in supporting enterprise applications. Alternatively, access to scheduling and event notification facilities through the iPlanet Calendar Server can only be provided to users who are authenticated through the iDS database.

TIP Many Solaris applications can use LDAP for authentication and authorization.

iDS does not use a proprietary protocol for storing user and group data or for communicating with clients; instead, iDS uses the LDAP standard for authenticating users. This is an open standard, meaning that a Solaris-based LDAP server can authenticate some Microsoft Windows clients. In addition, it means that iDS can act as a drop-in replacement for any other LDAP-compliant server, enabling you to standardize directory services across a single platform. Alternatively, multiple server types from different vendors can be combined to form an integrated solution. For example, you might choose to use iDS in mission-critical applications because of its clustering and high-availability features, which might be overkill in other situations. It is also possible to use the LDAP client software supplied with Solaris to connect to an LDAP server running on a different platform.

Two of the key benefits in switching from NIS/NIS+ are the ease of replication and the assurance of high availability. While NIS/NIS+ architecture is based on the idea of a primary server backed up by some slaves, LDAP servers can be replicated across subnets and domains to servers known as replicas, increasing the number of servers available for authoritative lookups and reducing the burden on any one server. In addition, updates occur rapidly between LDAP servers, rather than relying on uploads of all data between primary and slave servers in a NIS/NIS+ architecture.

Although LDAP has many features (and the iDS implementation implements all of the most important operations defined in the protocol), LDAP has a number of limitations. It does not have an interface defined to store data in a relational database, nor does it store data internally in a relational way. Although queries can be performed on the directory, these are not executed by using a query language (like SQL). LDAP is better designed for a reference data environment, where the types of lookups are well defined and data updates are infrequent.

However, its power lies in the flexibility to store and manage names and data in a flexible way. While there are predefined schema elements, such as users and organizations, other elements can be added where necessary. In addition, developers can write client programs that can easily access the directory and retrieve authoritative data.

TIP Since most networked applications perform some kind of authentication, a single, centralized source of authentication data can be accessed, reducing administrative overhead.

In this chapter we examine how to configure LDAP servers and configure a wide range of client services.

Exercise 31-1 LDAP Review Go to **www.sun.com**, review the Sun ONE architecture, and see where LDAP fits into the picture.

LDAP Overview

Since LDAP is a directory service, its basic data element is known as an "entry." Like a phone book entry, there are a number of attributes that are associated with the entry when regarded as an object. For example, a phone directory object has a surname, first name, address, and phone number that together comprise a single entry when instantiated. The overall organization of entries in an LDAP directory is defined by a schema, which consists of a ruleset that determines what attributes can be associated with different object types. Although it is possible to define your own schemas and data models, all LDAP servers support a standard schema that promotes interoperability—and is the basis for the LDAP standard as proposed in RFC 2307. Alternatively, your application can extend the standard schema with some additional object attributes, although these may not be accessible by other servers.

LDAP is used in Solaris 9 as a naming service that is compatible with existing NIS and NIS+ services. This allows integration at the present time, but also suggests future deprecation of the NIS and NIS+ services. iDS contains a set of objects and their attributes that are able to store all of the data contained within NIS/NIS+ maps and tables.

NOTE Additional schema data must also be stored within the LDAP directory to support client operations.

The directory structure for LDAP is arranged hierarchically, from a single top node within the Directory Information Tree (DIT) to as many levels of abstraction as are required to support an organization's directory requirements. The tree structure might, for example, be based on purely geographical information, with the top node representing a country. Or, it might be based on organizational lines, with the top node corresponding to a company name. All entries within the tree can be identified by their Distinguished Name (DN), and each attribute of the entry can be described as a Relative Distinguished Name (RDN). Figure 31-1 shows an example DIT, with all of the common elements found therein.

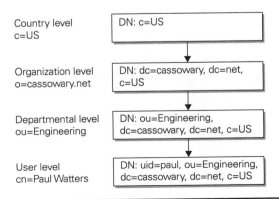

Figure 31-1   Example Directory Information Tree (DIT)

At the first level, the country c is defined as US, so the DN would simply be c=US. At the second level, the organization o is defined as cassowary.net, so the DN is defined as dc=cassowary, dc=net, c=US, where dc represents the Domain Component (DC). On the third level, the organizational unit ou is defined as Engineering, so the DN is defined as ou=Engineering, dc=cassowary, dc=net, c=US. On the fourth level, an individual user is identified by a Common Name (CN) of Paul Watters, and a corresponding UID of paul. Thus, the DN is uid=paul, ou=Engineering, dc=cassowary, dc=net, c=US. Thus, it is possible to clearly distinguish individuals belonging to organizations and departments in specific countries from each other by simply using a DN if the DIT is defined at a fine-grained level, assuming that no two users in the same department have exactly the same name.

EXAM TIP   You should be able to identify and interpret elements of a DIT for the exam.

Exercise 31-2 DIT Creation   Create a sample DIT for yourself and your organization, following the example given previously.

iDS stores all data in LDIF files. This standard is used by all LDAP directory servers and many messaging systems to store user and group data. Thus, it is possible to export an LDIF file with an organization's data from a previous version of iDS and import it here. Alternatively, third-party products may be able to export LDIF files, which can also be read into iDS, to initialize the directory structure. Let's look at an example entry in an LDIF file for the directory entry we've defined previously:

```
dn: cn=Paul Watters, o=cassowary.net, c=US
cn: Paul Watters
sn: Watters
mail: paul@cassowary.net
objectClass: people
```

As you can see, the LDIF file structure simply reflects the attributes that are defined within the directory, written sequentially to the file immediately following the DN.

EXAM TIP   You should be able to identify and interpret elements of an LDIF for the exam.

Installing and Configuring iDS

Configuring iDS is a two-stage process: the first stage involves installing and configuring the server to run iDS, and the second stage involves setting up iDS to support LDAP clients (as described in the next section). In order to begin the process of configuring the server to run iDS, the directoryserver program must be executed:

```
# /usr/sbin/directoryserver setup
```

You can install either the iPlanet Directory Server (iDS) or the stand-alone iPlanet Console. After selecting iDS, you are presented with three different installation options: express, which presents few opportunities for customization, but is very fast; typical, which offers some configuration before installation; and custom, which offers maximum flexibility but is the slowest installation method.

There are three packages that comprise the iDS installation:

- Server Core Components, comprising all of the common objects used by iDS

- iPlanet Directory Suite, which contains the management console and the iDS software

- Administration Server, which contains packages for system administration and directory management

After selecting the appropriate packages to install, you need to indicate if the current installation will store configuration information, or whether this will be stored in another server. If data will be stored in another server, the hostname, port number, username, and password must all be entered so that the correct target iDS installation for configuration can be identified.

Following the selection of the configuration iDS target, you need to indicate if the current installation will store user and group information, or whether this will be stored in another server. Again, if data will be stored in another server, the hostname, port number, Distinguished Name (DN), password, and suffix must all be entered so that the correct target iDS installation for user and group data can be identified.

Next, the new iDS server must be set up with a unique server identifier, a port number that is not used by any other application, and the appropriate suffix for the local installation.

NOTE The default port number for LDAP is 389, while LDAP over SSL typically runs on port 636.

The administrator ID and password for the local iDS installation must be selected and entered next. This ID and password are also used for managing the local LDAP server using the management console.

CAUTION Since the administrator ID and password can be used to gain access to the iDS server, and modify user and group data without restriction, it's important that these credentials are chosen carefully so as to avoid easy guessing by rogue users.

The Administration Domain must be entered next. Since iDS can manage multiple domains simultaneously from a single server, it's important that their data is kept functionally and physically separate. Typically, the Administration Domain matches the

Internet domain name. However, each server needs to have a separate Administration Domain if they are located underneath a top-level domain. For example, if there are two separate iDS servers running in the **cassowary.net** domain, one for Engineering, and one for Sales, then the Administration Domains could be **engineering.cassowary.net** and **sales.cassowary.net**, respectively.

The Directory Manager's password for the local iDS installation must be selected and entered next. Since the Directory Manager ID and administrator ID password can be used to gain access to the iDS server and modify user and group data with few restrictions, it's important that these credentials are chosen carefully so as to avoid dictionary-based cracking.

The Administration Server for iDS is used to manage all aspects of the LDAP service. The Administration Server runs as a web server, meaning that any HTML browser can be used to view and configure all current settings for the iDS server. A port must be chosen to access the iDS Administration Server. The URL for the Administration Server is then given by appending the port number with a colon to the hostname. For example, the URL **http://ldap.cassowary.net:38575/** suggests an LDAP server running on port 38575 of the host **ldap.cassowary.net**.

Supporting LDAP Clients

In order to configure iDS to provide services to clients, the `idsconfig` command is used. The service configuration can either be manually entered on the command line or supplied from an external file when the `-i` option is passed. Alternatively, a configuration file from one system (generated by passing the `-o` option) can also be read in from an external file. If multiple iDS instances are installed, configuration information from the first installation can be used by subsequent installations. `idsconfig` can be started with the following command:

```
# /usr/lib/ldap/idsconfig
```

The following output shows a sample `idsconfig` session for **sales.cassowary.net**. In the first section, you are required to review the basic configuration of the directory service, including the port number and directory manager DN (and its password):

```
Enter the port number for iDS (h=help): [389]
Enter the directory manager DN: [cn=Directory Manager]
Enter passwd for cn=Directory Manager :
Enter the domainname to be served (h=help): [sales.cassowary.net]
```

Next, you need to review the directory and server details, including the BaseDN, profile name, and list of servers:

```
Enter LDAP BaseDN (h=help): [dc=sales,dc=cassowary,dc=net]
Enter the profile name (h=help): [default]
Are you sure you want to overwrite profile cn=default? y
Default server list (h=help): [192.64.18.1]
Preferred server list (h=help):
Choose desired search scope (one, sub, h=help): [one]
```

Security choices must be made next, including the credential level and authentication method:

```
The following are the supported credential levels:
1 anonymous
2 proxy
3 proxy anonymous
Choose Credential level [h=help]: [1] 1
The following are the supported Authentication Methods:
1 none
2 simple
3 sasl/DIGEST-MD5
4 tls:simple
5 tls:sals/DIGEST-MD5
Choose Authentication Method (h=help): [1] 2
Current authenticationMethod: simple
Do you want to add another Authentication Method? N
```

After reviewing the server configuration, you now need to configure client access. This includes setting timeouts for profile and directory access, password formats, and time and size limits:

```
Do you want the clients to follow referrals (y/n/h)? [n] n
Do you want to modify the server timelimit value (y/n/h)? [n] n
Do you want to modify the server sizelimit value (y/n/h)? [n] n
Do you want to store passwd's in "crypt" format (y/n/h)? [n] y
Do you want to setup a Service Authentication Methods (y/n/h)? [n] n
Search time limit in seconds (h=help): [60]
Profile Time To Live in seconds (h=help): [3600]
Bind time limit in seconds (h=help): [10] 2
Do you wish to setup Service Search Descriptors (y/n/h)? [n] n
```

Finally, you are presented with a configuration summary before any actions are performed by idsconfig:

```
Summary of Configuration
1 Domain to serve : sales.cassowary.net
2 BaseDN to setup : dc=sales,dc=cassowary,dc=net
3 Profile name to create : default
4 Default Server List : 192.64.18.1
5 Preferred Server List :
6 Default Search Scope : one
7 Credential Level : anonymous
8 Authentication Method : simple
9 Enable Follow Referrals : FALSE
10 iDS Time Limit :
11 iDS Size Limit :
12 Enable crypt passwd storage : 1
13 Service Auth Method pam_ldap :
14 Service Auth Method keyserv :
15 Service Auth Method passwd-cmd:
16 Search Time Limit : 30
17 Profile Time to Live : 43200
18 Bind Limit : 2
19 Service Search Descriptors Menu
```

Exercise 31-3 idsconfig Configuration Review your idsconfig configuration. Are there any options that you would need to set differently from the previous example?

Creating LDAP Entries

The `ldapaddent` command is used to create entries in the LDAP container for all of the standard system databases stored in files underneath the */etc* directory. All of the following Solaris databases (with the corresponding ou) can be transferred into LDAP by this method:

- *aliases* (ou=Aliases)
- *bootparams* (ou=Ethers)
- *ethers* (requires bootparams database to be installed first) (ou=Ethers)
- *group* (ou=Group)
- *hosts* (ou=Hosts)
- *netgroup* (ou=Netgroup)
- *netmasks* (requires *networks* database to be installed first) (ou=Networks)
- *networks* (ou=Networks)
- *passwd* (ou=People)
- *shadow* (requires *passwd* database to be installed first) (ou=People)
- *protocols* (ou=Protocols)
- *publickey* (ou=Hosts)
- *rpc* (ou=Rpc)
- *services* (ou=Services)

Starting a Client

The ldapclient program can be used for several purposes, including starting LDAP client services on client systems and reviewing the LDAP cache. In order to initialize a client you will need the address of the LDAP server and where its profile is stored. The LDAP cache manager (ldap_cachemgr) is responsible for ensuring that the correct configuration data is returned to a client upon initialization, especially if changes have been made to the profile. One of the following subcommands must be supplied on the command line to specify the behavior of ldapclient:

- **genprofile** Creates an LDIF format configuration file that can exported to another system, or imported at some future time.
- **init** Initializes an LDAP client from an LDAP server using a profile.
- **list** Prints a list of entries stored in the client cache to standard output.
- **manual** Initializes an LDAP client from an LDAP server using parameters specified on the command line.

- **mod**   Permits the modification of parameter values after initialization has been completed.
- **uninit**   Uninitializes an LDAP client from an LDAP server.

The following parameters can be modified by using the `ldapclient mod` command, or passed directly for manual initialization using the `ldapclient manual` command:

- **attributeMap**   Used to modify the default schema for a specific service.
- **authenticationMethod**   Stipulates the authentication method to be used (none, simple, sasl/CRAM-MD5, sasl/DIGEST-MD5, tls:simple, tls:sasl/CRAM-MD5, or tls:sasl/DIGEST-MD5). None means no security at all, while simple means that a password is sent in the clear and is vulnerable to interception. The other methods use a message digest algorithm to enhance security.
- **bindTimeLimit**   Maximum number of seconds allowed for a bind operation to be performed.
- **certificatePath**   Full path to the certificate database.
- **credentialLevel**   Specifies the type of credential required for authentication (either anonymous or proxy).
- **defaultSearchBase**   Specifies the BaseDN for searching.
- **defaultSearchScope**   Determines the scope for searching on the client side.
- **domainName**   Fully qualified domain name.
- **followReferrals**   Determines whether the referral setting is used.
- **objectclassMap**   Used to designate a different schema.
- **preferredServerList**   Lists a set of alternative LDAP servers to be contacted prior to the default.
- **profileName**   Determines the name of the client profile.
- **profileTTL**   Refresh epoch for the client cache to obtain new information from the server.
- **proxyDN**   Specifies the DN for the proxy server.
- **proxyPassword**   States the password for the proxy server.
- **searchTimeLimit**   Restricts the amount of time for each LDAP search.
- **serviceAuthenticationMethod**   Determines the authentication method for the passwd-cmd, keyserv, and pam_ldap services.
- **serviceCredentialLevel**   Specifies the type of credential required for service authentication (either anonymous or proxy). Proxy access for clients can occur only if a proxy account has previously been created in the directory and the proxyDN and proxyPassword attributes have been defined. Anonymous is not recommended, because it provides no security at all.
- **serviceSearchDescriptor**   Allows a different BaseDN to be specified on a per-service basis.

PART III

Let's look at some different examples of how LDAP clients can be initialized by using `ldapclient`. In the first example, the LDAP server 192.64.18.1 will be used to initialize the local client by using the `init` subcommand:

```
# ldapclient init 192.64.18.1
```

No additional parameters are necessary. However, a manual installation is much more complex, as all nondefault parameters must be specified. Sometimes only a single parameter will differ from the default; for example, if simple authentication was required, instead of no authentication (the default), the following command would be used:

```
# ldapclient manual -a authenticationMethod=simple \
      -a defaultServerList=192.64.18.1
```

Alternatively, if a higher-level search base needed to be specified, the following command could be used:

```
# ldapclient manual -a authenticationMethod=simple \
      -a defaultSearchBase=dc=cassowary,dc=net    \
      -a defaultServerList=192.64.18.1
```

To generate an LDIF format configuration file, we would use the `genprofile` subcommand, and redirect the output to a file (*/tmp/default.ldif*):

```
# ldapclient genprofile -a profileName=default \
-a defaultSearchBase=dc=cassowary,dc=net \
-a defaultServerList=192.64.18.1 \
> /tmp/default.ldif
```

Using the LDAP-NIS+ Interface

The `nisldapmaptest` command is used to operate on data stored within LDAP by using a NIS+ interface. This is particularly important when testing to see that NIS+ and LDAP services are correctly integrated. It can also be useful for experienced NIS+ administrators who want to add, delete, or modify LDAP records by using a familiar NIS+ interface. There are several options that can be passed to the `nisldapmaptest` command, including

- **-d** Enables deletion of data
- **-r** Updates data or add new data
- **-s** Searches for existing data
- **-t** Name of the target NIS+ object

Let's look at some examples of how the `nisldapmaptest` command can be used. First, we will examine how to determine whether a user entry ("pwatters") exists in the password table:

```
# nisldapmaptest -t passwd.org_dir name=pwatters
```

Any of the following tables can be queried in this way:

- auto_home
- auto_master
- bootparams
- client_info
- cred
- ethers
- group
- hosts
- mail_aliases
- netgroup
- netmasks
- networks
- passwd
- protocols
- rpc
- sendmailvars
- services
- timezone

For example, to obtain a list of hosts stored in the hosts table, we would use the following command:

```
# nisldapmaptest -t hosts.org_dir
```

If a host was found in the table that was no longer valid, it could be deleted by using the following command:

```
# nisldapmaptest -d -t hosts.org_dir name=oldhost
```

Using iDS

In this example, we will demonstrate how to manage iDS by using the console. Once the iDS server has been installed, you should be able to start the console by using the command:

```
# directoryserver startconsole
```

The appropriate admin port number and hostname will be displayed on the login window, as shown in Figure 31-2. In this case, 14462 is the admin port for the LDAP

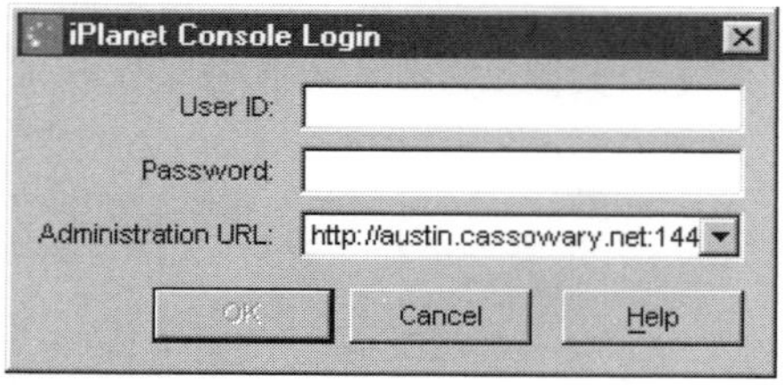

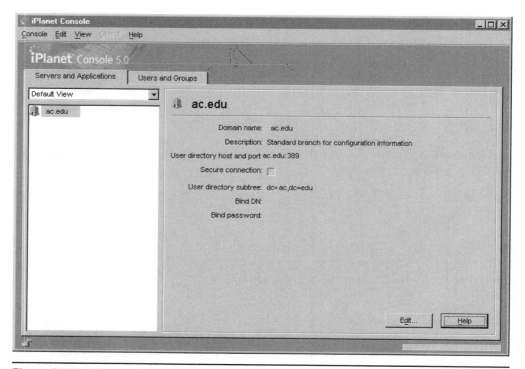

Figure 31-2   Authentication for the Administration Server

server that was specified during install. The administration user ID and corresponding password must be entered in order to bring up the main administration window.

The main iDS console is then displayed, as shown in Figure 31-3. There are two tabs that are used to separate the two main functions of the console: Servers and Applications, and Users and Groups. The Servers and Applications tab has two separate panes: the first pane is a hierarchical object list of all servers and their respective databases that have been configured for the network. The local server group is displayed, along with entries for the local administration server and the actual directory server. By selecting the icon associated with the localhost, the hostname, description, physical location, platform, and operating system will be displayed.

Figure 31-3   Main console window

NOTE Selecting the server group icon displays the group name, description, and installation path.

The second pane shows the domain name, description, port number, and user directory structure for the iDS server. In addition, the DN and password are displayed, as well as an option to encrypt connections to the server. It is possible to edit these details by clicking the Edit button.

By selecting the Directory Server icon in the Servers and Applications tab, a list of configured items for the local server is displayed, as shown in Figure 31-4. For example, the server name, description, installation date, product name, vendor name, version number, build number, revision level, security level, server status, and port are all displayed.

By double-clicking on the Directory Server icon, a new window is displayed, as shown in Figure 31-5, which is used to configure the directory server's operation. There are four tabs available, each with a number of different operations. The Tasks tab defines nine different operations:

1. Start Directory Server, which initializes the local iDS server and launches it.

2. Stop Directory Server, which shuts down all local services, and stops the iDS processes.

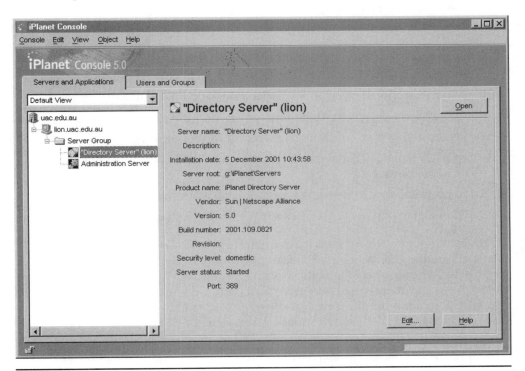

Figure 31-4　Main Directory Server window

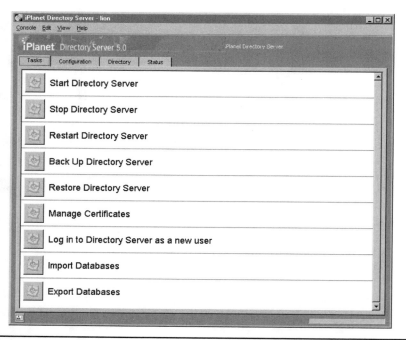

Figure 31-5 Directory Server Configuration window

3. Restart Directory Server, which shuts down all local services, stops the iDS processes, initializes the local iDS server and relaunches it.

4. Back Up Directory Server, which backs up the local iDS database.

5. Restore Directory Server, which restores the local iDS database from a backup.

6. Manage Certificates, which manages certificates for security.

7. Log In To Directory Server As A New User, which allows you to log in to iDS as a different user.

8. Import Databases, to import a new iDS database from a different system.

9. Export Databases, to export an existing local iDS database to a different system.

The Configuration tab contains a hierarchical list of objects associated with the iDS database, including tables, replication features, the database schema, logs, and optional plug-ins. In addition, a set of tabs allows various options to be configured. The Settings subtab allows the unencrypted port, encrypted port, and referrals to be set, as shown in Figure 31-6. In addition, the server can be set up as read-only and entry modification times can be tracked, along with various schema checks.

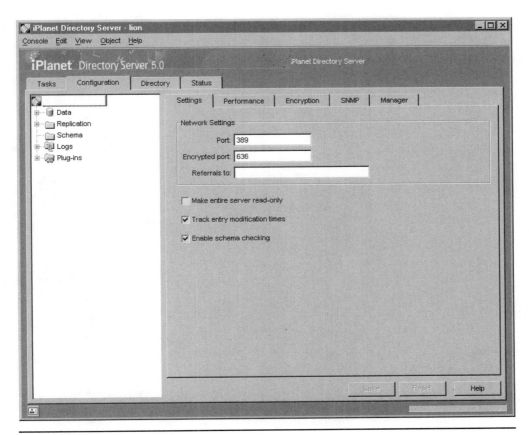

Figure 31-6 Settings Configuration window

The Performance subtab sets limits on the size of the directory, a time limit for access, and an idle timeout, as shown in Figure 31-7. These settings will need to be modified for local use, but are set at 2000 entries, one hour, and zero, respectively.

The Encryption subtab has two main tasks: setting options for server security and for client authentication, as shown in Figure 31-8. On the server side, access can be granted using SSL, thereby protecting authentication tokens from interception by a third party. In this case, RSA options need to be set, including the name of the security device (by default, internal/software-based), the certificate location, and the cipher. On the client side, authentication can be disallowed, allowed, or required, depending on the application's requirements. In addition, using SSL can be made mandatory within the iPlanet console.

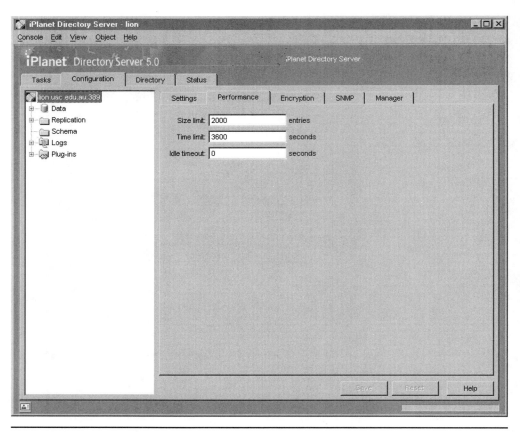

Figure 31-7   Performance configuration window

The SNMP subtab, as shown in Figure 31-9, provides an interface to the Simple Network Management Protocol (SNMP), allowing service status to be remotely monitored by a third-party SNMP monitoring product. When alarm events are triggered because of runtime errors, administration staff can be notified by pager, phone, or e-mail, and appropriate action can be taken to rectify the problem. Descriptive properties, including the organization, location, and support contact, can be entered from the SNMP subtab, as well as three buttons allowing the service to be started, stopped, and/or restarted.

The Manager subtab, as shown in Figure 31-10, sets several options for the Directory Manager role. This includes the Distinguished Name of the Directory Manager, the algorithm used to encrypt the Directory Manager's password (by default, the Secure Salted Hashing Algorithm, SSHA), and the Directory Manager's password. It's also possible to enter a new password into the New Password field and confirm it in the Confirm Password field.

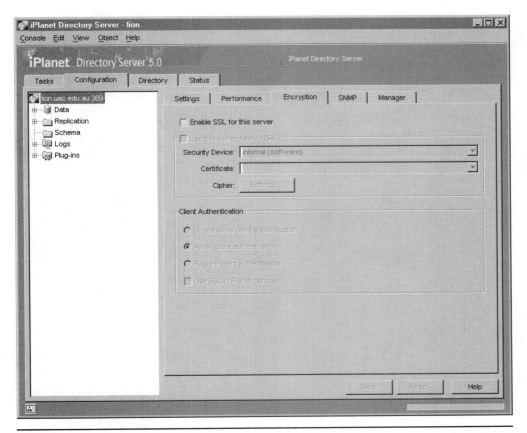

Figure 31-8   Encryption Configuration window

The administration server can be configured by double-clicking the administration server icon in the Servers and Applications tab, as shown in Figure 31-11, which is used to configure the directory server's operation. There are four tabs available, each with a number of different operations. The Tasks tab defines five different operations:

1. Start directory server, which initializes the local iDS server and launches it.

2. Restart directory, which shuts down all local services, stops the iDS processes, initializes the local iDS server, and relaunches it.

3. Configure the local administration server.

4. Set up local logging options.

5. Manage certificates for security.

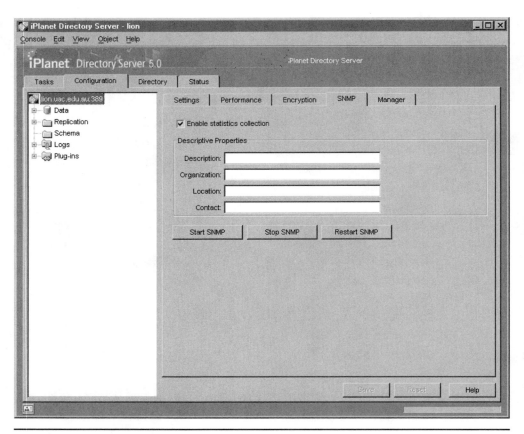

Figure 31-9 SNMP Configuration window

The console provides an interface for querying the directory, as well as adding new entries at the user, group, and organizational unit levels. The search facility allows a search string to be entered and searched, where the string is a full or partial username, group name, or organizational unit. For example, to find the user "Paul Watters" in the directory, you could search on "Paul" or "Watters". Figure 31-12 shows the searching interface, and the result of a search on "Watters" (no matches were found in the directory). If a match had been found, the name, user ID, e-mail address, and phone number would have been displayed. In addition, each entry found as the result of a search can be modified by selecting the Edit button.

If an entry is not found, it can be easily created by clicking on the Create button, as shown in Figure 31-13. A drop-down list of all possible entry types is shown, including users, groups, and organizational units.

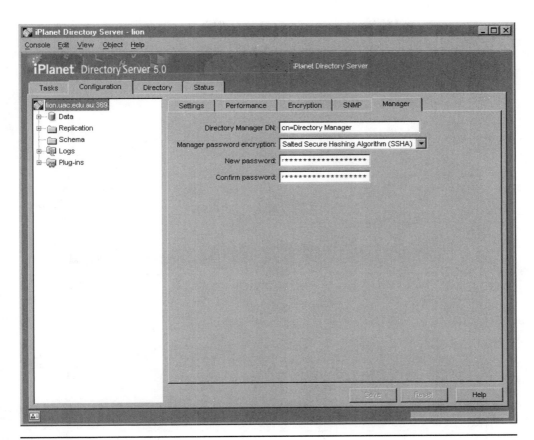

Figure 31-10   Manager Configuration window

After choosing to create a new user, group, or organizational unit, you need to indicate the directory subtree under which the entry will appear, as shown in Figure 31-14. There are four options: the Base Distinguished Name (that is, the top level of the directory), Groups, People, and Special Users.

A new user can be created by using the Create User screen, as shown in Figure 31-15. The user's first name, last name, common name, user ID, password, e-mail address, phone number, and fax number can be entered into their respective fields. In addition, a target language can be entered for the user, and Windows NT or POSIX-specific user data can be stored. Since this iDS installation is based on Solaris, Posix should be selected.

Once the user's detail have been entered, it should be possible to return to the user search screen, enter in the name of the user whose details have been stored, and retrieve their complete record, as shown in Figure 31-16. Once retrieved, the user's details can be modified, or their record can be deleted.

PART III

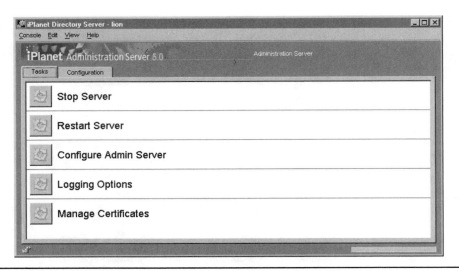

Figure 31-11   Administration Server Configuration window

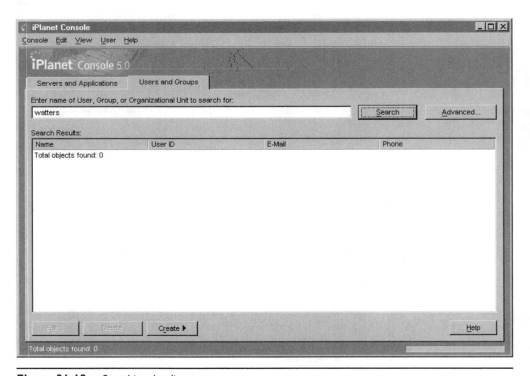

Figure 31-12   Searching the directory

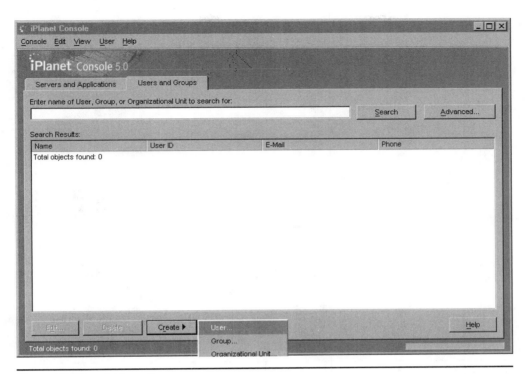

Figure 31-13   Adding a directory entry

A key user characteristic is group membership. Thus, once a number of users have been created in a directory, it makes sense to create a group to store them in, rather than entering them at the top level of the directory. Defining a new group requires a group name, as well as a group description. These can be entered into the Create Group window, as shown in Figure 31-17. The languages required to be used by group members can also be entered by selecting Languages from the left-hand pane.

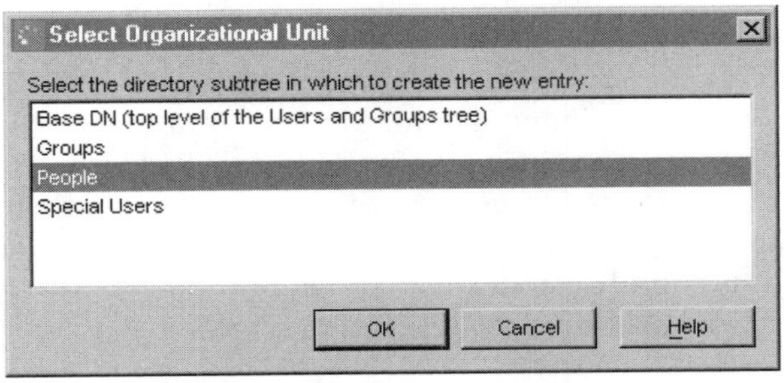

Figure 31-14   Selecting a directory subtree

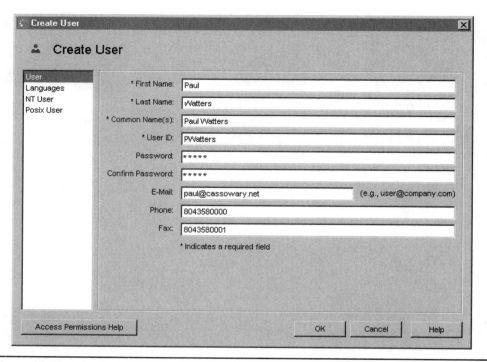

Figure 31-15   Creating a new user

Once a group has been defined, members can be added individually, by selecting Members from the left-hand pane and clicking the Add button, as shown in Figure 31-18. Alternatively, group members, once created using this screen, can be easily removed by clicking the Remove button.

After members have been added to groups, it's then possible to search on a user and group basis, rather than just a user basis, as shown in Figure 31-19. The search string can either be a group name or a username. Once group members have been selected on the basis of the search term, their details are displayed sorted by name, with user ID, e-mail address, and phone number appearing.

At the top level, it's possible to define a new organizational unit. The unit's entry can contain the unit's name, a description, phone number, fax number, alias, and full address, as shown in Figure 31-20. In addition, the language support required for the organizational unit can be defined by selecting Languages from the left-hand pane.

If you are unfamiliar with LDAP, you may need to consult a specialized book on the topic to be able to fully understand the administrative and security issues associated with creating organizational units, groups, and members.

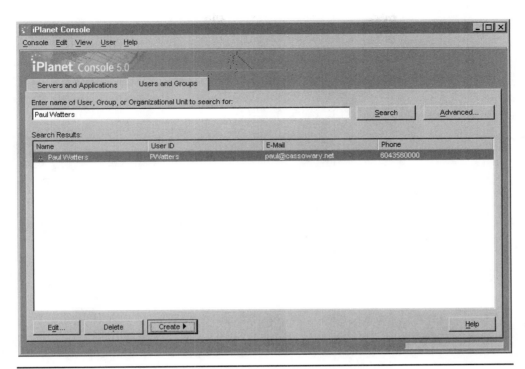

Figure 31-16 Finding an existing user

ldapsearch

The `ldapsearch` command is used to query the directory for a specific entry from the command line, and to display the attributes of an entry once located. A query string composed of a logical condition is passed on the command line, along with a set of attributes that are to be displayed. For example, to search for the common name "Paul Watters" and display the results, the following command would be used:

```
$ ldapsearch -u "cn=Paul Watters" cn
cn=Paul A Watters, ou=Engineering, o=cassowary.net, c=US
cn=Paul Watters
```

Alternatively, if the UID of the user you were searching for was known and you wanted to look up the common name, the following command could be used:

```
$ ldapsearch -u -t "uid=paul" cn
cn=Paul A Watters, ou=Engineering, o=cassowary.net, c=US
cn=Paul Watters
```

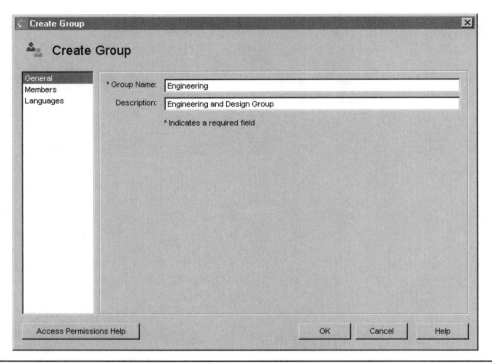

Figure 31-17   Creating a group

It's possible to perform a wider area search than just looking for a single individual. For example, to print a description of all organizations lying below the country "US" in the DIT, the following command would be used:

```
$ ldapsearch -L -b "c=US" description
dn: o=cassowary.net, c=US
description: Cassowary Computing Pty Ltd
```

ldapmodify

The ldapmodify command is used to create, read, update, or delete entries in the directory. There is also an ldapadd command, which is used to create new directory entries. However, this command is equivalent to invoking ldapmodify with the -a (add) option. In addition, while it is possible to enter data using standard input, most users will perform actions based on data stored in a file (after all, if you make a mistake when typing and you have to cancel the data entry, all of the input will be lost).

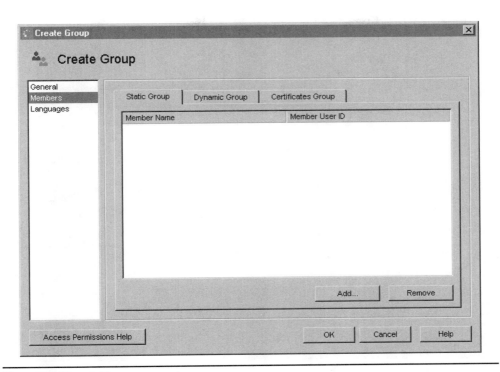

Figure 31-18   Adding group members

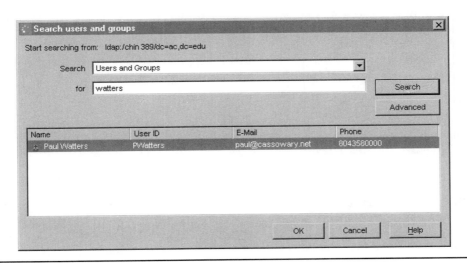

Figure 31-19   Searching users and groups

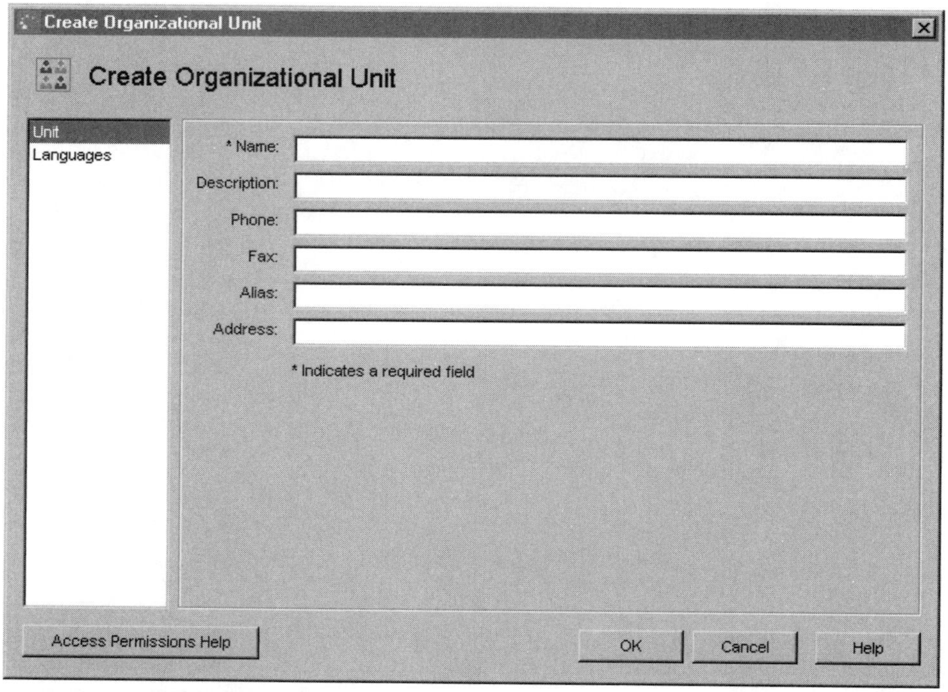

Figure 31-20   Creating an organizational unit

If we want to create a new entry for Moppet Watters in the directory, the following data should be inserted into a file called *newdata.txt*:

```
dn: cn=Moppet Watters, o=cassowary.net, c=US
objectClass: person
cn: Mopster Watters
sn: Watters
title: Mascot
mail: moppet@cassowary.net
uid: moppet
```

In order to insert this data into the directory, the following command would be used:

```
# ldapmodify -a -f newdata.txt
```

To delete this entry from the directory, we would first insert the following data into *delentry.txt*:

```
dn: cn=Moppet Watters, o=cassowary.net, c=US
changetype=delete
```

We could then delete the entry from the directory by using the following command:

```
# ldapmodify -f delentry.txt
```

Summary

LDAP is commonly used by large organizations as a standard directory service, and most used-based Solaris applications can now use LDAP. Although LDAP is a complex service to configure and administer, it certainly simplifies the management of large user bases.

Questions

1. What is the purpose of the `ldapsearch` command?

   A. Query the directory for a specific entry.

   B. Query the network for a LDAP server.

   C. Query the server for an IP address.

   D. Retrieve a list of LDAP clients.

2. What is LDAP?

   A. Green pages

   B. Yellow pages

   C. White pages

   D. Pink pages

3. How is the organization of entries in an LDAP directory defined?

   A. Directory

   B. Table

   C. Row

   D. Schema

4. How can all entries within the directory be identified?

   A. Directory Name (DN)

   B. Distinguished Name (DN)

   C. Relative Distinguished Name (RDN)

   D. Relative Directory Name (RDN)

5. How can attributes of an entry be identified?

   A. Directory Name (DN)

   B. Distinguished Name (DN)

   C. Relative Distinguished Name (RDN)

   D. Relative Directory Name (RDN)

6. Which of the following is the correct BaseDN for **engineer.paulwatters.com**?

   A. dc=engineer,dc=paulwatters,dc=com

   B. dc=com,dc=paulwatters,dc=engineer

   C. dc=com,paulwatters,engineer

   D. dc= engineer, paulwatters,com

7. What is the default port for LDAP services?

   A. 80

   B. 1024

   C. 389

   D. 264

8. Which of the following organizational units is not supported by Solaris?

   A. *group* (ou=Group)

   B. *hosts* (ou=Hosts)

   C. *netgroup* (ou=Netgroup)

   D. *db* (ou=metadb)

9. Which of the following cannot be used with the `ldapclient mod` command?

   A. certificatePath

   B. credentialLevel

   C. certificateKey

   D. defaultSearchBase

10. What command is used for configuring iDS?

   A. `idsconfig`

   B. `iDSconfig`

   C. `configiDS`

   D. `DSconf`

Answers

1. **A.** The `ldapsearch` command is used to query the directory for a specific entry.

2. **C.** LDAP is a "white pages" type of service.

3. **D.** The organization of entries in an LDAP directory is defined by a schema.

4. **B.** All entries in the directory are identified by a Distinguished Name (DN).

5. **C.** All attributes of an entry in the directory can be identified by a Relative Distinguished Name (DN).

6. **A.** dc=engineer,dc=paulwatters,dc=com is the correct BaseDN for **engineer.paulwatters.com**.

7. **C.** The default port for LDAP services is 389.

8. **D.** The *db* organizational unit is not supported by Solaris.

9. **C.** certificateKey cannot be used with the `ldapclient mod` command.

10. **A.** The `idsconfig` command is used to configure iDS.

OSI/IP Network Models

In this chapter, you will

- Describe the OSI networking model
- Describe the TCP/IP protocol suite
- List the properties of Ethernet
- Describe the mapping between hardware and software interface addresses
- State the properties of the Transmission Control Protocol (TCP), User Datagram Protocol (UDP), and Internet Protocol (IP)

Sun's view is that "The Network Is The Computer." However, while users often consider the "network" to be a single heterogeneous medium, the process of transferring a packet of data from one host to another is not a trivial task. This is where conceptual protocol stacks like the general Open System Interconnect (OSI) networking model are useful in encapsulating and dividing the labor associated with physical network transmission and its management by software. Solaris uses the four-layer TCP/IP suite of network protocols to carry out network operations, including the Transmission Control Protocol (TCP), User Datagram Protocol (UDP), and Internet Protocol (IP). These protocols and the layer in which they reside will be covered in depth in the following chapters. In this chapter, we'll examine how TCP/IP is implemented on Solaris, including the configuration of network interfaces, daemons, addresses, ports, and sockets. Finally, we'll examine how to configure the Internet daemon (inetd) to support a number of separate network services that are centrally managed.

Network Concepts

A network is a combination of hardware and software that enables computers to communicate with each other. At the hardware level, building a network involves installing a network interface into each system ("host") to be networked and implementing a specific network topology by using cables, such as Ethernet or wireless. At the software level, representations of network devices must be created and protocols for exchanging data between hosts must be established. Data is exchanged by dividing it into packets that have a specific structure, enabling large data elements to be exchanged between hosts by using a small amount of wrapping. This wrapping, based on various protocols, contains information about the order in which packets should be assembled when transmitted from one host to another, for example.

By supporting many different types of hardware devices and connection technologies, and by implementing standards-based networking software, Solaris provides a flexible platform for supporting high-level network services and applications. These will be explored in detail in the following chapters.

Network Topologies

The two most common forms of network topology are the star network and the ring network. The ring topology, as shown in Figure 32-1, is a peer-to-peer topology where neighboring hosts are connected and data is exchanged between distant hosts by passing data from the source host to the target host through all intermediate hosts. Ring networks are most suitable for networks where long distances separate individual hosts. However, if only one of the links between hosts is broken, then data transmission between all hosts can be interrupted.

In contrast, a star network has a centralized topology, where all hosts connect to a central point and exchange data at that point, as shown in Figure 32-2. This has the advantage of minimizing the number of hops that data must travel from a source to a target host, compared to a ring network. In addition, if one link is broken, only data originating from or sent to the host on that link will be disrupted. However, if the point at which hosts are connected breaks down, then all data transmission will cease.

In practice, most modern high-speed networks are based on star topologies. When connecting local area networks together to form internets, a star topology has the advantage of being able to interconnect networks by their central connection points. This means that data sent from a host on one network must travel to its central point, which then sends the data to the connection point on a remote network, which then passes the data to the remote target host. Thus, only three hops are required to exchange data between hosts on two networks when using a star topology. This data flow is shown in Figure 32-3.

Let's look at a specific example of how an internet can be laid out before examining how OSI and the Solaris implementation of TCP/IP make this possible. Imagine that a web server runs on the host 203.54.68.21, while a web client (such as Netscape Navigator) runs on the host 203.54.67.122. Because these two hosts are located on two different local area (Class C) networks, they must be interconnected by a router. In the star topology, a connection point must allow a link to each host on the local network—in this example, a hub is used to connect each host, as well as forwarding all data bound for nonlocal addresses to the router. Thus, when a high-level HTTP request is sent from the client 203.54.67.122 to the server 203.54.68.21, a packet is sent to the hub, which detects that the destination is nonlocal and forwards the packet to the router. The router

Figure 32-1
Ring network topology

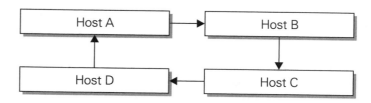

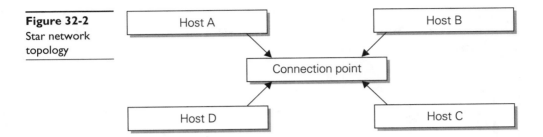

Figure 32-2
Star network
topology

then forwards the packet to the router for the remote network, which detects that the destination is local and passes it to the hub, which in turn passes it to the server. Because HTTP is a request/response protocol, the backwards path is traced when a response to the request is generated by the server. The configuration for this example is shown in Figure 32-4.

If this example seems complex, you'll be pleased to know that the implementation of many of these services is hidden from users, and most often from developers. This makes implementing networking applications very simple when using high-level protocols like HTTP. For example, consider the following Java code, which uses HTTP to make a connection to a remote server running an application called StockServer. After passing the name of a stock in the URL, the current price should be returned by the server. The code fragment shows the definition for the URL, and a declaration for an input stream, which reads a line from the stream and assigns the result to a variable (stockPrice), and then closes the stream. If this code was contained in an applet, for example, the stockPrice for SUNW could then be displayed.

```
String stockURL="http://data.cassowary.net/servlet/StockServer?code=SUNW";
URL u = new URL(stockURL);
BufferedReader in = new BufferedReader(new InputStreamReader(u.openStream()));
String stockPrice=in.readLine();
in.close();
```

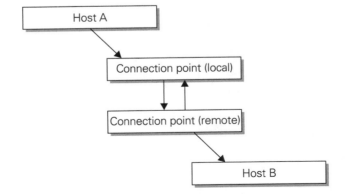

Figure 32-3
Interconnecting
networks

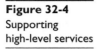

Figure 32-4
Supporting
high-level services

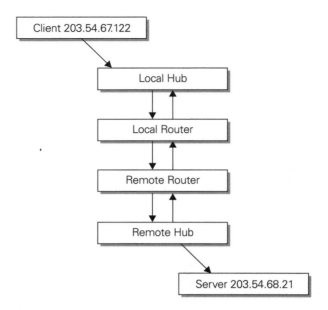

A further level of abstraction is provided by Web Services and the Simple Object Access Protocol (SOAP), which uses HTTP as a transport for transmitting requests to execute Remote Procedure Calls (RPC) in a platform-independent way. This approach has some similarities to working directly at the HTTP level, because a URL can be used to execute the SOAP request but the data is returned in a standard XML format. The following URL, for example, is used to retrieve the stock price for Sun Microsystems from XML Today: **http://www.xmltoday.com/examples/stockquote/getxmlquote.vep?s=*SUNW***

The data returned from this request can be parsed, and its tags can be interpreted by a client program:

```
<stock_quotes>
     <stock_quote>
          <symbol>SUNW</symbol>
          <when>
               <date>10/30/2002</date>
               <time>3:06pm</time>
          </when>
          <price type="ask" value="2.50" />
          <price type="open" value="2.60" />
          <price type="dayhigh" value="2.60" />
          <price type="daylow" value="2.49" />
          <change>-0.10</change>
          <volume>5768644</volume>
     </stock_quote>
</stock_quotes>
```

Web Services will become more commonly used in future versions of Solaris and related enterprise applications, so it's useful to understand how they work and how they relate to underlying networking protocols.

Open System Interconnect (OSI) Networking

Building networks is complex, given the wide array of hardware and software that can be used to implement them. The OSI networking model, as shown in Figure 32-5, provides a framework for defining the scope of different layers of networking technology, which can be used to understand how different protocols and suites (such as TCP/IP) operate. Each layer of the model, starting from the bottom, supports the functionality required by the top levels. Moving from bottom to top, operations become more and more abstracted from their physical implementation. It is this abstraction that allows HTTP and other high-level protocols to operate without being concerned about low-level implementations.

 TIP　The OSI networking model allows for different instantiations of lower levels, without higher-level code needing to be rewritten.

Starting from the bottom, the first level is the Physical Layer, which defines both how data is exchanged at its very basic level (bits and bytes) and cabling requirements. The second level is the Data Link Layer, which defines the apparatus for transferring data, including error checking and synchronization. The third level is the Network Layer, which specifies operational issues such as how networks can exchange data, as shown in Figures 32-3 and 32-4. The fourth level is the Transport Layer, which specifies how individual computers are

Figure 32-5
The Open System
Interconnect
(OSI) networking
model

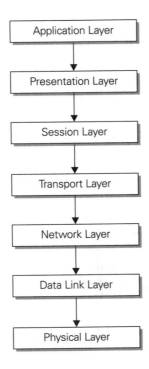

to interpret data received from the network. The fifth level is the Session Layer, which determines how data from different sources can be separated, and how associations between hosts can be maintained. The sixth level is the Presentation Layer, which specifies how different types of data are formatted and how it should be exposed. The seventh level is the Application Layer, which describes how high-level applications can communicate with each other in a standard way.

TCP/IP Networking

The TCP/IP suite of protocols forms the basis of all Internet communications and was originally devised as part of the Defense Advanced Research Projects Agency (DARPA) for the ARPANET. While TCP/IP is the default networking protocol supported by Solaris, other operating systems also support TCP/IP, even if it is not their primary protocol. For example, Microsoft Windows networks support NetBEUI and IPX/SPX, while MacOS supports AppleTalk. Linux administrators should already be familiar with TCP/IP because, like Solaris, it is the default networking protocol.

TCP/IP presents a simpler interface than OSI, since only the Application, Transport, Network and Link layers need to be addressed. This can be seen in the following packet intercept performed by the snoop application, which reads raw packet data from a network interface operating in promiscuous mode. The following example shows ETHER (Link), IP (Network), TCP (Transport), and TELNET (Application) sections respectively:

```
# snoop -v tcp port 23
Using device /dev/hme0 (promiscuous mode)
ETHER:  ----- Ether Header -----
ETHER:
ETHER:  Packet 1 arrived at 14:13:22.14
ETHER:  Packet size = 60 bytes
ETHER:  Destination = 1:58:4:16:8a:34,
ETHER:  Source      = 2:60:5:12:6b:35, Sun
ETHER:  Ethertype = 0800 (IP)
ETHER:
IP:   ----- IP Header -----
IP:
IP:   Version = 4
IP:   Header length = 20 bytes
IP:   Type of service = 0x00
IP:        xxx. .... = 0 (precedence)
IP:        ...0 .... = normal delay
IP:        .... 0... = normal throughput
IP:        .... .0.. = normal reliability
IP:   Total length = 40 bytes
IP:   Identification = 46864
IP:   Flags = 0x4
IP:        .1.. .... = do not fragment
IP:        ..0. .... = last fragment
IP:   Fragment offset = 0 bytes
IP:   Time to live = 255 seconds/hops
IP:   Protocol = 6 (TCP)
IP:   Header checksum = 11a9
IP:   Source address = 64.23.168.76, moppet.paulwatters.com
IP:   Destination address = 64.23.168.48, miki.paulwatters.com
```

```
IP:     No options
IP:
TCP:    ----- TCP Header -----
TCP:
TCP:    Source port = 62421
TCP:    Destination port = 23 (TELNET)
TCP:    Sequence number = 796159562
TCP:    Acknowledgement number = 105859685
TCP:    Data offset = 20 bytes
TCP:    Flags = 0x10
TCP:          ..0. .... = No urgent pointer
TCP:          ...1 .... = Acknowledgement
TCP:          .... 0... = No push
TCP:          .... .0.. = No reset
TCP:          .... ..0. = No Syn
TCP:          .... ...0 = No Fin
TCP:    Window = 8760
TCP:    Checksum = 0x8f8f
TCP:    Urgent pointer = 0
TCP:    No options
TCP:
TELNET:  ----- TELNET:    -----
TELNET:
TELNET:  "a"
TELNET:
```

TCP/IP is layered, just like the OSI reference model. Thus, when a client application needs to communicate with a server, a process is initiated of passing data down each level on the client side, from the Application Layer to the Physical Layer, and up each level on the server side, from the Physical Layer to the Application Layer. Data is passed between layers in service data units. However, it's important to note that each client layer logically only ever communicates with the corresponding server layer, as demonstrated by the Java code presented previously: the Application Layer is not concerned with logically communicating with the Physical Layer, for example.

 TIP   Abstraction is the core benefit of TCP/IP in development and communication terms, since each level is logically isolated, while methods for supporting service data are also well defined.

Exercise 32-1 Running snoop   As root, run the snoop command and examine the headers for each network layer.

The ETHER header defines many of the characteristics of the packet. In the snoop example, the packets arrival time, size (in bytes), destination, and source addresses (Ethernet format) are all noted. In addition, the network type is supplied. This leads into the IP header, which shows the IP version (IPv4), the length of the header (in bytes), destination and source addresses (IP format), and a checksum to ensure data integrity. Also, the protocol for transport is defined as TCP. The TCP header shows the port on which the data is being sent and on which it should be received, in addition to the application type (TELNET). The sequence and acknowledgement numbers determine how packets are ordered at the receiving end, because TCP is connection-oriented and guarantees data delivery, unlike other transport protocols (for example, UDP) that are connectionless and do not guarantee the delivery of data. Finally, the data being transported is displayed: "a". In addition to TELNET, other application protocols include the Simple Mail Transfer Protocol (SMTP), the File Transfer Protocol (FTP), and the Network File System (NFS).

We'll now review each of these layers as they are implemented in the Solaris TCP/IP stack.

EXAM TIP   You should be able to relate definitions of different OSI layer functionality to specific layer names.

Ethernet Layer

Ethernet is the most commonly used link technology supported by Solaris and comes in five different speeds, including:

- 10Base-2   2 Mbps
- 10Base-5   5 Mbps
- 10Base-T   10 Mbps
- 100Base-T   100 Mbps
- 1000Base-FX   1Gbps

Solaris systems are typically supplied with a single Ethernet card, supporting 10/100 Mbps; however, server systems (such as the 420R) are supplied with quad Ethernet cards, supporting four interfaces operating at 10/100 Mbps. Although Ethernet (specified by the IEEE 802.3 standard) is the most common link type, other supported link types on Solaris include the Fiber Distributed Data Interface (FDDI) and Asynchronous Transfer Mode (ATM). FDDI networks use a ring topology based on a transmitting and receiving ring, using high-quality fiber-optic cable to support high-speed redundant connections. However, FDDI is expensive compared to Ethernet, and gigabit FDDI is not available. ATM is designed for high quality of service applications, like video and audio streaming, which require a constant amount of bandwidth to operate. Data is transmitted in fixed-size cells of 53 bytes, and a connection is maintained while required between client and server.

CAUTION   Although ATM does not approach the speeds of Gigabit Ethernet, its quality of service provisions benefit certain types of data transmission.

Note that the address used in the ETHER is the hardware address, otherwise known as the Media Access Control (MAC) address. This address is used to distinguish hosts at the link level and is mapped to an IP address at the network level by using the Address

Resolution Protocol (ARP). You can check the table of IP address to MAC address mappings by using the `arp` command:

```
$ arp -a
Net to Media Table
Device IP Address            Mask            Flags Phys Addr
------ -------------------- --------------- ----- ---------------
hme0   www.cassowary.net    255.255.255.255        00:19:cd:e3:05:a3
hme0   mail.cassowary.net   255.255.255.255        08:11:92:a4:12:ee
hme0   ftp.cassowary.net    255.255.255.255 SP     08:12:4e:4d:55:a2
hme0   BASE-ADDRESS.MCAST.NET 240.0.0.0     SM     01:01:4e:00:00:00
```

Here, the network device is shown with either the fully qualified hostname or IP address, the netmask, any flags, and the MAC address. The flags indicate the status of each interface, including "SP" for the localhost, where an entry will be published on request, and "SM" for the localhost, supporting multicast. Alternatively, a specific host can be queries by passing its name on the command line:

```
$ arp mail
mail (204.67.34.12) at 08:11:92:a4:12:ee
```

Conversely, the Reverse Address Resolution Protocol (RARP) is used to map MAC addresses to IP addresses. RARP is typically used to supply IP addresses from boot servers to diskless clients.

TIP A database of Ethernet addresses is maintained in the */etc/ethers* table to support this activity.

Exercise 32-2 Running arp Run `arp -a` on your local system. Are there any flags displayed that are not described here? If so, read the man page for arp and interpret them.

IPv4

The basic element of the Internet Protocol version (IPv4) is the IP address, which is a 32-bit number (4 bytes) that uniquely identifies network interfaces on the Internet. For "single-homed" hosts, which have only one network interface, the IP address identifies the host. However, for "multihomed" hosts, which have multiple network interfaces, the IP address does not uniquely identify the host. Even the domain name assigned to a multihost can be different, depending on which network the interface is connected to. For example, a router, as a host that contains at least two interfaces, supports the passing of data between networks.

The IP address is usually specified in dot decimal notation, in which each of the bytes is displayed as an integer separated by a "dot." An example IP address is 192.205.76.123, which is based on a Class C network. There are five "classes" of networks defined by IP

(A, B, C, D, E), although only three of these (A, B, C) are actually used for the identification of hosts. Network classes can be identified by a discrete range of values; thus, if an address lies within a specific range, it can be identified as belonging to a network of a specific class. The following ranges are defined by IP:

- **Class A**   0.0.0.0–127.255.255.255
- **Class B**   128.0.0.0–191.255.255.255
- **Class C**   192.0.0.0–223.255.255.255
- **Class D**   224.0.0.0–239.255.255.255
- **Class E**   240.0.0.0–247.255.255.255

The different classes allow for ever-decreasing numbers of hosts in each network, starting from Class A, where networks can support millions of hosts, to Class C networks, which can only support up to 254 hosts. Some address ranges have special purposes: the network 10.0.0.0 is reserved for private use and is commonly used to define IP address for internal networks. This is a security feature, because 10.0.0.0 addresses are not resolvable from the Internet. In addition, the 127.0.0.0 addresses are used to refer to the localhost, with the most commonly used value being 127.0.0.1.

Subnets allow large networks to be divided up into smaller logical networks by using a subnet mask. For Class A networks, the mask is 255.0.0.0; for Class B networks, the mask is 255.255.0.0; and for Class C networks, the mask is 255.255.255.0.

TIP   Solaris 9 now provides complete support for IPv6 and IPSec, discussed in Chapter 36. These innovations are designed to increase the capacity of the Internet, and secure packets transmitted by using transport protocols.

TCP

TCP is a connection-oriented protocol that guarantees delivery of packets, where data has been segmented into smaller units. The benefit of transmitting small units in a guaranteed delivery scheme is that if checksum errors are detected or some data is not received, the amount of data that needs to be retransmitted is very small. In addition, if packet delivery "times out," packets can then be retransmitted. By using sequence numbers, TCP always manages to reassemble packets in their correct order. Port numbers for TCP (and UDP) services are defined in the */etc/services* database. A sample database is shown here:

```
tcpmux          1/tcp
echo            7/tcp
echo            7/udp
discard         9/tcp           sink null
discard         9/udp           sink null
systat          11/tcp          users
daytime         13/tcp
daytime         13/udp
netstat         15/tcp
chargen         19/tcp          ttytst source
chargen         19/udp          ttytst source
```

```
ftp-data          20/tcp
ftp               21/tcp
telnet            23/tcp
smtp              25/tcp          mail
time              37/tcp          timserver
time              37/udp          timserver
name              42/udp          nameserver
whois             43/tcp          nickname
domain            53/udp
domain            53/tcp
bootps            67/udp
bootpc            68/udp
hostnames        101/tcp          hostname
pop2             109/tcp          pop-2
pop3             110/tcp
sunrpc           111/udp          rpcbind
sunrpc           111/tcp          rpcbind
imap             143/tcp          imap2
ldap             389/tcp
ldap             389/udp
ldaps            636/tcp
ldaps            636/udp
tftp              69/udp
rje               77/tcp
finger            79/tcp
link              87/tcp          ttylink
supdup            95/tcp
```

Reading from left to right is the service name, port number transport type, and service aliases. For example, the sunrpc service is also known as rpcbind and is essential for supporting Remote Procedure Call (RPC) applications like NFS. Other services defined previously include the echo service, which simply sends back the segment transmitted to it; daytime, which returns the current local time at the server; ftp, which supports the File Transfer Protocol (FTP) service; and smtp, which supports the Simple Mail Transfer Protocol (SMTP). If services are not to be supported on the localhost, their entries should be commented in the service database. For example, to disable the service definition for the finger service, which allows remote users to check local user details, the finger entry would be modified as follows:

```
#finger           79/tcp
```

Port numbers between 1 and 1024 are standard, as defined by Request For Comment (RFC) memos (**http://www.rfc-editor.org/rfc.html**). Nonstandard services can be run on ports above 1024.

Application Protocols

Services are implemented by daemons that listen for connections and generate responses based on specific requests. Many of the TCP service definitions match up with an application supported by a daemon (server) process. There are two types of daemons supported by Solaris: stand-alone daemons and inetd daemons. Stand-alone daemons internally manage their own activities, while inetd allows daemons to be run through a single central server. This allows for centralization of administration and reduced need for processes running on a system, because inetd can listen for connections and

invoke daemon processes as required. Definitons for services are contained in the
/etc/inetd.conf file. A sample */etc/inetd.conf* file is shown here:

```
ftp       stream  tcp     nowait  root    /usr/sbin/in.ftpd     in.ftpd -l
telnet    stream  tcp     nowait  root    /usr/sbin/in.telnetd  in.telnetd
name      dgram   udp     wait    root    /usr/sbin/in.tnamed   in.tnamed
shell     stream  tcp     nowait  root    /usr/sbin/in.rshd     in.rshd
login     stream  tcp     nowait  root    /usr/sbin/in.rlogind  in.rlogind
exec      stream  tcp     nowait  root    /usr/sbin/in.rexecd   in.rexecd
comsat    dgram   udp     wait    root    /usr/sbin/in.comsat   in.comsat
talk      dgram   udp     wait    root    /usr/sbin/in.talkd    in.talkd
uucp      stream  tcp     nowait  root    /usr/sbin/in.uucpd    in.uucpd
tftp      dgram   udp     wait    root    /usr/sbin/in.tftpd    in.tftpd
 -s /tftpboot
finger    stream  tcp     nowait  nobody  /usr/sbin/in.fingerd  in.fingerd
systat    stream  tcp     nowait  root    /usr/bin/ps           ps -ef
netstat   stream  tcp     nowait  root    /usr/bin/netstat      netstat -f
inet
time      stream  tcp     nowait  root    internal
time      dgram   udp     wait    root    internal
echo      stream  tcp     nowait  root    internal
echo      dgram   udp     wait    root    internal
discard   stream  tcp     nowait  root    internal
discard   dgram   udp     wait    root    internal
daytime   stream  tcp     nowait  root    internal
daytime   dgram   udp     wait    root    internal
chargen   stream  tcp     nowait  root    internal
chargen   dgram   udp     wait    root    internal
```

Reading from left to right are the service name, socket type, transport protocol, flags,
executing user, and daemon program to execute upon request. Socket types include
streams or datagrams, transports include TCP and UDP, and flags include wait (wait
after response) and nowait (exit after response).

A sample inetd application is the talk service. By examining its definition in */etc/inetd
.conf*, we can see that it uses datagram sockets, runs on UDP, waits until timeout, is run
by root, is implemented by the command `/usr/sbin/in.talkd`, and has the name
in.talkd. The talk service supports instant communications between users on the local
system, or between any two systems on the Internet. To issue a talk request to a remote
user, a local user would issue the `talk` command followed by the user's username and
fully qualified domain name. For example, to talk to the user shusaku at the host **users
.cassowary.net**, the following command would be used:

```
$ talk shusaku@users.cassowary.net
```

If the host **users.cassowary.net** is running inetd, and inetd supports *in.talkd*, the following talk request would appear on the user shusaku's login shell:

```
Message from Talk_Daemon@db.cassowary.net at 10:50 ...
talk: connection requested by yasuanri@db.cassowary.net.
talk: respond with:  talk yasunari@db.cassowary.net
```

If the user shusaku wished to "talk" with yasunari, the following command would be used by shusaku:

```
$ talk yasunari@db.cassowary.net
```

If a service is to be disabled for security purposes, then its entry can simply be commented out, just like for the services database. For example, to disable the finger service, the finger entry would be commented as follows:

```
#finger  stream  tcp    nowait  nobody  /usr/sbin/in.fingerd    in.fingerd
```

Once changes have been made to *inetd.conf*, a SIGHUP signal should be sent to the inetd process, causing it to reread the *inetd.conf* file. To restart inetd with a PID of 186, the following command would be used:

```
# kill -1 186
```

Many of the services supported by inetd support remote access and can possibly be deemed security risks.

Network Interfaces

Because all network operations require access to a network interface, it's important to understand how to manage the interface and troubleshoot it when necessary. In the following sections, we examine how to configure a network interface, manually stop and start interfaces, and set key transmission parameters. In addition, we investigate the use of the `netstat` command to troubleshoot network configurations with respect to the IP, TCP, UDP, and ICMP protocols.

Interface Configuration

The current configuration for a network interface can always be displayed by using the `ifconfig` command. For example, to display the parameters for all of the interfaces installed on a local system, the following command could be used:

```
# ifconfig -a
lo0: flags=849<UP,LOOPBACK,RUNNING,MULTICAST> mtu 8232
        inet 127.0.0.1 netmask ff000000
hme0: flags=863<UP,BROADCAST,NOTRAILERS,RUNNING,MULTICAST> mtu 1500
        inet 192.68.24.16 netmask ffffff00 broadcast 192.68.24.255
```

This example shows two interfaces: the loopback interface, which handles internal connections, and the hme0 interface, which handles all external connections. The hme0 interface has the IP address 192.68.24.16, clearly belonging to the Class C network 192.68.24.0. Thus, a Class C netmask is specified in hex (ffffff00), and the broadcast address is given as the highest numbered slot in the 192.68.24.0 network (that is,

192.68.24.255). In addition, the interface is noted as UP as opposed to DOWN. To display information for a specific interface, the following command could be used:

```
# ifconfig hme0
hme0: flags=863<UP,BROADCAST,NOTRAILERS,RUNNING,MULTICAST> mtu 1500
        inet 192.17.128.16 netmask ffffff00 broadcast 192.17.128.255
        ether 8:0:18:6:e1:b2
```

In this example, the /etc/ethers database contains an entry for 192.17.128.16, so a MAC address for the interface is also displayed. In addition to displaying the configuration and status of a network interface, the ifconfig command can be used to bring an interface up, or take it down. While this operation is typically performed manually at boot time, there are occasions where it is necessary to perform this operation manually. For example, if an attack is detected through a remote access connection, the interface can be disabled rapidly, after which patches can be applied or some other remedial action performed before the interface is bought back up. For example to bring the hme0 interface down, the following command is used:

```
# ifconfig hme0 down
```

To verify the status of the interface, the ifconfig command can be used once again:

```
# ifconfig hme0
hme0: flags=863<DOWN,BROADCAST,NOTRAILERS,RUNNING,MULTICAST> mtu 1500
        inet 192.68.24.16 netmask ffffff00 broadcast 192.68.24.255
```

The DOWN flag is now noted in the status, and no incoming or outgoing connections will be accepted. Bringing an interface down will impact on all services that use that interface. Some daemons will handle the disruption gracefully, while others may terminate after a connection timeout. To bring the interface back up again, the following command is used:

```
# ifconfig hme0 up
```

Again, the UP status of the network interface can be verified by using the ifconfig command:

```
# ifconfig hme0
hme0: flags=863<UP,BROADCAST,NOTRAILERS,RUNNING,MULTICAST> mtu 1500
        inet 192.68.24.16 netmask ffffff00 broadcast 192.68.24.255
```

If you want to modify the operational settings of the TCP device /dev/tcp, the ndd command can be used. A wide range of parameters can be set, including IP forwarding, various connection intervals and timeouts, and buffer sizes. To view the current values, the following command can be used:

```
# ndd /dev/tcp \?
```

Parameters can also be set to new values by using the -set option. For example, to disable IPv4 packet forwarding, the following command would be used:

```
# ndd -set /dev/ip ip_forwarding 0
```

If you make changes that need to be made permanent, the */etc/rc2.d/S69inet* file should be modified to include the new ndd line.

Network Troubleshooting

One of the most difficult issues in network troubleshooting is determining exactly where the problem lies. For example, a user may complain that they've lost Internet access, but there may potentially be 20 or 30 hosts lying between the client and server systems: how is it possible to determine where the fault lies? The first step is to use the ping command to see if a host is reachable. This command attempts to make a connection to a remote host by sending off an ICMP echo request and waiting 20 seconds for a response. If no response is received, an error message is reported. However, if the host is reachable, the following message will be displayed:

```
$ ping cyclops.cassowary.net
cyclops.cassowary.net is alive
```

It is also possible to examine relative response latencies by pinging the remote host every second and seeing if there is a lot of variability:

```
$ ping -s cyclops.cassowary.net
PING cyclops.cassowary.net: 56 data bytes
64 bytes from cyclops.cassowary.net (192.128.205.2): icmp_seq=0. time=1. ms
64 bytes from cyclops.cassowary.net (192.128.205.2): icmp_seq=1. time=0. ms
64 bytes from cyclops.cassowary.net (192.128.205.2): icmp_seq=2. time=10. ms
...
---- cyclops.cassowary.net PING Statistics----
3 packets transmitted, 3 packets received, 0% packet loss
round-trip (ms) min/avg/max = 0/2/10
```

Here, we can see that there is a lot of variability in response times, with some taking up to ten times longer than others. This may indicate a high level of traffic, which is causing collisions. One solution would be to upgrade the speed of the local cabling and network interfaces used. Alternatively, subnets could be created to reduce the amount of data being transmitted around the local network.

If the connection is believed to be broken, the traceroute command can be used to isolate which intermediate host is failing. The following traceroute command shows a successful connection to the Sun web server:

```
$ traceroute www.sun.com
Tracing route to wwwwseast.usec.sun.com [192.9.49.30]
over a maximum of 30 hops:
  1   184 ms    142 ms    138 ms   202.10.4.131
  2   147 ms    144 ms    138 ms   202.10.4.129
  3   150 ms    142 ms    144 ms   202.10.1.73
  4   150 ms    144 ms    141 ms   atm11-0-0-11.ia4.optus.net.au [202.139.32.17]
  5   148 ms    143 ms    139 ms   202.139.1.197
  6   490 ms    489 ms    474 ms   hssi9-0-0.sf1.optus.net.au [192.65.89.246]
  7   526 ms    480 ms    485 ms   g-sfd-br-02-f12-0.gn.cwix.net [207.124.109.57]
```

```
 8    494 ms    482 ms    485 ms   core7-hssi6-0-0.SanFrancisco.cw.net
[204.70.10.9]
 9    483 ms    489 ms    484 ms   corerouter2.SanFrancisco.cw.net [204.70.9.132]
10    557 ms    552 ms    561 ms   xcore3.Boston.cw.net [204.70.150.81]
11    566 ms    572 ms    554 ms   sun-micro-system.Boston.cw.net
[204.70.179.102]
12    577 ms    574 ms    558 ms   wwwwseast.usec.sun.com [192.9.49.30]
Trace complete.
```

If one or more intermediate hosts fails to respond within 5 seconds, then a * would be displayed. For example, if the host xcore3.Boston.cw.net did not respond to three requests, that line of display would look like this:

```
10    * * *   xcore3.Boston.cw.net [204.70.150.81]
```

Alternatively, if the host was completely unreachable, the following output would be displayed:

```
10    * * !H  xcore3.Boston.cw.net [204.70.150.81]
```

The administrator of **xcore3.Boston.cw.net** should then be contacted to determine the nature of the problem.

If the connection fails on the first hop, the problem might be local. In this case, the netstat command should be used to determine the status of all network interfaces on the local system. Let's look at an example:

```
# netstat -i
Name Mtu  Net/Dest      Address     Ipkts     Ierrs   Opkts     Oerrs Collis
Queue
lo0  8232 loopback      localhost   434332    0       434332    0     0        0
hme0 1500 192.128.205.2 chaos       43234544  554533  43789077  0     0        0
```

This example shows the host chaos with the IP address 192.128.205.2. Although there were no outbound packet errors (Oerrs), there were a number of inbound packet errors (Ierrs). An alternative view is provided on a per-protocol basis for the TCP, ICMP, and UDP protocols:

```
# netstat -s
UDP
        udpInDatagrams    =502856     udpInErrors       =      0
        udpOutDatagrams   =459357
TCP     tcpRtoAlgorithm   =      4    tcpRtoMin         =    200
        tcpRtoMax         =240000     tcpMaxConn        =     -1
        tcpActiveOpens    = 33786     tcpPassiveOpens   = 12296
        tcpAttemptFails   =    324    tcpEstabResets    =    909
        tcpCurrEstab      =    384    tcpOutSegs        =19158723
        tcpOutDataSegs    =13666668   tcpOutDataBytes   =981537148
        tcpRetransSegs    = 33038     tcpRetransBytes   =41629885
        tcpOutAck         =5490764    tcpOutAckDelayed  =462511
        tcpOutUrg         =     51    tcpOutWinUpdate   =    456
```

```
          tcpOutWinProbe        =    290      tcpOutControl          = 92218
          tcpOutRsts            =   1455      tcpOutFastRetrans      = 18954
          tcpInSegs             =15617893
          tcpInAckSegs          =9161810      tcpInAckBytes          =981315052
          tcpInDupAck           =4559921      tcpInAckUnsent         =         0
          tcpInInorderSegs      =5741788      tcpInInorderBytes      =1120389303
          tcpInUnorderSegs      = 25045       tcpInUnorderBytes      =16972517
          tcpInDupSegs          =4390218      tcpInDupBytes          =4889714
          tcpInPartDupSegs      =    375      tcpInPartDupBytes      =130424
          tcpInPastWinSegs      =     17      tcpInPastWinBytes      =1808990872
          tcpInWinProbe         =    162      tcpInWinUpdate         =    270
          tcpInClosed           =    313      tcpRttNoUpdate         = 28077
          tcpRttUpdate          =9096791      tcpTimRetrans          = 18098
          tcpTimRetransDrop     =     26      tcpTimKeepalive        =    509
          tcpTimKeepaliveProbe=       76      tcpTimKeepaliveDrop    =      1
          tcpListenDrop         =      0      tcpListenDropQ0        =      0
          tcpHalfOpenDrop       =      0
IP        ipForwarding          =      2      ipDefaultTTL           =    255
          ipInReceives          =16081438     ipInHdrErrors          =      8
          ipInAddrErrors        =      0      ipInCksumErrs          =      1
          ipForwDatagrams       =      0      ipForwProhibits        =      2
          ipInUnknownProtos     =    274      ipInDiscards           =      0
          ipInDelivers          =16146712     ipOutRequests          =19560145
          ipOutDiscards         =      0      ipOutNoRoutes          =      0
          ipReasmTimeout        =     60      ipReasmReqds           =      0
          ipReasmOKs            =      0      ipReasmFails           =      0
          ipReasmDuplicates     =      0      ipReasmPartDups        =      0
          ipFragOKs             =   7780      ipFragFails            =      0
          ipFragCreates         =  40837      ipRoutingDiscards      =      0
          tcpInErrs             =    291      udpNoPorts             =144065
          udpInCksumErrs        =      2      udpInOverflows         =      0
          rawipInOverflows      =      0
ICMP      icmpInMsgs            =  17469      icmpInErrors           =      0
          icmpInCksumErrs       =      0      icmpInUnknowns         =      0
          icmpInDestUnreachs    =   2343      icmpInTimeExcds        =     26
          icmpInParmProbs       =      0      icmpInSrcQuenchs       =      0
          icmpInRedirects       =     19      icmpInBadRedirects     =     19
          icmpInEchos           =   9580      icmpInEchoReps         =   5226
          icmpInTimestamps      =      0      icmpInTimestampReps    =      0
          icmpInAddrMasks       =      0      icmpInAddrMaskReps     =      0
          icmpInFragNeeded      =      0      icmpOutMsgs            =  11693
          icmpOutDrops          =140883       icmpOutErrors          =      0
          icmpOutDestUnreachs   =   2113      icmpOutTimeExcds       =      0
          icmpOutParmProbs      =      0      icmpOutSrcQuenchs      =      0
          icmpOutRedirects      =      0      icmpOutEchos           =      0
          icmpOutEchoReps       =   9580      icmpOutTimestamps      =      0
          icmpOutTimestampReps=        0      icmpOutAddrMasks       =      0
          icmpOutAddrMaskReps =        0      icmpOutFragNeeded      =      0
          icmpInOverflows       =      0
```

Again, specific error counters such as icmpOutErrors, udpInErrors, and tcpInDupBytes should be regularly reviewed to ensure that error rates do not approach the total number of packets being transferred in or out of an interface.

Summary

In this chapter, the basic elements of the OSI and TCP/IP protocol stacks have been developed. The abstract elements of the OSI architecture are realized in the four-layer TCP/IP stack supported by Solaris. In the following chapters, each of these layers will be examined in more detail.

Questions

1. Which of the following is a valid network topology?

   A. Star

   B. Box

   C. Square

   D. Circle

2. Which of the following is a valid network topology?

   A. Cube

   B. Angle

   C. Cross

   D. Ring

3. What is OSI?

   A. A network protocol

   B. A framework for defining the scope of different layers of networking technology

   C. A cube network

   D. A networking software package

4. What is the role of the Physical Layer?

   A. Defines how data is exchanged at its very basic level

   B. Defines the apparatus for transferring data, including error checking and synchronization

   C. Defines specifies operational issues, such as how networks can exchange data

   D. Specifies how individual computers are to interpret data received from the network

5. What is the role of the Data Link Layer?

   A. Defines how data is exchanged at its very basic level

   B. Defines the apparatus for transferring data, including error checking and synchronization

   C. Defines specifies operational issues, such as how networks can exchange data

   D. Specifies how individual computers are to interpret data received from the network

6. What is the role of the Network Layer?

   A. Defines how data is exchanged at its very basic level

   B. Defines the apparatus for transferring data, including error checking and synchronization

   C. Defines specifies operational issues, such as how networks can exchange data

   D. Specifies how individual computers are to interpret data received from the network

7. What is the role of the Transport Layer?

   A. Defines how data is exchanged at its very basic level

   B. Defines the apparatus for transferring data, including error checking and synchronization

   C. Defines specifies operational issues, such as how networks can exchange data

   D. Specifies how individual computers are to interpret data received from the network

8. What is the role of the Session Layer?

   A. Defines how data is exchanged at its very basic level

   B. Determines how data from different sources can be separated

   C. Specifies how different types of data are formatted

   D. Describes how high-level applications can communicate with each other

9. What is the role of the Presentation Layer?

   A. Defines how data is exchanged at its very basic level

   B. Determines how data from different sources can be separated

   C. Specifies how different types of data are formatted

   D. Describes how high-level applications can communicate with each other

10. What is the role of the Application Layer?

    A. Defines how data is exchanged at its very basic level

    B. Determines how data from different sources can be separated

    C. Specifies how different types of data are formatted

    D. Describes how high-level applications can communicate with each other

11. What link speeds are not supported by Solaris?

    A. 10Base-T – 10 Mbps

    B. 100Base-T – 100 Mbps

    C. 1000Base-FX – 1Gbps

    D. 10000Base-T – 10Gbps

12. What command is used to modify */dev/tcp* settings?

    A. `tcp`

    B. `ar`

    C. `netstat`

    D. `ndd`

13. What command is used to disable IP forwarding?

    A. `ndd -forwarding 0`

    B. `ndd -set /dev/ip ip_forwarding 0`

    C. `ndd -set /dev/ip ip_-forwarding +0`

    D. `ndd -noforward`

14. What command is used to verify the status of a network interface?

    A. `netview`

    B. `netlook`

    C. `ifconfig`

    D. `hmelook`

15. What command is used to check the table of IP address to MAC address mappings?

    A. `arp`

    B. `ar`

    C. `ndd`

    D. `netstat`

Answers

1. **A.** Star is a valid network topology.

2. **D.** Ring is a valid network topology.

3. **B.** OSI is a framework for defining the scope of different layers of networking technology.

4. **A.** The Physical Layer defines how data is exchanged at its very basic level.

5. **B.** The Data Link Layer defines the apparatus for transferring data, including error checking and synchronization.

6. **C.** The Network Layer defines specifies operational issues, such as how networks can exchange data.

7. **D.** The Transport Layer specifies how individual computers are to interpret data received from the network.

8. **B.** The Session Layer determines how data from different sources can be separated.

9. **C.** The Presentation Layer specifies how different types of data are formatted.

10. **D.** The Application Layer describes how high-level applications can communicate with each other.

11. **D.** 10000Base-T – 10Gbps is not currently supported.

12. **D.** ndd is used to modify */dev/tcp* settings.

13. **B.** `ndd -set /dev/ip ip_forwarding 0` disables IP forwarding.

14. **C.** `ifconfig` is used to verify the status of a network interface.

15. **A.** `arp` is used to check the table of IP address to MAC address mappings.

## CHAPTER 33

Ethernet

In this chapter, you will
- Learn the fundamentals of Ethernet
- Discover the operational characteristics of Ethernet
- Learn about frames and addresses

Ethernet is a type of physical network that supports virtually any type of computer system, unlike previous networks that supported only certain types of computers. The "ether" part of the name comes from the material that was thought, in the 19th century, to surround the earth and provide a medium for the transmission of radio waves. In the same way that radio became a ubiquitous mode for transmitting data, Ethernet has become the most commonly used medium for network transmission.

Ethernet Fundamentals

Ethernet is the most commonly used link technology supported by Solaris, and comes in five different speeds, including:

- **10Base-2**   2 Mbps
- **10Base-5**   5 Mbps
- **10Base-T**   10 Mbps
- **100Base-T**   100 Mbps
- **1000Base-T/FX**   1 Gbps

The 10, 100, and 1000 here indicate the signaling frequency in MHz. There are different types of media that are supported for each baseband, such as 10Base. For example, the 10Base family, supports the following media types:

- Thick coaxial cable
- Thin coaxial cable
- Twisted-pair cable
- Optical fiber cable

Coaxial cable is a shielded, single strand copper cable that is generally surrounded by an aluminum insulator. It is a highly insulated, reliable transmission medium. In contrast, twisted-pair cables can either be shielded or unshielded. Optical fiber cable uses light as the transmission medium and typically achieves the highest bandwidth. However, your choice of transmission media may depend on the distances that need to be covered for interconnection. The following restrictions are imposed on the most commonly used transmission media:

- **10Base-2**   185 meters
- **10Base-5**   500 meters
- **10Base-T**   150 meters

So, in a building where 500-meter cabling is required, only 10Base-5 will be suitable unless a repeater is used. Single-mode fiber may be used where long distances of 10–15 km are involved. Also, there are limitations on the number of hubs that can be used to extend the logical length of a segment—a packet cannot be transmitted through more than four hubs or three cable segments in total to ensure successful transmission.

 TIP   There are some other restrictions that should be kept in mind when using specific media. For example, some types of cabling are more sensitive to electrical interference than others.

Ethernet on Solaris

Solaris systems are typically supplied with a single Ethernet card, supporting 10/100 Mbps; however, server systems (such as the 420R) are supplied with quad Ethernet cards, supporting four interfaces operating at 10/100 Mbps. Although Ethernet (specified by the IEEE 802.3 standard) is the most common link type, other supported link types on Solaris include the Fiber Distributed Data Interface (FDDI) and Asynchronous Transfer Mode (ATM). FDDI networks use a ring topology based on a transmitting and receiving ring, using high-quality fiber-optic cable, to support high-speed, redundant connections. However, FDDI is expensive compared to Ethernet, and gigabit FDDI is not available. ATM is designed for high quality of service applications like video and audio streaming that require a constant amount of bandwidth to operate. Data is transmitted in fixed-size cells of 53 bytes, and a connection is maintained while required between client and server. Although ATM does not approach the speeds of Gigabit Ethernet, its quality of service provisions benefit certain types of data transmission.

In terms of the OSI networking model, Ethernet comprises both the Physical Layer (Layer 1) and the Data Link Layer (Layer 2), although a logical link control protocol is not logically defined. Robert Metcalfe at Xerox PARC developed Ethernet during the 1970s, although the major standards for Ethernet were not published until the 1980s.

 TIP   TCP/IP only implements a subset of the OSI reference model.

Ethernet Characteristics

Ethernet has become the technology of choice for local area networks (LANs). Originally designed to transmit 3 Mbps, a base network interface using Ethernet can now transmit data at 10 Mbps. The latest Ethernet technology supports data transmission at 10 Gbps! Supported media for Ethernet includes thick and thin coaxial, fiber-optic, and twisted-pair cables.

The major reason for the success of Ethernet in industry was the adoption of the Ethernet standard (IEEE 802.3), allowing for interoperability between different vendor's products (Carrier Sense Multiple Access with Collision Detection CSMA/CD, Access Method and Physical Layer Specifications). This specification allowed many different vendors to produce network interfaces and media that supported Ethernet.

 TIP Ethernet is a very flexible system because interfaces operating at different transmission rates can be connected to the same LAN.

There are three elements that comprise Ethernet:

1. Physical media segments, which are used to interconnect systems

2. The Media Access Control (MAC) rules that implement access to Ethernet channels

3. A frame that organizes data to be transmitted in a standard way

Systems connected to the Ethernet are technically known as stations. Every station on the network is independent—access is not centrally controlled, because the medium allows signaling to be received and interpreted by all stations. Transmission across Ethernet occurs in bitwise form.

 CAUTION When transmitting data, a station must wait for the channel to be free of data before sending a packet formatted as a frame.

If a station has to wait for the channel to be free before sending its own packets, you can appreciate the potential for traffic congestion and a "broadcast storm" if one station had a lot of data to send. However, after transmitting one packet, each station then competes for the right to transmit each subsequent frame. The MAC access control system prevents traffic congestion from occurring. It is quite normal, for example, for collision rates of 50 percent to exist without any noticeable impact on performance.

A more insidious problem occurs with so-called late collisions. These are collisions that occur between two hosts that are not detected because the latency for transmission between the two hosts exceeds the maximum time allowed to detect a collision. If this occurs at greater than 1 percent of the time, serious problems may emerge in terms of data throughput and potential corruption.

The mechanism for preventing packet collision is the Carrier Sense Multiple Access with Collision Detection (CSMA/CD) method specified by the IEEE standard. Prior to data being transmitted, a station must enter Carrier Sense (CS) mode. If no data is detected on the channel, all stations have an equal opportunity to transmit a frame, a condition known as Multiple Access (MA). If two or more stations begin transmitting frames and detect that they are transmitting at the same time, a state known as Collision Detection (CD), then the stations halt transmission, enter the CS mode and wait for the next MA opportunity. Collisions can occur because there is a time difference between when two stations might detect MA, depending on their "distance" in the network. When a collision occurs, the frames must be re-sent by their respective parties. The process flow for CSMA/CD is shown in Figure 33-1.

When systematic problems emerge in a LAN, demonstrated by much lower than theoretical transmission rates, a design flaw in the network layout could be causing a large number of collisions. You might be wondering how, if a CD event occurs, two stations can prevent retransmitting at the same time in the future, thereby repeating their previous collision—the answer is that the delay between retransmission is randomized for each network interface. This prevents repetitive locking, and delivery of a packet will always be attempted 16 times before a failure occurs. When more stations are added to a single LAN, the number of collisions occurring will also increase. With high-speed networks, the delay caused by retransmission of a packet is usually in the order of microseconds rather than milliseconds. If the number of retransmission escalates, then there is a planned, exponential reduction in network traffic, affecting all stations, until stable operation is restored.

One of the important things to note about Ethernet, with respect to quality of service issues, is that Ethernet is not a guaranteed delivery system, unlike some other networking systems. This is because Ethernet operates on the principle of best effort, given the

Figure 33-1
Process flow
for CSMA/CD

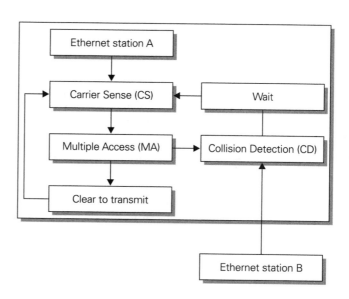

available resources. Ethernet is susceptible to electrical artifacts, interference, and a number of other problems that may interfere with data transmission. However, for most practical purposes, Ethernet performs very well. If assured delivery is required, higher-level application protocols (based on message queuing, for example) would need to be implemented across Ethernet to have guaranteed delivery.

 TIP Transport layer protocols like the Transmission Control Protocol (TCP) label each packet with a sequence number to ensure that all packets are received and reassembled in the correct order.

Ethernet has a logical topology, or tree-like structure, that is distinct from the set of physical interfaces that are interconnected using networking cable. One of the implications of this tree-like structure is that individual branches can be segmented in order to logically isolate structural groups. This structure also allows a large number of unrelated networks to be connected to each other, forming the basis of the Internet as we know it. Individual network branches can be linked together by using a repeater of some kind, such as a hub or a switch. In either case, the Ethernet channel can be extended beyond the local boundaries imposed by a single branch. A hub only connects interfaces on a single segment, while a switch can interconnect multiple LANs.

Ethernet Frame

The main data structure utilized by Ethernet is the frame. The frame has a number of defined fields that specify elements like the MAC addresses for the destination and originating hosts in a packet transmission. The advantage in this ordering is that only the first 48 bits of a packet need to be read by a host to determine whether a packet received has reached its ultimate destination. If the destination MAC address does not match the local MAC address, the contents of the packet do not need to be read. However, the snoop command can be used to extract the content of packets that are not destined for the local MAC address, assuming that you are using a hub and not a switch. This is why it's important to encrypt the contents of packets being transmitted across the Internet—because they can be trivially "sniffed" by using programs like snoop. In addition to the destination and originating MAC addresses, the frame also contains a data field of 46–1500 bytes and a cyclic redundancy check of 4 bytes. The data field contains all of the data encapsulated by higher-level protocols, such as the Internet Protocol (IP).

Exercise 33-1 Identifying Ethernet traffic   Log in to your system as root. Use the snoop command to sniff network packets. Can you discern the data field within the Ethernet frame?

Ethernet Addresses

One of the best features of Ethernet is the ability for a group of interfaces on a specific network to listen for broadcasts being transmitted to a specific group address, known as a multicast address. This allows a single host to originate a packet to be read by a number of different hosts without having to retransmit the packet multiple times. In addition, each interface listens on its normal MAC address, as well as the multicast address.

A MAC address is a hexadecimal number that is set in the factory for every network interface manufactured. It contains elements that allow an interface to be distinguished from those manufactured by other companies, and also allows individual interfaces from the same manufacturer to be distinguishable. It is possible with SPARC systems to set the MAC address manually in the PROM. However, this is generally not advisable except in systems with multiple interfaces, where they might have the same MAC address by default. The format of the MAC is usually a set of hexadecimal numbers delimited by colons. The MAC address 11:22:33:44:55:AA is one example. The initial three bytes identify a specific manufacturer—the list of manufacturers and their codes can be downloaded from **ftp://ftp.lcs.mit.edu/pub/map/ethernet-codes**.

In order to support IP and higher-level transport and application protocols, a mapping must be made between the MAC address and the IP address. This is achieved by the Address Resolution Protocol (ARP) and Reverse Address Resolution Protocol (RARP). The hardware address, otherwise known as the Media Access Control (MAC) address, is used to distinguish hosts at the link level. This is mapped to an IP address at the network level by using ARP and RARP. You can check the table of IP address to MAC address mappings by using the `arp` command:

```
$ arp -a
Net to Media Table
Device IP Address              Mask             Flags Phys Addr
------ --------------------- --------------- ----- ---------------
hme0   www.cassowary.net     255.255.255.255        00:19:cd:e3:05:a3
hme0   mail.cassowary.net    255.255.255.255        08:11:92:a4:12:ee
hme0   ftp.cassowary.net     255.255.255.255 SP     08:12:4e:4d:55:a2
hme0   BASE-ADDRESS.MCAST.NET 240.0.0.0       SM     01:01:4e:00:00:00
```

Here, the network device is shown with either the fully qualified hostname or IP address, the netmask, any flags, and the MAC address. The flags indicate the status of each interface, including "SP" for the localhost, where an entry will be published on request, and "SM" for the localhost, supporting multicast. Alternatively, a specific host can be queried by passing its name on the command line:

```
$ arp mail
mail (204.67.34.12) at 08:11:92:a4:12:ee
```

ARP works by broadcasting in order to identify the appropriate channel on which to locate the target host. Conversely, the Reverse Address Resolution Protocol (RARP) is used to map MAC addresses to IP addresses. RARP is typically used to supply IP addresses from boot servers to diskless clients. A database of Ethernet addresses is maintained in the /etc/ethers table to support this activity.

Exercise 33-2 Using arp   Log in to your system as root. Use the `arp` command to review the IP address to MAC address mappings. Can you identify any flags that you don't recognize?

EXAM TIP You should be able to interpret arp output for specific hosts and for address mappings.

Summary

In this chapter, we examined the basic characteristics of Ethernet, which is the underlying network system used to support most TCP/IP systems. Ethernet is very flexible, supporting multiple speeds, bandwidths, and transmission media, and is mostly reliable. Ethernet can detect and remedy problems occurring because of multiple simultaneous transmissions on the same channel.

Questions

1. What is the bandwidth for 10Base-2?

    A. 2 Mbps

    B. 5 Mbps

    C. 10 Mbps

    D. 100 Mbps

2. What is the bandwidth for 10Base-5?

    A. 2 Mbps

    B. 5 Mbps

    C. 10 Mbps

    D. 100 Mbps

3. What is the bandwidth for 10Base-T?

    A. 2 Mbps

    B. 5 Mbps

    C. 10 Mbps

    D. 100 Mbps

4. What is the bandwidth for 100Base-T?

    A. 2 Mbps

    B. 5 Mbps

    C. 10 Mbps

    D. 100 Mbps

5. What is the role of physical media segments?

    A. To interconnect systems

    B. To implement access to Ethernet channels

PART III

C. To organize data to be transmitted in a standard way

D. To act as stations

6. What is the role of Media Access Control (MAC) rules?

A. To interconnect systems

B. To implement access to Ethernet channels

C. To organize data to be transmitted in a standard way

D. To act as a station

7. What is the role of a frame?

A. To interconnect systems

B. To implement access to Ethernet channels

C. To organize data to be transmitted in a standard way

D. To act as a station

8. What is the generic title of each host connected to Ethernet?

A. Interconnected system

B. Ethernet channel

C. Data system

D. Station

9. In what form does transmission across Ethernet occur?

A. Integer

B. Hex

C. Bitwise

D. Char

10. What is the mechanism for preventing packet collision?

A. Super Collision Detection System (SCDS)

B. Internet Protocol eXtension (IPX)

C. Carrier Sense Multiple Access with Collision Detection (CSMA/CD)

D. Collision Detection Management Access (CDMA)

11. If a CD event occurs, how can two stations prevent retransmitting at the same time?

A. Randomize delay between retransmission for each network interface.

B. Synchronize all future retransmissions for the next 128 accesses.

C. Initiate a "push me pull me" sequence of asynchronous communication.

D. Activate a "C" class subnet broadcast emergency event.

12. When more stations are added to a single LAN, what is the likely impact on the number of collisions?

    A. The number of collisions occurring will increase.

    B. The number of collisions occurring will decrease.

    C. The number of collisions occurring will stay the same.

    D. The rate of collisions occurring will actually decrease.

13. How many times will the delivery of a packet be attempted before a transmission failure occurs?

    A. 2

    B. 4

    C. 8

    D. 16

14. What is the range of the data field in an Ethernet frame?

    A. 1–1500 bytes

    B. 46–1500 bytes

    C. 1–1500 bits

    D. 46–1500 bits

15. Which of the following is a valid MAC address?

    A. 11:22:33:44:55:AA

    B. 22:33:44:55:AA

    C. 33:44:55:AA

    D. 145.128.43.22

Answers

1. **A.** The bandwidth for 10Base-2 is 2 Mbps.

2. **B.** The bandwidth for 10Base-5 is 5 Mbps.

3. **C.** The bandwidth for 10Base-T is 10 Mbps.

4. **D.** The bandwidth for 100Base-T is 100 Mbps.

5. **A.** The role of physical media segments is to interconnect systems.

6. **B.** The role of Media Access Control (MAC) rules is to implement access to Ethernet channels.

7. **C.** The role of a frame is to organize data to be transmitted in a standard way.

8. **D.** The generic title of each host connected to Ethernet is station.

9. **C.** Transmission across Ethernet occurs in bitwise form.

10. **C.** The mechanism for preventing packet collision is Carrier Sense Multiple Access with Collision Detection (CSMA/CD).

11. **A.** Two stations can prevent retransmitting at the same time by randomizing the delay between retransmission for each network interface.

12. **A.** When more stations are added to a single LAN, the number of collisions occurring will increase.

13. **D.** The delivery of a packet will be attempted 16 times before a transmission failure occurs.

14. **B.** The range of the data field in an Ethernet frame is 46–1500 bytes.

15. **A.** Only 11:22:33:44:55:AA is a valid MAC address.

Internet Layer

In this chapter, you will
- Learn about the properties of the Internet Protocol v4
- Discover the structure of IP datagrams
- Learn about IPv4 security levels

The Internet Layer involves four different protocols: the Internet Protocol (IP), the Address Resolution Protocol (ARP), and the Internet Control Message Protocol (ICMP). In the following sections, we'll investigate each of these protocols.

Internet Protocol

The Internet Protocol (IP) layer sits between the Ethernet and Transport layers in the stack. Thus, it provides the interface between the underlying physical transport and the logical transport used by applications. It manages the mapping between hardware (MAC) addresses and software addresses for network interfaces. To connect a local area network to the Internet, it is necessary to obtain an IP network number from the InterNIC. However, since most Solaris software uses TCP/IP for network operations, even when not connected to the Internet, it is necessary to become familiar with IP, its configuration, and its major operational issues. Although IPv6 is the new version of IP, IPv4 is still widely deployed, so all of the material in this chapter relates to IPv4 (IPv6 is covered in Chapter 36).

IP carries out the following functions in the stack: addressing, routing, formatting, and fragmentation. Addressing involves mapping hardware addresses to software addresses, while routing involves finding a path to transmit a packet from a source network interface to a destination network interface. Formatting involves inserting specific types of data into a packet to ensure that it reaches its destination, and fragmentation involves the division of packets into fragments where a packet is too large to be transmitted using the underlying medium.

IP relies on three other protocols for its operation: the Address Resolution Protocol (ARP) ensures that datagrams are sent to the correct destination network interface from a source network interface by mapping IP addresses to hardware addresses. The Reverse Address Resolution Protocol (RARP) is responsible for mapping hardware addresses to IP addresses. The Internet Control Message Protocol (ICMP) is involved with the identification and management of network errors, which result from packets being dropped, physical disconnection of intermediate and destination routers, or a redirection directive issued by an intermediate or destination router.

 TIP   The `ping` command is typically used as the interface to check for errors on the network.

The key data structure used by IP is the datagram. Details about the datagram are recorded in the packet's header, including the addresses of the source and destination hosts, the size of the datagram, and the order in which datagrams are to be transmitted or received. The structure of the IP datagram is shown in Figure 34-1.

The IP Version is an integer which defines the current IP version (that is, 4). The IP Header Length specifies the size, in bytes, of the packet header—generally, the header is 20 bytes in length, because IPv4 options are not often used. The Type of Service specifies, in 8 bits, what type of data is being handled. This allows packets to be designated as requiring high speed, high reliability, or maximum bandwidth. Bits 0–2 are responsible for determining the message priority, with the following values being supported:

- **000**   Normal traffic
- **001**   Priority traffic
- **010**   Immediate traffic
- **011**   Flash traffic
- **100**   Flash override traffic
- **101**   Critical traffic
- **110**   Internet control traffic
- **111**   Network control traffic

Figure 34-1
Structure of
IP datagrams

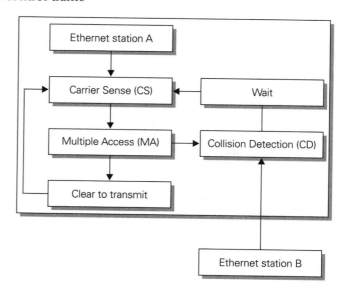

Bits 3–5 specify whether low (0) or high (1) priority be given to speed, bandwidth, or reliability, respectively, while the last two bits are reserved.

The total packet length is specified by a 16-bit number, which has a maximum of 65,535 bytes. However, this value is largely theoretical because framing through hardware layers (such as Ethernet and modems) sets this value to be much lower in practice. Large packets need to be fragmented—that's where the identification, fragmentation flags, and fragmentation offset come into play. The identification field is a 16-bit identifying number for reassembly. The fragmentation flag is a 3-bit number that indicates whether a packet may or may not be fragmented and whether the current fragment is the last fragment or other fragments are to be transmitted. The fragment offset is a 13-bit number that indicates where a fragment lies in the sequence of fragments to be reconstructed.

The time to live specifies the number of hops permitted before the packet expires and is dropped. The protocol number (defined in */etc/protocols*) specifies which protocol is to be used for data definition. The supported protocols are shown in Table 34-1. The header checksum determines whether the packet header has been corrupted by using a cyclic redundancy check. The origin and target addresses are the IP addresses of the source and destination hosts, respectively, for the packet.

A set of options up to 40 bytes can also be specified in the header, although these are not always used. The following options are available:

- **End of Option list** Marks the end of the list of options, because it can be a variable length list.

- **No Operation** Defines the boundary between options.

- **Security** Used to specify security levels for the traffic.

- **Loose Source Routing** Origin provides routing that may be followed.

- **Strict Source Routing** Origin provides routing that must be followed.

- **Record Route** Stores the route of a datagram.

Name	Number	Acronym	Description
ip	0	IP	Internet Protocol
icmp	1	ICMP	Internet Control Message Protocol
ggp	3	GGP	Gateway-Gateway Protocol
tcp	6	TCP	Transmission Control Protocol
egp	8	EGP	Exterior Gateway Protocol
pup	12	PUP	PARC Universal Packet Protocol
udp	17	UDP	User Datagram Protocol
hmp	20	HMP	Host Monitoring Protocol
xns-idp	22	XNS-IDP	Xerox NS IDP
rdp	27	RDP	Reliable Datagram Protocol

Table 34-1   Supported Solaris Protocols

- **Stream Identifier**   Used to support streaming.
- **Internet Timestamp**   Records the time in milliseconds since the start of UT.

The following security levels are defined:

- **00000000 00000000**   Unclassified
- **11110001 00110101**   Confidential
- **01111000 10011010**   EFTO
- **10111100 01001101**   MMMM
- **01011110 00100110**   PROG
- **10101111 00010011**   Restricted
- **11010111 10001000**   Secret
- **01101011 11000101**   Top Secret

The correct interpretation of these levels can be determined from the Defense Intelligence Agency Manual DIAM 65-19. A more accessible reference is MIL-STD-2411-1, the Registered Data Values For Raster Product Format specification (**http://www.nima.mil/publications/specs/printed/2411/2411_1.pdf**).

Exercise 34–1 Security Levels   Check the MIL-STD-2411-1 document and make a list of all available security levels.

The packet can be padded to ensure that the length of the header is 32 bits where necessary and separates the header from the packet data.

In order to check whether IP packets are being transmitted correctly between a source and destination network interface, and all intermediate routers, the traceroute command can be used.

 TIP   The traceroute command does not display the contents of packet headers and data like the snoop command.

Summary

In this chapter we have examined the structure of IP datagrams, and how IP addresses can be best managed by using the Dynamic Host Configuration Protocol (DHCP). Although Chapter 38 covered some operational aspects of IP, it's important to understand the structure of IP datagrams for troubleshooting.

Questions

1. What functions does IP not carry out in the stack?

    A. Addressing

   B. Routing

   C. Formatting

   D. Securitization

2. What protocols does IP not rely upon for its operation?

   A. Address Resolution Protocol (ARP)

   B. Reverse Address Resolution Protocol (RARP)

   C. Simple Mail Transfer Protocol (SMTP)

   D. Internet Control Message Protocol (ICMP)

3. What command is typically used as the interface to check for errors on the network?

   A. `snoop`

   B. `watch`

   C. `in.rarpd`

   D. `ping`

4. What does the Type of Service not specify?

   A. Packets are designated as requiring high speed.

   B. Packets are designated as requiring TCP.

   C. Packets are designated as requiring high reliability.

   D. Packets are designated as requiring maximum bandwidth.

5. If bits 0–2 of the Type of Service were 000, what would be the message priority?

   A. Normal traffic

   B. Priority traffic

   C. Immediate traffic

   D. Flash traffic

6. If bits 0–2 of the Type of Service were 001, what would be the message priority?

   A. Normal traffic

   B. Priority traffic

   C. Immediate traffic

   D. Flash traffic

7. If bits 0–2 of the Type of Service were 010, what would be the message priority?

   A. Normal traffic

   B. Priority traffic

   C. Immediate traffic

   D. Flash traffic

8. If bits 0–2 of the Type of Service were 011, what would be the message priority?

    A. Normal traffic

    B. Priority traffic

    C. Immediate traffic

    D. Flash traffic

9. What is the maximum total packet length in bytes?

    A. 1500

    B. 16636

    C. 32675

    D. 65535

10. What type of packets must be fragmented?

    A. Small packets

    B. Medium packets

    C. Large packets

    D. All packets

11. What is the protocol number for IP?

    A. 0

    B. 1

    C. 3

    D. 6

12. What is the protocol number for ICMP?

    A. 0

    B. 1

    C. 3

    D. 6

13. What is the protocol number for GGP?

    A. 0

    B. 1

    C. 3

    D. 6

14. What is the protocol number for TCP?

    A. 0

    B. 1

    C. 3

    D. 6

15. What command is used to check whether IP packets are being transmitted correctly between a source and destination network interface?

    A. `inetd`

    B. `snell`

    C. `traceroute`

    D. `openlook`

Answers

1. D. IP does not carry out securitizarion in the stack.

2. C. IP does not rely upon SMTP for its operation.

3. D. The `ping` command is typically used as the interface to check for errors on the network.

4. B. The Type of Service does not specify that packets are designated as requiring TCP.

5. A. The message priority for 000 is normal traffic.

6. B. The message priority for 001 is priority traffic.

7. C. The message priority for 010 is immediate traffic.

8. D. The message priority for 011 is flash traffic.

9. D. The maximum total packet length is 65536 bytes.

10. C. Large packets must be fragmented.

11. A. The protocol number for IP is 0.

12. B. The protocol number for ICMP is 1.

13. C. The protocol number for GGP is 3.

14. D. The protocol number for TCP is 6.

15. C. The `traceroute` command is used to check whether IP packets are being transmitted correctly between a source and destination network interface.

Routing

In this chapter, you will

- Learn about network structures
- Discover the role of routers
- Learn how to configure a router
- Review the role of firewalls and network security
- Discover static and dynamic routing protocols

In this chapter we will examine how to connect multiple machines in subnets and how to connect subnets to form local area networks (LANs) through routers. Inter-router connection allows the formation of wide area networks (WANs), and ultimately the Internet. Communication between different machines, through the transmission of data packets, can only take place through the process of routing. Routing involves finding a route between two hosts, whether they exist on the same network or are separated by thousands of miles and hundreds of intermediate hosts. Fortunately, the basic principles are the same in both cases. However, for security reasons, many sites on the Internet have installed packet filters, which deny certain packet transmissions on a host or port basis. In this chapter we will examine static and dynamic methods for configuring routes between hosts, and examine the mechanisms of IP filtering and firewalls.

Routing Concepts

Solaris supports many different kinds of network interfaces, for both local area and wide area transmission. Ethernet and FDDI are commonly used for creating networks of two or more systems at a single site through a LAN, while supporting high-speed, wide area connections through T1 and X.25 lines—and most recently, ATM (Asynchronous Transfer Mode) networks. A hub is a device that can interconnect many devices so that they can be channeled directly to a router for wide area connection. For example, each physical floor of a building may have a hub, and each of these hubs then connects to a single hub for the whole building. This hub is connected to an Internet service provider (ISP) through a router (**router.company.com**) and a dedicated ISDN service. A general rule of thumb for connecting routable networks is not to have more than three levels of connection between a server and a router; otherwise, the number of errors increases dramatically. Figure 35-1 shows a possible Class C network configuration for this building.

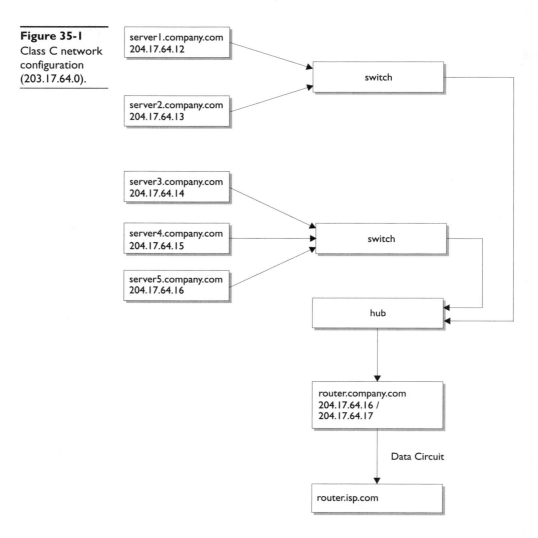

Figure 35-1
Class C network configuration (203.17.64.0).

This configuration is fine if a single company (**company.com**) owns and occupies this building and both use the same ISP. However, let's imagine that **company.com** downsizes and leases the second floor to a government department, **department.gov**. The government department wants to make use of the existing ISP arrangements and is happy to share the cost of the ISDN connection. However, they want to logically isolate their network from that of **company.com** for security purposes—they intend to install a packet filter on their own router, which explicitly denies or allows packets to cross into the government department's network.

This logical separation can be easily achieved by separating the existing network into two subnets, allowing the government department to install their own router, and then connecting the two networks through that router. Traffic to the ISP can still flow through the existing connection—even though from the hosts on the second floor, they are now separated from the router. The way that the department's traffic can "find" the ISP is the kind of problem that routing can solve. More generally, routing allows one host to find a path to any other host on the internet. Figure 35-2 shows the revised configuration for this building, incorporating the changes required by the government department, forming two Class C networks whose routers are connected to each other.

It should be clear from these examples that from a network perspective, a host must either be a router or a host. A router can be a Solaris server, which performs other functions (for example, DNS server or NIS server), however, it can also be a dedicated, hardware-based system supplied by another manufacturer (for example, Cisco or Ascend). In this chapter we will examine ways of setting up and configuring a Solaris host to be a router, although it may be that your organization prefers to use a dedicated system for routing.

The basic function of a router, as displayed in Figures 35-1 and 35-2, is to pass information from one network to another. In the examples, information is passed from one Class C network to another, but also to the router of an ISP. The ISP's router then

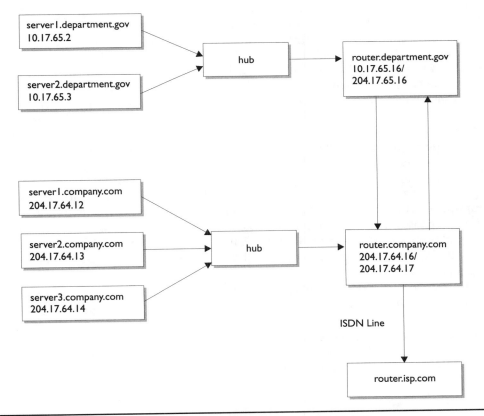

Figure 35-2   Connecting two Class C networks (203.17.64.0 and 203.17.65.0).

connects with many other ISP's routers, eventually giving global coverage. The information passed between networks is contained in discrete packets, and since the router passes this information along, it follows that the router can potentially make a copy of the data and save it to a local disk. This is the basis of many security-related problems on the Internet, because usernames and passwords are also transmitted as packets and can be intercepted by any intermediate router between client and server.

To be a router, a system must have multiple physical network interfaces. This is distinct from a system having one or more virtual interfaces defined for a single physical interface card. Thus, the router for **company.com** has the interfaces 204.17.64.16 and 204.17.64.17. The first interface accepts traffic from the internal network and passes it to the second interface, while the second interface accepts traffic from the other routers and passes it to the internal network or to other routers, as appropriate. Having two network interfaces allows data to be passed through the machine and exchanged across different networks. In the previous example, the **company.com** router was able to exchange information between the **department.gov** router and the ISP's router. Thus, many routers can be interconnected to form networks in which packets can be passed from a source to a destination host transparently.

Because the **department.gov** router serves as a packet-filtering firewall, it is likely that the network has a nonroutable, internal structure, which is not directly accessible to the external network but is visible from the router (the 10.17.65.0 network). Thus, a rogue user from **company.com** will be able to "see" the external interface for the **department.gov** router, but will not be able to see the internal interface or any of the hosts beyond, unless he or she manages to break into the router through the external interface. This adds a second layer of protection against intrusion. A packet filter can then be used to explicitly deny connections to machines in the internal network, except for very specific system or network services. For example, a departmental mail server may reside on **server1.department.gov**, and external machines will ultimately need access to the sendmail ports on this server. This can be achieved by port forwarding, or the ability of the router to map a port on its external interface to a port on a machine on the internal network. For example, a web server on **server1.department.gov:80** could be accessed from the external network by connecting to **router.department.gov:8080** if the mapping was enabled. These techniques can achieve the necessary logical isolation between external users and actual network configuration, which can be useful for security planning. Packet filtering, port forwarding, and nonroutable networks are discussed later in the chapter.

A machine with more than one network interface may not be configured to act as a router, in which case it is referred to a multihomed host.

TIP   Multihoming can be useful for performing such functions as load balancing and directly serving different Class C networks, without passing information between them.

IP Routing

Now that we have discussed how to install, configure, and tune network interfaces, we shall turn our attention to setting up routing and explain how packets are transferred from hosts to routers, and exchanged between routers. We will also examine how to troubleshoot routing problems with traceroute, and introduce the different routing protocols that are currently being used on the Internet.

There are two kinds of routing: static routing and dynamic routing. Static routing is common in simple networks with only a few hosts and networks interconnected. Static routing is much simpler to implement than dynamic routing, which is suitable for large networks where the routes between networks cannot be readily specified. For example, if your organizational network has only two routers connecting three networks, the number of routes that need to be installed statically is four (that is, the square of the number of routers). In contrast, for a building with five routers, the number of routes that need to be specified statically is 25. If a router configuration changes, all of the static configuration files on all of the routers need to be changed (that is, there is no mechanism for the "discovery" of routes). Alternatively, if a router fails because of a hardware fault, packets may not be able to be correctly routed. Dynamic routing solves all of these problems, but requires more processing overhead on each router.

NOTE   There are two related dynamic routing daemons—in.rdisc, the router discovery daemon, and in.routed, the route daemon—whose configuration will be discussed at length in this section.

Overview of Packet Delivery

Before we examine the differences between static and dynamic routing in detail, let's take a step back and consider how information is passed between two systems, whether the exchange is host to host, host to router or router to router. All information is exchanged in the form of discrete packets, which is the smallest unit of information that is transmitted between hosts using TCP/IP. A packet contains both a header and a message component, as shown in Figure 35-3. In order to deliver packets from one host to another host successfully, each packet contains information in the header (which is similar to an envelope)—among many other fields, it contains the address of the destination machine and the address of the source machine. The message section of the packet contains the actual data to be transferred. Packets are often transferred on the transport layer using the Transmission Control Protocol (TCP), which guarantees the delivery of packets. Some applications use User Datagram Protocol (UDP), where the continuity of a connection cannot be guaranteed. In normal TCP transmission mode, only 64KB of data can be transferred in a single session unless large window support is enabled, in which case up to 1GB of data may be transmitted. The header may also have information inserted by the source machine, which is referred to as data encapsulation.

NOTE The action of passing a packet is referred to as a "hop," so routing involves enabling packets to "hop" from a source host to any arbitrary host on the Internet.

In order for packets to be delivered correctly between two hosts, all intermediate routers must be able to determine where the packets have come from, and where they must be delivered. This can be achieved by referring to a host by using its IP address (for example, 203.16.42.58) or it's fully-qualified domain name (for example, **server.company.com**). Although it is also possible to refer to a machine by its Ethernet (hardware) address, it is often preferred in TCP/IP to use a logical rather than a physical representation of a machine's network interface card.

Sending a packet across a network makes full use of all network layers. For example, if a telnet session is to be established between two machines, the application protocol specifies how the message and header are to be constructed, information which is then passed to the transport layer protocol. For a telnet session, the transport layer protocol is TCP, which proceeds with encapsulation of the packet's data, which is split into segments. The data is divided based on the size of the TCP window allowed by the system. Each segment has a header and a checksum, which is used by the destination host to determine whether a received packet is likely to be free of corruption. When a segment is due to be transmitted from the source host, a three-way handshake occurs between source and destination: a SYN segment is sent to the destination host requesting a connection, and an acknowledgement (ACK) is returned to the source when the destination host is ready to receive. When the ACK is received by the source host, its receipt is acknowledged back to the destination and transmission proceeds with data being passed to the IP layer, where segments are realized as IP datagrams. IP also adds a header to the segment and passes it to the physical networking layer for transport. A common method of enacting a "denial of service" attack on a remote host involves sending many SYN requests to a remote host, without completing the "three-way handshake." Solaris now limits the maximum number of connections with handshake incomplete to reduce the impact of the problem. When a packet finally arrives at the destination host, it travels through the TCP/IP protocol stack in the reverse order from that which it took on the sender: just like a deck of cards that has been dealt onto a playing table and retrieved from the top of the pack.

Figure 35-3
A packet has both a message and a header.

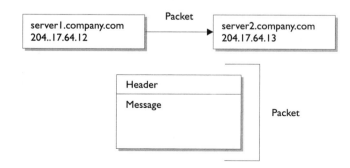

The story becomes more complicated when packets need to be passed through several hosts to reach their ultimate destination. Although the method of passing data from source to destination is the same, the next hop along the route needs to be determined somehow. The path that a packet takes across the network depends on the IP address of the destination host as specified in the packet header. If the destination host is on the local network, it can be delivered immediately without intervention of a separate router. For example, a source host 204.12.60.24 on the Class C network 204.12.60.0 can directly pass a packet to a destination 204.12.60.32. However, once a packet needs to be delivered beyond the local network, the process becomes more complicated. The packet is passed to the router on the local network (which may be defined in */etc/defaultrouter*), and a router table is consulted. The router table contains a list of the hosts on the local network and other routers to which the router has a connection. For example, the router for the 204.12.60.0 network might be 204.12.60.64. Thus, a packet from 204.12.60.24 would be passed to 204.12.60.64 if the destination host was not on the 204.12.60.0 network. The router 204.12.60.64 may have a second interface, 204.12.61.64, which connects the 204.12.60.0 and 204.12.59.0 networks. If the destination host was 204.12.59.28, the packet could now be delivered directly to the host because the router bridges the two networks. However, if the packet is not deliverable to a host on the 204.12.59.0 network, it must be passed to another router defined in the current router's tables.

IP Filtering and Firewalls

After going to all the trouble of making routing easy to use and semiautomated with the dynamic routing protocols, there are some situations requiring that the smooth transfer of packets from one host to another via a router be prevented. This is usually because of security concerns about data that is contained on hosts on a particular network. For example, Windows networks broadcast all kinds of information about workgroups and domains that is visible to any computer that can connect through the network's router. However, if the network's router prevents a computer on another network from listening to this information, it can still be broadcast internally but is not visible to the outside world. Fortunately, this kind of packet filtering is selective: only specific ports are blocked at the router level, and they can also be blocked in only one direction. For example, a database listener operating on a router could accept connections from machines internal to the network, but external access would be blocked. For large organizations that have direct connections to the Internet, setting up a corporate firewall at the router level has become a priority to protect sensitive data while providing employees with the access to the Internet that they require. In this section, we examine the basics of packet filtering. In the examples section, we review the installation and configuration of the popular ipfilter package for Solaris 9.

IP filtering involves the selective restriction and permission of access to TCP and UDP ports on a system. IP filtering is commonly used for two purposes: to secure a network from attacks and intrusion from rogue users on outside hosts and to prevent the broadcast and transmission of unauthorized data from an internal network to the rest of the

Internet. In the former case, an attacker may attempt to gain entry to your system by using an application like telnet or may try to insert or retrieve data from a database by connecting to a database listener, and issuing SQL commands from a client application. Both of these scenarios are common enough to motivate many sites to restrict all incoming traffic to their networks, except on a very small number of specific ports. Commonly allowed ports include

- Secure shell (ssh) on port 22
- Secure copy (scp) on port 24
- Mail server (sendmail) on port 25
- WWW server (apache) on port 80

This may seem like a very minimal list to many administrators, but the fact is that almost every UNIX daemon has been discovered to suffer from "buffer overflow" problems in recent years, leaving systems open to exploitation. A rule of thumb is to only allow services that users definitely need to be productive and that have been approved by management. Some users might argue that allowing the finger service is useful, but it also gives away a lot of information about home directories and valid usernames that can be exploited by rogue users. In addition, some users may set up web and ftp servers without permission. As Solaris only restricts ports less than 1024 for the superuser and system accounts, all ports above 1024 are available for users to engage in unauthorized activities for which your company may be held responsible. For example, a user might run a web server that distributes pirate software on port 8080: if a software manufacturer discovers this operation, they will most likely sue your company rather than the individual involved.

 TIP Blocking access to all ports unless they are specifically required or sanctioned limits these kinds of problems.

What is less intuitive than restricting incoming traffic is the notion of also restricting outgoing traffic. Firewalls are able to manage both because a firewall may also act as a router, and recall that routers always have at least two network interfaces. One good reason to consider blocking outgoing network on some ports is that users may engage in leisure activities, such as playing networked adventure games and talk, when they should be working. Since you don't really want to be the policeman "patrolling" the system for violators, it is best just to restrict any access in the first place to avoid any problems down the track. It's also possible to use a firewall to accept or deny connections based on IP address: obviously, a machine making a connection from the external network but pretending to have an address from inside the network should be identified and their attempts rejected (this is known as "IP spoofing"). Figure 35-4 summarizes the functions of a router that acts as a packet-filtering firewall. Permitted ports are shown with the label "OK," while denied ports are shown with "NO." All connections for sendmail (25) are accepted, as are ssh connections. However, external connections to a

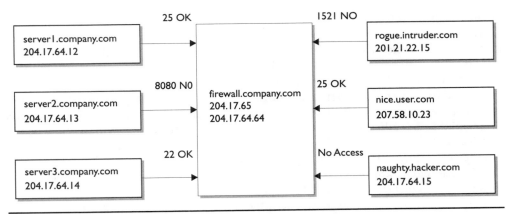

Figure 35-4 Basic firewall configuration blocking incoming and outgoing ports

database listener are rejected (port 1521), and an external machine spoofing an internal network IP address has all its connections rejected.

The Kernel Routing Table

The routing table maintains an index of routes to networks and routers that are available to the local host. Routes can be determined dynamically (by using RDISC, for example) or added manually by using the `route` or `ifconfig` command. These commands are normally used at boot time to initialize network services. There are three kinds of routes: host routes, which map a path from the local host to another host on the local network; network routes, which allow packets to be transferred from the local hosts to other hosts on the local network; and default routes, which pass the task of finding a route to a router. Both RIP and RDISC daemons can use default routes. Dynamic routing often causes changes in the routing table after booting, when a minimal routing table is configured by ifconfig while initializing each network interface, as the daemons manage changes in the network configuration and router availability.

Router Configuration

In order to configure routing, it is necessary to enable the appropriate network interfaces. In this chapter we will assume that an Ethernet network is being used; thus, each system that acts as a router must have at least two Ethernet interfaces installed. In addition, Solaris also supports multiple Ethernet interfaces to be installed on a single machine. These are usually designated by files like

```
/etc/hostname.hmen
```

or, for older machines,

```
/etc/hostname.len
```

where *n* is the interface number. Interface files contain a single IP address (or fully qualified domain name), with the primary network interface being designated with an interface number of zero. Thus, the primary interface of a machine called server would be defined by the file */etc/server.hme0*, which might contain the IP address 203.17.64.28 or the fully qualified domain name **external.server.com**. A secondary network interface, connected to a different subnet, might be defined in the file */etc/server.hme1*. In this case, the file might contain the IP address 10.17.65.28, or **internal.server.com**. Note that it is preferable to use fully qualified domain names to IP addresses, as the latter may be dynamically allocated using DHCP or a similar protocol. This setup is commonly used in organizations that have a provision for a failure of the primary network interface or to enable load balancing of server requests across multiple subnets (for example, for an intranet web server processing HTTP requests).

A system with a second network interface can act as either a router or as a multihomed host. Hostnames and IP addresses are locally administered through a naming service, which is usually the Domain Name Service (DNS) for companies connected to the Internet, and the Network Information Service (NIS/NIS+) for companies with large internal networks that require administrative functions beyond what DNS provides, including centralized authentication. It is also worth mentioning at this point that it is quite possible to assign different IP addresses to the same network interface, which can be useful for hosting "virtual" domains that require their own IP address, rather than relying on application-level support for multihoming (for example, when using the Apache web server). Simply create a new */etc/hostname.hmeX:Y* file for each IP address required, where *X* represents the physical device interface and *Y* represents the virtual interface number.

In the examples presented previously, each of the routers had two interfaces: one for the internal network and one for the external internet. The subnet mask used by each of these interfaces must also be defined in */etc/netmasks*. This is particularly important if the interfaces lie on different subnets or if they serve different network classes. In addition, it might also be appropriate to assign a fully qualified domain name to each of the interfaces, although this will depend on the purpose to which each interface is assigned. For the system **router.department.gov**, there will be two hostname files created in the */etc* directory. The */etc/hostname.hme0* file will contain the entry 10.17.65.16, while the */etc/hostname.hme0* file will contain the entry 204.17.65.16.

When installing a system as a router, it is necessary to determine which network interface to use as the external interface for passing information between networks. This interface must be defined in the file */etc/defaultrouter* by including that interface's IP address. These addresses can be matched to hostnames if appropriate. For example, the interfaces for **router.department.gov** will be defined in */etc/hosts* as

```
127.0.0.1     localhost    loghost
10.17.65.16     internal
204.17.65.16     router    router.department.gov
```

If the server is to be multihomed instead of being a router, ensure that */etc/ defaultrouter* does not exist and create an */etc/notrouter* file:

```
server# rm /etc/defaultrouter
server# touch /etc/notrouter
```

Exercise 35-1 /etc/notrouter check   Check to see if you have a *notrouter* file.

Exercise 35-2 Network Interface Status   Check your network interface settings using ifconfig. Is your interface up or down?

Static Routes

On hosts, routing information can be extracted in two ways: by building a full routing table, exactly as it does on a router, or by creating a minimal kernel table containing a single default route for each available router (that is, static routing). The most common static route is from a host to a local router, as specified in the */etc/defaultrouter* file. For example, for the host 204.12.60.24, the entry in */etc/defaultrouter* might be

```
204.12.60.64
```

This places a single route in the local routing table. Responsibility for determining the next hop for the message is then passed to the router. Static routes can also be added for servers using in.routed by defining them in the */etc/gateways* file. When using static routing, routing tables in the kernel are defined when the system boots and do not normally change unless modified by using the `route` or `ifconfig` command.

NOTE   When a local network has a single gateway to the rest of the Internet, static routing is the most appropriate choice.

Routing Protocols

The Routing Information Protocol (RIP) and the Router Discovery Protocol (RDISC) are some of the standard routing protocols for TCP/IP networks, and Solaris supports both. RIP is implemented by in.routed, the routing daemon, and is usually configured to start during multiuser mode startup (see Chapter 5 for more information). The route daemon always populates the routing table with a route to every reachable network, but whether or not it advertises its routing availability to other systems is optional.

Hosts use the RDISC daemon (in.rdisc) to collect information about routing availability from routers. in.rdisc typically creates a default route for each router that responds to requests: this "discovery" is central to the ability of RDISC-enabled hosts to dynamically adjust to network changes. Routers that only run in.routed cannot be discovered by RDISC-enabled hosts. For hosts running both in.rdisc and in.routed, the latter will operate until an RDISC-enabled router is discovered on the network, at which time RDISC will take over routing.

Viewing the Routing Table (netstat -r)

The command `netstat -r` shows the current routing table. Routes are always specified as a connection between the local server and a remote machine via some kind of gateway. The output from the `netstat -r` command contains several different flags: flag U indicates that the route between the destination and gateway is up, while flag G shows that the route passes through a gateway. Flag H indicates that the route connects to a host, while the D flag signifies that the route was dynamically created using a redirect. There are three other columns shown in the routing table: Ref indicates the number of concurrent routes occupying the same link layer, while Use indicates the number of packets transmitted along the route (on a specific Interface).

The following example shows an example server (**server.company.com**) that has four routes: the first is for the loopback address (lo0), which is Up and is connected through a host, and the second route is for the local Class C network (204.16.64.0), through the gateway **gateway.company.com.**, which is also Up. The third route is the special multicast route, which is also Up, while the fourth route is the default route, pointing to the local network router, which is also Up.

```
bash-2.01$ netstat -r

Routing Table:
  Destination            Gateway              Flags  Ref   Use   Interface
-------------------- -------------------- ----- ----- ------ ---------
127.0.0.1              localhost            UH     0     877   lo0
204.17.64.0           gateway.company.com  U      3      85   hme0
BASE-ADDRESS.MCAST.NET host.company.com    U      3       0   hme0
default               router.company.com   UG     0     303
```

Manipulating the Routing Table (route)

The `route` command is used to manually manipulate the routing tables. If dynamic routing is working correctly, it should not normally be necessary to do this. However, if static is being used, or the RDISC daemon does not discover any routes, it may be necessary to add routes manually. In addition, it may also be necessary to delete routes explicitly for security purposes. You should be aware, though, that except for interface changes, the routing daemon may not respond to any modifications to the routing table that may have been enacted manually. It is best to shut down the routing daemon first before making changes, and then restart it after all changes have been initiated.

Adding Host Routes

To add a direct route to another host, the `route` command is used with the following syntax:

```
route add -host destination_ip local_ip -interface interface
```

Thus, if we wanted to add a route between the local host (for example, 204.12.17.1) and a host on a neighboring Class C network (204.12.16.100) for the primary interface hme0, we would use this command:

```
add -host 204.12.16.100 204.12.17.1 -interface hme0
```

Adding Network Routes

To add a direct route to another network, the route command is used with this syntax:

```
route add -net destination_network_ip local_ip" -netmask mask
```

If we wanted to add a route between the local host (for example, 204.12.17.1) and the same network as the host we specified previously (that is, the 204.12.16.0 network), for the Class C netmask (255.255.255.0), we would use the following command:

```
route add -net 204.12.16.0 204.12.17.1 -netmask 255.255.255.0
```

Adding a Default Route

To add a default route, the route command can be used with this syntax:

```
route add default hostname -interface interface
```

For example, to add a default route to a local router (204.54.56.1) for a secondary interface hme1, you can use this command:

```
route add default 204.54.56.1 -interface hme1
```

Dynamic Routing

In this section, we will look more closely at the RIP and RDISC dynamic routing protocols. A prerequisite for dynamic routing to operate is that the */etc/defaultrouter* file should be empty.

routed

in.routed is the network routing daemon and is responsible for dynamically managing entries in the kernel routing tables, as described previously. It is usually started from a line during multiuser boot (*/etc/rc2.d/S69inet*) using the following command:

```
/usr/sbin/in.routed -q
```

The routing daemon uses port 520 to route packets and to establish which interfaces are currently Up and which are Down. in.routed listens for requests for packets and for known routes from remote hosts. This supplies hosts on a network with the information they need to determine how many hops to a host. When it is initialized, the routing daemon checks both gateways specified in */etc/gateways*. It is also possible to run the routing daemon in a special memory-saving mode that retains only the default routes in the routing table. While this may leave a system at the mercy of a faulty router, it does save memory and reduces the resources that in.routed requires to maintain lists of active routes, which are periodically updated. This can be enabled by initializing in.routed with the -S parameter.

PART III

rdisc

The rdisc daemon uses the ICMP router discovery protocol and is usually executed on both hosts and routers at boot time, at which time routers broadcast their availability and hosts start listening for available routers. Routers broadcast their availability using the 224.0.0.1 multicast address. Routers that share a network with a host are selected first as the default route, if one is found. Another approach is for the host to send out a broadcast on the 224.0.0.2 multicast address, to solicit any available routers. In either case, if a router is available, it will accept packet-forwarding requests from the host concerned.

Configuring the IPFilter Firewall

IPFilter is a popular freeware packet-filtering package for Solaris and is a kernel-loadable module that is attached at boot time. This makes IPFilter very secure because it cannot be tampered with by user applications. However, as we will see next, there are also problems with this approach because loading modules that are unstable into the kernel can cause a Solaris system to crash. The IPFilter distribution is available from **http:// coombs.anu.edu.au/~avalon/**.

The first step in creating an IPFilter configuration file is to consult with users and managers to determine a list of acceptable services. Many companies will already have an acceptable use policy that will govern which ports should be available and what permissions should be given for user-initiated services. After a list of ingoing and outgoing port requirements is determined, it is best to write a rule that first denies all packets and then to write rules that explicitly allow the services you identify. It is also important to enable allowed services in both directions: for example, it is usually necessary for users to both receive and send electronic mail, so an inbound and outbound rule needs to be included for sendmail (port 25).

IPFilter rules are processed in the order that they are specified in the configuration file. Every rule is processed, which means that more general rules (like blocking all connections) should precede specific rules (like allowing bidirectional sendmail connections) in the configuration file. If you have a very complicated configuration, it is also possible to specify that processing terminate at any point in the file if a condition is met by using the quick keyword. Other important keywords include block, to, and from to construct rules for limiting packet transmission. The block command blocks packets from a particular source to a particular destination. The from command specifies the source of these packets, while the to command specifies the destination of these packets. The following example prevents any packets from the Class B network 178.222.0.0:

```
block in quick from 178.222.0.0/16 to any
```

The pass command allows packets to pass the firewall. For example, the rule

```
pass in all
```

allows all packets to pass. Since routers by definition have more than two interfaces, it is also possible to specify a network interface to which a specific rule applies. For example, the rule

```
block in quick on hme2 all
```

prevents all transmissions on the hme2 interface. An interface specification can be mixed with a normal rule, so that one interface accepts traffic from one Class C network (178.222.1.0) but another interface may accept traffic only from a different Class C network (178.221.2.0):

```
block in quick on hme2 from 178.222.1.0/24 to any
block in quick on hme1 from 178.222.2.0/24 to any
```

All of our examples so far have focused on inbound traffic using the in command. As we mentioned earlier, it is also possible to restrict outbound traffic in the same way by using the out command. The following example prevents traffic from the internal, nonroutable network (10.222.1.0) to pass through:

```
block out quick on hme0 from 10.222.1.0/24 to any
```

This rule would only be applied to organizations that didn't want their employees using the Internet. Perhaps it could be combined with a cron job, which would reconfigure the firewall to allow access during lunchtime and after work. It is also possible to limit particular protocols so that TCP applications (like SSH) would be allowed, but UDP applications (like some streamed audio applications) would be banned, by specifying proto udp in the rule:

```
block in quick on hme0 proto udp from 10.222.1.0/24 to any
```

The most complicated rule comes in the form of a port-by-port specification of what is allowed and disallowed on a protocol-by-protocol basis. For example, the following rule blocks all web server requests from the internal network from reaching their destination:

```
block in quick on hme0 proto tcp from any to 10.222.1.0/24 port = 80
```

This would allow telnet and FTP connections to proceed freely, as TCP is only restricted on port 80.

Although this technology is very comprehensive, and is very useful in placing very specific restrictions on network transmission, there are some drawbacks with configuring firewalls in general—and IPFilter in particular. Since firewall configuration involves writing rules, the syntax of the commonly used rule languages is often difficult to understand; thus, packet filters can be difficult to configure correctly. Once you've created a configuration, there is also no testbed provided that determines if your configuration is satisfactory. There may be contention between one or more rules that is incorrectly resolved. There are also bugs in packet-filtering packages, which means that administrators should not just rely on them to protect their network—other measures, like disabling unrequired services in /etc/services and commenting out all unwanted daemons in /etc/inetd.conf, go a long way toward protecting a system. Bugs are more serious in IPFilter because it is a kernel-loadable module. Thus, instead of an application-level filtering program crashing and dumping core, IPFilter will sometimes crash the kernel and cause a panic. Be aware that some versions of IPFilter will cause panics on Solaris kernels, while others work happily. The output from a crash looks like this:

```
BAD TRAP: cpu=1 type=0x31 rp=0x3b103003 addr=0xe1 mmu_fsr=0x0
BAD TRAP occurred in module "ipf" due to an illegal access to a user
address.
sched: trap type = 0x31
addr=0x1e
pid=0, pc=0x60bc8607, sp=0x33ba0300, tstate=0x1e02f000, context=0x0
g1-g7: 1c, 13578104, 0, 0, 0, 0, 333e8000
Begin traceback... sp = 3033ba00
Called from 1005cb74, fp=30033c20, args=0 60760b14 20 10418440 0 0
Called from 1005cc90, fp=30033c80, args=60098aa0 600992c0 60098ac0
40000000 60099328 8c2421a
Called from 10026a48, fp=30033ce0, args=60098aa0 60098ab4 10418440
10418440 d 0
Called from 1005cc48, fp=0, args=60098aa0 0 0 0 0 0
```

This kind of problem is always a risk when installing kernel-loadable modules. However, Solaris does provide some tools to determine which modules are at fault. To examine the cause of the IPFilter problem, the following steps can be used:

1. Create the system crash directory, and enable the savecore facility in the system startup file (/etc/init.d/sysetup).

2. Wait for a crash, and then let the system reboot.

3. Enter the crash directory and analyze the crash file with the iscda.sh script available from SunSolve (**http://sunsolve1.sun.com.au/sunsolve/us/ iscda.html**).

4. Identify the offending command that caused the kernel panic. If it is IPFilter, download and test the most recent version.

Fortunately, there is a very active discussion group on IPFilter, with searchable archives available at **http://false.net/ipfilter/**. The firewall mailing list is also good for more general discussion of firewall-related issues, and the contents are available at **http://www.greatcircle.com/firewalls/**. If you are more interested in commercial firewall products, check out the comparisons with freeware at **http://www.fortified .com/fwcklist.html/**.

Configuring the SunScreen Firewall

The best system for users who are new to Solaris is Sun's own SunScreen firewall (**http://www.sun.com/software/securenet/lite/download.html**). It comes in both a free and a commercial edition, with the latter more than adequate for protecting small networks. It is available for both Solaris Intel and Solaris SPARC. The current release version is 3.1, which supports Gigabit Ethernet, SNMP management, and direct editing of security policy tables. However, it does not currently support IPv6. The firewall may be administered locally or remotely by using a secure session.

There are several important limitations that are placed on the Lite version of SunScreen:

- It is designed to work with a system that is already acting as a router (if it wasn't, why would you want SunScreen anyway?).

- It does not operate in the special "stealth" mode employed by the commercial edition.

- It does not support any of the High Availability features of the commercial version.

- It does not support more than two network interfaces. However, as most routers only have two interfaces, this should not be an issue for small networks.

- It does not provide support for proxying.

SunScreen can be operated in either GUI mode, through a standard web browser such as Netscape, or by directly editing the system's configuration files. It is easy to install using the Web Start Wizard, which is provided with the installation package.

To install the software, you need to run the */opt/SUNWicg/SunScreen/bin/ss_install* script. There are several options that you need to configure for SunScreen to operate as desired:

- Routing or stealth mode operation

- Local or remote administration

- Restrictive, secure, or permissive security level

- Support for DNS resolution

After choosing the appropriate options for your system, the following message will be displayed:

```
--Adding interfaces & interface addresses
--Initialize 'vars' databases
--Initialize 'authuser' & 'proxyuser' databases
--Initialize 'logmacro' database
--Applying edits
--Activating configuration
loading skip keystore.
Successfully initialized certificate database in /etc/skip/certdb
starting skip key manager daemon.
Configuration activated successfully on cassowary.
Reboot the machine now for changes to take effect.
```

After rebooting the system, the firewall software will be loaded into the kernel, and you will then need to add rules to the firewall by using your browser to set the appropriate administration options. Figure 35-5 shows the browser starting on port 3852 on the localhost.

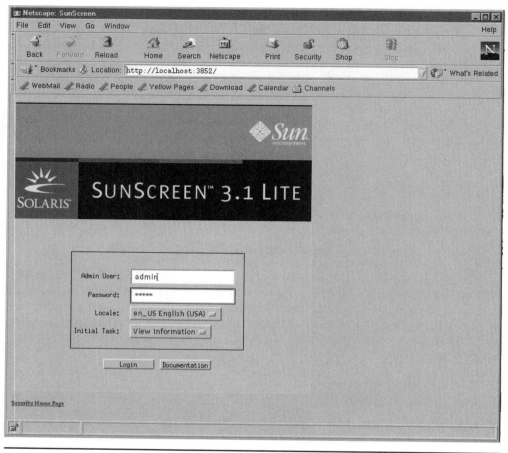

Figure 35-5   Starting the SunScreen administrative interface

When first installed, the SunScreen username and password will be admin and admin, respectively. These should be entered into the Admin User and Password fields. After clicking the Login button, the SunScreen Information page is displayed, as shown in Figure 35-6. There are several options available at this point: firewall logs may be viewed, as may connection statistics. However, most users will want to create a set of security policies immediately upon starting the firewall service.

Security policies are based on rules that either ALLOW or DENY a packet to be transmitted from a source to a destination address. Alternatively, an address class may be specified by using wildcards. The main actions associated with ALLOW rules are as follows:

- LOG_NONE
- LOG_SUMMARY

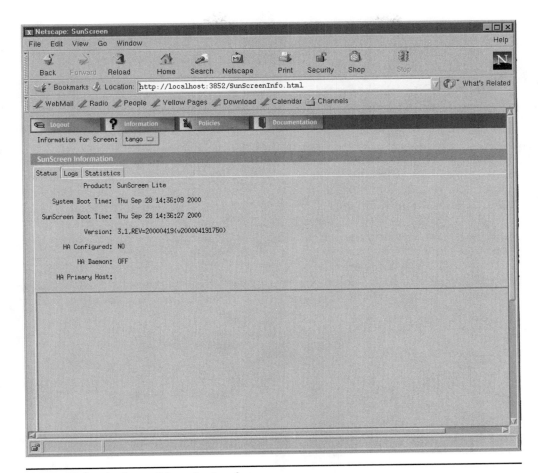

Figure 35-6 SunScreen Information interface

- LOG_DETAIL
- SNMP_NONE
- SNMP

The main actions associated with DENY rules are as follows:

- LOG_NONE
- LOG_SUMMARY
- LOG_DETAIL
- SNMP_NONE
- SNMP

- ICMP_NONE
- ICMP_NET_UNREACHABLE
- ICMP_HOST_UNREACHABLE
- ICMP_PORT_UNREACHABLE
- ICMP_NET_FORBIDDEN
- ICMP_HOST_FORBIDDEN

Figure 35-7 shows how to define a rule with actions for the SMTP service, which is operated by sendmail. This allows mail to be transferred from local users to remote hosts. However, it we wanted to block all mail being sent to and from our network, we could create a DENY action within the rule for the SMTP service. The rule could be applied selectively to specific local subnets or remote destinations. Another useful feature is the ability to apply rules only for specific time periods. For example, if you worked in a bank, you could prevent all e-mails from being sent externally after 5:00 P.M. at night and before 9:00 A.M. in the morning.

Once the new rule has been entered, it can be viewed on the Policy Rules panel, along with any other rules, as shown in Figure 35-8. The panel allows new rules to be added

Figure 35-7

Rule definition

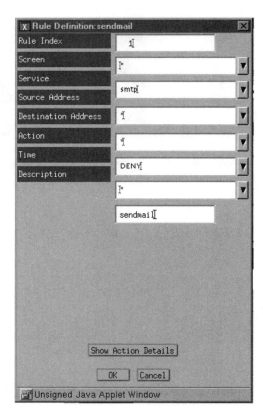

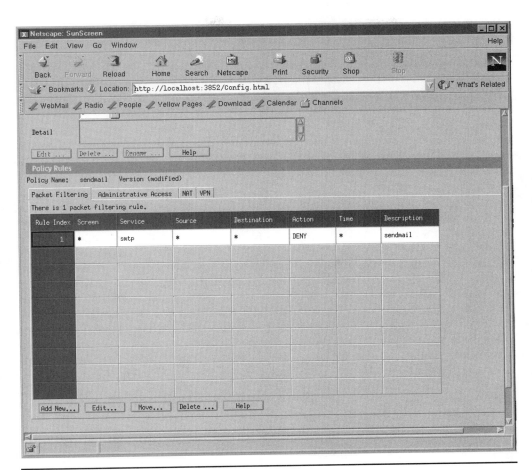

Figure 35-8 Policy Rules interface

and existing rules to be edited, moved, or deleted. For each packet-filtering rule, the service, source address, destination address, action timeframe, and name are shown.

SunScreen performs more than just packet filtering—it can be used to set up a virtual private network (VPN) and can perform advanced network address translation (NAT) functions.

Viewing Router Status

For both routing and multihomed hosts, the status of all network interfaces can be checked by using the netstat -i command:

```
router# netstat -i
Name  Mtu   Net/Dest    Address      Ipkts   Ierrs Opkts  Oerrs Collis Queue
                        localhost    199875  0     199875 0     0      0
lo0   8232  loopback    localhost    199875  0     199875 0     0      0
```

```
hme0  1500 203.17.65.0 department.gov 16970779 623190 19543549 0     0       0
hme1  1500 10.17.65.0 internal.gov 68674644 54543 65673376 0     0       0
```

In this example, Mtu is the maximum transfer rate, which is much higher for the loopback address than the network interface (as would be expected), and the number of Ipkts (inbound packets) and Opkts (outbound packets) is equivalent for lo0 (as one would hope). The loopback interface significantly increases the efficiency of a host that transmits packets to itself: in this example, there is an almost sixfold increase in the Mtu for the lo0 interface over either of the standard network interfaces. The primary network interface hme0 is connected to the 203.17.65.0 network, and transmitted a large number of packets in and out since booting (16970779 and 19543549, respectively). There have been a number of inbound errors (623190), but no outbound errors or collisions. Examining how these figures change over time can indicate potential problems in network topology, which may need to be addressed. For example, if you are testing a web server and it doesn't appear to be working, the Ipkts count can reveal whether or not the connections are actually being made—if the counter does not increase as expected, it may indicate an intermediate hardware failure (for example, a dead hub). Another example of identifying intermittent hardware failure might be revealed by a large number of inbound packets, representing requests, but only a small number of outbound packets. In the following example, there are 1000847 inbound packets, but only 30159 outbound packets since boot. Because it is unlikely in most situations that a 33:1 imbalance exists in the ratio of inbound to outbound packets, the hme0 network interface should be checked. There are also many collisions being experienced by the hme0 interface—between packets render them useless, and the figure reported here indicates a significant loss of bandwidth. If the interface is working as expected, it can also be worthwhile to investigate other causes arising from software (for example, incorrect configuration of a packet filter):

```
router# netstat -i
Name  Mtu   Net/Dest      Address         Ipkts  Ierrs Opkts  Oerrs Collis Queue
lo0   8232  loopback      localhost       7513   0     7513   0     0      0
hme0  1500  204.17.64.0   1000847 5       30159  0     3979   0
```

netstat –s also allows these per-interface statistics to be viewed on a per-protocol basis, which can be very useful in determining potential problems with routing, especially if the router is packet filtering. The following example shows output from the netstat –s command, which displays the per-protocol statistics for the UDP, TCP, and ICMP protocols:

```
router# netstat -i
UDP
        udpInDatagrams      =502856    udpInErrors      =     0
        udpOutDatagrams     =459357
```

The output from netstat –s begins with the UDP statistics, including the number of datagrams received and the number transmitted. The in/out ratio is fairly even at 1.09, and the networking appears to be working well—there were no detected UDP errors (that is, udpInErrors=0):

```
TCP   tcpRtoAlgorithm     =       4    tcpRtoMin           =     200
      tcpRtoMax           =240000       tcpMaxConn          =      -1
      tcpActiveOpens      = 33786       tcpPassiveOpens     = 12296
      tcpAttemptFails     =     324     tcpEstabResets      =     909
      tcpCurrEstab        =     384     tcpOutSegs          =19158723
      tcpOutDataSegs      =13666668     tcpOutDataBytes     =981537148
      tcpRetransSegs      = 33038       tcpRetransBytes     =41629885
      tcpOutAck           =5490764      tcpOutAckDelayed    =462511
      tcpOutUrg           =      51     tcpOutWinUpdate     =     456
      tcpOutWinProbe      =     290     tcpOutControl       = 92218
      tcpOutRsts          =    1455     tcpOutFastRetrans   = 18954
      tcpInSegs           =15617893
      tcpInAckSegs        =9161810      tcpInAckBytes       =981315052
      tcpInDupAck         =4559921      tcpInAckUnsent      =       0
      tcpInInorderSegs    =5741788      tcpInInorderBytes   =1120389303
      tcpInUnorderSegs    = 25045       tcpInUnorderBytes   =16972517
      tcpInDupSegs        =4390218      tcpInDupBytes       =4889714
      tcpInPartDupSegs    =     375     tcpInPartDupBytes   =130424
      tcpInPastWinSegs    =      17     tcpInPastWinBytes   =1808990872
      tcpInWinProbe       =     162     tcpInWinUpdate      =     270
      tcpInClosed         =     313     tcpRttNoUpdate      = 28077
      tcpRttUpdate        =9096791      tcpTimRetrans       = 18098
      tcpTimRetransDrop   =      26     tcpTimKeepalive     =     509
      tcpTimKeepaliveProbe=      76     tcpTimKeepaliveDrop =       1
      tcpListenDrop       =       0     tcpListenDropQ0     =       0
      tcpHalfOpenDrop     =       0
```

The TCP statistics more mixed. There were 324 `tcpAttemptFails`, but given that there were 33,786 `tcpActiveOpens` at the time netstat was run, this is quite reasonable. The ratio of `tcpInInorderSegs` to `tcpInUnorderSegs` (that is, received in order versus not received in order) was 229:1, which is not uncommon:

```
IP    ipForwarding        =       2    ipDefaultTTL        =     255
      ipInReceives        =16081438    ipInHdrErrors       =       8
      ipInAddrErrors      =       0    ipInCksumErrs       =       1
      ipForwDatagrams     =       0    ipForwProhibits     =       2
      ipInUnknownProtos   =     274    ipInDiscards        =       0
      ipInDelivers        =16146712    ipOutRequests       =19560145
      ipOutDiscards       =       0    ipOutNoRoutes       =       0
      ipReasmTimeout      =      60    ipReasmReqds        =       0
      ipReasmOKs          =       0    ipReasmFails        =       0
      ipReasmDuplicates   =       0    ipReasmPartDups     =       0
      ipFragOKs           =    7780    ipFragFails         =       0
      ipFragCreates       = 40837      ipRoutingDiscards   =       0
      tcpInErrs           =     291    udpNoPorts          =144065
      udpInCksumErrs      =       2    udpInOverflows      =       0
      rawipInOverflows    =       0
```

There are some IP errors but they were quite minor. There were eight `ipInHdr Errors` but only one `ipInCksumErrs`, and two `udpInCksumErrs`.

```
ICMP  icmpInMsgs          = 17469      icmpInErrors        =       0
      icmpInCksumErrs     =       0    icmpInUnknowns      =       0
      icmpInDestUnreachs  =    2343    icmpInTimeExcds     =      26
      icmpInParmProbs     =       0    icmpInSrcQuenchs    =       0
      icmpInRedirects     =      19    icmpInBadRedirects  =      19
      icmpInEchos         =    9580    icmpInEchoReps      =    5226
```

PART III

```
icmpInTimestamps      =      0    icmpInTimestampReps =      0
icmpInAddrMasks       =      0    icmpInAddrMaskReps  =      0
icmpInFragNeeded      =      0    icmpOutMsgs         = 11693
icmpOutDrops          =140883    icmpOutErrors       =      0
icmpOutDestUnreachs   =   2113    icmpOutTimeExcds    =      0
icmpOutParmProbs      =      0    icmpOutSrcQuenchs   =      0
icmpOutRedirects      =      0    icmpOutEchos        =      0
icmpOutEchoReps       =   9580    icmpOutTimestamps   =      0
icmpOutTimestampReps=        0    icmpOutAddrMasks    =      0
icmpOutAddrMaskReps   =      0    icmpOutFragNeeded   =      0
icmpInOverflows       =      0
```

On the ICMP front, `icmpOutErrors` and `icmpInErrors` are both zero, although there were 2,113 `icmpOutDestUnreachs`, indicating that at some point a network connection was not able to made when requested. This can be checked with the traceroute utility described in the following section. It also is often useful to run a cron job to extract these figures to a file, and then write a Perl script to compare the values of concern. This is because it is possible that errors could be masked by integers being "wrapped around" and starting at zero after they reach values that are greater than the maximum available for a machine's architecture. However, this should not be a problem for the new 64-bit kernels available with Solaris 7, 8, and 9.

traceroute

If the process of finding a route is difficult to conceptualize, Solaris provides the traceroute tool to literally display the route taken by a packet between two hosts. The traceroute utility measures the time taken to reach each intermediate host from source to destination. If an intermediate host cannot be reached in a specified time period (usually the ttl "time to live" field), an error message is reported. A maximum number of hops (usually 30) is specified to prevent traceroute from looping infinitely if an operational route cannot be found. traceroute is also very useful for determining network points of failure due to misconfiguration and hardware problems. Here is an example of a traceroute between a host on the AT&T network and a host on the Sun network:

```
client% traceroute www.sun.com
Tracing route to wwwwseast.usec.sun.com [192.9.49.30]
over a maximum of 30 hops:
  1    184 ms    142 ms    138 ms   202.10.4.131
  2    147 ms    144 ms    138 ms   202.10.4.129
  3    150 ms    142 ms    144 ms   202.10.1.73
  4    150 ms    144 ms    141 ms   atm11-0-0-11.ia4.optus.net.au [202.139.32.17]
  5    148 ms    143 ms    139 ms   202.139.1.197
  6    490 ms    489 ms    474 ms   hssi9-0-0.sf1.optus.net.au [192.65.89.246]
  7    526 ms    480 ms    485 ms   g-sfd-br-02-f12-0.gn.cwix.net [207.124.109.57]
  8    494 ms    482 ms    485 ms   core7-hssi6-0-0.SanFrancisco.cw.net [204.70.10.9]
  9    483 ms    489 ms    484 ms   corerouter2.SanFrancisco.cw.net [204.70.9.132]
 10    557 ms    552 ms    561 ms   xcore3.Boston.cw.net [204.70.150.81]
 11    566 ms    572 ms    554 ms   sun-micro-system.Boston.cw.net [204.70.179.102]
 12    577 ms    574 ms    558 ms   wwwwseast.usec.sun.com [192.9.49.30]
Trace complete.
```

Summary

In this chapter, we examined the basics of routing in the Solaris environment. Since routing underlies all remote packet delivery, it's important for administrators to understand the complex processes involved, especially the configuration of firewalls.

Questions

1. Which three major types of subnet are supported by Solaris?

    A. Class 1, Class 2, Class 3

    B. Class A, Class, Class C

    C. T1, broadband, cable

    D. None of the above

2. What is the purpose of a router?

    A. To pass information from one network to another

    B. To pass information between two hosts only

    C. To provide two independent network interfaces on a single host

    D. None of the above

3. What is the main requirement of a router?

    A. To be connected to the Internet

    B. To run Solaris 8

    C. To have multiple network interfaces

    D. None of the above

4. What would be contained in the file */etc/hostname.hme0* (choose two)?

    A. A hostname

    B. A fully qualified domain name

    C. An IP address

    D. The default router's hostname

5. What is contained in the file */etc/defaultrouter*?

    A. The local router's hostname

    B. The local router's IP address

    C. The local router's hostname or IP address

    D. The local router's netmask

PART III

6. What file should be created for a nonrouting, multihomed host?

   A. /etc/noroute

   B. /etc/notrouter

   C. /etc/notroute

   D. /etc/!route

7. What command is used to set parameters for network protocols?

   A. tcp

   B. ip

   C. tip

   D. ndd

8. What command is used to display parameters for network protocols?

   A. tcp /dev/tcp \?

   B. ip /dev/tcp \?

   C. tip /dev/tcp \?

   D. ndd /dev/tcp \?

9. What command is used to trace a network route?

   A. net route

   B. trace -route

   C. traceroute

   D. net -route

10. What protocol does rdisc use?

    A. ICMP router discovery protocol

    B. RTD router discovery protocol

    C. RDP router discovery protocol

    D. RDSC router discovery protocol

Answers

1. **B.** The three types of subnet supported by Solaris are Class A, Class B, and Class C.

2. **A.** The purpose of a router is to pass information from one network to another.

3. **C.** A router must have multiple network interfaces

4. **A, C.** A hostname or an IP address could be contained in the file /etc/hostname.hme0.

5. **C.** The local router's hostname or IP address is contained in */etc/defaultrouter*.

6. **B.** The */etc/notrouter* file should be created for a nonrouting, multihomed host.

7. **D.** The `ndd` command should used to set parameters for network protocols.

8. **D.** The `ndd /dev/tcp \?` command should used to display parameters for network protocols.

9. **C.** The `traceroute` command is used to trace a network route.

10. **A.** rdisc uses the ICMP router discovery protocol.

Internet Layer (IPv6)

In this chapter, you will

- Cover IPv6 addressing
- Learn the characteristics of IPv6 routing
- Learn the properties of IPSec security
- Go over the various standard and optional headers supported by IPv6 packets

The TCP/IP protocol suite relies on the Internet Protocol to provide the lower-level services required to support transport and application layers in the stack. However, the current version of IP (IPv4) is now approximately 20 years old, and much has changed in the network world since that time—the Internet has become globally distributed, commercial transactions are conducted on the Internet, and the sheer number of connected hosts has given rise to routing, configuration, and address allocation problems. If these problems are not fixed, the Internet in its present form may cease to function at some future time as it reaches capacity. The IETF predicts that this may occur in 2008.

IPv6 Motivation

The maximum number of IP addresses that can be created using IPv4 is 4,300,000,000. While this number must have seemed very large when IPv4 was developed, it now represents a fraction of the potential human users of the Internet. While the Dynamic Host Configuration Protocol (DHCP) has alleviated the address availability problem, by leasing out addresses dynamically instead of assigning them statically, the "always connected, always available" broadband world will consume these leases in the long-term. In addition, with the introduction of "smart spaces" filled with embedded devices with their own IP address, one human may potentially be associated with dozens if not hundreds of different devices. So, one key requirement for an improved IP is the ability to massively increase the pool of available IP addresses.

A related requirement has arisen by the effective breaking of end-to-end communication through the introduction of Network Address Translation (NAT). Like DHCP, NAT was introduced to alleviate the IP address availability problem, by assigning a router a public routable IP address, while assigning all hosts behind the router a private nonroutable IP address. This reduced the number of public IP addresses required by organizations to connect their hosts to the Internet. NAT also shielded private computers from attacks originating from the Internet, because their IP addresses were nonroutable.

However, NAT also made it impossible to perform machine-to-machine authentication, because the router running NAT software essentially acts as a proxy for the client system. Thus, while security initiatives like the IP Security Protocol (IPSec) that require source and destination IP addresses can be used for integrity checking, using NAT can potentially break IPSec. Another requirement for an improved IP is to remove the reliance on NAT for building secure networks.

A more practical problem also exists at the hardware level for IPv4 routers—because routing tables are growing exponentially, as new networks are added to the Internet the physical memory capacity of many routers to hold and process this information is limited. If the routing structure is not simplified, many routers may simply fail to route any packets correctly.

IPv6 attempts to address the core issues of the small IP address space, end-to-end communication, and the unwelcome mass of routing data. IPv6 is based on a 128-bit address space, rather than a 32-bit address space, providing a large pool of addresses for future computer systems and embedded devices to utilize. The 128 bits are divided into 8×16 byte integers expressed using hexadecimal (for example, 1072:3B:BED3:1:0:2:220:B6EB). In addition, end-to-end communications can be preserved by the use of flow labels that can be used to identify the true end parties for a specific real-time communication.

 NOTE Routing has been dramatically overhauled to ensure that addresses and routes can be more efficiently stored and utilized.

IPv6 has been supported by Sun since Solaris 8 in the form of a dual stack, whereby IPv4 and IPv6 traffic can be supported on a single network. This ensures that new applications requiring the use of IPv6 can coexist alongside legacy IPv4 applications. In the following sections, we will examine each of the key areas of IPv6 and discuss their implementation in Solaris.

Addressing

IPv6 sees the IP address size for each network interface increased from 32 bits to 128 bits, giving a total address space of 2^32 and 2^128, respectively. To give you an idea of the difference between these two spaces, 2^32 = 4,294,967,296 (about 1 billion less than the world's population, while 2^128 = 3.402 × e^38! This expansion will not only support the massive expansion of the Internet through the connection of billions of embedded devices, it will also ensure that many stopgap measures such as DHCP and NAT can be disbanded if they serve no other purpose in a specific environment. Although some competing proposals argued for only a 64-bit IPv6 address space, this would not have enabled some of the useful features of IPv6, including the ability to do away with subnet masks. This allows autoconfiguration of network interfaces without the user having to know what class of subnet (A, B, or C) their local area network belongs to.

Using 128-bit addressing makes autoconfiguration much easier in IPv6 compared to IPv4: the lower 64 bits are composed of the hardware (MAC) address for the network interface, while the upper 64 bits comprise a router message. Since every subnet now has an equivalent sized subnet prefix, it is no longer used to distinguish different subnet classes.

IPv6 has three different interface types that addresses can be identifiers for:

- **Unicast** An identifier for a single, specific interface.
- **Multicast** A broadcast-like identifier for all interfaces belonging to a set.
- **Anycast** Identifier for only one interface that belongs to a set, usually the member that is closest to the source.

While unicast and multicast addressing are readily identifiable from IPv4, the inclusion of anycast addressing provides the foundation for significant advances in the areas of high availability, redundancy, and network storage, since any member of a set of interfaces designated by their addresses can be selected based on some distance metric or availability at runtime. For example, a storage area network (SAN) may support distributed backup services for a multinational organization. When a client has a backup scheduled, it is directed to the nearest server node based on geographical distance. If that node is unavailable, the next available server node in the set of server nodes is selected, and so on. While this sort of decision logic can be programmed in at the application layer, its inclusion in the Internet layer makes it ubiquitous across all applications and services operating on a network.

Like IPv4, IPv6 has a number of special addresses that have specific purposes and that administrators should be aware of:

- **Loopback address** 0:0:0:0:0:0:0:1
- **IPv4 address** 96 bits zero-padded to the 32-bit original address
- **Local site address** 1111 1110 11
- **Local link address** 1111 1110 10
- **Multicast address** 1111 1111
- **Unspecific address** 0:0:0:0:0:0:0:0

IPv6 addresses are being allocated by using a simple formula:

Field Name	Provider-based	Registry	Provider	Subscriber	Subnet	Interface
Number of bits	3 (e.g., 010)	a	b	c	d	128-b-a-c-d

In this scheme, the registry is one of the following organizations, which caters to a specific region:

- **10000**   Multiregional (IANA)
- **01000**   RIPE NCC (Europe)
- **11000**   INTERNIC (North America)
- **10100**   APNIC (Asia/Pacific)

The provider is some network service provider within a specific region, and the subscriber is the end-user organization. Within the organization subnets can still exist, within which individual network interfaces will belong.

 TIP   At present, provider-based prefixes are being used to utilize a subset of all available address sets for the current range of networks connected to the Internet.

IPv6 addresses are much longer than IPv4 addresses, so they are difficult for humans to learn and use. Because the address space is so large, there are also large portions of the address that are presently zero padded. Thus, a notation has been introduced to simplify the representation of repeated sections of zeros. In order to eliminate any ambiguity in the resolution of zero-padded sections, only one set of zeros may be represented by the dual-colon token :: in each address. For example, the address 1080:0:0:0:0:711:100D:306B could also be represented as 1080::711:100D:306B, or the address 1080:0:0:0:0:0:100D:306B could be represented by 1080::100D:306B. However, it would not be possible to represent the address 1080:0:208:0:711:0:0:306B as 1080::208::711::306B because the position of each nonzero bit is ambiguous.

For further information, read the IP Version 6 Addressing Architecture RFC at **ftp://ftp.isi.edu/in-notes/rfc2373.txt**.

Exercise 36-1 IPv6 Addresses   How else could the address 1080:1:0:0:0:611:100 E:305B be represented?

Routing

Internet routing is based on the idea that optimal paths can be dynamically calculated because routers carry information about all network paths in memory. With the massive number of possible paths and new networks being introduced daily, it's impractical to do this, so most routers fall back on a set of default routes to handle most of their traffic. While a system to optimize routing is theoretically possible, the very flat organization of networks and domains means that it's not practically possible with IPv4. The exception here is the set of backbone Internet servers that must carry the load and determine all network paths that cannot be computed by individual nodes, placing an onerous burden on some service providers.

IPv6 aims to change this situation by implementing a hierarchical model for addressing, providing an explicit set of domains in the address to ensure that destinations can be resolved at a more local level. Thus, a router does not need to have knowledge of a large set of possible network destinations—the appropriate destination router can be determined from the address. The provider field in the address takes on the role of providing a first-glance indication of a packet's ultimate destination. At the same time, changes in the structure of the Internet cannot be reliably predicted, so any routing system must be flexible enough to support structural changes down the line.

A number of different routing algorithms are supported by IPv6, including a number that are compatible with IPv4:

- Open Shortest Path First (OSPF)
- Routing Information Protocol (RIP)
- Inter-Domain Routing Protocol (IDRP)
- Intermediate System to Intermediate System Protocol (ISIS)

Routing extensions are also available through a header in the IPv6 extended header segment. These extensions include the ability to specify intermediate hosts or specific packet paths, which can then be reversed to ensure that a reply packet is delivered back to the sender using the same path. This approach has great benefits to users of mobile telecommunications technologies such as mobile phones, because the highly dynamic path back to its source does not need to be recomputed by intermediate routers.

Headers

IPv6 introduces a number of changes to the format of headers contained in a standard IPv4 packet. The following fields are common to IPv4 and IPv6:

- Version
- Length
- Service Type
- Packet Length
- Identification
- Fragment Offset
- TTL
- Transport
- Header Checksum
- Source Address
- Destination Address

- Options
- Padding

However, there are several brand new headers that contain important information in standard format:

- **Version Number** A "6" identifies IPv6.
- **Priority** Sets a priority value, depending on whether a packet is noncongestion (priority) or congestion-controlled.
- **Flow Label** Sets a QualityOfService parameter for the packet.
- **Payload Length** Size of the packet's data.
- **Next Header** Determines whether an extension header follows.
- **Hop Limit** Sets a limit on the number of nodes that can handle the packet (graceful degradation).

Several extensions to the standard headers are available in the extended header if flagged in the Next Header field of the standard header. The following extensions are currently being developed:

- Authentication and security
- Confidentiality
- Destination data
- Extending routing
- Hop-by-hop processing
- Reassembly

Quality of Service

Quality of service (QoS) is very much a missing component of IPv4. When IPv4 was developed, there was no such thing as "mission critical e-commerce data" being exchanged between organizations on the Internet. However, with the rise of B2B e-commerce and the development of digital virtual enterprises, ensuring QoS is critical to the operation of certain classes of applications and services (such as Web Services).

IPv6 provides QoS through a priority and flow label system of packet prioritization defined within the packet header. There are several different priority values that have been suggested for congestion-controlled traffic, which has a lower priority than noncongestion-controlled traffic:

- **0** Unclassified
- **1** Bulk traffic

- **2**   Noninteractive bulk data transfer
- **3**   Undefined
- **4**   Interactive bulk data transfer
- **5**   Undefined
- **6**   Interactive nonbulk data transfer
- **7**   Control traffic

Security

All IPv6 stacks must implement Internet Protocol Security (IPSec). IPSec provides for security to be provided at the Internet layer, rather than at the transport layer (like the Secure Socket Layer currently provides for secure e-commerce). IPSec provides facilities for encryption, authentication, implementing security policies, and data compression. The two main components of IPv6 security are packet encryption through the Encapsulated Security Payload (ESP) and source authentication through the Authentication Header (AH).

The ESP provides confidentiality, authentication, and integrity checks, while the AH only supports authentication and integrity, and works at the packet level—it uses strong cryptography to ensure that a packet can be authentically exchanged between two interfaces by the sharing a secret key. This allows the two parties to be assured that the packet has not been tampered with in transit, and that the packet originated from the source interface as described in the packet's header.

The ESP provides a different level of security than the AH by ensuring that the data contained within a packet has not been intercepted and decrypted by a third party, as long as the secret key protecting the data has not been given to a third party.

Key management is clearly a central issue in the provision of a secure platform for IPv6. That's why the Internet Key Exchange (IKE) system is important to the success of IPSec. IKE makes it possible for two systems to share secret keys in a secure environment. However, if a cracker discovers a secret key, all of the traffic previously protected by the key will be open for reading by that hacker. This is why secret keys cannot be used indefinitely, and should be regularly modified. One of the benefits of using Solaris IPSec is that it incorporates IKE—Solaris 8 IPSec did not support IKE because it was not part of the IPSec standard at the time, leading to cross-platform incompatibilities. This is done automatically after the session is started with a public-key exchange.

Summary

In this chapter we have examined the future of the Internet Protocol (IP) as embodied by IPv6, which is the next-generation IP. The areas in which IPv6 introduces the greatest changes are the areas of security, addressing, routing, and quality of service. Much of the detail in IPv6 differs from IPv4, and these changes were covered in detail in this chapter.

PART III

Questions

1. What is the limit of the IPv4 address pool?

   A. 4,300,000,000 hosts

   B. 300,000,000 hosts

   C. 30,000,000 hosts

   D. 43,000,000 hosts

2. What stopgap measure has been used to limit the problems caused by the IPv4 address pool size?

   A. Network Address Translation

   B. Domain Name Service

   C. Internet Protocol Security

   D. Network Information Service

3. Which of the following is not a serious limitation of IPv4?

   A. Breaking of end-to-end communication

   B. 128-bit IP addresses

   C. Massive routing tables

   D. IP address availability

4. What issue does IPv6 not explicitly address?

   A. Providing a large pool of addresses

   B. Preserving end-to-end communications

   C. Simplified routing

   D. Fewer IP headers

5. In what form does Solaris 9 support IPv6?

   A. It does not support IPv6

   B. It supports IPv6 but not IPv4

   C. It supports IPv6 and IPv4 in separate stacks

   D. It supports IPv6 and IPv4 in the same stack

6. Name one immediate benefit for autoconfiguration of interfaces provided by IPv6?

   A. More IP addresses

   B. Not having to know the subnet mask

   C. Fewer network administrators

   D. Faster transmission rates

7. Which of the following is an identifier for a single specific interface?

    A. Unicast

    B. Multicast

    C. Anycast

    D. Broadcast

8. Which of the following is an identifier for all interfaces in a set?

    A. Unicast

    B. Multicast

    C. Anycast

    D. Broadcast

9. Which of the following is an identifier for a single interface that is the member of a set?

    A. Unicast

    B. Multicast

    C. Anycast

    D. Broadcast

10. What is the IPv6 loopback address?

    A. 0:0:0:0:0:0:0:1

    B. 96 bits zero-padded to the 32-bit original address

    C. 1111 1110 11

    D. 1111 1110 10

11. What is the IPv6 version of an IPv4 address?

    A. 0:0:0:0:0:0:0:1

    B. 96 bits zero-padded to the 32-bit original address

    C. 1111 1110 11

    D. 1111 1110 10

12. What is the IPv6 local site address?

    A. 0:0:0:0:0:0:0:1

    B. 96 bits zero-padded to the 32-bit original address

    C. 1111 1110 11

    D. 1111 1110 10

13. What is the IPv6 local link address?

    A. 0:0:0:0:0:0:0:1

     B. 96 bits zero-padded to the 32-bit original address

     C. `1111 1110 11`

     D. `1111 1110 10`

14. How else could the address 1080:0:0:0:0:151:200A:305C be represented?

     A. 1080::151:200A:305C

     B. 1080:0:0:0: 151:200A:305C

     C. 1080:0:0:0:*:151:200A:305C

     D. 1080:*:151:200A:305C

15. Which routing protocol is supported by IPv6?

     A. Open Shortest Path First (OSPF)

     B. Routing Information Protocol (RIP)

     C. Inter-Domain Routing Protocol (IDRP)

     D. All of the above

Answers

1. **A.** The limit of the IPv4 address pool is 4,300,000,000 hosts.

2. **A.** Network Address Translation has been used as a stopgap measure to limit the problems caused by the IPv4 address pool size.

3. **B.** IPv4 addresses only have 32 bits.

4. **D.** IPv6 actually increases the number of headers.

5. **D.** Solaris 9 supports a dual-stack implementation.

6. **B.** Autoconfiguration does not require knowledge of the subnet mask.

7. **A.** Unicast is an identifier for a single specific interface.

8. **B.** Multicast is an identifier for all interfaces in a set.

9. **C.** Anycast is an identifier for a single interface that is the member of a set.

10. **A.** 0:0:0:0:0:0:0:1 is the IPv6 loopback address.

11. **B.** 96 bits zero-padded to the 32-bit original address is the IPv6 version of an IPv4 address.

12. **C.** `1111 1110 11` is the IPv6 local site address.

13. **D.** `1111 1110 10` is the IPv6 local link address.

14. **A.** The address 1080:0:0:0:0:151:200A:305C could be represented by 1080::151:200A:305C.

15. **D.** All of these routing protocols are supported by IPv6.

Transport Layer

In this chapter, you will
- Identify the key properties of the TCP protocol
- Identify the key properties of the UDP protocol
- Describe the transport requirements of applications that use TCP or UDP
- Review higher-level protocols that require TCP or UDP

The interface between the application and the Internet layers in the TCP/IP stack is the transport layer. This layer implements protocols to transport packets in application-specific ways, depending on the individual requirements of the application. The two most commonly used transports are the Transmission Control Protocol (TCP) and the User Datagram Protocol (UDP). TCP aims to provide reliable transmission but is more heavyweight, while UDP is lightweight but does not guarantee the delivery of packets. Thus, applications that are error tolerant in terms of data transmission tend to use UDP, while applications that require the reliable transmission of data use TCP. In this chapter we will examine the key characteristics of TCP and UDP and review several applications that use either TCP or UDP as the underlying transport.

TCP and UDP

Transmission Control Protocol (TCP) and the User Datagram Protocol (UDP) are the two main transport protocols that support higher-level application protocols like the Simple Mail Transfer Protocol (SMTP) and the Hypertext Transfer Protocol (HTTP). In turn, TCP and UDP sit on top of the Internet Protocol (IP). The main feature of TCP is that it guarantees reliable delivery of packets, to the extent that dropped packets are retransmitted as required. However, reliable delivery in transport terms is different from reliable delivery assured by asynchronous messaging as might be implemented by a message queue. It is up to the application to provide for the storing and forwarding of packets if the network connection is broken. However, it's important to note that while TCP aims for guaranteed delivery, UDP makes no such promises—indeed, the "User Datagram" Protocol may well be described as the "Unreliable Delivery" Protocol! The trade-off here is between guaranteed delivery and efficiency—UDP is more lightweight than TCP and can significantly reduce bandwidth requirements. In some applications where bandwidth is limited and connectivity is transient, such as noisy wireless signals, UDP is much more appropriate for use at the transport level. However, as broadband, highly reliable Ethernet is rolled out, fewer applications will use UDP compared to TCP. TCP is best suited to situations where a reliable network is always available, and where real-time interactions are necessary. For example, the telnet daemon uses TCP transport because interactive commands are issued in real time. In contrast, the biff daemon, which lets the user know that new mail has arrived, doesn't really require real-time access because no interactive commands are issued. In this case, UDP is more appropriate than TCP.

In technical terms, TCP is a connection-oriented protocol, while UDP is a connectionless protocol. This means that where services use TCP to transmit data, a persistent connection must be maintained between the client and the server. There are some important differences in the way that data is packed using TCP and UDP—in TCP, sequence numbers are issued to ensure that packet delivery is consistent. UDP has much less restrictive requirements, which reduces the amount of bandwidth required to carry UDP traffic compared to equivalent services that utilize TCP.

All TCP and UDP services operate through a specific port. Sometimes, a service is offered over both TCP and UDP ports, such as the LDAP daemon, which operates on port 389 TCP and port 389 UDP. However, many services operate only on TCP or UDP. One service may operate on a specific TCP port, while a separate service may operate on the same numbered port for UDP. There are conventions for operating services on specific ports, although these may be modified on a local system. For example, the default port number for operating the Apache web server is port 80 TCP; however, any other TCP port may be used as long as it is not being used by another service. When a remote client connects to a locally operated service, a port listener receives the connection for the appropriate service as defined by the port number. This prevents data destined for one service from being diverted to another (inappropriate) service. A server socket is formed by the service port and the local IP address for the server. A client socket is formed in the same way, by the client's IP address and the appropriate port. In this way, client/server interactions can be described by the two sockets. The kernel has a port table that it maintains to match up client and server ports and IP addresses, which can be viewed by using the netstat command:

```
# netstat

TCP: IPv4
   Local Address      Remote Address       Swind Send-Q Rwind Recv-Q  State
--------------- -------------------- ----- ------ ----- ------ -------
ivana.telnet       austin.1040           8550      1 24820      0 ESTABLISHED
ivana.32807        ivana.32782          32768      0 32768      0 TIME_WAIT

Active UNIX domain sockets
Address  Type          Vnode      Conn   Local Addr      Remote Addr
30000b0dba8 stream-ord 300006cb810 00000000 /tmp/.X11-unix/X0
30000b0dd48 stream-ord 00000000 00000000
```

In this example, a socket comprised of the host ivana and the telnet port is servicing a telnet session for the client austin with the remote port 1040. All of the standard services are mapped in the services database (*/etc/services*). These ports are defined as part of the work of the Internet Engineering Task Force (IETF), and the Request For Comment

(RFC) process for defining Internet standards (**http://www.rfc-editor.org/rfc.html**). Generally, standard services are defined for ports 1–1024, which correspond to privileged ports on UNIX because only the superuser may execute services that operate in this range.

 TIP   Any user may execute services that operate on ports 1025 and above.

Exercise 37-1 Using netstat   Execute the `netstat` command on your local system. Can you identify any services that have active sockets that should be closed for security?

An example entry in */etc/services* is shown here:

```
telnet          23/tcp
```

This entry defines the telnet service to run on port 23 TCP. A number of possible tokens can be contained within each service definition:

- Name of service
- Service port number
- Service transport type
- Aliases for service

Another convention in UNIX systems is to operate Internet services through a single superdaemon known as inetd. One advantage of running through inetd is that daemons can be configured using a single file (*/etc/inetd.conf*). However, with complex services like a web servers, it's often preferable to configure them through their own configuration file.

sendmail

Electronic mail was one of the first applications to be widely adopted across the Internet, and despite changes in technology and a shift toward information delivery via the World Wide Web (WWW), "e-mail" has managed to hold its ground. E-mail has undergone many changes is recent years: instead of plaintext messages being sent from command-line clients (or mail user agents, MUA), there are many different mail protocols for remote clients to retrieve their mail from a centralized server (for example, POP, IMAP), as well as multimedia content being supported through MIME extensions.

Although desktop clients are technically capable of running mail servers, most organizations still prefer to run a single main mail server, running a mail transport agent (MTA), such as the traditional sendmail daemon or a newer replacement (for example, qmail). This is because server systems such as Solaris have high uptime and better security features than the average desktop client and because the security of mail services can be managed centrally. For example, if a security flaw is revealed in sendmail, a patch can be freely downloaded from SunSolve and applied to the server with minimal disruption to users. If everyone ran their own mail server, new security problems could take weeks if not months per incident to rectify in a large organization.

In this section we will examine the background to understanding how e-mail is addressed and delivered, by using the TCP transport protocol, and examine the configuration of the popular sendmail mail transport agent.

Understanding E-Mail Protocols

Transferring electronic mail between servers on the Internet is largely conducted using the Simple Mail Transfer Protocol, or SMTP. The advantage of using SMTP is that mail transfer can be initiated by a local third-party mail user agent, such as elm or pine, or it can be performed manually by a user using telnet. This makes installing sendmail somewhat easier because all mail commands can be tested interactively by a human operator, and the response to each command can be evaluated appropriately.

If your users are not logged in through a shell on the local mail server, it will be necessary for you to provide a means by which they can send and retrieve mail through the server by using a remote mail client. There are two protocols that support this: the Post Office Protocol (POP), which is the oldest client/server mail transfer protocol and only supports offline mail reading, and IMAP (the Internet Message Access Protocol), which supports both offline and online mail reading. The choice between the two will often come down to which mail user agents your users are comfortable with, and which protocol their favorite client supports. However, there can be other considerations like authentication, authorization, and security that would sway an administrator to stipulate that IMAP be used over POP, even for offline mail reading.

 TIP   It should be noted that POP is generally easier to install and configure than IMAP.

SMTP

SMTP is the Simple Mail Transfer Protocol (SMTP), which allows servers to exchange mail with each other on a message-by-message basis. Standardized since the publication of RFC 821, SMTP has become the dominant Internet mail transfer protocol at the expense of earlier transfer methods such as the ancient UUCP (Unix-to-Unix copy program) and the X.400 protocol, which is still popular with intranet and LAN-based e-mail. SMTP allows sendmail and other mail transport agents such as qmail to accept connections on port 25 and "speak" to each other in a language that is interpretable by humans. In fact, as we will see later, it is actually possible for an administrator to manually test sendmail by telnetting to port 25 and issuing SMTP commands directly. This is very useful for troubleshooting and testing existing configurations. Unfortunately, SMTP is almost too simple, because it can be used by malicious users to forge e-mail headers so as to make an e-mail appear to come from another user.

SMTP supports a sender/receiver model of host-to-host e-mail transactions: a host, such as **mail.companyA.com**, may wish to transfer a message to **mail.companyB.com**. The server **mail.companyA.com** first makes a connection to port 25, which **mail .companyB.com** acknowledges. Then, **mail.companyA.com** identifies the sender of the message, and again, **mail.companyB.com** acknowledges. Next, **mail.companyA.com** states the recipient of the message, and again **mail.companyB.com** acknowledges. If the local user exists, or is listed in the */etc/aliases* database, the acknowledgement is in the affirmative. However, if no local user can be matched to the intended recipient, the acknowledgement is in the negative. If a user is found, the message is transmitted from **mail.companyA.com** to **mail.companyB.com**, and the latter acknowledges receipt (with a receipt number). **mail.companyA.com** then requests a disconnection, and **mail.companyB.com** complies. Mail is held on the MTA until the RECV command to retrieve the message is sent by the MUA. This transaction is shown in Figure 37-1.

This kind of transaction is conducted millions of times every day on mail servers around the world and is very fast. In the example, each of the acknowledgements from **mail.companyB.com** is associated with a three-digit numeric code: for example, a successful command from **mail.companyA.com** is always acknowledged with a code "250" from **mail.companyB.com**. Alternatively, if a user is not local, the code "551" is returned.

There are a number of standard SMTP commands, which are summarized here:

- **HELO** Identifies the mail sending host to the mail receiving host.
- **MAIL** Identifies the remote user who is sending the mail to the mail receiving host.
- **RCPT** Indicates the local user to whom the mail is to be delivered.
- **DATA** Precedes the body of the mail message.
- **VRFY** Checks that a particular local user is known to the mail system.
- **EXPN** Expands local mailing lists.
- **QUIT** Terminates a session.

Figure 37-1

Mail exchange transaction between **mail.companyA .com** and **mail.companyB .com**

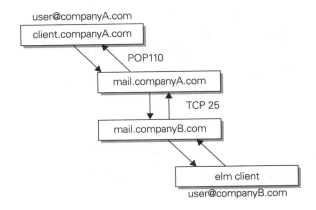

In addition to the standard SMTP commands presented here, RFC 1869 proposed extensions to SMTP, called ESMTP. ESMTP allows developers to extend the services currently provided by SMTP. MTAs that support ESMTP commands will attempt to greet each other with the EHLO command. If ESMTP is supported, a list of implemented commands on the remote server is returned. For example,

```
server% telnet server.companyB.com 25
Trying 192.68.232.45...
Connected to server.companyB.com.
Escape character is '^]'.
220 server.companyB.com ESMTP Sendmail 8.9.1a/8.9.1; Fri, 18 Feb 2000
13:05:14 +1100 (EST)
EHLO server.companyA.com
250-server.companyB.com Hello pwatters@server.companyA.com [192.68.231.64],
pleased to meet you
250-EXPN
250-VERB
250-8BITMIME
250-SIZE
250-DSN
250-ONEX
250-ETRN
250-XUSR
250 HELP
```

One example of an ESMTP command is Delivery Status Notification (DSN), which was proposed in RFC 1891 and reports on the status of remote mail deliveries to local users, just like a certified letter.

POP

Many users today do not log in directly to an interactive shell on a mail server or run a local mail client like mailx or elm; instead, they are able to use a GUI-based mail reading client that runs locally on their PC, contacting the mail server directly to retrieve and send their mail. One of the client/server protocols that facilitates this kind of mail delivery is the Post Office Protocol (POP), as codified in RFC 1725. POP supports offline mail delivery to remote clients when mail addressed to a user account is delivered via a centralized mail server. POP supports many useful features, including the ability to retain copies of e-mail on the server and transmit a copy to the client. This can be very useful for auditing and backup purposes, as a client machine may have to be reinstalled, or it may crash, in which case all of the user's mail (including unread mail) might be lost.

 TIP   Reliability of service is still one of the main arguments for using a centralized mail server.

To retrieve mail from a POP server, a client machine makes a TCP connection to port 110. The client then greets the server and receives an acknowledgement, and then the session continues until it is terminated. During this time, a user may be authenticated. If a user is successfully authenticated, they may begin conducting transactions in the form of retrieving messages until the QUIT command is received by the server, in which case the session is terminated. Errors are indicated by status codes like "-ERR" for negative responses and "+OK" for positive responses. POP is deliberately SMTP-like in its command set and operation, making it easier for administrators to apply their skills to configuring both kinds of systems.

One of the drawbacks of POP is its lack of security: although users are authenticated using their username and password on the mail server, this exchange is not encrypted—which means that anyone "snooping" the network might be able to retrieve this username and password. This would allow a rogue user to log in to the mail server as the mail user, perhaps without the mail user realizing this for a long time because they themselves never log in directly to the mail server. Since telnet and ftp use exactly the same method of authentication, it's certainly no worse than the standard networking toolset.

To obtain a free POP server for Solaris, download the freeware Qpopper server from Qualcomm at **http://www.eudora.com/qpopper/index.html**. Alternatively, Netra systems are supplied with the SUNWipop package that provides a POP service for that platform. Qualcomm also has a free POP mail user agent called Eudora that is very popular in educational institutions, and it is available for both the Macintosh and Windows platforms. Figure 37-2 shows the main user screen from Eudora: users can retrieve their mail from a remote server and display it ordered by date, sender, and subject. In addition, files from the local Macintosh or Windows file system can be sent as attachments by using the MIME extensions. Software like Eudora makes it easy for Macintosh or Windows users to have the convenience of local file access and GUI-based interfaces while retaining the security and reliability of the Solaris server platform. However, it should be noted that browsers such as Netscape and other command-line MUAs (such as elm or pine) may be more appropriate than Eudora for some environments.

IMAP

The Internet Message Access Protocol (IMAP), codified in RFC 2060, is intended to be a replacement for the POP protocol. While IMAP can perform offline processing, it is primarily intended for remote clients to retain some of the features of online processing enjoyed by MUAs like mailx and elm. A remote MUA using IMAP has the ability to perform more sophisticated transactions than a POP-based client: while POP works for requests like retrieving all new messages on the server and passing them to the client, IMAP supports requests of just header, just message bodies, or both. In addition, a search can be made for messages matching a particular criterion—for example, a request could be made to find all messages received by a particular user, or all messages received on a particular day. Although a POP-based MUA can perform these operations on its local copy of mail messages, IMAP can perform these operations remotely on the server. In addition, server-side messages can be marked with different flags indicating whether they have been replied to, for example. Again, this reflects the kind of functionality often supplied by server-side MUAs like mailx or elm, but allows these operations to be performed by remote, easy-to-use GUI interfaces. Even if IMAP users want to store their files locally, like a POP-based service, this is also supported—but significantly, there is a

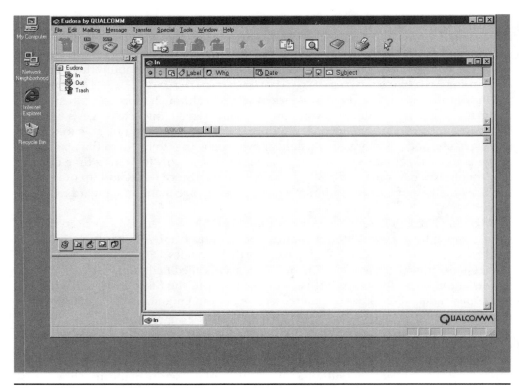

Figure 37-2 The POP-based Eudora client for Microsoft Windows, which receives mail from a centralized and secure Solaris mail server

synchronization feature whereby the local mailbox contents can be regularly matched with the mailbox on the server. This ensures that no data corruption occurs due to errors on the client machine. Remote mail folders are also possible.

In summary, POP and IMAP offer significantly different functions, and the use of either protocol depends on the mail user agents that are supported and the needs of the users.

 TIP Many mail clients only support POP, and it may be that your organization keeps with the POP platform because of this reason alone, even though IMAP offers many more features.

Mail Headers

When a mail message is delivered into a user's mailbox, it contains a history of its delivery process in the headers that precede the message body. These headers include

- **From** Records the mail sending user, and the date and time at which the mail was received.

- **Received** Provides details of how the mail was received by the MTA on the mail server, including the remote computer's name, MTA name, and identification.

- **Date** Indicates the time and date at which the message was received.

- **Message-Id** A unique number generated by the sending host that identifies the message.

- **To** Indicates the user to whom the message was addressed—usually a user on the local machine.

- **Content-Type** Indicates the MIME type in which the message was encoded. This is usually text, but could contain multimedia types as well.

- **Content-Length** The number of lines making up the body of the message.

- **Subject** The subject of the mail message as entered by the sender.

Mail Transport

Now that we have reviewed how mail is transferred between the client and the server, we turn our attention to server-to-server mail communications. Mail exchange between servers is performed by using mail transport agents (MTAs) such as sendmail, which implement the SMTP protocol. sendmail is the most popular mail transport agent for Solaris and many other UNIX systems, even though newer systems, such as qmail make configuring an MTA easier. In this section we cannot cover all material relating to sendmail, because it is one of the most complex UNIX programs to master; however, we provide sufficient detail so that most administrators working in a standard environment will be able to configure and test their mail transfer environment.

sendmail is the standard mail transport agent that is supported by default under Solaris, although it is certainly possible to install an alternative third-party MTA like qmail (see **http://www.qmail.org/** for details).

EXAM TIP As installed, Solaris 9 supports sendmail version 8.

In most Solaris installations, the sendmail MTA relies on a single configuration file (*sendmail.cf*), which contains sets of rules to determine how e-mail is to be sent from the local host to any arbitrary remote host, and which mailer is to be used (for example, for local vs. remote delivery). The rules are used to choose the mechanism by which each message is delivered, while mail addresses are often rewritten to ensure correct delivery. For example, a mail message sent from a server command line may not include the fully qualified domain name in the Reply-to field. This would mean that a remote user would not be able to reply to a message sent to them.

TIP The sendmail MTA ensures that the "virtual envelopes" that contain e-mail messages are addressed correctly by inserting headers where appropriate to identify senders and recipients.

Although sendmail is highly customizable, it is also difficult to configure and test because a single error in the rules can produce unexpected results. sendmail reads and processes every rule in *sendmail.cf*, so in order to speed up the process, the rules are written in a "computer friendly" format. Unfortunately, like assembly language, computer-friendly rules are rarely human friendly! In this section we will review the configuration of sendmail, and highlight some of the security issues that continue to surround its deployment. Fortunately, the public version of sendmail allows you to use simple configuration rules to create a *sendmail.mc* file, which is easier than working directly on the *sendmail.cf* file.

The *sendmail.cf* file consists of single-line commands, which can range from rules and macros to options and headers. Some of these commands must appear only once if they specify a directive that affects the interpretation of rules (there can, however, be many rules in a *sendmail.cf* file). The main kinds of commands in a *sendmail.cf* file are

- **C** Specifies a class that can contain more than one item. For instance, "C{MAILCLIENTS} mars venus pluto" specifies an array that contains a list of mail clients (mars, venus, and pluto).

- **D** Specifies a macro. For example, "DR mail.companyA.com" specifies a macro named "R" whose contents is "mail.companyA.com."

- **E** Specifies an environment variable. As a security measure, sendmail does not use environment information passed to it, preferring to use values specified in the *sendmail.cf* file. To set the location of a Java Virtual Machine (VM), which may be used to support some mail-related applications, use the variable specification "EJVM=/usr/local/java/bin/java."

- **H** Specifies a header, such as the "Received:" header. These definitions can be now very complex because of the inclusion of multipart MIME messages.

- **M** Specifies the mail delivery agent. For instance, "Mlocal,   P=/bin/mail" specifies that */bin/mail* is the mail delivery agent, which is usually the case under Solaris.

- **O** Specifies an option. For example, setting "O SendMimeErrors=True" enables the sending of MIME-encapsulated error messages.

- **P** Sets message precedence. For example, first class mail is set with a precedence of zero (Pfirst-class=0), while junk mail is set with a precedence of –100 (Pjunk=-100).

- **R** Specifies a rule. For example, the rule "R$- $@ $1 @ ${Mydomain} Rewrite address" appends the FQDN defined by the macro ${Mydomain} to a username.

- **S** Indicates the start of a ruleset, which can either be specified as a number (for example, "S2" for rule-set two) or with a label (for example, "SDomainRules" for the DomainRules ruleset).

There are six kinds of system-defined rulesets that are contained in the *sendmail.cf* file:

- **S0**   Handles basic address parsing. For example, if a user address is not specified, an error message "user address required" is returned.

- **S1**   Processes the e-mail sender's address.

- **S2**   Processes the e-mail recipient's address.

- **S3**   Performs name canonicalization and initiates the rewriting rules. For example, invalid addresses are checked (for example, those with colons), and any angle brackets <> are stripped from the address.

- **S4**   Performs the final output postrewriting, including conversion of expanded addresses like **pwatters%mail @companyA.com** to **pwatters@mail .companyA.com**.

- **S5**   The final rewriting ruleset, which occurs after all aliases, defined in */etc/aliases*, have been expanded.

User-defined rulesets can occupy S6 and above. For example, ruleset 33 is defined in Solaris to support Sun's RemoteMode. A typical sendmail rule takes the form

```
Rlhs      rhs       description
```

where *R* indicates that the line is a rule, lhs is the left-hand side of the rule, rhs is the right-hand side of the rule, and description is a comment that is useful for humans to interpret what action the rule performs. The left-hand side is a specification for matching a particular mail header, while the right-hand side specifies the action to be taken if a match is found for the rule.

In the same way that lex, yacc, and JavaCC can be used for specifying actions based on matched tokens, so does the sendmail parser. When the *sendmail.cf* file is parsed by sendmail, it recognizes several specifiers on the left-hand side:

- **$-**   Matches a single token.

- **$***   Matches any number of tokens, including zero tokens.

- **$+**   Matches any number of tokens greater than zero.

- **$=character**   Matches any token equal to character.

If any rule stated using these specifiers finds a match, then one or more actions may be performed by one or more right-hand side specifiers:

- **$@**   Rewrite and return.

- **$>integer**   Rewrite using the ruleset specified by integer.

- **$#**   Deliver through the specified mailer.

PART III

- **$character** and **$integer**   Actions can be performed on variables defined on the left-hand side.

As an example, we examine a rule that adds a fully qualified domain name onto a mail server username, where a message is destined for external delivery. In this case, $h (host) is set to "mail" and $d (domain) is set to "companyA.com". Thus, a rule to match a username with no FQDN specified would be

```
R$+      $@$1@$h.$d      Add a FQDN to username
```

Thus, any valid Solaris username like "pwatters" will have "mail," "." and "companyA.com" appended to it for external delivery, giving

```
paul@mail.companyA.com
```

A more complex rule for a more complex organization that has multiple internal networks might have a second level in the FQDN above the company name (for example, the mail server for the sales department of **companyA.com** would have the FQDN **mail.sales.companyA.com**). In this case, we define $o (organization level), set $o to "sales," and change the rule to

```
R$+      $@$1@$h.$o.$d      Add a FQDN to username, including organization level
```

Hence, any valid Solaris username like "neil" will have "mail," "." "sales,""."and "companyA.com" appended to it for external delivery, giving

```
neil@mail.sales.companyA.com
```

Thus, the combination of rules, macros, and options can successfully create and resolve most e-mail addresses. If all of the rule writing and option setting seems daunting to a first-time sendmail administrator, it is possible to use GUI-based configuration tools to ease the burden. One of the easiest ways to run and configure sendmail is to use webmin, which is freely available at **http://www.webmin.com/webmin/**. webmin is a web-based interface for system administration for Solaris, including sendmail. Using any browser that supports tables and forms, you can make use of the "sendmail configuration" module that allows administrators to manage sendmail aliases, masquerading, address rewriting, and other features. webmin can also use SSL to secure connections between your web browser and the webmin server, which is especially useful for remote administration. Figure 37-3 shows the webmin interface and the options it supports for configuring sendmail.

Running sendmail

sendmail is started as a daemon process from scripts that are usually activated during multiuser startup (*/etc/rc2*). To stop sendmail manually, use the following command:

```
/etc/init.d/sendmail stop
```

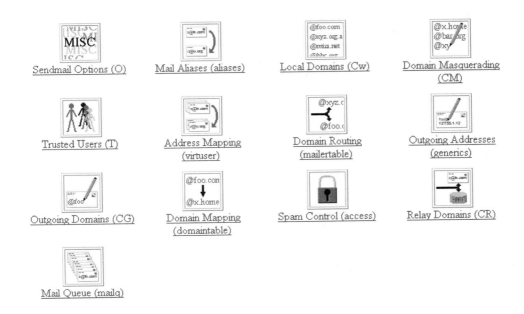

Figure 37-3   Webmin GUI interface for configuring sendmail.

To start sendmail, use this command:

```
/etc/init.d/sendmail start
```

Troubleshooting

Since sendmail can be a difficult program to configure, sendmail also includes some provision for troubleshooting. For example, the command

```
server# sendmail -bt
```

causes sendmail to execute in address-testing mode, which is very useful for testing rulesets interactively before including them in a production system. Keep in mind that ruleset 3 is no longer invoked automatically in address-testing mode; thus, to test the address

```
Paul.Watters.1996@pem.cam.ac.uk
```

you should use the test string

```
"3,0 Paul.Watters.1996@pem.cam.ac.uk"
```

instead of just using

```
"0 Paul.Watters.1996@pem.cam.ac.uk"!
```

As a complete example:

```
ADDRESS TEST MODE (ruleset 3 NOT automatically invoked)
Enter <ruleset> <address>
> 0 Paul.Watters.1996@pem.cam.ac.uk
rewrite: ruleset    0   input: Paul . Watters . 1996 @
pem . cam . ac . uk
rewrite: ruleset 199   input: Paul . Watters . 1996 @
pem . cam . ac . uk
rewrite: ruleset 199 returns: Paul . Watters . 1996 @
pem . cam . ac . uk
rewrite: ruleset  98   input: Paul . Watters . 1996 @
pem . cam . ac . uk
rewrite: ruleset  98 returns: Paul . Watters . 1996 @
pem . cam . ac . uk
rewrite: ruleset 198   input: Paul . Watters . 1996 @
pem . cam . ac . uk
rewrite: ruleset 198 returns: $# local $: Paul . Watters . 1996 @
pem . cam . ac . uk
rewrite: ruleset    0 returns: $# local $: Paul . Watters . 1996 @
pem , cam . ac . uk
> 0,3 Paul.Watters.1996@pem.cam.ac.uk
rewrite: ruleset    0   input: Paul . Watters . 1996 @
pem . cam . ac . uk
rewrite: ruleset 199   input: Paul . Watters . 1996 @
pem . cam . ac . uk
rewrite: ruleset 199 returns: Paul . Watters . 1996 @
pem . cam . ac . uk
rewrite: ruleset  98   input: Paul . Watters . 1996 @
pem . cam . ac . uk
rewrite: ruleset  98 returns: Paul . Watters . 1996 @
pem . cam . ac . uk
rewrite: ruleset 198   input: Paul . Watters . 1996 @
pem . cam . ac . uk
rewrite: ruleset 198 returns: $# local $: Paul . Watters . 1996 @
pem . cam . ac . uk
rewrite: ruleset    0 returns: $# local $: Paul . Watters . 1996 @
pem . cam . ac . uk
rewrite: ruleset    3   input: $# local $: Paul . Watters . 1996 @
pem . cam . ac . uk
rewrite: ruleset    3 returns: $# local $: Paul . Watters . 1996 @
pem . cam . ac . uk
```

In addition to sendmail-based troubleshooting, the mailx MUA has a -v (verbose) switch, which tracks the process of mail delivery directly after mail has been sent. For example, if a message is sent from **user@companyA.com** to **user@companyB.com**, from the machine **client.companyA.com**, the process of delivery is displayed to the sender:

```
client% mailx -v user@companyB.com
Subject: Hello
Hi user@companyB.com. This is a test.
^D
EOT
client% user@companyB.com... Connecting to mailhost (mail)...
```

```
220 mail.serverB.com ESMTP Sendmail 8.9.1a/8.9.1; Sat,
19 Feb 2000 12:13:22 +1100 (EST)
>>> HELO mail.companyA.com
250 mail.serverB.com Hello mail.companyA.com (moppet.companyA.com),
pleased to meet you
>>> MAIL From:<user@companyA.com>
250 <user@companyA.com>... Sender ok
>>> RCPT To:<user@companyB.com>
250 <user@companyA.com>... Recipient ok
>>> DATA
354 Enter mail, end with "." on a line by itself
>>> Hi user@companyB.com. This is a test.
>>>.
250 Ok
>>> QUIT
221 mail.companyB.com closing connection
user@companyB.com... Sent (Ok)
```

In the previous example, the local mail server (**mail.companyA.com**) contacts the remote mail server (**mail.companyB.com**) and delivers the mail correctly to the user. Used in this way, mailx can provide immediately useful hints for users and administrators to identify delivery problems with particular user addresses or remote network problems.

Since e-mail is a key Internet service, and since sendmail is the most widely deployed MTA, it is often associated with security warnings and issues. This has led some developers to develop alternative MTA systems like qmail, while many organizations worldwide devote the appropriate resources to tracking down and solving bugs in sendmail. If you are a sendmail administrator, it pays to watch the headlines at sites like the Sendmail Consortium (**http://www.sendmail.org/**).

For example, sendmail has been shown to suffer from the "buffer overflow" problem that allows remote users to execute arbitrary commands on a server running sendmail. This is a common problem for UNIX applications written in the C language, but only if proper bounds checking on array sizes is not correctly implemented. In the case of sendmail, very long MIME headers could be used to launch an attack—a patch is available that allows sendmail to detect and deny messages that might be associated with such an attack. If you need to apply the patch, it is available at **ftp:// ftp.sendmail.org/pub/sendmail/sendmail.8.9.1a.patch**.

m4 Configuration

The m4 macro language can be used to create a *sendmail.cf* file by making use of a set of predefined macros that have been developed for use with sendmail. In order to create a *sendmail.cf* file using m4 macros, a text file containing a list of macros to run (and the appropriate parameter values for your site) needs to be created in a text file, typically called *sendmail.mc*. Once this file has been installed into the *cf/cf* subdirectory underneath the main *sendmail* directory, the following command can be used from that directory to build a new *sendmail.cf* file:

```
# cp /etc/sendmail.cf /etc/sendmail.orig
# m4 ../m4/cf.m4 sendmail.mc > /etc/sendmail.cf
```

The first command backs up the current production *sendmail.cf* file, while the next command builds a new production *sendmail.cf* file. Once sendmail has been started, by using the command defined in the previous section, sendmail will be running with the new configuration.

Let's take a closer look at the macros and parameters that can be used to configure sendmail, before examining a sample *sendmail.mc* file.

Macros

The following macros are defined for use with *sendmail.mc*:

- **DOMAIN**   Used to define common elements for mail servers with the same domain name.
- **EXPOSED_USER**   Prevents domain masquerading for specific users.
- **FEATURE**   Enables a specific sendmail feature.
- **MAILER**   Specifies the mail delivery program to use on the server (local, smtp, or procmail).
- **MASQUERADE_AS**   Inserts an effective domain on all outgoing e-mail rather than the real domain.
- **OSTYPE**   Defines the host operating system type.

Features

Once the basic domain and operating system parameters have been generated, the next step is to enable specific sendmail features by using the FEATURE macro. One instance of FEATURE is required for every feature that is to be enabled. Commonly used features include

- **accept_unqualified_senders**   Accepts messages for delivery from users with e-mail addresses that do not have a fully qualified domain name.
- **accept_unresolvable_domains**   Accepts messages for delivery from users with e-mail addresses whose fully qualified domain name is not resolvable.
- **access_db**   Enables a database of senders and domains to be maintained from whom mail is automatically bounced or rejected.
- **always_add_domain**   Inserts the domain onto all e-mails sent through sendmail, even those that are being delivered to local users.
- **blacklist_recipients**   Defines a list of recipients who are not allowed to receive e-mail.
- **domaintable**   Substitutes a new domain name for a previous domain name.
- **mailertable**   Allows a different mail server to be associated with each virtual domain supported.

- **nullclient**   Allows local sendmail instances to forward all messages to a single outbound sendmail server for delivery.

- **promiscuous_relay**   Allows relaying of mail from any site through the local server. This should never be used because of the risk that SPAM merchants will find your server and use it to relay SPAM, thereby obscuring its true origin.

- **redirect**   Redirects messages destined for users who no longer exist on the system. Requires a corresponding entry in */etc/aliases* with the name of the former user and his or her new e-mail address.

- **relay_based_on_mx**   Uses the MX record defined in DNS to determine if the local sendmail server is the correct server to relay messages from other servers.

- **relay_entire_domain**   Permits all hosts within the local domain to route e-mail through the local sendmail server.

- **smrsh**   A functionally limited shell that can be used to restrict system access by the sendmail daemon.

- **use_ct_file**   Prevents users from changing the username part of their e-mail addresses on outbound e-mails.

- **use_cw_file**   Contains a list of all DNS aliases for the mail server.

- **virtusertable**   Supports routing of e-mail for user accounts with the same username that actually belong to different virtual domains. Thus, **joe@domainone.com** is not confused with **joe@domaintwo.com**, even though both domains use the same sendmail instance.

Parameters

Specific parameters can be set for sendmail's operation with the m4 `define` command. Although most of the values set by default within sendmail will be satisfactory for normal use, you may occasionally need to change a value. sendmail defines a very large number of parameters, but we'll only examine some of the most commonly modified parameters here:

- **confDOMAIN_NAME**   If your DNS server is unreliable, you might want to set the default domain name here.

- **confLOG_LEVEL**   Specifies the logging level for sendmail from 0 (minimal) to 13 (everything).

- **confMAILER_NAME**   The alias used for returning messages and other automatically generated mails sent by the system. This is generally set to MAILER-DAEMON, which is typically aliased to root. (So, it's possible to just set the value to root.)

- **confMAX_MESSAGE_SIZE**   The maximum size, in bytes, of any message that is accepted for delivery. Although large attachments are common these days, an upper limit of a few megabytes should be set to prevent a denial of service attack.

- **confSMTP_LOGIN_MSG**   Replaces the standard sendmail version banner with a local (usually nondescript) message. Can be useful in preventing would-be crackers from attempting an exploit that is specific to your version of sendmail.

Sample sendmail.mc File

Here, we define a sample *sendmail.mc* file that contains some of the parameters, features, and macros that we've discussed previously:

```
OSTYPE('solaris2')
define('confDOMAIN_NAME', 'cassowary.net')
define('confLOG_LEVEL', '13')
define('confMAILER_NAME', 'root')
define('confMAX_MESSAGE_SIZE', '1048576')
define('confSMTP_LOGIN_MSG', 'No Name Mail Server')
FEATURE('smrsh','/usr/sbin/smrsh')
FEATURE(redirect)
FEATURE(always_add_domain)
FEATURE(blacklist_recipients)
FEATURE('access_db')
```

There are more extensive examples for many different configuration files supplied with the sendmail source. In particular, Eric Allman's excellent README file should be read by anyone who is seriously contemplating extensive sendmail configuration.

Example SMTP Transaction

In this section we will walk through an actual SMTP session so that you can see how straightforward the procedure is. For example, it is possible to initiate message transfer from a client machine to a user on **server.companyB.com** by using the following commands:

```
client% telnet mail.serverB.com 25
Trying 192.68.232.41...
Connected to mail.serverB.com.
Escape character is '^]'.
220 mail.serverB.com ESMTP Sendmail 8.9.1a/8.9.1;
Fri, 18 Feb 2000 10:25:59 +1100 (EST)
```

If you now type

```
help
```

you will receive a list of SMTP commands that can be used to transfer mail interactively:

```
214-This is Sendmail version 8.9.1a
214-Topics:
214-    HELO    EHLO    MAIL    RCPT    DATA
214-    RSET    NOOP    QUIT    HELP    VRFY
214-    EXPN    VERB    ETRN    DSN
```

```
214-For more info use "HELP <topic>".
214-To report bugs in the implementation send email to
214-    sendmail-bugs@sendmail.org.
214-For local information send email to Postmaster at your site.
214 End of HELP info
```

To actually send a message, you can use a combination of the HELO, MAIL, RCPT, and QUIT commands. HELO introduces the hostname that you are connecting from:

```
HELO client.companyB.com
250 server.companyB.com Hello client.companyB.com [192.68.232.45],
pleased to meet you
```

Next, you need to specify a sender using the MAIL command:

```
MAIL FROM: <pwatters@companyB.com>
250 <pwatters@companyB.com>... Sender ok
```

A recipient for the mail should then be specified by the RCPT command:

```
RCPT TO: <postmaster@server.companyB.com>
250 <postmaster@server.companyB.com>... Recipient ok
```

After transmitting the sender and recipient information, it's then time to actually send the body of the message by using the DATA command:

```
DATA
354 Enter mail, end with "." on a line by itself
Hello,
My mail client is not working so I had to send this message
manually - can you help?
Thanks.
.
250 KAA11543 Message accepted for delivery
```

After the message has been accepted for delivery, you can then terminate the session by using the QUIT command:

```
QUIT
221 server.company.com closing connection
Connection closed by foreign host.
```

The message has now been successfully transmitted.

Mail Headers

These headers are useful in understanding how mail is transferred. For example, if a message is sent from a mail client on the local server to another user on the local server, the headers are easy to interpret:

```
From pwatters@companyA.com Fri Feb 18 13:31 EST 2000
Received: (from pwatters@localhost)
        by mail.companyA.com (8.9.1a/8.9.1) id NAA17837
        for pwatters; Fri, 18 Feb 2000 13:31:34 +1100 (EST)
```

```
Date: Fri, 18 Feb 2000 13:31:34 +1100 (EST)
From: WATTERS Paul Andrew <pwatters@companyA.com>
Message-Id: <200002180231.NAA17837@mail.companyA.com>
To: pwatters@companyA.com
Subject: Testing Local Delivery
Content-Type: text
Content-Length: 5
This is a test of local delivery.
```

These headers can be interpreted thus: the local user "pwatters@localhost" sent the remote user "pwatters@companyA.com" a five-line message, encoded as text, on the subject of "Testing Local Delivery". The message had an ID of **200002180231.NAA17837 @mail.CompanyA.com**, and was serviced by the sendmail MTA version 8.9.1a/8.9.1. If mail is forwarded from another host, the headers become more complicated but follow the same general principles.

Using the Multipurpose Internet Mail Extensions (MIME)

As we saw in the previous example concerning mail headers, there was a "Content-Type" that was text, but which could have conceivably been any kind of digital medium, thanks to the Multipurpose Internet Mail Extensions (MIME), as proposed in RFC 2045. MIME is very useful for sending multimedia files through e-mail, without having to worry about the specifics of encoding. Since many multimedia files are binary, and e-mail message bodies are transmitted as text, MIME suggests that these files be encoded as text and sent as a normal message. In addition, MIME supports the notion of multipart messages—that is, a single e-mail message may contain more than one encoded file. This is very useful for sending a number of documents to another user. It is not necessary to overburden sendmail by sending a new message for each document (recall that sendmail processes e-mail messages one at a time).

 TIP MIME also provides supports for languages that are encoded in ASCII but need to be displayed in another script (for example, Japanese kanji).

MIME defines how a Content-Type header can be used to specify a particular character set or other nontextual data type for an e-mail message. For example, the e-mail header

```
Content-Type: text/plain; charset=us-ascii
```

indicates that the message consists of plaintext in the US-ASCII character set. MIME also specifies how to encode data when necessary. In addition, MIME stipulates that it is the responsibility of the receiving user to interpret the encoded information, in order to correctly display an encoded message in a form that will be understood by the user. Here is example MIME-encoded message:

```
This is a multi-part message in MIME format.
------=_NextPart_000_01A6_01BF7314.FF804600
Content-Type: text/plain;
```

```
                charset="iso-8859-1"
Content-Transfer-Encoding: 7bit
Joe,
Just confirmed the latest sales figures.
See the attached report.
Jane
------=_NextPart_000_01A6_01BF7314.FF804600
Content-Type: application/msword;
        name="report.doc"
Content-Disposition: attachment;
        filename="report.doc"
Content-Transfer-Encoding: base64
```

```
0M8R4KGxGuEAAAAAAAAAAAAAAAAAAAAAPgADAP7/CQAGAAAAAAAAAAAACAAAAmQAAAAAAAAA
EAAAmwAAAAEAAAD+////AAAAJcAAACYAAA//////////////////////////////////////
///////////////////////////////////////////////////////////////////////
///////////////////////////////////////////////////////////////////////
///////////////////////////////////////////////////////////////////////
///////////////////////////////////////////////////////////////////////
///////////////////////////////////////////////////////////////////////
///////////////////////////////////////////////////////////////////////
```

After the headers are printed, indicating the number and type of attachments, the actual encoded data is printed (which is what all the forward slashes represent, in case you were wondering!). When you run metamail on this file, because it contains MIME encoded data, the user is prompted to save any detected attachments:

```
This message contains data in an unrecognized format, application/msword,
which can either be viewed as text or written to a file.
What do you want to do with the application/msword data?
1 -- See it as text
2 -- Write it to a file
3 -- Just skip it
```

At this point, the user enters **2**, and they are then prompted to save the file:

```
Please enter the name of a file to which the data should be written
(Default: report.doc) >
```

The data is then saved to the file specified. MIME is thus very useful for encoding data from several binary files into a portable format that can be transmitted as an e-mail message. Of course, handling MIME manually is not as easy as GUI mail readers, where attachments can be decoded automatically. However, this automation has led to the proliferation of viruses and numerous Trojan horses on some operating systems.

Apache Web Server

Apache is a multiprocess web server that is supplied with the Solaris 9 distribution. It is used by the majority of web servers in the world to serve HTTP (insecure) and HTTPS (secure) content. Apache also performs a number of different tasks, including

- Providing a Common Gateway Interface (CGI) to provide client access to server-side processes and applications. CGI applications can be written in C, C++, Perl, Bourne shell, or the language of your choice.

PART III

- Supporting the hosting of multiple sites on a single server, where each site is associated with a unique fully qualified domain name. Thus, a single Solaris system in an ISP environment can host multiple web sites, such as **www .java-support.com**, **www.paulwatters.com**, and so forth using a single instance of Apache.

- Securing the transmission of credit card details and other sensitive data by supporting the Secure Socket Layer (SSL). This allows for key-based encryption of the HTTP protocol (called HTTPS), with key sizes of up to 128 bits.

- A full-featured proxy/cache server, which provides an extra level of protection for clients behind a firewall and also keeps a copy of the most commonly retrieved documents from the WWW.

- Customized access, agent, and error logs, which can be used for marketing and reporting purposes.

The main Apache configuration file is *httpd.conf*, which contains three sections:

- The global environment section, which sets key server information, such as the root directory for the Apache installation, and several process management settings, such as the number of concurrent requests permitted per server process.

- The main server configuration section, which sets runtime parameters for the server, including the port on which the server listens, the server name, the root directory for the HTML documents and images that comprise the site, and the server authorization configuration (if required).

- The virtual hosts configuration section, which configures the Apache server to run servers for multiple domains. Many of the configuration options that are set for the main server can also be customized for each of the virtual servers.

We will now examine the configuration options in each of these sections in detail.

Global Environment Configuration

The following options are commonly set in the global environment configuration section:

```
ServerType standalone
ServerRoot "/opt/apache1.3"
PidFile /opt/apache1.3/logs/httpd.pid
ScoreBoardFile /opt/apache1.3/logs/apache_status
Timeout 300
KeepAlive On
MaxKeepAliveRequests 100
KeepAliveTimeout 15
MaxRequestsPerChild 0
LoadModule auth_module        modules/mod_auth.so
```

The server configuration shown here does not run as a service of the Internet superdaemon (inetd); rather, Apache runs as a stand-alone daemon. This gives Apache more flexibility in its configuration, as well as better performance than running through inetd. Since Apache is able to service more than one client through a single process (using the KeepAlive facility), no production system should ever use the inetd mode.

The ServerRoot for the Apache installation is set to */opt/apache1.3* in this installation. All of the key files required by Apache are located below this directory root, such as the lock file, the scoreboard file, and the file that records the PID of the current Apache process.

Each of the clients that connect to the server has an expiry date, in the form of a timeout. In this configuration, the timeout is set to 300 seconds (5 minutes). This is the period of inactivity after which a client is deemed to have timed out. Requests are kept alive, with up to 100 requests. There is no limit to the number of requests per child process

Main Server Configuration

The options that are commonly set in the main server configuration are as follows:

```
Port 80
ServerAdmin paul@paulwatters.com
ServerName www.paulwatters.com
DocumentRoot "/opt/apache1.3/htdocs"
<Directory/>
    Options FollowSymLinks
    AllowOverride None
</Directory>
<Directory "/opt/apache1.3/htdocs">
    Options Indexes FollowSymLinks MultiViews
    AllowOverride None
    Order allow,deny
    Allow from all
</Directory>
UserDir "/opt/apache1.3/users/"
DirectoryIndex index.html
AccessFileName .htaccess
<Files .htaccess>
    Order allow,deny
    Deny from all
</Files>
```

The parameters in this section determine the main runtime characteristics of the Apache server. The first parameter is the port on which the Apache server will run. If the server is being executed by an unprivileged user, this port must be set at port 1024 and higher. However, if a privileged user like root is executing the process, any unreserved port may be used (you can check the services database, */etc/services*, for ports allocated to specific services). By default, port 80 is used.

Next, some details about the server are entered, including the hostname of the system, which is to be displayed in all URLs, and a contact e-mail address for the server. This address is usually displayed on all error and CGI misconfiguration pages. The root directory for all HTML and other content for the web site must also be supplied. This allows for both absolute and relative URLs to be constructed and interpreted by the server. In this case, the *htdocs* subdirectory underneath the main Apache directory is used. Thus, the file *index.html* in this directory will be the default page displayed when no specific page is specified in the URL. There are several options that can be specified for the *htdocs* directory, including whether or not to ignore symbolic links to directories that do not reside underneath the *htdocs* subdirectory. This is useful when you have files available on CD-ROMs and other file systems that do not need to be copied onto a hard drive, but simply to be served through the WWW.

Apache has a simple user authentication system available, which is similar to the Solaris password database (*/etc/passwd*) in that it makes use of encrypted passwords, but it does not make use of the Solaris password database. This means that a separate list of users and passwords must be maintained. Thus, when a password-protected page is requested by a user, a username and matching password must be entered using a dialog box.

TIP   Any directory that appears underneath the main *htdocs* directory can be password protected using this mechanism.

Next, the various MIME types that can be processed by the server are defined, in a separate file called *mime.types*. Let's look at some examples of the MIME types defined for the server:

```
application/mac-binhex40      hqx
application/msword            doc
application/x-csh             csh
```

We can see the file types defined here for many popular applications, including compression utilities (Macintosh BinHex, *application/mac-binhex40*, with the extension *hqx*), word processing documents (Microsoft Word, *application/msword*, with the extension *doc*), and C shell scripts (*application/x-csh*, with the extension *csh*).

The next section deals with log file formats, as shown here:

```
HostnameLookups Off
ErrorLog /opt/apache1.3/logs/error.log
LogLevel warn
LogFormat "%h %l %u %t \"%r\" %>s %b \"%{Referer}I
\" \"%{User-Agent}i\"" combined
LogFormat "%h %l %u %t \"%r\" %>s %b" common
LogFormat "%{Referer}i -> %U" referrer
LogFormat "%{User-agent}i" agent
CustomLog /opt/apache1.3/logs/access.log common
CustomLog /opt/apache1.3/logs/access.log combined
```

The first directive switches off hostname lookups on clients before logging their activity. Since performing a reverse DNS lookup on every client making a connection is a CPU- and bandwidth-intensive task, many sites prefer to switch it off. However, if you need to gather marketing statistics on where your clients are connecting from (for example, by geographical region or by second-level domain type), you may need to switch hostname lookups on. In addition, an error log is specified as a separate entity from the access log. A typical set of access log entries looks like this:

```
192.64.32.12 - - [06/Jan/2002:20:55:36 +1000]
"GET /cgi-bin/printenv HTTP/1.1" 200 1024
192.64.32.12 - - [06/Jan/2002:20:56:07 +1000]
"GET /cgi-bin/Search.cgi?term=solaris&type=simple HTTP/1.1" 200 85527
192.64.32.12 - - [06/Jan/2002:20:58:44 +1000]
"GET /index.html HTTP/1.1" 200 94151
192.64.32.12 - - [06/Jan/2002:20:59:58 +1000]
"GET /pdf/secret.pdf HTTP/1.1" 403 29
```

The first example shows that the client 192.64.32.12 accessed the CGI application printenv on January 6th, 2002, at 8:55 P.M. The result code for the transaction was 200, which indicates a successful transfer. The printenv script comes standard with Apache, and displays the current environment variables being passed from the client. The output is very useful for debugging, and looks like this:

```
DOCUMENT_ROOT="/usr/local/apache-1.3.12/htdocs"
GATEWAY_INTERFACE="CGI/1.1"
HTTP_ACCEPT="image/gif, image/x-xbitmap, image/jpeg, image/pjpeg,
application/vnd.ms-excel, application/msword, application/vnd.
ms-powerpoint, */*" HTTP_ACCEPT_ENCODING="gzip, deflate"
HTTP_ACCEPT_LANGUAGE="en-au"
HTTP_CONNECTION="Keep-Alive"
HTTP_HOST="www"
HTTP_USER_AGENT="Mozilla/4.75 (X11; I; SunOS 5.9 i86pc; Nav)"
PATH="/usr/sbin:/usr/bin:/bin:/usr/ucb:/usr/local/bin:
/usr/openwin/bin:/usr/dt/bin:/usr/ccs/bin"
QUERY_STRING=""
REMOTE_ADDR="209.67.50.55"
REMOTE_PORT="3399"
REQUEST_METHOD="GET"
REQUEST_URI="/cgi-bin/printenv"
SCRIPT_FILENAME="/usr/local/apache/cgi-bin/printenv"
SCRIPT_NAME="/cgi-bin/printenv"
SERVER_ADDR="209.67.50.203"
SERVER_ADMIN="paul@paulwatters.com"
SERVER_NAME="www.paulwatters.com"
SERVER_PORT="80"
SERVER_PROTOCOL="HTTP/1.1"
SERVER_SIGNATURE="Apache/1.3.12 Server at www.paulwatters.com Port 80\n"
SERVER_SOFTWARE="Apache/1.3.12 (Unix)" TZ="Australia/NSW"
```

The second example from the log shows that a client running from the same system successfully executed the CGI program Search.cgi, passing two GET parameters: a search term of 'solaris' and a search type of 'simple.' The size of the generated response page was 85,527 bytes. The third example shows a plain HTML page being successfully retrieved, with a response code of 200 and a file size of 94,151 bytes.

The fourth example demonstrates one of the many HTTP error codes being returned, instead of the 200 success code. In this case, a request to retrieve the file /pdf/secret.pdf is denied with a 403 code being returned to the browser. This code would be returned if the file permissions set on the /pdf/secret.pdf file did not grant read access to the user executing Apache (for example, nobody).

PART III

Virtual Hosts Configuration

The following options are commonly set in the main server configuration section:

```
<VirtualHost www.cassowary.net>
    ServerAdmin webmaster@paulwatters.com
    DocumentRoot /opt/apache1.3/htdocs/www.cassowary.net
    ServerName www.cassowary.net
    ErrorLog /opt/apache1.3/logs/www.cassowary.net-error_log
    CustomLog /opt/apache1.3/logs/www.cassowary.net-access_log common
</VirtualHost>
```

Here, we define a single virtual host (called **www.cassowary.net**), in addition to the default host for the Apache web server. Virtual host support allows administrators to keep separate logs for errors and access, as well as a completely separate document root to the default server. This makes it very easy to maintain multiple virtual servers on a single physical machine.

Starting Apache

Apache is bundled with a control script (apachectl) that can be used to start, stop, and report on the status of the server. To obtain help on the apachectl script, the following command is used:

```
$ /opt/apache1.3/apachectl help
usage: /opt/apache1.3/apachectl (start|stop|restart|fullstatus|
status|graceful|configtest|help)

start       - start httpd
stop        - stop httpd
restart     - restart httpd if running by sending a SIGHUP or start if
              not running
fullstatus - dump a full status screen; requires lynx and mod_status
enabled
status      - dump a short status screen; requires lynx and mod_status
enabled
graceful   - do a graceful restart by sending a SIGUSR1 or start if
not running
configtest - do a configuration syntax test
help        - this screen
```

To start Apache, you simply need to issue the following command from the same directory:

```
$ /opt/apache1.3/apachectl start
```

In order to stop the service, the following command may be used from the same directory:

```
$ /opt/apache1.3/apachectl stop
```

If you change the Apache configuration file and you need to restart the service so that the server is updated with the changes, you can simply use the following command from the same directory:

```
$ /opt/apache1.3/apachectl restart
```

Once Apache is running on port 80, clients will be able to begin requesting HTML pages and other content. However, in recent times, Apache has grown to be more than a simple web server. When answering client requests, a HTTP status code is returned from the server, as shown in Table 37-1.

	Code Type	Code	Description
Table 37-1 HTTP Response Codes	Successful Transmission	200	OK
		201	Created
		202	Accepted
		203	Non-Authoritative Information
		204	No Content
		205	Reset Content
		206	Partial Content
	Client Errors	400	Bad Request
		401	Unauthorized
		402	Payment Required
		403	Forbidden
		404	Not Found
		405	Method Not Allowed
		406	Not Acceptable
		407	Proxy Authentication Required
		408	Request Timeout
		409	Conflict
		410	Gone
		411	Length Required
		412	Precondition Failed
		413	Request Entity Too Large
		414	Request-URI Too Long
		415	Unsupported Media Type
		416	Expectation Failed
	Server Errors	500	Internal Server Error
		501	Not Implemented
		502	Bad Gateway
		503	Service Unavailable
		504	Gateway Timeout
		505	HTTP Version Not Supported

PART III

Summary

In this chapter we have examined the characteristics of the TCP and UDP protocols, which implement transport in the TCP/IP stack. In addition, we have examined how these protocols underlie higher-level application protocols such as SMTP and HTTP. Without reliable delivery provided by TCP and lightweight delivery provided by UDP, application protocols would be unable to function.

Questions

1. What is the purpose of the DATA command?

   A. Indicates that the data being sent is message data.

   B. Indicates that the host speaks ESMTP.

   C. Lists local members of a mailing list.

   D. Indicates that the host speaks SMTP.

2. What is the purpose of the EHLO command?

   A. Indicates that the data being sent is message data.

   B. Indicates that the host speaks ESMTP.

   C. Lists local members of a mailing list.

   D. Indicates that the host speaks SMTP.

3. What is the purpose of the EXPN command?

   A. Indicates that the data being sent is message data.

   B. Indicates that the host speaks ESMTP.

   C. Lists local members of a mailing list.

   D. Indicates that the host speaks SMTP.

4. What is the purpose of the HELO command?

   A. Indicates that the data being sent is message data.

   B. Indicates that the host speaks ESMTP.

   C. Lists local members of a mailing list.

   D. Indicates that the host speaks SMTP.

5. The QUIT command is used for what purpose?

   A. Contains the address of the sender.

   B. Ends a session.

   C. Contains the address of the recipient.

   D. Verifies that a recipient address exists as a user account on the system.

6. The RCPT command is used for what purpose?

   A. Contains the address of the sender.

   B. Ends a session.

   C. Contains the address of the recipient.

   D. Verifies that a recipient address exists as a user account on the system.

7. The VRFY command is used for what purpose?

   A. Contains the address of the sender.

   B. Ends a session.

   C. Contains the address of the recipient.

   D. Verifies that a recipient address exists as a user account on the system.

8. The MAIL command is used for what purpose?

   A. Contains the address of the sender.

   B. Ends a session.

   C. Contains the address of the recipient.

   D. Verifies that a recipient address exists as a user account on the system.

9. What is the correct description of the HTTP code 200?

   A. OK

   B. Created

   C. Accepted

   D. Non-Authoritative Information

10. What is the correct description of the HTTP code 201?

    A. OK

    B. Created

    C. Accepted

    D. Non-Authoritative Information

11. What is the correct description of the HTTP code 202?

    A. OK

    B. Created

    C. Accepted

    D. Non-Authoritative Information

12. What is the correct description of the HTTP code 203?

    A. OK

    B. Created

  C. Accepted

  D. Non-Authoritative Information

13. What is the correct description of the HTTP code 204?

  A. No Content

  B. Reset Content

  C. Partial Content

  D. Bad Request

14. What is the correct description of the HTTP code 205?

  A. No Content

  B. Reset Content

  C. Partial Content

  D. Bad Request

15. What is the correct description of the HTTP code 206?

  A. No Content

  B. Reset Content

  C. Partial Content

  D. Bad Request

Answers

1. **A.** The `DATA` command indicates that the data being sent is message data.

2. **B.** The `EHLO` command indicates that the host speaks ESMTP.

3. **C.** The `EXPN` command lists local members of a mailing list.

4. **D.** The `HELO` command indicates that the host speaks SMTP.

5. **B.** The `QUIT` command ends a session.

6. **C.** The `RCPT` command contains the address of the recipient.

7. **D.** The `VRFY` command verifies that a recipient address exists as a user account on the system.

8. **A.** The `MAIL` command contains the address of the sender.

9. **A.** The HTTP code 200 indicates "OK."

10. **B.** The HTTP code 201indicates "Created."

11. **C.** The HTTP code 202 indicates "Accepted."

12. **D.** The HTTP code 203 indicates "Non-Authoritative Information."

13. **A.** The HTTP code 204 indicates "No Content."

14. **B.** The HTTP code 205 indicates "Reset Content."

15. **C.** The HTTP code 206 indicates "Partial Content."

DHCP

In this chapter, you will

- Learn DHCP key concepts
- Review the runtime operation of a DHCP server
- Learn how to configure a Solaris DHCP client
- Learn how to configure a Windows DHCP client

In this chapter, we examine the Dynamic Host Configuration Protocol (DHCP), which is an easy way to dynamically manage IP addresses in Class A, Class B, and Class C networks, using time-based leases for client addresses. Since at any one time only a few IP addresses on a network may be in use, it makes sense to organize their allocation dynamically, rather than statically assigning them to individual hosts. This is particularly important for popular Class C networks, where less than 300 addresses are available. In this chapter, readers will learn the background to DHCP and similar protocols (like RARP and BOOTP). In addition, we walk through how to install a Solaris DHCP server, and how to configure DHCP clients.

Overview of DHCP

The Internet is a worldwide, networked environment through which information can be exchanged by using a number of well-defined network protocols, such as TCP and UDP. Each host on the Internet can be identified by a single machine friendly number (for example, 128.43.22.1), which is mapped to a human-friendly fully qualified domain name (for example, **www.paulwatters.com**). This mapping is provided by a globally distributed database, known as the Domain Name Service (DNS), which allows local networks to statically assign IP address ranges to all their local hosts.

When DNS was first introduced, the exponential growth of networks and hosts connected to the Internet was not anticipated. This means that IP addresses allocations initially reserved for Class A, B, and C networks were rather generous in hindsight—many address ranges were not used to their full capacity. Nowadays, there is a critical shortage of available IP address space using the current IPv4 standard. Although the new IPv6 protocol (supported by Solaris 9) will provide many more potential addresses, organizations worldwide are seeking solutions to use their existing resources more efficiently. While IPv6 is currently being adopted by many organizations, widespread deployment is not anticipated in the near future.

As an alternative to static IP address allocation, a practical alternative IP address management strategy is to use the Dynamic Host Configuration Protocol (DHCP). This protocol allows a server to dynamically allocate IP addresses from a central DHCP server, to all configured DHCP clients on the local network. DHCP provides a mechanism by which computers using TCP/IP can obtain protocol configuration parameters automatically by using a lease mechanism, without having to rely on static addresses (which could be incorrect or outdated). This means that only hosts that are up will be taking an IP address from the pool of existing addresses assigned to a particular network, by requesting and accepting an IP address lease from the DHCP server. However, if a machine has been assigned an IP address, it is possible that the lease on that machine has still not expired. Thus, the machine is not up but still has an IP address. For a Class C network, the pool of available addresses is (at most) 254, excluding the broadcast address, which is insufficient for many growing organizations. In addition, if an organization changes ISPs, they ordinarily need to change the network configuration parameters for each client system, a manual and inefficient process that consumes the valuable time of network administrators.

DHCP is not the only protocol to lease out IP addresses in this way. Previously, Solaris clients used the Reverse Address Resolution Protocol (RARP) to obtain an IP address dynamically from a RARP server. This protocol is particularly important for diskless clients that cannot store their IP address locally. However, DHCP is better than RARP because it supports clients from Solaris, Linux, and Microsoft Windows, as well as being able to serve more parameters than just an IP address. In addition, RARP servers can only provide addresses to a single network, while DHCP is capable of serving multiple networks from a single server—provided that routing is correctly set up. On the other hand, Microsoft Windows administrators will be familiar with the Bootstrap Protocol (BOOTP), which provided IP addresses dynamically in the same way that DHCP does. In fact, DHCP can be considered a superset of BOOTP, and DHCP servers are generally backward compatible with BOOTP. The relationship between DHCP and BOOTP is historical: the BOOTP protocol is the foundation on which DHCP was built. Many similarities remain: the packet formats for DHCP and BOOTP are the same, although BOOTP packets are fixed length and DHCP packets are variable length. The DHCP packet length is negotiated between the client and the server.

Another advantage of DHCP over proprietary protocols is that it is an open network standard, developed through the Internet Engineering task Force (IETF). It is based on a client/server paradigm, in which the DHCP client (for example, a PC running Microsoft Windows), contacts a DHCP server (for example, a server running Solaris) for its network configuration parameters. The DHCP server is typically centrally located and is under the control of the network administrator. Since the server is secure, DHCP clients can obtain reliable information for dynamic configuration, with parameters that reflect up-to-date changes in the current network architecture. For example, if a client is moved to a new network, it must be assigned a new IP address for that new network. DHCP can be used to manage these assignments automatically. Readers interested in finding out more about how DHCP works can refer to RFC 2131. There is also a reference implementation of a DHCP server, a client, and a relay agent available from ISC (**http://www.isc.org/**). The ISC implementation uses a modular API, which is designed to work with both POSIX-compliant and non-POSIX-compliant operating systems. It also includes source code, making it useful for understanding how DHCP works behind the scenes.

In addition to dynamically allocating IP addresses, DHCP also serves other key network configuration parameters, such as the subnet mask, default router, and Domain Name System (DNS) server. Again, this goes beyond the capabilities of competing protocols like RARP. By deploying a DHCP server, network administrators can reduce repetitive client-based configuration of individual computers, often requiring the use of confusing operating system–specific setup applications. Instead, clients can obtain all their required network configuration parameters automatically, without manual intervention, from a centrally managed DHCP server.

Both commercial and freeware versions of DHCP clients and servers are available for all platforms. For example, Checkpoint's DHCP server can be integrated with its firewall product Firewall-1 to maximize the security potential of centralized network configuration management. Advanced network management protocols like the Simple Network Management Protocol (SNMP) are supported by DHCP. In addition, configuration change management issues like IP mobility and managing addresses for multiple subnets can all be handled from a single DHCP server. Implementation of DHCP should always be evaluated in the context of other network management protocols (like SNMP) and other directory services, like the Lightweight Directory Access Protocol (LDAP). Both LDAP and SNMP are crucial to the management of hosts and users in large and distributed networks. Since DHCP is responsible for the allocation of network configuration parameters, it is essential that SNMP agents obtain the correct information about hosts that they manage. In addition, LDAP servers need to be aware that host IP addresses will change over time.

This chapter will cover practical issues associated with installing DHCP servers and configuring DHCP clients on Windows, Linux, and Solaris systems. It is assumed that most readers will be familiar with the Domain Name Service and with TCP/IP stacks implemented on either Solaris, Linux, or Windows systems. Starting with a description of the DHCP protocol and its historical roots in the BOOTP protocol, the chapter aims to provide a reference for DHCP and practical installation and configuration procedures for heterogeneous environments.

Running DHCP

The basic DHCP process is a straightforward two-phase process involving a single DHCP client and at least one DHCP server. When the DHCP client (dhcpagent) is started on a client, it broadcasts a DHCPDISCOVER request for an IP address on the local network, which is received by all available servers running a DHCP server (in.dhcpd). Next, all DHCP servers that have spare IP addresses answer the client's request through a DHCPOFFER message, which contains an IP address, a subnet mask, a default router name, and a DNS server IP address. If there are multiple DHCP servers that have IP addresses available, it is possible that multiple servers will respond to the client request. The client simply accepts the first DHCPOFFER that it receives, upon which it broadcasts a DHCPREQUEST message indicating that a lease has been obtained. Once the server has received this second request, it confirms the lease with a DHCPACK message. After a client has finished using the IP address, a DHCPRELEASE message is sent to the server.

In the situation where a server has proposed a lease in the first phase that it is unable to fulfill in the second phase, it must respond with a DHCPNACK message. This means that the client will then broadcast a DHCPDISCOVER message, and the process will start again. A DHCPNACK message is usually sent if a timeout has occurred between the original DHCPDISCOVER request and the subsequent reception at the server side of a DHCPREQUEST message. This is often due to network outages or congestion. The list of all possible DHCP messages is shown in Table 38-1.

The DHCPOFFER message specifies the lease period, after which the lease will be deemed to have expired and made available to other clients. However, clients also have the option of renewing an existing lease so that their existing IP address can be retained. The DHCP protocol defines fixed intervals prior to actual lease expiry, at which time a client should indicate whether or not it wishes to extend the lease. If these renewals are not made in time, a DHCPRELEASE message will be broadcast and the lease will be invalid.

DHCP has three ways to allocate leases to client. Automatic allocation grants an IP address permanently to a client. This is useful for granting IP addresses to servers that require a static IP address. A DNS server typically requires a static IP address that can be registered in host records lodged with InterNIC. The majority of clients will have addresses assigned dynamically by the server, which allows the greatest reuse of addresses. Alternatively, an administrator may manually assign an address to a specific client.

The process of allocating a DHCP lease is shown in Figure 38-1.

Configuring a Solaris DHCP Server

The Solaris client (dhcpagent) and server (in.dhcpd) solution features backward compatibility with other methods already in use, particularly the Reverse Address Resolution Protocol (RARP) and static configurations. In addition, the address of any workstation's network interfaces can be changed after the system has been booted. The dhcpagent client for Solaris features caching and automated lease renewal and is fully

Table 38-1	Code	Description
DHCP Codes and Their Meanings	DHCPDISCOVER	Broadcast from client to all reachable servers.
	DHCPOFFER	Server responds to DHCPDISCOVER requests.
	DHCPREQUEST	Client accepts lease proposal from only one server.
	DHCPACK	Server acknowledges lease.
	DHCPNACK	Server refuses to accept DHCPREQUEST.
	DHCPRELEASE	Lease no longer required.

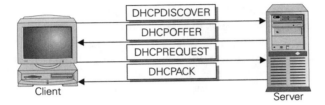

Figure 38-1
How DHCP
leases IP
addresses

DHCPDISCOVER
DHCPOFFER
DHCPREQUEST
DHCPACK
Client
Server

integrated with IP configuration (ifconfig). The in.dhcpd server for Solaris can provide both primary and secondary DHCP services and is fully integrated with the NIS+ Network Information Service. The Solaris DHCP server has the ability to handle hundreds of concurrent requests and also has the ability to boot diskless clients. Multiple DHCP support is provided through the Network File System (NFS). Although we won't cover these advanced features in this chapter, it's worthwhile considering them when making a decision to use RARP or DHCP (or some other competing dynamic IP allocation method).

The main program used to configure DHCP under Solaris is */usr/sbin/dhcpconfig*, which is a shell script that performs the entire configuration for you. Alternatively, you can use the dhtadm or pntadm applications to manage the DHCP configuration table (*/var/dhcp/dhcptab*). The dhcpconfig program is menu-based, making it easy to use. The first menu displayed when you start the program looks like this:

```
***                DHCP Configuration             ***
    Would you like to:
    1)          Configure DHCP Service
    2)          Configure BOOTP Relay Agent
    3)          Unconfigure DHCP or Relay Service
    4)          Exit
    Choice:
```

The first menu option allows the DHCP service to be configured for initial use. If your system has never used DHCP before, you must start with this option. You will be asked to confirm DHCP startup options, such as the timeout periods made on lease offers (that is, between sending DHCPOFFER and receiving a DHCPREQUEST) and whether or not to support legacy BOOTP clients. You will also be asked about bootstrapping configuration, including the following settings:

- Time zone
- DNS server
- NIS server
- NIS+ server
- Default router
- Subnet mask
- Broadcast address

PART III

These settings can all be offered to the client as part of the DHCPOFFER message. The second menu option allows the DHCP server to act simply as a relay agent. After entering a list of BOOTP or DHCP servers to which requests can be forwarded, the relay agent should be operational. Finally, you may choose to unconfigure either the full DHCP service or the relay service, which will revert all configuration files.

If you selected option 1, you will first be asked if you want to stop any current DHCP services:

```
Would you like to stop the DHCP service? (recommended) ([Y]/N)
```

Obviously, if you are supporting live clients, you should not shut down the service. This is why DHCP configuration needs to take place outside normal business hours, so that normal service is not disrupted. If you have ensured that no clients are depending on the in.dhcpd service, you can answer yes to this question and proceed. Next, you will be asked to identify the datastore for the DHCP database:

```
### DHCP Service Configuration ###
### Configure DHCP Database Type and Location ###
Enter datastore (files or nisplus) [nisplus]:
```

The default value is the NIS+ Network Information Service, covered in Chapter 27. However, if you are not using NIS+ to manage network information, you may choose the files option. If you choose the files option, you will need to identify the path to the DHCP datastore directory:

```
Enter absolute path to datastore directory [/var/dhcp]:
```

The default path is the */var/dhcp* directory. However, if your */var* partition is small or running on low on space, and you have a large network to manage, you may wish to locate the datastore directory somewhere else. You will then be asked if you wish to enter any nondefault DHCP options:

```
Would you like to specify nondefault daemon options (Y/[N]):
```

Most users will choose the standard options. However, if you wish to enable additional facilities like BOOTP support, you will need to answer yes to this question. You will then be asked whether you want to have transaction logging enabled:

```
Do you want to enable transaction logging? (Y/[N]):Y
```

Transaction logs are very useful for debugging, but grow rapidly in size over time—especially on a busy network. The size of the file will depend on the syslog level that you wish to enable as well:

```
Which syslog local facility [0-7] do you wish to log to? [0]:
```

Next, you will be asked to enter expiry times for leases that have been offered to client:

```
How long (in seconds) should the DHCP server keep outstanding OFFERs? [10]:
```

The default is 10 seconds, which is satisfactory for a fast network. However, if you are operating on a slow network or expect to be servicing slow clients (like 486 PCs and below), you may wish to increase the timeout. In addition, you can also specify that the *dhcptab* file be reread during a specified interval, which is useful only if you have made manual changes using dhtadm:

```
How often (in minutes) should the DHCP server rescan the dhcptab? [Never]:
```

If you wish to support BOOTP clients, you should indicate this at the next prompt:

```
Do you want to enable BOOTP compatibility mode? (Y/[N]):
```

After configuring these nondefault options, you will be asked to configure the standard DHCP options. The first option is the default lease time, which is specified in days:

```
Enter default DHCP lease policy (in days) [3]:
```

This value is largely subjective, although it can be estimated from the address congestion of your network. If you are only using an average 50 percent of the addresses on your network, then you can probably set this value to 7 days without concern. If you are at the 75 percent level, you may wish to use the default value of 3 days. If you are approaching saturation, you should select daily lease renewal.

 TIP If the number of hosts exceeds the number of available IP addresses, you may need to enter a fractional value to ensure the most equitable distribution of addresses.

Most sites will wish to allow clients to renegotiate their existing leases:

```
Do you want to allow clients to renegotiate their leases? ([Y]/N):
```

However, just like a normal landlord, you may sometimes be compelled to reject requests for lease renewal—especially if your network is saturated. You must now enable DHCP support for at least one network for DHCP to operate:

```
Enable DHCP/BOOTP support of networks you select? ([Y]/N):
```

For an example local network of 192.65.34.0, you will be asked the following questions:

```
Configure BOOTP/DHCP on local LAN network: 192.65.34.0? ([Y]/N):
```

You should (of course!) answer yes if this is the network that you wish to configure DHCP for. Next, you will need to determine whether you wish DHCP to insert hostnames into the hosts file for you, based on the DHCP data:

```
Do you want hostnames generated and inserted in the files hosts table? (Y/[N]):
```

Most sites will use DNS or similar for name resolution, rather than the hosts file, so this option is not recommended. One situation where you may wish to generate hostnames is a terminal server or web server pool, where the hostnames are arbitrary and frequently change in number. In this case, you simply need to enter a sensible basename for the hostnames to generated from:

```
What rootname do you want to use for generated names? [yourserver-]:
```

For a web server bank, you could use a descriptive name like "www-." Next, you will be asked to define the IP address range that you want the DHCP server to manage, beginning with the starting address:

```
Enter starting IP address [192.65.34.0]:
```

Next, you must specify the number of clients. In our Class C network, this will be 254:

```
Enter the number of clients you want to add (x < 65535):
```

Once you have defined the network that you wish to support, you're ready to start using DHCP. An alternative method for invoking dhcpconfig is from the command line, passing key parameters as arguments. For example, to set up a DHCP server for the domain **paulwatters.com**, with the DNS server 204.56.54.22 and a lease time of 14,400 seconds (4 hours), the following command would be used:

```
# dhcpconfig -D -r SUNWbinfiles -p /var/dhcp -l 14400 \
  -d paulwatters.com -a 204.56.54.22 -h dns -y paulwatters.com
```

To unconfigure a DHCP server, the following command should be executed:

```
# dhcpconfig -U -f -x -h
```

This command removes host entries from the name service, the dhcptab, and the network tables.

An alternative to the dhcpconfig command is the dhcpmgr GUI interface, which performs the following operations:

- Configure DHCP
- Configure BOOTP
- Administer DHCP
- Administer BOOTP
- Administer DHCP addresses and macros
- Administer DHCP options
- Migrate DHCP data stores
- Move data from one DHCP server to another

Figure 38-2 shows the GUI interface for dhcpmgr.

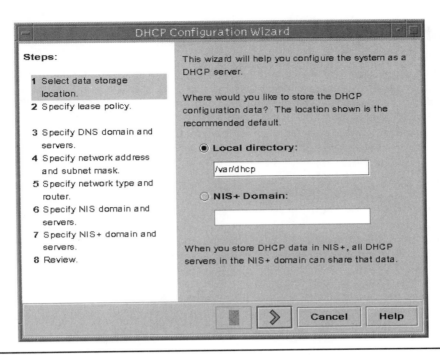

Figure 38-2   DHCP client for Microsoft Windows

EXAM TIP   You should be able to identify the main functions of dhcpmgr.

Manual DHCP Server Configuration

Although most administrators will use dhcpconfig or dhcpmgr to manage DHCP services, it is also possible to manually edit the DHCP configuration database, dhcptab, by using the dhtadm command. Macros can be installed and server options can be set by using the dhtadm command.

In the first instance, dhtadm can be used to create a new *dhcptab* file:

```
# dhtadm -C
```

The following options can be passed to dhtadm to perform various tasks:

- **-A**   Define a macro or symbol
- **-B**   Perform batch processing
- **-C**   Create the service configuration database
- **-D**   Remove a macro or symbol
- **-M**   Update a macro or symbol

Configuring a Solaris DHCP Client

Once the DHCP server has been configured, it is then very easy to configure a Solaris client. When installing the client, you will be asked whether you wish to install DHCP support. At this point, you should answer yes. Accordingly, you will not be asked to enter a static IP address as per a normal installation, as this will be supplied by the DHCP server with a DHCPOFFER message.

If you wish to enable support for DHCP on a client that has already been installed, you will need to use the `sys-unconfig` command, which can be used on all systems to reconfigure network and system settings without having to manually edit configuration files. The `sys-unconfig` command reboots the system in order to perform this task, so users should be given plenty of warning before reconfiguration commences. Again, you will be asked during configuration to install DHCP support, to which you should answer yes.

When configured, the DHCP client (dhcpagent) is managed by ifconfig—although dhcpagent can be started manually, it is most often started by ifconfig with respect to a specific interface. This process allows a lease to be initially obtained and subsequently renewed if the interface is still in use.

Configuring a Windows DHCP Client

Setting up support for a Microsoft Windows client is easy—you simply select the DHCP support option in the TCP/IP section of the Network Control Panel, which can be found in most versions of Windows. A DHCP client for Windows 95 is shown in Figure 38-3. Once DHCP support is enabled, it is no longer necessary to enter any static IP address information.

Exercise 39-1: Configuring and Unconfiguring a DHCP Service   This exercise requires you to configure and unconfigure a DHCP service. For example, to set up a DHCP server for the domain **paulwatters.com**, with the DNS server 204.56.54.22 and a lease time of 14,400 seconds (4 hours), the following command sequence would be

1. Identify the IP address of the local DNS server:
   ```
   # grep nameserver /etc/resolv.conf
   ```

2. Identify the local DNS domain:
   ```
   # cat /etc/defaultdomain
   ```

3. Configure the service:
   ```
   # dhcpconfig -D -r SUNWbinfiles -p /var/dhcp -l 14400 \
   -d paulwatters.com -a 204.56.54.22 -h dns -y paulwatters.com
   ```

4. Unconfigure the service:
   ```
   # dhcpconfig -U -f -x -h
   ```

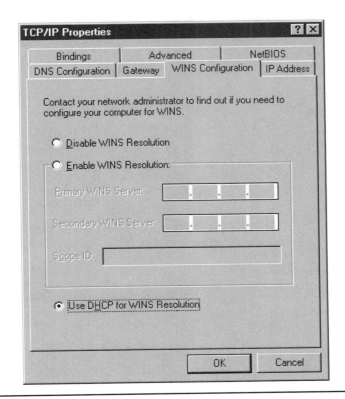

Figure 38-3   DHCP client for Microsoft Windows

PART III

Summary

In this chapter, we examined how to easily set up a Solaris DHCP server that can be used to dynamically allocate IP addresses to clients from several different operating systems. Although DHCP server setup involves making some complex decisions about your network architecture, setting up DHCP clients is easy. It's generally considered easier to configure a single server per subnet than 254 clients that all require their settings to be entered manually! However, DHCP administrators should be aware of a number of important security issues, such as the possibility of IP spoofing occurring, and watch the CERT site (**http://www.cert.org/**) for any advisories.

Questions

1. What is the DHCP server command?

   A. dhcp

   B. in.dhcpd

    C. `dhcp_server`

    D. `server_dhcp`

2. What is the DHCP client command?

    A. `dhcpagent`

    B. `in.dhcpd`

    C. `dhcp_client`

    D. `client_dhcp`

3. When configuring DHCP services, which of the following parameters are you *not* prompted for?

    A. Time zone

    B. NIS server

    C. NIS+ server

    D. LDAP server

4. What command is used to manually update the contents of dhcptab?

    A. `dhtadm`

    B. `dhtconfig`

    C. `dhcpd.in`

    D. `dhcpadm`

5. What Internet Protocol provides the greatest number of IP addresses?

    A. IPv4

    B. IPv6

    C. IPv8

    D. None of the above

6. What Internet Protocols are supported by Solaris 9?

    A. IPv4 and IPv6

    B. IPv6 and IPv8

    C. IP4 and IPv8

    D. None of the above

7. What does DHCP provide?

    A. Static IP addresses

    B. Multiple IP addresses per network interface

    C. Leased IP addresses

    D. Firewalls

8. What is the relationship between BOOTP and DHCP?

    A. DHCP is a superset of BOOTP.

    B. BOOTP is for Windows; DHCP is for Solaris.

    C. BOOTP is for Linux; DHCP is for Solaris .

    D. DHCP is a subset of BOOTP.

9. What other protocols does DHCP integrate with?

    A. LDAP

    B. SNMP

    C. BOOTP

    D. All of the above

10. What message is broadcast by a client looking for an IP address?

    A. DHCPACK

    B. DHCPFIND

    C. DHCPDISCOVER

    D. DHCP_TX

11. What message is broadcast by a server providing IP addresses?

    A. DHCPOFFER

    B. DHCPSERVE

    C. DHCPSERVICE

    D. DHCP_SRV

12. What message is broadcast by a client finished with an IP address?

    A. DHCPEND

    B. DHCPFINISH

    C. DHCPRELEASE

    D. DHCP_END

13. What message is broadcast by a server that can't provide IP addresses as specified?

    A. DHCPFAIL

    B. DHCPNACK

    C. DHCPOFF

    D. DHCP_NO_CAN_DO

14. What message is sent by a server acknowledging a lease?

    A. DHCPOK

    B. DHCPGOOD

    C. DHCPACK

    D. DHCPBACK

15. What command is used to by clients to specify interface configuration using DHCP?

    A. dhcp

    B. dhcpd

    C. ifconfig

    D. route

Answers

1. **B.** The DHCP server command is in.dhcpd.

2. **A.** The DHCP client command is dhcpagent.

3. **D.** When configuring DHCP services, you are *not* prompted for the LDAP server name.

4. **A.** The dhtadm command is used to manually update the contents of dhcptab.

5. **B.** IPv6 provides the greatest number of IP addresses.

6. **A.** IPv4 and IPv6 are both supported by Solaris.

7. **C.** DHCP provides leased IP addresses.

8. **A.** DHCP is a superset of BOOTP.

9. **C.** DHCP integrates with BOOTP.

10. **C.** DHCPDISCOVER is broadcast by a client looking for an IP address.

11. **A.** DHCPOFFER is broadcast by a server providing IP addresses.

12. **C.** DHCPRELEASE is broadcast by a client finished with an IP address.

13. **B.** DHCPNACK is broadcast by a server that can't provide IP addresses as specified.

14. **C.** DHCPACK is sent by a server acknowledging a lease.

15. **C.** The ifconfig command is used to by clients to specify interface configuration using DHCP.

Network Time Protocol

In this chapter, you will

- Learn the characteristics of Network Time Protocol (NTP)
- Learn how NTP is used by enterprise systems and networks
- Review the procedure for configuring an NTP server
- Review the procedure for configuring an NTP client
- Learn the access control and authentication methods supported by NTP

The Network Time Protocol (NTP) provides a framework for standardizing and synchronizing the accurate setting of time and date on individual systems and networks of systems.

Network Time Protocol (NTP)

Time may be relative to the observer, but keeping accurate and consistent time provides a critical frame of reference for applications running on a local server and across the network. For example, imagine a database application that records bank balances in a temporary database for an Internet banking system. The most recent bank balance for each account, when updated, would be always inserted into the column "balance" of the table "accounts," with two primary keys to identify the balances: account_name and timestamp. Whenever the latest balance is to be entered, a new row is inserted into the accounts table with the account_name, balance, and timestamp. All other transactions, such as withdrawals, require that the most recent balance be determined from the timestamp (no updates of rows are permitted for security reasons). If dates and times are not maintained consistently on the system, there is the potential for the true bank balance at the present time to be missed for selection based on the incorrect timestamp it may have been assigned.

This disparity would clearly render the application useless. Figure 39-1 demonstrates this scenario in action—two balances have been inserted into the table accounts for account_name 95639656 with $18,475.90 being the balance at January 1st, 2002, 18:54:21, and $17,475.90 being the balance at January 1st, 2002, 18:59:22. This set of entries indicates that a withdrawal of $1,000 occurred one second after the first transaction. What if the system clock did not have accuracy to within one second? The incorrect balance of $18,475.90 might then be reported when future queries are run.

Figure 39-1

Inserting database records using timestamps requires accurate timekeeping.

account_name	Balance	timestamp
95639656	18475.90	01012002185421
95639656	17475.90	01012002185422

accounts

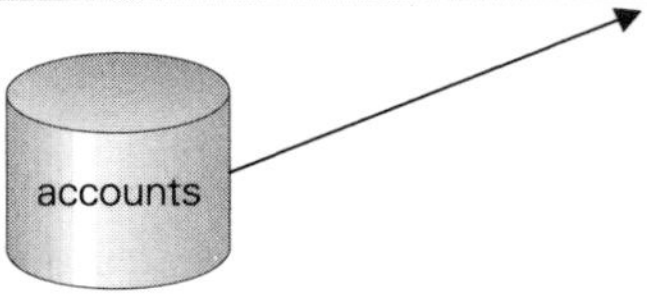

While most systems are capable of maintaining millisecond accuracy for time, a more complex situation arises when high availability and clustering becomes involved, and different systems in the cluster have different times and dates. For example, imagine that a single database server receives updates from six Java 2 Enterprise Edition (J2EE) application servers on six different machines. These servers process requests from clients in a round-robin fashion, and all update the same table on the database server. This allows each application server to always retrieve the most up-to-date information for each client. However, if each server has a different date and time, they would be writing balances into the accounts table with varying timestamps. Again, the fact that the timestamps varied would prevent the application from being used seriously.

Figure 39-2 again demonstrates this scenario—two balances have been inserted into the table accounts for account_name 95639656 by server1, with $18,475.90 being the balance at January 2002 1st, 18:54:21, and server2 with $17,475.90 being the balance at January 2002 1st, 18:59:21. This set of entries indicates that a withdrawal of $1,000 occurred one second after the first transaction. If the two clocks of system1 and system2 were not synchronized with millisecond accuracy, we would never know which balance ($18,475.90 or $17,475.90) was actually correct. What if a leap second was observed on one server and not another? Clearly, there is a need for systems to be able to regularly synchronize their clocks to ensure consistency in enterprise applications.

Figure 39-2

Inserting database records from multiple servers using timestamps requires even more accurate timekeeping.

account_name	Balance	timestamp
95639656	18475.90	01012002185421
95639656	17475.90	01012002185422

server1

server2

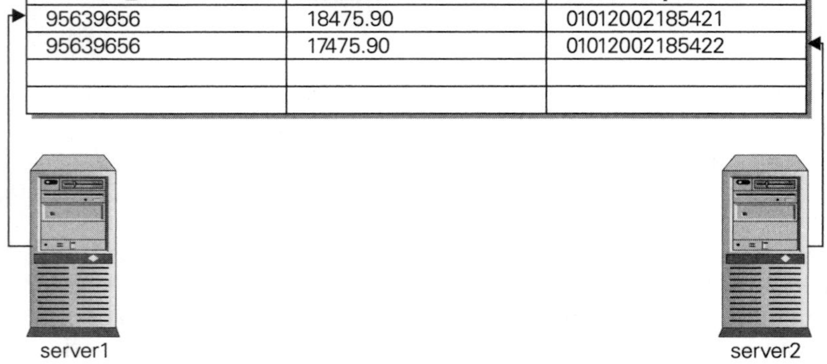

One solution that solves the accuracy problem for single systems and for networks is the Network Time Protocol (NTP). The current version of NTP is v3, specified in RFC 1305, which allows time to be synchronized between all systems on a network by using multicast, and also permits high-precision external hardware clock devices to be supported as authoritative time sources. These two approaches ensure that potential data consistency problems caused by timestamps do not hamper online transaction processing and other real-time data processing applications. By using a master-slave approach, one server on the network can be delegated the authority for timekeeping for all systems on that network.

 TIP Using a master-slave approach ensures that multiple, potentially conflicting sources of authoritative time do not interfere with each other's operation.

NTP v3 provides a number of enhancements over previous versions. It supports a method for servers to communicate with a set of peer servers to average offsets and achieve a more accurate estimation of current time. This is a similar method to that used by national measurement laboratories and similar timekeeping organizations. In addition, network bandwidth can be preserved because the interval between client/server synchronizations has been substantially increased. This improvement in efficiency has been achieved because of the improvements to the local-clock algorithm's accuracy. In any case, NTP uses UDP to communicate synchronization data, minimizing any network overhead. In order for clients to access server data, the IP address or hostname of the server must be known—there is no mechanism for automatic discovery of a time server defined by NTP.

While NTP has a simple client/server interface, individual servers also have the ability to act as secondary servers for external, authoritative time sources. For example, a network might have a designated time server from which all clients retrieve the correct time—which time the server in turn authoritatively receives from a national measurement laboratory. In addition, hardware clocks can be used as a backup in case of network failure between the local network and the measurement laboratory. When a connection is reestablished, the local server's time can simply be recalibrated with the authoritative time received from the laboratory.

In this chapter we will examine how to configure NTP servers and clients to synchronize their timekeeping and examine strategies for maintaining accurate time on the server side.

NTP Server

The Solaris NTP daemon is xntpd. It operates by listening for requests from NTP clients, and sends responses appropriately. The server processes a request, modifies the appropriate fields with the correct time and so forth, and then returns the modified request data as a response. The response allows the client to modify its clock settings appropriately. In addition, the server is able to provide data from a number of different authoritative sources.

The accuracy of a client's time can be improved by selecting the most accurate server. Fortunately, there are measurements available to determine which clocks provide the most accurate data. Reliability and accuracy data is returned in the response data when a client makes a request to the server.

In a more complex network, where a time server must be highly available, it may be more appropriate to create a hierarchical system of NTP servers where dynamic reconfiguration is possible. This is only necessary where hardware or software failures can affect a single production system's reliability. In this case, multiple servers can act as peers to each other. A primary time server in this setup obtains its time from a reference such as an external clock device, which it transmits to other secondary servers. Alternatively, there may be multiple primary time servers, and secondary servers must determine which course is most accurate. Clients then access secondary sources directly.

Of course, this creates a stratum of accuracy, with primary servers (1) being the most accurate, secondary servers (2) being the next most accurate, and clients (3) being the least accurate. Millisecond accuracy should be possible at least at level 2. However, errors can be estimated at lower levels and corrections made to improve the overall accuracy of the time estimation.

The timestamp lies at the core of the NTP data model. It is represented by a 64-bit unsigned floating-point number, and is the number of seconds that have elapsed since 01/01/1900 00:00. The first 32 bits represent the integer portion of the number, while the last 32 bits represent the fractional portion of the number.

The number of seconds in one nonleap year is 31536000. Given that only 64 bits are available to store time data in the NTP timestamp format, the maximum value will be reached in the year 2036. Given the number of legacy applications even now that use timestamping, a significant amount of planning will be required in around 30 years time to develop a new, high-capacity timestamp format that is backward compatible with existing formats.

A sample NTP server configuration file is located in */etc/inet/ntp.server*. This file provides a pro forma template for configuring an NTP server that utilizes an external clock device, provides for local clock synchronization, and broadcasts times across the network. A sample file is shown here:

```
server 127.127.XType.0 prefer
fudge 127.127.XType.0 stratum 0
broadcast 224.0.1.1 ttl 4
enable auth monitor
driftfile /var/ntp/ntp.drift
statsdir /var/ntp/ntpstats/
filegen peerstats file peerstats type day enable
filegen loopstats file loopstats type day enable
filegen clockstats file clockstats type day enable
keys /etc/inet/ntp.keys
trustedkey 0
```

```
requestkey 0
controlkey 0
```

The server entry indicates the primary server that this system prefers. The broadcast entry directs the server to broadcast messages to clients. The driftfile relates to a local clock's accuracy and its frequency offset.

EXAM TIP   You should be able to interpret a NTP server configuration file.

In both cases where "XType" appears, a legal value for a clock device must be inserted. The clock device could be one of the devices shown in Table 39-1.

XType	Device	RefID	Description
1	local	LCL	Undisciplined local clock
2	trak	GPS	TRAK 8820 GPS receiver
3	pst	WWV	PSTI/Traconex WWV/WWVH receiver
4	wwvb	WWVB	Spectracom WWVB receiver
5	true	TRUE	TrueTime GPS/GOES receivers
6	irig	IRIG	IRIG audio decoder
7	chu	CHU	Scratchbuilt CHU receiver
8	parse	----	Generic reference clock driver
9	mx4200	GPS	Magnavox MX4200 GPS receiver
10	as2201	GPS	Austron 2201A GPS receiver
11	arbiter	GPS	Arbiter 1088A/B GPS receiver
12	tpro	IRIG	KSI/Odetics TPRO/S IRIG interface
13	leitch	ATOM	Leitch CSD 5300 master clock controller
15	*	*	TrueTime GPS/TM-TMD receiver
17	datum	DATM	Datum precision time system
18	acts	ACTS	NIST automated computer time service
19	heath	WWV	Heath WWV/WWVH Receiver
20	nmea	GPS	Generic NMEA GPS receiver
22	atom	PPS	PPS clock discipline
23	Ptb	TPTB	PTB automated computer time service
24	Usno	USNO	USNO modem time service
25	*	*	TrueTime generic receivers
26	Hpgps	GPS	Hewlett Packard 58503A GPS receiver
27	Arc	MSFa	Arcron MSF receiver

Table 39-1   XTypes Available Through xntpd

PART III

Once the settings for the NTP server have been modified, they should be saved in the file */etc/inet/ntp.conf*. When started in debug mode, the NTP server produces the following output:

```
/usr/lib/inet/xntpd -d
tick = 10000, tickadj = 5, hz = 100
kernel vars: tickadj = 5, tick = 10000
adj_precision = 1, tvu_maxslew = 495, tsf_maxslew = 0.002070b9
create_sockets(123)
bind() fd 19, family 2, port 123, addr 00000000, flags=1
bind() fd 20, family 2, port 123, addr 7f000001, flags=0
bind() fd 21, family 2, port 123, addr 0a401203, flags=1
init_io: maxactivefd 21
getconfig: Couldn't open </etc/inet/ntp.conf>
report_event: system event 'event_restart' (0x01) status 'sync_alarm,
 sync_unspe
c, 1 event, event_unspec' (0xc010)
```

In this output, an error message is generated because the file */etc/inet/ntp.conf* could not be found—it's a common mistake not to copy across the template */etc/inet/ntp.server* file to */etc/inet/ntp.conf*! To observe the set of internal variables used by xntpd during its operation, the ntpq command can be used.

NTP Client

If a system is going to act as an NTP client, creating the configuration file is much simpler. Instead of copying the template */etc/inet/ntp.server* file to */etc/inet/ntp.conf*, the template */etc/inet/ntp.client* file is copied to */etc/inet/ntp.conf*. By default, this file contains a list that listens for multicast broadcasts on the local subnet:

```
multicastclient 224.0.1.1
```

NTP clients send and receive NTP message data in a specific format. The main fields transmitted include the following:

- **Leap Indicator**   Flag that indicates a leap year at the end of the day.
- **Version Number**   NTP v3.
- **Mode**   Determines whether the message is symmetric active, symmetric passive, client, server, broadcast, or an NTP control message.
- **Stratum**   Level of accuracy for the message, with 1 being a primary server and 2–255 indicating secondary servers of decreasing accuracy.
- **Poll Interval**   Maximum time separating messages.
- **Precision**   Local clock precision.
- **Root Delay**   Delay anticipated between the primary and other sources.

- **Root Dispersion**   Error estimate from the primary source.
- **Reference Clock Identifier**   Allows the primary source clock to be identified.
- **Reference Timestamp**   The last time the local clock was updated.
- **Originate Timestamp**   The time at which the message was transmitted from a client.
- **Receive Timestamp**   The time at which the message was received.
- **Transmit Timestamp**   The time at which the message was transmitted from a server.
- **Authenticator**   Specifies the authentication method used.

NTP Security

One of the main problems in tying all production time management operations to a single primary server is the potential for crackers to either spoof a legitimate primary server and pretend to be the primary server or to undertake a denial of service attack. Fortunately, NTP provides authentication procedures to ensure that only authorized servers and clients can access their peers and/or the primary server. In addition, the use of multiple authoritative sources, including a backup external hardware clock, can remove some of the problems associated with denial of service attacks—after all, if an external network port is being blocked by an attacker or group of attackers, the local standby can always be used.

NTP security is ultimately based on trust relationships that are developed as part of an overall network design. In addition, a number of innovations in the NTP authentication system make it very difficult for a cracker to spoof a primary server. For example, the original timestamp is equivalent to a one-time pad, although if the cracker has knowledge of previous timestamps, it may be possible (with sufficient CPU power) to successfully spoof a server. However, given the error estimation procedures and methods for clients to select the most accurate server, it's unlikely that an attack would succeed.

Summary

In this chapter we have examined the core NTP protocols and configuration information, as well as how to configure NTP clients and servers. Given that NTP is a central service that ensures data integrity, we've also examined the security implications of running an NTP service and how it may be protected with appropriate access control and authentication mechanisms.

Questions

1. Why is there a need for production systems to be able to regularly synchronize their clocks?

   A. To ensure data consistency in enterprise applications

   B. To ensure that time is printed correctly to users

   C. To ensure that machines can independently estimate time

   D. To ensure that an external hardware clock is required for every system

2. What is the purpose of NTP?

   A. To allow every system to have their own external hardware clock

   B. To allow time to be synchronized between all systems on a network by using multicast

   C. To prevent access to primary time servers by network clients

   D. To filter timestamps and prevent their dispersion at the router level

3. What kind of approach allows one server on the network to be delegated the authority for timekeeping for all systems on that network?

   A. Peer-to-peer

   B. Star topology

   C. Net topology

   D. Master-slave

4. What is the major new feature of NTP v3?

   A. It supports a method for servers to communicate with a set of peer servers to average offsets and achieve a more accurate estimation of current time.

   B. It supports native public-key cryptography.

   C. It supports packet filtering firewalls.

   D. It permits up to 1,024 secondary servers per primary server.

5. What is the name of the Solaris NTP daemon?.

   A. ntp

   B. ntpd

   C. xntpd

   D. nntpd

6. Where is the sample NTP server configuration file located?

   A. /etc/inet/ntp.server

   B. /etc/inet/ntp.server.sample

   C. */etc/inet/ntp.sample*

   D. */etc/inet/ntp.conf.sample*

7. What is the name of the command to start the NTP daemon in debug mode?

   A. `ntp -d`

   B. `ntpd -d`

   C. `xntpd -d`

   D. `nntpd -d`

8. What is the Leap Indicator?

   A. Flag that indicates a leap year at the end of the day.

   B. NTP v3.

   C. Determines whether the message is symmetric active, symmetric passive, client, server, broadcast, or an NTP control message.

   D. Level of accuracy for the message, with 1 being a primary server and 2–255 indicating secondary servers of decreasing accuracy.

9. What is the Version Indicator?

   A. Flag that indicates a leap year at the end of the day.

   B. NTP v3.

   C. Determines whether the message is symmetric active, symmetric passive, client, server, broadcast, or an NTP control message.

   D. Level of accuracy for the message, with 1 being a primary server and 2–255 indicating secondary servers of decreasing accuracy.

10. What is the Mode?

   A. Flag that indicates a leap year at the end of the day.

   B. NTP v3.

   C. Determines whether the message is symmetric active, symmetric passive, client, server, broadcast, or an NTP control message.

   D. Level of accuracy for the message, with 1 being a primary server and 2–255 indicating secondary servers of decreasing accuracy.

11. What is the Stratum?

   A. Flag that indicates a leap year at the end of the day.

   B. NTP v3.

   C. Determines whether the message is symmetric active, symmetric passive, client, server, broadcast, or an NTP control message.

   D. Level of accuracy for the message, with 1 being a primary server and 2–255 indicating secondary servers of decreasing accuracy.

PART III

12. What is the Poll Interval?

    A. Maximum time separating messages

    B. Local clock precision

    C. Delay anticipated between the primary and other sources

    D. Error estimate from the primary source

13. What is the Precision?

    A. Maximum time separating messages

    B. Local clock precision

    C. Delay anticipated between the primary and other sources

    D. Error estimate from the primary source

14. What is the Root Delay?

    A. Maximum time separating messages

    B. Local clock precision

    C. Delay anticipated between the primary and other sources

    D. Error estimate from the primary source

15. What is the Root Dispersion?

    A. Maximum time separating messages

    B. Local clock precision

    C. Delay anticipated between the primary and other sources

    D. Error estimate from the primary source

Answers

1. **A.** To ensure data consistency in enterprise applications, there is a need for production systems to be able to regularly synchronize their clocks.

2. **B.** The purpose of NTP is to allow time to be synchronized between all systems on a network by using multicast.

3. **D.** A master-slave approach allows one server on the network to be delegated the authority for timekeeping for all systems on that network.

4. **A.** The major new feature of NTP v3 is a method for servers to communicate with a set of peer servers to average offsets and achieve a more accurate estimation of current time.

5. **C.** The Solaris NTP daemon is xntpd.

6. **A.** The sample NTP server configuration file is located in */etc/inet/ntp.server*.

7. **C.** The name of the command to start the NTP daemon in debug mode is `xntpd -q`.

8. **A.** The Leap Indicator is the flag that indicates a leap year at the end of the day.

9. **B.** The Version Number is NTP v3.

10. **C.** The Mode determines whether the message is symmetric active, symmetric passive, client, server, broadcast, or an NTP control message.

11. **D.** The Stratum is the level of accuracy for the message, with 1 being a primary server and 2–255 indicating secondary servers of decreasing accuracy.

12. **A.** The Poll Interval is the maximum time separating messages.

13. **B.** The Precision is the local clock precision.

14. **C.** The Root Delay is the delay anticipated between the primary and other sources.

15. **D.** The Root Dispersion is the error estimate from the primary source.

INDEX